C O N T E N T S

Tele-Tunes 2000 © Mike Preston Music 2000

TELE-TUNES 2000 : THE REFERENCE BOOK OF MUSIC FOR TV
COMMERCIALS, TV PROGRAMMES, FILMS AND SHOWS

18TH COMPLETELY REVISED EDITION OF TELE-TUNES

W H A T   I S   I N   T E L E - T U N E S ?

TELE-TUNES IS INTENDED AS A GUIDE TO TV AND FILM MUSIC
CURRENTLY AVAILABLE IN RETAIL MUSIC OUTLETS

RECENT DELETIONS ARE GIVEN FOR REFERENCE ONLY, AND SOME
ITEMS MAY ONLY BE AVAILABLE FROM SPECIALIST SUPPLIERS

TV ADS, PROGRAMMES, FILMS & SHOWS *NOT LISTED* PLUS ITEMS
DELETED FROM PREVIOUS EDITIONS ARE HELD FOR REFERENCE
IN THE MIKE PRESTON MUSIC INFORMATION DATABASE, IT
CONTAINS DETAILS OF TV AND FILM MUSIC COVERING A FAR
WIDER SPECTRUM THAN WE CAN HOPE TO PUBLISH IN THIS BOOK
ACCESS TO THIS INFORMATION IS AVAILABLE TO SUBSCRIBERS
TO THE TELE-TUNES SUBSCRIPTION SERVICE. *SEE PAGE 357*

TELEVISION COMMERCIALS

ALPHABETICAL PRODUCT-MUSIC TITLE-(COMPOSER if Known)-
ARTIST-LABEL-(DISTRIBUTOR)-CATALOGUE NUMBER-(FORMAT)

TELEVISION PROGRAMMES, FILMS AND SHOWS (Integrated A-Z)

TV PROGRAMME TITLE-TV COMPANY-T/X DATE-MUSIC TITLE-
COMPOSER-ARTIST-LABEL (DISTRIBUTOR)-CAT.NUMBER-(FORMAT)
TV themes are cross referenced to COLLECTIONS.

FILM TITLE-YEAR-SCORE COMPOSER -S/T- OTHER INFO-LABEL
(DISTRIB)-CATALOGUE NUMBER-(FORMAT)

SHOWS TITLE-COMPOSER/LYRICIST-ORIG.CAST-YEAR-LEADING
CAST-LABEL (DIST)-CATALOGUE NUMBER-(FORMAT)

COLLECTIONS

410 COLLECTIONS NUMBERED FROM 1 UP BY TITLE AND ARTIST
ALPHABETICALLY. COLLECTION NUMBER-TITLE-ARTIST-RECORD
LABEL-(DISTRIBUTOR)-CATALOGUE NUMBER-(FORMAT)-YEAR +
CROSS REFERENCED TRACKS INCLUDED IN MAIN TEXT

JAMES BOND / ELVIS PRESLEY / WALT DISNEY / EUROVISION

JAMES BOND AND ELVIS PRESLEY CHRONOLOGICAL FILM INDEX
WALT DISNEY CD & VIDEO INDEX / EUROVISION SONG CONTEST

A.A.INSURANCE "You Make Me Feel Like Dancing" LEO SAYER
on 'Endless Flight' *CHRYSALIS-HIT: AHLCD 35 (CD)*

ADDICTION (Faberge) "Gopher Tango" PEREZ PRADO & HIS
ORCH 'Cha Cha Cha D'Amour' (Ultra Lounge Volume 9)
CAPITOL (EMI): CDEMS 1596 (CD)

ADIDAS 6 "Memory Gospel" by MOBY *unavailable*

ADIDAS 5 "Soul Surfin'" by FATBOY SLIM *unavailable*

ADIDAS 4 "Right Here Right Now" mixed by FAT BOY SLIM
from the album 'You've Come A Long Way Baby'
SKINT (3MV-Pinn): BRASSIC 11(CD)(MC)(LP)(MD)

ADIDAS 3 (D.Beckham ad) "Step On" by HAPPY MONDAYS
from 'Pills 'n' Thrills and Bellyaches' on
FACTORY TOO (Pinn): 828 223-2 (CD)

ADIDAS 2 (Soccer Re-invented) special production by
MASSIVE ATTACK from existing uncredited MA track

ADIDAS 1 "Dive" by The PROPELLERHEADS *WALL OF SOUND*
(Vital): WALLT 034 (12"s limited edit of 5000)

AIR FRANCE "Asleep From Day" by The CHEMICAL BROTHERS
from the album 'Surrender'
FREESTYLE DUST (EMI): XDUST(CD)(MC)(LP) 4

ALL GOLD (Terry's) "Will You" by HAZEL O'CONNOR feat
WESLEY MacGOOGHAN (sax) 'Live In Berlin' on
START (DISC): SRH 804 (CD)

ALLIED DUNBAR "Let's Face The Music And Dance" (Irving
Berlin) NAT KING COLE on 'ULTIMATE COLLECTION'
CAPITOL-EMI: 499 575-2 (CD) -4 (MC)

ALPEN 3 "Ocean Drive" LIGHTHOUSE FAMILY 'Ocean Drive'
POLYDOR (UNIV): 523 787-2 (CD) -4 (MC)

ALPEN 2 based on "Reasons To Be Cheerful Pt.3" (Dury)
orig by IAN DURY & THE BLOCKHEADS on 'Sex Drugs and
Rock'n'Roll' *DEMON (Pinn): FIENDCD 69 (CD)*

ALPEN 1 "Sun Rising" from 'Happiness' by The BELOVED
WEA: WX 299(C)(CD) also on Coll 'NEW PURE MOODS'

ALTON TOWERS "In The Hall Of The Mountain King" from
'PEER GYNT SUITE' (GRIEG) *many recordings*

AMBROSIA 3 "In The Navy" (based on) original by
VILLAGE PEOPLE *MUSIC CLUB (THE): MCCD 004 (CD)*

AMBROSIA 2 "Go West" original by The PET SHOP BOYS
on 'Disco Vol.2' *PARLOPHONE (EMI): CDPCSD 159 (CD)*

AMBROSIA 1 (Art compet.ad) "Left Bank Two" (Vision On
Picture Gallery music) NOVELTONES on 'THIS IS THE
RETURN OF CULT FICTION' *VIRGIN (EMI): VTCD 112 (CD)*

AMERICAN EXPRESS BLUE CARD "Blue Monday" by NEW ORDER
'Best Of' *FACTORY (UNIV): 828 580-2 (CD) -4 (MC)*

ANCHOR BUTTER 4 "Born Free" (John Barry-Don Black)
TV arrangement unavailable

ANCHOR BUTTER 3 based on "My Girl" (William Robinson
Ronald White) orig TEMPTATIONS on *MOTOWN (UNIV):*
530015-2(CD) -4(MC) -5(DCC) OTIS REDDING 'Dock Of
The Bay' *ATLANTIC (TEN): 9548 31708-2(CD) -4(MC)*

ANCHOR BUTTER 2 "In The Mood" (Andy Razaf-J.Garland)
GLENN MILLER ORCH *RCA (BMG): PD 89260 (CD)*

ANCHOR BUTTER 1 "Day Trip To Bangor" (Fiddlers Dram)
FIDDLERS DRAM *DINGLES: SID 211 (7"s)*

APPLE COMPUTERS "She's A Rainbow" (M.Jagger-K.Richard) ROLLING STONES from album 'Their Satanic Majesties Request' *LONDON (UNIV): 844 470-2 (CD) -4 (MC)*

APPLETISE "Tempted" performed by SQUEEZE on 'Greatest Hits' *A.& M. (UNIV): 397 181-2 (CD)*

ASDA 2 (main theme) composed by ROGER GREENAWAY and arranged by Graham Preskett *unavailable*

ASDA 1 "Perfect" (Mark E.Nevin) FAIRGROUND ATTRACTION 'First Of A Million Kisses' *RCA: 74321 13439-2 (CD)*

AUDI A4 "La Mer" (Trenet) CHARLES TRENET on 'Very Best' *EMI: CDP 794 464-2 (CD)*

AUDI A8 Moon Vehicle 2 "Moonlight Sonata" (BEETHOVEN) *TV version unavailable*

AUDI A8 Moon Vehicle 1 "Mooncar" (Vince POPE) Music Gallery *unavailable*

AUDI TT "The Very Thought Of You" (Ray Noble) ELLA FITZGERALD on 'The Incomparable Ella' on *POLYGRAM: 835 610-2 (CD) -4 (MC)* NANCY WILSON on 'Sophisticated Ladies' (Collect) *TRIO-EMI GOLD (EMI): 522 714-2 (3CDs)*

AXA EQUITY & LAW "Don't Worry Be Happy" BOBBY McFERRIN 'Walking On Sunshine' *KENWEST (THE): KNEWCD 742 CD* 'Best Of B.M.' *BLUENOTE (EMI): CDP 853329-2 (CD)*

AXA INSURANCE "Love Theme" from 'The MISSION' by ENNIO MORRICONE -S/T- *VIRGIN (EMI): CDV 2402 (CD)*

B.& Q. "Walk This Land" (Banks-Hurren-Richards) by EZ ROLLERS from 'Lock Stock and 2 Smoking Barrels" *ISLAND (UNIV): CID 8077 (CD) SHADOW 130CD1 (CDs)*

B.T.Cellnet 3 "Jelleyfish" JOHN ALTMAN *unavailable*

B.T.Cellnet 2 "Love Potion Number 9" (Jerry Leiber-Mike Stoller) *original version by* The COASTERS *ATLANTIC (Ten): 7567 90386-2 (CD)*

B.T.Cellnet 1 "Beat Goes On" (S.Bono) ALL SEEING I *LONDON FFFR (UNIV): FFCD 334 (CDs) FFCS 334 (MC)*

B.T.5 "Flying" (E.T.theme) by JOHN WILLIAMS *various recordings available*

B.T.4 "Hold On I'm Coming" (I.Hayes-David Porter) by SAM & DAVE *Stax Records*

B.T.3 'Second Line Offer' "Nojahoda" by NOJAHODA *S2: 666745 (CDs)*

B.T.2 Second line "A Man And A Woman" -S/T- (1966) *DRG (New Note-Pinn): DRGCD 12612 (CD)*

B.T.1 "CALL ME" (Tony Hatch) sung by Chris Montez *V.ARTS COLL* 'THIS IS EASY' *VIRGIN: VTDCD 80 (2CD) also on IMPORT through CD ONESTOP: DZS 056 CD)*

B.T.0 "Make Me Smile (Come Up And See Me)" sung by STEVE HARLEY & COCKNEY REBEL *EMI: CZ 385 (CD)*

BACARDI 2 (Prison cell) original music by VINCE POPE *unavailable*

BACARDI 1 (Casino) "Jive Samba" by JACK CONSTANZO and GERRY WOO from Coll 'EL RITMO LATINO VOLUME 1' on *MCI (THE-Disc): MCCD 025 (CD) MCTC 025 (MC)*

BAILEYS IRISH CREAM 2 "Big Bamboozle" (B.Adamson)
BARRY ADAMSON from 'Oedipus Schmoedipus'
MUTE-RTM (Disc): CDSTUMM 134 (CD)
BAILEYS IRISH CREAM 1 "Barcarolle"(Tales Of Hoffmann)
(OFFENBACH) Elizabeth Schwarzkopft-Jeanine Collard
'CLASSIC EXP.' *EMI (CD)(TC)EMTVD 45 (2CD/MC) 94TV*
BARCLAY'S BANK Cashpoint "Ride On" by LITTLE AXE on
WIRED (3MV-Sony): WIRED 27 (CD) WIRED 47 (MC)
BATCHELORS CUPA SOUP (office affair ad) "Racetrack" by
JACKIE MITTOO *Jet Star Records*
BBC Learning Zone - see TV SECTION
BBC Internet ads - see TV SECTION
BECKS BEER "Naturally" by CHRIS SMITH & SIMON STEVEN
(Final Touch Productions) *unavailable*
BEEFEATER RESTAURANTS "Moment Scale" SILENT POETS 'CAFE
DEL MAR IBIZA' VOL.2 *REACT (Vital): REACTCD 062(CD)*
BELLS WHISKY "Young At Heart" (C.Leigh-J.Richards) sung
by IAN McCULLOGH (Echo & Bunnymen) *unavailable*
BENDICKS MINTS (Bendicks Of Mayfair) "Missing You"
(Romeo-Law-Mazelle) SOUL II SOUL feat KYM MAZELLE
'New Dance Decade' *VIRGIN (EMI): DIXCD 90 (CD)*
BENYLIN "Nessun Dorma" 'Turandot' (Puccini) *TV version*
by ANTONIO NAGORE and R.P.O. *unavailable*
BIC SOFT FEEL "Funeral March Of A Marionette" (Charles
Gounod) on 'EUROPEAN LIGHT MUSIC CLASSICS' on
HYPERION: CDA 66998 (CD)
BIRDS CUSTARD based on "Bloop Bleep" (Frank Loesser)
orig DANNY KAYE *LIVING ERA (Koch): CDAJA 5270 (CD)*
BIRDS-EYE CRISPY CHICKEN "Chicken Rhythm" (Slim Gaill
ard) SLIM GAILLARD on 'The Legendary McVouty" on
HEP (New Note/Pinn): HEPCD 6 (CD)
BIRDS EYE FROZEN HERBS "Scarboro' Fayre" *TV version*
unavailable. SIMON & GARFUNKEL vers.on -S/T- to
THE GRADUATE. *COLUMBIA (Ten): CBSCD 32359 (CD)*
BISTO "Save The Best For Last" by VANESSA WILLIAMS
'The Comfort Zone' *POLYDOR: 511267-2 (CD) -4(MC)*
BLACK & DECKER 3 (WORKMATE +) "Acroche Toi Caroline"
(from VISION ON) PARIS STUDIO GROUP *COLL* 'THIS IS
THE RETURN OF CULT FICTION' *VIRGIN: VTCD 112 (CD)*
BLACK & DECKER 2 (DUSTBUSTER) "Blockbuster" (Chapman-
Chinn) orig The SWEET *RCA (BMG): ND 74313 (CD)*
BLACK & DECKER 1 (SNAKELIGHT) based on "The Wanderer"
DION on 'Runaround Sue' *ACE (Pinn): CDCHM 148 (CD)*
BLACK MAGIC 2 "Love Is The Sweetest Thing" (R.Noble)
AL BOWLLY & RAY NOBLE ORCH. *EMI:CDP 794341-2 (CD)*
BLACK MAGIC 1 (It's The Black Magic) 'Stranger Theme'
CHRISTOPHER GUNNING *unavailable*
BLACKTHORN CIDER "Faces" ad. music by PETER LAWLOR for
WATER MUSIC PRODUCTIONS *unavailable*
BLOCKBUSTER VIDEO "Sound and Vision" (Bowie) by DAVID
BOWIE 'SINGLES COLL' *EMI: CD(TC)EM 1512 (CD/MC/LP)*
BN BISCUITS - see McVITIES
BODDINGTONS 3 'Horror' ad original music composed by
JOHN ALTMAN *unavailable*

BODDINGTONS 2 'Cattle Market' ad "Back By Dope Demand"
    KING BEE from 'Hip Hop Volume 2' *deleted*
BODDINGTONS 1 'Cow-Ma-Sutra' "If Loving You Is Wrong"
    FAITHLESS from 'REVERENCE' *CHEEKY: CHEKCD 500 (CD)*
BOOTS Double Points "You're A Wonderful One" (H-D-H)
    sung by MARVIN GAYE on 'Motown's Early Hits'
    MOTOWN (Univ): 552 118-2 (CD)
BOOTS New Health & Travel Cover "Kyoko's Home" from
    'MISHIMA' composed by PHILIP GLASS -S/T- originally
    NONESUCH (Warner): 7559 79113-2 (CD)
BOOTS Xmas 96/7 "Make Someone Happy" sung by PAUL YOUNG
    EAST WEST (TEN): EW 148CD (CDs) EW 148C (MC) also
    JIMMY DURANTE *from* 'SLEEPLESS IN SEATTLE' *EPIC-Sony
    473 594-2 (CD)* + *WB (TEN): W.0385CD(MC) (CDs/MC)*
BOOTS NO.7 -1a "La Cumparsita" (G.Matos Rodriguez) *TV
    vers.arr.by Jeff Wayne (unavailable)* orig recording
    by XAVIER CUGAT ORCHESTRA on 'Mundo Latino' collect
    on *SONY: SONYTV2CD (CD) SONYTV2MC (MC)*
BP-MOBIL "Sing Sing Sing" (Louis Prima) *TV Version not
    available.* orig. by BENNY GOODMAN & HIS ORCHESTRA
    feat.GENE KRUPA (drs) on '16 Most Requested Songs'
    COLUMBIA (Ten): 474 396-2 (CD) -4 (MC)
BRANSTON PICKLE "Left Bank 2" (Vision On TV Picture
    Gallery music) NOVELTONES on 'THIS IS THE RETURN
    OF CULT FICTION' *VIRGIN (EMI): VTCD 112 (CD)*
BRITANNIC INSURANCE "Swan Lake Ballet" by TCHAIKOVSKY
BRITISH AIRWAYS (P.J.O'Rourke ad) "Jupiter" from 'The
    Planets Suite' (Gustav HOLST) *various recordings*
BRITISH AIRWAYS (1991-1997/98/99) main music theme used:
    "Dome Epais" (Flower Duet) from 'Lakme' (DELIBES)
    7.HELEN REEVES *unavailable*
    6.LESLEY GARRETT 'Diva' *Sil.Screen: SONGCD 903 (CD)*
    5.VARD SISTERS on 'HEAVENLY' *SONY: 488 092-2 (CD)*
    4.MADY MESPLE-DANIELLE MILLET & PARIS OPERA ORCH
      'Most Famous Movie Class.2' *EMI: 568 307-2 (CD)*
    3.MALCOLM McLAREN "Aria On Air" *Virg: VTCD 28 (CD)*
      'NEW PURE MOODS' *see COLL.262.*
    2.ZBIGNIEW PREISNER "Fashion Show No.2" from 'Three
      Colors Red') on *VIRGIN (EMI): VTCD 87 (CD)*
    1.YANNI (eye on the beach) "Aria" 'In The Mirror'
      PRIVATE MUSIC (BMG): 74321 47125-2 (CD)
BRITISH GAS 5 ('6' ad) "German Stroll" *Carlin Music
    Library unavailable*
BRITISH GAS 4 "Wipeout" by The SURFARIS on 'More
    Dirty Dancing' *RCA (BMG): 74321 36915-2 (CD)*
BRITISH GAS 3 2001 "Chinese Dance" (NUTCRACKER SUITE)
    (TCHAIKOVSKY) *various versions available*
BRITISH GAS 2 "The Universal" by BLUR from 'The Great
    Escape' *FOOD-EMI (EMI): FOOD(CD)(TC) 14*
BRITISH GAS 1 "Dance A Cachucha Fandango Bolero"
    from act 2 of 'The Gondoliers' GILBERT & SULLIVAN
    MFP (EMI): CDCFP 4609 (CD) TCCFP 4609 (MC)
BRITISH HEART FOUNDATION 3 "Liquidator" HARRY J.ALL
    STARS on 'SKA ARCHIVE' *RIALTO (Dir): RMCD 202 (CD)*

BRITISH HEART FOUNDATION 2 "Waiting For The Miracle" LEONARD COHEN from 'The Future' *SONY: 472 498-2 (CD) -4 (MC) -1 (LP) -3 (MD)*

BRITISH HEART FOUNDATION 1 "Stop In The Name Of Love" (Holland-Dozier-Holland) DIANA ROSS AND SUPREMES *MOTOWN (UNIV): 530 013-2 (CD) -4 (MC)*

BRITISH MEAT 3 (Lamb) "Way We Were" (M.Hamlisch-A.& M. Bergman) *TV version unavailable.* original by Barbra Streisand *(COLUMBIA)*

BRITISH MEAT 2 "I Got You Babe" by SONNY & CHER *ATLANTIC (TEN): 9548 30152-2 (CD) -4 (MC)*

BRITISH MEAT 1 "Let There Be Love" (I.Grant-L.Rand) NAT KING COLE '20 Golden Greats' *EMI: CD(TC)EMTV 9*

BRITISH MIDLAND "Easy Muffin" by EAMON TOBIN from album 'The Bricolage' *NINJA (Vital): (CD)*

BRITISH NUCLEAR FUELS "Last Stand" by ALOOF from album 'Sinking' *EAST WEST (W): 0630 17739-2 (CD)*

BRITISH TELECOM - *see* BT

BROOKE BOND HOT DRINKS "Tomorrow's Just Another Day" (Smith-Barson) MADNESS on 'Divine Madness' Coll. *VIRGIN (EMI): CDV 2692 (CD) TCV 2692 (MC)*

BRYLCREEM (D.Beckham ad)"Beautiful Ones" by SUEDE from 'COMING UP' *NUDE (Vit):NUDECD 6 (CD) NUDE 23CD CDs*

BUBBALOO "Babalu" (Lecuona-Russell) XAVIER CUGAT ORCH. feat MIGUELITO VALDEZ 'Hit Sound Of XAVIER CUGAT' *CHARLY (Koch): CDHOT 631 (CD)*

BUDWEISER 9 (Crocodile) "Ooh La La" (Theo Keating) by WISEGUYS from album 'The Antidote' *WALL OF SOUND (Vital): WALL(CD)(C)020 (CD/MC) / WALLD 038X (CDs)*

BUDWEISER 8 (World Cup 98) orig commission by FINAL TOUCH PRODUCTIONS *unavailable*

BUDWEISER 7 (poker game) "Dirt" by DEATH IN VEGAS on *CONCRETE (RTM/DISC): HARD 27CD (CDs)*

BUDWEISER 6 (money suitcase/taxi) "Crawl" composed and produced by ROBERT WHITE *unavailable*

BUDWEISER 5 "St.James Infirmary Blues" (Irving Mills adapt.from trad.folk song) sung by SNOOKS EAGLIN *cat.no.unconfirmed. vers.by* CAB CALLOWAY on 'Hi De Hi De Ho' *RCA (BMG): 74321 26729-2 + 18524-2 (CD)*

BUDWEISER 4 (Ants) "Get Down Tonight" KC & SUNSHINE BAND 'Get Down Tonight' *EMI: 494 019-2 (CD) -4 (MC)*

BUDWEISER 3 "Connection" ELASTICA *DECEPTIVE (Vital): BLUFF 014(CD)(MC)(LPN)*

BUDWEISER 2 "The Passenger" (Iggy Pop-Rick Gardiner) by MICHAEL HUTCHENCE on -S/T- 'Batman Forever' on *ATLANTIC (TEN): 7567 82759-2 (CD) -4 (MC)*

BUDWEISER 1 (Blues Train ad) "Smokestack Lightning" HOWLIN'WOLF "Smokestack Lightning" *INSTANT-CHARLY CDINS 5037 (CD) TCINS 5037 (MC) INSD 5037 (2LP)*

BURGER KING 10 "Temptation" by HEAVEN 17 feat CAROL KENYON. 'Best Of HEAVEN 17' *VIRGIN: VVIPD 118 (CD)*

BURGER KING 9 "I Like It" by the BLACKOUT ALLSTARS from FILM 'I LIKE IT LIKE THAT' (1994) -S/T- *COLUMBIA (Ten): 477 334-2 (CD) -4 (MC)*

BURGER KING 8 "Crazy" (Willie Nelson) by PATSY CLINE
  'Very Best Of' *MCA: MCD 11483 (CD) MCC 11483 (MC)*
BURGER KING 7 "Ride On Time" (Dan Hartman) BLACK BOX
  '80s Extended' *RCA CAMDEN (BMG): 74321 64790-2 (CD)*
BURGER KING 6 "Hungry Like The Wolf" by DURAN DURAN
  from 'Rio' *EMI: CDPRG 1004 (CD)*
BURGER KING 5 "You Ain't Seen Nothin'Yet" (R.Bachman)
  BACHMAN TURNER OVERDRIVE 'Roll On Down The Highway'
  MERCURY (UNIV): 550 421-2 (CD) -4 (MC)
BURGER KING 4 "Two Tribes" FRANKIE GOES TO HOLLYWOOD
  ZTT (Warner): 4509 93912-2 (CD) -4 (MC) -1 (LP)
BURGER KING 3 (WHOPPER) "Fire!" (Brown-Crane) CRAZY
  WORLD OF ARTHUR BROWN on 'CLASSIC ROCK' *SPECTRUM
  (UNIV): 550 645-2 (CD) -4(MC)* also on 'LIVE 1993'
  VOICEPRINT (Pinn): VP144CD (CD)
BURGER KING 2 "Who Do Ya Love" by GEORGE THOROGOOD &
  THE DESTROYERS from 'Move It On Over'
  DEMON (Pinn): FIENDCD 58 (CD)
BURGER KING 1 "Double Vision" by FOREIGNER on 'Best'
  ATLANTIC-E.WEST (TEN): 7567 80805-2(CD) WX 469C(MC)

C.& A. 1999 ads music composed by RICHARD WARMSLEY
  Pure Digital Nature Productions unavailable
C.& A. "Ya Ho He" by NC TRIBE *WOLFEN (German import
  through ZYX dist): WOL 00308 (CDs)*
CABLE AND WIRELESS "Homes" CHARLIE SPENCER-IAN RITCHIE
  Candle Music Productions unavailable
CADBURY (tastes like heaven) "Show Me Heaven" (M.McKee-
  J.Rifkin-E.Rackin) from film 'Days Of Thunder' orig
  MARIA McKEE on Coll 'Number One Movies Album' on
  POLYGRAM TV: 525 962-2 (CD)
CADBURY'S JESTIVE BISCUITS "Special Brew" BAD MANNERS
  'Best Of' *BLUEBEAT (UNIV): BBS(CD)(MC) 010 (CD/MC)*
CADBURY'S HIGHLIGHTS 2 "I'll Put You Together Again"
  (Don Black-Geoff Stephens) sung by ERROL BROWN orig
  HOT CHOCOLATE 'Greatest Hits' *EMI: CD(TC)EMTV 73*
CADBURY'S HIGHLIGHTS 1 "Sweet And Lovely" (G.Arnheim
  -Harry Tobias-Jules Lemare) sung by AL BOWLLY on
  "Very Thought Of You" *EMI CEDAR (EMI): CZ 306 (CD)*
CADBURY'S - *see also various brand names:'ROSES' etc*

CAFINESSE (DOUWE EGBERTS) Music composed by GARRY BELL
  Jeff Wayne Music Productions unavailable
CAFFREY'S ALES 4 (Storm Brewing ad) "Clubbed To Death"
  from 'THE MATRIX' *MAVERICK TEN: 9362 47419-2 (CD)*
  also from 'CLUBBED TO DEATH' by ROB D (DUGGAN) on
  VIRGIN IMPORT: 844 062-2 (CD)
CAFFREY'S ALES 3 "Brim Full Of Asha" by CORNERSHOP on
  WIIIJA (Vital): WIJ 81CD (CDs) WIJ 81 (7"s)
CAFFREY'S ALES 2 "Jump Around" (Muggeraud-Shrody) by
  HOUSE OF PAIN on *XL (TEN): XLS 32 CD (CDs) XLT 32
  (12"s) XLC 32 (MC)* + 'HOUSE OF PAIN' *XLCD(MC) 111*
CAFFREY'S ALES 1 'MILLER'S CROSSING' (Carter BURWELL)
  -S/T- *VARESE (Pinn): VSD 5288 (CD) deleted*

CALOR GAS CENTRAL HEATING "Reach Out I'll Be There"
(Holland-Dozier-Holland) *TV vers.unavailable* orig
FOUR TOPS on 'MOTOWN'S G.HITS' *POLY: 530 016-2 (CD)*

CAMPARI "Get Carter" (main theme from film) by ROY BUDD
-S/T- 1998 reissue: *ESSENTIAL (BMG): CINCD 001 (CD)*
*Colls: "Rebirth of The Budd" SEQUEL (BMG) NEMCD 927
(CD)* 'SOUND SPECTRUM' *WENCD 005 (CD)* 'THIS IS EASY'
VIRGIN: VTDCD 80 (CD) 'THIS IS CULT FICTION ROYALE'
VIRGIN: VTDCD 151 (CD)

CANDEREL "Perhaps Perhaps Perhaps" sung by DORIS DAY on
'LATIN FOR LOVERS' *COLUMBIA (Ten): 481 018-2 (CD)*
also on 'MUSIC TO WATCH GIRLS BY' (Collection) on
SONYMUSIC: SONYTV 67(CD)(MC) (2CDs/MC)

CAREX BODYWASH "Raindrops Keep Falling On My Head" from
'Butch Cassidy & The Sundance Kid'(Bacharach-David)
TV vers.unavailable orig -S/T- *POLY: 551 4330-2(CD)*

CARLING PREMIER 6 Medieval ad. "Vin-Da-Loo" (K.Allen)
FAT LES *TURTLENECK Telstar: CDSTAS 2982 (CDs)*

CARLING PREMIER 5 (high-wire cycle) "6 Underground"
SNEAKER PIMPS *CLEAN UP (Vital): CUP 036CD (CDs)*

CARLING PREMIER 4 "Tonight" by SUPERGRASS from 'IN IT
FOR THE MONEY' *PARLOPHONE (EMI): CD(TC)PCS 7388*

CARLING PREMIER 3 "Machine Gun" by The COMMODORES on
'14 Greatest Hits' *MOTOWN (UNIV): 530 096-2 (CD)*

CARLING PREMIER 2 "California Dreamin'" (J.Phillips)
MCA (BMG): MCSTD 48058 (CDs) also on 'MAMAS & PAPAS
Golden Greats' *MCA (BMG): DMCM 5001 CD*

CARLING PREMIER 1 "Cars" (Gary Numan) by GARY NUMAN
'Peel Sessions' *STRANGE FRUIT Rio (UNIV): SFMCD
202 (CD) SFMAC 202 (MC)*

CARLSBERG (Copenhagen ad) "They All Laughed" (G.& I.
Gershwin) sung by FRANK SINATRA
WARNER: W.469CD (CDs) W.469C (MC) also on COLLECT:
'COMPLETE REPRISE RECORDINGS' *9362 46013-2 (20CDs)*

CARTE NOIR Kenco "Try To Remember" fr.'The Fantasticks'
(H.Schmidt-T.Jones) *1998 TV version sung by* NORMAN
GROULX *unavailable* / previous version by RICHARD
DARBYSHIRE *VIRGIN (EMI): VSCDT(VSC) 1584 deleted*

CASTLEMAINE XXXX "Your Cheatin' Heart" (H.Williams)
GLEN CAMPBELL 'Country Classics' collection
MFP (EMI): CDMFP 6321 (CD) TCMFP 6321 (MC)

CELEBRATION MARS "Celebration" sung by KOOL & THE GANG
'Collection' *SPECTRUM-POLY: 551 635-2 (CD) -4 (MC)*

CELEBRATION MINI-BARS "Montok Point" (WILLIAM ORBIT) by
STRANGE CARGO 'Hinterland Strange Cargo Volume 4'
WEA: 4509 99295-2 (CD)

CELLNET - see under B.T.

CENTER PARCS "Don't Fence Me In" (Cole Porter) by BING
CROSBY & The ANDREWS SISTERS on 'Singing Detective'
Conn.Coll (Pinn): POTTCD 200 (2CD) also on'You Must
Remember This' *HAPPY DAYS (BMG): CDHD 2652 (2CD)*

CESAR DOG FOOD "If You Leave Me Now" (Peter Cetera) by
CHICAGO *COLUMBIA (Ten): CD 32391(CD) 40-32391 (MC)*

CGU INSURANCE "Heroes" comp.& performed by DAVID BOWIE
from 'HEROES' *EMI PREMIER: CDP 797 720-2 (CD)*

CHANEL ALLURE "Spiritual High" (Anderson-Vangelis) by
MOODSWINGS featuring CHRISSIE HYNDE on 'Moodfood'
ARISTA-BMG (BMG): 74321 11170-2 (CD) -4 (MC) -1(LP)

CHANEL "L'EGOISTE" "Dance Of The Knights" from Act.1 of
'Romeo & Juliet' Op.64 (PROKOFIEV) *many recordings*

CHANNEL TUNNEL - see 'EUROTUNNEL'/'EURSTAR'

CHAT MAGAZINE "Girls Just Want To Have Fun" (R.Hazard)
TV version unavailable. original by CYNDI LAUPER on
'12 Deadly Cyns' *EPIC: 477 363 (CD) -4 (MC) -8 (md)*

CHELTENHAM & GLOUCESTER B.SOC. ('diver' ad) by ADIEMUS
"Cantus Song Of Tears" (K.Jenkins) KARL JENKINS and
LONDON PHILHARMONIC ORCH with MIRIAM STOCKLEY on
'THE JOURNEY - THE BEST OF ADIEMUS' on
VIRGIN (EMI): (CD)(TC)(MD) 946 (CD/MC/MD) also on
'NEW PURE MOODS' *VIRGIN (EMI): VTDCD 158 (2CD)*

CHILD IMMUNISATION - see HEALTH EDUCATION AUTHORITY

CHRISTIAN AID 2 "Get A Life" SOUL II SOUL feat CARON
WHEELER *TEN-VIRGIN: CDV 2724 (CD) and DISCD 90 (CD)*

CHRISTIAN AID 1 "First Time Ever I Saw Your Face"
(Ewan MacColl) ROBERTA FLACK on 'Best Of Roberta
Flack' *ATLANTIC (TEN): 250840 (CD) 450840 (MC)*

CHRISTIE'S AGAINST CANCER APPEAL "Angels" performed by
ROBBIE WILLIAMS *CHRYSALIS: CD(TC)CHS 5072 (CDs/MC)*

CITIZEN WATCHES "Kyrie" from 'Misa Criolla' Mass (Ariel
RAMIREZ) sung by JOSE CARRERAS with A.Ramirez,
Laredo Choral Salve and Bilbao Choral Society on
PHILIPS (UNIV): 420 955-2PH (CD) 420 955-4PH (MC)

CITROEN SAXO "Counter Clockwise Circle Dance" (Ly-O-Lay
Ale-Loya) from 'SACRED SPIRIT' Collection on
VIRGIN EMI: CDV 2753 (CD) TCV 2753 (MC)

CITROEN SAXO VTS "Possessed" arr.by BARRINGTON PHELOUNG
sung by ENGLISH CHAMBER CHOIR *unavailable*

CITROEN XANTIA "For A Few Dollars More" ENNIO MORRICONE
SILVA SCREEN (Koch): FILMCD 171 (CD)

CITROEN XSARA (CLAUDIA SCHIFFA strip ad) "Rise" by
CRAIG ARMSTRONG from 'The Space Between Us' on
MELANKOLIC-VIRGIN (EMI): CDSAD 3 (CD) SADD 3 (CDs)

CLOVER MARGARINE "Love Is In The Air (H.Vanda-G.Young)
TV vers: BOB SAKER *unavailable / original by* JOHN
PAUL YOUNG *LASERLIGHT (Target-BMG): 1221-2 (CD)*

CLUB MED "There'll Be Some Changes Made" (Higgins) sung
by DINAH WASHINGTON from 'Complete Dinah Washington
on Mercury Volume 4' *MERCURY IMPORT*

COCA-COLA 8 "When I Get Thirsty I Reach For.." (orig
commissioned track) *unavailable*

COCA-COLA 7 Soccer ad 1 "Dedicated To The One I Love"
MAMAS & PAPAS *MCA (BMG): DMCM 5001 (CD)*

COCA-COLA 6 Soccer ad 2 "Atomic" by BLONDIE
CHRYSALIS (EMI): CCD 1817 (CD) ZCHR 1817 (MC)

COCA COLA 5 (boys cricket) "Mustt Mustt" NUSRAT FATEH
ALI KHAN on 'Mustt Mustt' *REAL WORLD-VIRGIN (EMI):
CDRW 15 (CD) RWMC 15 (MC)*

COCA COLA 4 (olympics 96) "Temple Head" by TRANSGLOBAL
EXPRESS from 'Dream Of A Hundred Nations' on *Nation
RTM (Disc): NR 021CD (CD) NR 021C (MC) NR 021L (LP)*

COCA COLA 3 "Eat My Goal" by COLLAPSED LUNG
Deceptive (Vital): BLUFF 029CD (CDs) also on Coll
'The Beautiful Game' (Official Album Of EURO 96)
RCA (BMG): 74321 38208-2 (CD) -4 (MC)

COCA COLA 2 "Always Coca-Cola" (Terry Coffey and John
Nettles) *USA production unavailable*

COCA COLA 1 "The First Time" (Spencer-Anthony-Boyle)
ROBIN BECK *Mercury: MER(X) 270 (7"/12") deleted*

COCA COLA early commercials collection (65 COCA-COLA
ads) *inc* SEEKERS-TOM JONES-ARETHA FRANKLIN-PETULA
CLARK-RAY CHARLES-SUPREMES-BEE GEES-DRIFTERS-JAN &
DEAN-MOODY BLUES *EAST ANGLIA PRODUCTIONS: CC1 (CD)*

COCA COLA - see also DIET COKE

COMFORT EASY IRON "T'ain't What You Do" by BANANARAMA &
FUN BOY THREE *POLYGRAM: 828B 146-2 (CD)*

COMFORT SILK "Feeling Good" (Leslie Bricusse-Anthony
Newley) sung by NINA SIMONE on 'Feeling Good - The
Very Best Of' *VERVE (UNIV): 522 669-2 (CD)*

COMFORT CONDITIONER (2) "Words Of Love" (Buddy Holly)
TV ver. by Lisa Millett unavailable orig BUDDY HOLLY
'20 Gold.Greats' *MCA (BMG): MCLD(MCLC) 19220(CD/MC)*

COMFORT CONDITIONER (1) "Air That I Breathe" (Hammond-
Hazlewood) by The HOLLIES on 'TOTALLY COMMERCIALS'
EMI (EMI): 495 475-2 (CD) / EMI: CDP 746 238-2 (CD)

COMPAQ COMPUTERS cartoon ad "Bang On" by PROPELLERHEADS
from album 'DECKSANDRUMSANMDROCKANDROLL' on *WALL OF
SOUND (Vital): WALL(CD)(C) 015 or WALLD 039 (CDs)*

CONTINENTAL TYRES "La La Means I Love You" (Bell-Hart)
The DELFONICS *ARISTA (BMG): 07822 18979-2 (CD)*

CO-OP BANK "Lid Of The Stars" by GANGER from 'Hammock
Style' *DOMINO (Vital): WIGCD 047 (CD) WIGLP 047(LP)*

CROWN PAINTS "What A Difference A Day Made" (M.Grever-
S.Adams) *TV vers.sung by* AMANDA WHITE *unavailable*
orig DINAH WASHINGTON *CHARLY (Koch): CPCD 8008 (CD)*

CRUNCHIE (Cadbury) "I'm So Excited" (Pointer-Lawrence)
ORIG (82) POINTER SISTERS on 'Break Out' *PLANET-RCA
(BMG): FD 89450 (CD) FK 89450 (MC)*

DAEWOO CAR INSURANCE "Adagietto" from 'Symphony No.5'
(MAHLER) vers.on 'CINEMA CLASSICS 1' *NAXOS (Select)
8551151 (CD)*

DAZ AUTOMATIC "Bod" composed & perf.by DEREK GRIFFITHS
unavailable

DE BEERS - *see under* 'DIAMONDS'

DEL MONTE 2 "Happiness" *original version* by PIZZAMAN
COWBOY (Pinn)

DEL MONTE 1 "Humming Chorus" from 'Madame Butterfly'
(PUCCINI) *many recordings available*

DELTA AIRLINES "Adiemus" (Karl Jenkins) by ADIEMUS *feat*
MIRIAM STOCKLEY & LONDON PHILHARMONIC *VIRGIN (EMI):
CD(TC)VE 925 (CD/MC) and VEND 4 (CDs) VENC 4 (MCs)
also* 'NEW PURE MOODS' *VIRGIN EMI: VTDCD 158 (2CD)*

DERBYSHIRE BUILD.SOC. "Everybody's Free (To Feel Good)"
   by ROZALLA *PULSE (BMG): PULSEMC 11 (MC)*
DIAMONDS (A Diamond Is Forever) (De Beers) "Palladio"
   (Karl Jenkins) LONDON PHILHARMONIC ORCH (K.Jenkins)
   on 'Palladio' *SONY CLASSICAL: SK(ST) 62276 (CD/MC)*
DIET COKE 3 "I Just Wanna Make Love To You" (Dixon)
   PATTI D'ARCY JONES *unavailable*
DIET COKE 2 "I Put A Spell On You" (Hawkins) sung by
   NINA SIMONE on Coll 'Feeling Good-The Very Best'
   VERVE (UNIV): 522 669-2 (CD) -4 (MC)
DIET COKE 1 "I Just Wanna Make Love To You" (Dixon)
   ETTA JAMES *MCA (BMG): MCSTD(MCSC) 48003 (CDs/MC)*
   also on COLL 'V.Best Of Blues Brother-Soul Sister'
   DINO (Pinn): DINCD(MC) 115 (CD/MC)
DIRECT DEBIT "Hit" by The WANNADIES from 'Bagsy Me" on
   INDOLENT (Vital): DIECD 008 (CD)
DISCOVERY - see LAND ROVER

DOCKERS LEVI 2 "Tu Vuo Fa L'Americano" (Nisa-Carosone)
   TV version arranged by JOHN ALTMAN for JEFF WAYNE
   MUSIC PRODUCTIONS *unavailable* / original version by
   RENATO CAROSONE (1959) *deleted*
DOCKERS LEVI 1 "I'm Sitting On Top Of The World" by
   BOBBY DARIN (Coll 'Totally Commercials') on
   EMI: E495 475-2 (CD)
DORITOS "Walk This Way" original by RUN DMC & AEROSMITH
   'Greatest Hits' *PROFILE (Pinn): FILECD 474 (CD)*
DULUX (Petals/Pastel shades) "Dulux Theme" composed
   by KEVIN SARGENT *unavailable*
DULUX ONCE "The Moldau" from 'Ma Vlast' (My Country) by
   SMETANA *vers* 'CLASSIC ADS' *EMI CLASS: 7243 568116-2*
DUNLOP TYRES 3 "Moonage Daydream" (Bowie) *TV version*
   unavailable. orig on -S/T- 'ZIGGY STARDUST T.MOTION
   PICTURE' by DAVID BOWIE - *EMI: CDP 780411-2 (CD)*
DUNLOP TYRES 2 "21st Century Schizoid Man" (R.Fripp)
   by KING CRIMSON 'In The Court Of The Crimson King'
   EG-VIRGIN (EMI): EGCD 1 (CD) EGMC 1 (MC)
DUNLOP TYRES 1 "Venus In Furs" (Lou Reed) VELVET
   UNDERGROUND 'Velvet Underground With Nico' *POLYDOR
   (UNIV): 823 290-2 (CD) 823 290-4 or SPEMC 20 (MC)
   SIRE (TEN): W0224CD (CDs) W0224C (MC) W0224 (7"s)*
DUSTBUSTER *see* 'BLACK & DECKER DUSTBUSTER'

EAGLE STAR INS.2 "You Spin Me Round (Like a Record)"
   by DEAD OR ALIVE on 'Youthquake' *EPIC (Ten):
   477 853-2 (CD)*
EAGLE STAR INS.1 "Driving In My Car" by MADNESS from
   'Divine Madness' *VIRGIN (EMI): (CD)(TC)(V) 2692*
EGYPT HOLIDAYS "Triumphal March" from 'AIDA' (VERDI)
   special arrangement-not available
ELIZABETH SHAW CHOCOLATES "Crazy" by WILLIE NELSON
   'Very Best Of' *MFP (EMI): CD(TC)MFP 6110 (CD/MC)*
ENERGY CENTRE - see BRITISH GAS

EUROMILK "The Clog Dance" from ballet 'LA FILLE MAL GARDEE' (HEROLD) *EMI EMINENCE: CDEMX 2268 (CD)*

EUROSTAR "Sway" (Ruiz-Gimbel) DEAN MARTIN 'Very Best' *EMI-CAPITOL: 496 721-2 (CD) -4 (MC)*

EUROTUNNEL (Le Shuttle) "Bean Fields" (Simon Jeffes) The PENGUIN CAFE ORCHESTRA on 'Signs Of Life' *EG (UNIV): EEGCD 50 (CD) EGEDC 50 (MC)*

FAMILY CREDIT TAX "WFTC" by VINCE POPE (Beat Route Productions) *unavailable*

FELIX CAT FOOD 4 "I Wanna Know" sung by JOHN E.PAUL on compilation 'Out On The Floor Tonight" on *GOLDMINE (Vital): GSCD 107 (CD)*

FELIX CAT FOOD 3 (RASCALS REWARD) "You've Been Away" by RUBIN on compilation 'WIGAN CASINO STORY' *GOLDMINE (Vital): GSCD 103 (CD)*

FELIX CAT FOOD 2 "Mambo No.5" (P.Prado) PEREZ PRADO 'King Of Mambo' *RCA (BMG): ND 90424 (CD) also on* 'OUR MAN IN HAVANA' *RCA (BMG): 74321 58810-2 (CD)*

FELIX CAT FOOD 1 "The Entertainer"(Scott Joplin)'The STING' *see under FILM* (2) "I'm The Leader Of The Gang (I Am)" (G.Glitter-Mike Leander) GARY GLITTER 'Back Again' *PICKWICK (Carlton): PWKS(PWKMC) 4052*

FERRERO ROCHER "The Ambassador's Party" dance version ROBERT FERRERA *KRUNCHIE (Pinn): KCD1(CDs) KT1(12")* *deleted.* orig music (Graham De Wilde) *unavailable*

FIAT BRAVO 2 / BRAVA "2:1" (Matthews) by ELASTICA 'Elastica' *DECEPTIVE (Vital): BLUFF 014(CD(MC)(LP)*

FIAT BRAVO *see also* FIAT PUNTO 1

FIAT CINQUENCENTO "But I Do" (Paul Gayten-R.Guidry) CLARENCE FROGMAN HENRY *MCA (BMG): MCSTD(MCSC) 1797 (CDs/MC)* 'But I Do' *CHESS (Charly): CDRED 13 (CD)*

FIAT PUNTO 3 "Wink and a Smile" from 'SLEEPLESS IN SEATTLE' sung by HARRY CONNICK JNR *COLUMBIA (Ten): 473 598-2 (CD) -4 (MC)*

FIAT PUNTO 2 "Music To Watch Girls By" (Velona-Ramin) sung by ANDY WILLIAMS on 'MUSIC TO WATCH GIRLS BY' *SONYMUSIC (Ten): SONYTV 67(CD)(MC) (2CDs/MC)* *also* 'BEST OF': *481 037-2 (CD) -4 (MC) 667 132-2*

FIAT PUNTO 1 "Amami Se Voui" sung by TANZIN DALLEY *TV vers.unavailable.* Coll (1) 'ITALY AFTER DARK' vers.by MARISA FIORDALISA *EMI: CDP 780023-2 (CD) TCEMS 1458 (MC)* / Coll (2) 'FESTIVAL DE SAN REMO VOL.1' vers. TONINA TORRIELLI *Butterfly Mus (Imp)*

FIAT SEICENTO "Cum on Feel The Noize" (Holder-Lea) by SLADE 'Very Best' *POLYDOR: 537 105-2 (CD) -4(MC)*

FIRST DIRECT (Bob Mortimer ads) "Gurney Slade theme" MAX HARRIS (1960) on Collect. 'NO.1 JAZZ ALBUM' *POLYGRAM TV: 553 937-2 (2CD)*

FISHERMAN'S FRIEND "I Want You" by the UTAH SAINTS *FFFR-LONDON (UNIV): FCD 213 (CDs) 828 379-2 (CD)*

FLORA 3 "Everybody Needs Somebody To Love (S.Burke-B. Berns-J.Wexler) from 'The BLUES BROTHERS' *TV vers. unavailable* (BLUES BROS. -S/T-) *(TEN) K.250715 CD*

FLORA 2 "You Make Me Feel So Young" (M.Gordon-Joseph
Myrow) *TV version by* TERESA JAMES *unavailable*
FLORA 1 "If I Love Ya Then I Need Ya" (Bob Merrill)
EARTHA KITT on 'BEST OF EARTHA KITT' on *MCA (BMG):
MCLD 19120 (CD) MCLC 19120 (MC)*
FORD (1999 global campaign) "Just Wave Hello" sung by
CHARLOTTE CHURCH from 'CHARLOTTE CHURCH' album
SONY CLASS: SK 64356 (CD)
FORD (1999 feature models) "Song Of Ancient Mariner"
by VANGELIS from -S/T- '1492 Conquest Of Paradise'
EAST WEST (War): 4509 91014-2 (CD) WX 497C (MC)
FORD COUGAR "Born To Be Wild" (Easy Rider) STEPPENWOLF
-S/T- EASY RIDER *MCA (BMG): MCLD 19153 (CD)*
FORD DIRECT (Insurance) "I Love Your Smile" by SHANICE
on 'Inner Child' *MOTOWN (UNIV): 530 008-2 (CD)*
FORD ESCORT 2 "Jeepers Creepers" *TV vers.unavailable*
LOUIS ARMSTRONG version on 'JEEPERS CREEPERS' on
MILAN (BMG): CDCH 602 (CD)
FORD ESCORT 1 "Lovely Day" (B.Withers) BILL WITHERS
COLUMBIA: 491 961-2 (CD) -8 (md) 'Best Of'
FORD FIESTA 2 "Roadrunner" by The ANIMALS on
EMI: 498 936-2 (CD)
FORD FIESTA 1 "My Favourite Game" by The CARDIGANS
'GRAN TURISMO' *STOCKHOLM (UNIV): 559 081-2 (CD)
559 081-4 (MC) 567 991-2 (CDs)*
FORD FOCUS "You Gotta Be" sung by DES'REE
SONY S2: 666 893-2 (CDs) -4 (MC) also on 'I Ain't
Movin' *SONY: 475 843-2 (CD) -4 (MC) -8 (md)*
FORD GALAXY "Light and Shadow" VANGELIS '1492 CONQUEST
OF PARADISE' *WARNER: 4509 91014-2 (CD) WX 497C (MC)*
FORD KA 2 track from 'Leftism' by LEFTFIELD *COLUMBIA
SONY: HANDCD 2 (CD) HANDMC 2 (MC) HANDLP 2 (LP)*
FORD KA 1 "Bright Red" (Anderson) *TV vers.unavailable*
original LAURIE ANDERSON version on "Bright Red"
WB (TEN): 9362 45534-2 (CD) -4 (MC)
FORD MONDEO 2 'Zetec' "Casta Diva" from opera 'NORMA'
(BELLINI) sung by MARIA CALLAS w.MILAN LA SCALA OR
"Legends Of The 20th Cent." *EMI: CDM 520 653-2 (CD)*
FORD MONDEO 1 "Speaking Of Happiness"(Radcliffe-Scott)
by GLORIA LYNNE *ISLAND (UNIV):CID(CIS) 659 (CDs/MC)
also on* -S/T- 'SEVEN' *EDEL (Pinn): 0022432CIN (CD)*
FORD PROBE 2 "Fly Me To The Moon" (Bart Howard) by
JULIE LONDON 'Best Of Liberty Years' *Liberty (EMI)
EMI CZ 150 (CD) also on Coll* 'THIS IS THE RETURN
OF CULT FICTION' *VIRGIN (EMI): VTCD 112 (CD) and on*
'TOTALLY COMMERCIALS' *EMI (EMI): 495 475-2 (CD)*
FORD PROBE 1 "You Can Go Your Own Way" (Chris Rea)
sung by CHRIS REA on 'Best Of Chris Rea' *EAST-WEST
(TEN): 4509 98040-2 (CD) -4 (MC)*
FORD PUMA "Bullitt" score from 1968 -S/T- LALO SCHIFRIN
W.BROS (Fra.imp)(TEN/Discovery): 9362 45008-2 (CD)
Black Dog remix *WEA: WESP 002(CD=CDs)(C=MC)(T=12s)*
FORD TRANSIT "Coz I Luv You" (N.Holder-J.Lea) by SLADE
'Very Best Of' *POLYDOR: 537 105-2 (CD) -4 (MC)*

FORTE (TRUSTHOUSE) "Le Lac De Come" (Galas) *(TV version unavailable)* vers.on 'Classics' by FRANCK POURCEL & HIS ORCHESTRA on *EMI: CZ 22(CD) TCEMS 1263 (MC)*

FOX'S BISCUITS "Gonna Be A Stranger" sung by SELAH *unavailable*

FRIEND'S PROVIDENT "Chi Mai" (also 'LIFE & TIMES OF DAVID LLOYD GEORGE' BBC) by ENNIO MORRICONE on *'PURE MOODS' VIRGIN (EMI): VTCD 28 (CD)* also *'FILM MUSIC OF ENNIO MORRICONE' VIRGIN: CD(TC)VIP 123*

FRIZZELL INSURANCE 2 "My Special Angel" (Jimmy Duncan) MALCOLM VAUGHAN on COLL 'Totally Commercials' *EMI: 495 475-2 (CD)*

FRIZZELL INSURANCE 1 "Everything Is Beautiful" (Ray Stevens) RAY STEVENS on 'Hit Singles Collectables' on *DISKY (THE): DISK 4510 (CD)*

FRUIT & NUT (Cadbury) "Dance Of The Mirlitons" from The 'Nutcracker Suite' (TCHAIKOVSKY) *many versions incl* 'The Classic Experience' *EMI: CDEMTVD 45 (2 CD's)*

FRUIT PASTILLES Rowntrees "Wheels" (Norman Petty) orig The STRING-A-LONGS *Ace (Pinn): CDCHD 390 (CD)*

FRUIT-TELLA 2 "Let's Talk About Sex" by SALT'n' PEPA feat PSYCHOTROPIC on 'Greatest Hits' *FFFR LONDON (UNIV): 828 291-2 (CD) 828 291-4 (MC)*

FRUIT-TELLA 1 "I'm Too Sexy" (Fred/Richard Fairbrass Rob Manzoli) RIGHT SAID FRED *TUG (BMG): CDSNOG 1 (CDs) CASNOG 1 (MC) 12SNOG 1 (12"s) SNOG 1 (7"s)*

FRUITOPIA music (Robin Guthrie-Simon Raymonde) by The COCTEAU TWINS *specially recorded and not available*

FUJI FILMS "Gorecki" by LAMB from 'LAMB' on *FONTANA (UNIV): 532 968-2 (CD) -4 (MC)*

GALAXY "Summertime" (Porgy and Bess) (G.& I.Gershwin) BILLIE HOLIDAY 'Essential Billie Holiday' on *COLUMBIA (Ten): 467 149-2 (CD) -4 (MC)*

GALAXY RIPPLE "Guns Of Navarone" The SKATALITES (1967) *Col* 'OLD SKOOL SKA' *SNAPPER (Pinn): SMDCD 139 (CD)*

GAP 7 "Just Can't Get Enough" *TV version unavailable* orig by DEPECHE MODE *MUTE (Vital): CDSTUMM 101 (CD)*

GAP 6 "Mellow Yellow" *TV version unavailable.* orig by DONOVAN *SEE FOR MILES (Pinn): SEECD 300 (CD)*

GAP 5 "Dress You Up" *TV version unavailable.* orig by MADONNA *SIRE (Warner): WX 20C (MC)*

GAP 4 Khaki-A-Go-Go "BLOW UP A-GO-GO"(Wild Elephants) by JAMES CLARKE *V2 (Pinn): VVR 5009523 (CDs) and VVR 5010073 (2CDs) VVR 5009525 (MC)* 'EXCLUSIVE BLEND VOL.2' *BLOWUP (SRD): BU 011CD*

GAP 3 Khaki Country "Crazy Little Thing Called Love" (F.Mercury) by DWIGHT YOAKAM *REPRISE: W497CD (CDs)*

GAP 2 Khaki Soul "Lovely Day" by BILL WITHERS 'Best Of' *COLUMBIA (Ten): 491 161-2 (CD) -8 (md) / ALSO* "I Hear Music On The Streets" by UNLIMITED TOUCH 'ESSENTIAL UNDERGROUND DANCEFLOOR CLASSICS VOL.2' *DEEP BEATS (BMG): DGPCD 705 (CD)*

GAP 1 (Khaki Swing) "Jump Jive & Wail" by LOUIS PRIMA *CAPITOL (EMI): CDP 794 072-2 (CD)*

GAS - *see under heading BRITISH GAS*

GEORGE AT ASDA 3 "Would You" by TOUCH AND GO
  V2 (3M-Pinn): VVR 500 308-2 (CDs) -4 (MC) -6 (12"s)
GEORGE AT ASDA 2 "Ready To Go" by REPUBLICA from
  1997 album 'Republica' *DE CONSTRUCTION (BMG):*
  74321 41052-2 (CD) -4 (MC)
GEORGE AT ASDA 1 "Get Ready For This" by 2 UNLIMITED
  'Get Ready' *PWL (TEN): HFCD 47 (CD) HFC 47 (MC)*
GIFTAID "Sunny Afternoon" (Ray Davies) The KINKS
  POLYDOR TV: 516 465-2 (CD) -4 (MC)
GILLETTE / GILLETTE CONTOUR PLUS "Looking Sharp" (Jake
  Holmes) and "The Best A Man Can Do" *unavailable*
GO AIRWAYS (a, Madrid) "Affair In Madrid" LALO SCHIFRIN
  'MISSION IMPOSSIBLE' *GNP (Greyhound) GNPD 8028 (CD)*
GO AIRWAYS (b, Italy) "Sequence Three" GIAN PIERO REVER
  BERI-FRANCO REVERBERI from 'EROTICA ITALIA' on
  RCA (BMG): 74321 54193-2 (CD)
GO AIRWAYS (c, Malaga) "Come Ray and Come Charles" by
  MICHEL LEGRAND from 'In Flight Entertainment Vol.1'
  DERAM (UNIV): 535 300-2 (CD) -4 (MC)
GOLF (VW) - see under VOLKSWAGEN GOLF
GORDON'S GIN "Hustler" by PETER LAWLOR (Water Music Pr)
  unavailable
GRATTAN'S CATALOGUE "I Get The Sweetest Feeling"
  (V.McCoy-A.Evelyn) JACKIE WILSON on 'Very Best'
  ACE (Pinn): CDCHK 913 (CD)
GREEN GIANT NIBLETS "The More I See You" sung by
  CHRIS MONTEZ on compilation 'And The Beat Goes On'
  POLYGRAM: 535 693-2 (CD)
GROLSCH "I'm Bored" by IGGY POP on 'PoP Music' on
  RCA CAMDEN (BMG): 74321 41503-2 (CD)
GUINNESS 10 (Surfer) "Phatt Planet" by LEFTFIELD
  HARD HANDS-HIGHER GROUND (Ten): HAND 057CD1 (CD1)
  HAND 057CD2 (CD2) HAND 057T (12"s) from the album
  'RHYTHM & STEALTH' *(Ten): HANDCD 4 (CD)*
GUINNESS 9 "Hear The Drummer Get Wicked" CHAD JACKSON
  BIG WAVE: BWR 36 (7"s) deleted
GUINNESS 8 Swimmer "Mambo No.5" *TV vers.unavailable*
  original by PEREZ PRADO ORCH on 'OUR MAN IN HAVANA'
  RCA (BMG): 74321 58810-2 (CD) also RCA: ND 90424 CD
GUINNESS 7 (Strange But Untrue) 'First Big Weekend' by
  ARAB STRAP *CHEMICAL UNDERGROUND (SRD):CHEM 007 (7")*
GUINNESS 6 (St.Patrick's Day) "I'm Sitting On Top Of
  The World'" (Young-Henderson-Lewis) by AL JOLSON
  PRESIDENT (BMG): PLCD 542 (CD)
GUINNESS 5 (old man) "Story Of My Life" (B.Bacharach-
  Hal David) sung by MICHAEL HOLLIDAY 'EP COLLECTION'
  SEE FOR MILES (Pinn): SEECD 311 (CD)
GUINNESS 4 (bicycle) "I'm Gonna Wash That Man Right
  Out Of My Hair" (R.Rodgers-O.Hammerstein II) sung
  by MITZI GAYNOR from -S/T- of 'South Pacific' *RCA*
  (BMG): ND 83681 (CD) NK 83681 (MC)

GUINNESS 3 (zoom) "We Have All The Time In The World"
(John Barry-Hal David) LOUIS ARMSTRONG from the
JAMES BOND -S/T- 'ON HER MAJESTY'S SECRET SERVICE'
EMI-LIBERTY (EMI): CZ 549 (CD) also on CDEMTV 89
GUINNESS 2a "Laudate Dominum" / 'Vesperae
Solennes De Confessore' (K.339) (Mozart) *vers:* KIRI
TE KANAWA-ST.PAUL'S CATHEDRAL CHOIR *PHILIPS (UNIV):
412 629-2 (CD)*   (2b)"Party Time" (L.Smith-Gerry Th
omas-Dave Gibson) FATBACK BAND on "Raising Hell" on
ACE-SOUTHBOUND (Pin): CDSEWM 028(CD) SEWC 028(MC)
GUINNESS 1 mambo dance "Guaglione" PEREZ PRADO ORCH.
'King Of Mambo' *RCA (BMG): ND 90424 (CD) also on*
'OUR MAN IN HAVANA' *RCA: 74321 58810-2 (CD)*

HAAGEN-DAZS ICE CREAM "Make Yourself Comfortable" (Bob
Merrill) sung by SARAH VAUGHAN on 'Golden Hits'
Mercury (UNIV): (CD/MC)
HALIFAX 9 "I and I Survive" by BURNING SPEAR 'Chant
Down Babylon' *ISLAND (UNIV): 524 190-2 (2CD set)*
HALIFAX 8 "Consider Yourself" from 'Oliver' (Lionel
Bart) *TV vers.unavailable* / see also under 'OLIVER'
HALIFAX 7 (Kaleidoscope) "Surfin'" by ERNEST RANGLIN
from 'Below The Bassline' *ISLAND (UNIV): IJCD4002
(CD) IJMC 4002 (MC) IJLP 4002 (LP) also CDsingle*
HALIFAX 6 Week In The Life "The Gift" (Wisternoff-
Warren-MacColl) by WAY OUT WEST and JOANNA LAW *De
CONSTRUCTION (BMG):74321 40191-2(CD) -4(MC) -1(12")*
HALIFAX 5 Financial Services (figures skating ad)
"Clock" by DAVID A.STEWART *unavailable*
HALIFAX 4 Financial Services "Moon River" (H.Mancini
Johnny Mercer) *TV vers.unavailable* / HENRY MANCINI
Coll 'IN THE PINK' on *RCA (BMG): 74321 24283-2 (CD)*
HALIFAX 3 Financial Services "Sentinel" (M.Oldfield)
from 'Tubular Bells II' MIKE OLDFIELD on *WEA (TEN)
4509 90618-2 (CD) -5 (DCC) WX 2002(C) (LP/MC)*
HALIFAX 2 "Let's Do It (Let's Fall In Love)"(Porter)
EARTHA KITT 'Best Of' *MCA (BMG): MCLD(MCLC 19120*
HALIFAX 1 "Our House" (Jenkins-Nash) CROSBY STILLS
NASH & YOUNG on 'Deja Vu' *ATLANTIC: K.250001 (CD)*
HALL'S MENTHOLYPTUS "Air That I Breathe" (A.Hammond-
Lee Hazlewood) The HOLLIES *EMI: CDP 746238-2 (CD)*
HALL'S SOOTHERS "Addicted To Love" by ROBERT PALMER on
'Addictions' *ISLAND: CID(ICT) 9944 (CD/MC) 4 (MC)*
HARVEY'S BRISTOL CREAM "The Clog Dance" from 'La Fille
Mal Gardee' (Louis HEROLD) ROYAL OPERA HOUSE ORCH.
(John Lanchbery) *DECCA (UNIV): 436 658-2 (CD)*
HEALTH EDUCATION : CHILD IMMUNISATION CAMPAIGN
"Sanvean: I Am Your Shadow" (Gerrard-Claxton) LISA
GERRARD from album 'The Mirror Pool' *4AD-B.Banquet
(RTM-DISC): CAD 5009CD (CD) CADC 5009 (MC)*
HEAT Magazine "Donaueschingen" by KRUDER & DORFMEISTER
'K.& D.Sessions' *STUDIO K7 (Vital): K7 073CD (2CD)*
HEINEKEN "Intermezzo" Cavalleria Rusticana" (MASCAGNI)
'OPERA AT THE MOVIES' *NAXOS (Select): 8.551164 (CD)*

HEINZ "Big Noise From Winnetka" (Crosby-Rodin) by the
   BOB CROSBY ORCHESTRA on '22 ORIGINAL RECORDINGS'
   HINDSIGHT (Target-BMG-Jazz Music): HCD 409 (CD)
HEINZ (Baked Beans/Tomato Soup etc) "Inkanyezi Nezazi"
   (J.Shambalala) THE LADYSMITH BLACK MAMBAZO 'Best
   Of LADYSMITH BLACK MAMBAZO' *POLYG 565 298-2 (CD)*
HEINZ WEIGHT-WATCHERS (Mexican Chili) "Leaving Rome"
   by JO JO BENNETT on Collection 'BLOW MR.HORNSMAN'
   TROJAN (USA IMPT.through CD1STOP): TJN 2572 (CD)
HELLMANNS MAYONAISSE 2 "Only Way To Dress" by BRUCE
   SMITH (ex Public Image) *unavailable*
HELLMANNS MAYONAISSE 1 "Waltz Of The Flowers" from
   'The Nutcracker Suite' (TCHAIKOVSKY) *var.records*
HIGHLIGHTS - *see under* 'CADBURY'S HIGHLIGHTS'
HONDA ACCORD 2 "Mystical Machine Gun" by KULA SHAKER
   COLUMBIA: KULA 22(CD)(CDX)(MC) taken from album
   'PEASANTS PIGS & ASTRONAUTS'*SHAKER 2(CD)(MC)(LP)*
HONDA ACCORD 1 "We've Gotta Get Out Of This Place"
   (Mann-Weil) *TV version by* SPACE *unavailable*
   orig by The ANIMALS *(EMI): CZ 10 (CD)*
HONDA SOLAR POWERED CAR "Stabat Mater Dolorosa" by
   PERGOLESI *TV version unavailable*
HOVIS BREAD "Largo" from Symphony No.9 in E.Min Op.95
   by DVORAK *many recordings available*
HP SAUCE 2 (HP Makes A Bacon Sandwich) "Soul Singer"
   unavailable library track
HP SAUCE 1 "That's The Way I Like It" (Casey-Finch)
   KC & SUNSHINE BAND 'Get Down Tonight - Very Best'
   EMI: 494 019-2 (CD) -4 (MC)
HSBC (MIDLAND BANK) "She's A Star" JAMES on 'Whiplash'
   FONTANA (UNIV): 534 354-2 (CD) JIMCD 16 (CDs)
HUGO BOSS (Bar model) "What It Means" by BARRY ADAMSON
   'As Above So Below' *MUTE (Vital): CDSTUMM 161 (CD)*
HYUNDAI "Adagietto" from 'Symphony No.5' (G.MAHLER)
   vers 'CINEMA CLASS.1' *NAXOS (Select):8.551151 (CD)*

ICELAND 2 "It Must Be Love" (Labi Siffre) by MADNESS
   on 'Divine Madness' *VIRGIN: CDV(TCV) 2692 (CD/MC)*
ICELAND 1 "Driving Home For Christmas" (Rea) CHRIS REA
   'BEST OF CHRIS REA' *MAGNET (TEN): 243841-2 (CD)*
IKEA "Walk Away" by The CAST from 'All Change'
   POLYDOR (Univ): 529 312-2 (CD)
IMPERIAL CANCER RESEARCH FUND "United We Stand" (Tony
   Hiller-Peter De Simmons) original by BROTHERHOOD
   OF MAN (1970) *DERAM (UNIV): 820 632-2 (CD)*
IMPULSE 4 ('Bar' ad) "Sugar Is Sweeter" (Bolland)
   C.J.BOLLAND from album 'ANALOGUE THEATRE'
   FFFR (UNIV): 828 909-2 (CD) -4 (MC)
IMPULSE 3 "Female Of The Species" by SPACE 'Spiders'
   GUT (BMG): GUTCD 1 (CD) GUTMC 1 (MC) GUTLP 1 (LP)
IMPULSE 2 (art class) "Pressure Drop" by The MAYTALS
   ISLAND Records (UNIV): number unconfirmed
IMPULSE 1 "Fever" (Cooley-Davenport) by PEGGY LEE on
   Coll 'TOTALLY COMMERCIALS' *EMI: 495-475-2 (CD)*

INTEL PENTIUM 3 "Song 2" by BLUR
  EMI: FOOD(CD)(MC)(LP) 19
INTEL PENTIUM 2 "Shake Your Groove Thing" PEACHES
  & HERB on Coll 'Then That's What They Call Disco'
  ELEVATE (3MV-SONY): CDELV 05 (CD)
INTEL PENTIUM 1 "Play That Funky Music" WILD CHERRY
  on 'Night Fever' *GLOBAL TV (Pinn): RADCD 24 (2CD)*
IONICA "Something In The Air" (John Keene) *TV Version:*
  OCEAN COLOUR SCENE *unavailable.(orig.by* THUNDERCLAP
  NEWMAN)'Golden Hits 60s' *PICKWICK: BOXD 16P CDx3*
IRELAND (TOURISM) ('Live A Different Life' ad) "Dream"
  by The CRANBERRIES from 'Everyone Else Is Doing It
  So Why Can't We' *ISLAND (UNIV): CID(ICT)(ILPS) 8003*
ITS INVESTMENT TRUST (S'Wonderful ad) "Via Con Mi" by
  PAOLO CONTI 'Best' *EAST WEST (Ten): 7559 79512-2 CD*
JAGUAR S.TYPE "History Repeating" The PROPELLERHEADS
  and SHIRLEY BASSEY *WALL OF SOUND (Vital):*
  WALLD 036 (CDs) WALLCS 036 (MC) WALLT 036 (12"s)
JEAN PAUL GAULTIER mus.from "Norma" (BELLINI) complete
  work on *EMI: CMS 763000-2 (3CD set)*
JJB SPORTS 2 "At The Sign Of The Swingin' Cymbal" by
  BRIAN FAHEY (Alan Freeman Pick Of The Pops Theme)
  'WORLD OF SOUND' *BBC W.WIDE (Koch): 33635-2 (CD)*
JJB SPORTS 1 "Everyone's A Winner" (Errol Brown) orig
  HOT CHOCOLATE 'Greatest Hits' *EMI: CD(TC)EMTV 73*
JOHN SMITH'S BITTER (Ladybirds ad) "Je T'aime Moi Non
  Plus" (S.Gainsbourg) JANE BIRKIN-SERGE GAINSBOURG
  (69) on 'Amoreuse' coll *PICKWICK: PWKS 539 (CD)*
JOHN SMITH'S EXTRA STRONG (Penguins) "Help Yourself"
  (Gli Occhi Miel)(C.Donida-J.Fishman) *TV vers.not
  available* TOM JONES *DERAM (UNIV): 820 559-2 (CD)*
JOHN SMITH'S MILLER LITE - *see* MILLER
JOHNSON'S PLEDGE "Humming Chorus" ('Madam Butterfly')
  (PUCCINI) *TV version unavailable*
KELLOGG'S 'Help Yourself' campaign "Keep Young and
  Beautiful" (Dubin-Warren) *TV version unavailable
  version by* HARRY ROY & HIS ORCHESTRA on
  MFP (EMI): CDMFP 6361 (CD)
KELLOGG'S BRAN FLAKES "Spirit In The Sky" (Greenbaum)
  orig by NORMAN GREENBAUM on 'Spirit In The Sky-Back
  Home Again' *EDSEL-DEMON (Pinn): ECDC 470 (CD) also*
KELLOGG'S CORN FLAKES 2 "Brideshead Revisited" theme
  GEOFFREY BURGON *SILVA SCREEN (Koch): FILMCD 117 CD)*
KELLOGG'S CORN FLAKES 1 "Oh What A Beautiful Mornin'"
  (Rodgers-Hammerstein) Glenn Miller **Army Air Forces**
  Training Command Or'CLASSIC THEMES FROM TV & RADIO'
  HAPPY DAYS (BMG): 75605 52283-2(CD) also '1943-44
  Rare Broadcast Perf.' *LASERLIGHT (BMG): 1571-2 (CD)*
KELLOGG'S NUTRI-GRAIN Overture to 'The Thieving Magpie'
  (La Gazza Ladra)(ROSSINI)*many recordings available*
KELLOGG'S RICE CRISPIES CHOCOLATE SQUARES "Buttons"
  (Thompson-Jarvis) MCCASSO PRODUCTIONS *unavailable*
KELLOGG'S SPECIAL K "Turning Ground" CAROLINE LAVELLE
  from 'Spirit' *WEA (TEN): 4509 98137-2(CD) -4(MC)*

KENCO CARTE NOIR "Try To Remember" fr.'The Fantasticks'
(H.Schmidt-T.Jones) *1998 TV version sung by* NORMAN
GROULX *unavailable* / previous version by RICHARD
DARBYSHIRE *VIRGIN (EMI): VSCDT(VSC) 1584 deleted*

KENCO COFFEE "Bailero" from 'Songs Of The Auvergne' by
(CANTELOUBE) ENGLISH CHAMBER ORCHESTRA on *VIRGIN:
VC 7907-14-2 (CD)* / LAMOUREUX CONCERT ORCHEST with
Victoria De Los Angeles - *EMI: CDC 747970-2 (CD)*

KENCO RAPPOR "She Sells Sanctuary" by The CULT on Coll
'Pure Cult' *BEGGARS BANQUET (TEN): BEGA 130CD (CD)*

KFC 4 "We Are Family" *originally by* SISTER SLEDGE on
'Very Best' *ATLANTIC-WEA: 9548 31813-2 (CD) -4(MC)*

KFC 3 "She's Not There" (Rod Argent) *original by* The
ZOMBIES *feat* COLIN BLUNSTONE on 'Singles A's& B's'
SEE FOR MILES (Pinn): SEECD 30 (CD)

KFC 2 (Fire Station) "Disco Inferno" from) 'SATURDAY
NIGHT FEVER' by TRAMMPS -S/T- *POLY: 825 389-2 (CD)*

KFC 1 "Canteloupe (Island)" (Herbie Hancock) version
US3 on Collection 'Jazz Moods' *TELSTAR (BMG): TCD
2722 (CD) STAC 2722 (MC) ALSO by* HERBIE HANCOCK on
'Best Of H.Hancock' *BLUENOTE (EMI): BNZ 143 (CD)*

KILKENNY IRISH BEER 2 "She Moves Through The Fair"
by SHANE McGOWAN *TV version unavailable. other
recordings inc.* FEARGAL SHARKEY on 'CELTIC MOODS'

KILKENNY IRISH BEER 1 "Need Your Love So Bad" (Green)
FLEETWOOD MAC on 'Greatest Hits' *SONY Nice Price
Collection: R.460704-2 (CD) -4 (MC)*

KINGSMILL 2 "Smile" (C.Chaplin) sung by NAT KING COLE
CAPITOL (EMI): CDS 795 129-2 (CD set)

KINGSMILL 1 GOLD "Storybook" composed & performed by
STEVE PARSONS *unavailable*

KISS 100 "Mucho Mambo" by SHAFT (based on 'Sway')
WONDERBOY-UNIVERSAL: WBOYD 015 (CDs) WBOYC 015 (MC)

KLEENEX Double Velvet "Blue Velvet" (Wayne-Morris)
TV version unavailable / orig BOBBY VINTON "16 MOST
REQUESTED SONGS' *COLUMBIA (Ten): 469 091-2 (CD)*

KNORR (various) "Perpetuum Mobile" by The PENGUIN CAFE
ORCHESTRA on 'Preludes Airs and Yodels' *AMBIENT-
VIRGIN (EMI): AMBT 15 (CD)*

KNORR TASTE BREAKS "Peckings" by the BALISTIC BROTHERS
unavailable

KP LOWER FAT CRISPS "It Started With A Kiss" (E.Brown)
HOT CHOCOLATE *RAK (EMI): CDP 746375-2 (CD)*

KRAFT "Mellow Yellow" DONOVAN on 'TOTALLY COMMERCIALS'
EMI (EMI): 495 475-2 (CD)

KRONENBERG 2 "She" sung by CHARLES AZNAVOUR
ENGLISH VERSION *EMI PREMIER: PRMTVCD 4 (CD)*
FRENCH VERSION *EMI: CDEMC 3716 (CD) deleted*

KRONENBERG 1 (French rap) "A La Claire Fontaine" by
MC SOLAAR on 'Prose Combat' *POLY: 521 289-2 (CD)*

KWIK-FIT song based on "The Thing" (Grean) original by
PHIL HARRIS *LIVING ERA-ASV (Koch): CDAJA 5191 (CD)*

L'EGOISTE AFTERSHAVE Chanel "Dance Of The Knights"
from Act.1 of 'Romeo And Juliet' Op.64 (PROKOFIEV)
LADYBIRD COLL 2 Woolworths "Into Each Life Some Rain
Must Fall" (Roberts-Fisher) by The INK SPOTS
CONNOISSEUR (Pinn): XPOTTCD 201 (CD)
LADYBIRD COLL 1 Woolworths "Q5 Theme"/"Ning Nang
Nong" (Spike Milligan) SPIKE MILLIGAN 'A Collect
ion Of Spikes' *EMI: CDECC 11 (CD) ECC 11 (MC)*
LANCOME PERFUME - see 'OUI'

LAND ROVER DISCOVERY "Mad Alice Lane (A Ghost Story)"
(Peter Lawlor) by LAWLOR *WATER (3MV-Sony) WAT 1CD
(CDs) WAT 1MC(MC) see COLL* 'SPIRITS OF NATURE'
LANSON CHAMPAGNE "Tipitina" PROFESSOR LONGHAIR 'Big Chi
ef' *TOMATO/PLAY IT AGAIN SAM (Vital):598109320 (CD)*
LE SHUTTLE - see 'EUROTUNNEL'
LEA & PERRINS WORCESTER SAUCE "Sorcerer's Apprentice"
(Paul DUKAS) *many recordings available*
LEE JEANS 3 (Hard To Be Parted From ad) music by
JOHN ALTMAN *Jeff Wayne Productions unavailable*
LEE JEANS 2 "Legends" by SACRED SPIRIT *VIRGIN (EMI):
VSCDT 1598 (CDs) VSC 1598 (MC) from album* 'SACRED
SPIRIT 2' *VIRGIN (EMI): CDV(TCV) 2827 (CD/MC)*
LEE JEANS 1 "Baby Lee" (J.L.Hooker) JOHN LEE HOOKER
with ROBERT CRAY on 'The Healer' *SILVERTONE (Pinn)
ORE(CD)(MC) 508 (CD/MC) / ORE(CD)(C) 81 (CDs/MC)*
LEMSIP 3 "Always Care For Me" (Mike Connaris for
MCASSO Productions) *unavailable*
LEMSIP 2 "Moon River" (Henry Mancini-Johnny Mercer)
HENRY MANCINI *see 'Henry Mancini' Collections*
LEMSIP 1 "Goodnight Sweetheart Well It's Time To Go"
(Calvin Carter-James Hudson) by The SPANIELS on
'Play It Cool' *CHARLY R&B: CDCHARLY 222 (CD)*
LEVI 31 (Sta-Prest) 'Guitar' based on "The Bass Walks"
(Bert Kaempfert) *original by* BERT KAEMPFERT ORCH
POLYDOR number unconfirmed
LEVI 30 (Sta-Prest) "Flat Beat" from 'Analogue Worms
Attack" (Quentin Dupieux) MR.OIZO *F.COMM (Vital)
F.104CD (CDs) /* note: Country song insert "What's
Happened To Me" sung by DON GIBSON *Hickory (USA)*
LEVI 29 'Shapes' "I'm Not a Fool" by COCKNEY REJECTS
'Great.Hits Vol 1.' *DOJO (DISC): DOJOCD 136 (CD)*
LEVI 28 'Tremor' "Whine 'n' Grine" by PRINCE BUSTER
ISLAND (UNIV):CID 691(CDs) CIS 691(MC) also 'WHINE
'N' GRINE-CLUB SKA '67' *ISLAND: IMCD 254(CD)*
LEVI 27 'White Tab' "Nanny In Manhattan" by the LILYS
CHE-COALITION (War): CHE 77CD (CDs) CHE 77C (MC)
LEVI 26 (kung-fu) "Stepping Stones" (Johnny Harris)
JOHNNY HARRIS ORCH *EMI: CD(TC)LIC 108 (CDs/MCs)*
LEVI 25 (mermaid) "Underwater Love" (Nina Miranda)
by SMOKE CITY *JIVE (Pinn): JIVECD 422 (CDs) JIVEC
422 (MC) JIVET 422 (12"s) deleted*
LEVI 24 "The Art Of Self Destruction Part 1" by
NINE INCH NAILS *ISLAND (UNIV): IMCD 8041 (CD)*

LEVI 23 (sci-fi) "Spaceman" (Jasbinder Mann) perform
by BABYLON ZOO from 'Boy With The X-Ray Eyes"
EMI:CD(TC)EMC 3742 (CD/MC)
LEVI 22 "Boombastic" (Shaggy-Robert Livingston) by
SHAGGY on *VIRGIN (EMI): VSCDT 1536 (CDs) VST
1536 (12"s) VSC 1536 (MC) / album: CD(TC)V 2782*
LEVI 21 "Novelty Ways" (Biosphere) BIOSPHERE on
APOLLO (Vital): APOLLO 020(CD)(MC) 020
LEVI 20 "Turn On Tune In Cop Out" (Norman Cook) by
FREAKPOWER on *4TH & BROADWAY (Isl-Poly): BRCD 606*
LEVI 19 (Accident/Hospital) "Fall" (Peter Lawlor)
p.White Water Music *unavailable*
LEVI 18 (Swimming Creek) "Inside" (Peter Lawlor) by
STILTSKIN on *WHITE WATER (3MV/Sony): LEV 1CD
(CDs) LEV 1C (MC) LEV 1 (7"s) LEV 1T (12"s) delet.*
LEVI 17 "Tackle" by CHRIS BLACKWELL *unavailable*
LEVI 16 "Ring Of Fire" (Merle Kilgore-June Carter) by
JOHNNY CASH 'Biggest Hits' Coll *SONY MUSIC:
CD 32304 (CD) 40.32304 (MC)*
LEVI 15 "Heart Attack And Vine" by SCREAMING JAY
HAWKINS *EPIC (Ten): 659109-2(CDs) -4(MC) deleted*
also on *DEMON (Pinn) FIENDCD(MC) 211 (CD/MC)*
LEVI 14 "Piece Of My Heart" (B.Berns-Jerry Ragavoy)
by ERMA FRANKLIN *EPIC (TEN): 472413-2 (CD)*
JANIS JOPLIN *CBS: CBS 32190-2 (CD) 40-(MC)*
LEVI 13 "Mad About The Boy" ('Words & Music') (Noel
Coward) DINAH WASHINGTON 'Best Of' *MERCURY (UNIV)
512214-2(CD) -4(MC)* / KEN MACKINTOSH & HIS ORCH
'Mac's Back' *PRESIDENT (Target): PLCD 532(CD)*
LEVI 12 "20th Century Boy" (Marc Bolan) by T.REX
'Ultimate Collect.' *TELSTAR (BMG): TCD(STAC) 2539*
LEVI 11 "Should I Stay Or Should I Go" The CLASH *CBS
SONY M:'Story Of The Clash' 460244-2 (CD) -4 (MC)*
LEVI 10 "The Joker" (S.Miller) the STEVE MILLER BAND
on *'The Joker' FAME-MFP (EMI): CDFA 3250 (CD)*
LEVI 9 "Can't Get Enough" by BAD COMPANY '10 From 6'
ATLANTIC (TEN): 781625-2 (CD) also 'Bad Company'
ISLAND: ILPS(ICT) 9279 (LP/MC)
LEVI 8 "Ain't Nobody Home" B.B.KING 'Best Of'
MCA: MCLC 1612 (MC) CMCAD 31040 (CD)
LEVI 7 "Be My Baby" (Phil Spector-E.Greenwich-Jeff
Barry) The RONETTES on 'Dirty Dancing' -S/T-
RCA (BMG): BK 86408 (MC) BD 86408 (CD)
LEVI 6 "Mannish Boy" by MUDDY WATERS
LEVI 5 "C'mon Everybody" (E.Cochran-Jerry Capehart)
EDDIE COCHRAN *LIBERTY (EMI): various collections*
LEVI 4 "When A Man Loves A Woman" (C.Lewis-A.Wright)
PERCY SLEDGE *OLD GOLD (Pinn): OG 9496 (7"s)*
LEVI 3 "Stand By Me" (B.E.King-M.Stoller-J.Leiber)
BEN E.KING *ATLANTIC: A.9361 (7"s)*
LEVI 2 "Wonderful World" (S.Cooke-L.Adler-H.Alpert)
SAM COOKE *RCA: PD 87127 (CD)*
LEVI 1 "I Heard It Through The Grapevine" (Whitfield
-Barrett Strong) orig MARVIN GAYE *MOTOWN*

LEVI DOCKERS 2 "Tu Vuo Fa L'Americano" (Nisa-Carosone)
TV version arranged by JOHN ALTMAN for JEFF WAYNE
MUSIC PRODUCTIONS *unavailable* / original version by
RENATO CAROSONE (1959) *deleted*
LEVI DOCKERS 1 "I'm Sitting On Top Of The World" by
BOBBY DARIN (Coll 'Totally Commercials') on
EMI: 495 475-2 (CD)
LEXUS - *see under* TOYOTA LEXUS
LILT "Come Dig It" (Machel Montano) by MACHEL *LONDON*
(UNIV): LONCD 386 (CDs) LONCS 386(MC) deleted
LINDT CHOCOLATE "Wild Is The Wind" (Tiomkin-Washington)
sung by NINA SIMONE on Coll 'TOTALLY COMMERCIALS'
EMI (EMI): 495 475-2 (CD)
LISTERINE MOUTHWASH "Kiss" (Prince) TOM JONES with Art
Of Noise on 'At This Moment' *JIVE (BMG): TOMCD 1*
(CD) TOMTC 1 (MC) TOMTV 1 (LP)
LITTLEWOODS (Berkertex Fashion Range) "Perdido" (Juan
Tizol-H.Lenk-E.Drake) DUKE ELLINGTON ORCHESTRA on
'16 Most Requested Songs' *COLUMBIA (Ten):*
476 719-2 (CD) 476 719-4 (MC)
LLOYDS TSB 2 "What Can I Do" 'Talk On Corners' The
CORRS *LAVA-ATLANTIC (TEN): 7567 83051-2(CD) -4(MC)*
LLOYDS TSB 1 "Let's Work Together" by CANNED HEAT
LIBERTY (EMI): CZ 226 (CD) TCGO 2026 (MC) 'Best Of'
LLOYDS BANK (Black Horse ad 2) music prod.by JOE & CO
based on Symph.No.1 (BRAHMS) *TV version unavailable*
LLOYDS BANK (Black Horse ad 1) "Zion Hears The Watchmen
Singing" ('Wachet Auf,Ruft Uns Die Stimme')
"Cantata No.BWV 140" (J.S.BACH) *various recordings*
LOCKETS "After The Storm" from 'Pastoral Symphony'
Number 9 (BEETHOVEN) *many recordings available*
LUCOZADE 4 "Lara Croft Goes To The Dogs" by ANTHONY
PARTOS *unavailable*
LUCOZADE 3 'Quadrophenia' "Louie Louie" by KINGSMEN
on 'SON OF CULT FICTION' *VIRGIN: VTCD 114 (CD)*
also on *CHARLY (Koch): CPCD 8160 (CD)*
LUCOZADE 2 (NRG) "Leave You Far Behind" LUNATIC CALM
MCA (BMG): MCSTD 40131 (CDs) deleted
LUCOZADE 1 "EVA" (Prilly-Perrault-Badale)JEAN JACQUES
PERREY *MOOG INDIGO BGP-ACE (Pinn): CDBGPM 103 (CD)*
LUNN POLY (THOMSON AT) "Love Is Just Around The Corner"
(Robin-Gensler) played by LEO ADDEO & HIS ORCH
RCA (BMG): 07863 66647-2 (CD)
LURPAK 2 "Flight Of The Bumblebee" (RIMSKY-KORSAKOV)
and part of "Requiem" (FAURE) *many recordings*
LURPAK 1 "Spread A Little Happiness" from the Musical
'Mr.Cinders' (V.Ellis-R.Myers-G.Newman) - STING on
A.& M.: AMS 8242 (7"s) see also 'Mr.Cinders' SHOWS
LYNX 4 (Pied-Piper ad) "Bentley's Gonna Sort You Out"
BENTLEY RHYTHM ACE from 1997 self titled album
PARLOPHONE EMI: (CD)(TC)PCS 7391 & PCS 7391 (2LP)
LYNX 3 (caveman) "Mini-Skirt" (D.J.Esquivel) ESQUIVEL
on 'LOUNGECORE' *RCA (BMG): 74321 57815-2 (CD) and*
'Cabaret Manana' *RCA (BMG): 07863 66657-2 (CD)*

LYNX 2 (elevator) original music produced by NOVA
    PRODUCTIONS (Paris, France) *unavailable*
LYNX 1 "Boom Shack-A-Lak" by APACHE INDIAN
    from 'Make Way For The Indian' on *ISLAND (UNIV):*
    CID 8016 (CD) ICT 8016 (MC) ILPSD 8016 (2LP)

M.& M.'s 2 "Nocturne in E.Flat" (CHOPIN)
    various recordings available
M.& M.'s 1 (fun pack) "Trip Your Trigger" by
    Stephen Williams *unavailable*
McCAINS HOME FRIES "I'm A Believer" (Neil Diamond) The
    MONKEES on 'Greatest Hits' *WEA: 0630 12171-2 (CD)*
McCAINS MICRO CHIPS "Yakety Yak" (Jerry Leiber-Mike
    Stoller) *originally by* COASTERS on 'Greatest Hits'
    ATLANTIC (TEN): 7567 90386-2 (CD)
McDONALDS 9 'Bacon Roll ad' "ALYA" MINISTRY OF SOUND
    compilation 'TRANCE NATION 2' on
    MINISTRY OF SOUND (3MV-TEN): TN(CD)(MC) 2 (CD/MC)
McDONALDS 8 'Straws' "BATMAN DANCING" (Jim Elliott)
    CRITICAL MASS (BMG): (-)
McDONALDS 7 & COKE "Everlasting Love" (Cason-Gayden)
    THE LOVE AFFAIR *COLUMBIA: 483 673-2 (CD)*
McDONALDS 6 "Three Steps To Heaven" (Eddie Cochran)
    TV version unavailable. original EDDIE COCHRAN on
    'EP COLLECT.' *SEE FOR MILES (Pinn): SEECD 271 (CD)*
McDONALDS 5 Money For Nothing) "Vissi D'arte" from
    'TOSCA' (PUCCINI) *TV Version unavailable*
McDONALDS 4 "Singin' In The Rain" (N.H.Brown-A.Freed)
    TV version by GAZEBO and DEE JACOBEE *EMI Records:*
    CDLIC 107 (CDs) TCLIC 107 (MC) deleted
    (b) "Don't Fence Me In" (Porter) *TV version by*
    Jeff Wayne Music Productions unavailable
McDONALDS 3 (Hat TRICK (football ad) "Life Of Riley"
    (I.Broudie) The LIGHTNING SEEDS from 'Sense' on
    VIRGIN (EMI): CDV 2690 (CD) TCV 2690 (MC)
McDONALDS 2 "Jungle Jamboree" by DUKE ELLINGTON ORCH
    on 'COMMERCIAL BREAK' *ASV (Koch): CDAJA 5281 (CD)*
McDONALDS 1 "Bottleneck Blues" by SYLVESTER WEAVER &
    WALTER BEASLEY on Collection 'COMMERCIAL BREAK'
    ASV (Koch): CDAJA 5281 (CD)
McEWANS LAGER ('Trainspotting' montage) "Do What You
    Wanna Do" EDDIE & THE HOT RODS on 'Best Of Eddie
    and The Hot Rods *ISLAND (UNIV): IMCD 156 (CD)*
McVITIES BN "Mah Na Ma Nah" (Piero Umiliani) orig.by
    The MUPPETS / PIERO UMILIANI *both versions deleted*
MALTESERS "Tease Me" by CHAKA DEMUS & PLIERS on 'Tease
    Me" *MANGO-ISLAND (UNIV): CIDMX(MCTX) 1102 (CD/MC)*
MARS BAR 2 "Lipsofa" by JOHN ALTMAN *unavailable*

MARS BAR 1" Crazy World" REDD KROSS on 'Phaseshifter'
    THIS WAY UP-ISLAND (UNIV): 518 167-2 (CD) -4 (MC)
MARTINI V2 2 (Italian Job ad) "Return Of The Carboot
    Techodisco Roadshow" from 'BRA' BENTLEY RHYTHM ACE
    PARLOPHONE-EMI: CD(PCS)7391 (CD/MC) PCS 7391 (2LP)

MARTINI V2 1 "Oceana" (Matt Fowler) by MUMBLES (USA) 'AUDIO ALCHEMY' *UBIQUITY (Timewarp): URCD 020 (CD)*

MASTERCARD "Angelina" (Allan Roberts-Doris Fisher-Paolo Citarella-L.Prima) perf.by LOUIS PRIMA ORCH *CAPITOL (EMI): CZ 423 (CDP 794072-2) (CD) also on CO11* 'TOTALLY COMMERCIALS' *EMI: 495 475-2 (CD)*

MASTERCARD (Football) "I Believe" by EMF from 'Schubert Dip' *EMI-PARLOPHONE: CD(TC)PCS 7353 (CD/MC)*

MAXWELL HOUSE 2 "Going Home" (M.Knopfler) from film 'Local Hero' -S/T- *VERTIGO (UNIV): 811 038-2 (CD) VERCD 81 (CDsigle)*

MAXWELL HOUSE 1 "The Mission" (Ennio Morricone) from film -S/T- of the 1986 Robert De Niro-Jeremy Irons movie *VIRGIN (UNIV): CDV 2402 (CD) TCV 2402 (MC)*

MAYNARDS JUST FRUITS based on "Gimme Dat Ding" (Mike Hazlewood-Albert Hammond) orig The PIPKINS (1970)

MAYNARDS WINE GUMS "Hoots Mon" (Harry Robinson) by LORD ROCKINGHAM'S XI (1959) on *DECCA (UNIV): 882 098-2 (CDs) 882 098-4 (MC) 882 098-7 (7")* also 'BRITISH 'BEAT BEFORE THE BEATLES VOL.3' *EMI CDGO 2048 (CD)*

MAZDA CARS "Double Concerto for Saxophone & Cello" (Michael NYMAN) + JOHN HARLE-JULIAN LLOYD WEBBER *EMI CLASSICS: CDC 556413-2 (CD)*

MERCEDES BENZ A Class "Fun Lovin' Criminal" by FUN LOVIN' CRIMINALS from 'Come Find Yourself' on *CHRYSALIS (EMI): CD(TC)CHR 6113 (CD/MC/LP)*

MERCEDES BENZ 2 "Blues Cruise" by SIMON PARK *library track unavailable*

MERCEDES BENZ 1 "Mercedes Benz" (Oh Lord Why Won't You Buy Me A MERCEDES BENZ) sung by JANIS JOPLIN 'Pearl' *COLUMBIA (Ten): CD 480 415-2 (CD)*

MERCURY ONE-TO-ONE "Telephone and Rubber Band" (Simon Jeffes) PENGUIN CAFE ORCHESTRA 'Penguin Cafe Orch' *EG-VIRGIN (EMI): EEGCD 11(CD) OVEDC 429(MC)*

MICHELOB LAGER 2 "Possente-Possente" (Act 1 'AIDA') VERDI *(TV version unavailable)* also on Coll 'Relaxing Opera' *CFP (EMI): CD(TC)CFP 4664 (CD/MC)*

MICHELOB LAGER 1 "Put A Little Love In Your Heart" (J De Shannon-Holiday-Myers) *by* JACKIE DE SHANNON 'Definitive Collect' *EMI LIBERTY: 829 786-2 (CD) also on* 'TOTALLY COMMERCIALS' *EMI: 495 475-2 (CD)*

MICROSOFT "Heroes" (D.Bowie) sung by DAVID BOWIE *EMI: CDP 797720-2 (CD)*

MICROSOFT WINDOWS 95 "Start Me Up" (M-Jagger-K.Richard) ROLLING STONES 'Tattoo You' *VIRGIN : CDV 2732 (CD)*

MILK 2 Dancing Bottles "Grasshopper's Dance" (Ernest BUCALSSI) PALM COURT THEATRE ORCH. 'Picnic Party' *CHANDOS: CHAN 8437 (CD) LBT 002 (MC)*

MILK 1 "Clog Dance" from ballet 'LA FILLE MAL GARDEE' (Louis HEROLD) *EMI EMINENCE: CDEMX 2268 (CD)*

MILK TRAY (Cadbury's) (orig)"The Night Rider" (Chris Adams) by ALAN HAWKSHAW on Coll 'SOUND GALLERY' on *EMI STUDIO TWO: CD(TC)TWO 2001 (CD/MC) also on* 'TOTALLY COMMERCIALS' *EMI (EMI): 495 475-2 (CD)*

MILLER 7 (Beer Breath) "Multi Family Garage Sale" by
LAND OF LOOPS *POP (Cargo-Greyhound): UP 011 (7"s)*
MILLER 6 (Honk Bobo) "900 NUMBER" (Jones) by 45 KING
TUFF CITY (Cargo): TUFFEP 3001 (12"s)
MILLER 5 (Opera) "Je Veux Vivre" from ROMEO & JULIET
(GOUNOD) *version by* INESSA GALANTI (debut album)
*CAMPION: RRCD 1335 (CD) / also available complete
version EMI: CDS5 56123-2 (CD)*
MILLER 4 (Rob) "Girl At The Bus Stop" by MY DRUG HELL
VOLTONE (Shellshock-Pinn-DISC): VTONECD 001X (CD)
MILLER 3 "Town Without Pity" (D.Tiomkin-N.Washington)
sung by EDDI READER on *BLANCO Y NEGRO
(TEN): NEG 90CD (CDs) NEG 90MC (MC)*
MILLER 2 Lite "Somewhere Down The Crazy River" ROBBIE
ROBERTSON *GEFFEN-MCA (BMG): GFLD 19294 (CD)*
MILLER 1 Lite "He Ain't Heavy He's My Brother" by The
HOLLIES *EMI: CDP 746238-2 (CD)*
MINUMUM WAGE "Fine Time" by The CAST from 'All Change'
POLYDOR: 529 312-2 (CD)
MITSUBISHI CARISMA "Zip-A-Dee-Doo-Dah" (Gilbert-Wrubel)
(Disney's 'Song Of The South') *orig* 'DISNEY'S HIT
SINGLES' *WALT DISNEY (UNIV): WD 11563-2 (CD)*
MOTOROLA (Wings) "You Can't Always Get What You Want"
(Jagger-Richards) The ROLLING STONES from 'Let It
Bleed' *DECCA (UNIV): 820 052-2 (CD)*
MULLERICE 2 "The Saint" by ORBITAL -S/T- 'THE SAINT'
VIRGIN: CDVUS 126 (CD)
MULLERICE 1 "(This Is The) Captain Of Your Ship"
original by REPARATA & The DELRONS *deleted*

N.S.P.C.C. "Pie Jesu" (Andrew LLoyd Webber) sung by
CHARLOTTE CHURCH on Coll 'Voice Of An Angel'
SONY CLASSICAL: SK 60957 (CD)
NAT.WEST 4 'Air Miles' ad "Maybe Tomorrow" sung by
TERRY BUSH from TV series 'The Littlest Hobo'
unavailable
NAT.WEST 3 'Apartments' ad music mix by HOWIE B
unavailable
NAT.WEST 2 'Breakaway' ad "Ghostrider" FAT MACHINE
recording unconfirmed
NAT.WEST 1 'Escape' ad "Self Preservation Society"
from 'THE ITALIAN JOB' *currently unavailable*
NATREL PLUS Flower Girl "Read My Lips (Saturday Night
Party)" (A.Party) ALEX PARTY *CLEVELAND CITY BLUE
(3MV Sony): CCICD 17000 (CDs) CCI 17000 (12"s)*
NATREL PLUS (Willow ad) "Sex Sleep Eat And Drink" by
KING CRIMSON *DISCIPLINE-VIRGIN (EMI): KCCDY1 (CDs)*
NESTLE - *see under* brand name e.g. 'LION BAR'
NIKE 5 TIGER WOODS ad "Straight Down The Middle"
(Burke-Van Huesen) BING CROSBY on 'Quintessential'
CASTLE (BMG): CTVMC 211 (MC)
NIKE 4 Roll on 2002, World Cup ad "You're Nobody Now"
EMBRACE from 'Good Will Out' *HUT-VIRGIN (EMI)
CDHUT 46 (CD) HUTMC 46 (MC) MDHUT 46 (MD)*

NIKE 3 (Brazil Football.airport ad) "Mas Que Nada"
   (a) TAMBA TRIO from 'NOVA BOSSA RED HOT AND VERVE'
   VERVE (UNIV): 535 884-2 (CD) and TLCD 34 (CDs)
   (b) SERGIO MENDEZ on 'MUNDO LATINO' *VERVE (UNIV):*
                         841 396-2 (CD) -4(MC)
   (c) RENALDO'S REVENGE (Re-mixed version) *(AM:PM)*
   (d) ECHOBEATZ (dance v) *ETERNAL: WEA176(CD)(T)(C)*
NIKE 2 Brazil Football.beach ad "Soul Bossa Nova" by
   QUINCY JONES 'MUNDO LATINO' *SONY:SONYTV2(CD)(MC)*
   also 'AUSTIN POWERS' *-S/T- POLYD: 162 112-2 (CD)*
NIKE 1 (Eric Cantona ad) "Parklife" by BLUR
   FOOD (EMI): FOOD(CD)(MC)(LP) 10
NIMBLE BREAD (orig ad) "I Can't Let Maggie Go" (Pete
   Dello) The HONEYBUS on 'At Their Best' on
   See For Miles (Pinn): SEECD 264 (CD)
NISSAN (theme) "Astrea" by JOHN HARLE on 'SILENCIUM'
   ARGO-DECCA (UNIV): 458 356-02 (CD)
NISSAN: (321 Committ:MICRA/ALMERA/PRIMERA) "Sugar Baby
   Love" (Bickerton-Waddington) RUBETTES 'Best Of'
   POLYDOR: 843 896-2 (CD) also 'It's The Sensation
   al Seventies' *MCI (THE-DISC): MCD 051 (CD)*
NISSAN ALMERA 2 "The Sweeney" theme by HARRY SOUTH
   see COLL.2,6,109,110,270,360,390,
NISSAN ALMERA 1 "The Professionals" (Laurie Johnson)
   see COLL.6,149,215,217,360,363,
NISSAN MICRA 3 "The Glory Of Love" (B.Hill) *version*
   JIMMY DURANTE *WB (TEN): 9362 45456-2 (CD)*
NISSAN MICRA 2 ('Hollywood') (Stuntman) "Beach Samba"
   ASTRUD GILBERTO on 'Beach Samba' *VERVE-POLYDOR*
   (UNIV.): 519 801-2 (CD)
NISSAN MICRA 1 "You Don't Love Me (No No No)" (Dawn
   Penn) DAWN PENN *deleted*
NISSAN PRIMERA 3 "Aquarium" 'Carnival Of The Animals'
   (SAINT-SAENS) I MUSICI DE MONTREAL (Turovsky)
   CHANDOS: CHAN 9246 (CD)
NISSAN PRIMERA 2 "Wild Thing" (Chip Taylor) TROGGS
   'Greatest Hits' *POLYGRAM: 522 739-2 (CD)*
NISSAN PRIMERA 1 New Primera 1996 "Lifted" sung by
   LIGHTHOUSE FAMILY from album 'Ocean Drive'
   POLDOR: 523 787-2(CD) -4(MC) / 851 669-2 CD s
NO.7 - see BOOTS NO.7

NOA by Cacherel "Song To The Siren" performed by
   THIS MORTAL COIL on album 'It'll End In Tears'
   4AD (Vital): CAD 411 (CD) CADC 411 (MC)
NOKIA "Gran Vals" (Francisco TARREGA) *version on COLL*
   '19th Century Guitar Fav.'played by NORBERT KRAFT
   NAXOS (Select): 8.553007 (CD)
NORWICH UNION "Part Of The Union" (Hudson-Ford)
   by the STRAWBS on 'Halcyon Days (Very Best Of)'
   A.& M. (UNIV): 540 662-2 (2CD)
NOUVELLE "Alla Hornpipe" from 'Water Music' (HANDEL)
   many recorded versions available

OLD SPICE 2 "I Feel Good" (Brown) JAMES BROWN 'Very Best of James Brown' *Poly: 845 828-2(CD) -4(MC)*

OLD SPICE 1 "Prima Vere" (Carmina Burana) (Carl ORFF) *various recordings available*

ONE-TO-ONE (Mercury) "Telephone and Rubber Band" (Simon Jeffes) PENGUIN CAFE ORCHESTRA on 'Penguin Cafe Orchestra' *EG-VIRGIN (EMI): EEGCD 11(CD) OVEDC 429(MC)*

OPEN UNIVERSITY "Lily Was Here" by DAVE STEWART and CANDY DULFER on compilation 'New Pure Moods' *VIRGIN VTDCD 158 (2CD)*

ORANGE 4 (dog ad) produced by HUM MUSIC PRODUCTIONS French vocal by CHRISTIAN MARTEC *unavailable*

ORANGE 3 "I Loves You Porgy" (Gershwin) from 'Porgy and Bess) by NINA SIMONE on 'TOTALLY COMMERCIALS' *EMI (EMI): 495 475-2 (CD)* also 'Blue For You-Very Best Of NINA SIMONE' *GLOBAL TV (BMG): RADCD 84*

ORANGE 2 "To Cure A Weakling Child" by The APHEX TWIN from the album 'Richard D.James LP' on *WARP (RTM-Disc):WARP(CD)(MC)43*

ORANGE 1 "Blow The Wind Southerly" arranged by JOCELYN POOK and featuring KATHLEEN FERRIER on *VIRGIN (EMI): VTDCD 158 (2CD)* 'New Pure Moods' orig= KATHLEEN FERRIER solo on 'World Of Kathleen Ferrier' *DECCA (UNIV): 430 096-2 (CD) -4 (MC)*

ORANGINA "Pida Me La" (Michel Berger) THE GYPSY KINGS "Greatest Hits" *COLUMBIA: 477242-2 (CD) -4 (MC)*

OUI Perfume (Lancome) "Everything's Gonna Be Alright" by SWEETBOX *RCA (BMG): 74321 60684-2 (CDs) -4 (MC)*

P.& O.STENA LINE "Riptide" (Gus Kahn-Walter Donaldson) by ROBERT PALMER taken from the album 'Riptide' *ISLAND (UNIV): IMCD 25 (CD)*

P.& O.FERRIES "Stompin'At The Savoy" (B.Goodman-A.Razaf E.Sampson-Chick Webb) BENNY GOODMAN on Collection 'TOTALLY COMMERCIALS' *EMI (EMI): 495 475-2 (CD)*

PANTENE SHAMPOO 2 "You and Me Song" by the WANNADIES 'Be A Girl' *INDOLENT-3MV (BMG): 74321 32546-2 (CD)*

PANTENE SHAMPOO 1 "Une Very Stylish Fille" by DIMITRI FROM PARIS on album 'Sacre Bleu' *EAST WEST (Warner) 0630 17832-2 (CD) -4 (MC)*

PEDIGREE PAL ('Dog Head' ad) "Jesus" music by the TIGER LILLIES *recording unconfirmed*

PENTIUM 2 "Song 2" by BLUR *EMI: FOOD(CD)(MC)(LP) 19 see also under* INTEL

PEPSI 6 MAX "Thank Heaven For Little Girls" (GIGI) by LUSCIOUS JACKSON *USA Studio session unavailable*

PEPSI 5 NEXT GENERERATION "Step To Me" SPICE GIRLS *PEPSI promotions only*

PEPSI 4 "Rhythm Of My Heart" by ROD STEWART *W.BROS (TEN): WO017(7")(T*

PEPSI 1 "It Takes Two" (William Stevenson-Sylvia
Moy) ROD STEWART & TINA TURNER (1990) *W.BROS.(TEN)*
ROD 1(T)(C)(CD) (7"/12"/MC/CD) /orig (1966) MARVIN
GAYE & KIM WESTON on *MOTOWN (UNIV): ZD 72397 (CD)*
PERRIER "Crossroads Blues" (Robert Johnson) on Collect
'King Of The Delta Blues Singers' *COLUMBIA (Ten):*
4844102 (CD) + *'Complete Rec.'Sony: 46222-2 (CD)* +
'CROSSROADS' The BRIDGE *ILC (Ten): ILC 1CDS (CDs)*
PERSIL Stain Release (based on 'Prelude in C.Minor')
(CHOPIN) TV ver:Paul Hart-Joe Campbell *unavailable*
PEUGEOT 106 2 KEY WEST/KEY LARGO (spec.edit.) "Open
Your Heart" (M.Ciccone-Gardner Cole-Peter Rafelson)
by MADONNA from 'True Blue' (86) *SIRE (TEN):*
925 442-2 (CD) WX 54C (MC) WX 54 (LP) & on single
PEUGEOT 106 1 "(We Want)The Same Thing" (R.Howells-
E.Shipley) BELINDA CARLISLE 'Best Of Belinda Vol.1'
VIRGIN (EMI): BELCD(MC)(MD)1 (CD/MC/md)
PEUGEOT 206 "Fly Away" by LENNY KRAVITZ from '5' on
VIRGIN (EMI): CDVUS 140 (CD) VUCMC 140 (MC) MDVUS
40 (md) also on VUSCD 141 (CDsingle) VUSC 141 (MC)
PEUGEOT 306 3 "Memories Are Made Of This" sung by
DEAN MARTIN *EMI-CAPITOL: 496 721-2 (CD) -4 (MC)*
PEUGEOT 306 2 "I Want Two Lips" by APRIL STEVENS on
'TEACH ME TIGER' *MARGINAL: MAR 086 (CD) deleted*
PEUGEOT 306 1 "Can't Take My Eyes Off You" sung by
ANDY WILLIAMS 'IN THE LOUNGE WITH ANDY' *COLUMBIA*
(Ten): 490 618-2(CD) -4(MC) + *481 037-2(CD) -4(MC)*
PEUGEOT 405 "Take My Breath Away"(Moroder-T.Whitlock)
BERLIN from -S/T- 'Top Gun' *COLUMBIA (Ten)*
PEUGEOT 406 3 "True Colors" sung by DOMINIQUE MOORE
unavailable (orig by CYNDI LAUPER)
PEUGEOT 406 2 (Kim Basinger) "Dream A Little Dream Of
Me" (Kahn-Schwandt-Andre) orig MAMAS AND PAPAS on
'20 GOLDEN GREATS' *MCA (BMG): MCLD 19125 (CD)*
PEUGEOT 406 1 "Search For The Hero" (Mike Pickering)
M.PEOPLE from 'Bizarre Fruit II' *De CONSTRUCTION*
(BMG): 74321 32817-2 (CD) -4 (MC)
PHILIPS PHILISHAVE FOR MEN "The Man Inside" by JOHN
SILVERMAN *unavailable*
PHILIPS RECORDABLE CDS "Jaan" (Talvin Singh) SOUNDS OF
THE ASIAN UNDERGROUND *Chrysalis*
PHILIPS STEREOS (TEST IT ON YOUR NEIGHBOURS) MOTORBASS
from 'PANSOUL' *DIFFERENT (Vital): DIF 001CD (CDs)*
PHILIPS WIDESCREEN "It's Getting Better All The Time"
(J.Lennon-P.McCartney) sung by GOMEZ *unavailable*
PHOSTROGEN (Dancing Hedgehogs) "Ma Belle Marguerita"
from 'Bless The Bride' (V.Ellis-AP.Herbert)sung by
GEORGES GUETARY *DRG (New Note-Pinn): CDXP 605 (CD)*
ROSSENDALE MALE VOICE CHOIR *CHANDOS: CHAN 6604 CD*
PHYSIO SPORTS 2 "Sound Of The Police" by KRS 1
specially recorded version
PHYSIO SPORTS 1 "Hersham Boys" by SHAM 69 'Best Of'
ESSENTIAL (BMG): ESMCD 512 (CD) also on 'First The
Best And The Last *POLYGRAM: 513 429-2 (CD)*

PILLSBURY THOMAS TOASTERS based on"Choo Choo Ch'Boogie"
  TV version unavailable original (1945) recorded by
  LOUIS JORDAN & HIS TYMPANI 5 on '5 Guys Name MOE'
  MCA (BMG): MCLD 19048 (CD) MCLC 19048 (MC)
PIRELLI TYRES 5 (Running Girl) "Elektrobank" CHEMICAL
  BROTHERS *FREESTYLE DUST-VIRGIN (EMI):CHEMSD 6 CDs*
PIRELLI TYRES 4 (Carl Lewis) music by Richard James
  performed by The APHEX TWIN *unavailable*
PIRELLI TYRES 3 (Sharon Stone) "Symph.No.9' BEETHOVEN
  + "Worldly Woman" by STEVE PARSONS *unavailable*
PIRELLI TYRES 2 "Riders On The Storm" (Densmore-Krieg
  er-Morrison-Manzarek) THE DOORS on 'L.A.Woman'
  ELEKTRA (WAR): K2-42090 (CD) K4 (MC)
PIRELLI TYRES 1 "Vesti La Giubba"'On With The Motley'
  from 'Pagliacci' (LEONCAVALLO) vers.inc: FRANCO
  CORELLI *EMI:CDC 747851-2(CD)* JOSE CARRERAS *HMV: EX
  290811-3 (2LP) EX 290811-5 (2MC)* LUCIANO PAVAROTTI
  DECCA:414590-2(2CD) JUSSI BJORLING *EMI:CDC 749503-2*
PIZZA HUT 2 'ITALIAN' "That's Amore" (Brooks-Warren)
  DEAN MARTIN 'Very Best' *EMI: 496 721-2 (CD) -4(MC)*
PIZZA HUT 1 "Hot Hot Hot" by ARROW on 'Sound Of Soul'
  BLATANT (Castle): BLATCD 11 (CD)
PLAN INTERNATIONAL (Charity) "Don't Give Up On Us"
  (Tony Macaulay) sung by DAVID SOUL on 'Best Of' on
  MUSIC COLLECTION INT (DISC/THE): MCCD 152 (CD)
PPP HEALTHCARE 2 "Boum!" CHARLES TRENET on 'PARIS..
  CAFE CONCERT' *FLAPPER (Pavilion-Pinn): PASTCD 9797
  also* 'Extraordinary Garden Best Of CHARLES TRENET'
  EMI: CDP 794 464-2 (CD) / also available on 'Boum'
  MUSIDISQUE (Target-BMG): MDF 10264 (CD)
PPP HEALTHCARE 1 "Someone To Watch Over Me" (George &
  I.Gershwin) *TV ver* DUSTY SPRINGFIELD *unavailable*

QUALITY STREET 2 "On The Street Where You Live" (Ler
  ner-Loewe) NAT KING COLE '20 Golden Greats' on
  CAPITOL (EMI): CDEMTV 9 (CD)
QUALITY STREET 1 "Magic Moments" (B.Bacharach-H.David)
  TV Version by NEIL INNES *unavailable*
QUITLINE (Anti-Smoking Campaign) "Ain't Go No - I Got
  Life" (Ragni-Rado-McDermott from 'Hair') sung by
  NINA SIMONE on "Feeling Good" *POLY: 522669-2 (CD)*

R.A.F. *see* **ROYAL AIR FORCE**

RADIO TIMES "Oriental Shuffle" by DJANGO REINHARDT and
  STEPHANE GRAPELLI Quintet Of The Hot Club Of France
  FLAPPER (Pav/Pinn): PASTCD 9738 (CD)
RAGU PASTA SAUCE 5 "Funiculi-Funicula" (DENZA) vers:
  JOSE CARRERAS *POLY: 400015-2 (CD)* LUCIANO PAVAROTTI
  DECCA: 410015-2 (CD) and 417011-2 (CD)
RAGU PASTA SAUCE 4 "Vesto La Guibba" ('I Pagliacci')
  (LEONCAVALLO) *various versions available)*
RAGU PASTA SAUCE 3 "La Donna E Mobile" ('Rigoletto')
  (VERDI) *various versions available*

RAGU PASTA SAUCE 2 "Anvil Chorus" from 'Il Travatore'
(VERDI) *various versions available*

RAGU PASTA SAUCE 1 Aria "Largo Factotem" from 'Barber
Of Seville' (ROSSINI) *various versions available*

RED MAGAZINE "Fun For Me" by MOLOKO 'Ladykillers Vol.1'
POLYGRAM TV: 535 536-2 (CD)

REEBOK 2 "Are You Experienced"JIMI HENDRIX EXPERIENCE
MCA (BMG): MCD 11608 (CD) MCC 116908 (MC)

REEBOK 1 (Raindrops ad) 2nd m/m Symphony No.7 in A.Maj
(BEETHOVEN) *TV ver: special arr.unavailable*

RENAULT CLIO (Nicole/Papa) "Johnny and Mary" (Robert
Palmer) by MARTIN TAYLOR on 'ONLY JAZZ ALBUM YOU'LL
EVER NEED' *RCA (BMG): 74321 66895-2 (2CD) -4 (2MC)*

RENAULT CLIO NEW (size matters) "Organ Grinder's Swing"
(Hudson-Parish-Mills) by JIMMY SMITH 'Jazz Masters'
VERVE (UNIV): 521 855-2 (CD)

RENAULT KANGOO 'Frisbee' "Run On" by MOBY from 'Play'
*MUTE (Pinn): CDSTUMM(CSTUMM) 172 (CD/MC) also on
CDMUTE 221 (CDs)*

RENAULT MEGANE SCENIC "Marvellous" The LIGHTNING SEEDS
'JOLLIFICATION' *SONY: 477 237-2 (CD) -4(MC) -8(MD)*

REVLON "Man I Feel Like A Woman" sung by SHANIA TWAIN
'Come On Over' *MERCURY (Univ): 170 081-2 (CD) -4MC*

RIBENA 3 'Robbie G' ad "I Feel Good" by JAMES BROWN
POLYDOR: 848 845-2 (CD)

RIBENA 2 'Smoothie' (1) "Norbert's Working" (2)"Bada
Bada Schwing" by FREDDIE FRESH & mixed by FATBOY
SLIM from CD 'Last True Family Man' on
EYE Q (Vital): EYEUKCD 017 (CD) EYEUK 040CD (CDs)

RIBENA 1 "Absurd" FLUKE *CIRCA-VIRGIN (EMI): YRCD 126
(CDs) YRT 126 (12"s)*

RIMMELL COSMETICS 2 "Girl Like You" by EDWYN COLLINS
'Gorgeous George'*SETANTA Vital: SET(CD)(MC) 014*

RIMMELL COSMETICS 1 "Allright" by SUPERGRASS from
'I Should Coco' *EMI PARLOPHONE: CD(TC)PCS 7373*

RIPPLE - *see* GALAXY RIPPLE

ROAD SAFETY (Don't Look Now) "Mysteries Of Love"
JULEE CRUISE from 'Floating Into The Night'
WB (TEN): 925 859-2 (CD) 925 859-4 (MC)

ROBERTSON'S GOLDEN SHRED "Jumping Bean" (R.Farnon)
'British Light Music Classics' NEW LONDON ORCH
HYPERION: CDA 66868 (CD)

ROBINSONS FRUIT DRINKS "Music Box Dancer" (Mills) by
FRANK MILLS on 'Happy Music-Best Of FRANK MILLS'
IMPORT (CD 1 STOP): MBD: MRC 1172CD and MRC 1172MC

ROCKY BAR (Fox's) based on "Rockin'Robin" *original by*
BOBBY DAY (58) 'Rockin'Robin' *ACE: CDCH 200 (CD)*
MICHAEL JACKSON (72) 'Best Of M.J.' *MOTOWN (BMG)*

ROLLING ROCK 2 "Drinking In L.A." by BRAN VAN 3000
CAPITOL-EMI: CDCL 811 (CDs) and TCCL 811 (MC)
from 'GLEE' *PARLOPHONE-EMI: 823 604-2 (CD) -4(MC)*

ROLLING ROCK 1 "Drifting Away" by FAITHLESS from
'Reverence' *CHEEKY (3MV-BMG):CHEKCD 500 (CD)*
CHEKK 500 (MC) CHEKLP 500 (2LP)

ROLO COOKIES "Skippy The Bush Kangaroo" (Eric Jupp) on
   coll 'TELEVISION'S GREATEST HITS VOLUME 5'
   EDEL-CINERAMA (Pinn): 002 274-2CIN (CD)
ROVER 75 "Proverb" by the STEVE REICH ENSEMBLE from
   'City Life' *NONESUCH-WARNER: 7559 79376-2 (CD)*
ROVER 200 3 "Downtown" (Hatch) sung by PETULA CLARK
   CASTLE (BMG): SELCD 508 (CD) SELMC 597 (MC)
ROVER 200 2 "This Town Ain't Big Enough For The Both
   Of Us" (Ron Mael) by SPARKS on 'Mael Intuition'
   ISLAND (UNIV): IMCD 88 (CD)
ROVER 200 1 "Englishman In New York" (Sting) by STING
   'Fields of Gold' *A.& M.(UNIV): 540307-2(CD) -4(MC)*
ROVER 400 4 "Ever Fallen In Love With Someone You
   Shouldn't 'ave" (P.Shelley) by The BUZZCOCKS on
   'SINGLES GOING STEADY' *EMI Fame: CDFA 3241 (CD)*
ROVER 400 3 "Donald, Where's Your Troosers" sung by
   ANDY STEWART *MFP (EMI): CDMFP 5700 (CD)*
ROVER 400 2 "Virginia Plain" (B.Ferry) ROXY MUSIC on
   'Thrill Of It All' *EG-VIRGIN (EMI): CDBOX 5 (CDx4)*
ROVER 400 1 "Rupert Bear" from 'The ENGLISH PATIENT'
   by GABRIEL YARED *FANTASY (Pinn): FCD 16001 (CD)*
ROVER 800 "Lullaby In Ragtime" (H.Nilsson) NILSSON
   on 'A Little Touch Of Schmilsson In The Night'
   RCA (BMG): ND 90582 (CD) NK 83761 (MC)
ROYAL AIR FORCE 3 "Keep Hope Alive" performed by
   CRYSTAL METHOD *SONY MUSIC: Sony CM3CD (CDs)*
ROYAL AIR FORCE 2 (Boredom) "Adagietto" from Symphony
   No.5 (G.MAHLER) *various recordings available*
ROYAL AIR FORCE 1 (Payload) "Crystal Method" special
   remix by 808 STATE *recording unconfirmed*
ROYAL BANK OF SCOTLAND mus.based on "Caravan Of Love"
   by HOUSEMARTINS *TV version unavailable.* Or.Vers.
   by HOUSEMARTINS *GO DISCS! (UNIV): 828 344-2 (CD)*
ROYAL LIVER ASSURANCE "Lean On Me" *TV vers unavailable*
   BILL WITHERS *SONY: 491 961-2 (CD) -8(md)* 'BEST OF'
ROYAL MAIL "Patricia" (Prado) *original by* PEREZ PRADO
   ORCH on 'KING OF MAMBO' *RCA (BMG): ND 90424 (CD)*
   and on 'OUR MAN IN HAVANA' *RCA: 74321 58810-2 (CD)*
ROYAL SUN AND ALLIANCE "Duo Seraphim"'L'Coronazione Di
   Poppea' (The Coronation Of Poppea) (MONTEVERDI) by
   JENNIFER LARMORE *HARM.MUNDI: HMC 901330-32 (3CDs)*
RSPCA CREDIT CARD "All Creatures Great and Small" by
   JOHNNY PEARSON *PLAY IT AGAIN (BMG): PLAY 006 (CD)*

SADOLIN WOOD PRESERVE "Air That I Breathe" (Hazlewood)
   TV version sung by CARRIE RYAN CARTER *unavailable*
SAFEWAY MILLENNIUM PARTY "I'm In The Mood For Dancing"
   (Mike Myers-Ben Findon-R.Puzey) sung by The NOLANS
   EPIC (Ten): 484 044-2 (CD)
SAINSBURYS (memories of..ad) "The Norville Suite" from
   film 'HUDSUCKER PROXY' composed by CARTER BURWELL
   -S/T- *(VARESE Import only)* - *(CD)*
SARSONS VINEGAR "Coronation Scott" (VIVIAN ELLIS)
   see COLL.147,

SCHWEPPES MALVERN WATER "Symphony No.1" (4th movement)
(ELGAR) *many recordings available*

SCOTTISH TOURIST BOARD 2 "Happiness" BLUE NILE feat:
PAUL BUCHANAN from the album 'PEACE AT LAST'
WARNER: 9362 45848-2 (CD) -4 (MC)

SCOTTISH TOURIST BOARD 1 "Wild Mountain Thyme" trad.
performed by THE SILENCERS on 'NEW PURE MOODS' on
VIRGIN (EMI): VTDCD 158 (2CD)

SCOTTISH WIDOWS "Looking Good" (Tony & Gaynor SADLER)
p.Logorythm Music *unavailable*

SCRUMPY JACK CIDER "The Moldau" 'Ma Vlast'(My Country)
Smetana *vers.*'CLASSIC ADS' *EMI: 7243 568116-2 (CD)*

SHAPE YOGHURT - *see under* ST.IVEL

SHEBA CAT FOOD 3 "There You Are" *unavailable*

SHEBA CAT FOOD 2 "When I Need You" (Albert Hammond-
Carole B.Sager) LEO SAYER - *CHRYSALIS RECORDS*

SHEBA CAT FOOD 1 "If" (David Gates) BREAD 'Sound Of
Bread' *ELEKTRA (WAR): K 252062 (CD) K 452062 (MC)*

SHELL "Going Home" from 'Local Hero' by MARK KNOPFLER
-S/T- *VERTIGO (Univ): 811 038-2 (CD)*

SHERIDANS "Love Hate" FLANAGAN-TARN PRODUCTIONS
unavailable

SHIPPAMS "Here You Come Again" (B.Mann-Cynthia Weil)
sung by DOLLY PARTON on 'Essential D.P.Volume 2'
RCA (BMG): 07863 66933-2 (CD)

SHREDDED WHEAT "Walking On Sunshine" (K.Rew) *orig.by*
KATRINA & T.WAVES 'Best Of' *EMI: CDEMC 3766 (CD)*

SHU UEMURA LIPSTICK "Ain't That A Kick In The Head"
(Sammy Cahn) sung by DEAN MARTIN on 'Very Best Of'
EMI-CAPITOL: 496 721-2 (CD) -4 (MC)

SIEMENS 2 SL10 "The Devil's Trill" (TARTINI) played
by VANESSA MAE *EMI: 498 082-2 (CD) -4 (MC)*

SIEMENS 1 S10 (Mobile P.) "Canon In D." (PACHELBEL)
'CLASSIC ADS' *EMI: 7243 568116-2 (CD)*

SILVIKRIN HAIR PRODUCTS "Saltibanco" (Rene Dupere) by
CIRQUE DU SOLEIL 'Il Sogno Du Volare' *RCA (BMG):
74321 25707-2 (CD) -4 (MC)*

SKODA OCTAVIA "Steppin' Out With My Baby" (Irv.Berlin)
from 'Easter Parade' *TV version unavailable*
FRED ASTAIRE -S/T- 'EASTER PARADE' *EMI: CDODEON 4*

SKY DIGITAL 5 "Express Yourself" by CHARLES WRIGHT &
103RD STREET RHYTHM BAND *WARNER (1970) deleted*

SKY DIGITAL 4 "Mack The Knife" - 'Threepenny Opera'

SKY DIGITAL 3 "As Time Goes By" *TV vers.unavailable*

SKY DIGITAL 2 "Ad Infinite" by GENOCIDE II *unavailable*

SKY DIGITAL 1 "Goin'Out Of My Head" by FAT BOY SLIM
'Better Living Through Chemistry' *SKINT (3MV-Vit)*
BRASSIC 2CD (CD) BRASSIC 2LP(2LP) BRASSIC 2MC(MC)

SKY FOOTBALL Sean Bean ad "Strings For Yasmin" by TIN
TIN OUT *VIRGIN (EMI): VCRD 20 (CDs) VCRT 20 (12")*

SKY PREMIER SOCCER TRAILER "Out Of Control" by The
CHEMICAL BROTHERS *remixed version*

SKY TV "Praise You" by FATBOY SLIM
SKINT (3MV-Pinn): SKINT 42(CD)(MC) (12"s/CDs/MCs)

SKYTOURS "We Are Family" (Rodgers-Edwards) orig SISTER SLEDGE *ATLANTIC (TEN): 9548 31813-2 (CD) -4 (MC)*

SMA PROGRESS (Babyfood) "Take Good Care Of My Baby" (Goffin-King) *TV Version unavailable.* original by BOBBY VEE 'Very Best' *MFP (EMI): CDMFP 6386 (CD)*

SMIRNOFF 4 (1999 ad) "Tame" by THE PIXIES 'DOOLITTLE' *4AD (Vital): GAD905CD (CD) GADC 905 (MC)*

SMIRNOFF 3 (GIRL IN GREEN ad) "Naked And Ashamed" DYLAN RHYMES on 'Attack Of The Killer DJ's' on *JUNIOR BOYS OWN (RTM/DISC): JBOCD 6 (CD)*

SMIRNOFF 2 (BLACK) "Conquest Of Paradise" -S/T- '1492 CONQUEST OF PARADISE' by VANGELIS *EAST WEST (TEN): 4509 91014-2 (CD) WX 497C (MC)*

SMIRNOFF 1 (Reflections in Bottle Ad) "Midnight The Stars And You" (H.Woods-J.Campbell-R.Connelly) *TV version not available* orig: RAY NOBLE ORCHESTRA & AL BOWLLY *MONMOUTH EVERGREEN Impt: MES 6816 (LP)*

SOFT & GENTLE DEODORANT "Move Closer" (Phyllis Nelson) TV vers: MASON JAMES *SOFT G (Pinn): SOFTGCD 001 (CD) SOFTGMC 001 (MC) SOFTGT001 (12"s) deleted*

SONY MINI-DISC 3 "Rude Boy Rock" (Robertson) LIONROCK *CONCRETE-DeCONSTRUCTION (BMG): HARD 31CD (CDs)* on 'CITY DELERIOUS' *(BMG): HARD 32LPCD (CD)*

SONY MINI-DISC 2 "Chinese Burn" by CURVE *ESTUPENDO Universal-MCA (BMG): UMD 80423 (CDs)*

SONY MINI-DISC 1 "Naked" by REEF on *SONY S2 (Ten): 662062-2 (CDs) 662062-7 (7"s) 662062-4 (MC)*

SONY PLAYSTATION 'DOUBLE LIFE: MUSIC FOR PLAYSTATION' incl.JAMIROQUAI "Canned Heat" CHEMICAL BROTHERS "Hey Boy Hey Girl" APOLLO 440 "Carrera Rapida" CHUMBAWUMBA "Tubthumping" RIDGE RACER etc. *SONY TV: SONYTV 65CD (2CD)*

SONY 'WEGA' TV music composed and arranged by DAVID MAURICE *unavailable*

SPECSAVERS OPTICIANS "Aquarium" ('Carnival Of The Animals') (SAINT-SAENS) *CHANDOS CHAN 9246 (CD)*

SPILLERS PRIME - *see under* 'WINALOT-PRIME'

SPRITE (COCA-COLA) "Freeze The Atlantic" by CABLE *INFECTIOUS (RTM-Disc): INFECT 38S (7")* from 'When Animals Attack' *INFECTIOUS (RTM-Disc): INFECT 35CD (CD) INFECT 35LP (ltd edit LP)*

STANDARD LIFE "Ring Telephone Ring" (Ram-Tinurin) sung by The INK SPOTS on album 'Bless You' *PRESIDENT (BMG): PLCD 535 (CD)*

STAKIS HOTELS "Time To Say Goodbye" sung by ANDREA BOCELLI and SARAH BRIGHTMAN from 'ROMANZA' on *PHILIPS (UNIV): 456 456-2 (CD) -4 (MC)*

STELLA ARTOIS 2 'Jean De Florette/Manon Des Sources' (JEAN CLAUDE PETIT) TOOTS THIELMANS *see Films*

STELLA ARTOIS 1 Oil Painting "La Forza Del Destino" (VERDI) as used in 'JEAN DE FLORETTE' *see FILM*

STENA LINE (P.& O.) "Riptide" (Gus Kahn-W.Donaldson) by ROBERT PALMER taken from the album 'Riptide' *ISLAND (UNIV): IMCD 25 (CD)*

STORK MARGARINE "Big Rock Candy Mountain" (McClintock)
ROBERT TEX MORTON on collection 'Yodelling Crazy'
EMI: CDP 798 656-2 (CD)

STREPSILS (Sword Swallower) "Waltz In Black" STRANGLERS
on 'Meninblack' *FAME (EMI): CDFA 3208 (CD)*

STRONGBOW CIDER 2 "Toccata & Fugue in D.Min" BWV 538
(BACH) *version* PETER HURFORD 'Great Organ Works'
DECCA (UNIV): 436 225-2 (CD)

STRONGBOW CIDER 1 "Smoke On The Water" (R.Blackmore-
Ian Gillan-Roger Glover) by DEEP PURPLE on 'Machine
Head' *FAME-MFP (EMI): CDFA 3158(CD) TCFA 3158(MC)*

SUN NEWSPAPER "Only The Strongest Will Survive" by
HURRICANE NO.1 *CREATION (3MV-Vit): CRESCD 285 (CDs)*

SUNKIST Solar Power "Krupa"(Noko-Gray-Gray) APOLLO 440
from album 'ELECTRO GLIDE IN BLUE' *STEALTH SONIC
(Ten): SSX 2440CDR (CD) SSX2440CR (MC)*

SUPERDRUG "Y'a D'La Joie" (C.Trenet) by CHARLES TRENET
on 'Very Best Of Charles Trenet' *EMI: CZ 314 (CD)*

SURE SENSIVE "Jeepers Creepers" (Harry Warren-Johnny Me
rcer) LOUIS ARMSTRONG from film 'Going Places' (38)
on 'Jeepers Creepers' *MILAN: CDCH 602 (CD) deleted*

SURE ULTRA DRY "Ultra Stimulation" by FINLAY QUAYE on
'Maverick A Strike' *EPIC:488 758-2(CD) -4(MC)-8(md)*

SWATCH 2 "Snow On The Sahara" by ANGGUN
EPIC (Ten): 6678762 (CDs) 6678765 (2CD)

SWATCH 1 "Breathe" by MIDGE URE from 'Breathe'
ARISTA (BMG): 74321 34629-2 (CD) -4 (MC)

TAKE A BREAK MAGAZINE "Don't Stop Moving" by LIVIN' JOY
on *MCA (BMG): MCD 60023 (CD) MCC 60023 (MC)*

TANGO BLACKCURRANT "Don't You Want Me" (Fexix-Ware-Wash
ington-Richardson-Jenkins) sung by FELIX (96 Remix)
DeCONSTRUCTION (BMG): 74321 41814-2 (CDs) -4 (MCs)

TATE & LYLE (Gary Rhodes ad) "Won't You Get Off It, Ple
ase" by FATS WALLER on collection 'You Rascal You'
ASV (Koch): CDAJA 5040 (CD) ZCAJA 5040 (MC)

TCP (Gargling Horse ad) "White Horses" (Carr-Nisbet)
TV ver.unavailable / original by JACKY on 'THIS IS
THE RETURN OF CULT FICTION' *VIRGIN: VTCD 112 (CD)*

TEACHER'S HIGHLAND CREAM WHISKY "Cement Mixer" (Slim
Gaillard-L.Ricks) SLIM GAILLARD 'Legendary McVouty'
HEP-N.NOTE (Pinn):HEPCD 6 (CD) + 'CEMENT MIXER
PUTTI PUTTI' *PRESIDENT-DELTA (BMG): PLCD 558 (CD)*

TENNENTS 2 (feminist ad) "The More I See You" (Warren-
Gordon) sung by CHRIS MONTEZ on Coll 'And The Beat
Goes On' (Vol.1) *DEBUTANTE (UNIV): 535 693-2 (2CD)*

TENNENTS 1 (Romeo & Juliet) "Can't Take My Eyes Off
You" (Crewe-Gaudio) ANDY WILLIAMS 'Can't Get Used
To Losing You' *COLUMBIA (Ten): 477 591-2(CD)*

TERRY'S - *see under brand* 'ALL GOLD' etc.

TETLEY BITTER (dog on beach) "Moanin'" CHARLES MINGUS
TV version unavailable. orig CHARLES MINGUS *vers.*
'Blues & Roots' *ATLANTIC (TEN): 81227 52205-2 (CD)*

TETLEY TEA 7 (Soft Pack) "Bend It" (Howard-Blaikley)
TV version unavailable. orig.version by DAVE DEE-
DOZY BEAKY MICK & TICH (1966) on 'Best Of' Collect
SPECTRUM (UNIV): 551 823-2 (CD)

TETLEY TEA 6 (Draw String Bags) "The Stripper" (Rose)
DAVID ROSE ORCH 'The Stripper and Other Favourites'
EMPORIO (THE-DISC): EMPRCD 501 (CD) also on
'TOTALLY COMMERCIALS' *EMI (EMI): 495 475-2 (CD)*

TETLEY TEA 5 "I've Got My Love To Keep Me Warm" (Irv.
Berlin) *TV vers.*sung by JOAN VISKANT *unavailable*

TETLEY TEA 4 "Reach Out I'll Be There" (H-D-Holland)
FOUR TOPS on 'Motown's Greatest Hits' on
MOTOWN-POLYDOR (UNIV): 530 016-2 (CD) -4 (MC)

TETLEY TEA 3 "I Won't Last A Day Without You" (Roger
Nichols-Paul Williams) *TV vers.unavailable* Orig by
CARPENTERS on 'Greatest Hits' *A.& M: CDA 1990 (CD)*

TETLEY TEA 2 "The Sorcerer's Apprentice" (Paul DUKAS)
CHANDOS: CHAN 8852 (CD) ABTD 1469 (MC)

TETLEY TEA 1 "Lovely Day" (Bill Withers) BILL WITHERS
COLUMBIA (Ten) 491 961-2 (CD) -8 (md) 'Best Of'

THOMPSON HOLIDAYS "SOAP" (theme from) (Geo.A.Tipton)
'TV's G.Hits Vol.6' *EDEL (Pinn): 0022752-CIN (CD)*

THOMSON AT LUNN POLY - *see* LUNN POLY

THOMSON LOCAL DIRECTORY "You Showed Me" by LIGHTNING
SEEDS on 'Like You Do' (Gr.Hits) *EPIC (Ten):*
489 034-2 (CD) -4 (MC) 884 328-2 (CDs) -4 (MCs)

THORNTONS ('Chocolate Home' ad) "Everloving" by MOBY
on 'PLAY' *MUTE (Vital): CD(CS)STUMM 172 (CD/MC)*

TIMES NEWSPAPER "Labyrinth" by PHILIP GLASS from '1000
Airplanes On The Roof' *VIRGIN (EMI): CDVE 39 (CD)*

TIMOTEI MINERALS SHAMPOO (Waterfalls ad) orig music by
KARL JENKINS & MIKE RATLEDGE *unavaliable*

TOFFEE CRISP "If I Were With Her Now" by SPIRITUALIZED
from 'Laser Guided Melodies' *DEDICATED (Vital):*
DEDCD 004 (CD) DEDMC 004 (MC)

TOYOTA AVENSIS 2 "Voodoo Chile (Slight Return)" from
'Electric Ladyland' by JIMI HENDRIX *MCA-UNIVERSAL*
(BMG): MCD 11600 (CD) MCC 11600 (MC)

TOYOTA AVENSIS 1 "The Passenger" (I.Pop-R.Gardiner)
IGGY POP on 'Lust For Life' *VIRGIN: CDOVD 278 (CD)*

TOYOTA LEXUS 2 "Pure Morning" PLACEBO 'Without You...'
ELEVATOR (Vital): CDFLOOR 8 (CD) FLOORMC 8 (MC)

TOYOTA LEXUS 1 "Ending (Ascent)" BRIAN ENO 'Apollo'
EG-Virgin (EMI): EGCD 53 (CD)

TOYOTA PICNIC "Cape Fear" (BERNARD HERRMANN) CITY OF
PRAGUE P.ORCH *SILVA SCREEN (Koch): FILMCD 162 (CD)*

TOYOTA YARIS "Wondrous Place" (Giant-Lewis) sung by
BILLY FURY *K-TEL: TOY 9051-2 (CDs) TOY 9051-4 (MC)*
BILLY FURY *DECCA-LONDON: 882 267-2 (CDs) -4 (MC)*

TWEED PERFUME "Pastoral" from 'Symphony No.6 in F.Maj
Op.68' (BEETHOVEN) *many recordings available*

TWIX 2 (Norman's car) "Beat Boutique" ALAN HAWSHAW
and KEITH MANSFIELD on 'GIRL IN A SPORTS CAR' on
Coliseum (TEN): 0630 18071-2 (CD) or HF 53CD

TWIX 1 "I Want It All" composed & performed by QUEEN 'Greatest Hits 2' *EMI: CDP 797971-2 (CD) -4 (MC)*
TYPHOO TEA "Fresh" (J.Taylor) orig by KOOL AND THE GANG 'Collect' *SPECTRUM (UNIV): 551 635-2 (CD) -4(MC)*

UNITED FRIENDLY INSURANCE "All Together Now" originally by The FARM on *PRODUCE (Vital): CDMILK 103 (MC)*
UNITED NATIONS (For Refugees) "Where Have All The Flowers Gone" (Pete Seeger) by MARLENE DIETRICH 'Essential Marlene Dietrich' *EMI: CDEMS 1399 (CD)*

VASELINE INTENSIVE CARE "Button Up Your Overcoat" (DeSylva-Brown-Henderson) sung by RUTH ETTING on 'Love Me Or Leave Me' *FLAPPER (Pinn): PASTCD 7061 (CD)*
VAUXHALL ASTRA string part of The VERVE's "Bitter Sweet Symphony" (Ashcroft) from 'URBAN HYMNS' The VERVE *HUT-VIRGIN (EMI): CDHUT 45 (CD) HUTMC 45 (MC)* also opening music on "Treat Infamy" REST ASSURED *LONDON-FFRR (UNIV): FCD(FCS) 333 (CDs/MC)*
VAUXHALL SINTRA "Pure" by The LIGHTNING SEEDS from 'Cloudcuckooland' *VIRGIN (EMI): CDOVD(OVDC) 436*
VAUXHALL TIGRA "Fiesta" (Pogues) The POGUES from 'If I Should Fall From Grace With God' on *WEA (TEN): 244493-2 (CD) WX 2434C (MC)*
VAUXHALL VECTRA 3 "Say What You Want" TEXAS on 'White On Blonde' *MERCURY (UNIV): 534 315-2 (CD) -4 (MC)*
VAUXHALL VECTRA 2 "Peter Gunn theme" (Henry Mancini) *TV version unavailable* / HENRY MANCINI vers: 'Best Of HENRY MANCINI' *RCA (BMG): 74321 47676-2 (CD)*
VAUXHALL VECTRA 1 "The Next Millenium" (Arnold) DAVID ARNOLD on 'Senses' *POLYGRAM: 516 627-2 (CD)* / voc. vers BJORK 'This Is Cult Fiction' *VIRGIN VTCD 59 (CD)* and 'NEW PURE MOODS' *VIRGIN see COLL.265.*
VIRGIN ATLANTIC AIRWAYS 2 "Crazy Horses" The OSMONDS on 'Very Best' *POLYDOR: CURCD 065 (CD)*
VIRGIN ATLANTIC AIRWAYS 1 "Sleep Walk" SANTO & JOHNNY on 'GOLDEN AGE OF AMERICAN ROCK'n'ROLL VOLUME 1' *ACE (Pinn): CDCHD 600 (CD)*
VODAPHONE "The Garden" (Rollo) performed by FAITHLESS from 'SUNDAY 8PM' *CHEEKY (3MV-BMG): CHEKCD 503 (CD)*
VOLKSWAGEN GOLF 2 "Gassenhauer" from 'SCHULWERK' (CARL ORFF-G.KEETMAN) 'BEST OF CARL ORFF' on *RCA (BMG): 75605 51357-2 (CD) -4 (MC)* also on 'MUSIC FOR KINDER' *RCA (BMG): 09026 68031-2 (6CDs)*
VOLKSWAGEN GOLF 1 "Left Bank Two" (Vision On TV Picture Gallery music) NOVELTONES on 'THIS IS THE RETURN OF CULT FICTION' *VIRGIN (EMI): VTCD 112 (CD)* also on 'A-Z OF BRITISH TV THEMES VOLUME 2' *PLAY IT AGAIN (Koch): PLAY 006 (CD)*
VOLVO S40 2 "One To One Religion" White Knuckle Remix by BOMB THE BASE (orig track on 'Clear') *FOURTH & BROADWAY-ISL.(UNIV): BRCD 611 (CD) BRCA 611 (MC)*
VOLVO S40 1 orig music composed and performed by VINCE POPE *unavailable*

VOLVO V40 2 "When Somebody Thinks You're Wonderful"
 sung by FATS WALLER on 'Ultimate Collection'
 PULSE-RCA (BMG): PDSCD 550 (2CD) PDSMC 550 (2MC)
VOLVO V40 1 "Butterfly 747" by MOLOKO from 'Do You
 Like My Tight Sweater' *ECHO (Pinn): ECH(CD)(LP) 7
 also on -S/T- 'TWIN TOWN' A.& M. (UNIV): 540 718-2*
VOLVO 850 ('Tornado' ad) by ANNE DUDLEY *unavailable*

W ALES (Tourism ad) "Design For Life" by MANIC STREET
 PREACHERS from 'Everything Must Go' on
 EPIC (Ten): 483 930-2 (CD) -4 (MC) -1(LP) -8(md)
WALL'S CALIPPO "My Generation" (Pete Townshend) WHO
 'The Singles' *POLYDOR: 815 965-2(CD) WHOHC 17(MC)
 854 637-2 (CDs) 863 918-4 (MC) -7 (7"s)*
WALLS CORNETTO "Help Yourself" *TV version unavailable*
 orig by TOM JONES *DERAM Poly: 820 559-2 (CD)*
WALKERS CHEESE & OWEN "Instant Karma" (J.Lennon) sung
 by JOHN LENNON on Collection 'LENNON LEGEND'
 EMI: 821 954-2 (CD) -4 (MC) -1 (LP)
WALKERS DORITOS "Walk This Way" by RUN DMC & AEROSMITH
 'Greatest Hits' *PROFILE (Pinn): FILECD 474 (CD)*
WEETABIX based on "Tragedy" orig.by The BEE GEES
 POLYDOR: 847 339-2 (CD)
WEIGHT-WATCHERS (Heinz) (Mexican Chili) "Leaving Rome"
 by JO JO BENNETT (1975) on Coll 'BLOW MR.HORNSMAN'
 TROJAN (Jetstar): CDTRL 257 (CD) TRLS 257 (LP)
WH SMITH 'Regression ad' "Tiger Feet" (Chinn-Chapmqan)
 MUD 'Gold Collection' *EMI: CD(TC) 1003 (CD/MC)*
WHICH MAGAZINE "Money" (Gordy-Bradford) sung by FLYING
 LIZARDS on 'Best Punk Album In The World..Ever' on
 VIRGIN (EMI): VTDCD 42 (2CD) VTDMC 42 (2MC)
WHISKAS 5 SINGLES "Lazybones" (H.Carmichael-J.Mercer)
 sung by HOAGY CARMICHAEL on 'Mr.Music Master'
 FLAPPER-PAVILION (Pinn): PASTCD 7004 (CD) also on
 'Sometimes I Wonder' *LIVING ERA: CDAJA 5345 (CD)*
WHISKAS 4 "On The Rebound" comp/perf.by FLOYD CRAMER
 on Collection 'THE ESSENTIAL FLOYD CRAMER' on
 RCA (BMG): 74321 66591-2 (CD) -4 (MC)
WHISKAS 3 "Hold Tight (I Want Some Sea Food Mama)" by
 FATS WALLER *CLASSICS (Discov): CLASSICS 943 (CD)*
WHISKAS 2 (Kittens) "Onions" (Sidney Bechet) *TV vers.*
 unavailable /HUMPHREY LYTTLETON BAND 'Parlophone
 Years' *DOORMOUSE (N.Note-Pinn): DM21CD deleted*
WHISKAS 1 "Teach Me Tiger" sung by APRIL STEVENS on
 'TOTALLY COMMERCIALS' *EMI: 495 475-2 (CD) also on*
 'Cocktail Capers-Ult.Lounge 8' *EMI:CDEMS 1595 (CD)*
WILDLIFE OF BRITAIN MAGAZ. "Victorian Kitchen Garden"
 (Paul Reade) EMMA JOHNSON on 'ENCORES' on
 ASV (Koch): CDDCA 800 (CD) ZCDCA 800 (MC)
WINALOT-PRIME "The Long March" (Chris Gunning) Barking
 Light *KENNEL (BMG): WOOF 1 (7"s) DELETED*
WINDOWS 95 - *see* MICROSOFT
WOODPECKER CIDER (car in puddle)"Mr.Vain" CULTURE BEAT
 'Serenity' *EPIC (TEN) 474 101-2 (CD)-4 (MC) -8(MD)*

WOOLWORTH'S LADYBIRD COLLECTION - *see* 'LADYBIRD'

WRANGLER JEANS 4 "Key To The Highway" (Monque'd) vers BIG BILL BROONZY on 'House Rent Stomp' on *BLUES ENCORE/TARGET (BMG): CD 52007 (CD)*

WRANGLER JEANS 3 'DJ Rap' (Ron-In) *unavailable*

WRANGLER JEANS 2 "You're Undecided" (D.Burnette-P. Burlisson) by JOHNNY BURNETTE TRIO on 'Rock-A-Billy Boogie' *BEAR FAMILY (Rollercoaster): BCD 15474 (CD)*

WRANGLER JEANS 1 "Cross Town Traffic" (Hendrix) JIMI HENDRIX 'Singles Album' *POLYDOR: 827 369-2 (2xCD)*

WRIGLEY'S SPEARMINT "All Right Now" (Andy Fraser-Paul Rodgers) by FREE on 'All Right Now' *ISLAND CITV 2 (CD) CID 486 (CDsingle) CIS 486 (MC single)*

YELLOW PAGES 4 "You're More Than A Number In My Little Red Book" (T.Macaulay-R.Greenway) orig by DRIFTERS *RCA (BMG): 74321 44674-2 (CD) -4 (MC)*

YELLOW PAGES 3 "Baby I Love You" (Spector-Greenwich-Barry) The RAMONES from 'End Of The Century' *SIRE (TEN): 7599 27429-2 (CD)* / *original vers.by* by The RONETTES 'Best Of' *EMI: PSCD 1006 (CD)*

YELLOW PAGES 2 "Days" (Ray Davies) by The KINKS on 'Best of Ballads' *ARISTA (BMG): 74321 13687-2 (CD)*

YELLOW PAGES 1 (J.R.Hartley book ad) (piano piece) composed and played by DICK WALTER *unavailable*

COMMERCIAL BREAK: Old Tunes from The New Ads - Various *ASV (Select): AJA 5281 (CD)* 1998
1.JEEPERS CREEPERS *(SURE SENSIVE)* Louis Armstong 2. HAPPY FEET *(CLARK'S SHOES)* Jack Hylton Orchestra 3. BOTTLENECK BLUES 4.JUNGLE JAMBOREE Duke Ellington 4.SWEET AND LOVELY *(CADBURY HIGH LIGHTS)* Al Bowlly 5.WON'T YOU GET OFF IT PLEASE *(TATE & LYLE)* Fats Waller 6.EGYPTIAN ELLA *(TERRY'S PYRAMINTS)*Ted Lewis 7.SUN HAS GOT HIS HAT ON *(BRITISH GAS)* Sam Browne 8 LOVE IS THE SWEETEST THING *(BLACK MAGIC)* Al Bowlly 9.TEDDY BEAR'S PICNIC *(PERSIL/SONY CAMCORDER)* Henry Hall Orch 10.LET'S FACE THE MUSIC AND DANCE *(ALLIED DUNBAR)* Fred Astaire 11.STOMPIN'AT THE SAVOY *(P.& O FERRIES)* Benny Goodman Orch 12.VERY THOUGHT OF YOU *(PRETTY POLLY)* Al Bowlly 13.PENNIES FROM HEAVEN*(BT)* Frances Langford, Bing Crosby & Louis Armstrong 14. ORIENTAL SHUFFLE *(RADIO TIMES)* Stephane Grappelli & Django Reinhardt 15.BOUM *(PPP HEALTHCARE)* Charles Trenet 16.IN THE MOOD *(RADION/ANCHOR BUTT/DORITOS)* Glenn Miller Or 17.LA CUMPARSITA *(No.7)* Dinah Shore 18.WHEN YHOU WISH UPON A STAR *(DISNEYLAND)* Cliff Edwards 19.GRASSHOPPERS DANCE *(MILK)*Alfredo Campoli 20.YES SIR THAT'S MY BABY *(JOHNSON'S BABY)* Eddie Cantor 21.TICO TICO *(WHISKAS)* Andrews Sisters 22. SENTIMENTAL JOURNEY *(CADBURY'S INSPIRATIONS)* Doris Day 23.ZIP-A-DEE-DOO-DAH *(MITSUBISHI CARISMA)* 24. AS TIME GOES BY *(NPI PENSIONS)* Dooley Wilson

2.4 CHILDREN (BBC1 3/9/91) theme music: HOWARD GOODALL
unavailable
7 *see under* SEVEN
8MM (1999) Music score by MYCHAEL DANNA -S/T- on
SILVA SCREEN (Koch): FILMCD 313 (CD)
9 songs by Maury Yeston
ORIG LONDON CONCERT CAST 1992 *with:* JONATHAN PRYCE
ELAINE PAIGE *TER (Koch): CDTER2 1193 (2CD)*
9 MONTHS (1995) Music sco HANS ZIMMER *feat* "Time Of
Your Life" sung by LITTLE STEVEN + tracks by MARVIN
GAYE-TYRONE DAVIS -S/T- *MILAN (BMG): 30110-2 (CD)*
9 TO 5 (Film-TV) Theme DOLLY PARTON *(BMG) ND 84830 (CD)*
9½ WEEKS (1986) Music score: JACK NITZSCHE -S/T- reiss
CAPITOL (EMI): CDP 746722-2 (CD)
9TH GATE The (1999) Music score by WOJCIEK KILAR
performed by CITY OF PRAGUE PHILHARMONIC & CHORUS
and featuring Soprano SUMI JO. -S/T-
SILVA SCREEN (Koch): FILMCD 321 (CD)
10 COMMANDMENTS The (1956) Music sco: ELMER BERNSTEIN
-S/T- *TSUNAMI Imp (Sil.Screen): TSU 0123 (CD) and*
-S/T- *MCA USA (Silva Screen): MCAD 42320 (CD)*
10 THINGS I HATE ABOUT YOU (1998) Music: RICHARD GIBBS
-S/T- *HOLLYWOOD-EDEL (Pinn): 010254-2HWR (CD)*
13TH FLOOR The (1999) Music score: HARALD KLOSER -S/T-
MILAN (BMG): 73138 35882-2 (CD)
13TH WARRIOR The (1999) Music score by JERRY GOLDSMITH
-S/T- *VARESE (Pinn): VSD 6038 (CD)*
20TH CENTURY BLUES: The Words and Music of Noel Coward
(BBC2 11/4/1998) featuring contemporary recordings
of his songs *EMI: 494 631-2 (CD) 494 631-2 (MC)*
20TH CENTURY FOX (Fanfare) (Alfred Newman)
see COLL.1,
21 JUMP STREET (USA) m: LIAM STERNBERG *see COLL.17,351*
24/7 (1997) Music sc: BOO HEWERDINE-NEIL MacCOLL -S/T-
songs by VAN MORRISON-TIM BUCKLEY-CHARLATANS etc.
INDEPENDIENTE (TEN): ISOM 6CD (CD) ISOM 6MC (MC)
26 MEN (USA TV) *see COLL.348,*
42nd STREET (1933 MUSICAL) *feat* DICK POWELL-RUBY KEELER
WARNER BAXTER-BEBE DANIELS *inc.songs* 'SKY'S THE LIM
IT'/'DUBARRY WAS A LADY' *TARGET (BMG):CD 60010 (CD)*
42nd STREET (MUSICAL 1980) Songs: AL DUBIN-HARRY WARREN
O.Broadway Rev.Cast *feat:* JERRY ORBACH-TAMMY GRIMES
LEE ROY REAMES-WANDA RICHERT-CAROLE COOK & Company
RCA Victor (BMG): BD 83891 (CD)
77 SUNSET STRIP (USA) *see COLL.345,375*
100 RIFLES (1968) Music score: JERRY GOLDSMITH
TARAN (Silver Sounds): W.9101 (CD)
101 DALMATIONS (1996) Music score: MICHAEL KAMEN -S/T-
DISNEY-EDEL (Pinn): WD 69940-2 (CD) see also p.362
110 IN THE SHADE (MUSICAL) songs by HARVEY SCHMIDT and
TOM JONES. *NEW RECORDING* JOHN OWEN EDWARDS (cond)
TER (KOCH): CDTER2 1255 (2CD)
187 (1997) VARIOUS ARTISTS -S/T- on
ATLANTIC (TEN): 7567 92760-2 (CD) -4 (MC)

200 MOTELS (1971) music by FRANK ZAPPA with The MOTHERS
   OF INVENTION and ROYAL PHILHARMONIC ORCH.AND CHORUS
   -S/T- *reiss with additional items RYKODISC (Vital)*:
   RCD 10513/14 (2CD) RAC 10513/14 (2MC)
633 SQUADRON (64) Music score by RON GOODWIN
   see COLL.70,142,168,170,384
999 / 999 INT / 999 LIFESAVERS (BBC1 25/06/1992)
   theme music by ROGER BOLTON *unavailable*
1492 CONQUEST OF PARADISE (1992) Music score: VANGELIS
   S/T- *EAST WEST (TEN)*: *4509 91014-2(CD) WX 497C(MC)*
   see COLL.70,72,380,381
1914-18 (BBC2 10/11/96) Music score: MASON DARING -S/T-
   'The Great War and The Shaping Of The 20th Century'
   DARING (Direct Dist): *DARINGCD 3029 (CD)*
1941 (1979) Music score: JOHN WILLIAMS -S/T- *reissue on*
   VARESE (Pinn): *VSD 5832 (CD)*
1969 (1988) Music score: MICHAEL SMALL -S/T- *reissue*
   POLY (IMS-Poly): *AA 837 362-2 (CD)*
1984 (1984) Mus.comp/perform by EURYTHMICS -S/T- *reiss*:
   VIRGIN-MFP (EMI): *CDVIP 135 (CD) TCVIP 135 (MC)*
1900 HOUSE The (C4 22/09/1999) series music by the
   FRATELLI BROTHERS *unavailable*
2000 THOUSAND YEARS (ITV 18/04/1999) title music by
   ROBERT HARTSHORNE -S/T- *feat Various Classics on*
   CONIFER CLASSICS (BMG): *75605 51353-2 (2CD)*
2001-A SPACE ODYSSEY (1968) Classical -S/T- featuring
   "Blue Danube"(J.STRAUSS) "Also Sprach Zarathustra"
   (R.STRAUSS) etc. -S/T- *EMI ODEON: CDODEON 28 (CD)*
   see COLL.71,77,105,131,229,298,308,333,362
2001-A SPACE ODYSSEY (REJECTED SCORE by ALEX NORTH)
   National Philharmonic Orchestra (JERRY GOLDSMITH)
   VARESE (Pinn): *VSD 5400 (CD)*
20,000 LEAGUES UNDER THE SEA (1996 TV Mini-Series)
   Music score: JOHN SCOTT.recording by UTAH STUDIO
   SYMPHONY ORCHESTRA on *PROMETHEUS: PCD 143 (CD)*
   Orig -S/T- *JOS RECORDS (S.Screen)*: *JSCD 122 (CD)*
A.TEAM The (USA) ITV from 29/7/83) theme by MIKE POST
   PETE CARPENTER *SIL.SCREEN (Koch)*:*SILVAD 3509 (CD)*
   see COLL.17,109,110,347
ABBOTT & COSTELLO SHOW The (USA TV) *see COLL.348*
   also available 'WHO'S ON FIRST' (comedy routine)
   ON THE AIR-DELTA (Target-BMG): *OTA 101913 (CD)*
ABOUT LAST NIGHT (1986) Music sc: MILES GOODMAN -S/T-
   EMI AMER (EMI): *CDP 746 560-2 (CD)*
ABOVE THE RIM (1993) M.sco: MARCUS MILLER -S/T- V/A
   INTERSCOPE-MCA (BMG): *IND 92359 (CD) also on*
   WEA: *6544-92359-2 (CD) -4 (MC)*
ABSOLUTE BEGINNERS (Film Musical 86) Score: GIL EVANS
   -S/T- *VIP (EMI)*: *CDVIP 112 (CD) TCVIP 112 (MC)*
   also Highlights on *VIRGIN: CDV 2386 (CD)*
ABSOLUTE POWER (1996) Music score: LENNIE NIEHAUS with
   CLINT EASTWOOD -S/T- *VARESE (Pinn)*: *VSD 5808 (CD)*
ABSOLUTE TRUTH (BBC2 27/9/1998) Music: DEBBIE WISEMAN
   BBC Worldwide (Pinn-Koch): *WMSF 60002 (CD)*

ABSOLUTELY FABULOUS (BBC2 12/11/92) theme "This Wheel's
On Fire" (Bob Dylan-Rick Danko) ABSOLUTELY FABULOUS
(aka PET SHOP BOYS) *EMI: CDR(TCR)(12R)6382 deleted*
1968 version JULIE DRISCOLL-BRIAN AUGER TRINITY on
'I WILL SURVIVE' *PICKWICK (Che): PWKS 4092 (CD)*

ABYSS The (Film 89) Music score: ALAN SILVESTRI -S/T-
VARESE (Pinn): VSD 5235 (CD)

ACE VENTURA PET DETECTIVE (93) Music sco: IRA NEWBORN
-S/T- *Poly: 523 000-2 (CD) DELETED / see COLL 88*

ACROSS 110TH STREET (1972) Mus score: J.J.JOHNSON with
addit.songs composed & performed by BOBBY WOMACK
-S/T- *RYKODISC (Vital): RCD 10706 (CD)* / see also
BOBBY WOMACK on *CHARLY (Charly): CPCD 8340 (CD)*

ACT The (1978) ORIG BROADWAY CAST *feat:* LIZA MINNELLI
ORIG CAST RECORDING *DRG (Pinn): CDDRG 6101 (CD)*

ADAM 12 (USA TV) *see COLL.345,*

ADDAMS FAMILY The (USA 64) Music from orig TV ser.by
VIC MIZZY *RCA IMP (S.Screen): 61057-2(CD) -4 (MC)*
see COLL.38,122,249,345

ADDAMS FAMILY The (1991) Music sco: MARC SHAIMAN -S/T-
CAPITOL (EMI): CDESTU 2161 (CD) TCESTU 2161 (MC)

ADDAMS FAMILY VALUES (1993) Music score: MARC SHAIMAN
SCORE -S/T- *VARESE (Pinn): VSD 5465 (CD)*
SONGS -S/T- *POLY: 521 502-2 (CD) deleted 1995*

ADIEMUS - *see COLL.12,*

ADJUSTER The (1991) Music score: MYCHAEL DANNA -S/T-
VARESE (Pinn): VSD 5674 (CD)

ADVENTURES IN PARADISE (USA TV) *see COLL.348,*

ADVENTURES OF AGGIE (ITV) theme music "High Stepper"
RONALD BINGE *see COLL.50,*

ADVENTURES OF BLACK BEAUTY The (LWT 23/9/72 & C4 1986)
theme "Galloping Home" (DENIS KING) London String
Chorale *see COLL.5,+ 149,* (NEW ADVENT.OF B.BEAUTY)

ADVENTURES OF DON JUAN (1948) *see COLL.338,*

ADVENTURES OF MARCO POLO (1937) Music: HUGO FRIEDHOFER
Suite on Coll "HUGO FRIEDHOFER" *with* 'THE LODGER'/
'RAINS OF RANCHIPUR'/'SEVEN CITIES OF GOLD' perf.
by The MOSCOW SYPHONY ORCH (cond: W.T.Stromberg)
MARCO POLO (Select): 8.223857 (CD)

ADVENTURES OF MARK TWAIN (1944) Music sc: MAX STEINER
score perf.by BRANDENBURG PHILHARMONIC ORCHEST
(William T.Stromberg) *with* 'PRINCE AND THE PAUPER'
(E.W.KORNGOLD) *RCA (BMG): 09026 62660-2 (CD)*

ADVENTURES OF NICHOLAS NICKLEBY *see COLL.7,*

ADVENTURES OF OZZIE AND HARRIET (USA TV) *see COLL.348,*

ADVENTURES OF PINOCCHIO (1996) Mus sco: RACHEL PORTMAN
& songs by STEVIE WONDER-JERRY HADLEY-SISSEL-BRIAN
MAY -S/T- *LONDON (Univ): 452 740-2 (CD)*
see also 'PINOCCHIO'

ADVENTURES OF PRISCILLA QUEEN OF THE DESERT (1994) Mus
sco: GUY CROSS -S/T- *MOTHER (Univ): 516 937-2 (CD)*

ADVENTURES OF ROBIN HOOD The (ITV 17/2/56-1960) theme
mus (Carl Sigman) DICK JAMES *EMI:TCEM 1307 (MC)*
CDS 791255-2 (CD) GARRY MILLER *see COLL.346,367,*

ADVENTURES OF ROBIN HOOD The (1938) Mus sco: ERICH
   WOLFGANG KORNGOLD -S/T- *TER (Koch): CDTER 1066 +*
   VARESE: VSD 47202 (CD) see COLL.71,90,221,327,338

ADVENTURES OF ROBINSON CRUSOE The (BBC1 12/10/65) Music
   score: ROBERT MELLIN-GIAN PIERO REVERBERI Original
   TV S/TRACK *reissued w.ADDITIONAL unreleased music*
   S.SCREEN (Koch): FILMCD 705 (CD) see COLL.121,

ADVENTURES OF WILLIAM TELL (ITC 15/9/58-1959) theme
   sung by DAVID WHITFIELD 'Sings Stage & Screen Fav'
   PICKWICK CARLTON PWK 096 (CD) SDTO 2004 (MC)

AFFLICTION (1997) Music score by MICHAEL BROOK -S/T-
   CITADEL (Hot): STC 77121 (CD)

AFRICAN SANCTUS 1 (BBC2 29/7/95) Music: DAVID FANSHAWE
   new digital rec.feat: WILHELMENIA FERNANDEZ and
   KATAMANTO + BOURNEMOUTH SYPH.CHORUS +CHORISTERS OF
   ST.GEORGE'S CHAPEL WINDSOR. *SILVA SCREEN (Koch):*
   SILKD 6003 (CD) SILKC 6003(MC) see also MISSA LUBA

AFRICAN SANCTUS 2 (BBC1 1978) A Mass For Love and Peace
   DAVID FANSHAWE *PHILIPS: 426 055-2 (CD) -4(MC)*
   also available Allmanna Sangen cond.by ROBERT SUND
   PROPRIUS Records: PR(C)(CD) 9984 (LP/MC/CD)

AFTER THE FOX (1966) Music score: BURT BACHARACH -S/T-
   RYKODISC (Vital): CD 10716 (CD)

AFTERGLOW (1997) Music score: MARK ISHAM -S/T- on
   SONY JAZZ (TEN): CK 67929 (CD)

AGAINST ALL ODDS (1984) Music sco: MICHEL COLOMBIER
   -S/T- *VIRGIN (MFP-EMI): CDVIP 112 (CD)*

AGATHA CHRISTIE'S POIROT (LWT from 8/1/89) Theme
   music by CHRISTOPHER GUNNING *see COLL.6,390,*

AGE OF INNOCENCE (1992) *see COLL.88,89,*

AGONY AND THE ECSTASY The (1965) Music sco: ALEX NORTH
   with 'PRIDE & THE PASSION' (George Antheil) 75mins
   CLOUD NINE (Import, S.Screen): CNS 5001 (CD)

AGONY AND THE ECSTACY The (1965) Mus score: ALEX NORTH
   New Record *VARESE (Pinn): VSD 5901 (CD, 10.1998)*

AIDA (1999) Musical songs by TIM RICE and ELTON JOHN
   "Written In The Stars" sung by ELTON JOHN & LeANN
   RIMES *MERCURY-ROCKET (Univ): EJSCD 45 (CDs)*
   -S/T- *feat* ELTON JOHN-LeANN RIMES-BOYZ II MEN
   SPICE GIRLS-TINA TURNER-JANET JACKSON-JAMES TAYLOR
   STING-SHANIA TWAIN-LENNY KRAVITZ-LULU-KELLY PRICE
   MERCURY-ROCKET (Univ): number to be confirmed

AIN'T MISBEHAVIN' (ITV 28/7/97) orig mus: NIGEL WRIGHT
   sgs "Ain't Misbehavin'"/"The Kiss Polka"/"A Night
   ingale Sang In Berkeley Square" on ROBSON & JEROME
   album 'Take Two' *BMG: 74321 42625-2 (CD) -4 (MC)*

AIN'T MISBEHAVIN' (ORIG LONDON CAST 1995)
   FIRST NIGHT (Pinn): ORCD 6053 (CD)

AIN'T MISBEHAVIN' (O.BROADWAY CAST 1979) Music: FATS
   WALLER with Andre de Shields-Nell Carter-Ken Page
   RCA Import (S.Screen): 2965-2 (2CD) CBK2 2965 (MC)

AIR FORCE ONE (1997) Music score: JERRY GOLDSMITH with
   additional music by JOEL McNEELY -S/T- on
   VARESE (Pinn): VSD 5825 (CD)

AIRPLANE (1980) Music score: ELMER BERNSTEIN. Suite on
'Disasters' *SILVA SCREEN (Koch): FILMCD 301 (CD)*

AIRPORT (1970) Music score: ALFRED NEWMAN -S/T- reiss
VARESE (Pinn): VSD 5436 (CD)

AIRPORT (BBC1 2/4/96) series title music composed and
performed by HAL LINDES *unavailable*

AIRWOLF (USA 84-ITV) Theme music: SYLVESTER LEVAY
see COLL.17,38,350

AKIRA (Cartoon 1991) Music sco: YAMASHIRO SHOJI *VIDEO
Manga:IWCV 1001VHS* -S/T- *DEMON (Pinn): DSCD 6 (CD)*

AKIRA 2 (1994) Animated Manga Video / Music score
YAMASHIRO SHOJI -S/T- *DEMON (Pinn): DSCD 7 (CD)*

ALADDIN (1993) Mus. & songs: ALAN MENKEN-HOWARD ASHMAN
TIM RICE -S/T- *feat* "A Whole New World" sung by
PEABO BRYSON-REGINA BELLE -S/T- *DISNEY (B.Vista):
WD 74260-2 (CD) WD 74260-4 (MC)*
see also WALT DISNEY INDEX p.362

ALAMO The (1960) Music sco: DIMITRI TIOMKIN title song
"Green Leaves Of Summer" (Tiomkin-Webster) sung by
BROTHERS FOUR -S/T- *COLUMBIA (S.Scre) CB 66138 (CD)*
ORCHESTRAL SUITE on 'HIGH NOON' (D.TIOMKIN Collect)
RCA VICTOR (BMG): 09026 62658-2 (CD)
see COLL.41,70,73,202,260,358,401,

ALCHEMIST The (1985) Music score: RICHARD BAND -S/T- on
INTRADA (S.Screen): MAF 7046D (CD) also contains
-S/T- *to* 'THE HOUSE ON SONORITY ROW' (Richard BAND)

ALEGRIA (Royal Albert Hall 01/1998) SHOW featuring the
Circus Troupe CIRQUE DU SOLEIL Music: RENE DUPERE
-S/T- *RCA (BMG): 09026 62701-2 (CD)*

ALEXANDER NEVSKY (1938 Eisenstein) Mus sco: S.PROKOFIEV
ST.PETERSBURG PHILHAR.ORCH *RCA: 09026 61926-2 (CD)*
also avail: Scottish National Orch (Neeme Jarvi) &
Linda Finnie (mezzo-sopr) *CHANDOS: CHAN 8584 (CD)*

ALEXANDER THE GREAT (1956) Music sco: MARIO NASCIMBENE
score WITH 'BARABBAS' *DRG (Pinn): DRGCD 32964 (CD)*

ALFIE (1966) Music sco: SONNY ROLLINS -S/T- score *reiss
IMPULSE-MCA-GRP-New Note (BMG): IMP 12242 (CD)*
Title song (Burt Bacharach-Hal David) *sung by* CHER
see COLL.52,259,278,

ALFRED HITCHCOCK PRESENTS (USA 55) / ITV 60's) Theme
"Funeral March Of A Marionette" (GOUNOD)
see COLL.68,146,197,

ALIAS SMITH AND JONES (USA 71/rpt.BBC2 1997/98 title
theme music by BILLY GOLDENBERG *see COLL.2,*

ALICE IN WONDERLAND (1950) -S/T-
DISNEY-EDEL (Pinn): 019 607-2DNY (CD)
see WALT DISNEY INDEX p.362

ALICE IN WONDERLAND (1998) Music score: RICHARD HARTLEY
VARESE (Pinn): VSD 6021 (CD)

ALICE IN WONDERLAND (1968 RECORDING reissued) *featuring*
Karen Dotrice-Kenneth Connor-Beryl Reid-Dorothy Squ
ires-Bruce Forsyth-Fenella Fielding-Tommy Cooper-Pe
ggy Mount-Ian Wallace-Arthur Haynes-Frankie Howerd-
EMI: CDEMS 1471 (CD) TCEMS 1471 (MC)

ALICE'S RESTAURANT (1969) music by GARRY SHERMAN feat
ARLO GUTHRIE *RYKODISC (Vital): RCD 10737 (CD)*
ALICE'S RESTAURANT (1969) Songs: ARLO GUTHRIE *feat* PETE
SEEGER -S/T- *REPRISE (TEN): K244045 (CD)*
30TH ANNIVERSARY EDITION *KOCH: 37959-2 (CD)*
ALIEN (1979) Music score by JERRY GOLDSMITH -S/T *delet.*
see COLL.121,166,264,267,308,328,362
ALIEN (2) ALIENS (1986) Music score: JAMES HORNER -S/T-
VARESE USA (Pinn): VCD 47263 (CD)
ALIEN 3 (92) Music score: ELLIOT GOLDENTHAL -S/T- on
MCA (BMG): MCD 10629 (CD)
ALIEN TRILOGY - The Royal Scottish National Orch
VARESE (Pinn): VSD 5753 (CD) Mus by JERRY GOLDSMITH
JAMES HORNER (ALIENS) ELLIOT GOLDENTHAL (ALIEN 3)
ALIEN 4 (97) Music score: JOHN FRIZZELL -S/T-
RCA (BMG): 09026 68955-2 (CD)
ALIEN NATION (USA/SKY1 13/6/94) mus: STEVE DORFF-LARRY
HERBSTRITT-DAVID KURTZ -S/T- on *GNP (ZYX)*
GNPD 8024 (CD) GNP5 8024 (MC)
ALIEN NATION (1988) Mus score: JOE HARNELL
see COLL.310,351,
ALL ABOUT EVE (1950) Music sco: ALFRED NEWMAN.Suite by
MOSCOW SYMPHONY ORCH.& CHOR.(William T.Stromberg) +
'BEAU GESTE' (1939) 'HUNCHBACK OF NOTRE DAME' 1939
MARCO POLO (Select): 8.223750 (CD) see.COLL.1,
ALL ABOUT MY MOTHER (1999) Music sco: ALBERTO IGLESIAS
-S/T- *UNIVERSAL MUSIC: 676 208-2 (CD)*
ALL CREATURES GREAT AND SMALL (UKGO 17/9/93 orig BBC1
8/1/78) Theme and incidental music: JOHNNY PEARSON
see COLL.5,74,100,180,248,261,
ALL OVER ME (1996) Music score: MIKI NAVAZIO -S/T- Impt
TVT (Cargo-Greyhound): 8110 (CD)
ALL PASSION SPENT (BBC2 9/12/86) *see COLL.193,*

ALL QUIET ON THE PRESTON FRONT (BBC1 4/1/94) theme mus
"Here I Stand" by The MILLTOWN BROTHERS on 'Slinky'
A.& M. (Univ): 395 346-2 (CD) 395 346-4 (MC)
ALL THAT JAZZ (1979) Mus sco: RALPH BURNS "On Broadway"
GEORGE BENSON -S/T- *SPECTRUM (Univ):551 269-2 (CD)*
ALL THAT MONEY CAN BUY (aka 'The Devil And Daniel Webs
ter')(1941) Music score: BERNARD HERRMANN National
Philharmonic Orchestra (B.Herrmann) Film Suite on
UNICORN-KANCHANA (Harmonia Mundi): UKCD 2065 (CD)
ALL THE BROTHERS WERE VALIANT (1953) Music sco: MIKLOS
ROSZA *PROMETHEUS (Silva Screen): PCD 131 (CD)*
ALL THE KINGS MEN (BBC1 00/11/1999) Music score by
ADRIAN JOHNSTSON and perf.by BBC CONCERT ORCHESTRA
-S/T- *BBC WORLDWIDE (Pinn): WMSF 6017-2 (CD)*
ALLAN QUATERMAIN AND THE LOST CITY OF GOLD (1986) Mus
score: MICHAEL LINN *also includes Suites from:*
'MANIFESTO' (88- Nicola Piovani) 'MAKING THE GRADE'
(84- Basil Poledouris) 'DOIN' TIME ON PLANET EARTH'
(87- Dana Kaproff) 'SEVEN MAGNIFICENT GLADIATORS'
(83- Dov Seltzer) *S.SCREEN: SIL 1528-2 (CD)*

ALLY McBEAL (USA/C4 3/6/1998) main theme "Searchin' My
  Soul" and other songs sung by VONDA SHEPARD -S/T-
  SONY: 491 124-2(CD) -4(MC) theme: 666 633-2 (CDs)
  'THE HEART & SOUL OF ALLY McBEAL' by VONDA SHEPARD
  EPIC (TEN): 495 091-2 (CD) -4 (MC)
ALMANAC (USA MUSICAL) Songs by JOHN MURRAY ANDERSON
  ORIG USA CAST *DRG (New Note-Pinn): DRGCD 19009 (CD)*
ALVIN'S SHOW (USA TV) *see COLL.347,378,*
ALWAYS (1990) Music score: JOHN WILLIAMS
  -S/T- *MCA USA (Silva Screen): MCAD 8036 (CD)*
AMADEUS (1984) Music (MOZART) Academy Of St.Martin-In
  The Fields (Neville Marriner) -S/T- *LONDON (Univ):*
  825 126-2 (CD) LONDON 511 126-2 (CD Boxed Set)
  see COLL.73,78,79,80,81,82,105
AMAHL AND THE NIGHT VISITORS (CHRISTMAS OPERA) Music &
  Libretto (Gian Carlo MENOTTI) Royal Opera House Orc
  & Chorus (David Syrus) with JAMES RAINBIRD as Amahl
  TER (Koch) CDTER 1124 (CD)
AMATEUR The (1982) Music score: KEN WANNBERG -S/T-
  select.with 'LATE SHOW'/'OF UNKNOWN ORIGIN' Imp
  PROMETHEUS (Silva Screen): PCD 137 (CD)
AMAZING STORIES (STEVEN SPIELBERG) USA Amblin/MCA-BBC1
  19/4/1992) theme by JOHN WILLIAMS. recording with
  ROYAL SCOTTISH NAT.ORCH.+ music by GEORGES DELERUE
  VARESE (Pinn): VSD 5941 (CD)
AMERICAN BANDSTAND (USA TV) *see COLL.347,*
AMERICAN GIGOLO (1980) Music sc: GIORGIO MORODER -S/T-
  with V/Arts *reiss SPECTRUM (Univ) 551 103-2 (CD)*
  "Seduction Love Theme" JAMES LAST *POLY:831786-2 CD*
AMERICAN GRAFFITI (1973) Music by VARIOUS ORIG ARTISTS
  MCA (BMG): MCLDD 19150 (CDx2)
AMERICAN HISTORY X (1998) Music score by ANNE DUDLEY
  -S/T- *EMI CLASSICS: CDQ 556 781-2 (CD)*
AMERICAN PIE (1999) Music score by DAVID LAWRENCE
  -S/T- *feat:* TONIC-THIRD EYE BLIND-BLINK 182-SUGAR
  RAY-SUPERTRANSATLANTIC-DISHWELLA-DAN WILSON etc.
  -S/T- *UNIVERSAL MUSIC: UND 53269 (CD)*
AMERICAN TWISTORY A HYSTERICAL LOOK AT AMERICA (SHOW)
  Songs: KEVIN KAUFMAN-JOHN EVEREST / ORIG.CAST REC
  DUCY LEE (Silver Sounds): DLR 900106 (CD)
AMERICAN VISIONS (BBC2 03/11/1996) Music score by
  DAVID FERGUSON *see COLL.151,*
AMISTAD (1998) Music score: JOHN WILLIAMS -S/T- on
  DREAMWORKS (BMG): DRD 50035 see COLL.3,
AMOS 'N' ANDY (USA TV) *see COLL.348,*
AN AMERICAN IN PARIS (1951) Songs:GEORGE & IRA GERSHWIN
  1.-S/T- *EMI-Soundtrack: CDODEON 20 (2CD) DELETED*
  2.import score with -S/T- of 'SINGIN' IN THE RAIN'
  BLUE MOON (Discovery): BMCD 7008 (CD)
  3.new recording on *VIRGIN (EMI): VM 561247-2 (CD)*
AN AMERICAN TAIL (1987) Music sco: JAMES HORNER song:
  "Somewhere Out There" (J.Horner-Barry Mann-Cynthia
  Weill) sung by LINDA RONSTADT & JAMES INGRAM -S/T-
  MCA (S.Screen): MCAD 39096 (CD) MCAC 39096 (MC)

AN AMERICAN TAIL 2: Fieval Goes West (1991) Mus score: JAMES HORNER -S/T- *MCA: MCAD(MCAC) 10416 (CD/MC)*

AN AMERICAN WEREWOLF IN LONDON (1981) Music sco: ELMER BERNSTEIN / "Blue Moon" (Rodgers-Hart) songs by MARCELS/BOBBY VINTON/SAM COOKE *-S/T- unavailable*

AN AMERICAN WEREWOLF IN PARIS (1996) Music sc: WILBERT HIRSCH -S/T- *EDEL-HOLLYW.(Pinn): 012131-2HWR (CD)*

AN ANGEL AT MY TABLE (1990) Music score: DON McGLASHAN -S/T- *DRG USA (Pinn): CDSBL 12603 (CD)*

AN AWFULLY BIG ADVENTURE (1994) Music: RICHARD HARTLEY -S/T- *FILMTRACKS (S.Screen): TRAXCD 2001 (CD)*

AN EVENING WITH ALAN JAY LERNER (ORIG LONDON CAST 1987) Song lyrics:Alan Jay Lerner / Music:Frederick Loewe L.Bernstein-B.Lane-C.Strouse) *Feat:* LIZ ROBERTSON-MARTI WEBB-PLACINDO DOMINGO-ELAINE PAIGE and others *FIRST NIGHT (Pinn): OCRCD 6012 (CD)*

AN IDEAL HUSBAND (1999) Music score: CHARLIE MOLE -S/T- *BMG SOUNDTRACKS: 74321 66992-2 (CD)*

AN OFFICER AND A GENTLEMAN (1982) Mus sc: JACK NITZSCHE "Up Where We Belong" (Jack Nitzsche-Buffy Saint Marie-Will Jennings) sung JOE COCKER-JENNIFER WARNES -S/T- *ISLAND (Univ.): IMCD 77 (CD) ICM 2041 (MC) see COLL.106,*

ANACONDA (1997) Music score: RANDY EDELMAN -S/T- *EDEL (Pinn): 002281-2CIN (CD)*

ANALYZE THIS (1998) Music score by HOWARD SHORE -S/T- *VARESE (Pinn): VSD 6016 (CD)*

ANASTASIA (1997) Music score: DAVID NEWMAN -S/T- *ATLANTIC (TEN): 7567 80753-2 (CD) -4 (MC)*

ANATOMY OF A MURDER (1959) Music score: DUKE ELLINGTON -S/T- *reiss: COLUMBIA (USA): CK 65569 (CD)*

ANCHORS AWEIGH (1945 MUSICAL) *feat:* FRANK SINATRA-GRACE KELLY-KATHRYN GRAYSON *TARGET (BMG): CD 60003 (CD) also abailable -S/T- Import with* 'ON THE TOWN' *BLUE MOON (Discovery): BMCD 7007 (CD) also on SANDY HOOK (Silver Sounds): CDSH 2024 (CD)*

AND DO THEY DO Music: MICHAEL NYMAN with MICHAEL NYMAN BAND *TER (Koch): CDTER 1123 (CD)*

AND THE BAND PLAYED ON (1993) Music sco: CARTER BURWELL -S/T- *VARESE (Pinn): VSD 5449 (CD)*

ANDORRA (BBC 1967) music: RON GRAINER *see COLL.8,367,*

ANDY GRIFFITH SHOW (USA) *see COLL.345,*

ANDY WARHOL'S DRACULA and **FRANKENSTEIN** (1974) Music sc CLAUDIO GIZZI -S/T- *IMPT (S.Screen): OST 119 (CD)*

ANGEL (USA 1983) music sco: CRAIG SAFAN -S/T- *INTRADA USA Imprt (Silva Screen-Koch): MAF 7047D (CD)*

ANGEL & THE SOLDIER BOY The (1989) BBC1 27/12/89 -S/T- *reissue BMG Kidz (BMG): 74321 25081-2 (CD)*

ANGEL BABY (1995) Music sco: JOHN CLIFFORD WHITE -S/T- *Import on ICON (Pinn.Import): ICON 19951 (CD)*

ANGEL HEART (1987) Music score: TREVOR JONES -S/T- on *ISLAND (Univ) IMCD 76 (CD) ICM(ILPM) 2025 (MC/LP)*

ANGELIQUE (1964) Music score: MICHEL MAGNE -S/T- *MOVIE SELECT AUDIO (Direct): MSA 99011 (CD)*

ANGELS (BBC1 1976-80) theme music "Motivation" by ALAN
   PARKER *see COLL.2,5,243,*
ANGELS AND INSECTS (1994) Mus sco: ALEX BALANESCU perf
   BALANESCU QUART.-S/T- *MUTE-RTM (Disc) CDSTUMM 147*
ANGIE (1993) Music sco: JERRY GOLDSMITH -S/T- *VARESE
   (Pinn): VSD 5469 (CD)*
ANGST (1986) Electronic Music sco: KLAUS SCHULZE -S/T-
   THUNDERBOLT-MAGNUM (MMG): CDTB 2.027 (CD)
ANIMAL E.R. (C5 15/02/1999) music by DAVID ARNOLD
   unavailable
ANIMAL FARM (1998) Music score by RICHARD HARVEY
   VARESE (Pinn): VSD 6082 (CD)
ANIMAL HOSPITAL (BBC1 5/1/95) theme music composed
   and arranged by RONALD DE JONG *unavailable*
ANIMAL HOUSE - *see under* 'National Lampoon's...'
ANIMAL MAGIC (BBC1 to 84) "Las Vegas" LAURIE JOHNSON
   see COLL.5,172,215,
ANIMAL PEOPLE (BBC1 25/07/1999) series title music by
   AL LETHBRIDGE *unavailable*
ANIMAL POLICE (BBC1 08/02/1999) music by NEIL ARTHUR
   unavailable
ANIMALS OF FARTHING WOOD The (BBC1/EBU 6/1/93) music
   DETLEV KUHNE & WDR ORC *BBC: YBBC 1452 (2MC)*
   see COLL.67,
ANIMANIACS (ITV 24/2/94) Songs from series *ATLANTIC
   (TEN): 8122 71570-2 (CD) -4 (MC)*
ANNA (FRENCH TV SERIES 1967) Music: SERGE GAINSBOURG
   MERCURY (Univ): 558 837-2 (CD)
ANNA AND THE KING *see COLL.1,*

ANNA KARENINA (1997) TCHAIKOVSKY-RACHMANINOV-PROKOFIEV
   w: St.Petersburg Phil.Orch cond.by Sir GEORG SOLTI
   with GALINA GORCHAKOVA sopr; MAXIM VENGEROV violin
   -S/T- *LONDON (Univ): 455 360-2 (CD) 455 360-4 (MC)*
ANNA OF THE FIVE TOWNS (BBC2 9/1/85) title music by
   NIGEL HESS London Film Orch *see COLL.193,*
ANNE OF GREEN GABLES (ORIG LONDON CAST 1969) Songs by
   NORMAN CAMPBELL-DONALD HARRON *featur* POLLY JAMES
   BARBARA HAMILTON on *SONY Broadway: SMK 53495 (CD)*
ANNIE - songs by Charles Strouse and Martin Charnin
   1. STUDIO RECORDING 1997 *feat:* KIM CRISWELL-RUTHIE
   HENSHALL-RON RAINES-SARAH FRENCH with NAT.SYMPH
   ORCHESTRA conducted by MARTIN YATES
   TER-Music Theatre Hour (Koch): CDTEH 6001 (CD)
   2. FILM MUSICAL 1982 *feat* ALBERT FINNEY-AILEEN QUINN
   CAROL BURNETT -S/T- *Sony: 467 608-2 (CD) -4 (MC)*
   3. ORIG BROADWAY CAST 1977 *feat:* ANDREA McARDLE-REID
   SHELTON-DOROTHY LOUDEN-SANDY FAISON-ROBERT FITCH
   COLUMBIA (Ten): SK 60723 (CD) see COLL.58,119,322,
ANNIE GET YOUR GUN songs: Irving Berlin-Dorothy Fields
   1. 1998 REVIVAL CAST STUDIO RECORDING *featuring:*
   BERNADETTE PETERS and The NEW BROADWAY CAST
   ANGEL (EMI): CDQ 556 812-2 (CD)
   2. LINCOLN CENTER EDIT.FIRST COMPLETE RECORDING *w:*

JUDY KAYE-BARRY BOSTWICK *TER (Koch): CDTER2 12292*
3. CARLTON SHOWS COLLECTION 1995 *feat:* GEMMA CRAVEN-
   with EDMUND HOCKRIDGE-STEVE BUTLER-ALISON COX
   CARLTON Shows Collect: 30362 0012-2 (CD) -4 (MC)
4. NEW LONDON CAST 1986 *feat:* SUZI QUATRO & Company
   FIRST NIGHT (Pinn): OCRCD 6024 (CD)
5. ORIG LONDON CAST 1947 *feat:* DOLORES GRAY-BILL JOHNS
   ON-HAL BRYAN-IRVING DAVIES-WENDY TOYE-PADDY STONE
   LASERLIGHT (Target-BMG): 12 449 (CD)
6. ORIG BROADWAY CAST 1946 *with* ETHEL MERMAN-BRUCE YAR
   NELL-BENAY VENUTA-JERRY ORBACH *BMG: RD 81124 (CD)*
7. STUDIO 1990 *feat:* KIM CRISWELL-THOMAS HAMPSON-JASON
   GRAAE-REBECCA LUKER-Ambrosian Chor-London Sinfonia
   (J.McGlinn) *EMI: CDANNIE 1 (CD) TCANNIE 1 (MC)*

ANOTHER DAWN (1937) Music sco: ERICH WOLFGANG KORNGOLD
   new version: MOSCOW S.ORCH (Stromberg) also featur:
   "Ballet Fantasy" from 'ESCAPE ME NEVER' on
   MARCO POLO (Select): 8.223871 (CD)
ANTARCTICA (HORIZON BBC2 30/10/97) o.score: PHILIP POPE
   unavailable   "Musica Poetica" (Carl Orff-G.Keetman)
   TOLZ BOYS CHOIR *RCA (BMG): 09026 68031-2 (CD)*
ANTARCTICA (1983) Music score: VANGELIS -S/T- POLYDOR
   815732-2 (CD) -4 (MC)
ANTHOLOGY - THE BEATLES (ITV 26/11/95) music and songs
   TV S/T *EMI Parloph: CD(PC)PCSP 727 (2CD/2MC/3LPs)*
ANTIQUES INSPECTORS The (BBC1 7/9/97) theme music "Hot
   Club Swing" by JOHNNY HAWKESWORTH *De Wolfe libr.*
ANTIQUES ROAD SHOW (BBC1 18/2/79-2000)
   1989-2000 series theme: PAUL READE *unavailable*
   1985-1989 series theme: ROGER LIMB *unavailable*
ANTONIA'S LINE (1995) Music score: ILONA SEKACZ -S/T-
   SILVA SCREEN (Koch): FILMCD 183 (CD)
ANTONIO CARLUCCI'S ITALIAN FEAST (BBC2 17/9/96) music:
   CROCODILE MUSIC *see COLL.342,*
ANTONY AND CLEOPATRA (1972) Music score by JOHN SCOTT
   Royal Philharmonic Orch (Scott) Symphonic score on
   JOHN SCOTT Records (Silva Screen): JSCDC 114 (CD)
ANTZ (1998) Music score: HARRY GREGSON WILLIAMS & JOHN
   POWELL -S/T- *EMI: CDANTZ 001 (CD)*
ANYONE CAN WHISTLE (ORIG BROADWAY CAST) Songs: STEPHEN
   SONDHEIM *with* Angela Lansbury-Lee Remick & Company
   CBS USA (S.Screen): CK 02480 (CD) JST 02480 (MC)
ANYTHING GOES - songs by Cole Porter
   1. FILM 1936 *feat:* BING CROSBY-ETHEL MERMAN etc
      recording also incl.extracts from 'PANAMA HATTIE'
      SANDY HOOK (Silver Sounds): CDSH 2043 (CD)
   2. ORIG LONDON CAST 1989 *feat:* ELAINE PAIGE-HOWARD
      McGILLIN-BERNARD CRIBBINS and Comp *FIRST NIGHT
      (Pinn): OCRCD 6038 (CD)*
   3. STUDIO RECORDING 1989 *feat:* FREDERICA VON STADE-KIM
      CRISWELL-CRIS GROENENDAAL-JACK GILFORD-LONDON SYMPH
      ONY ORCHESTRA and AMBROSIAN CHORUS (John McGlynn)
      EMI: CDC 749848-2 (CD) EL 749848-4 (MC)

APOCALYPSE NOW (1979) Music: CARMINE & FRANCIS COPPOLA
   inc.'Die Walkure' (WAGNER) + V.Art -S/T- *reissued*
   WEA (TEN): 7559 60689-2 (2CD)
   see COLL.77,105,198,273,274,275,
APOLLO 13 (1994) Music score by JAMES HORNER
   -S/T- *MCA (BMG): MCD 11241*
   see COLL.49,71,205,206,207,267,306,328,
APPLE TREE The (ORIG BROADWAY CAST 66) Songs JERRY BOCK
   SHELDON HARNICK *featuring* BARBARA HARRIS-LARRY BLYD
   DEN-ALAN ALDA *SONY MUSIC: CD 48209 (CD)*
APRIL MORNING - *see* IRONCLADS

AQUA MARINA (ATV 60's) theme music by BARRY GRAY with
   vocal by GARRY MILLER *see COLL.171,360,*
ARABESQUE (1966) Music sco: HENRY MANCINI -S/T- with
   score from 'BREAKFAST AT TIFFANYS' (1961)
   RCA CAMDEN (BMG): 74321 69878-2 (CD)
ARCHIES The (USA TV) *see COLL.347,*

ARCTIC BLUE (1993) Music score: PETER MELNICK -S/T-
   NARADA (New Note-Pinn): ND 63030 (CD)
ARE YOU LONESOME TONIGHT (ORIG LONDON CAST 1985) Play:
   Alan Bleasdale / *ELVIS PRESLEY songs sung by* MARTIN
   SHAW-SIMON BOWMAN *FIRST NIGHT (Pinn): OCRCD 6027*
ARENA (BBC2) Theme "Another Green World" by BRIAN ENO
   EG (Univ): EGMC 21 (MC) EGCD 21 (CD) see COLL.262,
ARISTOCATS The (1970) Songs: RICHARD and ROBERT SHERMAN
   -S/T- *DISNEY (B.Vista): WD 74250-2 (CD) -4 (MC)*
   see WALT DISNEY INDEX p.362
ARISTOCRATS The (BBC 1999) Music score: MARK THOMAS
   BBC (Pinn): WMSF 6011-2 (CD)
ARLINGTON ROAD (1998) Music score: ANGELO BADALAMENTI
   -S/T- (V.ARTISTS) *RCA (BMG): 74321   65152-2 (CD)*
ARMAGEDDON (1997) Music score: TREVOR RABIN
   -S/T- *COLUMBIA (Ten): 491 384-2 (CD) -4 (MC)*
   also available 'MUSIC INSPIRED BY THE FILM' (Coll)
   BGRM (Silver Sounds): 1096 34011-2 (CD)
ARMY OF DARKNESS (1992) Music sco: JOSEPH LoDUCA -S/T-
   VARESE (Pinn): VSD 5411 (CD) VSC 5411 (MC)
ARMY GAME The (ITV Granada 57-62) Theme feat ALFIE BASS
   MICHAEL MEDWIN-BERNARD BRESSLAW on 'Hits Of 58' col
   MFP Hour Of Pleasure (EMI): HR 8175 (MC only)
AROUND THE WORLD IN 80 DAYS (1956) Music: VICTOR YOUNG
   -S/T- *MCA (S.Scr) MCAD 31164 (CD) see COLL.298,*
AROUND THE WORLD IN 80 DAYS (Michael Palin BBC1 14/7/91
   (11/10/89) Orig music: PADDY KINGSLAND *unavailable*
ARRIVAL (1991) Music score: RICHARD BAND -S/T- *INTRADA*
   (Silva Screen): MAF 7032CD (CD)
ARRIVAL The (1996) Mus: ARTHUR KEMPEL feat NORTHWEST
   SINFONIA *SILVA SCREEN (Koch): FILMCD 182 (CD)*
ARTHUR (1980) Theme 'Best That You Can Do' sung by
   CHRISTOPHER CROSS *see COLL.13,36,303,*

ARTHUR C.CLARKE'S MYSTERIOUS UNIVERSE (USA)/Discovery/
Satellite) Music sco: ALAN HAWKSHAW -S/T- music on
HUNGRY HAWK (Grapevine/Polygram): HHCD 101 (CD)

AS GOOD AS IT GETS (1997) Mus score: HANS ZIMMER -S/T-
COLUMBIA (Ten): 489 502-2 (CD) see COLL.3,

AS THOUSANDS CHEER (SHOW with songs by IRVING BERLIN)
ORIGINAL CAST STUDIO RECORDING on
VARESE (Pinn): VSD 5999 (CD)

AS TIME GOES BY (BBC1 12/1/92) theme "As Time Goes By"
(Herman Hupfeld) by JOE FAGIN on Coll 'Best Of on
Westmoor (BMG): CDWM 107(CD) CWM 107(MC)
CDS 1(CDs) see also under 'CASABLANCA'

AS YOU LIKE IT (1936) Music sc: WILLIAM WALTON select.
'Walton Film Music' LONDON PHILHARMONIC ORCHESTRA
conduct: CARL DAVIS *EMI: CDM 565585-2 (CD) also*
ACADEMY of ST.MARTIN-IN-THE-FIELDS (N.Marriner)
and 'HAMLET' *CHANDOS: CHAN 8842 (CD)*

ASK THE FAMILY (BBC2) *see COLL.7,*

ASPECTS OF LOVE -songs by Andrew Lloyd Webber-Charles
Hart and Don Black
  1. ORIG LONDON CAST 1989 *feat:* MICHAEL BALL-ANN CRUMB
     DIANA MORRISON-KEVIN COLSON *POLY: 841 126-2 / -4*
  2. SHOWS COLLECTION Studio 1993 *feat:* PAUL JONES with
     STEPHANIE LAWRENCE-DAVE WILLETTS-FIONA HENDLEY-CARL
     WAYNE-WEST END CONCERT ORCH. *plus music of* 'PHANTOM
     OF THE OPERA' *CARLTON: PWKS(PWKMC) 4164 (CD(MC)*
  3. ROYAL PHILH.ORCH *PLAY SUITES from* Aspects Of Love
     Cats/Joseph and The Amazing Technicolor Dreamcoat
     Carlton: PWKS(PWKMC) 4115 (CD(MC)
  4. Classic Musicals series *feat:* JOHN BARROWMAN-JANIS
     KELLY-SHONA LINDSAY-JOHN DIEDRICH + 'JESUS CHRIST
     SUPERSTAR' *KOCH INT: 34083-2 (CD)*

ASSASSIN The: Point Of No Return (1992) Music sco: HANS
ZIMMER includes songs by NINA SIMONE -S/T- *MILAN*
(BMG): 14302-2 (CD)

ASSASSINATION BUREAU The (1968) Music sco: RON GRAINER
see COLL.8,

ASSASSINS (ORIG USA CAST 1991) Songs: STEPHEN SONDHEIM
William Parry-Terence Mann *(BMG): RD 60737 (CD)*

ASSAULT ON PRECINCT 13 (1976) Music sc: JOHN CARPENTER
see COLL.121,

ASSAULT The (1986) - *see under* 'CRY IN THE DARK'

ASTERIX IN BRITAIN (1986) Music score: VLADIMIR COSMA
-S/T- including 'CAESAR'S GIFT' on
POMME (Discovery): 95129-2 (CD)

ASTEROID (ITV1/3/97) music: SHIRLEY WALKER *unavailable*

ASTRO BOY (USA TV) *see COLL.311,348,*

ASTRONAUT'S WIFE The (1998) Music sco: GEORGE S.CLINTON
-S/T- *SIRE (USA Impt): SIRE 31084 (CD)*

ASTRONOMERS The (USA TV) Music score: J.A.C.REDFORD
INTRADA USA (Silva Screen): MAF 7018D (CD)

AT FIRST SIGHT (1998) Music score: MARK ISHAM -S/T-
MILAN (BMG: 74321 65510-2 (CD)

AT THE DROP OF A HAT (Musical Revue 1958 Fortune)
featuring MICHAEL FLANDERS and DONALD SWANN on
EMI: CDP 797465-2(CD) / AT THE DROP OF ANOTHER HAT
(Musical Revue 1960 Haymarket) MICHAEL FLANDERS-
-DONALD SWANN *EMI: CDP 797466-2 (CD) ECC (2MC)*

ATHLETICS (BBCTV 79-96) "World Series" KEITH MANSFIELD
Also used "Fanfare For The Common Man" (A.Copland)
see COLL.176

ATLANTIC CITY (1981) Music score: MICHEL LEGRAND -S/T-
MUSIDISC Import (Discovery): 11907-2 (CD)

ATLANTIC REALM (BBC1 8/1/89) Music comp.& performed by
CLANNAD -S/T- *reis: RCA (BMG): 74321 31867-2 (CD)*

ATLANTIS (1991) Music score: ERIC SERRA -S/T- *VIRGIN
Impt (Silva Screen): 869462 (CD) 50867 (MC)*

ATOM ANT SHOW (USA TV) *see COLL.311,349,*

ATOMIC CAFE The (1982) PRO-NUCLEAR FILM DOCUMENTARY
-S/T- *FUTURE (Timewarp): FR 996 (CD)*

ATTACK ON THE IRON COAST 1967 Music: GERARD SCHURMANN
'Coastal Command' *S.SCREEN (Koch): FILM(C)(CD) 072*

AU REVOIR LES ENFANTS 1987 *see COLL.84,*

AUF WIEDERSEHEN, PET (C4 11/3/95 orig ITV 11/11/83)
"That's Livin' Alright"/"Breakin'Away" (David Mac
Kay-Ian La Frenais) sung by JOE FAGIN 'BEST OF AUF
WIEDERSEHEN PET' *PRESTIGE (ELSE): CDSGP 0201 (CD)*
+ WESTMOOR: CDWM 107(CD) see COLL.5,7,19,

AUGUST (1995) Music sco: ANTHONY HOPKINS arr/orch and
conducted by GEORGE FENTON *featur: ANTHONY HOPKINS
(piano) -S/T- DEBONAIR (Pinn): CDDEB 1003 (CD)*

AUSTIN POWERS:INTERNATIONAL MAN OF MYSTERY (1997) -S/T-
Various Artists *POLYDOR (Univ): 162 112-2 (CD)*

AUSTIN POWERS 2: THE SPY WHO SHAGGED ME (1999) V.ARTS
-S/T-(1) *MAVERICK-WB (TEN):9362 47348-2 (CD) -4(MC)*
-S/T-(2) *MAVERICK-WB (TEN):9362 47538-2 (CD) -4(MC)*

AUTUMN SONATA (1978) Music by CHOPIN *see COLL.86,87,*

AVALON (90) Music score: RANDY NEWMAN -S/T- on *WARNER
BROS IMP (S.Screen): 926 437-2 (CD) 926 437-4(MC)*

AVENGERS The (1998) Music sco: JOEL McNEELY -S/T- *incl*
MARIUS DE VRIES-GRACE JONES-MERZ-ASHTAR COMMAND-
BABY BIRD-ANNIE LENNOX-STEREO MC'S-IGGY POP & UTAH
SAINTS-VERVE PIPE-SUGAR RAY-SUGGS-SINEAD O'CONNOR
-S/T- (songs) *WB: 7567 83118-2 (CD) -4 (MC)*
-S/T- (score) *SILVA SCREEN (Koch): FILMCD 304 (CD)*

AVENGERS The (ABCTV 65-69) music by LAURIE JOHNSON
*see COLL.2,4,23,38,109,110,121,149,150,215,216
217,337,344,346,360,367,369,377,*

AVENUE X (MUSICAL SHOW) with music by RAY LESLEE and
lyrics by JOHN JILER / ORIG USA CAST RECORDING on
RCA VICTOR (BMG): 09026 63208-2 (CD)

BABE (THE GALLANT PIG) (1995) Music: NIGEL WESTLAKE
"If I Had You" adapted from Symphony No.3 Op.78
(Saint-Saens) by YVONNE KEELY-SCOTT FITZGERALD
-S/T- *VARESE (Pinn): VSD 5661 (CD) deleted*

BABE 2: PIG IN THE CITY (1998) Music score:
-S/T- *GEFFEN (BMG): GED 25310 (CD)*

BABE (1992) Music score: ELMER BERNSTEIN -S/T- Import
 MCA (S.Screen): MCAD 10576 (CD) MCAC 10576 (MC)
BABES IN ARMS (1939) Songs: RICHARD RODGERS-LORENZ HART
 -S/T- *with* JUDY GARLANDO-MICKEY ROONEY *NEW WORLD
 (Harmonia Mundi): NW 386-2 (CD) NW 386-4 (MC)*
BABETTE'S FEAST (1988) Music score: PER NORGARD -S/T-
 MILAN (Pinn): CDCH 333 (CD)
BABY (ORIG BROADWAY CAST 1983) Mus: DAVID SHIRE Lyrics
 RICHARD MALTYBY JNR *feat:* Liz Callaway-Beth Fowler
 James Congdon-T.Graff *TER (Koch): CDTER 1089*
BABY IT'S YOU (C4 25/5/94) theme music "Spiritu" by
 JOHN HARLE on 'Silencium' - *see COLL.182,*
BABY OF MACON The (1993) Classical music by MONTEVERDI
 CORELLI-TALLIS-BACH-CLAMER-FRESCOBALDI etc. -S/T-
 KOCH International (Koch): 34014-2 (CD)
BABYLON 5 (USATV/C4 1994-97)Music by CHRISTOPHER FRANKE
 *SONIC IMAGES (Greyhound-Cargo-Silver Sounds) CD's :
 SI 8403-2 (VOLUME 1) SI 8502-2 (VOLUME 2)
 SI 8602-2 (VOLUME 3: MESSAGES FROM EARTH)
 SI 0312 (DELIVERY FROM AVALON) SI 0318 (WALKABOUT)
 SI 0513 (RAGGED EDGE) SI 0310 (SEVERED DREAMS)
 SI 0321 (SHADOW DANCING) SI 0222 (FALL OF NIGHT)
 SI 0417 (FACE OF THE NIGHT) SI 0406 (INTO THE FIRE)
 SI 0315 (INTERLUDES AND EXAMINATIONS)
 SI 0415 (NO SURRENDER NO RETREAT)
 7828 278900-2 (THIRDSPACE)
 SID 0516 (CD) (DARKNESS ASCENDING)
 SID 0404 (CD) 'FALLING TOWARDS..)
 SID 8900 (CD) 'THIRDSPACE)
 see COLL.121,267,270,308,312,362,*
BACK TO THE FUTURE (Trilogy) Music from all 3 movies
 VARESE (Pinn): VSD 5950 (CD)
BACK TO THE FUTURE (1985) Music score: ALAN SILVESTRI
 -S/T- *MCA MCLD 19151 (CD) see COLL.334,*
BACK TO THE FUTURE 3 (1990) Mus: ALAN SILVESTRI -S/T-
 VARESE (Pinn): VSD 5272 (CD)
BACKBEAT (1994) Beatles Early Years -S/T- songs:
 VIRGIN (EMI): CD(TC)V 2729 (CD/MC/LP) -S/T-
 score: (Don Was) *Virgin CDV(TCV)2740 (CD/MC)*
BAD BOYS (1995) Music score: MARK MANCINA -S/T- on
 COLUMBIA (Ten): 480 453-2(CD) -4(MC)
BAD CHANNELS (1992) Music by BLUE OYSTER CULT -S/T-
 ANGEL AIR (Direct): SJPCD 046 (CD)
BAD GIRLS (ITV 01/06/1999) music by NINA HUMPHREYS
 unavailable
BAD INFLUENCE (1990) Music score: TREVOR JONES -S/T- +
 V.Arts *reissued SPECTRUM (Univ): 551 102-2 (CD)*
BAD MOON (1996) Music score: DANIEL LICHT -S/T- on
 SILVA AMERICA (Koch): SSD 1068 (CD)
BAD TASTE (1988) Music by various artists -S/T- on
 NORMAL (Topic/Proj/Dir): QDKCD 002 (CD)
BADGER (BBC1 11/07/1999) music by NIGEL HESS on
 'NIGEL HESS TV THEMES' *CHANDOS: CHAN 9750 (CD)*
 see COLL.193,

BADLANDS (1973) music inc. "Gassenhauer" ('SCHULWERK')
   (CARL ORFF-G.KEETMAN) on 'THE BEST OF CARL ORFF' on
   RCA (BMG): 75605 51357-2 (CD) -4 (MC)
BAGDAD CAFE (1988) Mus (B.Telson-P.Adlon-O.Ebner-L.Brue
   hr-Bach) Theme "Calling You" sung by JEVETTA STEELE
   -S/T- *ISLAND: IMCD 102 (CD) ICM 2005 (MC)*
BAGPUSS (BBC1 12/02/1974) music & songs by SANDRA KERR
   & JOHN FAULKNER *SMALLFOLK (Dir): SMF 1 (CD)*
BALLAD OF LITTLE JO The (1993) Mus sco: DAVID MANSFIELD
   featuring songs by KATE & ANNA McGARRIGLE -S/T- on
   INTRADA (Silva Screen): MAF 7053D (CD)
BALLYKISSANGEL (BBC1 11/2/96-1999)
   1996/1997 series music and theme by SHAUN DAVEY on
   -S/T- *VIRGIN (EMI): VTCD 17 (CD) VTMC 17 (MC)*
   1998 series music by DOMINIC CRAWFORD COLLINS
BALTO (1995) Music score: JAMES HORNER -S/T- *MCA Impt*
   (EMS): MCAD 11388 (CD)
BAMBI (1942) Songs (Frank Churchill-Edward Plumb) -S/T-
   DISNEY-EDEL (Pinn): 010 880-2DNY (CD)
   see WALT DISNEY INDEX p.362
BANANA SPLITS (aka BANANA BUNCH) (USA68) theme "Tra La
   La Song" (Adams-Barkan) *see COLL.349,373,*
BAND OF GOLD (ITV 12/3/95) theme and music score by
   HAL LINDES *unavailable* song "LOVE HURTS" (Bryant)
   by BARBARA DICKSON from 'Dark End Of The Street'
   TRANSATLANTIC-CASTLE (Pinn): TRA(CD)(MC)117 (CD/MC)
BANDIT QUEEN (1993) Music score: NUSRAT FATEH ALI KHAN
   -S/T- *MILAN (BMG): 74321 37811-2 (CD)*
BAPS (B.A.P.S.) (1997) Mus sc: STANLEY CLARKE -S/T- inc
   KOOL & THE GANG-KINSUI-VERONICA and CRAIG MACK-ALEC
   BROWN-GYRL etc. *MILAN (BMG): 74321 48684-2 (CD)*
BARABBAS (1962) Mus: MARIO NASCIMBENE + 'ALEXANDER THE
   GREAT' *DRG (Pinn): DRGCD 32964 (CD) see COLL.261,*
BARAKA (1993) Music score: MICHAEL STERNS -S/T- on
   MILAN (BMG): 15306-2 (CD) 15306-4 (MC)
BARBARA (ITV 27/06/1999) mus by PETE BAIKIE *unavailable*
BARBARELLA (1967) Music score: CHARLES FOX-BOB CREWE
   -S/T- *reissue DYNOVOICE (Greyhound): DY 31908 (LP)*
BARBARIANS The (Film) Music score: PINO DONAGGIO -S/T-
   INTRADA (Koch): MAF 7008D (CD)
BAREFACED CHIC (1999) MUSICAL SHOW *feat* FASCINATING ADA
   FIRST NIGHT (Pinn): SCENECD 25 (CD)
BAREFOOT CONTESSA The (1954) Mus sco: MARIO NASCIMBENE
   -S/T- inc.scor: *'ROOM AT THE TOP'/'QUIET AMERICAN'*
   DRG (Pinn): DRGCD 32961 (CD) see also COLL
BARETTA (USA) *see COLL.347,382,*
BARMY AUNTY BOOMERANG (BBC1 Scotland 16/09/1999)
   series music by GREGOR PHILP with vocal by
   TOYAH WILLCOX *unavailable*
BARNABY JONES (USA) *see COLL.17,347,*
BARNARDO'S CHILDREN (BBC2 4/7/95) theme and incidental
   music "Dives and Lazarus" (Vaughan Williams) *vers:*
   ACADEMY OF ST.MARTIN-IN-THE FIELDS (N.Marriner) on
   PHILIPS (Univ.): 442 427-2 (CD)

BARNEY MILLER (USA 82 / C4 9/1/88) theme: JACK ELLIOT
and ALLYN FERGUSON *see COLL.19,347,*

BARON The - *see COLL.360,*

BARRIO (Neighbourhood)(1998) m: HECHOS CONTRA EL DECORO
-S/T- *KARONTE (Silver Sounds-Discovery): EQ 137CD*

BARRY LYNDON (1975) MD: LEONARD ROSENMAN *feat.Classics*
-S/T- *reiss: WB (TEN): 7599 25984-2 (CD) SONY Fra.
(Disc): SK(ST) 61684 (CD/MC) see COLL.79,86,131,*

BARTON FINK (1991) Mus.sco: CARTER BURWELL *with 'FARGO'*
-S/T- *SNAPPER (Pinn): SMACD 808 (CD)*

BASIC INSTINCT (1992) Music sco: JERRY GOLDSMITH -S/T-
VARESE (Pinn): VSD(VSC) 5360 (CD(MC) note: disco
track "Rave The Rhythm" by CHANNEL X *not on -S/T-*

BASKETBALL DIARIES The (1994) Music sco: GRAEME REVELL
-S/T- *ISLAND Poly (Univ.): 524 093-2 (CD) -4(MC)*

BASQUIAT (1996) Music score by JOHN CALE -S/T- on
ISLAND (Univ.): 524 260-2 (CD) 524 260-4 (MC)

BAT MASTERSON (USA TV) *see COLL.346,*

BATHING BEAUTY (1944 MUSICAL) *feat* ESTHER WILLIAMS and
RED SKELTON *incl.songs from* 'HERE COMES THE WAVES'
+ 'THIS GUN FOR HIRE' *TARGET (BMG): CD 60001 (CD)*

BATMAN (USATV 1966) Music: NEAL HEFTI - ORIG TV S-/T-
*RAZOR & TIE (Koch): RE 2153 (CD) see COLL.38,121,
122,150,267,311,345,367,378,382,*

BATMAN (FILM 1989) *Songs* comp & sung by PRINCE -S/T-
*W.BROS (TEN): K.7599 25936-2 (CD) WX 281C (MC)
Score:* DANNY ELFMAN *WEA 925977-2 CD deleted*

BATMAN AND ROBIN (1997) Music score: ELLIOT GOLDENTHAL
V.ARTS -S/T- *W.BROS (TEN): 9362 46620-2 (CD) -4(MC)*

BATMAN FOREVER (1994) Music: ELLIOT GOLDENTHAL -S/T-
score: *ATLANTIC (TEN): 7567 82776-2 (CD) deleted*
songs: *inc.*U2-P.J.HARVEY-BRANDY-SEAL-MASSIVE ATTACK
-S/T- *ATLANTIC (TEN) 7567 82759-2 see COLL.49,145,*

BATMAN: MASK OF PHANTASM (1993) Music: SHIRLEY WALKER
-S/T- *WARNER Impt (S.Scr): WA 45484-2 (CD)*

BATMAN RETURNS (1992) Music: DANNY ELFMAN *see COLL.311,*

BATMAN TRILOGY / JOEL McNEELY & ROYAL SCOTTISH N.ORCH
VARESE (Pinn): VSD 5766 (CD)   *1997*
featuring music from 'BATMAN' and 'BATMAN RETURNS'
(DANNY ELFMAN) 'BATMAN FOREVER' *(ELLIOT GOLDENTHAL)*
'BATMAN' TV THEME *(NEAL HEFTI/NELSON RIDDLE)* and
'BATMAN AND ROBIN' *(ELLIOT GOLDENTHAL)*

BATTERSEA DOGS HOME (BBC1 07/12/1998) theme music based
on "Perfect Day" (Lou Reed) & "Always Look On The
Bright Side Of Life" (Eric Idle) Doggy arrangement
by JANE ELLER *unavailable*

BATTLE OF BRITAIN (1969) Music score by RON GOODWIN.
"Air Battle Sequence" by WILLIAM WALTON -S/T- reiss
RYKODISC (Vital): RCD 10747 (CD)

BATTLE OF BRITAIN 1969 Mus: WILLIAM WALTON-RON GOODWIN
selection of WALTON music *EMI: CDM 565585-2 (CD)*
see COLL.187,383,

BATTLE OF BRITAIN 1969 Mus: RON GOODWIN-WILLIAM WALTON
    Academy of St.Martin-in-the-Fields (N.Marriner) and
    'Escape me Never'/'Three Sisters'/'Spitfire Prelude
    & Fugue'/'Wartime Sketchbook' *CHANDOS:CHAN 8870*

BATTLE OF NERETVA (1969) Music score: BERNARD HERRMANN
    selection on Coll 'BERNARD HERRMANN AT THE MOVIES'
    including 'SISTERS' (1973) / 'NIGHT DIGGER' (1971)
    LABEL X (Hot): ATMCD 2003 (CD)

BATTLESHIP POTEMKIN 1925 Mus.sco: EDMUND MEISAL + music
    from 'THE HOLY MOUNTAIN' Orch della Svizzera Italia
    na (Mark Abeas) *EDEL (S.Screen) 0029062EDL (2CD)*

BATTLESTAR GALACTICA (USA 78/ITV) Music score by STU
    PHILLIPS. New Recording by ROYAL SCOTTISH NATIONAL
    ORCHESTRA on *VARESE (Pinn): VSD 5949 (CD)*
    see COLL.17,38,122,267,308,329,

BAYWATCH (USA/ITV 13/1/90) Theme (95) "I'm Always Here"
    JIM JAMISON *unavailable* Theme 93 "Current Of Love"
    DAVID HASSELHOFF *Arista BMG 74321 17618-2 (CD)*
    orig theme "Save Me" by PETER CETERA on 'One More
    Story' *FULL MOON-TEN: WX161(C)(CD) see COLL.17,270,*

BBC Learning Zone 1999 "Rundadinella" from 'Schulwerk'
    on 'BEST OF CARL ORFF' *RCA BMG: 75605 51357-2 (CD)*
    also a 6 CD set *RCA (BMG): 09026 68031-2 (6CDs)*

BBC Internet trails 1999 "That's Life" (1) by SHIRLEY
    BASSEY 'Let Me Sing & I'm Happy' *MFP (EMI): CZ 98*
    (2) 'That's Life' sung by FRANK SINATRA *Reprise*

BBC On Line trailer 1999 "Walk On The Wild Side" by
    LOU REED on 'TRANSFORMER' *RCA (BMG): 74321 60181-2*
    (CD) -4 (MC) / also 'BEST OF' *ND(NK) 83753 (CD/MC)*

BBC PROMS 1999 (BBC1/2 JUL/AUG/SEP 1999)
    'BBC PROMS 99' VARIOUS ARTISTS (2CD SELECTIONS)
    TELDEC: 9548 37591-2 (2CD)

BBC SPORTS PERSONALITY OF THE YEAR "The Challenge" by
    CHARLES WILLIAMS *see COLL.176,*

BBC YOUNG MUSICIAN OF THE YEAR (UK) 1998
    (BBC2 29/3/1998, from BELFAST)
    winner: ADRIAN SPILLETT (percussion) playing the
    'Percussion Concerto' (Joseph SCHWANTER)

BBC YOUNG MUSICIAN OF THE YEAR (EUROPE) 1998
    (BBC2 14/6/1998, from VIENNA) *winner:* LIDIA BAICH
    (Austria) 1st mm 'Violin Conc.No.5' (H.VIEUXTEMPS)

BEACH The (1999) Music score by
    -S/T- *LONDON: cat.number to be confirmed*

BEACHES (1989) BETTE MIDLER (songs: Cole Porter-Randy
    Newman etc)"Wind Beneath My Wings" (Henley-Silbar)
    -S/T- *ATLANTIC (TEN): K.781933-2 (CD) -4 (MC)*
    see COLL.125,145,

BEAN (1997) Music sc: HOWARD GOODALL -S/T- with V.Arts
    MERCURY-POLYGRAM TV: 553 774-2 (CD) -4 (MC)

BEAST The (USA TV mini-series) Music score: DON DAVIS
    -S/T- *VARESE (Pinn): VSD 5731 (CD)*

BEAST WITH FIVE FINGERS The (1947) Music: MAX STEINER
    new rec: MOSCOW S.O.(Stromberg)+ 'VIRGINIA CITY'
    /'LOST PATROL' *MARCO POLO (Select): 8.223870 (CD)*

BEAT GIRL (1960) Music score: JOHN BARRY Featuring:
Adam Faith-John Barry Seven + 4-Shirley Anne Field
-S/T- *PLAY IT AGAIN (Koch): PLAY 001 (CD) also
contains* John Barry's 1961 "Stringbeat" album

BEATLES - *see* 'ANTHOLOGY'

BEATRIX POTTER TV animated s -*see also* 'WORLD OF PETER
RABBIT AND FRIENDS' *and* 'TALES OF BEATRIX POTTER'

BEAU GESTE (1939) Music score: ALFRED NEWMAN. Suite by
MOSCOW SYMPH.ORCH.& CHORUS (William T.Stromberg)
'HUNCHBACK OF NOTRE DAME'(1939) 'ALL ABOUT EVE'
MARCO POLO (Select): 8.223750 (CD)

BEAUTIFUL GIRL LIKE ME, A (1972-'Belle Fille.') Mus sc
GEORGES DELERUE *on COLL* 'TRUFFAUT & DELERUE ON
THE SCREEN' *DRG (Pinn): 32902 (CD)*

BEAUTIFUL THING (1997) Music score: JOHN ALTMAN with
songs sung by MAMA CASS and The MAMAS & The PAPAS
-S/T- *MCA (BMG): MCD 60013 (CD)*

BEAUTY AND THE BEAST
Songs: Alan Menken-Howard Ashman-Tim Rice
1.FILM 1992 -S/T- *WALT DISNEY (B.Vista): WD 71360-2
(CD) -4(MC)* see also DISNEY FILM INDEX p.362
2.ORIGINAL BROADWAY CAST 1994
EDEL-DISNEY (Pinn): 010861-2DNY (CD) -4(MC)

BEAUTY AND THE BEAST (Belle Et La Bette, La) (1946) M.
score: GEORGES AURIC *new record:* MOSCOW SYMPHONY
ORCH.(Adriano) *MARCO POLO (Select): 8.223765 (CD)*

BEAUTY AND THE BEAST (USA TV) *see COLL.39,130,169,*

BEAVIS AND BUTTHEAD (USA/C4 13/1/95)'Beavis & Butthead
Experience' -S/T- *GEFFEN-MCA (BMG): GED 24613 (CD)*

BEAVIS AND BUTTHEAD DO AMERICA (1996) M: JOHN FRIZZELL
-S/T- songs: *GEFFEN (BMG): GED(GEC) 25002 (CD/MC)*
-S/T- score: *MILAN (BMG): 74321 47536-2 (CD)*

BECOMING COLLETTE (1991) Music score by JOHN SCOTT
JOHN SCOTT RECORDS (Silva Screen): JSCD 115 (CD)

BED OF ROSES (1995) Music sc: MICHAEL CONVERTINO songs
"Independent Love Song" SCARLET & "Ice Cream" by
SARAH MacLACHLAN -S/T- *MILAN (BMG): 74321 34863-2*

BEDKNOBS AND BROOMSTICKS *see* WALT DISNEY INDEX p.362

BEDLAM (1946) Music score: ROY WEBB *see COLL.398,*

BEETLEJUICE (1988) Music score: DANNY ELFMAN -S/T- +
HARRY BELAFONTE *GEFFEN-MCA (BMG):GFLD 19284 (CD)*
see *COLL.122,309,313,*

BEGGAR BRIDE The (BBC1 24/8/97) music sco: COLIN TOWNS
theme song "She's A Star" performed by JAMES on
FONTANA (Univ): JIMCD 16 (CDs)

BEGGAR'S OPERA The (LIGHT OPERA by John Gay) *featur:*
WARREN MITCHELL-MICHAEL HORDERN-JOAN SUTHERLAND-
KIRI TE KANAWA-ANGELA LANSBURY-STAFFORD DEAN-
ALFRED MARKS-JAMES MORRIS-REGINA RESNIK & National
Phil.Orch (Richard Bonynge) *DECCA:430 066-2 (2CDs)*

BEIDERBECKE AFFAIR The (C4 4/93 o.1985) music of BIX
BEIDERBECKE performed by FRANK RICOTTI ALL-STARS
& KENNY BAKER -S/T- *DOORMOUSE (C.Wellard): DM20CD
also 'Collection' CASTLE (Pinn): CCSCD 350 (CD)*

BEIDERBECKE CONNECTION see COLL.6,

BEING HUMAN (1993) Music score: MICHAEL GIBBS -S/T- on
VARESE (Pinn): VSD 5479 (CD)

BELFRY WITCHES The (BBC1 29/09/1999) series music by
KIRSTEN MORRISON with title theme performed by The
ATOMIC KITTEN unavailable

BELIZAIRE THE CAJUN -S/T- Music score by HOWARD SHORE
Arhoolie USA (Topic/Proj): ARHC 5038 (MC)

BELLE ET LA BETTE, LA - see 'BEAUTY AND THE BEAST'

BELLE OF NEW YORK The (1952) feat FRED ASTAIRE and VERA
ELLEN BLUE MOON (Discov): BMCD 7011 (CD) including
'BAND WAGON'

BELLY VARIOUS HIP-HOP ARTISTS
DEF JAM (Univ): 558 952-2 (CD) -1 (2LP)

BELLY OF AN ARCHITECT (1987) Music score: WIM MERTENS
-S/T- CREPUSCULE (Discovery) TWI 8132 (CD)

BELOVED (1998) Music score by RACHEL PORTMAN -S/T- feat
V.Arts. on EPIC (Ten): 492 679-2 (CD) see COLL.3,

BEN CASEY (USA)(C4 4/1/97)m: DAVID RAKSIN see COLL.346,

BEN-HUR (silent 1925) New score: CARL DAVIS -S/T-
SILVA SCREEN (Koch): FILMCD 043 (CD)

BEN HUR (1959) (1) Music score: MIKLOS ROSZA digitally
re-mastered 75m.CD EMI ODEON: CDODEON 18 (CD)
(2) MIKLOS ROSZA Orig sco + unissued material MGM
Imp (S.Screen): A2K 47020 (2CDs) (3) MY KIND OF MU
SIC' (4) Choral Pieces BEN HUR Coll 'MIKLOS ROZSA
FILM MUS V.1' PROMETHEUS (S.Scr): PCD 122 (CD) (5)
see COLL.18,70,169,204,302,385,

BENEATH THE 12 MILE REEF see COLL.1,

BENEATH THE VALLEY OF THE ULTRA VIXENS 1979, RUSS MEYER
includes music from Russ Meyer Films "UP" and "Mega
Vixens" NORMAL-QDK (Pinn): QDK(CD)(LP) 009 (CD/LP)

BENNY AND JOON (1993) music sco: RACHEL PORTMAN -S/T-
MILAN (BMG): 15168-2 (CD)

BENNY HILL SHOW see COLL.270,350,

BENSON (USA TV) see COLL.350,

BERGERAC (BBC1 from 18/10/81) theme by GEORGE FENTON
see COLL.5,19,46,69,109,110,270,390,

BERTHA (BBC TV) see COLL.186,

BESIEGED (1998) Music score by ALESSIO VLAD -S/T- on
ARISTA (BMG): 74321 64027-2 (CD)

BEST FOOT FORWARD (ORIG OFF-BROADWAY CAST 1963) Songs
(Hugh Martin-Ralph Blane) feat LIZA MINNELLI-RONALD
CHRISTOPHER WALKEN etc. DRG USA (Pinn) CD15003 (CD)

BEST IN FOOTBALL (TV) m: TONY HATCH see COLL.184,281,

BEST LAID PLANS (1999) Mus: CRAIG ARMSTRONG -S/T- incl:
NENEH CHERRY/MASSIVE ATTACK/PATSY CLINE/MAZZY STAR
VIRGIN (EMI): CDVUS 157 (CD)

BEST LITTLE WHOREHOUSE IN TEXAS (82)M: PATRICK WILLIAMS
Songs: CAROL HALL feat: DOLLY PARTON-BURT REYNOLDS
-S/T- MCA USA (Silva Screen): MCAD 31007 (CD)

BEST OF EVERYTHING see COLL.1,

BEST SHOT 'Hoosiers' (1987) Mus: JERRY GOLDSMITH -S/T-
TER (Koch): CDTER 1141 (CD)

BETTY BLUE (1986) Music score: GABRIEL YARED -S/T- on
VIRGIN: (TC)V 2396 (MC/LP) CDV 2396 (CD)

BETWEEN THE LINES (BBC1 from 4/9/92) theme music: HAL
LINDES *see COLL.356,*

BEVERLY HILLBILLIES The (USA 62) Theme "The Ballad Of
Jed Clampett" sung by LESTER FLATT & EARL SCRUGGS
see COLL.270,345,

BEVERLY HILLS COP (1985) Music Sco: HAROLD FALTERMEYER
-S/T- *MCA (BMG): MCLD 19087 (CD)*

BEVERLY HILLS 90210 (ITV 12/1/91) theme: JEFFREY Skunk
BAXTER & STACY WIDELITZ -S/T- inc.theme: JOHN DAVIS
'Vol.1' *GIANT (BMG):74321 14798-2(CD) /* Volume 2 on
74321 20303-2(CD) see COLL.17,270,351,

BEWITCHED (USA 60's) theme music by JACK KELLER and
HOWARD GREENFIELD *see COLL.256,346,363,378,*

BEYOND THE CLOUDS (C4 28/2/94) music: GEORGE FENTON
-S/T- *WESTMOOR (Target/BMG): CDWM(CWM) 109 (CD/MC)*
note: also used for C4 'SPIRITS GHOSTS AND DEMONS'
see COLL.19, 'AS SEEN ON TV'

BEYOND THE FRINGE (The Complete) *REVUE 1961 Fortune The
atre London)* feat PETER COOK-DUDLEY MOORE-ALAN BENN
ETT-JONATHAN MILLER-PAXTON WHITEHEAD *and also ORIG
BROADWAY CAST 1962) feat:* PETER COOK-DUDLEY MOORE-
ALAN BENNETT-JONATHAN MILLER *EMI: CDBTF 61 (3CDs)*

BEYOND THE VALLEY OF THE DOLLS (1970) mus: STU PHILLIPS
-S/T- (V.Arts) *reissued with* 'GROUPIE GIRL' (1970)
SCREEN GOLD (Greyhound): SGLDCD 0010 (CD)

BIG BAD WORLD (ITV 20/06/1999) Music by HAL LINDES
SONGS INSPIRED BY AND FROM SERIES *INC.THEME MUSIC
VIRGIN (EMI): VTDCD 257 (2CD) VTDMC 257 (2MC)*

BIG BLUE The (1988) Music sco: ERIC SERRA -S/T- *VIRGIN
CDV 2541 (CD) MDV 2541 (MiniD)* Imprt: *SILVA SCREEN:*
VOL.1 *30145 (CD) 50145 (MC)* VOL.2 *30667 (CD) 50667
(MC) COMPLETE 30193 (2CDs) 40065 (2MC)*

BIG BREAK (BBC1 30/4/91) theme "The Snooker Song"
(Mike Batt) sung by CAPTAIN SENSIBLE *deleted*

BIG CHILL The 1984 Music: MARVIN GAYE-TEMPTATIONS-FOUR
TOPS etc. -S/T- *MOTOWN (Univ): 636 062-2 (CD) also*
'MORE SONGS FROM BIG CHILL' *636 094-2 (CD)*

BIG CITY RHYTHM Songs: BARRY KLEINBORT
ORIGINAL CAST with The Original Songs of BARRY
KLEINBORT *HARBINGER (Pinn): HCD 1401 (CD)*

BIG COUNTRY The (1958) Music score: JEROME MOROSS New
Digital Rec.- Philharmonia Orch *SILVA SCREEN (Koch)
FILMCD 030 (CD) see COLL.41,47,70,400,401,*

BIG DADDY (1999) -S/T- *feat:* SHERYL CROW-GARBAGE-BIG
AUDIO DYNAMITE-MEL C-SHAWN MULLINS-YVONNE ELLIMAN
COLUMBIA: 494 395-2 (CD)

BIG DEAL (BBC1 14/10/84) title song composed/sung by
BOBBY G. *see COLL.7,*

BIG EASY The (1987) Music score: BRAD FIEDEL + V.Arts
-S/T- *re-issue SPECTRUM (Univ): 551 159-2 (CD)*

BIG GUNDOWN The (1966) Music sco ENNIO MORRICONE *Import
with* 'FACE TO FACE' *Mask (S.Screen): MK 701 (CD)*

BIG JAKE (1971) Music score: ELMER BERNSTEIN suite on
VARESE (Pinn): VCD 47264 (CD)
BIG KEVIN LITTLE KEVIN (BBC2 04/05/1999) orig music by
JOHN PAED *unavailable*
BIG LEBOWSKI The (1998) Music score: CARTER BURWELL
-S/T- *MERCURY (Univ): 536 903-2 (CD)*
BIG MATCH The (ITV) Themes include "Aztec Gold" ROD
ARGENT-PETER VAN HOOKE *see also COLL.7,176,325*
BIG NIGHT, A (1996) Music score: GARY De MICHELE -S/T-
V.Arts on *EDEL-CINERAMA (Pinn): 002278-2CIN (CD)*
BIG SWAP The (1996) Mus: JASON FLINTER & CRAIG JOHNSON
-S/T- *OCEAN DEEP (Univ): OCD 011 (CD)*
BIG TEASE The (1999) Music score by MARK THOMAS -S/T-
VIRGIN (EMI): CDVUS 165 (CD)
BIG TROUBLE IN LITTLE CHINA *see COLL.51,203,*
BIG VALLEY (USA) *see COLL.349,*
BIG WOMEN (C4 02/7/1998) Various chart songs: "Power To
The People" by JOHN LENNON; "Big Girls Don't Cry"
FOUR SEASONS; "White Rabbit" JEFFERSON AIRPLANE
BIKER MICE FROM MARS (1993) Music Various Artists -S/T-
GASOLENE ALLEY/MCA (BMG): MCD 10948 (CD)
BILITIS (1977) Music score by FRANCIS LAI -S/T- *reiss:*
MILAN (BMG): 74321 64881-2 (CD) theme also on
'FRANCIS LAI-A MAN AND A WOMAN' *COLL*
BILL The (Thames 16/10/84-96 also UKGold from 2/11/92)
theme "Overkill" ANDY PASK-CHARLIE MORGAN
see COLL.46,109,110,270,390,
BILL AND TED'S BOGUS JOURNEY (1991) Music: DAVID NEWMAN
-S/T- *feat* STEVE VAI-MEGADETH-SLAUGHTER-KISS-WINGER
PRIMUS *reiss: INTERSCOPE-MCA (BMG): IND 91725 (CD)*
BILL BRYSON'S NOTE FROM A SMALL ISLAND (ITV 10/01/1999)
title music by DEREK HOLT *unavailable*
BILLY (O.LONDON CAST 1974) Songs: JOHN BARRY-DON BLACK
feat: MICHAEL CRAWFORD-ELAINE PAIGE-AVIS BUNNAGE-
BILLY BOYLE and Company *SONY: 472818-2(CD)*
BILLY BUNTER OF GREYFRIARS SCHOOL (BBC 1950's) theme
"Sea Songs" (VAUGHAN WILLIAMS) *see COLL.172,*
BILLY CONNOLLY'S WORLD TOUR OF AUSTRALIA (BBC Sc/Sleepy
Dumpling/ BBC1 28/10/96) end theme song "Dreamtime"
(Ralph McTell) sung by BILLY CONNOLLY *unavailable*
other commiss.music by GRAHAM PRESKETT-RALPH McTELL
BILLY CONNOLLY'S WORLD TOUR OF SCOTLAND (BBC Sco/Sleepy
Dumpling/ BBC1 12/7/94) end theme mus "Irish Heartb
eat" sung by BILLY CONNOLLY on 'Musical Tour Of Sco
tland' *POLYGRAM TV: 529 816-2 (CD) -4(MC)* also by
VAN MORRISON *POLYDOR (Univ): 839 604-2 (CD) -4 (MC)*
BIOGRAPH GIRL The (O.LONDON CAST 1980) Songs: David
Heneker-Warner Brown *feat:* SHEILA WHITE-BRUCE BARRY
KATE REVILL-GUY SINER *TER (Koch): CDTER 1003 (CD)*
BIONIC WOMAN (USA TV) *see COLL.311,349,*
BIRD (1988) Music score: LENNIE NIEHAUS *feat music of*
CHARLIE PARKER 1949 RECORDING: *POLY 837176-2 (CD)*
BIRD OF PREY (BBC1 22/4/82) theme mus: DAVE GREENSLADE
see COLL.7,

BIRD WITH THE CRYSTAL PLUMAGE (1969) Music sco: ENNIO
 MORRICONE -S/T- inc 'FOUR FLIES ON GREY VELVET'
 'CAT O'NINE TAILS' *DRG (Pinn): DRGCD 32911 (CD)*
BIRDCAGE The (1995) Music arr./adapt.by JONATHAN TUNICK
 -S/T- *EDEL-Cinerama (Pinn): 002257-2 MCM (CD)*
BIRDMAN (BBC 14/05/1999) Music by SIAN JAMES -S/T-
 BBC WORLDWIDE MUSIC (Pinn): WMSF 6007-2 (CD)
BIRDS OF A FEATHER (BBC1 16/10/1989-1998) Theme song
 "What'll I Do" (Irving Berlin) *TV vers.by* PAULINE
 QUIRKE-LINDA ROBSON *unavailable see COLL.279,*
BIRDY (1985) Music score: PETER GABRIEL -S/T- *CHARISMA
 VIRGIN (EMI): CASCD 1167 (CD)*
BIRTHS MARRIAGES AND DEATHS (BBC2 22/02/1999) music by
 NICK BICAT *unavailable*
BITTER SWEET (Musical Show 1988) Songs: NOEL COWARD New
 Sadlers Wells Opera VALERIE MASTERSON *TER (Koch):
 Highlights CDTEO 1001 (CD)*
BJ AND THE BEAR (USA TV) *see COLL.350,*

BLACK AND WHITE MINSTREL SHOW The (BBC1 1950's-60's)
 'Down Memory Lane' *MFP (EMI):CC 223 (CD)* 'The Black
 & White Minstrel Show' *EMI: CD(TC)IDL 105 (CD(MC)*
BLACK BEAUTY *(TV) see* 'ADVENTURES OF BLACK BEAUTY' and
 COLL 'GREATEST TV THEMES'
BLACK CAESAR (1973) Mus by JAMES BROWN inc.LYNN COLLINS
 POLYDOR (Univ): 517 135-2 (CD) -1 (LP)
BLACK EAGLE (86) Music score: TERRY PLUMERI -S/T- on
 Edel (Pinn): 0022202CIN (CD)
BLACK HOLE (1979) JOHN BARRY *see COLL.308,*
 see WALT DISNEY FILM INDEX p.362
BLACK MASK (1999) VARIOUS ARTISTS -S/T-
 TOMMY BOY (Pinn): TBCD 1343 (CD)
BLACK RAIN (1989) Music score HANS ZIMMER songs by V/A
 VIRGIN: CDV 2607 (CD)
BLACK ROBE (1991) Music score: GEORGES DELERUE -S/T-
 VARESE (Pinn): VSD 5349 (CD)
BLACK SHIELD OF FALWORTH (1954) Mus: Hans J.Salter +
 mus.'HITLER' (61) 'INCREDIBLE SHRINKING MAN' (57)
 INTRADA (Koch): MAF 7054CD (CD) see COLL.309,357,
BLACK WINDMILL The (1974) Music score by ROY BUDD -S/T-
 CINEPHILE-CASTLE (Pinn): CINCD 004 (CD)
BLACKADDER (BBC2 began 5/9/84) music by HOWARD GOODALL
 BBC Radio Coll (Techn): ZBBC 2227 (6 AUDIO CASS)
BLACKBEARD'S GHOST - *see* WALT DISNEY FILM INDEX p.362
BLACKOUT The (1998) Music: SCHOOLLY D and JOE DELIA
 -S/T- *POLYDOR (Univ): 537 854-2 (CD) -4 (MC)*
BLACULA (1972) Music score by GENE PAGE -S/T-
 RAZOR & TIE (Koch): RE 82179-2 (CD)
BLADE (1998) Music score by MARK ISHAM
 -S/T- (score) *VARESE (Pinn): VSD 5976 (CD)*
 -S/T- (songs) *EPIC (Ten): 492 884-2 (CD)*
BLADE RUNNER (1982) Music score: VANGELIS origin -S/T-
 EAST WEST (TEN): 4509 96574-2 (CD) -4 (MC)
 see COLL.51,121,144,203,267,307,308,360,362,380,381

BLAIR WITCH PROJECT The (1999) -S/T- includes music by
PUBLIC IMAGE LTD/BAUHAUS/LYDIA LUNCH/SKINNY PUPPY/
CREATURES/FRONT LINE ASSEMBLY/LAIBACH/AFGHAN WHIGS
TYPE O NEGATIVE/MEAT BEAT MANIFESTO/TONES ON TAIL
GOLD CIRCLE (Direct): GC 0120-2 (CD)

BLAKE'S 7 (UKGO 4/6/94 orig BBC1 2/1/78) Theme music
DUDLEY SIMPSON *see COLL.6,38,121,267,270,333,362,*

BLEAK HOUSE (BBC2 1985) music scored and conducted by
GEOFFREY BURGON *see COLL.61,*

BLIND DATE (LWT 30/11/85-1999) theme: LAURIE HOLLOWAY
see COLL.270,

BLISS (1997) Music score: JAN A.P.KACZMAREK -S/T- on
VARESE (Pinn): VSD 5836 (CD)

BLONDEL - songs: Stephen Oliver and Tim Rice
ORIG CAST 1983 *feat:* PAUL NICHOLAS-SHARON LEE HILL
DAVID ALDER-CANTABILE-TRACY BOOTH-STEPHEN LANGHAM-
ROGER LLEWELLYN *reissue: MCA (BMG): MCD 11486 (CD)*

BLOOD AND GUNS (1969) Music sco: ENNIO MORRICONE -S/T-
'Western Quintet' *DRG (Pinn): DRGCD 32907 (2CD)*

BLOOD AND SAND (70's) Music score ENNIO MORRICONE
ENNIO MORRICONE ORCH on Coll 'An Ennio Morricone
Quintet' *DRG USA (Pinn): DRGCD 32907 (CD)*

BLOOD BROTHERS - songs by Willy Russell
  1.ORIG LONDON CAST 1995 *feat:* STEPHANIE LAWRENCE & Co
   FIRST NIGHT (Pinn): CASTCD 49 (CD) CASTC 49 (MC)
  2.INTERNATIONAL CAST 1995 PETULA CLARK-DAVID & SHAUN
   CASSIDY & Co *FIRST NIGHT (Pinn): CASTCD 50 (CD)*
  3.ORIG LONDON CAST 1988 *feat:* KIKI DEE and Comapny
   FIRST NIGHT (Pinn): CASTCD 17 (CD)
  4.ORIG LONDON CAST 1983 *feat:* BARBARA DICKSON & Comp.
   CASTLE CLASS.(Pinn): CLACD 270 (CD)

BLOOD IS STRONG The (C4/Grampian 1/9/88) music composed
& performed: CAPERCAILLE with KAREN MATHESON -S/T-
SURVIVAL (Pinn): SURCD 014 (CD) SURMC 014 (MC)

BLOOMER GIRL (O.BROADWAY CAST 1944) Music: HAROLD ARLEN
Lyrics: E.Y.HARBURG *MCA USA Imp (Silva Screen)*
MCAD 10522 (CD) MCAC 10522 (MC)

BLOSSOM (USA TV) *see COLL.351,*

BLOTT ON THE LANDSCAPE (BBC2 6/2/85) music: DAVE MACKAY
performed by VIV FISHER *see COLL.6,19,*

BLOW-UP (1966) Music score: HERBIE HANCOCK / Songs by
YARDBIRDS and TOMORROW -S/T- *EMI: CDODEON 15 (CD)*

BLUE (1993) Music score: SIMON FISHER TURNER + V.Arts.
-S/T- *MUTE (Pinn): CDSTUMM 49 (CD)*

BLUE COLLAR (1978) Mus sco: JACK NITZSCHE -S/T- V.Arts
CAPTAIN BEEFHEART-HOWLIN'WOLF-LYNYRD SKYNYRD-IKE &
TINA TURNER on *EDSEL-DEMON (Pinn): EDCD 435 (CD)*

BLUE HAWAII (1961) feat: ELVIS PRESLEY remast. -S/T-
(BMG): 07863 67459-2 (ltd CD) 07863 66959-2 (CD)
see also ELVIS PRESLEY FILM INDEX p.360

BLUE LAGOON The (1980) Music score: BASIL POLEDOURIS
-S/T- *SOUTHERN CROSS (HOT): SCCD 1018 (CD)*

BLUE MAX The (1966) Music score: JERRY GOLDSMITH -S/T-
COLUMBIA Music): CK 57890 (CD)

BLUE PETER (BBC1 27/10/58-1999) Theme "Barnacle Bill"
(Hornpipe) 95-98 heme by YES/NO PEOPLE *unavailable*
Orig SIDNEY ORCH ORCH *EMI* MIKE OLDFIELD *VIRGIN*
EMI CDMOC 1 (2CD) original theme on COLL 186,
BLUE SKIES (1946) VARIOUS -S/T- SELECTIONS on
GREAT MOVIE THEMES: (Targ-BMG): CD 60025 (CD)
BLUE STREAK (1999) VARIOUS ARTISTS -S/T-
COLUMBIA (Ten): 495 491-2 (CD) -4 (MC) -1 (LP)
BLUE TRAIN The (ORIG LONDON CAST 1927) Songs (Robert St
oltz-Reginald Arkell) Addit.Songs (Ivy St.Helier)
PEARL-PAVILION: GEMMCD 9100 (CD)
BLUE VELVET (1987) Music sco: ANGELO BADALEMENTI -S/T-
VARESE (Pinn): VCD 47277 (CD) see COLL.143,258,359,
BLUE WILDERNESS (C4 17/3/96) Music score: TANIA ROSE
theme music from 'Coral Sea Dreaming' courtesy of
NATURAL SYMPHONIES (Australia) *unavailable in UK*
BLUEBEARD (1972) Music score: ENNIO MORRICONE -S/T-
including music from 'LADY OF MONZA' (1969) on
POINT IMP (Silva Screen): PRCD 121 (CD)
BLUES ARE RUNNING The / KING MACKEREL (USA MUSICALS)
SUGAR HILL USA (Koch): SHCD 8503 (CD) SH 8503(MC)
BLUES BROTHERS (1980) *Featur:* RAY CHARLES-JAMES BROWN
ARETHA FRANKLIN-CAB CALLOWAY-BLUES BROTHERS -S/T-
WEA: K4 50715 (MC) K2 50715 (CD) 756781471-5 (DCC)
BLUES BROTHERS 2000 VAR.ARTISTS inc: PAUL BUTTERFIELD
BLUES BAND-MATT MURPHY-JOHN POPPER-DAN AYKROYD-
LONNIE BROOKS-JUNIOR WELLS & BLUES BROTHERS BAND
UNIVERSAL (BMG): UND 53116 (CD)
BLUES IN THE NIGHT (ORIG DONMAR WAREHOUSE THEATRE 1987)
DEBBY BISHOP-MARIA FRIEDMAN-CLARKE PETERS-CAROL WOO
DS & Co.*reiss FIRST NIGHT (Pinn): OCRCD 6029 (CD)*
BOAT The (DAS BOOT) (BBC2 17/9/89 orig 21/10/84) music
KLAUS DOLDINGER *see COLL.51,384*
BOB AND MARGARET (C4 18/11/1998) BOB'S BIRTHDAY (1993)
theme & incid.music by PATRICK GODFREY *unavailable*
BOB NEWHART SHOW (USA TV) *see COLL.347,*
BOCCACCIO '70 (1962) Music sco: NINO ROTA with ARMANDO
TROVAIOLI-PIERO UMILIANI "Soldi Soldi Soldi" sung
by Sophia Loren *ITALIAN IMP (S.Scr): OST 116 (CD)*
BODY The (1970) Mus: ROGER WATERS-RON GEESIN -S/T-
EMI Premier (EMI): CZ 178 (CD)
BODY BAGS (1993) Music score: JOHN CARPENTER-JIM LANG
-S/T- *VARESE (Pinn): VSD 5448 (CD)*
BODY HEAT (1981) Music score: JOHN BARRY. new recording
VARESE Pinn: VSD 5951 (CD) see COLL.29,30,121,329,
BODY SHOTS (1999) Music score by MARK ISHAM -S/T- on
MILAN (BMG): 74321 35898-2 (CD)
BODYGUARD (1992) *Songs:* WHITNEY HOUSTON-LISA STANSFIELD
JOE COCKER-SASS JORDAN-CURTIS STIGERS-KENNY G-AARON
NEVILLE -S/T- *ARISTA (BMG): 07822 18699-2CD -4MC*
BODYWORK (LIGHT OPERA MUSICAL 1988) Mus/Lyrics: RICHARD
STILGOE featuring *The National Youth Music Theatre*
with LONNIE DONEGAN-CHAS & DAVE and JAKE THACKRAY
FIRST NIGHT (Pinn): CASTCD 15 (CD) CASTC 15 (MC)

BOLERO (1984) Music score: PETER BERNSTEIN -S/T- incl:
   Elmer Bernstein prev.unreleased material *cond* Chris
   topher Palmer *PROMETHEUS (S.Scr): PCD 124 (CD)*
BONANZA (USA 59) theme: DAVID ROSE (lyrics: Jay Living
   ston-Ray Evans) *see COLL.2,260,270,345,358,*
BONE COLLECTOR The (1999) Music score: CRAIG ARMSTRONG
   -S/T- *DECCA (Univ): 466 804-2 (CD)*
BOOGIE NIGHTS (1998 SHOW) 70's music ORIG CAST RECORD.
   BEECHWOOD MUSIC (BMG): BOOGIE(CD)(MC) 1 (2CD/2MC)
BOOGIE NIGHTS (1997 FILM) Mus MICHAEL PENN -S/T- w.ERIC
   BURDON-MARVIN GAYE-EMOTIONS-JOHN C.REILLY & MARK WA
   HLBERG-CHAKACHAS-COMMODORES-WALTER EGAN-McFADDEN &
   WHITEHEAD-MELANIE-BEACH BOYS-NIGHT RANGER-E.L.O.
   Volume 1 - *EMI PREMIER: 855 631-2 (CD) -4 (MC)*
   Volume 2 - *EMI PREMIER: 493 076-2 (CD) -4 (MC)*
BOON (Central 14/1/86-1992) theme "Hi Ho Silver" (Jim
   Diamond-Chris Parren) sung by JIM DIAMOND on 'Jim
   Diamond' *POLYDOR (Univ): 843 847-2 (CD) -4 (MC)*
BOOTY CALL (1996) -S/T- with Various Arts on
   JIVE-ZOMBA (Pinn): CHIP 182 (CD) HIP 182 (2LP)
BORGIAS The (BBC1 14/10/81) music sco: GEORGES DELERUE
   PROMETHEUS (S.Screen): PCD 109 (CD)
BORN AND BRED (Thames 13/9/78) mus: RON GRAINER *COLL 7*
BORN FREE (1965) Mus sco JOHN BARRY t.song (J.Barry-D.
   Black) MATT MONRO *see COLL.28,29,30,31,34,70,259,*
BORN TO DANCE (1936) *feat* ELEANOR POWELL -S/T- selec.+
   'GOING MY WAY' *GREAT MOVIE THEMES (BMG): CD 60031*
BORN TO RUN (BBC1 25/5/97) "Hang It On Your Heart" sung
   by MARIANNE FAITHFULL on *EMI UK: CDDISC 010 (CDs)*
BORSALINO (1970) Music sco: CLAUDE BOLLING selection on
   AUVIDIS (Harmonia Mundi): K.1505 (CD)
BOSTON KICKOUT (1996) Music score: DAVID ARNOLD -S/T-
   SILVERTONE (Pinn): ORECD 543 (CD)
BOTTOM (BBC2 17/9/91) theme music "BB's Blues" (B.B.
   King) / "Last Night" (Mar-Keys) by The BUM NOTES
   -S/T- *BBC (Techn): ZBBC 1875CD (CD) ZBBC 1875 (MC)*
BOUNTY The (Mutiny On The Bounty) (1984) Mus: VANGELIS
   theme *Coll* 'THEMES' *POLYDOR: 839518-2 (CD) -4 (MC)*
BOWFINGER (1999) Music score by DAVID NEWMAN -S/T-
   VARESE (Pinn): VSD 6040 (CD)
BOX OF DELIGHTS The (BBC1 21/11/84) Theme "Carol Sympho
   ny" (Hely-Hutchinson) PRO-ARTE ORCH (Barry Rose) on
   EMI: CDM 764131-2 (CD) -4 (MC)
BOY FROM MERCURY The (1997) Music: Various Arts -S/T-
   OCEAN DEEP (Grapev/Polyg): OCD 004 (CD)
BOY MEETS GIRL (BBC 67) m. RON GRAINER *see COLL.8,13,*
BOY WHO GREW TOO FAST The (OPERA) Music &Libretto (Gian
   Carlo Menotti) Royal Opera House Orch/Chorus (David
   Syrus) - *TER (Koch): CDTER 1125 (CD)*
BOYFRIEND The - songs by Sandy Wilson
   1.30TH ANN.REVIV.LONDON CAST 1984 *feat:* ROSEMARY ASHE
   SIMON GREEN-JANE WELLMAN-ANNA QUAYLE-PETER BAYLISS
   PADDIE O'NEIL-DEREK WARING and Company
   <u>Highlights</u>: *SHOWTIME (MCI-THE): SHOW(CD)(MC) 027*

Complete: *TER (Koch): CDTER 1095 (CD)*
2. ORIG BROADWAY CAST 1954 *feat:* JULIE ANDREWS & Comp.
   RCA (BMG): GDGK 60056 (CD)
3. CLASSIC MUSICALS SERIES *featur:* JANE WELLMAN-SIMON
   GREEN-ANNA QUAYLE-DEREK WARING-PETER BAYLIS *plus*
   songs from 'ME AND MY GIRL' *KOCH INT: 34080-2 (CD)*
BOYS FROM SYRACUSE -songs: Richard Rodgers-Lorenz Hart
   OFF-BROADWAY REV.CAST 63 *Angel EMI ZDM 764695-2 CD*
BOYS ON THE SIDE (1994) M.sco: DAVID NEWMAN -S/T- V.Art
   ARISTA (BMG): 07822 18748-2 (CD)
BOYZ UNLIMITED (C4 05/02/1999) Music by PHIL HARDING &
   IAN CURNOW. *theme* "I Say A Little Prayer For You"
BRADY BUNCH The (USA TV) *see COLL.256,346,*
BRAINDEAD (1992) Music sco: PETER DASENT Var Artists:
   -S/T- *NORMAL (Topic/Project/Dir): QDKCD 006 (CD)*
BRAINSPOTTING (C4 11/8/96) closing theme mus "Concerto
   For Cootie" by DUKE LELLINGTON ORCHESTRA / version
   'Great Paris Concert' *WB (TEN): 7567 81303-2 (CD)*
BRANDED (USA) *see COLL.345,*
BRASSED OFF (1996) Music score TREVOR JONES *feat* The
   GRIMETHORPE COLLIERY BAND conductor: JOHN ANDERSON
   -S/T- *RCA-CONIFER (BMG): 09026 68757-2 (CD)*
   see COLL.75,144,286,
BRAVEHEART (1995) Music sco: JAMES HORNER with London
   S.Orch -S/T- *ICON-LONDON (Univ): 448 295-2 (CD)*
   see COLL.3,49,71,106,165,205,207,385,
BRAVO TWO ZERO (BBC1 03/1/1999) Music: DAVID FERGUSON
   main theme on Coll 'The View From Now' *CHANDOS:.
   CHAN 9679 (CD) see COLL.151,*
BRAZIL (1985) Music score: MICHAEL KAMEN -S/T-
   MILAN (BMG): 11125-2 (CD) 11125-4 (MC)
BREAD (UKGO 3/11/92 / BBC 1/5/86-91) Theme mus "Home"
   DAVID MacKAY sung by The CAST *see COLL.5,19,46,*
BREAKFAST AT TIFFANY'S (1961) Music sco: HENRY MANCINI
   song "Moon River" (Lyr: Johnny Mercer) -S/T- with
   'ARABESQUE' *RCA CAMDEN (BMG): 74321 69878-2 (CD)*
   -S/T- *RCA: ND 89905 (CD)*
   see COLL.37,41,71,106,128,211,238,239,298,
BREAKFAST CLUB (1985) Music sco: KEITH FORSEY songs:
   Simple Minds-Wang Chung-Karlo De Vito-J.Johnson
   -S/T- *A.& M. (Univ): CDMID 179 (CD) AMC 5045 (MC)*
BREAKING AWAY (1979) music by PATRICK WILLIAMS
   see COLL.81,
BREAKING GLASS (1980) mus.comp/perf by HAZEL O'CONNOR
   -S/T- *reis: SPECTRUM (Univ): 551 356-2 (CD)*
BREAKING THE WAVES (1995) Music sco: JOACHIM HOLBEK
   -S/T- Var.Art *POLLYANNA (Pinn): POLLYPREM 001 (CD)*
BRIDE OF CHUCKY (1997)-S/T- *SPV (Koch): 0851858-2 (CD)*
BRIDE OF FRANKENSTEIN The (1935) Mus sco: FRANZ WAXMAN
   see COLL.68,70,208,392,395,
BRIDE OF THE RE-ANIMATOR (1990) Music sc: RICHARD BAND
   +'RE-ANIMATOR' -S/T- *S.SCREEN Koch: FILMCD 082(CD)*

BRIDESHEAD REVISITED (C4 24/1/1998 or: GRAN 12/10/1981)
music score: GEOFFREY BURGON -S/T- re-iss on *MFP*
(EMI) CD(TC)MFP 6172 (CD/MC) see COLL.61,262,270,
BRIDGE The (1990) Music sco: RICHARD G.MITCHELL -S/T-
DEMON (Pinn): DSCD 5 (CD) DSCASS 5 (MC)
BRIDGE ON THE RIVER KWAI (1957) Music: MALCOLM ARNOLD
LSO (R.Hickox) *CHANDOS: 9100 (CD)* "Colonel Bogey"
(Kenneth Alford) *see COLL.20,41,70,198,255,*
BRIDGE TOO FAR, A (1977) Muisic score by JOHN ADDISON
-S/T- reissue *RYKODISC (Vital): RCD 10746 (CD)*
BRIDGES OF MADISON COUNTY The (1995) Music sc: LENNIE
NIEHAUS -S/T- *MALPASO-WB (TEN): 9362 45949-2 (CD)*
see COLL.43,74,
BRIEF ENCOUNTER (1945) Mus: RACHMANINOV new collect:
'BRIEF ENCOUNTER: THE VERY BEST OF RACHMANINOV'
ERATO (TEN): 0630 18061-2 (CD) -4 (MC)
see COLL.78,100,105,106,388,
BRIGADOON - songs - Alan Jay Lerner & Frederick Loewe
  1.ORIG 1954 FILM -S/T- w:GENE KELLY-CYD CHARISSE-VAN
JOHNSON / 23 tracks *EMI PREMIER: CDODEON 16 (CD)*
  2.ORIG BROADWAY CAST 1947 w:DAVID BROOKS-MARION BELL
PAMELA BRITTON-LEE SULLIVAN *(BMG): GD(GK) 81001*
  3.ORIG LONDON CAST 1988 *feat:*ROBERT MEADMORE-JACINTA
MULCAHY-MAURICE CLARK-LESLEY MACKIE-ROBIN NEDWELL-
IAN MACKENZIE STEWART *FIRST NIGHT (Pin) OCRCD 6022*
  4.STUDIO RECORDING 1991 Ambrosian Chorus & London
Sinfonietta (John McGlynn) *EMI: CDC 754481-2 (CD)*
  5.STUDIO RECORDING 1997 *SHOWTIME (Disc): SHOWCD 056*
  6.HIGHLIGHTS STUDIO RECORDING 1998) *feat* JANIS ELLIS
ETHAN FREEMAN-MAURICE CLARKE-MEG.KELLY & N.S.O.
(JOHN OWEN EDWARDS) *TER (Koch): CDTEH 6003 (CD)*
BRIGHT LEAF (1950) Music score by VICTOR YOUNG
NEW RECORD.by MOSCOW SYMPHONY ORCH + 'UNINVITED'
/'GREATEST SHOW ON EARTH'/'GULLIVER'S TRAVELS'
MARCO POLO (Select): 8225063 (CD)
BRING ON THE NIGHT (1986) Music by STING
A.& M. (Univ): BRIND 1 (2CD) BRINC 1 (2MC)
BRITISH SONG CONTEST 1999 (BBC1 3/1999) *Winning song*
(entry chosen for Eurovision Song Contest 1999)
1st "Say It Again" composed by Paul Varney, sung
by **PRECIOUS** *recorded on EMI:CD(TC)EM 544 (CDs/MC)*
2nd "So Strange" performed by **ALBERTA** *unavailable*
3rd "Until You Saved My Life" **SISTER SWAY**   "
4th "You've Taken My Dreams" **JAY**   "
BRITISH SONG CONTEST 1998 (BBC1 3/1998) *Winning song*
(entry chosen for Eurovision Song Contest 1998)
"Where Are You" (Scott English-Phil Manikiza-Simon
Sterling) sung by **IMAANI** *EMI:CD(TC)EM 510 (CDs/MC)*
2nd "Don't It Make You Feel So Good"(Mike Connaris
Paul Brown) **ALBERTA** *RCA (BMG): 74321 57158-2 (CDs)*
3rd "I'll Never Be Lonely Again" (R.Louie-Stephen
Christopher) **SAPPHIRE** *ETERNAL TEN: WEA 158CD (CDs)*
4th "When We're Alone" (Collective) THE COLLECTIVE
RCA (BMG): 74321 57468-2 (CDs)

BRITS The (BRITANNIA MUSIC AWARDS) VARIOUS ARTISTS
1999 SONY MUSIC: SONYTV 61CD (CD) SONYTV 61MC (MC)
1998 SONY MUSIC: SONYTV 36CD (CD) SONYTV 36MC (MC)
1997 SONY MUSIC: SONYTV 23CD (CD) SONYTV 23MC (MC)
BROADWAY MELODY OF 1936 (1935 MUSICAL) *feat:* JACK BENNY
ELEANOR POWELL-ROBERT TAYLOR + 'BRO.MELODY OF 1940'
GREAT MOVIE THEMES (TARGET-BMG): CD 60007 (CD)
BROADWAY MELODY OF 1938 (1937) -S/T- *f:* ELEANOR POWELL
JUDY GARLAND *contains mus.from* 'Moon Over Miami'
GREAT MOVIE THEMES (Target-BMG): CD 60030 (CD)
BROADWAY MELODY OF 1940 (40 MUSICAL) *feat:* FRED ASTAIRE
GEORGE MURPHY-ELEANOR POWELL + 'BRO.MELODY OF 1936'
GREAT MOVIE THEMES (TARGET-BMG): CD 60007 (CD)
BROKEDOWN PALACE (1999) Music score: DAVID NEWMAN -S/T-
VARIOUS ARTISTS *MERCURY (Univ): 546 390-2 (CD)*
BROKEN ARROW (1996) Music sco: HANS ZIMMER -S/T- reiss:
MILAN (BMG): 74321 34865-2 (CD)
BRONCO (USA tv 1950's/60's) *see COLL.178,348,*
BROOKSIDE (C4 2/11/82-2000) Theme music: DAVE ROYLANCE
STEVE WRIGHT *see COLL.150,270,376,*
BROTHER FROM ANOTHER PLANET (1984) Music score: MASON
DARING -S/T- *Daring (Direct): DRCD 1007 (CD)*
BROTHERS The (UKGold 6/11/92 orig BBC1 71) Theme music
DUDLEY SIMPSON *see COLL.2,46,*
BROTHERS McMULLEN The (1995) Music score: SEAMUS EGAN
-S/T- includ "I Will Remember You" sung by SARAH
McLACHLAN   *ARISTA (BMG): 07822 18803-2 (CD) -4(MC)*
BRUSH STROKES (BBC1 12/10/87) theme "Because Of You" by
DEXYS MIDNIGHT RUNNERS on 'Very Best Of Dexys..' on
MERCURY (Univ): 846 460-2 (CD) -4(MC) -1(LP)
BUBBLING BROWN SUGAR (ORIG LONDON CAST 1977) VAR ARTS.
DRG (Pinn): CDSBL 13106 (CDx2)
BUCK ROGERS IN THE 25TH CENTURY (USA 79 ITV) theme mus:
STU PHILLIPS *see COLL.17,38,267,308,*
BUDDAH OF SUBURBIA The (BBC 3/11/93) title song and inc
idental music (David Bowie) sung by DAVID BOWIE and
ERDAL KIZILCAY feat LENNY KRAVITZ gtr -S/T- **reissue**
ARISTA (BMG): 74321 17004-2 (CD) -4 (MC)
BUDDY (1997) Music score: ELMER BERNSTEIN -S/T- on
VARESE (Pinn): VSD 5829 (CD)
BUDDY (ORIG LONDON CAST 95 'LIVE' RECORDING) on
FIRST NIGHT (Pinn): CASTCD 55 (CD) CASTC 55 (MC)
BUDDY (ORIG LONDON CAST 89) PAUL HIPP-Gareth Marks-Enzo
Squillino *FIRST NIGHT (Pinn):QUEUECD 1 (CD)*
BUDDY - A LIFE IN MUSIC (SHOWS COLLECTION 1999) *with*
MIKE BERRY-JERRY ALLISON-SONNY CURTIS. 40TH YEAR
ANNIVERSARY TRIBUTE *CARLTON: 30362 00422 (CD)*
SHOWS COLLECTION (CHE): 3036 20042-2 (CD)
BUDDY'S SONG (90) Featur: Chesney Hawkes-Roger Daltrey
-S/T- *CHRYSALIS (EMI): CCD21 (CD) ZDD21 (MC)*
BUDGIE (LWT 9/4/71-72) theme "The Loner" NEIL HARRISON
see COLL.5,281,363,
BUDGIE THE LITTLE HELICOPTER (Sleepy Kid/HTV/ 4/1/94)
theme: PAUL K.JOYCE *MFP (EMI): TCMFP 6117 (MC)*

BUFFY THE VAMPIRE SLAYER (TV USA 1996)(SKY1/BBC2 1999) theme by NERF HERDER, score by WALTER MURPHY -S/T- inc:GARBAGE-GUIDED BY VOICES-HEPBURN-ALISON KRAUSS *COLUMBIA (Ten): 496 633-2 (CD) -4 (MC)*

BUGS (BBC1 1/4/95) original series music composed by GAVIN GREENAWAY *unavailable*

BUGS BUNNY SHOW (Cart.USA) *see COLL.331,345,*

BUG'S LIFE, A (1998) Music & songs: RANDY NEWMAN "The Time Of Your Life" performed by RANDY NEWMAN -S/T- *DISNEY-EDEL (Pinn): 010634-2DNY (CD) -4DNY (MC)*

BUGSY MALONE (Show 1997) Music & songs: PAUL WILLIAMS Or.London National Youth Theatre Cast *with* MICHAEL STURGES-SHERIDAN SMITH-STUART PIPER-JANEE BENNETT-ALEX LEA-PAUL LOWE-HANNAH SPEARITT-MALINDA PARRIS *TER (Koch): CDTER 1246*

BUGSY MALONE (Film 1976) Music & songs: PAUL WILLIAMS -S/T- *reissue RSO-POLYDOR (Univ): 831 540-2 (CD)*

BULLETS OVER BROADWAY (1994) dir: WOODY ALLEN / -S/T- *SONY CLASSICAL: SK 66822 (CD)*

BULLITT (1968) Music sco: LALO SCHIFRIN -S/T- **reissue** *W.BROS (TEN): 9362 45008-2 (CD)* see COLL.52,143,195,360,

BULWORTH (1998) Music score: ENNIO MORRICONE -S/T- (songs) *INTERSCOPE (TEN): INTD 90160 (CD)* -S/T- (score) *RCA VICTOR (BMG): 09026 63253-2 (CD)*

BURGLED (BBC1 13/09/1999) series theme music by BARRIE BIGNOLD *unavailable*

BURKE'S LAW (USA) *see COLL.122,348,378,*

BURN THE FLOOR (MUSIC INSPIRED BY THE STAGE SHOW) *MCA (Univ): MCD 60071 (CD)*

BUSTER (1988) Music score: ANNE DUDLEY w. PHIL COLLINS -S/T- *VIRGIN (EMI): CDV 2544 (CD) OVEDC 398 (MC)*

BUTCH CASSIDY AND THE SUNDANCE KID (1969) Music: BURT BACHARACH "Raindrops Keep Falling On My Head" (B. Bacharach-H.David) sung by B.J.THOMAS -S/T- *reiss: SPECTRUM (Univ): 551 433-2(CD)*

BUTCHER BOY The (1998) Music score: ELLIOT GOLDENTHAL -S/T- *inc:* SINEAD O'CONNOR-SANTO & JOHNNY-DION AND THE BELMONTS-EDDIE CALVERT-B.BUMBLE & THE STINGERS *EDEL-CINERAMA (Pinn): 0022892CIN (CD)*

BUTTERFLY (1981) Music score ENNIO MORRICONE -S/T- on import on *PROMETHEUS (Silva Screen): PCD 108 (CD)*

BUTTERFLY BALL The (Film Musical 1974) Music sc: ROGER GLOVER / Roger Glover & Friends -S/T- *CONNOISSEUR (Pinn): VSOPCD 139 (CD) VSOLP(MC) 139 (Dbl LP/MC)*

BUTTERFLY KISS (BBC2 14/6/97) Music score: JOHN HARLE *see COLL.182,*

BY JEEVES! (MUSICAL) Songs: ANDREW LLOYD WEBBER-ALAN AYCKBOURN *feat:* STEVEN PACEY-MALCOLM SINCLAIR & Co *POLYDOR (Univ.): 533 187-2 (CD)*

CABARET - songs by John Kander and Fred Ebb
  1.NEW BROADWAY CAST 1997 *w:* NATASHA RICHARDSON-ALAN CUMMING-MARY LOUISE WILSON and Company *RCA VICTOR (BMG): 09026 63173-2 (CD)*

2. NEW LONDON CAST 1986 *feat:* WAYNE SLEEP-VIVIENNE MARTIN-CAROLINE CLARE-GRAZINA FRAME-KELLY HUNTER-OSCAR QUITAK etc.*FIRST NIGHT (Pinn): OCRCD 6010 (CD)*
3. STUDIO RECORDING *featur:* JONATHAN PRYCE-JUDI DENCH MARIA FRIEDMAN-GREGG EDELMAN-JOHN MARK AINSLEY
   Complete: *TER (Koch): CDTER2 1210 (2CD)*
   Highlights: *SHOWTIME (MCI-THE): SHOW(CD)(MC) 021*
4. BROADWAY CAST 1966 *with* JILL HAWORTH-LOTTE LENYA-JACK GILDORD-JOEL GREY-BERT CONVY-PEG MURRAY-EDWARD WINTER *COLUMBIA (Ten): SMK 60533 (CD)*
5. ORIG LONDON CAST 1968 *feat:* JUDI DENCH-LILA KEDROVA KEVIN COLSON-BARRY DENNEN *SONY: SMK 53494 (CD)*
6. FILM MUSICAL 1972 *featuring* LIZA MINNELLI -S/T- *MCA (BMG): MCLD 19088 (CD)*
7. SHOWS COLLECTION 1997 *feat:* TOYAH WILLCOX-NIGEL PLANER & Comp.*CARLTON Shows: 3036 20039-2 (CD) -4 (MC)*
8. (UNKNOWN SOURCE)
   VARESE (Pinn): VSD 5945 (CD)

CABIN IN THE SKY (1943) *feat* LOUIS ARMSTRONG-LENA HORNE ETHEL WATERS-EDDIE ANDERSON *re-mastered -S/T- on EMI SOUNDTRACKS (EMI): CDODEON 31 (CD)*
Songs by VERNON DUKE and JOHN LaTOUCHE *selection on DEFINITIVE (Discovery): SFCD 33504 (CD)*
CABOBLANCO (1980) Music score: JERRY GOLDSMITH -S/T- *PROMETHEUS Imp (Silva Screen): PCD 127 (CD)*
CADFAEL (ITV from 29/5/1994) music score by COLIN TOWNS -S/T- *SOUNDTRACKS EMI GOLD: 521 945-2 (CD)*
CAESAR SMITH see *COLL.215,217,*
CAGNEY AND LACEY (USA81 BBC1 9/7/82) theme: BILL CONTI see *COLL.17,109,110,270,350,390,*
CAINE MUTINY (1954) Music score: MAX STEINER see *COLL.65,71,*
CAL (1984) Music score: MARK KNOPFLER -S/T- *VERTIGO-Poly: VERHC 17 (MC) 822 769-2 (CD)*
CALAMITY JANE - songs: Sammy Fain-Paul Francis Webster
1. STUDIO RECORDING 1996 *featuring:* GEMMA CRAVEN *CARLTON Shows Collect 30362 0030-2 (CD) -4 (MC)*
2. STUDIO R.1995 *w:* DEBBIE SHAPIRO-TIM FLAVIN-SUSANNAH FELLOWS Complete: *TER (Koch): CDTER2 1215 (2CD)*
3. FILM MUSICAL 1953 DORIS DAY -S/T- *SONY: 467610-2 (CD)* + -S/T- *songs from* 'THE PAJAMA GAME' also *ENTERTAINERS: CD 343 (CD)*
CALIFORNIA DREAMS (USA C4 25/4/93) Rock Drama TV Ser -S/T- *re-issue: GEFFEN MCA (BMG): GFLD 19301 (CD)*
CALL ME MADAM - songs by Irving Berlin
1. ORIG LONDON CAST 1994 *feat:* TYNE DALY-DAVID KERNAN JOHN BARROWMAN *DRG Pinn: DRGCD(DRGMC) 94761*
CALL MY BLUFF (BBC1 13/5/96 revived ser.) theme music "Ciccolino" *unavailable*
CALLAN (ITV 1967) see *COLL.2,*
CAMBERWICK GREEN (BBC1 1966) see *COLL.186,*
CAMELOT - songs by Alan Jay Lerner & Frederick Loewe
1. FILM MUSICAL 1967 RICHARD HARRIS-VANESSA REDGRAVE -S/T- *W.Bros (TEN): 7599 27325-2 (CD)*

CAMELOT - songs by Alan Jay Lerner & Frederick Loewe
  1.FILM MUSICAL 1967 RICHARD HARRIS-VANESSA REDGRAVE
    -S/T- *W.Bros (TEN): 7599 27325-2 (CD)*
  2.REVIVAL LONDON CAST 1982 RICHARD HARRIS-FIONA FULL
    ERTON-ROBERT MEADMORE-ROBIN BAILEY-MICHAEL HOWE
    Complete: *TER (Koch): CDTER 1030 (CD)*
  3.ORIG LONDON CAST 1964 *w:* LAURENCE HARVEY-ELIZABETH
    LARNER-NICKY HENSON-JOSEPHINE GORDON-KIT WILLIAMS
    BARRY KENT *FIRST NIGHT: OCRC 4 (MC) deleted*
  4.ORIG BROADWAY CAST 1961 *feat:* JULIE ANDREWS-RICHARD
    BURTON-ROBERT GOULET-R.McDOWELL *SONY: SK 60542 (CD)*
  5.CLASSIC MUSICALS SERIES *featuring:* RICHARD HARRIS
    FIONA FULLERTON-ROBERT MEADMORE-MICHAEL HOWE etc.+
    songs from 'MY FAIR LADY' *Koch Int: 34079-2 (CD)*
CAMILLE CLAUDEL (1989) Music sco: GABRIEL YARED -S/T-
  VIRGIN FRANCE (Discovery): 88098-2 (CD)
CAMOMILE LAWN The (C4 5/3/92) music by STEPHEN EDWARDS
  based on 'String Quartet in F' (RAVEL). Recordings
  BRITTEN QUART.*EMI: CDC 754346-2 (CD) EL 754346-4
  (MC)* CHILINGIRIAN QUARTET *EMI: (CD)(TC)EMX 2156*
CAMPION (UKGO 9/1/93 orig BBC1 22/1/89) theme music by
  NIGEL HESS *see COLL.7,193,*
CAN-CAN (ORIG BROADWAY CAST 1953) Songs (Cole Porter)
  feat: GWEN VERDON-LILO-PETER COOKSON-HANS CONREID
  ERIK RHODES *ANGEL (EMI): ZDM 764664-2 (CD)*
CANDID CAMERA (1960's/70's) 'JONATHAN ROUTH'S CLASSIC
  CANDID CAMERA' *PULSE (BMG): PLS(CD)(MC) 272*
  see COLL.348,
CANDIDE -songs by Leonard Bernstein-Stephen Sondheim
        Richard Wilbur and John Latouche
  1.ORIG BROADWAY CAST 1956 *w:* BARBARA COOK-MAX ADRIAN
    ROBERT ROUNSEVILLE-IRRA PETINA-WILLIAM OLVIS-LOUIS
    EDMONDS-C.BAIN *SONY Broadway: SK 48017 (CD)*
  2.MUSICAL OPERA 1988 Studio *feat:* SCOTTISH OPERA CAST
    TER (Koch): CDTER 1156 Highlights: *CDTER 1006*
  3.MUSICAL OPERA 1991 Studio Recording *w:* JERRY HADLEY
    JUNE ANDERSON-CHRISTA LUDWIG-ADOLPH GREEN-NICOLAI
    GEDDA-DELLA JONES-KURT OLLMANN & L.S.O.(Bernstein)
    DG (Univ): 429734-2 (2CDs) -4 (2MC)
  4.NEW BROADWAY CAST 1997 *RCA (BMG):0902 668835-2 (CD)*
CANNON (USA TV) *see COLL.349,*
CAPEMAN The (MUSICAL 1997/8) All songs by PAUL SIMON
  featuring RUBEN BLADES-MARC ANTHONY-EDNITA NAZARIO
  W.BROS (TEN): 9362 46814-2 (CD) -4 (MC)
CAPITAL CITY (Thames 26/9/89) theme music: COLIN TOWNS
  -S/T- *FIRST NIGHT (Pinn): SCENE(CD)(C) 18 (CD/MC)*
CAPRICORN ONE (1978) Music sco: JERRY GOLDSMITH -S/T-
  so containing music from 'OUTLAND') on *GNP USA
  (ZYX): GNPD 8035 (CD) GNP-5 8035 (MC)*
  see COLL.166,167,267,328,330,
CAPTAIN BLOOD (1935) *see COLL.204,221,330,338,*
CAPTAIN BLOOD (1952) Mus.sco: VICTOR YOUNG new record:
  BRANDENBURG S.ORCH.(Kaufman) with other items on
  MARCO POLO (Select): 8.223607 (CD

CAPTAIN FROM CASTILLE *see COLL.1,*
CAPTAIN FUTURE (1995) Music score: CHRISTIAN BRUHN
  -S/T- *COLOSSEUM (Pinn): CST 8051 (CD)*
CAPTAIN KANGAROO (USA) *see COLL.345,*
CAPTAIN MIDNIGHT (USA TV) *see COLL.348,*
CAPTAIN SCARLET AND THE MYSTERONS (BBC2 1/10/93 orig
  ITV 29/9/67) music by BARRY GRAY *see COLL.4,23,38,*
  122,171,270,311,360,362,367,369,377,
CAPTIVE (1986) Music sco: MICHAEL BERKLEY-The EDGE
  -S/T- *VIRGIN (EMI): CDV 2401 (CD)*
CAR 54 WHERE ARE YOU (USA TV) *see COLL.346,*
CAR WASH (1976) T.theme: NORMAN WHITFIELD sung by ROSE
  ROYCE -S/T- reissue: *MCA (BMG): MCD 11502 (CD)*
CARAVAGGIO 1610 (1986) Music: SIMON FISHER TURNER
  -S/T- *reissued on DEMON (Pinn): DSCD 10 (CD)*
CARD The - songs by Tony Hatch and Jackie Trent
  ORIG LONDON CAST 1973 *w:* JIM DALE-MILLICENT MARTIN
  JOAN HICKSON-MARTI WEBB-ELEANOR BRON-ALAN NORBURN
  JOHN SAVIDENT *FIRST NIGHT (Pinn): OCRCD 6045 (CD)*
CARDIAC ARREST (Island World/BBC1 21/4/94) music and
  sound design: DAVID MOTION & BOB LAST *unavailable*
CAREER GIRLS (1998) featuring music by The CURE -S/T-
  TWEED COUTURE (New Note-Pinn): TWEEDCD 8 (CD)
CAREFREE (1938) FILM MUSICAL *feat* FRED ASTAIRE-GINGER
  ROGERS -S/T- *selection on* 'Let's Swing and Dance'
  +songs fr.'FOLLOW THE FLEET'/'TOP HAT'/'SWINGTIME'
  GREAT MOVIE THEMES (Target-BMG): CD 60015 (CD)
  also available -S/T- + songs from 'SHALL WE DANCE'
  IRIS Mus-Chansons Cinema (Discov): CIN 007 (CD)
CARIBBEAN HOLIDAY (BBC1 04/05/1999) original music
  composed and performed by EDDY GRANT *unavailable*
CARIBBEAN UNCOVERED (SKY1 01/3/1998) Mus: VARIOUS ARTS
  'CARIBBEAN UNCOVERED 45 HOTTEST CARNIVAL HITS' *2CDs*
CARLA'S SONG (1996) Music score: GEORGE FENTON -S/T-
  DEBONAIR Records (Pinn): CDDEB 1005 (CD)
CARLITO'S WAY (1993) Mus sco: PATRICK DOYLE Songs V/A
  -S/T- (Songs) *EPIC (Ten): 474 994-2 (CD) deleted*
  -S/T- (Score) *VARESE (Pinn): VSD(VSC) 5463 CD/MC*
CARMEN - *mus:* Georges Bizet *libr:* H.Meilhac-L.Halevy
  1.FILM MUSICAL 1983 *w:* LAURA DEL SOL-PACO DE LUCIA
    ANTONIO GADES-CRISTINA HOYOS -S/T- *POLY (IMS):*
    E.817 247-2 (CD)
  2.FILM MUSICAL 1984 *w:* PLACIDO DOMINGO-JULIA MIGENES
    JOHNSON *ERATO: MCE 75113 (3MC) ECD 88037 (3CD)*
  3.STUDIO RECORDING *with* MARILYN HORNE as Carmen
    DG (Univ): 427 440-2 (3CD's)
CARMEN JONES songs by G.Bizet & Oscar Hammerstein II
  1.FILM MUSICAL 1954 *feat:* MARILYN HORNE-PEARL BAILEY
    LaVERN HUTCHINSON-MARVIN HAYES-OLGA JAMES-BERNICE
    PETERSON-BROCK PETERS -S/T- *(BMG): GD(GK) 81881*
  2.ORIG LONDON CAST 1991 *Direct:* SIMON CALLOW *with*
    WILHELMINA FERNANDEZ-SHARON BENSON-DAMON EVANS-
    MICHAEL AUSTIN-GREGG BAKER-KAREN PARKS-CLIVE ROWE
    DANNY JOHN JULES *EMI: CDJONES 1 (EL 754351-2)*

CARNIVAL OF SOULS (1998) *BIRDMAN (Cargo): BMR 012 (CD)*
CARO DIARIO - see under DEAR DIARY
CAROL VORDERMAN'S BETTER HOMES (ITV 04/01/1999) music:
DAVID KESTER *unavailable*
CAROUSEL - songs: Richard Rodgers-Oscar Hammerstein II
1.FILM MUSICAL 1956 *feat:* GORDON McRAE-SHIRLEY JONES
-S/T- Reissue *EMI ANGEL: ZDM 764 692-2 (CD)*
2.ORIG LONDON CAST 1993 JOANNA RIDING-KATRINA MURPHY
FIRST NIGHT (Pinn): OCRCD 6042 (CD) CASTC 40 (MC)
3.SHOWS COLLECTION 1993 *feat:* DAVE WILLETTS-CLAIRE
MOORE-SU POLLARD-IAN WALLACE-LINDA HIBBERD
CARLTON Shows: PWKS 4144 (CD) PWKMC 4144 (MC)
4.REVIVAL BROADWAY CAST 1965 *with* JOHN RAITT
Import (SILVA SCREEN): 6395-2 (CD)
5.ORIG BROADWAY CAST 1945 *with* JOHN RAITT-JAN CLAYTON
JEAN DARLING-C.JOHNSON *MCA: MCLD 19152 (CD deleted)*
also Imp (SILVA SCREEN): MCAD(MCAC) 10048 (CD/MC)
CARRIE (1976) Music score: PINO DONAGGIO -S/T- *reiss +*
additional items RYKODISC (Vital): RCD 10701 (CD)
CARRIED AWAY (1996) Music score: BRUCE BROUGHTON -S/T-
INTRADA (Koch): MAFCD 7068 (CD)
CARRINGTON (1995) Music sco: MICHAEL NYMAN -S/T- incl:
'Adagio' from String Quintet in C. (SCHUBERT) on
ARGO-DECCA (Univ): 444 873-2(CD)
CARRY ON... (UK COMEDY FILM SERIES FROM 1958-1991)
Music by ERIC ROGERS-BRUCE MONTGOMERY + Var.Arts
CITY OF PRAGUE PHILHARMONIC ORCH: Gavin Sutherland
WHITE LINE-ASV (Select): WHL 2119 (CD) see COLLS.
CASABLANCA (1943) Mus: MAX STEINER *vocal:* DOOLEY WILSON
-S/T- + *dialogue EMI: 823 502-2 (CD)* see COLL.41,
65,70,90,106,120,128,211,214,282,298,383
CASINO (1995) Songs by Various Artists
-S/T- (31 Tracks) on *MCA (BMG): MCAD 11389 (2CD)*
CASINO ROYALE (1967) Music score: BURT BACHARACH -S/T-
VARESE (Pinn): VSD 5265 (CD) also COLL.128,259,
CASPER (1995) Music sco: JAMES HORNER / "Remember Me
This Way" JORDAN HILL "Casper The Friendly Ghost"
by LITTLE RICHARD -S/T- *MCA (BMG): MCD 11240 (CD)*
CASPER THE FRIENDLY GHOST (USA TV) *see COLL.345,*

CASSANDRA CROSSING The (1977) Music sc: JERRY GOLDSMITH
feat song "I'm Still On My Way" sung by Ann Turkel
-S/T- *CITADEL Imp (Silva Screen): OST 102 (CD)*
CASTLE FREAK (1995) Music score: RICHARD BAND -S/T-
INTRADA (Silva Screen): MAF 7065 (CD)
CASUALTY (BBC1 1998) Main theme by KEN FREEMAN + song
"EVERLASTING LOVE"(Cason-Gayden) CAST FROM CASUALTY
WARNER ESP (TEN): WESP 003CD (CDs) WESP 003C (MC)
see COLL.46,243,270,407,
CAT O'NINE TAILS (1980) Music: ENNIO MORRICONE -S/T-
inc 'FOUR FLIES ON GREY VELVET'/'BIRD WITH THE CRYS
TAL PLUMAGE' on *DRG (Pinn): DRGCD 32911 (CD)*
CATHEDRAL (BBC1 7/9/97) theme "Anna Of The Five Towns"
by NIGEL HESS *see COLL.193,*

CATLOW (1971) Music score: ROY BUDD -S/T- Collect also
feat 'SOLDIER BLUE' (1970) & 'ZEPPELIN' (1971) on
CINEPHILE (Pinn): CINCD 022 (CD)

CATS - songs by Andrew Lloyd Webber and Trevor Nunn
1. ORIG LONDON CAST 1981 *feat:* ELAINE PAIGE & Comp
POLYDOR: 817 810-2 (2CD) 817 810-4 (2MC)
'Highlights' 839415-2(CD) -1(LP) -4(MC) -5 (DCC)
2. ROYAL PHILH.ORCH *PLAY SUITES from* Aspects Of Love
Cats/Joseph and The Amazing Technicolor Dreamcoat
CARLTON Int: PWKS(PWKMC) 4115 (CD/MC)
3. CLASSIC MUSICALS SERIES *feat:* MARIA FRIEDMAN and
CLIVE CARTER w. MUNICH SYMPHONY ORCH (J.O.Edwards)
+songs 'PHANTOM OF THE OPERA' *KOCH Int: 34078-2CD*
4. SHOWS COLLECTION *CARLTON: PWKS(PWKMC) 4192 (CD/MC)*

CATWEAZLE (LWT 1/3/70-71) theme music: TED DICKS
see COLL.4,

CAUGHT UP (1998) *VIRGIN: CDVUS 139 (CD) VUSLP 109 (LP)*

CELEBRITY (1999) WOODY ALLEN'S SELECTION OF 30s and 40s
songs *feat:* ERROLL GARNER/CARMEN CAVALLARO/JACKIE
GLEASON & HIS ORCHESTRA/LITTLE JACK LITTLE/JANET
MARLOW/LIBERACE/RAY COHEN/TEDDY WILSON
MILAN (BMG): 74321 64071-2 (CD)

CELL BLOCK 4 (1992) Music score (John Barnes) -S/T-
MCA (BMG): MCD 10758 (CD)

CELTS The (BBC2 14/5/87) Music score comp/performed by
ENYA -S/T/- WEA: 4509 91167-2 (CD) WX 498C (MC)

CENTRAL STATION (Central Do Brasil) (1998) Music score:
ANTONIO PINTO-JAQUES MORELEMBAUM -S/T- issued on
BMG SOUNDTRACKS: 74321 63196-2 (CD)

CENTURY (1993) Music score: MICHAEL GIBBS -S/T- *with*
'CLOSE MY EYES' *IONIC-MUTE (Pinn): IONIC 10 (2CD)*

CENTURY ROAD (BBC2 09/01/1999) music by JOHN EACOTT
add.music by GREAT YARMOUTH BRASS *unavailable*

CESAR (1936) MARCEL PAGNOL'S TRILOGY (3) / music sco.by
VINCENT SCOTTO on Coll 'Films Of Marcel Pagnol' on
EMI FRA.(Discov): 855 883-2 (CD) / see also 'FANNY'

CHAIRMAN The (1969) Music sc: JERRY GOLDSMITH -S/T- inc
'Ransom' (75) *S.SCREEN (Koch): FILMCD 081 (CD)*

CHALLENGE The (ORIGINAL LONDON CAST RECORDING)
TER (Koch): TERCD 1201 (2CD)

CHAMPION THE WONDER HORSE (USA 56)(BBC1 7/11/92) theme
song (Norman Luboff-Marilyn Keith) sung by FRANKIE
LAINE *BEAR FAMILY (Rollecoaster): BCD 15632 (CDs)*

CHAMPIONS (1984) Music score: CARL DAVIS -S/T- *deleted*
vocal version "Sometimes" Elaine PAIGE *see COLL 278*

CHAMPIONS The (ITC 25/9/68 - 4/69) theme: EDWIN ASTLEY
see COLL.4,23,

CHAMPIONS LEAGUE FOOTBALL *see* EUROPEAN CHAMPIONS LEAGUE

CHANCER (Central 6/3/90) theme (Jan Hammer) JAN HAMMER
'Escape From Television' inc: 'Crockett's Theme'
MCA (BMG): MCAD 10410 (CD) MCAC 10410 (MC)

CHANGE OF HABIT *see* ELVIS PRESLEY INDEX p.360

CHANGING ROOMS (BBC2 4/9/96-2000) theme music by
JIM PARKER *unavailable*

CHAPLIN (1992) Music sco JOHN BARRY -S/T- reissue *EPIC*
(SM): 472 602-2 (CD DELETED) see COLL.29,30,43,
CHARADE (1964) Music score: HENRY MANCINI
see COLL.238,239,246,
CHARGE OF THE LIGHT BRIGADE (1936) Music score: MAX
STEINER *new recording* SLOVAK STATE PHILHARMONIC
(Barry COLEMAN, cond) also with 'TREASURE OF THE
SIERRA MADRE' *CENTAUR (Comp/Pinn): CRC 2367 (CD)*
CHARIOTS OF FIRE (1981) Music score: VANGELIS -S/T-
POLYDOR (Univ): POLDC (MC) 800 020-2 (CD) see also
see COLL.41,70,84,204,331,339,380,
CHARLIE BROWN (A BOY NAMED) (USA 80's/BBC1) Mus score
composed and performed by The VINCE GUARALDI TRIO
FANTASY (Complete): FCD 8430-2 (CD)
CHARLIE GIRL - songs by David Heneker and John Taylor
1. NEW LONDON CAST 1986 *w:* PAUL NICHOLAS-CYD CHARISSE
MARK WYNTER-DORA BRYAN-NICHOL.PARSONS-KAREN DAVIES
LISA HULL *FIRST NIGHT (Pinn): OCRCD 6009(CD)*
CHARLIE'S ANGELS (USA 76) theme: JACK ELLIOTT & ALLYN
FERGUSON *see COLL.109,110,347,363,382,*
CHARRO! *see* ELVIS PRESLEY INDEX p.360
CHASING THE DEER (1993) Music by JOHN WETTON -S/T- on
BLUEPRINT (Pinn): BP 282CD (CD) and BLUEPRINT (Sil
ver Sounds): 6043 88124-2 (CD) theme also on Coll.
'Battle Lines" *CROMWELL (THE): CPCD 020 (CD)*
CHE! (1969) Music score: LALO SCHIFRIN -S/T- *reissue*
ALEPH (Koch): ALEP 006 (CD)
CHECKMATE (USA TV) *see COLL.348,*
CHEERS (USA C4 6/1/84-93) theme "Where Everybody Knows
Your Name" GARY PORTNOY *see COLL.17,256,270,347,*
CHELSEA FLOWER SHOW The (BBC2 var.dates) music sel.inc:
'Lakme'"The Flower Duet" (DELIBES) sung by MADY MES
PLE and DANIELLE MILLET with Paris Opera Orchestra
EMI: 568 307-2 (CD) 1994 (BBC2 25/5/94) theme music
from 'The Celts' composed & performed by ENYA *WEA
4509 91167-2(CD)* WX 498C(MC) 1993 (BBC2 26/5/93)
closing mus. "The Mission" by ENNIO MORRICONE -S/T-
VIRGIN (EMI):CDV(TCV)(MDV)2402 (CD/MC/MD) also used
"Pomp And Circumstance No.2" (ELGAR) **1992 & 1991**
(BBC2) mus.inc: PENGUIN CAFE ORCHEST "From The Colo
nies"(Broadcasting From Home) *EG-VIRGIN: EGCD 38CD*
"Air A Dancer"/"A Telephone And A Rubber Band"
from 'When In Rome'*EGCD 56 (CD)* "Sketch"/"Perpetuum
Mobile" from 'Signs Of Life' *EGCD 50 (CD) other mus
ic used* "Prelude" ('Holberg Suite Op.40) (E.GREIG)
CHELTENHAM FESTIVAL (BBC1 14/3/89-1998) theme music
"Odissea" (G.Reverberi-L.Giordiano) RONDO VENEZIANO
BMG (Discovery): 610.535 (CD)
CHERRY HARRY & RAQUEL (1969, RUSS MEYER) -S/T- inc:
'MONDO TOPLESS' (66) 'GOOD MORNING & GOODBYE' (67)
NORMAL/QDK (Dir/Greyhound/Pinn): QDK(CD)(LP) 014
CHESS *see under* 'WORLD CHESS CHAMPIONSHIPS 1993'
CHESS - songs: Benny Andersson-Bjorn Ulvaeus-Tim Rice
1. 1986 Chess Pieces: The Best Of Chess *feat:* ELAINE

PAIGE-BARBARA DICKSON-MURRAY HEAD-TOMMY KORBERG-DEN
IS QUILLEY-BJORN SKIFS-LONDON SYMPHONY ORCH-AMBROSI
AN SINGERS *RCA (BMG): 74321 15120-2 (CD) -4 (MC)*
  2.ORIG BROADWAY CAST: *POLYDOR (Univ): 847 445-2 (CD)*
CHEYENNE (USA TV 1958) *see COLL.348,*
CHEYENNE AUTUMN (1964) Music score by ALEX NORTH.
  SELECTION WITH 'CINERAMA SOUTH SEAS ADV. (1958) and
  'DRAGONSLAYER' (81) *LABEL X (Hot): ATMCD 2004 (CD)*
CHICAGO - songs: John Kander and Fred Ebb
  1.ORIG LONDON CAST (1997) *feat:* UTE LEMPER-RUTHIE
  HENSHALL-HENRY GOODMAN-NIGEL PLANER-MEG JOHNSON etc
  RCA (BMG): 09026 63155-2 (CD, 09.1998) -4 (MC)
  2.ORIG BROADWAY CAST (1996) *featuring:* ANN REINKING
  BEBE NUEWIRTH-JAMES NAUGHTON-JOEL GRAY and Company
  RCA (BMG): 09026 68727-2 (CD) -4 (MC)
  3.ORIG NEW YORK CAST (1975, re-mastered 1998)
  RCA (BMG): 07822 18952-2 (CD)
CHICAGO BLUES (Film 'Blues' Document) Muddy Waters &
  J.B.Hutto-Junior Wells-Mighty Joe Young-Koko Taylor
  Johnnie Young *CASTLE COMM (Pinn): CLACD 425 (CD)*
CHICAGO HOPE (BBC1 1/4/1995) Mus: MARK ISHAM-JEFF RONA
  -S/T- *SONIC IMAGES (Greyhound-Cargo): SI 8702 (CD)*
  see COLL.243,
CHICO AND THE MAN (USA 74) theme (Jose Feliciano) JOSE
  FELICIANO on *RCA: ND 90123 (CD) NK 89561 (MC)*
  CARLTON Ess.Gold (CHE): 30359 00232 (CD) -4(MC)
CHIGLEY (BBC1 1969) *see COLL.186,*
CHILDREN IN NEED (BBC1 20/11/1998) song "PERFECT DAY"
  (L.Reed) V.ARTS *CHRYSALIS (Univ): CDNEED 001 (CDs)*
  TCNEED 001 (MC) 7NEED 001 (7"s) / song 1996 "When
  Children Rule The World"(A.Lloyd Webber-J.Steinman)
  by RED HILL CHILDREN *POLYD: 579726-2 (CDs) -4 (MC)*
  theme 1989-95 "If You Want To Help-Help Children In
  Need"(David Martin) FINCHLEY CHILDREN'S MUSIC GROUP
  recording unconfirmed (previous entries in TT 1991)
CHILDREN OF A LESSER GOD (1986) "Largo Ma Mon Tanto"
  2nd m/m 'Concerto D.Min For Violins' (BACH) / Music
  sco: MICHAEL CONVERTINO -S/T- *GNP (ZYX)*
  GNPD(GNP5)(GNPS)8007 (CD/MC/LP)   *see COLL.81,*
CHILDREN'S HOSPITAL (BBC1 19/10/93) Theme mus.by DEBBIE
  WISEMAN on *BMG INT (BMG): 74321 47589-4 (MC*
  see COLL.243,407,
CHILDREN'S THIEF The (Film Italy) Music score: FRANCO
  PIERSANTI -S/T- contains mus from 'ON MY OWN'(92)
  -S/T- *OST (Silva Screen): OST 117 (CD)*
CHIMERA (Anglia 7/9/91) theme music "Rosheen Du" by
  NIGEL HESS sung by CHAMELEON *see COLLS 138,191,192*
CHIMPANZEE DIARY (BBC2 17/01/1999) music by DAVID POORE
  unavailable
CHINA 9 LIBERTY 37 (1978) Music sco: PINO DONAGGIO
  -S/T- *Import (SILVA SCREEN): PCD 117 (CD)*
CHINATOWN (1974) Music score: JERRY GOLDSMITH -S/T-
  VARESE (Pinn): VSD 5677 (CD)
CHIPS (USA TV 1980) theme: JOHN PARKER *see COLL.350,*

CHITTY CHITTY BANG BANG (1968) Music and songs by
RICHARD & ROBERT SHERMAN -S/T- *reissue + add.items*
DICK VAN DYKE-SALLY ANN HOWES-LIONEL JEFFRIES etc.
RYKODISC (Vital): RCD 10702 (CD) RAC 10702 (MC)

CHORUS LINE, A   songs: Marvin Hamlisch-Edward Kleban
1. FILM SOUNDTRACK 1985 *feat:* MICHAEL DOUGLAS-TERENCE
MANN-ALYSON REED *reissue BGO (BMG): BGOCD 360 (CD)*
2. ORIGINAL BROADWAY CAST 1975 *w:* KELLY BISHOP-PAMELA
BLAIR-WAYNE CILENTO-KAY COLE-PATRICIA GARLAND and
DONNA McKECHNIE *COLUMBIA (Ten): SK 65282 (CD)*

CHRISTINE (1984) Music score: JOHN CARPENTER -S/T-
John Carpenter's original music only on import
VARESE (Pinn): VSD 5240 (CD)

CHRISTOPHER COLUMBUS (1949)   Music by Sir ARTHUR BLISS
new recording by SLOVAK RADIO S.O. (Adriano) plus
Music from film and from 'Seven Waves Away' (1956)
MARCO POLO (Select): 8.223315 (CD)

CHRISTOPHER COLUMBUS: THE DISCOVERY (1992) Music score
CLIFF EIDELMAN -S/T- *VARESE (Pinn): VSD 5389 (CD)*

CHRONICLES OF NARNIA (BBC1 13/11/88)
theme mus by GEOFFREY BURGON *see COLL.61,*
also avail BBC (Techn): ZBBC 1109 & ZBBC 1110 (2MC)

CIDER WITH ROSIE (ITV 27/12/1998) Music score: GEOFFREY
BURGON -ST- on *SILVA SCREEN (Koch): FILMCD 306 (CD)*

CIMARRON STRIP (USA TV) *see COLL.349,*

CINDERELLA (Disney 1950) *see* WALT DISNEY INDEX p.362

CINDERELLA (MUSICAL SHOW 1957) with JULIE ANDREWS *Col.*
(Silva Screen): CK 02005 (CD) JST 02005 (MC)

CINDERELLA (SONGS FROM THE CLASSIC FAIRY TALE)
NEW RECORDINGS *VARESE (Pinn): VSD 5875 (CD)*

CINEMA PARADISO (1990) Music score ENNIO MORRICONE
DRG (Pinn): CDSBL 12598 (CD) SBLC 12598 (MC)
see COLL.43,69,89,106,144,239,251,254,330

CINERAMA SOUTH SEAS ADVENTURE (1958) Music score by
ALEX NORTH. *SELECTION WITH* 'CHEYENNE AUTUMN' (1964)
'DRAGONSLAYER' (81) *LABEL X (Hot): ATMCD 2004 (CD)*

CIRCUS The (1928) Music sco: CHARLES CHAPLIN *see COLL*
'FILM MUS.OF CHARLES CHAPLIN' *RCA: 09026 68271-2*

CIRQUE DU SOLEIL - *see* 'ALEGRIA' and 'SALTIMBANCO'

CITIZEN KANE (1941) Music: BERNARD HERRMANN *(complete)*
AUSTRALIAN P.O.(TONY BREMNER) *feat* ROSAMUND ILLING
PREAMBLE-5th CONT (HOT-S.Screen): PRCD 1788 (CD)
also recored on VARESE (Pinn): VSD 5806 (CD)
see COLL.70,188,189,192,

CITY HALL (1995) Music score: JERRY GOLDSMITH -S/T- on
VARESE (Pinn): VSD 5699 (CD)

CITY LIGHTS (1931) Original Music composed by CHARLES
CHAPLIN. New recording reconstructed from the orig
manuscripts. City Lights Orch conductor: CARL DAVIS
S.SCREEN (Koch):FILMCD 078 see COLL.66,70,

CITY OF ANGELS (O.LONDON CAST 1993) Songs (Cy Coleman-
Larry Gelbart) *feat:* MARTIN SMITH-ROGER ALLAM-HENRY
GOODMAN-HADYN GWYNNE-SUSANNAH FELLOWS-JOANNE FARREL
FIRST NIGHT (Pinn): OCRCD 6034 (CD)

CITY OF ANGELS (1998) Music score: GABRIEL YARED -S/T-
ALANIS MORRISETTE-SARAH McLACHLAN-PETER GABRIEL etc
WB (TEN): 9362 46867-2 (CD) -4 (MC)

CITY OF FEAR (1958) Music score: JERRY GOLDSMITH
TARAN (Silver Sounds): W 9104 (CD)

CITY OF INDUSTRY (1996) Music score: STEPHEN ENDELMAN
-S/T- with MASSIVE ATTACK-BOMB THE BASS-LUSH-TRICKY
PHOTEX etc. *QUANGO-ISLAND (Univ): 524 308-2 (CD)*

CITY OF THE WALKING DEAD (1970) Music score: STELVIO
CIPRIANI -S/T- *LUCERTOLA (SRD): EFA 04362-2 (CD)*

CITY OF VIOLENCE (Citta Violenta) Music score: ENNIO
MORRICONE -S/T- *IMPT (Silva Screen): OST 127 (CD)*

CITY SLICKERS (1991) Music score: MARC SHAIMAN -S/T-
VARESE (Pinn): VSD 5321 (CD)

CIVIL ACTION, A (1998) Music score by DANNY ELMAN -S/T-
HOLLYWOOD-EDEL (Pinn): 010087-2HWR (CD)

CIVIL WAR The (BBC2 30/3/91) theme "Ashokan Farewell"
by JAY UNGAR -S/T- incl: "Shenandoah"/"When Johnny
Comes Marching Home" & others - KEN BURNS -S/T- on
ELEKTRA-NONESUCH (TEN): 7559-79256-2(CD) -4(MC)
ALSO AVAILABLE: "The Civil War-It's Music & Sounds"
IMS-POLY E.432 591-2 (CD) also see COLL.155,

CLAMBAKE see ELVIS PRESLEY INDEX p.360

CLANDESTINE MARRIAGE The (1999) Music score: STANISLAS
SYREWICZ -S/T- *VENTURE-VIRGIN (EMI): CDVE 949 (CD)*

CLARISSA EXPLAINS IT ALL (USA TV) see COLL.351,

CLASH OF THE TITANS (1981) Music sc: LAURENCE ROSENTHAL
reissue with LONDON SYMPHONY ORCHEST (L.Rosenthal)
FANTASY IMP (S.Screen): PNDL 14 and PEG A28693 (CD)

CLASSIC ADVENTURE (BBC1 11/5/92) mus: NIGEL HESS
see COLL.149,193,

CLERKS (1994) Music sco: SCOTT ANGLEY -S/T- with V.Arts
COLUMBIA (Ten): 477 802-2 (CD)

CLIVE ANDERSON ALL TALK (BBC1 6/10/96) title music "All
Talk" by ELVIS COSTELLO & ATTRACTIONS *unavailable*

CLIVE BARKER'S A-Z OF HORROR (BBC2 4/10/97) t.music by
TOT TAYLOR on the 'WATERLAND' album
TWEED (Pinn/Vital): TWEEDCD 001 (CD)

CLOCKERS (1995) Music score by STANLEY CLARKE-TERENCE
BLANCHARD -S/T- *MCA (BMG): MCD 11304 (CD)*

CLOCKWORK ORANGE, A (1971) Electronic music sco WALTER
'Wendy' CARLOS V.Classics -S/T- *WB: CD 246127 (CD)*
K.446127 (MC) see COLL.78,79,80,122,131,144,309,

CLOSE ENCOUNTERS OF THE THIRD KIND (1977) music by
JOHN WILLIAMS *-S/T- COLLECTOR SPECIAL EDITION
ARISTA (BMG): 07822 19004-2*

CLOSE ENCOUNTERS OF THE THIRD KIND (1977) Music score
JOHN WILLIAMS Nat.Phil.Orch *RCA: RCD 13650 (CD)*
see COLL.175,201,267,307,310,328,333,403,

CLOSE MY EYES (1991) Music sco: MICHAEL GIBBS -S/T- +
'CENTURY' on *IONIC-MUTE (Pinn): IONIC 10 (2CD)*

CLOSE RELATIONS (BBC1 17/5/1998) orig theme and score
music by ROB LANE *unavailable* / song "Feeling Good"
sung by NINA SIMONE on 'Movie Killers' *TCD 2836 CD*

CLOSE SHAVE, A (Wallace & Gromit) (1995) Mus by JULIAN
    NOTT *Video: BBC (Pinn): BBCV 5766 (VHS) see also*
    'GRAND DAY OUT'/'WRONG TROUSERS'
CLOSE UP (BBC2 Doc.ser.from 9/9/1998) theme "Teardrop"
    by MASSIVE ATTACK *VIRGIN Records*
CLOTHES SHOW The (BBC1 13/10/87-98)theme "In The Night"
    by PET SHOP BOYS (re-mix version *unavailable*) orig
    on 'Disco' *EMI: CDP 746 450-2 (CD) TC-PRG 1001 (MC)*
CLUB The (BBC1 08/11/1999) music by DEBBIE WISEMAN
    unavailable
CLUELESS (1995) Music sco: DAVID KITAY -S/T- w. V.Arts
    CAPITOL (EMI): CDEST 2267 (CD)
COASTAL COMMAND (1942) Music score: VAUGHAN WILLIAMS
    on 'Film Music' RTE CONCERT ORCH (Andrew Penny) on
    MARCO POLO (Sel):8.223665 (CD) see COLL.94,173,187,
COCKTAIL (1988) Music score: J.PETER ROBINSON -S/T- on
    ELEKTRA (TEN): 960806-2 (CD)
COCOON (1985) Music: JAMES HORNER inc: Michael Sembello
    IMP (Silva Screen): PNDL 13 (CD)
    see COLL.205,264,328,334,
COCOON 2 'The Return' (1989) Music score: JAMES HORNER
    -S/T- *VARESE Pinn: VSD 5211 (CD) see COLL.207,313,*
COLBY'S The (USA TV) *see COLL.350,*
COLD FEET (ITV 15/11/1998) music score by MARK RUSSELL
    theme "Female Of The Species" re-mix by SPACE
    -S/T- *GLOBAL TV (BMG): 74321 72607-2 (2CDs) -4(2MC)*
    orig SPACE track from 'SPIDERS' GUT (BMG): GUTCD 1
COLD HEAVEN (1992) Music score: STANLEY MYERS Suite on
    INTRADA (S.Screen): MAF 7048D (CD) also includes
    Suite from film 'TRUSTING BEATRICE' (S.MYERS)
COLD LAZARUS (BBC1 5/96) Music sco: CHRISTOPHER GUNNING
    -S/T- includes music from 'KARAOKE' and feat tracks
    by BING CROSBY-HANK WILLIAMS-CRAIG DOUGLAS etc.
    SILVA SCREEN (Koch): FILM(CD)(C) 181 (CD/MC)
COLD ROOM The (1994) Music score: MICHAEL NYMAN -S/T-
    SILVA SCREEN (Koch): FILMCD 157 (CD)
COLDITZ (BBC1 19/10/72) "Colditz March" ROBERT FARNON
    see COLL.2,281,
COLOR OF MONEY The (1986) Mus: ROBBIE ROBERTSON +songs
    -S/T- *MCA USA Imp (Silva Screen): MCAD 6189 (CD)*
    see COLL.364,
COLOR PURPLE The (1986) Music sco: QUINCY JONES +Songs
    Tata Vega -S/T- *QWEST Imp (S.Scr): 925389-2 (2CDs)*
COLT 45 (USA TV) *see COLL.348,*
COLUMBO (USA) - *see COLL.2,*
COMEDY PLAYHOUSE (BBC1 1960s) theme "Happy Joe" by RON
    GRAINER *see COLL.8,23,367,*
COMIN' ATCHA (ITV 05/02/1998) music by CLEOPATRA and
    EVERIS PELLIUS *unavailable*
COMMITMENTS The (1991) -S/T- (Various Atists covers)
    MCAD 10286 (CD) MCAC 10286 (MC)
    COMMITMENTS 2 Second Album incl: "Hard To Handle"
    "Show Me"/"Too Many Fish In The Sea"/"Nowhere To
    Run" + 7 new tracks *MCA (BMG): MCLD 19312 (CD)*

COMPANEROS (1970) Music score (E.Morricone) ENNIO MORR
  ICONE ORCHESTRA on Collection 'An Ennio Morricone
  Quintet' *DRG USA (Pinn): DRGCD 32907 (CD)*
COMPANY - songs: Stephen Sondheim
  1. ORIG LONDON CAST 1995/6 *w:*ADRIAN LESTER-SHEILA GISH
    SOPHIE THOMPSON-CLIVE ROWE-PAUL BENTLEY and Company
    FIRST NIGHT (Pinn): CASTCD 57 (CD) CASTC 57 (MC)
  2. ORIG BROADWAY CAST 1995
    EMI PREM.West End (EMI): PRMFCD 2 (CD) DELETED
  3. ORIG LONDON CAST 1972 *w:* ELAINE STRICH-BETH HOWLAND
    GEORGE COE-SUSAN BROWNING-LARRY KERT *SONY*
    Broadway: SMK 53496 (CD) deleted
  4. ORIGINAL BROADWAY CAST 1970 *with* ELAINE STRITCH-
    DEAN JONES-BARBARA BARRIE-DONNA McKECHNIE and Comp
  5. COMPANY IN JAZZ by The TROTTER TRIO
    VARESE (Pinn): VSD 5673 (CD)
COMPANY OF WOLVES The (1984) Mus: GEORGE FENTON -S/T-
  TER (Koch): CDTER 1094 (CD)
COMPASS (BBC2 5/1/1998) mus: DAVID STEPHENS *unavailable*
CON AIR (1997) Music score: MARK MANCINA & TREVOR RABIN
  song "How Do I Live" sung by TRISHA YEARWOOD on
  MCA (BMG): MCSTD 48064 (CDs) MCSC 48064 (MC)
  -S/T- (import only) *POLY: E.162 099-2 (CD)*
CONAN THE ADVENTURER (TV) music score: CHARLES FOX
  -S/T- *SONIC IMAGE (Cargo): 78282 78801-2 (CD)*
CONAN THE BARBARIAN (1981) Music sco: BASIL POLEDOURIS
  -S/T- *MILAN (BMG): 111 262 (CD)*
  see COLL.70,72,304,305,385,
CONAN THE DESTROYER (1983) Music sco: BASIL POLEDOURIS
  VARESE (S.Screen): VSD 5392 (CD) see COLL.304,
CONFESSIONS OF A POLICE CAPTAIN (1971-Italy) *see under*
  'IN THE GRIP OF THE SPIDER'
CONFIDENTIALLY YOURS (1983 'Vivement Dimanche') Music
  GEORGES DELERUE *on Coll* 'TRUFFAUT & DELERUE ON
  THE SCREEN' *DRG (Pinn): 32902 (CD)*
CONFORMIST The (1970) Music sco: GEORGES DELERUE -S/T-
  with -S/T- score from 'TRAGEDY OF A RIDICULOUS MAN'
  DRG (Pinn): DRGCD 32910 (CD)
CONNECTION The (1961) Mus.by FREDDIE REDD-JACKIE McLEAN
  -S/T- *re-iss BOPLICITY (Complete): CDBOP 019 (CD)*
CONQUEST OF THE AIR (1938) *see COLL.94,187,*
CONRACK (1974) Music score: JOHN WILLIAMS main theme on
  Collection 'POSEIDON ADVENTURE' (limited edit.) on
  RETROGRADE (Silva Screen/MFTM): FSMCD 2 (CD)
CONSPIRACY THEORY The (1997) Music sco: CARTER BURWELL
  -S/T- (score) - *SNAPPER (Pinn): SMACD 805 (CD)*
  -S/T- (songs, V.Art) *TVT (Pinn): TVT 81302 (CD)*
CONTACT (1997) Music score: ALAN SILVESTRI -S/T- V.Arts
  WB (TEN): 9362 46811-2 (CD) -4 (MC)
COOK THE THIEF HIS WIFE AND HER LOVER The (1989) Music:
  MICHAEL NYMAN -S/T- *VIRGIN (EMI): (CD)(TC)VE 53*
COOKIE'S FORTUNE (1998) Music score: DAVE STEWART
  "Cookie's Blues" by DAVE STEWART with CANDY DULFER
  -S/T- *ARISTA (BMG): 74321 66110-2 (CD)*

COOL HAND LUKE see COLL.52,298,

COOL McCOOL (USA TV) see COLL.349,

COOL RUNNINGS (1993) Music score: HANS ZIMMER songs by:
WAILING SOULS-JIMMY CLIFF-DIANA KING-TIGER etc.
-S/T- reissue: COLUMBIA (Ten): 474 840-2 (CD)

COOL WORLD (1992) Music score: MARK ISHAM -S/T- score
VARESE (Pinn): VSD 5382 (CD)

COOLEY HIGH (1975) Music sc: FREDDIE PERREN -S/T- feat
SMOKEY ROBINSON & MIRACLES-TEMPTATIONS-MARY WELLS-
SUPREMES etc. SPECTRUM (Univ): 551 547-2 (CD)

COP LAND (1997) Music score: HOWARD SHORE -S/T-
RCA-MILAN (BMG): 74321 53128-2 (CD)

COPACABANA (ORIG LONDON CAST 1994) Songs: BARRY MANILOW
feat GARY WILMOT FIRST NIGHT (Pinn): OCRCD 6047(CD)

COPYCAT (1996) Music score: CHRISTOPHER YOUNG -S/T-
MILAN (BMG): 74321 33742-2 (CD)

CORNBREAD EARL AND ME -S/T- feat: The BLACKBYRDS on
BGP/ACE (Pinn): CDBGPM 094 (CD) BGPD 1094 (LP)

CORONATION STREET (Granada 9/12/1960-2000) theme music:
ERIC SPEAR see COLL.2,150,270,367,376,
'THE CORONATION STREET ALBUM' feat The CAST with
guests CLIFF RICHARD-HOLLIES-MICHAEL BALL & DEUCE
EMI PREM: CD(TC)COROTV 1 (CD/MC) also '25TH ANNI
VERSARY ALB' K-TEL: ECD 3115 (CD) EMC 2115 (MC)
'Best Of' V.Arts EMI GOLD: CD(TC)MFP 6310 (CD/MC)

CORONER The (C4 16/02/1999) Music sco: HOWARD DAVIDSON
unavailable

CORRUPTOR The (1998) Music score by CARTER BURWELL
-S/T- score VARESE (Pinn): VSD 6014 (CD)
-S/T- songs JIVE (Pinn): 052 311-2 (CD)

COSBY SHOW The (USA C4 20/1/85) series theme mus by:
STU GARDNER-BILL COSBY see COLL.17,351,

COSI (1996) Music score: STEPHEN ENDELMAN -S/T- Imp
ICON (Pinn.Imports): ICON 19961 (CD)

COTTON CLUB The (1985) Music score: JOHN BARRY -S/T-
reissue: GEFFEN-MCA (BMG): GED 24062 (CD)
see COLL.30,71,

COUNT DRACULA (1970) Music sco: BRUNO NICOLAI -S/T-
PAN Imprt (Silva Screen): PAN 2502 (CD)

COUNT OF LUXEMBOURG The (OPERETTA) Music: FRANZ LEHAR
English lyr:ERIC MASCHWITZ New Sadlers Wells Cast
English Highlights TER (Koch): CDTER 1050 (CD)

COUNT OF MONTE CRISTO The (1976) Mus: ALLYN FERGUSON
-S/T- includes 'MAN IN THE IRON MASK' mus (Allyn
Ferguson) PROMETHEUS (Sil.Screen): PCD 130 (CD)

COUNTDOWN (C4 from 2/11/82-99) theme and incidental
music by ALAN HAWSHAW unavailable

COUNTESS MARITZA (OPERETTA) Mus: EMERICH KALLMANN Engl
ish lyr: NIGEL DOUGLAS New Sadlers Wells Cast
English Highlights TER (Koch): CDTER 1051 (CD)

COUNTRY PRACTICE (Australian TV) see COLL.150,243,

COUNTRYMAN (1982) Reggae music -S/T- feat: BOB MARLEY &
WAILERS-ASWAD-TOOTS & MAYTALS-LEE SCRATCH PERRY-
-S/T- Reggae Refresh-ISLAND (Univ): RRCD 44(CD)

COURAGEOUS CAT AND MINUTE MOUSE (USA TV) *see COLL.346,*
COURIER The (88) Music sco: DECLAN McMANUS (Elvis Cost
    ello) Songs: U2-Something Happens-Hothouse Flowers
    Cry Before Dawn -S/T- *VIRGIN (EMI):CDV 2517 (CD)*
COURT JESTER The (1955) Songs (Sylvia Fine-Sammy Cahn)
    with DANNY KAYE -S/T- also incl.songs from 'HANS
    CHRISTIAN ANDERSEN' *VARESE (Pinn): VSD 5498 (CD)*
COUSIN BETTE (1998) Music score: SIMON BOSWELL -S/T-
    RCA VICTOR (BMG): 09026 63168-2 CD)
COVER GIRL (1944) Songs: JEROME KERN-IRA GERSHWIN
    -S/T- selection with 'GOOD NEWS' on
    GREAT MOVIE THEMES (BMG): CD 60035 (CD)
COWBOYS The (1971) Music score: JOHN WILLIAMS -S/T-
    VARESE (Pinn): VSD 5540 (CD)
COX AND BOX (OPERETTA by GILBERT and SULLIVAN)
    LEON BERGER (bar) IAN KENNEDY (ten) DONALD FRANCKE
    (bass) KENNETH BARCLAY (piano) *COMPLETE OPERETTA
    DIVINE ART (Celtic Music): 2.4104 (CD, 1998)*
CRACKER: To Be A Somebody (Gran 10/10/1994) score music
    by DAVID FERGUSON *see COLL.151*
CRAFT The (1995) Music sco: GRAEME REVELL 2 soundtracks
    music score -S/T- *VARESE (Pinn): VSD 5732 (CD)*
    songs V.Art -S/T- *SONY: 484 152-2 (CD) -4 (MC)*
CRANE (TV 1963) *see COLL.23,*
CRASH (1996) Music score: HOWARD SHORE -S/T- on
    MILAN (BMG): 74321 40198-2 (CD)
CRAZY FOR YOU - songs by George and Ira Gershwin
  1.ORIG LONDON CAST 1993 *w:* RUTHIE HENSHALL-KIRBY WARD
    FIRST NIGHT (Pinn): OCRCD 6055 (CD)
  2.ORIG BROADWAY CAST 1992 *EMI: CDC 754618-2 (CD)*
CRAZY IN ALABAMA (1999) Music score by MARK SNOW -S/T-
    SILVA SCREEN (Koch): FILMCD 322 (CD)
CREATURE (Peter Benchley's) (1997) Music score by JOHN
    VAN TONGEREN -S/T- *INTRADA (USA): MAF 7081 (CD)*
CREATURE FROM THE BLACK LAGOON (54) Mus: Hans J.Salter
    +mus.from 'HITLER' (61) 'BLACK SHIELD OF FALWORTH'
    (54) 'INCREDIBLE SHRINKING MAN'(57)(Hans J.Salter)
    INTRADA (Koch): MAF 7054CD (CD) see COLL.310,357,
CREATURES THE WORLD FORGOT - *see COLL.248,261,*
CRICKET (1) - see **TEST CRICKET (C4)**
CRICKET (2) - see **WORLD CUP CRICKET 1999 (BBC/SKY)**
    BBC Theme "Soul Limbo" by BOOKER T.& MG's
    see COLL.148,257,
CRIES AND WHISPERS (1972) *see COLL.88,*
CRIME STORY (USA 1989) Theme "Runaway" (Del Shannon-
    Max Crook) re-recorded by DEL SHANNON on Collect:
    'DEL SHANNON-A COMPLETE CAREER ANTHOLOGY 1961-1990
    RAVEN (Australian Import): RVCD 51 (2CD)
CRIMES OF PASSION (1984) Music score by RICK WAKEMAN
    "It's A Lovely Life" (theme) (R.Wakeman-N.Gimbel)
    "Dangerous Woman" (Bell-Crumley) by MAGGIE BELL
    -S/T- *PRESIDENT (BMG): RWCD 3 (CD)*
CRIMETIME (1996) Music: DAVID A.STEWART -S/T- inc V/A
    POLLYANNA Prod (Pinn): POLLYPREM 002 (CD)

CRIMEWATCH UK (BBC1 7/6/84-1999) series theme music
   "Rescue Helicopter" (Emergency) by JOHN CAMERON
   see COLL.7,270,
CRIMSON PIRATE (1952) *see COLL.173,338,*
CRIMSON TIDE (1995) Music score by HANS ZIMMER -S/T-
   EDEL-HOLLYWOOD (Pinn): 012025-2 (CD)
CRISSCROSS (1991) Music score: TREVOR JONES -S/T-
   INTRADA USA (Silva Screen): MAFCD 7021 (CD)
CROCODILE DUNDEE (1986) Music score: PETER BEST -S/T-
   SILVA SCREEN (Koch): FILMCD 009 (CD)
CROCODILE SHOES (BBC1 10/11/94) music: TONY McANANEY
   "Crocodile Shoes" sung by JIMMY NAIL -S/T- on
   EAST WEST (TEN): 4509 98556-2 (CD) -4 (MC) title
CROCODILE SHOES 2 (BBC1 14/11/96) *featur* JIMMY NAIL
   -S/T- *EAST WEST (TEN): 0630 16935-2 (CD) -4 (MC)*
CROSSFIRE (1947) Music score: ROY WEBB *see COLL.398,*
CROSSING DELANCEY (1988) Music sc: PAUL CHIHARA -S/T-
   VARESE (Pinn) VSD 5201 (CD)
CROSSROADS (Central 2/11/64 - 4/4/88 | 4510 episodes)
   Orig theme 'Crossroads' TONY HATCH 1964-1987 *also*
   by PAUL McCARTNEY & WINGS on 'VENUS and MARS'*(EMI)*
   see COLL.2,4,23,150,184,185,281,367,369,376,
CROW The (1993) Music score: GRAEME REVELL + Var.Arts
   -S/T- (score) *VARESE (Pinn): VSD 5499 (CD)*
   -S/T- (songs) *WB (TEN): 7567 82519-2(CD) 4(MC)*
CROW The (2): CITY OF ANGELS (1996) Music sco: GRAEME
   REVELL -S/T- with V.Arts: HOLE/FILTER/BUSHG/WHITE
   ZOMBIE/SVEN MARY THREE/ABOVE THE LAW with FROST
   HOLLYWOOD-POLYDOR (Univ): 533 147-2 (CD) -4 (MC)
CROW ROAD The (BBC2 4/11/96) theme & incidental music
   composed and performed by COLIN TOWNS *unavailable*
CROWN COURT (Granada 1972) closing theme mus "Distant
   Hills" (Reno-Haseley) *see COLL.360,*
CROWN GREEN BOWLS *see COLL.176,*
CROWS - *see COLL* 'SIMONETTI PROJECT' *see COLL 319,*
CRUEL INTENTIONS (1998) Music score: EDWARD SHEARMUR
   -S/T- V.Arts: PLACEBO/BLUR/FATBOY SLIM/FAITHLESS-
   CRAIG ARMSTRONG/VERVE/SKUNK ANASIE/AIMEE MANN etc
   VIRGIN (EMI): CDVUS 158 (CD)
CRUEL SEA The (1953) *see COLL.223,*
CRUISE The (BBC1 12/1/98) title mus: JOHN HARLE sung
   by BBC CONCERT ORCHESTRA & BBC SINGERS.JOHN HARLE
   album 'SILENCIUM' *ARGO (Univ): 458 356-3 (CD)*
   JANE McDONALD album "Jane McDonald" on *FOCUS-GUT*
   (Vital) FMCD 001 (CD) FMMC 001 (MC)
CRUMB (BBC2 26/12/96) Music: DAVID BOEDDINGHAUS-CRAIG
   VENTRESCO -S/T- *RYKODISC (Vital): RCD 10322 (CD)*
CRY BABY (1989) Music score: PATRICK WILLIAMS -S/T-
   MCA: MCLD 19260 (CD)
CRY FREEDOM (1987) Music: GEORGE FENTON-JONAS GWANGWA
   -S/T- *MCA (SIlva Screen): MCAD 6224 (CD)*
CRYING GAME The (1992) Music score: ANNE DUDLEY "The
   Crying Game" (Geoff Stevens) -S/T- feat Var.Arts
   reissue: POLYDOR: 517024-2 (CD)

CURSE OF THE CAT PEOPLE (1944) Music score: ROY WEBB
CLOUD NINE (Silva Screen): CNS 5008 (CD)
see COLL.398,

CUTTHROAT ISLAND (1995) Mus sco: JOHN DEBNEY w. LONDON
SYMPHONY ORCH *SILVA SCR (Koch): FILMCD 178 (CD)*
see COLL.49,338,

CYBERCITY OEDO 808 (Animated 94 MANGA/C4 19/8/95) Mus
score (-) -S/T- issued *DEMON (Pinn): DSCD 8 (CD)*

CYCLO (95) Music score: TON-THAT TIET with V.Artists
-S/T- *MILAN (BMG): 74321 30108-2 (CD) see COLL*

CYRANO DE BERGERAC (1950) Music score: DIMITRI TIOMKIN
on Coll 'HIGH NOON' *RCA (BMG): 09026 62658-2 (CD)*

CYRANO DE BERGERAC (1990) Music sco: JEAN-CLAUDE PETIT
-S/T- *COLOSSEUM (Pinn): CST 348046 (CD)*
see also 'JEAN DE FLORETTE' and see COLL 69,

DAD (BBC1 25/9/97) theme "Tijuana Taxi" HERB ALPERT &
HIS TIJUANA BRASS 'The Very Best Of HERB ALPERT'
A.& M.(Univ): CDMID 170 (CD) CMID 170 (MC)
(2nd Series BBC1 11/01/1999) theme "Go Daddy Go"
arranged by JULIAN STEWART LINDSAY *unavailable*

DAD'S ARMY (BBC1 31/7/68-77) theme "Who Do Think You
Are Kidding Mr.Hitler" (J.Perry-D.Taverner) by
BUD FLANAGAN O.Cast Rec *BBC (Tech): ZBBC 1140 (MC)*
see COLL.2,4,23,270,

DADDY LONG LEGS *see COLL.1,*

DAKTARI (USA TV) *see COLL.346,*

DALES DIARY The (YTV only) theme music "Overture" from
'The Wasps' (VAUGHAN WILLIAMS) complete version on
EMI CLASSICS: CDM 565 130-2 (CD)

DALLAS (UKGO 2/11/93 USA80 / BBC1 1978-6/10/91) theme:
JERROLD IMMEL *see COLL.46,150,169,270,347,376,*

DALZIEL AND PASCOE (BBC1 16/3/96-1999) orig music by
BARRINGTON PHELOUNG *unavailable*

DAMAGE (1993) Music score: ZBIGNIEW PREISNER -S/T-
VARESE (Pinn): VSD 5406 (CD)

DAMES (1934) *COLLECTION with 'SAN FRANCISCO'/'SUZY'*
GREAT MOVIE THEMES (Targ-BMG): CD 60022 (CD)

DAMES AT SEA - songs by Jim Wise with George Haimsohn
and Robin Miller. ORIG UK TOURING CAST 1989 *with*
BRIAN CANT-SANDRA DICKINSON-JOSEPHINE BLAKE etc.
TER (Koch): CDTER 1169 (CD)

DAMBUSTERS The (1955) Theme music: ERIC COATES
see COLL.41,138,142,173,

DAMN YANKEES (FILM MUSICAL 1958) Songs: RICHARD ADLER-
JERRY ROSS -S/T- *RCA Austr (S.Scr): 1047-2 (CD) -4*

DAMNED The (1969) Music sco: MAURICE JARRE on 'MAURICE
JARRE TRILOGY' *DRG (Pinn): DRGCD 32906 (2CD)*

DANCE A LITTLE CLOSER (Musical) Music: CHARLES STROUSE
Lyrics: ALAN JAY LERNER *Original Broadway Cast* on
TER (Koch): CDTER 1174 (CD)

DANCE TO THE MUSIC OF TIME, A (C4 9/10/97) Music score
by CARL DAVIS / theme song "20th Century Blues" by
NOEL COWARD (1931) Orig music and V.Artists songs
-S/T- *MCI-C4 (DISC-Pinn): MPRCD 002 (CD)*

DANCE WITH ME (1998) Music score: MICHAEL CONVERTINO
    V.ARTS -S/T- *EPIC (Ten): 491 125-2 (CD) -4 (MC)*
DANCES WITH WOLVES (1990) Music sco: JOHN BARRY -S/T-
    EPIC (SM): 467591-2(CD) -4(MC) ZK 66817 (CD spec)
    see COLL.29,30,34,35,70,106,111,202,255,286,327,
    400,401,
DANCING AT LUGHNASA (1998) Music score: BILL WHELAN
    -S/T- *SONY CLASSICS: SK 60585 (CD)*
DANCING IN THE STREET: Rock'n'Roll History (BBC2 15/6/
    96) featuring VAR ARTISTS -S/T- *ELITE-CARLTON:*
    (CHE): 30364 0016-2 (2CD) 30364 0016-4 (2MC)
DANGER MAN (ITV 11/9/1960-68) Theme mus "High Wire" by
    EDWIN ASTLEY -S/T-*RAZOR & TIE (Koch): RE 21512(CD)*
    see COLL.4,5,23,185,270,344,360,365,369,
DANGERFIELD (2) BBC1 1998/1999 ser) theme & incidental
    music by RAY RUSSELL *unavailable*
DANGERFIELD (1) (BBC1 1995-1998 ser)theme & incidental
    music by NIGEL HESS *see COLL.6,193,243,270,*
DANGEROUS BEAUTY (1997) Music sco: GEORGE FENTON -S/T-
    RST (Silva Screen): RST 72958 (CD)
DANGEROUS GROUND (1997) Music sc: STANLEY CLARKE -S/T-
    CHIPS-ZOMBA (Pinn): CHIP 181 (CD) HIP 181 (2LP)
DANGEROUS LIAISONS (1988) Music Score: GEORGE FENTON
    -S/T- *VIRGIN (EMI): CDV 2583 (CD)*
    see COLL.74,84,144,273,
DANGEROUS MINDS (1995) Music score composed/performed
    by WENDY and LISA -S/T- *feat:* Various Artists
    MCA (BMG): MCD 11228 (CD)
DANGEROUS MOONLIGHT (1941) Theme 'Warsaw Concerto' by
    RICHARD ADDINSELL *see COLL.11,170,383,386,387,388,*
DANIEL BOONE (USA) *see COLL.345,*
DANTE'S PEAK (1997) Music score: JOHN FRIZZELL with
    main theme composed by JAMES NEWTON HOWARD -S/T-
    VARESE (Pinn): VSD 5793 (CD)
DANZON (1992) Music sco: DANZONERA DIMAS-FELIPE PEREZ
    -S/T- *DRG (Pinn): CDSBL 12605 (CD)*
DARK ADAPTED EYE, A (BBC1 02/01/1994) Music score by
    DAVID FERGUSON *see COLL.151,*
DARK CITY (1997) Music score: TREVOR JONES -S/T- on
    SNAPPER (Pinn): SMACD 810 (CD)
DARK CITY (1950) *see COLL.309,394,*
DARK EYES (1987) Music score: FRANCIS LAI -S/T- on
    DRG (Pinn): CDSBL 12592 (CD)
DARK HALF The (1992) Music sc: CHRISTOPHER YOUNG -S/T-
    VARESE (Pinn): VSD 5340 (CD)
DARK SHADOWS (USA Soap 1966-70) "Quentin's Theme" by
    Charles Randolph Green / ROBERT COBERT ORCHESTRA
    -S/T-*VARESE: VSD 5702 (CD) see COLL*
DARK SKIES (USA96 / C4 13/1/97) theme: MICHAEL HOENIG
    see COLL.267,389,
DARK STAR (1974) Music score: JOHN CARPENTER -S/T-
    VARESE (Pinn): VSD 5327 (CD) see COLL.62,267,306,
DARKMAN (1990) Music score: DANNY ELFMAN -S/T- *Impt.*
    MCA USA (Silva Screen): MCAD 10094 (CD)

DARLING BUDS OF MAY The (YTV 07/04/1991) theme music
   PIP BURLEY. score by BARRIE GUARD + ENGLISH LIGHT
   ORCH -S/T- *SOUNDTRACKS EMI GOLD: 520 685-2 (CD)*
DARLING LILI (1970) Music score by HENRY MANCINI
   -S/T- RCA EUROPE (Discovery): 74321 66500-2 (CD)
DARTS (BBC1/2 All Competitions) Theme mus "Cranes" by
   by DOUGLAS WOOD GROUP *see COLL.176,*
DAS BOOT (W.Germany) - *see under* 'BOAT The'
DASTARDLY AND MUTTLEY *see COLL.347,373,*
DATELINE LONDON theme "Cutty Sark" *see COLL.28,32,*
DAVE ALLEN (Carlton/Noel Gay 7/1/93) theme "Blarney's
   Stoned" ALAN HAWKSHAW *see COLL.185,326,*
DAVY CROCKETT (1955) Theme s "Ballad Of Davy Crockett"
   sung by FESS PARKER on 'Americana'
   COLUMBIA (SM): 468 121-2(CD) -4(MC) see COLL.260,
DAWN OF THE DEAD (Film) - *see under* ZOMBIES
DAWSON'S CREEK (USA) (C4 2/5/1998) theme mus "I Don't
   Want To Wait" composed & performed by Paula Cole.
   score music by DANNY LUX other songs by JANN ARDEN
   with incidental music by ADAM FIELDS.
   'Songs from Dawson's Creek' *feat* PAULA COLE-CURTIS
   STEIGERS-SEAN MULLINS-SIXPENCE NONE THE RICHER etc
   COLUMBIA (Ten): 494 369-2 (CD) -4 (MC)
DAY AT THE RACES, A (1937) feat The MARX BROTHERS
   DEFINITIVE (Discovery): SFCD 33503 (CD)
DAY THE EARTH STOOD STILL The (1951) Music sc: BERNARD
   HERRMANN Suite on 'Great Film Music'l *DECCA PHASE4*
   (Univ): 443 899-2 (CD) also incl JOURNEY TO
   THE CENTRE OF THE EARTH-SEVENTH VOYAGE OF SINBAD
   FAHRENHEIT 451-THREE WORLDS OF GULLIVER *also avail*
   able: Symphonic Suite (Nat.P.O.-Fred Steiner) with
   'The Kentuckian' *Imp PREAMBLE (S.Scr): PRCD 1777*
DAY THE FISH CAME OUT (1967) Music: MIKIS THEODORAKIS
   -S/T- SAKKARIS (Pinn): SR 50088 (CD)
DAYS AND NIGHTS OF MOLLY DODD (USA TV) *see COLL.351,*
DAYS OF HOPE (Musical 91) Songs: HOWARD GOODALL Orig.
   London Cast *TER (Koch): CDTER 1183 (CD)*
DAYS OF WINE AND ROSES The (1962) *see COLL.32,239,*
DAZED AND CONFUSED (1994) ALICE COOPER-DEEP PURPLE-
   KISS-ZZ TOP -S/T- *GIANT (BMG): 74321 16675-2 (CD)*
DEAD MAN (1995) Music score: NEIL YOUNG
   -S/T- WB (TEN): 9362 46171-2 (CD)
DEAD MAN ON CAMPUS (1998) Music sco: MARK MOTHERSBAUGH
   -S/T- sgs: MARILYN MANSON/BLUR/ELASTICA/GOLDFINGER
   DUST BROTHERS/AUDIOWEB/SUPERGRASS
   DREAMWORKS: DRMD 5003-2 (CD)
DEAD MAN WALKING (1995) T.song by BRUCE SPRINGSTEEN *w*
   JOHNNY CASH-SUZANNE VEGA-L.LOVETT-MICHELLE SHOCKED
   -S/T- (songs) *COLUMB (Ten): 483 534-2(CD) -4(MC)*
DEAD MEN DON'T WEAR PLAID (1981) Music: MIKLOS ROZSA
   -S/T- PROMETHEUS (Silva Screen): PCD 126 (CD)
DEAD POETS SOCIETY (1989) Music score: MAURICE JARRE
   -S/T- MILAN (BMG): CDCH 558 (CD) inc:'THE YEAR OF
   LIVING DANGEROUSLY' (M.Jarre) *see COLL.85,*

DEAD PRESIDENTS (1995) Music score by DANNY ELFMAN
-S/T- (score) *CAPITOL (EMI): 7248 35818-2 (CD)*
-S/T- (songs 1) *EMI PREM: PRDCD 4 (CD)*
-S/T- (songs 2) *EMI PREM: PRMDCD 5 (CD)*
DEAD SOLID PERFECT (1991) Music score: TANGERINE DREAM
-S/T- *SILVA SCREEN (Koch): FILMCD 079 (CD)*
DEADFALL (1968) Music sco: JOHN BARRY / song "My Love
Has Two Faces" (John Barry-Jack Lawrence) sung by
SHIRLEY BASSEY. solo guitar: RENATA TARRAGO -S/T-
RETROGRADE (Silv.Sounds/Pinn/HOT): FSC 80124-2 (CD)
DEADLOCK (aka 'WEDLOCK') see COLL.51,
DEADLY CARE (1992) M: EDGAR FROESE-CHRISTOPHER FRANKE
TANGERINE DREAM-S/T- *S.SCREEN Koch: FILMCD 121(CD)*
DEAN MARTIN SHOW The (USA TV) *see COLL.349,*
DEATH AND THE MAIDEN (1994) Music sco: WOJCIECH KILAR
-S/T- on *ERATO (BMG): 4509 99727-2 (CD)*
DEATH BEFORE DISHONOUR (1987) Music sc: BRIAN MAY
-S/T- *PROMETHEUS (Silva Screen): PCD 118 (CD)*
DEATH IN VENICE (1971) Music: GUSTAV MAHLER (Symphony
numbers 3 & 5) -S/T- *SONY Fra (Discov): SK 70097
(CD) ST 70097 (MC)* see COLL.77,105,
DEATH OF A SCOUNDREL (1956) *see under* 'KING KONG' 1933
DEATH RIDES A HORSE (1969) Music score ENNIO MORRICONE
-S/T- also inc.'A PISTOL FOR RINGO' + 'THE RETURN
OF RINGO' *Import (SILVA SCREEN): OST 107 (CD)*
DEATH WISH (1974) Music score: HERBIE HANCOCK
-S/T- *reissue SONY JAZZ: 491 981-2 (CD)*
*DEATH WISH (1974) Music: HERBIE HANCOCK sel.also
incl 'DEATH WISH 4' (87-John Bisharat-Val McCallum
'TEN TO MIDNIGHT' (84-Robert O Ragland) 'MURPH'S
LAW' (86-Marc Donahue-Val McCallum) 'TOUGH GUYS
DON'T DANCE' (87-Angelo Badalamenti) 'X-RAY'
(80-Arlon Ober) SILVA SCREEN: 1529-2 (CD)*
DEEP BLUE SEA (1999) Music score by TREVOR RABIN
Songs: *WARNER (TEN): 9362 47485-2 (CD) -4 (MC)*
Score: *VARESE (Pinn): VSD 6063 (CD)*
DEEP END OF THE OCEAN (1999) Music score composed and
conducted by ELMER BERNSTEIN -S/T- on
RCA BMG SOUNDTRACKS: 74321 66520-2 (CD)
DEEP IMPACT (1997) Music score: JAMES HORNER -S/T- on
SONY Classics: SK 60690 (CD) ST 60690 (MC)
DEEP RED (Profondo Rosso) see COLL.210,319,
DEEP RISING (1998) Music score: JERRY GOLDSMITH -S/T-
EDEL-HOLLYWOOD (Pinn): 012120-2HWR
DEEP SPACE - *see* **STAR TREK**
DEERHUNTER The (1978) Music sco: STANLEY MYERS -S/T-
CAPITOL (S.Screen) 92058-2(CD) -4(MC) 'Cavatina'
perf.by John WILLIAMS *see COLL.71,88,262,286,364,*
DEF-CON 4 (1985) Music sco: CHRISTOPHER YOUNG -S/T-
incl.Music from "Avenging Angel" (85) "Torment"
(85) "The Telephone" (88) Mus.by CHRISTOPHER YOUNG
on *INTRADA USA (Sil.Screen): MAF 7010D (CD) and*
DEFENCE OF THE REALM (BBC1 8/8/96) theme mus "School Of
Mysteries" JOHN HARLE on 'SILENCIUM' *see COLL*

DEKALOG (The Ten Commandments) (1988) Music: ZBIGNIEW
PREISNER -S/T- *AMPLITUDE (Discov): AMP 709 (CD)*
DELERIA (1987) Music s: SIMON BOSWELL-STEFANO MAINETTI
LUCITOLA MEDIA (Backtrack/S.Scr): LMCD 002 (CD)
DELIA'S HOW TO COOK (BBC2 13/10/1998) music: GUY DAGUL
original theme by FATHER JAMES WALSH *unavailable*
DELIVERANCE (1972) M: ERIC WEISSBERG "Duelling Banjos"
feat STEVE MANDELL -S/T- *WB (TEN): K246214*
(CD/MC/LP) see COLL.364,
DELUSION (1991) Music sco: BARRY ADAMSON *MUTE:*
IONIC 4 (LP) IONIC 4C (MC) IONIC 4CD (CD)
DEMOLITION MAN (1993) Music s: ELLIOT GOLDENTHAL
-S/T- *VARESE (Pinn): VSD 5447 (CD)*
DEMON KNIGHT (1994) Various Artists -S/T-
ATLANTIC WEA 7567 82725-2 (CD) -4 (MC)
DEMPSEY & MAKEPEACE (LWT 11/1/85) theme: ALAN PARKER
see COLL.6,360,
DENNIS THE MENACE (USA TV) *see COLL.345,*
DEPARTMENT S (ITC 9/3/69) theme music: EDWIN ASTLEY
see COLL.2,23,360,369,
DEPUTY The - *see COLL.2,23,216,*
DER SILBERSEE - *see* SILVER LAKE The
DESERT ISLAND DISCS (BBC) theme "By The Sleepy Lagoon"
by ERIC COATES. compilation "CASTAWAY'S CHOICE' on
BBC AUDIO INT. (Pinn): WMEF 00267 (2CDs)
DESERT OF THE TARTARS (1976) Music sco: ENNIO MORRICONE
-S/T- *IMPRT (Silva Screen): CDST 309 (CD)*
DESERT SONG - songs by Sigmund Romberg - Oscar Hammer
stein II and Otto Harbach
1.ORIG LONDON CAST 1927 *w:* EDITH DAY-PHEBE BRUNE-GENE
GERRARD-CLARICE HARDWICKE-DENNIS HOEY-BARRY MACKAY
plus music from 'NEW MOON (1929) 'BLUE TRAIN' (27)
PEARL (Pavilion): GEMMCD 9100(CD)
2.STUDIO RECORDING *w:* GORDON MacRAE & DOROTHY KIRSTEN
+ music from 'New Moon' and 'The Student Prince'
HMV (EMI): CDM 769052-2 (CD)
3.STUDIO RECORDING *with:* MARIO LANZA *also music from*
The STUDENT PRINCE RCA (BMG) GD(GK)60048 (CD/MC)
DESPERATELY SEEKING SUSAN (1985) Score: THOMAS NEWMAN
+'Making Mr.Right' *VARESE (Pinn): VCD 47291 (CD)*
DESTRY RIDES AGAIN (O.LONDON CAST 1979) Songs: HAROLD
ROME *featuring* JILL GASCOINE and Co. / Recording
TER (Koch): CDTER 1034
DETECTIVE The (BBC 1968) Mus: RON GRAINER *see COLL.8,*
DETROIT ROCK CITY (1999) Music score by
VAR.ARTISTS -S/T- *MERCURY (Univ): 546 389-2 (CD)*
DEUX ANGLAISES ET LE CONTINENT *see* 'TWO ENGLISH GIRLS'
DEVIL AND DANIEL WEBSTER The (aka 'All That Money Can
Buy) (1941) music score: BERNARD HERRMANN / Suite
UNICORN KANCHANA (Harmonia Mundi): UKCD 2065 (CD)
also on 'CONCERTO MACABRE' *KOCH INT: 37609-2 (CD)*
DEVIL DOLL The (1936) *see COLL.394,*
DEVIL IN MISS JONES The (1972) SOUNDTRACK on
OGLIO (Direct): OGL 81597-2 (CD)

DEVIL RIDES OUT The (1968) Music score: JAMES BERNARD
  see COLL.180,208,209

DEVIL'S ADVOCATE (1997) Music sco: JAMES NEWTON HOWARD
  -S/T- *MADFISH-SNAPPER (Pinn): SMACD 803 (CD)*

DEVIL'S OWN The (1996) Music sco: JAMES HORNER -S/T-
  TOMMY BOY (RTM-Disc): TBCD 1204 (CD)

DEVIL'S TOOTHPICK The (1992) Doc.Brazilian/USA music:
  GILBERTO GIL-BILLY COBHAM-KENIA-LARRY CORYELL etc.
  CTI-KUDU (New Note-Pinn): CTI 10122 (CD)

DEVOTION (1943) Music score by ERICH WOLFGANG KORNGOLD
  New Rec: MOSCOW SYMPHONY ORCH (William T.Stromberg)
  MARCO POLO (Select): 8.225038 (CD)

DIABOLIQUE (1996) Music score: RANDY EDELMAN -S/T- on
  EDEL-CINERAMA (Pinn): 002258-2CIN

DIAL M.FOR MURDER (1954) Music by DIMITRI TIOMKIN
  see COLL.194,197,

DIAMONDS (1975) Music score by ROY BUDD -S/T- *reissue*
  CASTLE (Pinn): CINCD 003 (CD) CINLP 003 (LP)

DIAMONDS ARE FOREVER (1971) Music sco: JOHN BARRY t.
  song (J.Barry-Don Black) sung by SHIRLEY BASSEY
  -S/T- *EMI: CZ 554 (CD) see COLL.27,28,34,37,53,54,*
  55,314, see also JAMES BOND FILM INDEX p.358

DIARY OF ANNE FRANK The (1959) Music sco: ALFRED NEWMAN
  TSUNAMI (Silva Screen): TSU 0122 (CD)

DICK (1999) Music score by JOHN DEBNEY -S/T- on
  VIRGIN (EMI): CDVUS 164 (CD)

DICK BARTON (ITV 78) theme mus "Devil's Galop" CHARLES
  WILLIAMS *see COLL.56.104,147,172,*

DICK POWELL THEATRE (USA TV 1961) *see COLL.184,*

DICK VAN DYKE SHOW (USA TV 1962) *see COLL.345,378,*

DIDIER (1997) Music score: PHILIPPE CHANY
  XIII BIZ (Discovery): LBS 1097010-2 (CD)

DIE HARD (1988) Music sco: MICHAEL KAMEN -S/T- *reissue*
  Fox (BMG): (unconfirmed) *see COLL.105,313,*

DIE HARD 2: DIE HARDER (1989) Mus: MICHAEL KAMEN -S/T-
  VARESE (Pinn): VSD 5273 see COLL.78,105,

DIE HARD 3: WITH A VENGEANCE (1995) Music sco: MICHAEL
  KAMEN w: V/A -S/T- *RCA (BMG): 09026 68306-2 (CD)*

DIFFERENT FOR GIRLS (1998) Music score: STEPHEN WARBECK
  VARIOUS ARTISTS -S/T- *OCEAN DEEP: OCD 010 (CD)*

DIFFERENT STROKES (USA TV) *see COLL.350,*

DIFFERENT WORLD, A (USA series C4 from 22/9/88) theme
  music (Stu Gardner-Bill Cosby-Dawnn Lewis) sung by
  ARETHA FRANKLIN (USA TV) *see COLL.351,*

DINOSAURS The (USA TV Ser 93) music by PETER MELNICK
  TV -S/T- *NARADA Cinema (Pinn): ND 66004 (CD)*

DIRTY DANCING (1987) Music score: JOHN MORRIS + V.Arts
  -S/T- *RCA: BD 86408 (CD) BK 86408 (MC)* DELETED
  'MORE DIRTY DANCING' *74321 36915-2 (CD) -4 (MC)*
  'LIVE' music *RCA (BMG): PK 90336 (MC)*
  'COLLECTORS EDIT' *RCA (BMG): 0786 367786-2 (2CDs)*

DIRTY HARRY (ANTHOLOGY) Music scores by LALO SCHIFRIN
  ALEPH (Koch): ALEP 003 (CD) also available on
  SIMPLY VINYL (Telstar): SVLP 82 (LP)

DISAPPEARANCE OF FINBAR The (1995) Music score by DAVY
SPILLANE -S/T- V.Artists *SNAPPER (Pinn): SMACD 504*
DISAPPEARANCE OF GARCIA LORCA (1997) Mus: MARK McKENZIE
-S/T- *INTRADA (Koch/S.Screen): MAF 7080CD (CD)*
DISCLOSURE (1994) Music score ENNIO MORRICONE -S/T- on
VIRGIN Movie Music (EMI): CDVMM 16 (CD)
DISCWORLD (TERRY PRATCHETT'S) (C4) 'SOUL MUSIC' album
PLUTO (Direct): TH 030746 (CD)
DISORDERLIES (1987) Music: RAY PARKER JNR & others
-S/T- *re-issued on SPECTRUM (Univ): 551 137-2 (CD)*
DIVA (1982) Music score: VLADIMIR COSMA *feat* 'La Wally'
WILHEMLMENIA FERNANDEZ -S/T- *MILAN Imp 950 622 (CD)*
see COLL.69,70,78,105,159,273,274,
DIVAS LIVE (MUSIC CONCERT, N.YORK USA)(BBC1 12/10/1998)
CELINE DION-MARIAH CAREY-GLORIA ESTEFAN-ARETHA
FRANKLIN-SHANIA TWAIN-CAROLE KING
SONY TV: SONYTV55(CD)(MD)(MC)
DIVORCE ME DARLING - Music and lyrics by SANDY WILSON
Chichester Festival Theatre 1997 *RECORDING featur:*
DAVID ALDER-SIMON BUTTERISS-KEVIN COLSON-TIM FLAVIN-
ROSEMARY FORD-ANDREW HALLIDAY-LINZI HATELY-RUTHIE
HENSHALL-LILANE MONTEVECCHI-JOAN SAVAGE-JACK TRIPP-
MARTIN WEBB *TER (Koch): CDTER 1245 (CD)*
DIXON OF DOCK GREEN (BBC1 50s-70s) theme "An Ordinary
Copper" (Jeff Darnell) *see COLL.2,*
DOBERMANN (1997) Music: SCHYZOMANIAC; FRANCOIS ROY-
JEAN JACQUES HERTZ-PHILLIPE MALLIER feat BRUNE
-S/T- *ISLAND France: (Discovery): 524 412-2 (CD)*
DOBIE GILLIS (USA TV) *see COLL.345,*
DOC HOLLYWOOD (1991) Music score: CARTER BURWELL -S/T-
VARESE (Pinn): VSD 5332 (CD)
DOCTOR AT LARGE (ITV 1971) theme "Bond Street Parade"
by ALAN TEW *see COLL.326,*
DOCTOR AT THE TOP (BBC1 21/2/91)
see also 'DOCTOR IN THE HOUSE' *see COLL.4,*
DOCTOR DOLITTLE (ORIGINAL LONDON CAST 1998) *featuring*
PHILLIP SCHOFIELD and Company
FIRST NIGHT (Pinn): CASTCD 68 (CD) CASTC 68 (MC)
DOCTOR DOLITTLE (FILM 1998) VARIOUS ARTISTS -S/T- on
ATLANTIC (TEN): 7567 83113-2 (CD) -4(MC) -1(LP)
DOCTOR DOLITTLE (1967) songs by LESLIE BRICUSSE -S/T-
feat: REX HARRISON-SAMANTHA EGGAR-ANTHONY NEWLEY
reissued -S/T- SPECTRUM (Univ): 554 527-2 (CD)
DOCTOR FAUSTUS (1967) Music sc: MARIO NASCIMBENE -S/T-
+ 'FRANCIS OF ASSISI' *DRG (Pinn) DRGCD 32965 (CD)*
DOCTOR FINLAY'S CASEBOOK (BBC1 1962-71) theme music
"March from 'A Little Suite' No 2 (TREVOR DUNCAN)
see COLL.2,6,23,57,172,243,
DOCTOR GIGGLES (1992) Music score (Brian May)
-S/T- score: *INTRADA (Silva Screen): MAF 7043CD*
-S/T- songs: *Victor USA (Import only)*
DOCTOR IN THE HOUSE (LWT 70) *see COLL 4,*
DOCTOR JEKYLL AND MS.HYDE (1994) Music: MARK McKENZIE
-S/T- *INTRADA (Silva Screen Imp): MAF 7063D (CD)*

DOCTOR KILDARE (USA 61) Theme music: JERRY GOLDSMITH
    see COLL.2,150,243,348,
DOCTOR NO (1962) Music score: MONTY NORMAN-JOHN BARRY
    -S/T- *reiss EMI PREM (EMI):CZ 558 (CD)*
    see COLL.53,55,71,also JAMES BOND FILM INDEX p.358
DOCTOR QUINN: MEDICINE WOMAN (USA/ITV 28/5/93) orig
    music by WILLIAM OLVIS -S/T- with Various Artists
    SONIC IMAGE (Cargo-Greyhound): SI 8804 (CD)
DOCTOR STRANGELOVE (1963) Music: LAURIE JOHSON
    see COLL.71,131,215,216,
DOCTOR WHO (1996) (BBC1 27/5/96) Music sc: JOHN DEBNEY
    (orig theme by RON GRAINER) + additional music by
    JOHN SPONSLER and LOUIS SERBE *unavailable*
DOCTOR WHO (BBC1 23/11/63-93) orig theme RON GRAINER
    see COLL.4,8,149,150,307,362, and also under:-

    'THIRTY YEARS AT THE RADIOPHONIC WORKSHOP' (BBC)
    Music Var.Arts *BBC (Pinn) BBCCD 871 (CD) see also*
    (1) 'DR.WHO - VARIATIONS ON A THEME' various comp.
    SILVA SCREEN (Koch): FILMCD 706 (CD)
    'DOWNTIME' (Doctor Who Video) music: IAN LEVENE
    SILVA SCREEN (Koch): FILMCD 717 (CD)
    'SHAKEDOWN' Music MARK AYRES
    SILVA SCREEN (Koch): FILMCD 718 (CD)
    DOCTOR WHO: EVOLUTION feat music by RON GRAINER-
    KEFF McCULLOCH and DOMINIC GREEN
    PRESTIGE (THE): RDSGP 0320 (CD)
    DOCTOR WHO: VENGEANCE ON VAROS
    BBC (Techn): ZBBC 1932 (2MC)
DOCTOR WILLOUGHBY (ITV 14/11/1999) theme music by
    DAVE MACKAY on 'AS SEEN ON TV' *see COLL.19,*
DOCTOR ZHIVAGO (1965) Music score: MAURICE JARRE
    -S/T- *reissue: EMI Premier (EMI): CDODEON 1 (CD)*
    see COLL.41,70,106,204,213,298,
DOCTORS The (BBC1 69) m: TONY HATCH *see COLL.23,184,*

---

*DOCUMENTARY SERIES: MUSIC FROM INDIVIDUAL DOCUMENTARY
PROGRAMME SERIES (eg: THE NATURAL WORLD / SECRET LIVES
TIMEWATCH / HORIZON / ARENA / WILDLIFE ON ONE etc.)
MUSIC INFO HELD ON DATABASE: DETAILS ON REQUEST FROM
MIKE PRESTON MUSIC*

DOGMA (1999) Music score by HOWARD SHORE -S/T- *IMPORT*
    MAVERICK-WARNER (TEN): 9362 47597-2 (CD)
DOIN' TIME ON PLANET EARTH - *see* 'ALLAN QUARTERMAIN'
DOLLY SISTERS The (1945) BETTY GRABLE-JUNE HAVER inc.
    songs from 'ROSE OF WASHINGTON SQUARE' and
    'GOLD DIGGERS OF 1933' *TARGET (BMG): CD 60009 (CD)*
DOLORES CLAIBORNE (1995) Music sco: DANNY ELFMAN -S/T-
    VARESE (Pinn): VSD 5602 (CD)
DON JUAN DE MARCO (1994) Music sc: MICHAEL KAMEN "Have
    You Ever Really Loved A Woman" (Adams-Lange-Kamen)
    by BRYAN ADAMS -S/T- *A.& M. (Univ): 540 357-2 (CD)*

DON QUIXOTE (Spanish TV mini-series) music score: LALO
    SCHIFRIN -S/T- *PROMETHEUS (S.Scr): PCD 132 (CD)*
DONNA REED SHOW (USA TV) *see COLL.345,*
DONNIE BRASCO (1997) Music score: PATRICK DOYLE
    -S/T- (songs) *HOLLYWOOD (Univ.): 162 102-2 (CD)*
    -S/T- (score) *VARESE (Pinnacle): VSD 5834 (CD)*
DON'T BE A MENACE (1995) Music score:
    -S/T- *Island (Univ): 524 146-2 (CD) -4 (MC)*
DON'T GO BREAKING MY HEART (1998) Music sc: ROLFE KENT
    -S/T- inc.t.track by ELTON JOHN & KIKI DEE + songs
    by FIVE-KOLONY-LEO SAYER-BEACH BOYS-GERRY & PACEM.
    SOUNDTRACK (Pinn): STRACK 101 (CD)
DON'T LOOK NOW (1973) Music sco: PINO DONAGGIO -S/T-
    TER (Koch): CDTER 1007
DOOGIE HOWSER MD (USA) *see COLL.17,283,351,*
DOORS The (1991) Music sco: BUDD CARR Orig songs by
    JIM MORRISON & DOORS -S/T- *ELEKTRA (TEN): 7599
    61047-2 (CD) EKT 85C (MC) EKT 85 (LP)*
DOUBLE IMPACT (1991) Music score: ARTHUR KEMPEL -S/T-
    S.SCREEN (Koch): FILMCD 110 (CD) see 'KICKBOXER'
DOUBLE INDEMNITY (1944) Music sco: MIKLOS ROZSA Suite
    on Coll *'FILM NOIR CLASSICS'* with 'THE KILLERS' +
    'THE LOST WEEKEND' *feat* NEW ZEALAND S.O.cond.by
    JAMES SEDARES on *KOCH INT (Koch): 37375-2 (CD)*
DOUBLE LIFE OF VERONIQUE (1991) Music sco: ZBIGNIEW
    PREISNER Choral music by VAN DEN BUDENMAYER -S/T-
    VIRGIN (EMI): CDVE 939 (CD)
DOUBLE TROUBLE *see* ELVIS PRESLEY INDEX p.360

DOWN BY LAW (1987) Music sco: JOHN LURIE & TOM WAITS
    also includes 'VARIETY' -S/T- music: JOHN LURIE
    MADE TO MEASURE (New Note-Pinn): MTM 14 (CD)
DOWN IN THE DELTA (1998) Music score: STANLEY CLARKE
    -S/T- STEVIE WONDER-LUTHER VANDROSS-THE LEVERTS-
    JANET-D'ANGELO-SUNDAY feat WHITNEY-CHAKA KHAN etc
    VIRGIN (EMI): CDVUS 153 (CD) VUSMC 153 (MC)
DR. *see under* DOCTOR

DRACULA - *see COLL.180,181,208,249,309,357,*

DRACULA (1931) CONTEMPORARY SCORE (1999) composed by
    Philip Glass *and featuring the* Kronos Quartet
    NONESUCH-WARNER (Ten): 7559 79542-2 (CD)
DRACULA (1992) Music sco: WOJCIECH KILAR -S/T- *featur*
    "Love Song For A Vampire" sung by ANNIE LENNOX
    COLUMBIA (Ten): 472 746-2 (CD)
DRACULA (HAMMER STORY featuring CHRISTOPHER LEE & The
    HAMMER CITY ORCHESTRA) *BGO (Pinn): BGOCD 240 (CD)*
DRAGNET (USA TV 1950s) theme: WALTER SCHUMANN
    see COLL.109,110,118,270,345,
DRAGON: THE BRUCE LEE STORY (1993) Mus: RANDY EDELMAN
    -S/T- *MCA (BMG): MCAD 10827 (CD)*
DRAGONHEART (1996) Music score: RANDY EDELMAN -S/T-
    MCA (BMG): MCAD 11449 (CD)

DRAGONSLAYER (1981) Music score: ALEX NORTH. *SELECTION
    WITH* 'CHEYENNE AUTUMN' (1964) 'CINERAMA SOUTH SEAS
    ADVENTURE' (1958) *LABEL X (Hot): ATMCD 2004 (CD)*
DRAT THE CAT! (MUSICAL) sgs: MILTON SCHAFER-IRA LEVIN
    ORIG 1997 USA STUDIO RECORDING *featur* SUSAN EGAN-
    JASON GRAAE-JONATHAN FREEMAN-JUDY KAYE on
    VARESE (Pinn):VSD 5721 (CD)
DRAUGHTSMAN'S CONTRACT The (1983) Mus: MICHAEL NYMAN
    -S/T- *CHARISMA (Virgin-EMI): CASCD 1158 (CD)*
DRAW! (1984) Music sc: KEN WANNBERG -S/T- inc.m.from
    'RED RIVER' *PROMETHEUS (Silva Scr):PCD 129 (CD)*
DREAM DEMON (1988) Mus: BILL NELSON Theme on 'Duplex'
    COCTEAU (Pinn): CDJCD 22(CD) TCJCD 22(MC) JCD 22
DREAM LOVER (1994) Music sco: CHRISTOPHER YOUNG -S/T-
    KOCH Screen Rec (Koch): 387002 (CD)
DREAM OF OLWEN The *see* 'WHILE I LIVE' +
    see COLL.170,386,387,
DREAM WHEELS (BBC1 08/09/1999) series title music by
    DOMINIC GLYNN *unavailable*
DREAM WITH THE FISHES (1998) VARIOUS ARTISTS -S/T- on
    SNAPPER (Pinn): SNACD 811 (CD)
DRIFTWOOD (1996) Music score: CARL DAVIS -S/T- on
    OCEAN DEEP (Grapev/Polyg): OCD 003 (CD)
DRIVING MISS DAISY (1989) Music sco HANS ZIMMER songs
    Eartha Kitt-Louis Armstrong -S/T- *VARESE (Pinn):
    VSD 5246 (CD) VSC 5246 (MC)*
    see COLL.88,159,273,274,
DROP DEAD GORGEOUS (1999) Music sc: MARK MOTHERSBAUGH
    -S/T- (VARIOUS ARTS) *SIRE (TEN): 4434 3106-2 (CD)*
DROP ZONE (1994) Music score HANS ZIMMER -S/T- on
    VARESE (Pinn): VSD 5581 (CD)
DROWNING BY NUMBERS (1988) Music score: MICHAEL NYMAN
    -S/T- *VENTURE (Virg-EMI): CDVE 23 (CD)*
DUBARRY WAS A LADY (1943) *feat:*LUCILLE BALL-GENE KELLY
    RED SKELTON-TOMMY DORSEY ORCH + *songs from* 'SKY'S
    THE LIMIT'/'42ND STREET' *TARGET (BMG):CD 60010 (CD)*
DUCHESS OF DUKE STREET The (UKGo 2/11/92 orig BBC 76)
    theme music: ALEXANDER FARIS *see COLL.2,46,281,*
DUCK SOUP (1933) Songs by BERT KALMAR and HARRY RUBY
    selection DEFINITIVE (Discovery): SFCD 33501 (CD)
DUCKMAN (USA TV) *see COLL.351,*
DUE SOUTH (Canada 94/BBC1 9/5/95) mus: (Jack Lenz-John
    -McCarthy-Jay Semko) **theme** performed by JAY SEMKO-
    CRASH TEST DUMMIES *other mus.by* THE NORTHERN PIKES
    SARAH MacLACHLAN-KLAATU-GUESS WHO-FIGGY DUFF-BLUE
    RODEO-LOREENA McKENNITT and PAUL GROSS etc.
    -S/T- VOLUME 1: (VARIOUS ARTISTS)
    NETTWERK (Pinn): 62428 40004-2 (CD) -4 (MC)
    -S/T- VOLUME 2: (VARIOUS ARTISTS)
    NETTWERK (Pinn): 62428 40007-2 (CD) -4 (MC)
DUEL AT DIABLO (1966) Music score: NEAL HEFTI / with
    'HORSE SOLDIERS' (1959, DAVID BUTTOLPH score)
    TARAN (Silver Sounds): W 9105 (CD)
DUEL IN THE SUN (1946) m: DIMITRI TIOMKIN *see COLL.368,*

DUEL OF HEARTS, A (1990) Music score: LAURIE JOHNSON
  see COLL.217,
DUELLISTS The (1977) *see COLL.173,338,*
DUKES OF HAZZARD (USA 79) Theme 'Good Ol'Boys' (WAYLON
  JENNINGS) *see COLL.350,*
DULCIMA (Film 1971) Music score: JOHNNY DOUGLAS Theme
  DULCIMA (THE-DISC): DLCD 110 (CD) DLCT 110 (MC)
DUMB AND DUMBER (1994) Music sc: TODD RUNGREN -S/T-
  Revised Re-is RCA (BMG): 74321 48059-2 (CD) -4(MC)
DUMBO (1941) -S/T-
  DISNEY-EDEL (Pinn): - (CD)
  - see WALT DISNEY INDEX p.362
DUNE (1984) Music score: BRIAN ENO and TOTO. Complete
  Score with 30m of previously unreleased music on
  IMPRT (Silva Screen): PNDL 15 (CD) also on
  POLYDOR (IMS-Poly): E.823 770-2 (CD)
  see COLL.229,267,329,362,
DUNGEONS AND DRAGONS (BBC2 83) theme: JOHNNY DOUGLAS
  'On Screen' with JOHNNY DOUGLAS STRINGS *DULCIMA*
  (THE): DLCD 110 (CD) DLCT 110 (MC)
DURANGO (-) Music score by MARK McKENZIE -S/T-
  INTRADA Import (Silva Screen): MAF 7087 (CD)
DUSTY SPRINGFIELD STORY The (ORIG CAST RECORDING)
  OCEAN DEEP (Univ): OCD 015 (CD)
DYING YOUNG (91) Music sco: JAMES NEWTON HOWARD theme:
  KENNY G.-S/T- also inc JEFFREY OSBORNE-KING CURTIS
  reissue: ARISTA (BMG): 261952 (CD) 411952 (MC)
DYNAMITE BROTHERS The (1973) Music by CHARLES EARLAND
  -S/T- *BEAT GOES PUBLIC (Pinn): CDBGPM 120 (CD)*
DYNASTY (UKGO 8/3/93 orig BBC1 82 (USA 80) theme music
  BILL CONTI *see COLL.46,150,169,270,347,376,*
E.R. (USA/C4 1/2/95) theme music: JAMES NEWTON HOWARD
  -S/T- *WEA (TEN): 7567 82942-2 (CD) -4 (MC)*
  see COLL.243,270, and 'HIT TV'
E.T. (The Extra Terrestrial) (1982) Music comp & cond
  JOHN WILLIAMS -S/T- *MCA (BMG): MCLD 19021 (CD)*
  see COLL.70,175,201,310,327,334,389,404,
EAGLE HAS LANDED The (1976) Music sco: LALO SCHIFRIN
  -S/T- *ALEPH (Koch): ALEP 009 (CD)*
EARLY TRAVELLERS IN NORTH AMERICA (BBC2 23/07/1992)
  Music score by TOT TAYLOR -S/T- on
  TWEED CULTURE (Pinn): TWEEDCD 12 (CD)
EARTH FINAL CONFLICT (USA/SKY1 1/1998) theme & incid.
  music: MICKY ERBE-MARIBETH SOLOMON *unavailable*
EARTH STORY (BBC2 1/11/1998) music composed,conducted
  and produced by DEBORAH MOLLISON (piano, synths)
  -S/T- BBC PRODUCTION *CHANDOS/BBC: CHAN 9688 (CD)*
EARTHQUAKE (1974) Music sco: JOHN WILLIAMS -S/T- *reiss*
  VARESE (Pinn): VSD 5262 (CD) see COLL.129,371,
EAST IS EAST (1998) Music score by DEBORAH MOLLISON
  -S/T- *feat* BLUE MINK/JIMMY CLIFF/DEEP PURPLE/DAVE
  & ANSELL COLLINS/GEORGIE FAME/HOLLIES/McGUINNESS
  FLINT/SUPERGRASS + *score cues by* DEBORAH MOLLINSON
  EMI RECORDS: 523 361-2 (CD)

EAST OF EDEN (1954) Music score: LEONARD ROSENMAN *new Recording* LONDON SINFONIETTA (J.ADAMS) *with* 'REBEL WITHOUT A CAUSE' (1955 Leonard Rosenman) *NONESUCH (TEN): 7559 79402-2 (CD) also available:* LEONARD ROSENMAN complete score + 'GIANT'/'REBEL WITHOUT A A CAUSE' *CINERAMA (S.Scr): CIN 2206-2(2CD) -4(2MC)*

EASTENDERS (BBC1 19/2/85-2000) *theme*: SIMON MAY-LESLIE OSBORNE *Orig version* SIMON MAY ORCHESTRA *see COLL.46,150,270,376,407,*

EASTER PARADE (FILM MUSICAL 1948) Songs by IRVING BERLIN *featuring* FRED ASTAIRE-JUDY GARLAND -S/T- *reiss EMI Prem: CDODEON 4 (CD) see COLL.272,355,*

EASY COME EASY GO *see* ELVIS PRESLEY INDEX p.360

EASY RIDER (1969) Music: STEPPENWOLF-ELECTRIC PRUNES-JIMI HENDRIX EXPERIENCE-BYRDS-ROGER McGUINN..-S/T- *MCA (BMG): MCLD 19153 (CD) MCLC 19153 (MC) SIMPLY VINYL (Telstar): SVLP 26 (LP)*

EAT DRINK MAN WOMAN (1993) Music score: MADER -S/T- *VARESE (Pinn): VSD 5528 (CD)*

ECHO FOUR-TWO (Assoc.Rediff.24/8/61-25/10/61) theme mus LAURIE JOHNSON *see COLL.23,216,*

ED TV (1998) Music score by RANDY EDELMAN -S/T- V.ART: *REPRISE (TEN): 93624 7310-2 (CD) -4 (MC)*

ED WOOD (1994) Music score: HOWARD SHORE -S/T- reissue *EDEL-HOLLYWOOD (Pinn): 012 002-2HWR (CD)*

EDGE The (1997) Music score: JERRY GOLDSMITH -S/T- on *RCA (BMG): 09026 68950-2 (CD)*

EDGE OF DARKNESS (BBC2 10/5/92 orig 4/11/85) Theme mus ERIC CLAPTON-MICHAEL KAMEN *see COLL.218,*

EDGE OF SEVENTEEN -S/T- *RAZOR & TIE (Koch): RE 82847-2 (CD)*

EDUCATING RITA (1983) Music sco: DAVID HENTSCHEL -S/T- *reissue C5 (Pinn): C5CD 587 (CD)*

EDWARD II (1991) Music score: SIMON FISHER TURNER -S/T- *MUTE (Pinn): IONIC 8CD (CD) IONIC 8LP (LP)*

EDWARD AND MRS.SIMPSON (ITV 8/11/78) Music: RON GRAINER *see COLL.8,*

EDWARD SCISSORHANDS (1990) Music score: DANNY ELFMAN -S/T- re-issued on *MCA (BMG): MCLD 19303 (CD) see COLL.73,122,249,309,*

EDWIN DROOD (MUSICAL 1986) *see* 'Mystery Of Edwin Drood'

EERIE INDIANA (USA) *see COLL.17,*

EIGER SANCTION The (1975) Music score: JOHN WILLIAMS -S/T- reissue *VARESE (Pinn): VSD 5277 (CD)*

EIGHT HEADS IN A DUFFELBAG (1997) Mus sco: ANDREW GROSS -S/T- *VARESE (Pinn): VSD 5835 (CD)*

EL CID (1961) Music score: MIKLOS ROZSA *New Recording COMPLETE SCORE* New Zealand Symphony Orchestra on *KOCH INTernat.Class (Koch): 37340-2 (CD) -4(MC) see COLL.71,202,302,330,385,*

ELIZABETH (1998) Music score: DAVID HIRSCHFLEDER -S/T- *DECCA (Univ): 460 796-2 (CD)*

ELECTION (1999) VARIOUS ARTISTS -S/T- on *SIRE (Ten): 4344 31057-2 (CD)*

ELECTRA (1975) Music score: MIKIS THEODORAKIS -S/T-
  SAKARIS (Pinn): SR 50090 (CD)
ELECTRIC DREAMS (1984) m: GIORGIO MORODER-PHILIP OAKEY
  -S/T- VIRGIN (EMI): CDVIP 127 (CD) TCVIP 127 (MC)
ELEGIES For Angels Punks & Raging Queens (ORIG LONDON
  CAST 1993) *First Night (Pinn): OCRCD 6035 (CD)*
ELEPHANT MAN The (1980) Music score: JOHN MORRIS plus
  'Adagio' (Samuel BARBER) sco *MILAN (BMG): 199 862
  (CD) see COLL.77,100,*
ELIZABETH (1998) Music score: DAVID HIRSCHFLEDER -S/T-
  DECCA (Univ): 460 796-2 (CD)
ELIZABETH AND ESSEX (1939) M: ERICH WOLFGANG KORNGOLD
  New: CARL DAVIS & Munich S.O. *MILAN: 873 122 (CD)*
ELMER GANTRY (1960) Music score: ANDRE PREVIN -S/T- on
  RYKODISC (Vital): RCD 10732 (CD)
ELVIRA MADIGAN (1987) 'Piano Con.No.21'K.467' (MOZART)
  see COLL.79,105,317,
ELVIS PRESLEY TV SPECIAL see ELVIS PRESLEY INDEX p.360
EMERGENCY WARD 10 (ATV 1957-1967) closing theme music
  "Silks and Satins" by PETER YORKE
  see COLL.2,6,172,
EMMA (1995) Music score by RACHEL PORTMAN -S/T- on
  EDEL-HOLLYWOOD (Pinn): 012 069-2HWR (CD)
EMMERDALE (FARM) (Yorkshire 16/10/72-2000) theme mus
  by TONY HATCH *see COLL.4,150,270,281,376,*
EMPIRE RECORDS (1997) Songs by VARIOUS ARTISTS -S/T-
  A.& M.(Univ): 540 437-2 (CD)
EMPIRE STRIKES BACK The (Star Wars 2) Music score by
  JOHN WILLIAMS / Special-Edition SOUNDTRACK (1997)
  RCA (BMG): 09026 68747-2 (Deluxe 2CD)
  RCA (BMG): 09026 68773-2 (Slimline 2CD) -4 (2MC)
  see also under 'STAR WARS 2'
  see COLL.267,306,308,328,329,334,335,403,404,
EMPTY NEST (USA TV) *see COLL.351,*
END OF DAYS (1999) Music score by JOHN DEBNEY
  -S/T- VARESE (Pinn): VSD 6099 (CD)
END OF THE VIOLENCE (1997) Music score: RY COODER
  -S/T- (score) OUTPOST (BMG): OPD 30007 (CD)
  -S/T- (songs) OUTPOST (BMG): OPD 30008 (CD)
ENDLESS HARMONY: The BEACH BOYS (ITV 6/9/1998)
  CAPITOL (EMI): 496 391-2 (CD)
ENEMY MINE *see COLL.328,*
ENEMY OF THE STATE (1997) Music sco: TREVOR RABIN and
  HARRY GREGSON WILLIAMS -S/T- issued on
  HOLLYW-EDEL (Pinn): 010200-2HWR (CD) HR 62160-2 CD
ENGLAND MY ENGLAND (C4 25/12/95) Music: HENRY PURCELL
  feat: MONTEVERDI CHOIR & ORCH (John Eliot Gardner)
  ERATO (TEN): 0630 10700-2 (CD) -4 (MC)
ENGLAND OF ELIZABETH The (1956 travel short) Music by
  VAUGHAN WILLIAMS *MARCO POLO (Select) 8.223665(CD)*
ENGLISH PATIENT The (1996) Music sco: GABRIEL YARED
  -S/T- FANTASY (Pinn): FCD 16001 (CD) also on Coll
  'SHINE'/'THE PIANO' *VARESE (Pinn): VSD 25982 (2CD)*
  see COLL.74,76,91,144,286,330,

ENTER THE DRAGON (1973) Music sco: LALO SCHIFRIN -S/T-
 WEA FRA (Discov): 7599 26380-2 (CD) see COLL.363,
ENTRAPMENT (1999) Music score: CHRISTOPHER YOUNG -S/T-
 RESTLESS USA (BMG): 74321 73518-2 (CD)
EQUALIZER The (USA 29/10/86) theme by STEWART COPELAND
 -TV S/T- *IRS: DMIRF 1029 (CD)   see COLL.17,351,*
EQUINOXE (1992) Music by Various Artists -S/T-
 VARESE (Pinn): VSD 5424 (CD)
EQUUS (1977) Music score: RICHARD RODNEY BENNETT -S/T-
 RYKODISC (Vital): RCD 10726 (CD)
ER - *see E.R.beginning of E's*
ESCAPE FROM L.A. (1996) Music sco: SHIRLEY WALKER-J.C.
 score -S/T- *MILAN (BMG): 74321 40951-2 (CD)*
 songs -S/T- *WEA: 7567 92714-2 (CD) -4 (MC)*
 Dance Re-mixes from the original score
 MILAN (BMG): 74321 42639-1 (12"vinyl)
ESCAPE FROM NEW YORK (1981) Music sco: JOHN CARPENTER-
 ALAN HOWARTH -S/T- *VARESE (Pinn): VCD 47224 (CD)*
ESCAPE ME NEVER (1947) Mus sc: ERICH WOLFGANG KORNGOLD
 "Ballet Fantasy" MOSCOW SYMPH.ORCH (Stromberg) and
 'ANOTHER DAWN' *MARCO POLO (Select): 8.223871 (CD)*
 suite also available on *CHANDOS: CHAN 8870 (CD)*
 see COLL.221,
ESCORT The - *see 'LA SCORTA'*
ESTATE AGENTS (ITV 2/9/1998) theme mus "Our House" by
 MADNESS on Collection 'Divine Madness' *VIRGIN EMI*
 CDV 2692 (CD) TCV 2692 (MC) MDV 2692 (MD)
ET - see beginning of 'E's
ETERNITY AND A DAY (1998) Music sco: ELENI KARAINDROU
 -S/T- *ECM Import: 465 125-2 (CD)*
EUREKA STREET (BBC1 13/09/1999) Mus.sco: MARTIN PHIPPS
 BBC WORLDWIDE (Pinn): WMSF 6016-2 (CD)
EUROPA (1992) Music sco: JOAKIM HOLBEK -S/T- *VIRGIN*
 FRANCE (Discovery): 87781-2 (CD)
EUROPA EUROPA (1991) Music score: ZBIGNIEW PREISNER
 -S/T- also inc.mus. 'OLIVIER OLIVIER' (Preisner)
 DRG (Pinn): DRGCD 12606(CD) DRGMC 12606(MC)
EUROPEAN CHAMPIONS LEAGUE Football (ITVSport 25/11/92)
 "Champion League Anthem" (TONY BRITTEN) *unavailable*
EUROPEAN FIGURE SKATING CHAMPIONSHIPS (BBC 1/2) theme
 music "Mornings At Seven" (James Last) JAMES LAST
 ORCHESTRA on 'By Request' *POLYDOR (Univ.):*
 831 786-2 (CD) -4 (MC) see also 'ICE SKATING'
EUROTRASH (C4 from 1993) theme mus "St.Tropez" (F.Lai)
 BRIDGET BARDOT on 'A SONG FOR EURTRASH'
 EMI UK: 495 062-2 (CD)
EUROVISION SONG CONTEST (1999) (UK) BBC1 29/5/1999)
 99 winning song: "Take Me To Your Heaven" sung by
 CHARLOTTE NILSSON **Sweden** scor.163pts (23 countries)
 ARISTA (BMG): 74321 68695-2 (CDs)
 99 UK entry: "Say It Again" performed by PRECIOUS
 placed joint 12th with 38pts. *EMI: CDEM 544 (CDs)*
 Austrian entry (placed 10th) "Reflection" sung by
 BOBBIE SINGER *available through KOCH*

EUROVISION SONG CONTEST (1998) (UK) BBC1 9/5/1998)
 98 winning song: "Diva" perf.by DANA INTERNATIONAL
 Israel scored 174pts (25 countries) recorded on
 DANCEPOOL (Ten): DANA 1CD (CDs)
 98 UK entry: "Where Are You" performed by IMAANI
 placed 2nd with 167pts. *EMI: CDEM 510 (CDs)*
 Other song entries unreleased in the UK

EUROVISION SONG CONTEST (1997) (Ireland) BBC1 3/5/1997)
 97 winning song: "Love Shine A Light" performed by
 KATRINA & THE WAVES UK scored 227pts (25 countries)
 on *ETERNAL (TEN): WEA 106(CD)(C)(T) (CDs/MC/12"s)*
 97 runner up: "Mysterious Woman" performed by MARC
 ROBERTS Ireland scored 157pts. recorded on *RITZ*
 (Pinn): RITZCD 305 (CDs) RITZC 305 (MC)
 Interval Music: composed by RONAN KEATING and perf.
 by BOYZONE *Other song entries unreleased in the UK*

EUROVISION SONG CONTEST (1996) (Norway) BBC1 18/5/96)
 96 winning song: "The Voice" perform: EIMEAR QUINN
 for IRELAND scored 162 pts (23 Countries) recorded
 POLYDOR (Univ): 576 884-2 (CD) 576 884-4 (MC)
 96 UK entry: "Ooh Aah Just A Little Bit" by GINA G.
 (77pts - 7th) *ETERNAL (TEN): WEA 041(CD)(C)(T)*
 Interval Music: composed by EGIL MONN-IVERSEN perf:
 NORWEGIAN RADIO ORCH cond: FRODE THINGNAES. song by
 MORTEN HARKET 'Heaven's Not For Saints Let It Go'

EUROVISION SONG CONTEST (1995) (Ireland) BBC1 13/5/95)
 95 winning song: "Nocturne" perform: SECRET GARDEN
 for NORWAY scored 148 pts (25 Countries) recorded
 POLYDOR: 856 978-2 (CD) 856 978-4 (MC)
 95 UK entry: "Love City Groove" by LOVE CITY GROOVE
 (76pts - 10th) *PLANET 3: GXY 2003CD (CDs)*
 Interval Music: "Lumen" by MICHEAL O'SUILLEABHAIN
 VENTURE VIRGIN (EMI): VENDX 5 (CDs) VENCX 5 (MC)

EUROVISION SONG CONTEST (1994) (Ireland) (BBC1 30/4/94)
 94 winning song: "Rock'n'Roll Kids"(Brendan Graham)
 by PAUL HARRINGTON & CHARLIE McGETTIGAN for IRELAND
 scored 226pts (25 Countries) *Roc Kids M (Grapevine*
 /Poly): RNRK(CD)(MC)(SP) 1 (CDs/MC/7"s) deleted
 94 UK entry: "Lonely Symphony" (De Angelis-Dean) by
 FRANCES RUFFELLE (63pts-10th) *VIRGIN: VSCCD(VSC)*
 (VS) 1499 (CDs/MC/7"s) / Interval Music (1994)
 "RIVERDANCE" by BILL WHELAN *see also* 'RIVERDANCE'

EUROVISION SONG CONTEST (1993) (Ireland) (BBC1 15/5/93)
 93 winning song: "In Your Eyes" (Jimmy Walsh) sung
 by NIAMH KAVANAGH for IRELAND scored 187 pts (25 Co
 untries) *ARISTA: 74321 15415-2(CDs) -4(MC) -7(7")*
 93 UK entry:"Better The Devil" (Dean Collinson-Red)
 SONIA (164 pts-2nd) *ARISTA (BMG): 74321 14687-2CDs*

EUROVISION SONG CONTEST (1992) (Sweden) (BBC1 9/5/92)
 92 winning song: "Why Me"(Johnny Logan)LINDA MARTIN
 scored 155 points (23 Countries) *Columbia deleted*
 92 UK entry: "One Step Out Of Time" (Tony Ryan-Paul
 Davies-Victor Stratton) MICHAEL BALL (139 pts- 2nd)
 Poly: PZCD 206 (CDs) PO 206 (7") POCS 206 deleted

EUROVISION SONG CONTEST (1991) (Rome) (BBC1-4/5/91)
91 winning song: "Fangad Av En Stormvind' (Captured
By A Love Storm) CAROLA (Sweden) scored 146 points
(22 Countries) *RCA: PB 44649(7") PD 44650(CDs)*
also "Le Dernier Qui A Parle" (Last One Who Speaks)
AMINA (France) 146 Pts *Philips: PH 45 (7") PHMC 45*
91 UK entry "A Message To Your Heart" (Paul Curtis)
SAMANTHA JANUS (47pts-11th) *Hollywood HWD(T)(CD)104*

EUROVISION SONG CONTEST (1990) (Yugoslav)(BBC1 5/5/90)
90 winning song "Insieme 1992" (All Together Now)by
TOTO COTUGNO (Italy) scored 149 pts (22 countries)
on *Odeon (EMI): (12)ODO 113 (12"s/7"s) deleted*
90 UK entry "Give A Little Love Back To The World"
(Paul Curtis) sung by EMMA (87 points placed 6th)
recorded on *Big Wave (BMG): BWR 33 (7"s) deleted*

EUROVISION THEME MUSIC "Te Deum In D.Major" (Marc-Antoi
ne Charpentier) Academy Of St.Martin-In-The Fields
(Neville Marriner) *EMI: CDC 754 284-2 (CD)* also
English Chamber Orch *EMI: CZS 767 425-2 (2CD)*

EVE'S BAYOU (1997) Music sco: TERENCE BLANCHARD -S/T-
SONIC IMAGES (Cargo-Greyhound): SI 8707 (CD)

EVEN COWGIRLS GET THE BLUES (1993) Music & songs (k.d.
lang) -S/T- *Sire-WB (TEN): 9362 45433-2(CD)*

EVENING SHADE (USA) *see COLL.17,351,*

EVENING STAR (1996) Music score: WILLIAM ROSS -S/T-
Import (Silva Screen): ANG 54567 (CD)

EVENT HORIZON (1997) Music sc: MICHAEL KAMEN + V.Arts.
-S/T- *INTERNAL (Univ): 828 939-2 (CD)*

EVER AFTER (1998) Music score: GEORGE FENTON -S/T- on
DECCA (Univ): 460 581-2 (CD)

EVER DECREASING CIRCLES (BBC1 29/1/84-1989) theme mus
"Prelude No.15 Op.34 Allegretto" (D.SHOSTAKOVICH)

EVERY SUNDAY (1936) DEANNA DURBIN-JUDY GARLAND -S/T-
selection with 'ZIEGFELD GIRL' on
GREAT MOVIE THEMES (BMG): CD 60026 (CD)

EVERY WOMAN KNOWS A SECRET (ITV 18/03/1999) Music by
NIGEL HESS *on* 'TV Themes of Nigel Hess' on
CHANDOS: CHAN 9750 (CD)

EVERYONE SAYS I LOVE YOU (1996) Mus: DICK HYMAN / Songs
on *RCA Victor (BMG): 09026 68756-2 (CD)*

EVIL OF FRANKENSTEIN *see COLL.181,*

EVIL UNDER THE SUN (1982) Music of COLE PORTER arranged
and conducted by JOHN LANCHBERRY *reissue -S/T- on*
DRG USA (Pinn): DRGCD 12615 (CD)

EVITA - songs by Tim Rice and Andrew LLoyd Webber
   1.FILM 1996 *feat* MADONNA-JONATHAN PRYCE-ANTONIO BANDE
     RAS-JIMMY NAIL etc.-S/T- *SIRE (TEN): 9362 463462-2*
     (CD) -4 (MC) / "Don't Cry For Me Argentina" MADONNA
     WEA: W.0384CD (CDs) W.0384C (MCs)
   2.STUDIO RECORDING 1976 *with* JULIE COVINGTON and Comp
     MCA (BMG): DMCXC 503 (CD)
   3.ORIG BROADWAY CAST 1979 *feat:* PATTI LuPONE-MANDY
     PATINKIN-BOB GUNTON-MARK SYERS-JANE OHRINGER & Comp
     MCA (BMG): MCDW 453 (2LP)

4.ORIG LONDON CAST 1978 *w:* ELAINE PAIGE-DAVID ESSEX
  MCA (BMG): DMCG 3527 (CD) MCGC 3527 (MC)
5.SHOWS COLL *w:* MARTI WEBB *CARLTON: PWKS(PWKMC) 4233*
  see COLL.42,43,119,214,231,242,279,
EXCALIBUR (1981) Music score incl.unused music cues
  TREVOR JONES *OLD WORLD MUSIC (Imp): OWM 9402 (CD)*
  see COLL.71,72,79,82,85,121,274,
EXECUTIVE DECISION (1995) Music score: JERRY GOLDSMITH
  VARESE (Pinn): VSD 5714 (CD)
EXISTENZ (1999) Music score by HOWARD SHORE -S/T- on
  RCA VICTOR (BMG): 09026 63478-2 (CD)
EXIT (Film) Music score: TANGERINE DREAM -S/T-
  VIRGIN (EMI): CDV 2212 (CD) OVEDC 166 (MC)
EXIT TO EDEN (1994) Music score: PATRICK DOYLE -S/T-
  VARESE (Pinn): VSD 5553 (CD)
EXODUS (1960) Music score: ERNEST GOLD + score from
  'Judith' (KAPLAN) *TSUNAMI (Sil.Sc): TSU 0115 (CD)*
  see COLL.204,214,
EXORCIST The (1973) Music sco: JACK NITZSCHE -S/T- inc.
  V.composers MIKE OLDFIELD-KRYSZTOF PENDERECKI-HANS
  WERNER HENZE-GEORGE CRUM-ANTON WEBERN-DAVID BORDEN
  WEA FRA (Discov): 9362 46294-2 (CD)
EXOTICA (1994) Music score: MYCHAEL DANNA -S/T- on
  VARESE (Pinn): VSD 5543 (CD)
EXPERIENCE (Rock 1968) JIMI HENDRIX EXPERIENCE feat:
  Jimi HENDRIX-Noel REDDING-Mitch MICTHELL *reissue*
  -S/T- *CHARLY (Koch): CDGR 246 (CD) / also on*
  NECTAR (Pinn): NTRCD 036 (CD) NTRC 036 (MC)
EXPOSED (1983) *see COLL.83,85,125,*
EXTREMELY DANGEROUS (ITV 11/11/1999) Music score by
  RUPERT GREGSON-WILLIAMS *unavailable*
EYE OF THE PANTHER Mus.sco: JOHN DEBNEY -S/T- incl 'NOT
  SINCE CASANOVA' *PROMETHEUS (S.Screen): PCD 140 (CD)*
EYES WIDE SHUT (1999) Music score: JOCELYN POOK -S/T-
  REPRISE (TEN): 9362 47450-2 (CD) -4 (MC)
  see COLL.144,
F 1 (Formula One Grand Prix) (ITV 7/3/97) theme music
  "Cosmic Girl" (Kay-Stone) by JAMIROQUAI on *S2 (SONY*
  Mus): 663829-2 (CDs) -4 (MC) TV version unavailable
F.B.I.(USA TV) *see COLL.345,*

FABULOUS BAKER BOYS The (1989) Music score: DAVE GRUSIN
  reissue -S/T- GRP USA (BMG): GRP 2002-2 (CD)
FACE (1997) Music sco: ANDY ROBERTS-PAUL CONROY-ADRIAN
  CORKER -S/T- *feat V/A ISLAND (Univ): CID 8061 (CD)*
FACE / OFF (1997) Music score: JOHN POWELL -S/T-
  EDEL-HOLLYWOOD (Pinn): 012125-2HWR (CD)
FACE TO FACE (BBC2 18/9/95) theme mus "Overture to Les
  Francs Juges" Op.3 (BERLIOZ) *version* Chicago S.Orch
  (Solti) *DECCA (Univers.): 417 705-2 (CD)*
FACE TO FACE (1967) Music score ENNIO MORRICONE *Import*
  with 'BIG GUNDOWN' *MASK (S.Screen): MK 701 (CD)*
FACULTY The (1998) Music score: MARCO BELTRAMI -S/T-
  COLUMBIA (Ten): 493 038-2 (CD) -4 (MC)

FAHRENHEIT 451 (1966) Music score by BERNARD HERRMANN
SEATTLE SO *VARESE (Pinn): VSD 5551 (CD)* ORIG -S/T-
TSUNAMI (Sil.Screen): TSU 0136 (CD) see COLL.190,

FALCON CREST (USA TV) *see COLL.350,376,*

FALL GUY The (USA TV) *see COLL.350,*

FALL OF BERLIN The (1949) *see COLL.316,*

FALL OF THE ROMAN EMPIRE The (1964) Music sco: DIMITRI
TIOMKIN -S/T- *CLOUD NINE (S.Screen): ACN 7016(CD)*

FALLEN IDOL (1948) Music score: WILLIAM ALWYN *suite by*
London S.O.(Richard Hickox) CHANDOS: CHAN 9243 (CD)

FALLING IN LOVE (1985) Music score: DAVE GRUSIN Select
by Dave Grusin *GRP USA (Pinn): GRPD 9018 (CD)*

FAME (USA/BBC1 82-12/2/85) *reissue of* KIDS FROM FAME on
RCA: (BMG): ND 90427 (CD) theme by ERICA GIMPEL
RCA: (BMG): PK 89257 (MC)

FAME (FILM MUSICAL 80) M: MICHAEL GORE-DEAN PITCHFORD
IRENE CARA *see COLL.350,*

FAME (THE MUSICAL)(ORIG LONDON CAST 95) *feat:* LORRAINE
VELEZ-RICHARD DEMPSEY-SONIA SWABY and Company on
POLYDOR-RUG (Univ): 529 109-2 (CD) -4 (MC)

FAME THE MUSICAL (Various) 1999 ORIG CAST RECORDING
DRG USA (Pinn): DRGCD 19010 (CD)

FAMILY AFFAIRS (C5 30/3/1997) m: RICK TURK *unavailable*

FAMILY AT WAR, A (Gra+6/10/96 orig ITV 12/5/70) Theme:
Ist m/m Symphony No.6 in E.Min. (VAUGHAN WILLIAMS)
London Symp Or (A.Previn) *RCA (BMG) RD 89883 (CD)*
New Phil Or (A.Boult) *HMV (EMI) CDC 747215-2(CD)*

FAMILY THING (95) -S/T- *Edel (Pinn): 0022602 (CD)*

FAMILY WAY The (66) Music score: PAUL McCARTNEY (arr.&
prod: George Martin) Suite on 'The Family Way'
PHILIPS (Univ): 454 230-2 (CD)

FAN The (1996) Mus.sc: HANS ZIMMER *feat* MASSIVE ATTACK
-S/T- *SNAPPER (Pinn): SMACD 806 (CD)*

FANNY (1932) MARCEL PAGNOL'S TRILOGY (2) / music sco:
VINCENT SCOTTO on 'The Films Of Marcel Pagnol' on
EMI FRA.(Discov): 855 883-2 (CD) see also 'MARIUS'

FANTASIA (1941) New Recording of complete classical
film music *NAXOS (Select): 8551166 (CD)*
see also WALT DISNEY INDEX p.362
see COLL.74,83,84,85,86,88,95,98,271,

FANTASIA 2000 (1999) Mus: SORCERER'S APPRENTICE *DUKAS*
PINES OF ROME *RESPIGHI*; 5TH SYMPH.*BEETHOVEN*; PIANO
CONC.NO.2 *SHOSTAKOVICH*; RHAPSODY IN BLUE *GERSHWIN*
CARNIVAL OF THE ANIMALS *SAINT-SAENS*; POMP AND CIRC
UMSTANCE MARCH *ELGAR*; FIREBIRD SUITE *STRAVINSKY*

FANTASTICK VOYAGE (1966) Music sco: LEONARD ROSENMAN
complete score on Ltd Ed.Imp Coll 'POSEIDON ADV.'
RETROGRADE (S.Screen/MFTM): FSMCD 3 (CD)

FANTASTICKS The - songs by Harvey Schmidt & Tom Jones
1.ORIG BROADWAY CAST 1960 *with:* JERRY ORBACH-RITA
GARDNER-KENNETH NELSON *TER (Koch): CDTER 1099*
2.JAPAN TOUR CAST REC. *DRG (Pinn) DRGCD 19005 (CD)*

FANTASY FOOTBALL LEAGUE (Avalon/Gr.Slam/BBC2 14/1/94)
music STEVE BROWN *unavailable* / *see also WORLD CUP*

FANTASY ISLAND (USA TV) *see COLL.350,*

FANTASY ROOMS (BBC2 20/10/1999) series theme music by BEN SALISBURY *unavailable*

FAR AND AWAY (1992) Music score: JOHN WILLIAMS also The Chieftains and ENYA ("Book Of Days") -S/T- on *MCA: MCAD(MCAC) 10628 CD/MC deleted* / end credits music on *SILVA SCREEN (Koch): FILMCD 152 (CD)*

FAR FLUNG FLOYD (BBC2 13/7/93) theme "Waltz In Black" The STRANGLERS on "Meninblack" *Fame (MFP-EMI): CDFA 3208 (CD) TCFA 3208 (MC)*

FAR FROM HOME: ADVENTURES OF YELLOW DOG (1996) Music: JOHN SCOTT -S/T- *JOHN SCOTT (S.Scr): JSCD 118(CD)*

FAREWELL TO ARMS, A (1957) Mus: MARIO NASCIMBENE -S/T- +'SONS AND LOVERS' *DRG (Pinn): DRGCSD 32962 (CD)* *also avail:* inc.mus. from 'The Barefoot Contessa' on *LEGEND Import (Silva Screen): LEGENDCD 11 (CD)*

FAREWELL TO MY CONCUBINE (1993) Music sco: ZHAO JIPING -S/T- *VARESE (Pinn): VSD 5454 (CD)*

FARGO (1996) Mus.sco: CARTER BURWELL + 'BARTON FINK' -S/T- *SNAPPER (Pinn): SMACD 808 (CD)*

FARINELLI: IL CASTRATO (1995) Classical music -S/T- *AUVIDIS Travelling (Harmonia Mundi): K.1005 CD)*

FARMING (BBC 1950's) theme music "A Quiet Stroll" CHARLES WILLIAMS *see COLL.172,*

FAST CHEAP AND OUT OF CONTROL (1996) M: CALEB SAMPSON -S/T- *ACCURATE (Direct): AC 5027 (CD)*

FAST SHOW The (BBC2 27/9/94) mus.d.PHIL POPE / theme: "Release Me" (Miller-Stevenson-Harris) arranged by Phil Pope *unavailable* orig vers: (USA) Ray Price

FASTER PUSSYCAT (1968,RUSS MEYER) V.Arts with 'LORNA'/ 'VIXEN' -S/T- *NORMAL-QDK MEDIA (Pinn/Greyh./Dir) QDKCD 008 (CD) QDKLP 008 (LP)*

FATAL ATTRACTION (1987) Music sco: MAURICE JARRE -S/T- *GNP USA (ZYX) GNPD 8011 (CD) GNP-5 8011 (MC) opera music:* "Un Bel Di" (Madam Butterfly) (PUCCINI) *see COLL.213,273,275,*

FATHER CHRISTMAS (C4-25/12/91) music: MIKE HEWER perf: Phoenix Chamber Orch (Julian Bigg) narrated by Mel Smith -S/T- *COLUMBIA (SM): 469475-2 (CD) -4(MC)*

FATHER OF THE BRIDE (1991) Music score: ALAN SILVESTRI -S/T- *VARESE (Pinn): VSD 5348 (CD)*

FATHER TED (C4 21/4/95-1998) series title music by the DIVINE COMEDY *unavailable*

FAWLTY TOWERS (BBC2 1975) theme music by DENNIS WILSON *see COLL.270,*

FEAR AND LOATHING IN LAS VEGAS (1998) VARIOUS ARTISTS -S/T- *GEFFEN (BMG): GED 25218 (CD)*

FEAR IS THE KEY (1972) Music score by ROY BUDD -S/T on *CINEPHILE (Pinn): CINCD 002 (CD) CINLP 002 (LP)*

FEARLESS (1993) music sco: MAURICE JARRE -S/T- *ELEKTRA NONESUCH (TEN): 7559 79334-2 (CD)*

FEARLESS VAMPIRE KILLERS The (1967) Music score by KRZYSTOF KOMEDA -S/T- includes 'ROSEMARY'S BABY' *POLONIA (Silva Screen): POLONIA CD 160 (CD)*

FEDS (1988) Music score and songs: RANDY EDELMAN -S/T-
   GNP (ZYX) GNPD 8014 (CD)
FEET OF FLAMES Music by RONAN HARDIMAN
   POLYGRAM TV: 559 562-2 (CD) -4 (MC)
FELICIA'S JOURNEY (1999) Music score by MYCHAEL DANNA
   -S/T- *MILAN (BMG): 74321 35896-2 (CD)*
FELIX THE CAT (USA TV) *see COLL.345,*
FENN STREET GANG The (LWT 24/9/71) theme "The Dandy"
   DENIS KING *see COLL.5,*
FEVER PITCH (1996) Mus sc: NEIL MacCOLL & BOB HEWERDINE
   -S/T- *BLANCO Y NEGRO (TEN): 0630 18453-2(CD) -4(MC)*
FIDDLER ON THE ROOF - songs Jerry Bock-Sheldon Harnick
   1.FILM MUSICAL 1971 *featuring:* TOPOL -S/T- *re-issue:*
   UNITED ARTISTS (EMI): CDP 746091-2 (CD)
   2.CARLTON SHOWS COLLECTION 1995 *feat:* ANTHONY NEWLEY
   TRACEY MILLER-MARION DAVIES-LINDA HIBBERT-NICK
   CURTIS-DAVID HITCHEN *CARLTON: 30362 0014-2(CD)*
   3.STUDIO RECORDING 1968 *featuring:*
   ROBERT MERRILL-MOLLY PICON-ROBERT BOWMAN-ANDY COLE
   LONDON FESTIVAL ORCHESTRA (Stanley Black) *reissue:*
   DECCA (Univ): 448 949-2 (CD)
   4.ORIG LONDON CAST 1967 *inc:* TOPOL-MIRIAM KARLIN-
   SANDOR ELES-HEATHER CLIFTON-LINDA GARDNER-
   SONY West End (Ten): SMK(SMT)53499 (CD/MC)
   5.ORIG BROADWAY CAST 1964 *with:* ZERO MOSTELL & MARIA
   KARNILOVA-BEATRICE ARTHUR-JULIA MIGENES *RCA (BMG):*
   RD 87060 CD also Silva Screen Imp: RCD1 7060 (CD)
FIDDLY FOODLE BIRD (BBC1 8/1/92) title song: BOB SAKER
   JONATHAN HODGE + Stuart Leathwood-Julian Littman
   MFP (EMI): CDMFP 5958 (CD) TCMFP 5958 (MC)
FIELDS OF AMBROSIA *sgs:* MARTIN SILVESTRI-JOEL HIGGINS
   ORIG LONDON CAST *feat:* CHRISTINE ANDREAS & Company
   FIRST NIGHT (Pinn): CASTCD 58 (CD)
FIERCE CREATURES-DON'T PET THEM (1996) Music score:
   JERRY GOLDSMITH -S/T- *VARESE (Pinn): VSD 5792 (CD)*
FIFTEEN-TO-ONE (C4 11/1/1988-2000) music directed by
   PAUL McGUIRE *unavailable*
FIFTH ELEMENT The (1997) Music sco: ERIC SERRA -S/T-
   VIRGIN (EMI): CDVIRX 63 (CD) MCVIRX 63 (MC)
FIFTY-FIVE DAYS AT PEKING (1961) Mus: DIMITRI TIOMKIN
      on 'HIGH NOON' RCA (BMG): 09026 62658-2 (CD)
FIGHT CLUB (1999) Music by the DUST BROTHERS
   RESTLESS-RCA (BMG): 74321 71643-2 (CD)
   SIMPLY VINYL (Vital): SVLP 161 (LP)
FILM 99 WITH JONATHAN ROSS (BBC1 1972-1999) *theme mus:*
   "I Wish I Knew How It Would Feel To Be Free"
   BILLY TAYLOR *see COLL.52,281,407,*
FINIAN'S RAINBOW - songs by Burton Lane & E.Y.Harburg
   1.ORIGINAL BROADWAY CAST 1947 *inc:* ELLA LOGAN-ALBERT
   SHARPE-DONALD RICHARDS-DAVID WAYNE-ANITA ALVAREZ
   COLUMBIA (S.Screen): CK 04062 (CD) JST 04062 (MC)
   2.REVIVAL BROADWAY CAST 1960 *with:* JEANNE CARSON
   RCA (Silva Screen): 1057-2 (CD) 1057-4 (MC)

FIORELLO (O.BROADWAY CAST 1959) Songs (Jerry Bock-Sheld
 on Harnick) *featuring:* TOM BOSLEY-PATRICIA WILSON-
 ELLEN HANLEY-HOWARD DA SILVA-MARK DAWSON & company
 EMI ANGEL: ZDM 565 023-2 (CD)
FIRE (1997 Deepa Mehta) Music score: A.R.RAHMAN -S/T-
 COLOSSEUM (Pinn): CST 348068 (CD)
FIRE IN THE SKY (1992) Music score: MARK ISHAM -S/T-
 VARESE (Pinn): VSD 5417 (CD)
FIREBALL XL5 (ATV/ITV 25/3/63) theme song: BARRY GRAY
 sung by DON SPENCER *see COLL.4,23,38,122,267,308,*
 345,360,369,
FIRELIGHT (1998) Music score: CHRISTOPHER GUNNING -S/T-
 SILVA SCREEN (Koch-S.Screen): FILMCD 198 (CD)
FIREMAN SAM (BBC/SC4-88) theme music: Ben HENEGHAN and
 IAN LAWSON *sung by* MALDWYN POPE *see COLL.186,*
FIRM The (1993) Music score: DAVE GRUSIN -S/T-*GRP USA*
 NEW NOTE-MCA (BMG): GRLD 19358 (CD)
FIRST BLOOD (82) Music: JERRY GOLDSMITH voc: DAN HILL
 -S/T- *INTRADA (S.Scr): FMT 8001D (CD) see* 'RAMBO'
FIRST GREAT TRAIN ROBBERY (1978) *see* 'WILD ROVERS'
FIRST LOVE LAST RITES (1998) Music by SHUDDER TO THINK
 -S/T- V.ARTS *EPIC (Ten): 491 610-2 (CD) -4 (MC)*
FIRST MEN IN THE MOON The (1964) Music score: LAURIE
 JOHNSON *CLOUD NINE (S.Screen-Conif): ACN 7015 (CD)*
 see COLL.215,217,
FIRST OF THE FEW (1942) Music incl: "Spitfire Prelude
 and Fugue" (WILLIAM WALTON) L.P.Orch (Sir A.Boult)
 HMV: ED 2911129-4 (MC) with 'Things To Come'
FIRST SNOW OF WINTER (BBC1 1998) *see COLL.19,*
FISHER KING The (1991) Music sco: GEORGE FENTON -S/T-
 arts include Harry Nilsson-Brenda Lee-Chill Rob.G
 MCA (BMG): MCAD 10249 (CD) MCAC 10249 (MC)
FIST GOES WEST, A (1980) Music score ENNIO MORRICONE
 ENNIO MORRICONE ORCH 'An Ennio Morricone Quintet'
 DRG USA (Pinn): DRGCD 32907 (CD)
FISTFUL OF DOLLARS, A (1964) Music sc: ENNIO MORRICONE
 -S/T- complete *inc* 'FOR A FEW DOLLARS MORE' (1965)
 /'ONCE UPON A TIME IN THE WEST' (1968)
 RCA (BMG): 74321 66040-2 (CD) also 'A FISTFUL OF
 SOUNDS' *SIMPLY VINYL (Telstar): SVLP 83 (LP)*
 see COLL.251,253,286,358,400,401,
FISTFUL OF DYNAMITE, A (Duck You Sucker!) (1971) Music
 ENNIO MORRICONE *DRG USA (Pinn) DRGCD 32907 (CD)*
 see COLL.250,
FIVE DAYS AND FIVE NIGHTS (FILM) Music: D.SHOSTAKOVICH
 mus.score inc.music from 'THE GADFLY' (1955)
 NAXOS (Select): 8.553299 (CD) see COLL.316,
FIVE EASY PIECES (1970) *see COLL.82,*
FIVE GUYS NAMED MOE (O.LONDON CAST 1991) Song & Dance
 Review w.music by LOUIS JORDAN *feat:* CLARKE PETERS
 FIRST NIGHT (Pinn): CAST(C)(CD) 23 DELETED 1998
 'Five Guys Named Moe'(L.JORDAN) *MCA:MCLD 19048 CD*
 L.JORDAN & TYMPANY 5 *BANDSTAND (H.Mund):BDCD 1531*

FIVE HEARTBEATS The (1991) Various Arts -S/T- *VIRGIN Movie Music (EMI): CDVMM 4 (CD) TCVMM 4 (MC)*

FIX The (Musical 1997) ORIG LONDON CAST RECORDING *feat* JOHN BARROWMAN-PHILIP QUAST and Company *FIRST NIGHT (Pinn): CASTCD 62 (CD) CASTC 62 (MC)*

FLAMING STAR *see* ELVIS PRESLEY INDEX p.360

FLAMINGO KID The (1984) Music sco: CURT SOBELL + V/A -S/T- *re-issue SPECTRUM (Univ): 551 539-2 (CD)*

FLASH GORDON (1980) Music & Songs: QUEEN -S/T- reiss: *EMI: CDP 789 499-2 (CD) TCPCSD 137 (MC)* see COLL.229,264,

FLASHDANCE (1983) Mus: GIORGIO MORODER t.song IRENE CARA -S/T- *CASABLANCA: 811 492-2(CD) PRIMC 111(MC)*

FLASHPOINT (1985) Music score: TANGERINE DREAM -S/T- *ONE WAY (Greyhound): 18507 (CD)*

FLEET'S IN (1942) DOROTHY LAMOUR-BETTY HUTTON -S/T- selections with 'YOLANDA AND THE THIEF' on *GREAT MOVIE THEMES (BMG): CD 60033 (CD)*

FLEMISH FARM The (1943) Music score: VAUGHAN WILLIAMS *MARCO POLO (Select): 8.223665 (CD)*

FLESH IS WEAK The *see* COLL.292,

FLETCH (1985) Music: HAROLD FALTERMEYER + STEPHANIE MILLS-KIM WILDE-DAN HARTMAN *MCA: DMCF 3284(CD)*

FLIGHT OF THE DOVES (1971) Music score by ROY BUDD song DANA -S/T- *CINEPHILE (Pinn): CINCD 010 (CD)*

FLINTSTONES The (USA 61/85) "Meet The Flinstones" (H. Curtin) TV-S/T- reiss: *MCI (MCI-THE): MCCD(MCTC) 181 (CD/MC) see COLL.373,*

FLINTSTONES The (FILM 1993) Music: HOYT CURTIN & oth) *MCA (BMG): MCD 11045 (CD) and MCA 11100 (CD)*

FLIPPER (USA 1964) *see* COLL.199,345,

FLORA THE RED MENACE - songs: John Kander & Fred Ebb OFF BROADWAY CAST 1987 *TER (Koch): CDTER 1159 (CD)*

FLORADORA (ORIG LONDON CAST 1899) Mus (Leslie Stuart) Lyrics (Ernest Boyd-Jones and Paul Rubens) Louis Bradfield-Kate Cutler-Ada Reeve-Syney Barraclough *PEARL (Harmonia Mundi): OPALCD 9835 (CD)*

FLOWER OF MY SECRET The (La Fleur De Mon Secret)(1995) Music sco: ALBERT IGLESIAS -S/T- *feat* MILES DAVIS CAETANO VELOSO *SQUATT Sony: SQT 481 444-2(CD)*

FLOWERING PASSIONS (C4 13/6/91) music by FRANCIS SHAW -S/T- *SILVA SCREEN (Koch): FILMCD 116 (CD)*

FLOWERS IN THE ATTIC (1988) Music: CHRISTOPHER YOUNG -S/T- *INTRADA USA (Silva Screen): MAF 7009D (CD)*

FLOYD COLLINS (Musical 1996 USA) Songs: ADAM GUETELL *w:* CHRISTOPHER INNVAR-JESSE LENAT-THERESA McCARTHY *NONESUCH (TEN): 7559 79434-2 (CD)*

FLOYD ON...(BBC2 1986-94) theme music "Waltz In Black" also used "Peaches" by THE STRANGLERS 'Collection' *Fame (EMI): (CD)(TC)FA 3230 (CD/MC)*

FLUBBER (1997) Music score by DANNY ELFMAN -S/T- reiss *EDEL-DISNEY (Pinn): 017 566-2DNY (CD) see p.362*

FLY The (1986) Music score: HOWARD SHORE -S/T- on *VARESE (Pinn): VCD 47272 (CD)*

FLYING DOWN TO RIO (1933 MUSICAL) FRED ASTAIRE-GINGER
    ROGERS-DOLORES DE RIO *incl.songs from* 'HOLLYWOOD
    HOTEL' *TARGET (BMG): CD 60008 (CD)*
FLYING VET (BBC2 4/9/96) orig music sco: ART PHILLIPS
    -S/T- *ABC Soundtracks (S.Screen): 479784-2 (CD)*
FOG The (1979) Music score: JOHN CARPENTER -S/T- Imp
    VARESE (Pinn): VCD 47267 (CD) see COLL.62,
FOLLIES - songs by Stephen Sondheim
    1.ORIG LONDON CAST 1987 *feat:* JULIA McKENZIE-DIANA
        RIGG-DANIEL MASSEY-DAVIE HEALEY-DOLORES GRAY & Co
        FIRST NIGHT (Pinn): OCRCD 6019 (CD)
    2.ORIG BROADWAY CAST 1971 ALEXIS SMITH-GENE NELSON
        DOROTHY COLLINS-JOHN McMARTIN-YVONNE DE CARLO & Co
        EMI ANGEL: ZDM 764666-2 (CD)
    3.LIVE STUDIO RECORD. 1985 *also featur:* 'STAVISKY'
        (Stephen Sondheim) *RCA (BMG): RD 87128 (2CD's)*
    4.REVIVAL USA LINCOLN CENTER 1985 *w:* BARBARA COOK-
        GEORGE HEARN-MANDY PATINKIN-LEE REMICK-ELAINE
        STRITCH-CAROL BURNETT & New York Philharmonic Orch
        RCA (BMG) BK 87128 (MC) BD 87128 (CD)
    5.TROTTER TRIO *VARESE (Pinn): VSD 5934 (CD)*
FOLLOW THAT DREAM *see* ELVIS PRESLEY INDEX p.360
FOLLOW THE BOYS (1944) VARIOUS -S/T- SELECTIONS on
    GREAT MOVIE THEMES: (Targ-BMG): CD 60032 (CD)
FOLLOW THE FLEET (1936) FILM MUSICAL *feat* FRED ASTAIRE
    GINGER ROGERS -S/T- *sel.on* 'Let's Swing and Dance'
    +songs from 'SWING TIME'/'TOP HAT'/'CAREFREE'
    GREAT MOVIE THEMES (Target-BMG): CD 60015 (CD)
    -S/T- + songs from 'SWING TIME' *IRIS Mus-Chansons
    Cinema (Discovery): CIN 006 (CD) see COLL.21,282,*
FOLLYFOOT (ITV 1971) theme "Lightning Tree" (Steve
    Fracis) sung by The SETTLERS *see COLL.7,*
    and "Meadow Mist" from Follyfoot *see COLL.132,*
FOOD & DRINK (BBC2 26/10/1999) 1999 series theme music
    by STEVE BROWN *unavailable* / 1993-98 theme: SIMON
    MAY *COLL* 'NEW VINTAGE' *ARC Total: CDART102 DELETED*
FOOTBALL *see* EUROPEAN CHAMPIONS LEAGUE/MATCH OF T.DAY
FOOTLIGHT PARADE (1933 MUSICAL) *inc:* JAMES CAGNEY-JOAN
    BLONDELL-RUBY KELLER DICK POWELL *incl.songs from*
    'STAR SPANGLED RHYTHM' *TARGET (BMG): CD 60013 (CD)*
FOOTLOOSE (Rock Film 1984) Music: KENNY LOGGINS *feat:*
    BONNIE TYLER "Holding Out For A Hero" + V/Arts
    -S/T- reissue *COLUMBIA: CBS 493 007-2 (CD)*
FOOTLOOSE (ORIGINAL BROADWAY CAST RECORDING)
    FIRST NIGHT (Pinn): CASTCD 74 (CD)
FOR A FEW DOLLARS MORE (1965) Music: ENNIO MORRICONE
    -S/T- complete with 'A FISTFUL OF DOLLARS' (1964)
    'ONCE UPON A TIME IN THE WEST' (1968)
    RCA VICTOR (BMG): 74321 66040-2 (CD)
    see COLL.137,251,253,358,
FOR LOVE OF THE GAME (1999) Music sc: BASIL POLEDOURIS
    -S/T- *VARESE (Pinn): VSD 6092 (CD)*
FOR ME AND MY GAL (1942) *feat:* JUDY GARLAND-GENE KELLY
    reissued -S/T- *EMI ODEON: CDODEON 12 (CD)*

FOR RICHER OR POORER (1997) Music score: RANDY EDELMAN
  -S/T- *VARESE (Pinn): VSD 5891 (CD)*
FOR ROSEANNA - *see* 'ROSEANNA'S GRAVE'
FOR THE BOYS (1991) Music sco: DAVE GRUSIN with BETTE
  MIDLER -S/T- *ATLANTIC WEA: 756782329-2(CD) -4(MC)*
FOR THE LOVE OF THE GAME (1998) Music score by BASIL
  POLEDOURIS -S/T- *VARESE (Pinn): VSD 6092 (CD)*
FOR THOSE I LOVED (BBC1 21/7/91) musis score: MAURICE
  JARRE *on 'Maurice Jarre Trilogy' with 'A Seas
  in Hell'/'The Damned'DRG (Pinn): DRGCD 32906 (2CD)*
FOR YOUR EYES ONLY - *see* JAMES BOND FILM INDEX p.358
  see COLL.54,55,
FORBIDDEN GAMES (1952) *see COLL.87,*
FORBIDDEN PLANET (1954) Music sco: LOUIS & BEBE BARRON
  -S/T- *GNP USA (Greyhound):PRD 001 (CD) PR 001 (LP)*
  see COLL.329,
FORCES OF NATURE (1998) Music score: JOHN POWELL -S/T-
  V/A: U2/PROPELLERHEADS/BLUE BOY/FAITHLESS/TRICKY
  DREAMWORKS-POLY: DRD 50111 or 450 111-2 (CD)
FOREVER AMBER (1947) Music score: DAVID RAKSIN. *NEW
  COMPLETE RECORDING on VARESE (Pinn): VSD 5857 (CD)*
FOREVER GREEN (LWT 26/2/89) theme: PATRICK GOWERS
  see COLL.149,
FOREVER KNIGHT (USA TV series) music sco: FRED MOLLIN
  -S/T- *GNP (ZYX): GNPD 8043 (CD)*
FOREVER PLAID (O.LONDON CAST RECORDING 1993) American
  Hit Musical with songs from the 50's/60's *featur*
  STAN CHANDLER-DAVID ENGEL-LARRY RABEN-GUY STROMAN
  and Company on *FIRST NIGHT (Pinn):CASTCD 33 (CD)*
FORGOTTEN (ITV 15/02/1999) Music score by ROB LANE
  unavailable
FORMULA 1 - *see* 'F1'
FORREST GUMP (1993) Music sco: ALAN SILVESTRI + V.Arts
  -S/T- (songs): *EPIC (Ten): 476 941-2 (2CD)*
  see COLL.43,120,255,
FORSYTE SAGA The (BBC1 1967) Theme "Elizabeth Tudor"
  Three Elizabeths Suite ERIC COATES *see COLL.4,23,*
FORTY-SECOND STREET - *see under* 42ND STREET
FOSSE THE MUSICAL (1999)
      (O.BROADWAY CAST) *RCA (BMG): 09026 63379-2 (CD)*
      (O.LONDON CAST 99) *RCA (BMG): 74321 72157-2 (CD)*
FOUR FEATHER FALLS (ITV 25/02/1960) t.song: BARRY GRAY
  MICHAEL HOLLIDAY 'EP Collect' *SEE FOR MILES (Pinn)
  SEECD 311 (CD) see COLL.5,18,*
FOUR FLIES ON GREY VELVET (1971) Mus: ENNIO MORRICONE
  Complete score *CINEVOX (S.Screen): CDMDF 325 (CD)*
  -S/T- inc 'BIRD WITH THE CRYSTAL PLUMAGE' +
  'CAT O'NINE TAILS' *DRG (Pinn): DRGCD 32911 (CD)*
FOUR IN THE MORNING (1965) Music sco: JOHN BARRY -S/T-
  reiss.with 'ZULU' -S/T- *RPM (Pinn): RPM 195 (CD)*
  also on PLAY IT AGAIN (Koch): PLAY 002 (CD)
FOUR JILLS IN A JEEP (1944) DICK HAYMES-BETTY GRABLE
  CARMEN MIRANDA-JIMMY DORSEY + *mus.* 'Lady Be Good'
  GREAT MOVIE THEMES (Target-BMG): CD 60029 (CD)

FOUR WEDDINGS AND A FUNERAL (1993) Music sco: RICHARD
    RODNEY BENNETT -S/T- *VERTIGO (Univ):516 751-2 (CD)*
    see *COLL.74,87,106,120,143,*
FOURTH KING The Music score by ENNIO MORRICONE -S/T-
    DRG (Pinn): DRGCD 12622 (CD)
FOX AND THE HOUND The - see WALT DISNEY INDEX p.362
FRANCES (1982) Music sco JOHN BARRY see *COLL.30,35,*
FRANCIS OF ASSISI (1961) Music: MARIO NASCIMBENE -S/T-
    with 'DOCTOR FAUSTUS' *DRG (Pinn): DRGCD 32965 (CD)*
FRANKENSTEIN see *COLL.249,* see also 'MARY SHELLEY'S..'
FRANKENSTEIN AND THE MONSTER FROM HELL - see *COLL.181,*
FRANKENSTEIN CREATED WOMAN (1966) Music: JAMES BERNARD
    see *COLL.181,*
FRANKENSTEIN MUST BE DESTROYED *see COLL.180,*
FRANKIE AND JOHNNY see ELVIS PRESLEY FILM INDEX p.360
FRANKIE STARLIGHT (1995) Music score: ELMER BERNSTEIN
    -S/T- *VARESE (Pinn): VSD 5679 (CD)*
FRASIER (USA 93/C4 20/4/94) title mus by BRUCE MILLER
    DARRYL PHINNESSEE per: KELSEY GRAMMER *unavailable*
    version on 'HIT TV' *VARESE (Pinn): VSD 5957 (CD)*
FRED (BBC2 1/10/84) **+FRED DIBNAH STORY** (BBC2 28/8/96)
    LIFE WITH FRED (BBC2 10/3/94) series theme music
    "Carnival Of Venice" Op.77 (BRICCIALDI) version by
    JAMES GALWAY,flute on 'Music For My Friends' on
    RCA (BMG): 09026 68882-2 (CD)
FRED DIBNAH'S INDUSTRIAL AGE (BBC2 18/02/1999) music
    by ADRIAN BURCH and DAVID WHITAKER *unavailable*
FREDDIE AS F.R.O.7 1992 M: DAVID DUNDAS-RICK WENTWORTH
    -S/T- *MCI (THE-DISC): FRO7 CD1(CD) FRO7 MC1(MC)*
FREDDY'S DEAD: THE FINAL NIGHTMARE (A NIGHTMARE ON ELM
    STREET 6)(1991) Mus: BRIAN MAY -S/T- *METAL BLADE*
    (Pinn): CDZZORRO 33 (CD) ZORRO 33 (LP)
FREE WILLY (1993) Mus sco: BASIL POLEDOURIS -S/T- *MJJ*
    (Ten): 474 264-2 (CD) Deleted see *COLL.43,255,*
FREE WILLY 2: The Adventure Home (1995) Music: BASIL
    POLEDOURIS -S/T- *SM: 480 739-2 / -4 deleted*
FREE WILLY 3: The Rescue (1997) Music: CLIFF EIDELMAN
    -S/T- *VARESE (Pinn): VSD 5830 (CD)*
FREEJACK (1991) Music score: TREVOR JONES -S/T- *reiss*
    MORGAN CREEK (Univ): 002247-2 (CD)
FREEWHEELERS The (ITV 70's) theme music "Private Eye"
    LAURIE JOHNSON see *COLL.5,215,*
FRENCH KISS (1995) Music score: JAMES NEWTON HOWARD
    -S/T- *MERCURY (Univ): 528 321-2 (CD) -4 (MC)*
FRENCH LIEUTENANT'S WOMAN The (1981) Music: CARL DAVIS
    'Adagio' Sonata in D.K576 (MOZART) John Lill (pno)
    -S/T-*DRG (Pinn): DRGCD 6106* see *COLL.80,*
FRENCH TWIST - see 'GAZON MAUDIT'
FRESH PRINCE OF BEL-AIRE (USA 1990/BBC2 14/1/91)
    music by WILL SMITH see *COLL.351,*
FREUD (1962) Music score: JERRY GOLDSMITH
    -S/T- *TSUNAMI Imp (Silva Screen): TSU 0129 (CD)*
FRIDAY (1994) Music sco: HIDDEN FACES -S/T- *PRIORITY*
    VIRGIN (EMI): CDPTY 117 (CD) PTYMC 117 (MC)

FRIDAY NIGHT'S ALL WRIGHT (ITV 13/11/1998) theme music
"Shaft" by ISAAC HAYES *orig version on* 'THIS IS
CULT FICTION' *VIRGIN (EMI): VTCD 59 (CD)*

FRIDAY THE 13TH (TV Series) (USA 89)(ITV-13/7/90) mus
score by FRED MOLLIN -S/T- on *GNP Crescendo USA
(Greyhound): GNPD 8018 (CD) GNPS(5) 8018 (LP/MC)*

FRIED GREEN TOMATOES (1992) Music score: THOMAS NEWMAN
-S/T- *MCA: MCAD 10461 (CD)*

FRIENDLY PERSUASION (1956) Music sco: DIMITRI TIOMKIN
t.song (D.Tiomkin-P.F.Webster) sung by PAT BOONE
-S/T- *VARESE (Pinn): VSD 5828 (CD)*

FRIENDS (NZ/C4 28/4/95) theme mus "I'll Be There For
You" (Michael Skloff-Allee Willis) by REMBRANDTS
-S/T- (TEN): 9362 46008-2 (CD) 9362 46008-4 (MC)
'FRIENDS AGAIN' *REPRISE: 9362 47100-2 (CD) -4(MC)*
see COLL.256,270,

FRITZ THE CAT (1971) Music sco: ED BOGAS-RAY SHANKLIN
CHARLES EARLAND -S/T- inc 'Heavy Traffic' score
*FANTASY (Pinn): FCD 24745 (CD) also available on
MOVING IMAGE (Cargo/Silver Sounds): MIE 003 (LP)*

FROG PRINCE The (1984) Music score: ENYA -S/T- *re-iss
SPECTRUM (Univ): 551 099-2 (CD)*

FROM DAWN TIL DUSK (1995) Music score: GRAEME REVELL
-S/T- *EPIC Soundtrax (Ten): 483 617-2 (CD) -4(MC)*

FROM RUSSIA WITH LOVE (1963) Music: JOHN BARRY title
song (L.Bart) MATT MONRO -S/T- *EMI: CZ 550 (CD)*
see COLL.33,34,41,52,53,54,55,118,140,314,356,
see also JAMES BOND FILM INDEX p.358

FUGITIVE The (USA ABC/QM 1963-66) theme music: PETE
RUGOLO *see COLL.23,122,150,270,348,369,377,378,*

FUGITIVE The (1993) Music: JAMES NEWTON HOWARD -S/T-
ELEKTRA (TEN): 7599 61592-2 (CD) see COLL 70,366,

FULL CIRCLE (The Haunting Of Julia) (1976) Music score
COLIN TOWNS -S/T- *KOCH Screen (Koch): 38703-2(CD)*

FULL CIRCLE WITH MICHAEL PALIN (BBC1 31/8/97) music:
by PETER HOWELL + orig music by ELIZABETH PARKER
BBC Radio Coll (Techn): ZBBC 2016 (MC)

FULL METAL JACKET (1987) Songs by various artists
-S/T- *W.BROS (TEN): 925 613-2 (CD) -4 (MC)*
also available with 'CLOCKWORK ORANGE' *on
WARNER ESP: 9362 47517-2 (3CD set)*

FULL MONTY The (1996) Music: ANNE DUDLEY -S/T- *feat:-*
HOT CHOCOLATE-TOM JONES-M.PEOPLE-SERGE GAINSBOURG-
STEVE HARLEY & COCKNEY REBEL-GARY GLITTER-WILSON
PICKETT-IRENE CARA-DONNA SUMMER-SISTER SLEDGE etc
Volume 1 *RCA (BMG): 09026 68904-2 (CD) -4 (MC)*
Volume 2 *RCA (BMG): 74321 60448-2 (CD) -4 (MC)*
see Coll 143,177,

FUN IN ACAPULCO *see* ELVIS PRESLEY INDEX p.360

FUNNY BONES (1995) Music score: JOHN ALTMAN -S/T- on
EDEL UK (Pinn): 002930-2EDL (CD)

FUNNY FACE (1957) Songs: GEORGE & IRA GERSHWIN *with:*
AUDREY HEPBURN-FRED ASTAIRE-KAY THOMPSON-MICHEL
AUCLAIR *VERVE (Univ): 531 231-2 (CD)*

FUNNY GIRL - songs by Jule Styne and Bob Merrill
  1. FILM SOUNDTRACK 1968 *feat:* BARBRA STREISAND -S/T-
    COLUMBIA (Ten): 462 545-2 (CD) -4 (MC)
  2. ORIG BROADWAY CAST 1964 BARBRA STREISAND-JEAN STAP
    LETON-S.CHAPLIN-K.MEDFORD *EMI: ZDM 764661-2 (CD)*
FUNNY LADY (FILM MUSICAL 1975) Songs: JOHN KANDER-FRED
  EBB *featuring:* BARBRA STREISAND -S/T- reissue on
  RCA (BMG): 07822 19006-2 (CD, 09.1998)
FUNNY THING HAPPENED ON THE WAY TO THE FORUM, A
  songs by Stephen Sondheim
  1. FILM 1966 -S/T- re-issue on
    RYKODISC (Vital): RCD 10727 (CD)
  2. ORIG LONDON CAST 1963 FRANKIE HOWERD-ISLA BLAIR-
    KENNETH CONNOR-JOHN RYE-JON PERTWEE-MON.EDDIE GRAY
    LEON GREENE *EMI Angel: CDANGEL3 (CD) DELETED 2.96*
  3. ORIG BROADWAY CAST 62 ZERO MOSTEL-JOHN CARRADINE
    JACK GILFORD-RAYMOND WALBURN-DAVID BURNS and Comp.
    EMI ANGEL: ZDM 764770-2 (CD)
  4. JAZZ VER: TROTTER TRIO *VARESE (Pinn):VSD 5707 (CD)*
FUNNY WOMEN (BBC2 4/10/97) theme "Funny Face" (G.& I.
  I.Gershwin) by FRED ASTAIRE 'FUNNY FACE' -S/-T
  VERVE (Univ): 531 231-2 (CD)
FURY The (1978) Music sc: JOHN WILLIAMS / LONDON S.O.
  -S/T- import *VARESE (Pinn): VSD 5264 (CD)*
G.B.H. (C4 6/6/91) mus: RICHARD HARVEY-ELVIS COSTELLO
  -S/T- music by ELVIS COSTELLO & RICHARD HARVEY
  DEMON (Pinn): DSCD 4(CD) DSCASS 4(MC) DSLP4 (LP)
G.I.BLUES (1960) feat ELVIS PRESLEY remastered -S/T-
  RCA (BMG): 07863 67460-2 (ltd ed) 07863 66960-2
  (CD) -4 (MC) see also ELVIS PRESLEY INDEX p.360
G.I.JANE (1997) Music score: TREVOR JONES -S/T- on
  POLYDOR: 162 109-2 (CD)
GADFLY The (1955) Music Suite Op.97A (D.SHOSTAKOVICH)
  score incl.music from 'FIVE DAYS AND FIVE NIGHTS'
  NAXOS (Select): 8.553299 (CD) recording also on
  CFP (EMI) CDCFP 4463 (CD) -4 (MC)
GADJO DILO (1998) Music score: TONY GATLIF -S/T-
  (VAR.ARTISTS) *LUAKA BOP (TEN): 3984 23045-2 (CD)*
GAELIC GAMES (C4 8/7/95) theme mus "The Celts" (Enya)
  ENYA *WEA (TEN): 4509 91167-2 (CD) WX 498C (MC)*
  also 1993 series "Book Of Days" (Enya-Roma Ryan)
  "Shepherd Moons" *WEA 9031 75572-2(CD)-4(MC)*
GALLIPOLI (1981) *see COLL.78,165,273,*
GAMBLER The (1997) Mus: TCHAIKOVSKY adapt: BRIAN LOCK
  -S/T- *VIRGIN CLASSICS (EMI): VC 545 312-2 (CD)*
GAME The (1997) Music score: HOWARD SHORE song "White
  Rabbit" (G.Slick) performed by JEFFERSON AIRPLANE
  -S/T- *LONDON (Univ): 458 556-2 (CD) -4 (MC)*
GAME OF DEATH (1979) Music score: JOHN BARRY c/w NIGHT
  GAMES (Barry) *SILVA SCREEN (Koch):FILMCD 123 (CD)*
GAME ON (Hat-Trick for BBC2 27/2/95) theme music "When
  I Find My Heaven" by The GIGOLO AUNTS on 'Flippin'
  Out' *FIRE Records (Pinn): FIRECD 35 (CD)* + on
  -S/T- 'DUMB & DUMBER' *RCA (BMG):07863 66523-2 (CD)*

GAMEKEEPER The (BBC1 28/7/95) Music by The IRON HORSE
   -S/T- 'Voice Of The Land'-THE IRON HORSE on *KLUB*
   (Gord.Duncan/Ross/Topic): CD(ZC)LDL 1232 (CD/MC)
GANG RELATED (1998) -S/T- featuring VARIOUS ARTISTS
   PRIORITY-VIRGIN (EMI): CDPTY(PTYMC) 149 (CD/MC)
GANGWAY (1937) md: Louis Levy / 4 songs on 'LOUIS LEVY
   MUSIC FROM T.MOVIES' *EMPRESS KOCH: RAJCD 884 (CD)*
GARDEN The (1990) Music sc: SIMON FISHER TURNER -S/T-
   IONIC (Pinn): IONIC 5C (MC) IONIC 5CD (CD)
GARDEN OF EVIL (1954) Music score: BERNARD HERRMANN
   new record: MOSCOW SYMPHONY ORCH. (W.Stromberg)
   also feat suite from 'PRINCE OF PLAYERS' (1955)
   MARCO POLO (Select): 8.223841 (CD) see COLL.1,
GARDEN OF THE FINZI-CONTINIS The (1970) Music: MANUEL
   DE SICA -S/T- *LEGEND (Silva Screen): OST 125 (CD)*
GARDENER'S WORLD (BBC2/Catalyst) theme music 1993-98
   series by NICK WEBB & GREG CARMICHAEL (ACCOUSTIC
   ALCHEMY) title track from "NATURAL ELEMENTS" on
   GRP (New Note-BMG): GRP 01412 (CD)
GAS FOOD AND LODGING (1992) Music sc: BARRY ADAMSON &
   V.Arts) *IONIC (RTM/Pinn): IONIC 9(C)(CD) (MC/CD)*
GATE TO THE MIND'S EYE The (1994)(Animated) Music by
   THOMAS DOLBY -S/T- *GIANT (BMG):74321 23386-2 (CD)*
GATTACA (1997) Music score: MICHAEL NYMAN -S/T-
   VIRGIN VENTURE (EMI): CDVE 936 (CD) TCVE 936 (MC)
GAZON MAUDIT (FRENCH TWIST) (1995) Music: MANUEL MALOU
   -S/T- *VIRGIN (EMI): CDVIR 49 (CD)*
GBH - see beginning of G's
GENDERQUAKE (C4 9/7/96) op.theme music "Ebben Ne Andro
   Lontano" from 'La Wally' (Catalini) sung by LESLEY
   GARRETT 'DIVA' *S.Screen (Koch): SONGCD 903 (CD)*
GENERAL The (1997) Music sco: RICHIE BUCKLEY songs by
   Var.Artists including VAN MORRISON-BRENDAN GLEESON
   -S/T- *HUMMINGBIRD (Dir/ADA/Polyg): HBCD 0015 (CD)*
GENERAL The (BBC1 6/4/1998) theme mus "The Way It Is"
   BRUCE HORNSBY and The RANGE on 'The Way It Is"
   RCA (BMG): 74321 144421-2 (CD) -4 (MC)
GENERAL HOSPITAL (ITV 70's series) *theme (1)* "Girl In
   The White Coat" DEREK SCOTT *theme (2)* "Red Alert"
   see COLL.243,280,
GENERAL HOSPITAL (USA TV) *see COLL.348,*
GENERAL WITH THE COCKEYED I.D. Music: JERRY GOLDSMITH
   TARAN (Silver Sounds): W.9103 (CD)
GENERAL'S DAUGHTER The (1999) Music by CARTER BURWELL
   -S/T- *MILAN (BMG): 74321 69474-2 (CD)*
GENERATION GAME *see* JIM DAVIDSON'S GENERATION GAME
GENEVIEVE (1953) Music score composed & performed by
   LARRY ADLER "Genevieve Waltz"/"Love Theme"/"Blues"
   'Best Of Larry Adler' *EMI GOLD: CD(TC)MFP 6259*
   "Genevieve Waltz" on *EMI: CD(TC)EMS 1543 (CD/MC)*
GENTLE BEN (USA TV) *see COLL.348,*
GENTLEMEN PREFER BLONDES - songs: Jule Styne-Leo Robin
   1.REVIVAL BROADWAY RECORDING 1995 *with:* K.T.SULLIVAN
   DRG (Pinn): DRGCD (DRGMC) 94762 (CD/MC)

GEORGE OF THE JUNGLE (1997) Music score: MARC SHAIMAN
-S/T- *EDEL-DISNEY (Pinn): 010 444-2DNY (CD)*
see COLL.345,

GERMINAL (1993) Music: JEAN LOUIS ROCQUES with ORCHES
TRE NAT.DE LILLE -S/T- *VIRGIN (EMI) CDVIR 28 (CD)*

GET CARTER (1971) Music score: ROY BUDD -S/T- re-issue
CINEPHILE-CASTLE (Pinn): CINCD 001 (CD) theme also
on *ESSPR 656 (CDs) ESSLP 656 (LP)* theme also on
'THIS IS CULT FICTION ROYALE' *VIRGIN: VTDCD 151*
see COLL.60,360,

GET ON THE BUS (1996) Music s: TERENCE BLANCHARD -S/T-
V/A: STEVIE WONDER-D'ANGELO-A TRIBE CALLED QUEST
CURTIS MAYFIELD *INTERSCOPE/MCA (BMG):IND 90089(CD)*

GET REAL (1997) Music score by JOHN LUNN -S/T- V.Arts.
ARISTA (BMG): 74321 66590-2 (CD)

GET SHORTY (1996) Music score: JOHN LURIE -S/T- V.Arts
US3-BOOKER T.& MG's-MORPHINE-GREYBOY etc.
ANTILLES-ISLAND (Univ): 529 310-2 (CD) -4 (MC)

GET SMART (USA TV 60s) *see COLL.345,363,382,*

GET WELL SOON (BBC1 2/11/97) title theme song "In Over
My Head" by CHRISTIE HENNESSEY sung by ALED JONES
COALITION (TEN): COLA 032CD (CDs) COLA 032C (MC)

GHOST (1990) Music sco: MAURICE JARRE feat "Unchained
Melody" (Alex North-Hy Zaret) - RIGHTEOUS BROTHERS
-S/T- re-issue *MILAN (BMG): 4321 34278-2 (CD)*
see COLL.70,71,106,128,213,266,

GHOST AND MRS.MUIR (1947) Music sco: BERNARD HERRMANN
1-*DEFINITIVE (Discovery): SFCD 33508 (CD)*
2-*VARESE (Pinn): VSD 5850 (CD)*
3-*SILVA SCREEN (Koch): FILMCD 162(CD) see COLL.192,*
4-*SILVA SCREEN (Koch): FILMXCD 308 (2CD) COLL.188,*
5-*VARESE (Pinn): VSD 5937 (CD) COLL.1,*

GHOST AND MRS.MUIR (USA TV) *see COLL.349,*

GHOST AND THE DARKNESS (1997) Music s: JERRY GOLDSMITH
-S/T- *EDEL-HOLLY (Pinn): 012 089-2HWR (CD) COLL.3,*

GHOST IN MONTE CARLO, A (1990) Music: LAURIE JOHNSON
see COLL.215,217,

GHOST SHIP The - *see COLL.398,*

GHOST SQUAD *see COLL.23,365,*

GHOSTBUSTERS (1984) Music sco: ELMER BERNSTEIN Title
song: Ray Parker Jnr. songs by Various Arts -S/T-
ARISTA (BMG) 258720 (CD) see COLL.264,

GHOSTBUSTERS 2 (1989) Music sco: RANDY EDELMAN -S/T-
also includes "Love Is A Cannibal" by Elton John
MCA (BMG): MCD 06056 (CD)

GHOSTS OF THE CIVIL DEAD (1991) Music: NICK CAVE-BLIXA
BARGOED-MICK HARVEY -S/T- *Mute (RTM/Pinn):(-)(CD)*

GI BLUES *see* ELVIS PRESLEY INDEX p.360

GIANT (1956) Music: DIMITRI TIOMKIN suite on 'Western
Film World Of D.Tiomkin' LONDON STUDIO S.ORCH.
(L.Johnson) *U.KANCHANA (H.Mundi) UKCD 2011 (CD)*
also avail: complete score + 'EAST OF EDEN'/'REBEL
WITHOUT A CAUSE' *TSUNAMI (S.Screen):TSU 0201 (CD)*

GIDGET (USA TV) *see COLL.346,*

GIGI - songs by Alan Jay Lerner and Frederick Loewe
  1.FILM MUSICAL 1958 LESLIE CARON-MAURICE CHEVALIER
    -S/T- *42 trks MGM (EMI Premier): CDODEON 10 (CD)*
  2.ORIG LONDON CAST 1985 *w:* SIAN PHILLIPS-BERYL REID-
    AMANDA WARING-JEAN PIERRE AUMONT-GEOFFREY BURRIDGE
    JOHN AARON *FIRST NIGHT (Pinn): OCRCD 6007 (CD)*
    see COLL.42,327,
GILBERT & SULLIVAN OVERTURES LIGHT OPERA PRO-ARTE ORCH
  (Sir M.Sargent) *CFP (EMI): CD(TC)CFP 4529 (CD/MC)*
GILLIGAN'S ISLAND (USA) *see COLL.345,*
GIMME GIMME GIMME (BBC2 08/01/1999) music: PHILIP POPE
  arrang.of "Gimme Gimme Gimme" (Andersson-Ulvaeus)
  TV version unavailable. ABBA version on *POLYDOR*
GIRL 6 (96) PRINCE -S/T- *WEA:9362 46239-2(CD) -4(MC)*
GIRL CRAZY (1943) Songs by GEORGE & IRA GERSHWIN *feat:*
  JUDY GARLAND-MICKEY ROONEY-TOMMY DORSEY ORCHESTRA
  EMI SOUNDTRACKS: CDODEON 30 (CD) new recording on
  VIRGIN (EMI): VM 561247-2 (CD)
GIRL FROM U.N.C.L.E. (USA TV) *see COLL.349,*
GIRL HAPPY *see* ELVIS PRESLEY INDEX p.360
GIRL ON A MOTORCYCLE (1968) Music by LES REED -S/T-
  RPM (Pinn): RPM 171 (CD) also available on
  DAGORED (Cargo/APex/Silver Sounds): RED 108 (LP)
GIRL WHO CAME TO SUPPER The - songs by Noel Coward
  1.NOEL COWARD SINGS HIS SCORE (1963)
    DRG (Pinn): DRGCD 5178 (CD)
GIRL WITH BRAINS IN HER FEET The (1998) Music score by
  ROB LANE -S/T- with VARIOUS ARTISTS inc: TOM JONES
  SYMPOSIUM-SLADE-SWEET-STEREOPHONICS and others
  V2 (Pinn): VVR 100265-2 (CD)
GIRLS GIRLS GIRLS *see* ELVIS PRESLEY INDEX p.360
GIVE MY REGARDS TO BROAD STREET (1984) PAUL McCARTNEY
  J.LENNON -S/T- *EMI:CDP 789 268-2 (CD)*
GLADIATORS (ITV 9/96) theme "Boys Are Back In Town"
  (P.Lynnot) GLADIATORS *RCA (BMG):74321 41699-2 CDs*
  (LWT 10/92 ser) theme by MUFF MURFIN *see COLL.270,*
GLASS MOUNTAIN The (1949) Music sc: NINO ROTA 'Legend
  Of The Glass Mountain' (NINO ROTA) MANTOVANI ORC
  HORATIO NELSON (THE): CDSIV 6128(CD) SIV 1128(MC)
  see COLL.170,387,
GLENN MILLER STORY The (1954) Universal Studio Orch
  -S/T- *MCA (BMG): MCLD 19025 (CD)*
GLOBAL SUNRISE (BBC 1/1/97) Music score: BRIAN BENNETT
  -S/T- *OCEAN DEEP (Grapev/Poly): OCD 002 (CD)*
GLORY (1989) Music score: JAMES HORNER w. Boys Choir
  Of Harlem -S/T- *VIRGIN: CDV(TCV)V 2614 (CD/MC)*
GLORY DAZE (1997) -S/T- featuring VARIOUS GROUPS
  KUNG FU (Greyh-Pinn): 78761-2 (CD) -4 (MC) -1 (LP)
GLORY OF MY FATHER (LA GLOIRE DE MON PERE)(90) Music:
  VLADIMIR COSMA + 'MY MOTHER'S CASTLE' (CHATEAU DE
  MA MERE)(90) -S/T-*Imp (S.Scr) 50050(CD) 40050(MC)*
GO! (1998) VARIOUS ARTS -S/T- *feat* NO DOUBT-LEFTFIELD-
  NATALIE IMBRUGLIA-FATBOY SLIM-AIR and others
  HIGHER GROUND SONY: HIGH 8CD (CD) HIGH 8MC (MC)

GO INTO YOUR DANCE (1935) Film Musical songs: AL DUBIN
   HARRY WARREN *feat* AL JOLSON and RUBY KEELER & Comp
   -S/T- including songs from 'MELODY FOR TWO'/'YOU
   CAN'T HAVE EVERYTHING'/'YOU'LL NEVER GET RICH' on
   GREAT MOVIE THEMES (Target-BMG): CD 60014 (CD)

GODFATHER The (1972) Mus sc: NINO ROTA -S/T- *MCA (BMG)*
   MCLD 19022 (CD) SUITE: *S.Screen (Koch): FILMCD 077*
   see COLL.41,70,71,211,239,298,300,

GODFATHER II (1974) Music sco: NINO ROTA -S/T- *reiss*
   MCA (BMG): MCAD 10232 (CD)

GODFATHER III (1991) M: CARMINE COPPOLA. Theme: NINO
   ROTA. voc, HARRY CONNICK JR -S/T- *SONY: 467 813-2*
   see COLL.79,105,106,274,275,286,

GODFATHER SUITE - The Milan Philharmonic Orchestra
   SILVA SCREEN (Koch): FILMCD (FILMC) 077 (CD/MC)
   CARMINE COPPOLA cond.Milan Philh.Orch music from 3
   GODFATHER Films (Mus: NINI ROTA & CARMINE COPPOLA)

GODMONEY (1997) -S/T-
   V2 (34MV-Pinn): VVR 100060-2 (CD)

GODS AND MONSTERS (1999) Music score: CARTER BURWELL
   -S/T- *RCA (BMG): 09026 63356-2 (CD)*

GODSPELL - songs by Stephen Schwartz
   1. FILM -S/T- 1973 *feat:* VICTOR GARBER-DAVID HASKELL-
      JERRY STOKA-LYNNE THIGPEN-ROBIN LAMONT -*S/T*-
      ARIOLA (S.Screen): ARCD 8337 (CD) ACB6 8337 (MC)
   2. ORIG BROADWAY CAST 1971 *feat:* DAVID HASKELL-LAMAR
      ALFORD-JOHANNE JONAS-ROBIN LAMONT-SONIA MANZANO
      JEFFREY MYLETT-STEPHEN NATHAN and Comp *Orig Cast*
      ARIOLA (S.Screen): ARCD 8304 (CD) ACB6 8304 (MC)
   3. CARLTON SHOWS: GODSPELL / JESUS CHRIST SUPERSTAR
      STUDIO HIGHLIGHTS 1994 Various Arts *CARLTON Shows*
      PWKS 4220 (CD) PWKMC 4220 (MC)
   4. STUDIO RECORDING 1993 JOHN BARROWMAN-CLAIRE BURT
      JACQUELINE DANKWORTH-RUTHIE HENSHALL-GLYN KERSLAKE
      PAUL MANUEL-CLIVE ROWE-SAMANTHA SHAW-DARREN DAY
      <u>Highlights</u>: *SHOWTIME (MCI-THE): SHOW(CD)(MC) 012*
      <u>Complete</u>: *TER (Koch): CDTER 1204 (CD)*

GODZILLA (Film Series) - *see COLL.229,247,248,249,*

GODZILLA (1954-1984) Var.music scores from Japanese
   monster series NEW SYMPHONIC DIGITAL RECORDINGS
   VARESE (Pinn): VSD 5920 (CD)

GODZILLA (1954-1984) Var.music from the TOHO FILMS
   Music by AKIRA IFUKUBE & others
   BEST OF GODZILLA 1 *SILVA SCREEN (Koch): FILMCD 201*
   BEST OF GODZILLA 2 *SILVA SCREEN (Koch): FILMCD 202*

GODZILLA (1998) Music score: DAVID ARNOLD / Var.Arts
   COLUMBIA-SONY (Ten): 489 610-2 (CD) -4 (MC) -8 (MD)

GOING FOR A SONG (BBC1 71) Theme "Prelude" 'The Birds'
   (RESPIGHI) *several classical recordings available*

GOING MY WAY (1944) *feat* BING CROSBY -S/T- select +
   'BORN TO DANCE' *GREAT MOVIE THEMES (BMG): CD 60031*

GOING STRAIGHT (BBC1 24/2/1978) - *see COLL.407,*

GOLD DIGGERS (1995) Music score: JOEL McNEELY -S/T-
   VARESE (Pinn): VSD 5633 (CD)

GOLD DIGGERS OF 1933 (33 MUSICAL) DICK POWELL-RUBY KEEL
ER-JOAN BLONDELL-GINGER ROGERS *includes songs from*
'ROSE OF WASHINGTON SQUARE' and 'THE DOLLY SISTERS'
TARGET (BMG): CD 60009 (CD)

GOLD RUSH The (1925) Music: CHARLES CHAPLIN *see*
'FILM MUS.OF CHARLES CHAPLIN' *RCA: 09026 68271-2*
MAX TAK ORCH *BASTER (Direct): BASTER 309050 (CD)*

GOLDEN APPLE The (MUSICAL 1954) Songs: JEROME MOROSS-
JOHN LATOUCHE *featuring:* PRISCILLA GILLETTE-STEPHEN
DOUGLASS-KAYE BALLARD-JONATHAN LUCAS-JACK WHITING
Broadway Cast Rec. *RCA (BMG): 09026 68934-2 (CD)*

GOLDEN BOY (SHOW 1964) Songs: CHARLES STROUSE-LEE ADAMS
O.BROADWAY CAST feat: SAMMY DAVIS JNR-BILLY DANIELS
PAULA WAYNE-LOUIS GOSSETT-LOLA FALANA-KENNETH TOBEY
RAZOR & TIE (Koch): RE 82202-2 (CD)

GOLDEN EARRINGS (1947) Music score by VICTOR YOUNG *feat*
MURVYN VYE with MARLENE DIETRICH-RAY MILLAND -S/T-
extracts including music from 'GONE WITH THE WIND'
GREAT MOVIE THEMES (Delta-BMG): CD 60050 (CD)

GOLDEN GIRLS The (USA)(C4 1/8/86) Theme "Thank You For
Being a Friend" (Andrew GOLD) *see COLL.350,*

GOLDEN MOUNTAINS (1931) *see COLL.316,*

GOLDEN VOYAGE OF SINBAD (1973) Music sco: MIKLOS ROSZA
Complete score: *PROMETHEUS (S.Screen): PCD 148 (CD)*
see COLL.302,338,

GOLDENEYE - *see* JAMES BOND FILM INDEX p.358
see COLL.54,55,

GOLDFINGER (1964) Mus: JOHN BARRY title song (J.Barry
L.Bricusse-A.Newley) sung by SHIRLEY BASSEY -S/T-
-S/T- *reissue EMI PREMIER (EMI): CZ 557 (CD)*
see COLL.27,28,32,34,36,37,41,53,54,55,204,
see also JAMES BOND FILM INDEX p.358

GOLF (BBC1/2) theme mus "Chase Side Shoot Out" (Brian
Bennett) by BRIAN BENNETT *deleted*

GOMER PYLE (USA TV) *see COLL.346,*

GONDOLIERS The - songs by Gilbert and Sullivan
  1. D'OYLY CARTE OPERA COMPANY - New Symph Orchestra
     (Isadore Godfrey) *LONDON (Univ): 425 177-2 (CDx2)*
  2. NEW SADLERS WELLS OPERA *TER: CDTER2 1187 (2CD)*
  3. PRO-ARTE ORCHESTRA (Malcolm Sargent) & GLYNDEBOURNE
     FESTIVAL CHOIR Soloists: Geraint Evans-Alexander Yo
     ung-Owen Brannigan-R.Lewis *EMI:CMS 764394-2 (2CDs)*

GONE TO TEXAS Music score: DENNIS McCARTHY -S/T- *IMPT.*
IMPRT (Silva Screen): PCD 142 (CD)

GONE WITH THE WIND (1939) Music sco: MAX STEINER -S/T-
with addition.unissued items *digitally re-mastered*
EMI ODEON (EMI): CDODEON 27 (2CD) also available:
National Philharmonic Orchestra (Charles Gerhardt)
RCA RED SEAL (BMG): GD 80452 (CD) GK 80452 (MC)

GONE WITH THE WIND (1939) Music score by MAX STEINER
-S/T- extracts including music & songs from movie
'GOLDEN EARRINGS' (1947) music by VICTOR YOUNG on
GREAT MOVIE THEMES (Delta-BMG): CD 60050 (CD)
see COLL.41,70,90,170,204,228,298,327,

GOOD GUYS The (Thames 3/1/92) mus: DEBBIE WISEMAN
   see *COLL.149,*
GOOD MORNING AND GOODBYE - see 'CHERRY HARRY & RAQUEL'
GOOD MORNING VIETNAM (1988) Music score: ALAN MASON +
   Var.Arts -S/T- *A.& M: CDMID 163 (CD) CMID 163 (MC)*
GOOD NEWS (1947) *feat* JUNE ALLYSON -S/T- selections +
   'COVER GIRL' *GREAT MOVIE THEMES (BMG): CD 60033*
GOOD NEWS! MUSIC THEATRE OF WICHITA Songs B.G.DeSylva
   Lew Brown-Ray Henderson *inc* KIM HUBER-ANN MORRISON
   LINDA MICHELE-MICHAEL GRUBER *TER (Koch):CDTER 1230*
GOOD ROCKIN'TONITE (O.LONDON CAST 1992) *JACK GOOD'S* no
   stalgic look back at the 50's *with* PHILIP BIRD-TIM
   WHITNALL-GAVIN STANLEY-JOE BROWN and Company on
   FIRST NIGHT (Pinn): OCRCD 6026 (MC/CD)
GOOD THE BAD & THE UGLY (1966) Music: Ennio Morricone
   -S/T- *LIBERTY (EMI): CDP 748 408-2 (CD)*
   see *COLL.137,250,251,253,256,258,*
GOOD WILL HUNTING (1997) Music sco: DANNY ELFMAN -S/T-
   feat ELLIOTT SMITH-THE WATERBOYS-GERRY RAFFERTY-
   LUSCIOUS JACKSON-HEART-DANDY WARHOLS-DANNY ELFMAN
   EMI PREMIER SOUNDTRACKS (EMI): 823 338-2 (CD)
GOODBYE AGAIN (1961) Music score: GEORGES AURIC
   see *COLL.82,294,*
GOODBYE GIRL O.LONDON CAST 1996 (Marvin HAMLISCH-Don
   BLACK) *featur* GARY WILMOT-ANN CRUMB and Company
   FIRST NIGHT (Pinn): CASTCD 63 (CD) CASTC 63 (MC)
   FIRST NIGHT (Pinn): SCORECD 44 (CDsingle)
GOOBYE MR.CHIPS (O.CHICHESTER CAST 1979) *w:* JOHN MILLS
   TER (Koch): CDTER 1025 see COLL.9,
GOODFELLAS The (1990) Music score: CHRISTOPHER BROOKS
   "Roses Are Red" (Al Byron-Paul Evans) Bobby VINTON
   -S/T- *ATLANTIC (TEN): 7567 82152-2 (CD)*
GOODNIGHT SWEETHEART (BBC1 18/11/93-1999) title song
   (RAY NOBLE) TV version by NICK CURTIS *unavailable*
   original by AL BOWLLY with RAY NOBLE ORCHESTRA on
   EMI: CDP 794 341-2 (CD) / incidental music by
   Anthony & Gaynor SADLER *unavailable*
   'GOODNIGHT SWEETHEART' and other songs sung by
   ELIZABETH CARLING (Phoebe) recorded on
   UNIVERSAL: 547 548-2 (CD) -4 (MC)
GOODTIME CHARLEY (MUSICAL) Songs: LARRY GROSSMAN & HAL
   HACKADY Broadway Cast *RCA (BMG): 09026 68935-2 CD*
GOOFY MOVIE The (1995) Music: DON DAVIS + V.Artsists
   -S/T- *W.DISNEY (Technic): WD 76400-2 (CD) -4 (MC)*
GORKY PARK (1983) Music sco: JAMES HORNER -S/T- reiss:
   VARESE (Pinn): VCD 47260 (CD)
GOSPEL ACCORDING TO ST.MATTHEW (1964) M: LUIS BACALOV
   and BACH/MOZART/PROKOFIEV *+ excerpts from* 'MISSA
   LUBA' *+ song* "Sometimes I Feel Like A Motherless
   Child" by ODETTA *IMPORT Silva Screen: OST 132 (CD)*
GOTHIC (1987) Music: THOMAS DOLBY feat Screaming Lord
   Byron (Tim Spall) -S/T- *VIRGIN (EMI): CDV 2417*
GOTHIC DRAMAS (1977 Italian TV) mus: ENNIO MORRICONE
   TV -S/T- *DRG/New Note (Pinn): DRGCD 32916 (CD)*

GOVERNESS The (1997) Music sco: EDWARD SHEARMUR -S/T-
   SONY CLASSICS: SK 60685 (CD)
GRADUATE The (1967) Songs: PAUL SIMON & ART GARFUNKEL
   -S/T- *COLUMBIA (Ten): 40-32359 (MC) CD 32359 (CD)*
   also on *SIMPLY VINYL (Telstar): SVLP 39 (LP)*
GRAFFITI BRIDGE (1990) Mus: PRINCE -S/T- *Paisley Park*
   WB (TEN): 759927493-2 (CD) WX(C) 361 (LP/MC)
GRAND The (Gran 4/4/97) orig music: JULIAN NOTT and
   ROGER BOLTON -S/T- incl orig 1920's hits performed
   by NOEL COWARD-HUTCH-SOPHIE TUCKER-PAUL ROBESON
   HAPPY DAYS (BMG-Con): 75605 52291-2 (2CD)
GRAND CANYON (1992) Music score: JAMES NEWTON HOWARD
   -S/T- *MILAN (BMG): 262493 (CD) 412493 (MC)*
GRAND DAY OUT,A (Wallace & Gromit) music: JULIAN NOTT
   v/o PETER SALLIS -S/T- with 'The Wrong Trousers'
   BBC (Techn): ZBBC 1947 (MC) BBC Video: BBCV 5155
   (Grand Fay Out) *BBCV 5155* (Wrong Trousers) *(VHS)*
GRAND NATIONAL (BBC Grandstand) opening music theme
   from film "Champions" 1983 (CARL DAVIS) *DELETED*
GRAND PRIX (BBC 78-96) theme "The Chain" originally
   FLEETWOOD MAC from 'Rumours' *WEA: K2 56344 (CD)*
   from 1997 see F1 (FORMULA 1) (ITV) *see COLL.148,*
GRANDSTAND (BBC1 began 8/10/58 - 1998) *THEME MUSIC*
   1976-98 KEITH MANSFIELD *see COLL.5,148,176,270,*
   1958 "News Scoop" LEN STEVENS *see COLL.7,176,*
GRANGE HILL (BBC1 1978-96) *theme mus (1978-1989)*
   "Chicken Man" (ALAN HAWKSHAW) *see COLL.363,*
   1990-2000 theme PETER MOSS *unavailable*
GRASS HARP The (USA BROADWAY MUSICAL PLAY)
   ORIG BROADWAY CAST *VARESE (Pinn): VSD 6010 (CD)*
GREASE - songs by Jim Jacobs-Warren Casey-Gibb Bros
   John Farrar-Louis St.Louis-S.Simon and others
   1.FILM MUS.1978 JOHN TRAVOLTA-OLIVIA NEWTON JOHN
     FRANKIE VALLI-STOCKARD CHANNING-FRANKIE AVALON
     POLYDOR (Univ): 044041-2 (CD) 044041-4 (MC) and
   2.O.LONDON CAST 1993 CRAIG McLACHLAN-DEBBIE GIBSON
     VOYD EVANS & Co *Epic (SM): 474 632-2 (CD) -4 (MC)*
   3.STUDIO RECORD 1994 JOHN BARROWMAN-SHONA LINDSAY
     ETHAN FREEMAN-MARK WYNTER & Company
     <u>Highlights</u>: *SHOWTIME (MCI-THE): SHOW(CD)(MC) 007*
     <u>Complete</u>: *TER (Koch): CDTER 1220 (CD)*
     see also Tele-Tunes 1995 p.188 for other records
   4.CARLTON SHOWS COLL (Studio 93) CARL WAYNE-MICHAELA
     STRACHAN *CARLTON: PWKS(PWKMC) 4176 (CD/MC)*
   5.NEW BROADWAY CAST 1994 *RCA (BMG): 09026 62703-2 CD*
   6.STUDIO RECORDING VARIOUS ARTISTS *HALLMARK (CHE):*
     30395-2 (CD) -4 (MC)
   7.ALL THE HIT SONGS VARIOUS ARTISTS
     CASTLE PIE (Pinn): PIESD 078 (CD)
GREAT CARUSO The (1950) Sung by MARIO LANZA   *RCA GOLD*
   SEAL (BMG): GD(GK)(GL) 60049 (CD/MC/LP)
GREAT COMPOSERS The (BBC2 7/12/1998) CLASSICAL MUSIC
   SELECTION *TELDEC/BBC/WARNER: 3984 21856-2 (2CD)*

GREAT DAY IN HARLEM, A (1995) Various Arts / spin-off
CD (not -S/T-) inc.tracks by ART BLAKEY-GENE KRUPA
DUKE ELLINGTON-DIZZY GILLESPIE-COUNT BASIE-CHARLES
MINGUS etc. on *SONY JAZZ (SM): 460500-2 (CD)*

GREAT ESCAPE The (1962) Mus sco: ELMER BERNSTEIN -S/T-
reiss RYKODISC (Vital): RCD 10711 (CD, 09.1998)
New recording by ROYAL SCOTTISH NATIONAL ORCHESTRA
conducted and produced by ELMER BERNSTEIN on
RCA VICTOR (BMG): 09026 63241-2 (CD)
also on *INTRADA USA (Koch Int): MAFCD 7025 (CD)*
see COLL.41,70,198,202,

GREAT EXPECTATIONS (BBC1 12/04/1999) Mus: PETER SALEM
BBC WORLDWIDE (Pinn): WMSF 6012-2 (CD)

GREAT EXPECTATIONS (1997) Music score: PATRICK DOYLE
-S/T- incl.songs by TORI AMOS-REEF-IGGY POP
ATLANTIC (TEN): 7567 83058-2 (CD) -4 (MC)

GREAT EXPECTATIONS (ORIG CAST THEATR CLWYD, MOLD 1993)
Songs: MIKE READ Adap:Christopher G.Sandford *feat*
DARREN DAY-CHRIS CORCORAN-ELIZABETH RENEHAN-TAMARA
USTINOV *TER (Koch): CDTER 1209 (CD)*

GREAT MUPPET CAPER The (1981) Mus & Songs: JOE RAPOSO
feat JIM HENSON-FRANK OZ-DAVE GOELZ -S/T- *ARISTA
KIDZ (BMG): 74321 18246-2 (CD) 74321 18246-4 (MC)*

GREAT ROCK AND ROLL SWINDLE (1980) Music: SEX PISTOLS
-S/T- *full VIRGIN (EMI): TCVD 2510(2MC) CDVD 2510
(2CDs) highlights: OVED 234 (LP) OVEDC 234 (MC)*

GREAT TRAIN ROBBERY (FIRST) - see COLL.108,167,

GREATEST AMERICAN HERO (USA TV) see COLL.347,

GREATEST SHOW ON EARTH The (1952) Music score: VICTOR
YOUNG *NEW RECORDING by* MOSCOW SYMPHONY ORCHESTRA
+ *suites from* 'THE UNINVITED'/'GULLIVER'S TRAVELS'
MARCO POLO (Select): 8225063 (CD)

GREATEST STORY EVER TOLD (1960) Music s: ALFRED NEWMAN
-S/T- *RYKODISC (Vital): RCD 10734 (CD)*

GREEN ACRES (USA TV) see COLL.256,345,

GREEN CARD (1991) Music score HANS ZIMMER -S/T-
VARESE (Pinn): VSD 5309 (CD) VSC 5309 (MC)

GREEN HORNET The (USA TV) see COLL.311,346,382,

GREENWICH MEAN TIME (1998) Music score: GUY SIGSWORTH
-S/T- (VAR.ARTISTS) *ISLAND (Univ): CID 8092 (CD)*

GREENWILLOW (ORIG N.Y.CAST 1960) Songs: FRANK LOESSER
feat: ANTHONY PERKINS-CECIL KELLAWAY-PERT KELTON-
ELLEN McKOWN-WILLIAM CHAPMAN-GROVER DALE *on*
DRG USA (Pinn): DRGCD 19006 (CD)

GREY FOX The (1982) Music score: MICHAEL CONWAY -S/T-
DRG (Pinn): CDSL 9515 (CD) see COLL.88,

GREYSTOKE: THE LEGEND OF TARZAN LORD OF THE APES
(1984) see COLL.86,

GRIDLOCK'D (1997) Mus score: STEWART COPELAND -S/T- on
MERCURY (Univ): 534 684-2 (CD) -4 (MC)

GRIND (O.BROADWAY CAST 1985) Songs (LARRY GROSSMAN and
ELLEN FITZHUGH) *with* Ben Vereen-Leilani Jones & Co
TER (Koch): CDTER 1103 (CD)

GRIZZLY ADAMS - *see* 'LIFE AND TIMES OF GRIZZLY ADAMS'

GROSSE POINT BLANK (1997) Music sco: JOE STRUMMER -S/T-
   (Various Artisrs) *LONDON (Univ): 828 867-2 (CD)*
GROUND FORCE (BBC2 19/07/1997) theme mus.by JIM PARKER
   performed by The BLACK DYKE MILLS BAND
   -S/T- *BBC MUSIC (Pinn): WMSF 6015-2 (CD) -4 (MC)*
GROUNDHOG DAY (1092) Music score: GEORGE FENTON -S/T-
   Imp: CB 53760 (CD) deleted / see COLL.105,271,388,
GROUPIE GIRL (1970) Various Artists -S/T- *reissue with*
   'BEYOND THE VALLEY OF THE DOLLS' (1970) V.Artists
   SCREEN GOLD (Greyhound): SGLDCD 0010 (CD)
GROWING PAINS (BBC1 16/5/92) theme music: NIGEL HESS
   see COLL.193,350,
GULLIVER'S TRAVELS (1939) Music score by VICTOR YOUNG
   NEW RECORDING by MOSCOW SYMPHONY ORCHEST.*+ suites*
   from 'THE UNINVITED'/'THE GREATEST SHOW ON EARTH'
   MARCO POLO (Select): 8225063 (CD)
GULLIVERS TRAVELS (C4 7/4/96) mus score: TREVOR JONES
   -S/T- *RCA IMPT (Silva Screen): RCA 68475-2 (CD)*
GUMBY SHOW The (USA TV) *see COLL.348,*
GUMMO (1998) VARIOUS ARTISTS -S/T- on
   DOMINO (Vital): WIGCD 052 (CD)
GUN LAW (also known as GUN SMOKE)(USA 55-75)
   theme music (Koury-Spencer) *see GUNSMOKE*
GUNS OF NAVARONE The (1961) Music sco: DIMITRI TIOMKIN
   -S/T- suite on *U.KANCHANA: DKPCD 9047 (CD) DELETED*
   see COLL.71,384,
GUNSMOKE *see COLL.348,*

GUYS AND DOLLS - songs by Frank Loesser
  1.REV.LONDON N.THEATRE CAST 1982: IAN CHARLESON-JULIE
    COVINGTON-DAVID HEALY-BOB HOSKINS-JULIA McKENZIE
    reiss MFP (EMI): CD(TC)MFP 5978 (CD/MC)
  2.ORIG BROADWAY CAST 1950 ROBERT ALDA-VIVIENE BLAINE
    STUBBY KAYE *MCA: MCLD 19155 / MCAD(MCAC) 10301*
  3.NEW BROADWAY CAST 1991 Walt Bobbie-John Carpenter-
    Steve Ryan-Ernie Sabella-Herschel Sparber
    RCA (BMG): 09026 61317-2(CD) -4(MC) -5(DCC)
  4.CARLTON SHOWS COLLECT.1995 DENNIS LOTIS-BARBARA
    WINDSOR-KEITH MICHELL-BERNARD CRIBBINS and Company
    CARLTON SHOWS Collect: 30362 0013-2 (CD) -4 (MC)
  5.STUDIO RECORDING 1995 EMILY LOESSER-GREGG EDELMAN
    TIM FLAVIN-DAVID GREEN-KIM CRISWELL-DON STEPHENSON
    <u>Complete:</u> *TER (Koch): CDTER 1228 (CD)*
    <u>Highlights:</u> *SHOWTIME (MCI-THE): SHOW(CD)(MC) 034*
  6.Songs by FRANK LOESSER / 'The Best Of'
    VARIOUS ARTISTS *EMPORIO (Disc): EMPRCD 802 (CD)*
  7.REPRISE MUSICAL REPERTORY THEATRE
    REPRISE (TEN): 9362 45014-2 (CD)
GYPSY - songs by Jules Styne and Stephen Sondheim
  1.ORIG BROADWAY CAST 1959 *w.*ETHEL MERMAN and Company
    COLUMBIA (S.Screen): CK 32607 (CD) JST 32607 (MC)
  2.ORIG LONDON CAST 1973 ANGELA LANSBURY-DEBBIE BOWEN
    JUDY CANNON-ZAN CHARISSE-BARRIE INGHAM on *RCA IMP*
    (Silva Screen): 60571-2 (CD) 60571-4 (MC)

HACKERS (1996) Music score: SIMON BOSWELL -S/T- *feat:*
STEREO MCs-ORBITAL-LEFTFIELD-UNDERWORLD-PRODIGY...
EDEL-CINERAMA (Pinn): 002256-2 CIN (CD)
HADLEIGH (Yorkshire 29/10/69-76) theme mus: TONY HATCH
see COLL.4,184,281,
HAIR - songs by Galt McDermott-Jerome Ragni-James Rado
  1.1979 Film Cast, Re-mastered 20th anniv.edition)
    RCA (BMG): 07863 67812-2 (CD)
  2.ORIG BROADWAY CAST 1968 STEVE CURRY-RONALD DYSON
    MELBA MOORE *RCA Victor (BMG): BD 89667 (CD)*
  3.ORIG LONDON CAST 1968 PAUL NICHOLAS-VINCE EDWARDS
    OLIVER TOBIAS *POLYDOR (Univ): 519 973-2 (CD)*
  4.REV. LONDON CAST 1993 *w:* PAUL HIPP-JOHN BARROWMAN-
    SINITTA-PEPSI LAWRIE DEMACQUE-ANDRE BERNARD-FELICE
    ARENA-PAUL J.MEDFORD *EMI: CDEMC 3663(CD) delet.96*
  5.CARLTON SHOWS COLLECTION 1995 CARL WAYNE-NICOLA
    DAWN-BOBBY CRUSH-JOHN HOWARD *prod:* Gordon Lorenz
    CARLTON Shows Collect: 30362 0015-2 (CD) -4 (MC)
  6.STUDIO RECORDING - SHOWS COLLECTION
    SHOWTIME (Disc): SHOWCD 055 (CD)
HAIR BEAR BUNCH (USA 1971) "Help It's The Hair Bear
  Bunch'(H.Curtain-Roland-Williams) *see COLL.373,*
HALF COCKED (1995) *feat* VARIOUS ARTISTS -S/T- *MATADOR
(Vital): OLE 152-2 (CD) -1 (LP)*
HALLOWEEN (THE BEST OF HALLOWEEN 1-6) S/track Master
  VARESE (Pinn): VSD 5773 (CD)
  see COLL.51,62,121,208,309,
HALLOWEEN 1 (1978) Music sc: JOHN CARPENTER -S/T- Imp
  VARESE USA (Pinn): VSD 5970 (CD) & VCD 47230 (CD)
HALLOWEEN 2 (1981) Music sco: JOHN CARPENTER -S/T- Imp
  VARESE USA (Pinn): VCD 47152 (CD)
HALLOWEEN 3 (1983) Mus: ALAN HOWARTH-J.CARPENTER -S/T-
  VARESE (Pinn): VSD 5243 (CD)
HALLOWEEN 4 (1988) Music sco: ALAN HOWARTH -S/T- Impt
  VARESE (Pinn): VSD 5205 (CD) see COLL.63,
HALLOWEEN 5 (1989) Music sco: ALAN HOWARTH -S/T- Impt
  VARESE (Pinn): VSD 5239 (CD) see COLL.63,
HALLOWEEN 6 (1995) Music score: ALAN HOWARTH -S/T-
  VARESE (Pinn): VSD 5678 (CD)
HAMISH MACBETH (BBC1 Scot 26/3/95) series music by
  JOHN LUNN *see COLL.270,*
HAMLET (1948) Music score: WILLIAM WALTON inc.mus.from
  'As You Like It' *CHANDOS (Chandos): CHAN 8842 (CD)*
  see COLL.173,
HAMLET (1964 USSR) Music: SHOSTAKOVICH score performed
  by BELGIAN RADIO SYMPHONY ORCHESTRA (Shostakovich)
  RCA Navigator Classics (BMG): 74321 24212-2 (CD)
  see COLL.299,315,316,
HAMLET (1990) Music score ENNIO MORRICONE -S/T-
  VIRGIN (EMI): CDVMM 3 (CD) see COLL.91,165,
HANA-BI (1998) Music score: JOE HISAISHI -S/T- on
  MILAN (BMG): 74321 57396-2 (CD)
HANCOCK (BBC1 60's) theme mus: DEREK SCOTT
  see COLL.4,23,367,369,

HAND THAT ROCKS THE CRADLE (1991) Music: GRAEME REVELL
   -S/T- *reiss EDEL-HOLLYWOOD (Pinn): 013 304HWR (CD)*
HANDFUL OF DUST, A (1988) Music score: GEORGE FENTON
   -S/T- *OCEAN DISQUE (Pinn): CDLTD 071 (CD)*
   also *DRG (Pinn): DRGCD 6110 (CD)*
HANDMAID'S TALE The (1990) Music sco: RYUICHI SAKAMOTO
   -S/T- *GNP (ZYX): GNPD 8020(CD) GNP-5 8020(MC)*
HANGED MAN The (ITV 1975) Music score: ALAN TEW feat:
   BULLET -S/T- *DC Records (Vital): DC 015(CD)(LP)*
HANGING GARDEN The (1998) Music score: JOHN ROBY -S/T-
   VIRGIN (EMI): CDVIR 72 (CD)
HANGOVER SQUARE (1945) Music score: BERNARD HERRMANN
   Suite on 'CONCERTO MACABRE' *KOCH INT: 37609-2 (CD)*
   -S/T- with 'HATFUL OF RAIN'/'ON DANGEROUS GROUND'
   TSUNAMI (S.Screen): TCI 0610 (CD) see COLL.189,387
HANNAH 1939 (ORIG USA CAST) Songs: BOB MERRILL
   TER (Koch): CDTER 1192 (CD)
HANNAH AND HER SISTERS (1986) Music: COUNT BASIE Orch
   + HARRY JAMES ORCH -S/T- *MCA (BMG): IMCAC 6190(MC)*
   see COLL.74,77,81,
HANNAY (ITV 06/01/1988) music: DENIS KING *see COLL.19,*
HANS ANDERSEN - songs by Frank Loesser
   1. FILM MUSICAL 1952 *feat:* DANNY KAYE 'Very Best Of
   MCA (BMG): MCLD 19049 (CD) MCLC 19049(MC) also on
   VARESE (Pin): VSD 5498 (CD) inc 'THE COURT JESTER'
   2. ORIG LONDON CAST 1974/77 TOMMY STEELE-SALLY ANN
   HOWES-ANTHONY VALENTINE-SIMON ANDREWS-LILA KAYE-
   MILO O'SHEA-COLETTE GLEASON-BOB TODD *reiss on 1CD*
   DRG-New Note (Pinn): DRGCD 13116 (CD)
HAPPY DAYS (USA 74 / re-run C4 27/2/89) *orig opening*
   theme "Rock Around The Clock" (Jimmy De Knight-Max
   Freedman) BILL HALEY & THE COMETS *MCA Rec (BMG)*
   Title theme "Happy Days" (Norman Gimbel-Chas Fox)
   PRATT & McLAIN *see COLL.270,347,*
HAPPY TRAILS (USA TV) *see COLL.345,*
HARBOUR LIGHTS (BBC1 18/02/1999) theme and score by
   JOE CAMPBELL and PAUL HART *unavailable*
HARD BOILED (1993) music score: MICHAEL GIBBS -S/T-
   IONIC-MUTE (RTM-Pinn): IONIC 11CD (CD)
HARD DAY'S NIGHT (1964) *Sgs* JOHN LENNON-PAUL McCARTNEY
   BEATLES & GEORGE MARTIN -S/T- *PARLOPHONE EMI:*
   CDP 746 437-2 (CD) PCS 3058 (LP) TCPCS 3058 (MC)
HARD RAIN (1998) Music by CHRISTOPHER YOUNG.conductor:
   PETE ANTHONY -S/T- *MILAN (BMG): 74321 56425-2 (CD)*
HARD TARGET (1993) Music score: GRAEME REVELL -S/T- on
   VARESE (Pinn): VSD 5445(CD) see COLL.87,
HARDCASTLE AND McCORMICK (USA TV) *see COLL.17,283,350,*
HARDER THEY COME The (1971) Music & songs: JIMMY CLIFF
   -S/T- *MANGO ISLAND: RRCD 11 (CD) RRCT 11 (MC)*
HARDY BOYS & NANCY DREW MYSTERIES (USA) *see COLL.350,*
HARMAGEDDON (1982) Music score by KEITH EMERSON -S/T-
   VOLCANO (Cargo): CPC 83003 (CD)
HARPIST The (1997) Music score: BRIAN BENNETT -S/T-
   OCEAN DEEP (Grapevine/Polyg): OCD 011 (CD)

HARRY AND THE HENDERSONS (USA 90 BBC1 27/9/91) theme "Your Feet's Too Big" (Ada Benson-F.Fisher & Ink Spots) TV vers.sung by LEON REDBONE *unavailable* INK SPOTS on *FLAPPER (Pinn): PASTCD 9757 (CD)*

HARRY ENFIELD'S TELEVISION PROGRAMME (BBC2 2/4/1992) mus: KATE ST.JOHN additional music by SIMON BRINT *BBC (Techn): ZBBC 15877CD (2CD)*

HARRY'S GAME (Yorkshire 25/10/82) music: PAUL BRENNAN CLANNAD 'Ultimate Coll.' *(BMG) 74321 48674-2 (CD)* see COLL.155,262,270,356,

HARRY'S MAD (Central 4/1/93) mus: NIGEL BEAHAM POWELL-BELLA RUSSELL *SPOK.WORD MC BBC (Tech):YBBC 1395*

HART TO HART (USA TV) see COLL.347,

HARUM SCARUM - see ELVIS PRESLEY FILM INDEX p.360

HARVEST (Regain) (1937) Music: ARTHUR HONEGGER suite on *MARCO POLO (Select): 8.223467 (CD)*

HARVEY GIRLS The (1946) Songs: HARRY WARREN-JOHNNY MERCER *feat:* JUDY GARLAND-RAY BOLGER-JOHN HODIAK -S/T- *reissue: EMI PREMIER: CDODEON 11 (CD)*

HATARI! (62) Music: HENRY MANCINI see COLL.71,238,

HAUNTED (1995) Music score: DEBBIE WISEMAN -S/T- *SILVA SCREEN (Koch): TRXCD 2002 (CD)*

HAUNTED SUMMER (1989) Music: CHRISTOPHER YOUNG -S/T- *SILVA SCREEN (Koch): FILMCD 037 (CD) see COLL*

HAUNTING The (1999) Music score: JERRY GOLDSMITH *VARESE (Pinn): VSD 6054 (CD)*

HAV PLENTY (1998) VARIOUS ARTISTS -S/T- on *EPIC (Ten): 491 004-2 (CD) -4 (MC)*

HAVE GUN-WILL TRAVEL (USA 57) "The Ballad Of Paladin" (Richard Boone-J.Western-S.Rolfe) JOHNNY WESTERN 'Americana' *COLUMB Ten 468121-2 (CD)* see COLL.346,

HAVE I GOT NEWS FOR YOU (BBC2 28/9/90-1998 theme tune performed by BIG GEORGE see COLL.407,

HAWAII 5-0 (USA 1968-80) theme music: MORTON STEVENS see COLL.2,109,110,121,270,281,344,345,359,382,

HAWAIIAN EYE (USA TV) see COLL.346,

HAZARD OF HEARTS, A (1987) Music by LAURIE JOHNSON see COLL.215,217,

HE GOT GAME (1998) Music score: AARON COPLAND -S/T- score: *SONY CLASSICS: SK 60593 (CD)* -S/T- songs: *MERCURY (Univ): 558 130-2 (CD)*

HE'S GOT THE GAME (1998) Mus: AARON COPLAND songs by PUBLIC ENEMY -S/T- *MERCURY: 558 130-2 (CD) -4(MC)*

HEAD (1968) Music performed by The MONKEES featuring: MICKEY DOLENZ-DAVY JONES-MIKE NESMITH-PETER TORK -S/T- *RHINO/ATLANTIC (TEN): 4509 97659-2 (CD)*

HEADS AND TAILS (BBC TV) see COLL.186,

HEAR MY SONG (1991) Music: JOHN ALTMAN Josef Locke's v/o VERNON MIDGLEY -S/T- *WEA: 7599 24456-2 (CD) -4 (MC)* JOSEF LOCKE recordings are on 'Hear My Song' *EMI: CDGO 2034 (CD) TCGO 2034 (MC)*

HEART CONDITION (1990) Music score: PATRICK LEONARD song "Have A Heart" sung by Bonnie Raitt from 'Nick Of Time' *CAPITOL EMI: CD(TC)EST 2095 (CD/MC)*

HEART IN WINTER, A (Un Coeur En Hiver) (1991) Music sc
    (Philippe Sarde)'Sonata for Piano,Violin & Cello'
    (RAVEL) Complete mus *ERATO (TEN): 4509 92408-2(CD)*
    see COLL.85,
HEART OF DARKNESS (1992) Music score: BRUCE BROUGHTON
    INTRADA-BALTIC (Silver Sounds): MAF 7085 (CD)
HEART OF MIDNIGHT (1988) Music score: YANNI -S/T-
    SILVA SCREEN (Koch): FILMCD 119 (CD) see COLL.51,
HEARTBEAT (YTV 10/4/92) theme "Heartbeat" (N.Petty-Bob
    Montgomery) TV version sung by NICK BERRY
    'HEARTBEAT THE GOLD COLLECTION' (Various Artists)
    GLOBAL TV (BMG): RADCD 90 (2CD) RADMC 90 (MC)
    see COLL.109,110,270,
HEARTBREAK HIGH (Aust.94/BBC2 27/9/94) Various Music
    -S/T- *WEA (TEN): 4509 99938-2 (CD)*
HEARTBREAKERS (1984) Music sco: TANGERINE DREAM -S/T-
    SILVA SCREEN (Koch): FILMCD 163 (CD)
HEARTBURN (1986) *see COLL.86,*
HEARTS AND SOULS (1993) Music score: MARC SHAIMAN
    -S/T- *MCA (S.Screen): MCAD(MCAC) 10919 (CD/MC)*
HEAT (1995) mus: ELLIOT GOLDENTHAL *WEA: 9362 46144-2*
HEAT AND DUST (1982) *see COLL.77,*
HEATHCLIFF - songs by John Farrar and Tim Rice
    1.LIVE 1996 RECORDING *feat* CLIFF RICHARD *with* HELEN
      HOBSON-SARA HAGGERTY and GORDON GILTRAP *(guitar)*
      EMI UK: CD(TC)EMD 1099 (2CD/MC)
    2.STUDIO ALBUM 1995 *featuring* CLIFF RICHARD *with*
      OLIVIA NEWTON JOHN-KRISTINA NICHOLS and others
      EMI: CD(TC)EMD 1091 (CD/MC)
HEAVENLY CREATURES (1994) Music: PETER DASENT + V.Art
    -S/T- *MILAN (BMG): 253 502-2 (CD)*
HEAVEN'S GATE (1980) Music score by DAVID MANSFIELD
    -S/T- *reissue RYKODISC (Vital): RCD 10749 (CD)*
    see COLL.121,401,
HEAVEN'S PRISONERS (1995) Music score: GEORGE FENTON
    -S/T- (songs) *CODE BLUE-WEA: 7567 82848-2 / -4*
    -S/T- (score) *DEBONAIR (Pinn): CDDEB 1004 (CD)*
HEAVY (1994) Music score: THURSTON MOORE -S/T- on
    CINERAMA-EDEL (Pinn): 0022642CIN (CD)
HEAVY METAL (1981) Mus.sco: ELMER BERNSTEIN + V/A:
    SAMMY HAGAR-RIGGS-DEVO-CHEAP TRICK-DONALD FAGEN-
    CHEAP TRICK-BLACK SABBATH-NAZARETH-JOURNEY-
    STEVIE NICKS -S/T- *reiss.COL.(Ten): 486 749-2 (CD)*
HEAVY TRAFFIC (1973) Music sco: ED BOGAS-RAY SHANKLIN-
    CHARLES EARLAND -S/T- inc 'Fritz The Cat' score on
    FANTASY (Pinn): FCD 24745 (CD)
HEIDI (1968) Music score: JOHN WILLIAMS -S/T- *Imp.on*
    COLUMBIA USA (Silva Screen): LXE 707 (CD)
HELLO AGAIN (1987) Music sco: WILLIAM GOLDSTEIN -S/T-
    MULTIMEDIA IMP (Silver Sounds): 7956 76005-2 (CD)
HELLO DOLLY - songs by Jerry Herman /
    1.FILM MUSICAL 1969 -S/T- *featur* BARBRA STREISAND
      CASABLANCA (S.Screen): 810368-2 (CD) -4 (MC)
    2.SHOWS COLLECT. *CARLTON: 30362 0025-2 (CD) -4 (MC)*

HELLO GIRLS (BBC1 5/9/1996) theme "Busy Line" (Murray
   Semos-Frank Stanton) *sung by* BBC CAST *unavailable*
HELLRAISER (1987) Music score: CHRISTOPHER YOUNG -S/T-
   S.SCREEN (Koch): FILMCD 021(CD) see COLL 309,
HELLRAISER 2 'Hellbound' (1988) Mus: CHRISTOPHER YOUNG
   -S/T- GNP (ZYX): GNP(C)(D) 8015 (LP/MC/CD)
HELLRAISER III 'Hell On Earth'(92) Music: RANDY MILLER
   *-S/T- (SCORE) GNP (ZYX): GNPD 8233 (CD) GNP5
   8233 (MC)* (SONGS) *S.Screen: 480007-2(CD) -4(MC)*
HELLRAISER IV: BLOODLINE (95) Music sco: DANIEL LICHT
   feat Northwest Sinfonia and Chorus (Pete Anthony)
   -S/T- SILVA SCREEN (Koch): FILMCD 179 (CD)
HELP (1965) Songs: JOHN LENNON-PAUL McCARTNEY -S/T-
   EMI: CDP 746 439-2 (CD) TC-PCS 3071 (MC) PCS (LP)
HEMINGWAY'S ADVENTURES OF A YOUNG MAN (1962) Music by
   FRANZ WAXMAN 'Sayanora' *BMG: 09026 662657-2 (CD)*
HENRY FOOL (1998) Music score: HAL HARTLEY -S/T- on
   ECHO STATIC (Cargo-Greyhound): ECHO 105 (CD)
HENRY PORTRAIT OF A SERIAL KILLER (1990) Music by JOHN
   McNAUGHTON-KEN HALE -S/T- *QDK (SRD):EFA 11910 (CD)*
HENRY V (1944) music by WILLIAM WALTON / *NEW RECORDING*
   RTE ORCHESTRA (Andrew Penny) narr.by MICHAEL SHEEN
   and ANTON LESSER *NAXOS (Select): 8553343 (CD)*
   see COLL.90,173,291,
HENRY V (1944) Music sco: WILLIAM WALTON *sel:* 'WALTON
   FILM MUSIC' LONDON PHILHARM.ORCH cond: CARL DAVIS
   EMI:CDM 565585-2 (CD) also BOURNEMOUTH SYMPH.ORCH.
   (Litton) *LONDON DECCA (Univ): 448 134-2(CD)*
HENRY V (1989) Music sco: PATRICK DOYLE C.B.S.O.(Simon
   Rattle) -S/T- *EMI: CDC(EL) 749919-2 (CD) -4(MC)*
   see COLL.74,299,
HENRY VIII (C4 15/3/1998) m: ADRIAN THOMAS *see COLL.19,*
HENRY'S CAT (BBC 1984) *see COLL.186,*
HERCULES (1997, WALT DISNEY) Music: ALAN MENKEN -S/T-
   DISNEY-EDEL (Pinn): WD 60864-2 (CD) **see COLL.130,**
   see also WALT DISNEY FILM INDEX p.362
HERCULES The Legendary Journeys (TV 95) mus sc: JOSEPH
   LoDUCA -S/T- *VARESE (Pinn): VSD 5660 (CD,Vol.1)
   VSD 5884 (CD,Vol.2) VSD 6032 (CD, Vol 3) VSD 5983
   (CD, 'Young Hercules')   see COLL.38,122,312,*
HERE COME THE WAVES (1945 MUSICAL) *feat* BING CROSBY +
   BETTY HUTTON *incl.songs from* 'BATHING BEAUTY' and
   'THIS GUN FOR HIRE' *TARGET (BMG): CD 60001 (CD)*
HERE WE GO ROUND THE MULBERRY BUSH (1967) Mus: STEVIE
   WINWOOD and The SPENCER DAVIS GROUP -S/T- re-iss:
   RYKODISC (Vital): RCD 10717 (CD)
HERE'S HARRY (BBC1 1960s) theme music "Comedy Hour"
   by IVOR SLANEY *see COLL.5,*
HETTY WAINTHROP INVESTIGATES (BBC1 3/1/96) ser.theme
   music by NIGEL HESS *on* 'A-Z OF BRITISH TV THEMES
   VOL.3' *PLAY IT AGAIN (Koch): PLAY 010 (CD) and*
   'WORLD OF SOUND' *BBC Worldw (Koch): 33635-2 (CD)*
   see COLL.6,193,407,
HEY LOVE ORIG USA CAST - *VARESE (Pinn): VSD 5772 (CD)*

HEY MR.PRODUCER! (C4 00/12/1998) CAMERON MACKINTOSH
    TRIBUTE CONCERT SUMMER 1998 with VARIOUS ARTISTS
    FIRST NIGHT (Pinn): ENCORE CD 9 (2CD, 10.1998)
HI-LO COUNTRY The (1997) Music score: CARTER BURWELL
    -S/T- *TVT (USA IMPORT) TVT 8290 (CD)*
HIDDEN IN SILENCE Music score: DENNIS McCARTHY -S/T-
    IMPRT *(Silva Screen): PCD 142 (CD)*
HIDEAWAY (1994) Music score: TREVOR JONES -S/T- on
    INOIC-MUTE/RTM (Disc): IONIC 12CD (CD)
HIDEOUS KINKY (1998) Music score: JOHN KEANE -S/T-
    incl.songs by JEFFERSON AIRPLANE-RICHIE HAVENS-
    INCREDIBLE STRING BAND-CANNED HEAT-NICK DRAKE- +
    Moroccan Music by JILL JALALA-KHALIFA OULD EIDE
    SILVA SCREEN (Koch): FILMCD 311 (CD)
HIDER IN THE HOUSE (1989) Music sc: CHRISTOPHER YOUNG
    -S/T- *INTRADA USA (Silva Screen): MAF 7007D (CD)*
HIGH AND THE MIGHTY The Music score: DIMITRI TIOMKIN
    RCA (BMG): 09026 62658-2 (CD)   see COLL.70,129,
HIGH ART (1997) Music by SHUDDER TO THINK -S/T- on
    REEL SOUNDS (Pinn): 63467 79735-2 (CD)
HIGH CHAPARRAL The (USA BBC1 67) music: DAVIS ROSE
    see COLL.178,349,
HIGH NOON (1952) Music score: DIMITRI TIOMKIN suite on
    'Western Film World Of D.Tiomkin' LONDON STUDIO SO
    (L.Johnson) *UN.KANCHANA (H.Mundi) UKCD 2011 (CD)*
    Song "Do Not Forsake Me" sung by TEX RITTER
    BEAR FAMILY: BCD 15625 (CD)   see COLL.260,358,368,
HIGH ROAD TO CHINA (1984) Music sco: JOHN BARRY -S/T-
    SOUTHERN CROSS (Hot): SCCD 1030 (CD)
HIGH SCHOOL HIGH (1996) Music: IRA NEWBORN *-S/T- feat*
    The BRAXTONS-BRAIDS-FAITH EVANS-JODECI and others
    BIG BEAT/EAST WEST (TEN): 7567 92709-2(CD) -4(MC)
HIGH SOCIETY - songs by Cole Porter
    1.FILM MUSICAL 1956 SOUNDTRACK *inc* BING CROSBY-GRACE
    KELLY-FRANK SINATRA-CELESTE HOLM and Company -S/T-
    CAPITOL EMI: CDP 793787-2 (CD)
    2.CARLTON SHOWS COLLECTION 1994 Studio Recording
    KENNY BALL & HIS JAZZMEN-DENNIS LOTIS-CARL WAYNE-
    TRACY COLLIER *CARLTON Shows : PWKS(PWKMC) 4193*
    3.ORIGINAL BROADWAY REVIVAL CAST 1998
    DRG (Pinn): DRGCD 19011 (CD)
HIGH SPIRITS (1988) Music score: GEORGE FENTON -S/T-
    GNP (ZYX) GNPD 8016 (CD) GNP5 8016 (MC)
HIGH SPIRITS (O.LONDON CAST 1964) Songs (Tim Gray-Hugh
    Martin) *inc.*Cicely Courtneidge-Dennis Quilley-Jack
    Waters-Marti Stevens *DRG (Pinn): CDSBL 13107 (CD)*
HIGH VELOCITY (1977) Music sco: JERRY GOLDSMITH -S/T-
    PROMETHEUS (Silva Screen): PCD 134 (CD)
HIGHER AND HIGHER (1943 MUSICAL) *inc* FRANK SINATRA-MEL
    TORME-VICTOR BORGE *includ.songs from* 'STEP LIVELY'
    TARGET (BMG): CD 60004 (CD)
HIGHLANDER (1986) Music score: MICHAEL KAMEN Songs by
    by Queen (6 from 'A Kind Of Magic' inc. title trk
    PARLOPHONE: (TC)EU 3509 (MC/LP) CDP 746267-2 (CD)

HIGHLANDER: Final Dimension (1994) Mus: PETER ROBINSON
  -S/T- *Edel (Pinn): EDL 28892 (CD)*
HIGHLANDER (TV series 1992) theme song "Princes Of The
  Universe" by QUEEN from album 'A Kind Of Magic'
  EMI: CDP 746 267-2 (CD)
HIGHWAY PATROL (USA TV 1950's) *see COLL.348,*
HIGHWAY TO HEAVEN (USA)(ITV 7/6/87) theme: DAVID ROSE
  see COLL.17,350,
HILARY AND JACKIE (1998) Music sc: BARRINGTON PHELOUNG
  -S/T- *SONY CLASSICS: SK 60394 (CD)*
HILL STREET BLUES (USA TV 1980) Music by MIKE POST
  O.TV -S/T- *SILVA SCREEN (Koch): SILVAD 3510 (CD)*
  see COLL.17,109,110,169,270,283,347,360,390,
HIP-HOP YEARS The (C4 23/09/1999) 'The Hip Hop Years
  -Music from the Channel 4 Series' (VARIOUS ARTS)
  VIRGIN-COLUMBIA/C4 (Ten): MOOD(CD)(C)66 (2CD/2MC)
HIPPIES (BBC2 12/11/1999) theme composed & performed
  by SIMON BRINT *unavailable*
HISTORY OF ALTERNATIVE COMEDY (BBC2 10/01/1999) theme
  music by DAVE STEWART *unavailable*
HISTORY OF MR.POLLY (1949) Music score: WILLIAM ALWYN
  Suite from film played by London Symphony Orch
  (Richard Hickox) on *CHANDOS: CHAN 9243 (CD)*
HITCHER The (1986) Music score: MARK ISHAM -S/T-
  SILVA SCREEN (Koch): FILMCD 118 (CD) see COLL
HITCHHIKERS GUIDE TO THE GALAXY (BBC2 81) *theme*: TIM
  SOUSTER *other mus*: PADDY KINGSLAND *BBC:ZBBC 1035*
  (MC set) BBCCD 6001(CD set)
HITLER (1961) Mus: HANS J.SALTER + mus. 'BLACK SHIELD
  OF FALWORTH' (54) 'INCREDIBLE SHRINKING MAN' (57)
  INTRADA (Koch): MAF 7054CD (CD) see COLL
HMS BRILLIANT (BBC1 26/7/95) music: JOHN HARLE. title
  theme "Light" sung by SARAH LEONARD *see COLL.182,*
HMS PINAFORE - (operetta) songs by Gilbert & Sullivan
  1.New Sadlers Wells 87 NIKOLAS GRACE-LINDA ORMISTON
    Highlights: *SHOWTIME (MCI-THE): SHOW(CD)(MC) 022*
    Complete: *TER (Koch): CDTER 1150 (2CD)*
  2.D'OYLY CARTE OPERA COMPANY - New Symphony Orchest
    (I.Godfrey) *LONDON (Univ): 414 283-2 (CDx2)*
  3.PRO-ARTE ORCH Malcolm Sargent GLYNDEBOURNE FESTIV.
    CHOIR +'TRIAL BY JURY' *EMI: CMS 764397-2 (2CD)*
HOBSON'S CHOICE (1953) Music sco: MALCOLM ARNOLD suite
  +other MALCOLM ARNOLD works *KOCH Int: 37266-2 (CD)*
  Suite 'Film Music' London Symphony Orch (Richard
  Hickox) *CHANDOS: CHAN 9100 (CD) see COLL.20,*
HOFFA (1992) Music sco: DAVID NEWMAN -S/T- on *FOX IMPT*
  (Silva Screen): FOX 11001-2 (CD) FOX 11001-4 (MC)
HOGAN'S HEROES (USA TV) *see COLL.346,*
HOLBY CITY (BBC1 12/01/1999) theme music composed and
  performed by KEN FREEMAN *unavailable*
HOLIDAY (BBC1 series from autumn 1999) theme music by
  STEVE BROWN *unavailable*
  (BBC1 series 1992-1999) theme by PAUL HARDCASTLE
  on 'FIRST LIGHT' *CONNOISSEUR COLL: NSPCD 516 (CD)*

HOLIDAY IN MEXICO (1946) *feat* JANE POWELL-XAVIER CUGAT
    plus 'WEEKEND IN HAVANA' selections on
    GREAT MOVIE THEMES (BMG): CD 60036 (CD)
HOLIDAY INN (1942) *feat* BING CROSBY & FRED ASTAIRE
    with 'TWO FOR TONIGHT' & 'ROAD TO MOROCCO'
    GREAT MOVIE THEMES (Target-BMG): CD 60027 (CD)
HOLIDAY PARK (C5 08/01/1999) music by COLIN WILLSHER
    unavailable
HOLIDAY REPS (BBC1 13/11/97) theme m "There She Goes"
    The LA'S *GO DISCS (Univ): 828 202-2 (CD) -4 (MC)*
HOLIDAY SWAPS (BBC1 12/04/1999) title theme music
    "Marvellous" LIGHTNING SEEDS from 'Jollification'
    COLUMBIA Sony: 477 237-2 (CD) -4 (NC)
HOLLY VS.HOLLYWOOD (1997) Music score: DOUGLASS FAKE
    -S/T- *INTRADA (USA): MAF 7082 (CD)*
HOLLYOAKS (Mersey Productions/C4 23/10/95) theme mus
    STEVE WRIGHT-GORDON HIGGINS *unavailable*
HOLLYWOOD CANTEEN (1944) VARIOUS -S/T- SELECTION on
    GREAT MOVIE THEMES (Targ-BMG): CD 60024 (CD)
HOLLYWOOD HOTEL (1937 MUSICAL) *w:* DICK POWELL-ROSEMARY
    & LOLA LANE *includ.songs from* 'FLYING DOWN TO RIO'
    TARGET (BMG): CD 60008 (CD)
HOME ALONE (1990) Music: JOHN WILLIAMS *see COLL.404,*
HOME ALONE 2 (1992) -S/T- Music sore by JOHN WILLIAMS
    ARISTA (BMG): 07822 11000-2(CD) -4
HOME ALONE 3 (1999) Music score: NICK GLENNIE SMITH
    -S/T- *EDEL-HOLLYWOOD (Pinn): 012138-2HWR (CD)*
HOME AND AWAY (Australia)(ITV from 13/2/1989) -S/T-
    theme by MIKE PERJANIK sung by KAREN BODDINGTON
    & MARK WILLIAMS *MUSHROOM (Pinn.Imps): D.93463 (CD)*
    MUSIC FROM THE TV SER.*S.T.W.(Pinn): STW 19CD (CD)*
    see COLL.150,270,376,
HOME FOR THE HOLIDAYS (1995) Music score: MARK ISHAM
    -S/T- feat V.Arts *MERCURY (Univ): 528 871-2 (CD)*
HOMEBOY (1988) Music score: ERIC CLAPTON-MICHAEL KAMEN
    -S/T- *VIRGIN (EMI): CDV 2574 (CD)*
HOMEGROWN (1996) Music score by TREVOR RABIN -S/T- on
    IMPORT (Silver Sounds): 7801 63365-2 (CD)
HOMEWARD BOUND (1993) Music sco: BRUCE BROUGHTON -S/T-
    INTRADA (Silva Screen): MAF 7041D (CD)
HOMICIDE: LIFE ON THE STREET (USA/C4 15/11/93) theme
    LYNN F.KOWAL + incid.score JEFF RONA *unavailable*
HONEY I BLEW UP THE KID (1992) Music: BRUCE BROUGHTON
    -S/T- *INTRADA (Koch/S.Screen): MAFCD 7030 (CD)*
HONEYMOONERS The (USA TV) *see COLL.346,*
HONG KONG PHOOEY (USA TV) *see COLL.349,373,*
HOODLUM (1996) Music score: ELMER BERNSTEIN -S/T-
    INTERSCOPE (BMG): INTD 90131 (CD)
HOOK (1991) *see COLL.175,201,338,403,404,*
HOOSIERS (1987) - *see* BEST SHOT
HOPALONG CASSIDY (USA TV) *see COLL.348,*
HOPE AND GLORY (BBC1 22/06/1999) CLASSICAL MUSIC -S/T-
    -S/T- *BBC MUSIC (Pinn): WMSF 6014-2 (CD)*

HOPE FLOATS (1998) Music score: DAVE GRUSIN
  -S/T- score: *RCA VICTOR (BMG): 09026 63255-2 (CD)*
  -S/T- songs: *EMI PREM: 493 402-2 (CD) -4 (MC)*
HORIZON (BBC2) title music: WILFRED JOSEPHS other mus
  ELIZABETH PARKER (BBC Radiop.Workshop) *unavailable*
  individual programme music details on request from
  MIKE PRESTON MUSIC
HORNBLOWER (ITV 7/10/1998) Music score: JOHN KEANE
  unavailable
HORRORS OF THE BLACK MUSEUM *see COLL.208,209,*
HORSE OF THE YEAR SHOW (BBC1) theme: "A Musical Joke"
  in F (K.522) 'Musikalischer Spass' 4th mm (MOZART)
  see COLL.148,
HORSE SOLDIERS (1959) Music: DAVID BUTTOLPH / score
  with 'DUAL AT DIABLO' (1966, NEAL HEFTI score)
  TARAN (Silver Sounds): W 9105 (CD)
HORSE WHISPERER The (1998) Music score: THOMAS NEWMAN
  -S/T- score *EDEL-HOLLYWOOD (Pinn): 012137-2 (CD)*
  -S/T- songs *UNIVERSAL (BMG): UMD 80503 (CD)*
HORSEMAN ON THE ROOF The (1995) Music sco: JEAN CLAUDE
  PETIT -S/T-*AUVIDIS-TRAVELLING (H.Mundi): 1139-2 CD*
HOSPITAL WATCH (BBC1 17/8/1986) theme "La Serenissima"
  (Gian P.Reverberi-L.Giordano) by RONDO VENEZIANO
  'Venezia 2000' *BMG Italy (Discovery): 610 299 (CD)*
  also on 'Scaramucce' *BMG (Discovery): 610 193 (CD)*
HOSTAGE (C4 10/01/1999) music by DAVID FERGUSON
  unavailable
HOT MIKADO (ORIG LONDON CAST 1995) *feat:* SHARON BENSON
  LAWRENCE HAMILTON-ROSS LEHMAN-PAULETTE IVORY & Co
  FIRST NIGHT (Pinn): OCRCD 6048 (CD)
HOT MILLIONS (1968) Music score: LAURIE JOHNSON
  see COLL.215,217,
HOT SHOE SHUFFLE (ORIG AUSTRALIAN CAST 1993) *inc* DAVID
  ATKINS-RHONDA BURCHMORE-JACK WEBSTER-TAP BROTHERS
  FIRST NIGHT (Pinn): OCRCD 6046 (CD)
HOT SHOTS (1991) Music score: SYLVESTER LEVAY -S/T-
  VARESE (Pinn): VSD 5338 (CD)
HOT SPOT The (1991) Music sco: JACK NITZSCHE + V/A
  -S/T- *ANTILLES (IMS): F.846 813-2 (CD)*
HOT TO TROT (1988) *see COLL.79,*
HOTEL DU NORD (1938) Music score by MAURICE JAUBERT
  selection on *AUVIDIS (Harmonia Mundi): K.1502 (CD)*
HOUR OF THE GUN (1967) Music score: JERRY GOLDSMITH
  -S/T- *INTRADA (Koch/Silva Screen): MAFCD 7020 (CD)*
HOUSE OF AMERICA (1997) Music score: JOHN CALE -S/T-
  EMI SOUNDTRACKS (EMI); PRMDCD 29 (CD)
HOUSE OF FRANKENSTEIN (1944) Music sco: HANS SALTER &
  PAUL DESAU *new rec:* MOSCOW SYMPH.ORCH.(Stromberg)
  MARCO POLO (Select): 8.223748 (CD) see COLL.357,
HOUSE ON HAUNTED HILL (1999) Music score by DON DAVIS
  -S/T- *VARESE (Pinn): VSD 6088 (CD)*
HOUSE ON SONORITY ROW (1985) Music: RICHARD BAND -S/T-
  INTRADA (S.Screen): MAF 7046D (CD) also cont
  ains -S/T- to 'THE ALCHEMIST' by RICHARD BAND

HOUSE PARTY 2 (1993) Music by Various Artists -S/T-
   MCA (BMG): MCLD 19246 (CD)
HOW DO YOU WANT ME (BBC2 24/2/1998) theme mus "Love's
   The Only Thing That's Real" and incidental music
   composed & performed by MICHAEL STOREY *unavailable*
HOW GREEN WAS MY VALLEY (1941) Music sco: ALFRED NEWMAN
   -S/T- *FOX-ARISTA (BMG): 07822 11008-2 (CD)*
HOW STELLA GOT HER GROOVE BACK (1998) VAR.ARTS -S/T-
   MCA (BMG): MCD 11806 (CD)
HOW THE WEST WAS WON (1962) Music score: ALFRED NEWMAN
   -S/T- *deleted / see COLL.73,358,400,401,*
HOW TO SUCCEED IN BUSINESS WITHOUT REALLY TRYING 1967
   Music: NELSON RIDDLE with songs by FRANK LOESSER
   RYKODISC (Vital): RCD 10728 (CD)
HOW TO BE A PLAYER (DEF JAM'S) (1997) VARIOUS ARTISTS
   DEF JAM (Univ): 537 973-2 (CD) -1 (2LP)
HOWARD GOODALL'S CHOIR WORKS (C4 8/3/1998)
   HOWARD GOODALL with Various Choirs and soloists
   ASV (Select): CDCCA 1028 (CD)
HOWARDS END (1992) Music score: RICHARD ROBBINS -S/T-
   NIMBUS (Nimbus): NI 5339 (CD) NC 5339 (MC)
HOWARDS' WAY (BBC1 1/9/85-25/11/90) theme: SIMON MAY-
   LESLIE OSBORNE / SIMON MAY ORCH "Barracuda" theme
   "Always There" sung by MARTI WEBB *see COLL.407,*
HOWDY DOODY! (USA TV) *see COLL.345,*
H.R.PUF'N STUFF (USA TV) *see COLL.349,*
HUCKLEBERRY HOUND (USA TV) *see COLL.373,*
HUDSON HAWK (1991) Music: MICHAEL KAMEN-ROBERT KRAFT
   -S/T- *VARESE (Pinn): VSD 5323 (CD)*
HUMAN JUNGLE The (ITC 63/C4 87) theme: BERNARD EBBING
   HOUSE by JOHN BARRY ORCH *see COLL.5,28,378,*
HUMAN TRAFFIC (1999) CLUB MUSIC -S/T- by PETE TONG +
   PRIMAL SCREAM-ORBITAL-PUBLIC ENEMY-PETE HELLER-
   UNDERWORLD-C.J.BOLLAND *FFRR (Uni): 556 109-2 (CD)*
HUMORESQUE (1946) Mus.score: FRANZ WAXMAN.*new record*
   LONDON SYMPHONY ORCHESTRA conduct: ANDREW LITTON
   feat: NADJA SALERNO-SONNENBERG (violin)
   NONESUCH-WB (TEN): 7559 79464-2 (CD)
HUNCHBACK OF NOTRE DAME The (1939) Mus: ALFRED NEWMAN
   Suite by MOSCOW SYMPHONY ORCH.& CHORUS (William T.
   Stroberg) 'BEAU GESTE' (1939) 'ALL ABOUT EVE' (39)
   MARCO POLO (Select): 8.223750 (CD)
HUNCHBACK OF NOTRE DAME (1996, Disney) Mus ALAN MENKEN
   Lyr STEPHEN SCHWARTZ *song* "Someday" by ETERNAL
   EMI FIRST AVENUE: CDEMS 439 (CDs) TCEM 439 (MC)
   -S/T- *W.DISNEY (Technic): WD 77190-2 (CD) -4(MC)*
   see also WALT DISNEY FILM INDEX p.362
HUNDRED ACRES, A (Antelope West/C4 23/2/90) theme by
   NIGEL HESS *see COLL.149,193,*
HUNGER The (1982) Music: MICHAEL RUBINI-DENNY JAEGER+
   music "Lakme" (DELIBES) "Solo Cello Suites" (BACH)
   VARESE (Pinn): VSD 47261(CD) -S/T- also available
   MILAN (BMG): CDCH 004 (CD) inc.'THE YEAR OF LIVING
   DANGEROUSLY' *see COLL.159,208,309,*

HUNT FOR RED OCTOBER The (1989) Music: BASIL POLEDOURIS
-S/T- *MCA (BMG): MCLD 19306 (CD) see COLL*
HUNTER (USA77)(ITV 5/85) mus: MIKE POST-PETE CARPENTER
see COLL.17,283,350,
HUNTERS: THE WORLD OF PREDATORS AND PREY (Discovery 95)
Mus: The RESIDENTS -S/T- *MILAN (BMG): 31169-2 (CD)*
HUNTING OF THE SNARK The (O.LONDON CAST 1991) Songs by
MIKE BATT.   Kenny EVERETT-David McCALLUM-Veronica
HART-John PARTRIDGE *FIRST NIGHT (Pinn): CASTCD 24*
HUNTING VENUS (ITV 31/03/1999) starring MARTIN CLUNES
TV -S/T- COLUMBIA (Ten): 494 300-2 (CD) -4 (MC)
HURLYBURLY (1998) Music score: DAVID BAERWALD -S/T-
USA INPORT: WILL 33658 (CD)
HURRICANE (1979) Music sc: NINO ROTA score select.with
'THIS ANGRY AGE' *LEGEND (S.Screen): LEGENDCD 22*
HURRICANE STREETS (1998) Music score: THEODORE SHAPIRO
-S/T- (VAR.ARTISTS) *POLYDOR (Univ): 557 067-2 (CD)*
HYPERSPACE (Film) Music score: DON DAVIS on *PROMETHEUS*
(S.Screen): PCD 120 (CD) also contains SUITE FROM
TV SERIES 'BEAUTY AND THE BEAST'
I AIM AT THE STARS (1960) Music score: LAURIE JOHNSON
see COLL.215,217,
I BURY THE LIVING (1957) *see under* 'RETURN OF DRACULA'
I DREAM OF JEANNIE (USA 60s) *see COLL.345,363,*
I KNOW WHAT YOU DID LAST SUMMER (1997) Mus: JOHN DEBNEY
-S/T- *incl:* KULA SHAKER-TOAD THE WET SPROCKET-TYPE
O NEGATIVE-SOUL ASYLUM-FLICK-ADAM COHEN-OFFSPRING-
COLUMBIA (Ten): 488 663-2 (CD) 488 663-2 (MC)
I LOVE LUCY (USA 1950s) *see COLL.256,345,*
I LOVE MY WIFE (O.BROADWAY CAST) Songs by CY COLEMAN-
MICHAEL STEWART *DRG (Pinn): CDRG 6109 (CD)*
I LOVE YOU PERFECT (TVM 1989) Music score: YANNI -S/T-
SILVA SCREEN (Koch): FILMCD 122 (CD) see COLL
I LOVE YOU YOU'RE PERFECT NOW CHANGE (USA REVUE 1996)
O.CAST RECORDING *VARESE (Pinn): VSD 5771 (CD)*
I MARRIED JOAN (USA TV) *see COLL.346,*

I REMEMBER MAMA (MUSICAL 1985) Songs: Richard Rodgers
Martin Charnin *World premiere record* Sally Anne
HOWES-George HEARN-Ann MORRISON-Sian PHILLIPS-Gay
SOPER-Patricia ROUTLEDGE *TER (Koch): CDTER 1102*
I SPY (USA TV) *see COLL.337,372,*

I STILL KNOW WHAT YOU DID LAST SUMMER (1998) Music sco:
JOHN FRIZZELL -S/T- (VARIOUS ARTISTS) on
WARNER (TEN): 9362 47276-2 (CD) -4 (MC
I WALK THE LINE (1970) Music by JOHNNY CASH and CARL
PERKINS *with* 'LITTLE FAUSS AND BIG HALSY' (1970)
BEAR FAMILY (Rollercoaster): BCD 16130 (2CD)
I WANT TO LIVE (1958) Music score: JOHN MANDEL -S/T-
feat: SHELLEY MANNE-GERRY MULLIGAN-RED MITCHELL etc
RYKODISC (Votal): RCD 10743 (CD)
I WENT DOWN (1997) Music score: DARIO MARIANELLI -S/T-
OCEAN DEEP (Grapevine-Polyg): OCD 008 (CD)

IBIZA UNCOVERED (SKY1 6/7/97) theme mus "Magic Carpet
    Ride" by The MIGHTY DUB KATZ on *LONDON-FRR (Univ):
    FCD 306(CDs) FX 306(12"s)* / 'IBIZA UNCOVERED' with
    V/A (Vol.1) *VIRGIN: VTDCD 168 (2CD) VTDMC 168 (MC)*
    V/A (Vol.2) *VIRGIN: VTDCD 202 (2CD) VTDMC 202 (MC)*
    IBIZA UNCOVERED: THE RETURN *VTDCD(MC) 255 (2CD/MC)*
ICE HOUSE The (BBC1 05/04/1997) Music score by
    DAVID FERGUSON *see COLL.151,*
ICE SKATING (BBC 1978-98) theme "Mornings At Seven" by
    JAMES LAST ORCH 'By Request' *POLY: 831 786-2 (CD)*
ICE STORM The (1996) Music: MYCHAEL DANNA -S/T- V.ARTS
    VELVET (Pinn): VEL 79713-2 (CD)
IDLE HANDS (1998) VARIOUS ARTISTS -S/T-
    TIMEBOMB (Cargo): 43526 (CD)
IF (1968) Music sco: MARC WILKINSON *score unavailable
    also used* "African Sanctus" from 'MISSA LUBA'
    (Congolese African Mass) available version on
    PHILIPS (Univ): 426 836-2 (CD) -4 (MC)
IF YOU CAN'T STAND THE HEAT (C4 06/10/1999) ser.title
    music by JIM MEACOCK *unavailable*
IGNATIO (Film) Music VANGELIS -S/T- *813 042-2 (CD)*
I'LL DO ANYTHING (1993) Music score HANS ZIMMER -S/T-
    VARESE (Pinn): VSD 5474 (CD)
I'LL FLY AWAY (USA TV) *see COLL*
IL POSTINO - *see* 'POSTMAN The'
ILLUSTRATED MAN The (1969) Music sco: JERRY GOLDSMITH
    TARAN (Silver Sounds): W.9102 (CD)
I'M GETTING MY ACT TOGETHER AND TAKING IT ON THE ROAD
    Songs: Nancy Ford-Gretchen Cryer O.LOND.CAST 1981
    DIANE LANGTON-BEN CROSS *TER (Koch): CDTER 1006*
I'M NO ANGEL (1933) *see COLL.399,*
IMAGINE - THE MOVIE (1988) Mus: JOHN LENNON -S/T- *EMI:
    CDP 790 803-2 (CD) TCPCSP 722 (MC) PCSP 722 (LP)*
IMMORTAL BELOVED (1994) Mus.extr.(Beethoven-Rossini)
    LONDON S.O.(Sir George Solti) + other arts -S/T-
    Sony: SK 66301 (CD) SM 66301 (MD) see COLL
IMPOSTERS The (1998) Music score: GARY DE MICHELE
    -S/T- V.ARTISTS *RCQ (BMG): 09026 63172-2 (CD)*
IN AN OUT (1997) Music score: MARC SHAIMAN -S/T- V/A
    MOTOWN (Univ): 530 841-2 (CD)
IN CUSTODY (1993) Trad.Indian Music by ZAKIR HUSSAIN-
    USTAD SULTAN KHAN -S/T- *EMI: CDQ 5550972(CD)*
IN DREAMS (1998) Music score: ELLIOT GOLDENTHAL -S/T-
    VARESE (Pinn): VSD 6001 (CD)
IN HARM'S WAY - *see COLL.384,*
IN LIKE FLINT (1967) Music score: JERRY GOLDSMITH also
    includes score to 'OUR MAN FLINT'
    VARESE (Pinn): VSD 5935 (CD)
IN LOVE AND WAR (1958) Music sco: HUGO FRIEDHOFER Symp
    honic Suite - National Philh.Orch (Fred Steiner)
    'The Kentuckian' *PREAMBLE (S.Scr) PRCD 1777 (CD)*
IN SEARCH OF HAPPINESS (BBC1 15/10/95) theme arrangem.
    of SIDNEY BECHET'S "Si Tu Vois Ma Mere" by
    BIG GEORGE *unavail* / orig: *VOGUE Imp: 600026 CD*

IN THE ARMY NOW (1993) Music score: ROBERT FOLK -S/T-
  INTRADA (Silva Screen): MAF 7058CD (CD)
IN THE BLOOD (BBC2 13/5/96) t.mus: GILES SWAYNE -S/T-
  RYKODISC (Vital): RCD 20172(CD) RACS 20174(MC)
IN THE GRIP OF THE SPIDER (*aka* WEB OF THE SPIDER)(72)
  Music (Riz Ortolani) inc 'CONFESSIONS OF A POLICE
  CAPTAIN' (71-Italy) *OST (S.Screen): OST 114 (CD)*
IN THE HEAT OF THE NIGHT (1967) Music sc: QUINCY JONES
  title sung by RAY CHARLES -S/T- inc.mus.from 'THEY
  CALL ME MR.TIBBS' *RYKODISC (Vital): RCD 10712 (CD)*
  also on TARAN (Silver Sounds): W.9106 (CD)
  see COLL.351,
IN THE LINE OF DUTY (IV) Music score: MARK SNOW -S/T-
  INTRADA (Koch Int): MAFCD 7034 (CD)
IN THE MOUTH OF MADNESS (1994) Music: JOHN CARPENTER
  -S/T- *DRG USA (Pinn): DRGCD 12611 (CD)*
IN THE NAME OF THE FATHER (1993) Music: TREVOR JONES
  -S/T- *ISLAND (Univ): IMCD 208 (CD) ICT 8026 (MC)*
IN TOO DEEP (1998) Music score: CHRISTOPHER YOUNG
  -S/T- (songs) *COLUMBIA (Ten): 495 295-2 (CD)*
  -S/T- (score) *VARESE (Pinn): VSD 6072 (CD)*
IN TOWN TONIGHT (BBC 1950s) *see COLL.57,147,172,*
INCOGNITO (1996) Music score by JOHN OTTMAN -S/T-
  RCA (BMG): 09026 68971-2 (CD)
INCREDIBLE HULK The (USA 1978) theme mus: JOE HARNELL
  see COLL.17,281,311,350,
INCREDIBLE SHRINKING MAN The (1957) mus: FRED CARLING
  & ED LAWRENCE + 'CREATURE FROM THE BLACK LAGOON
  (54) 'HITLER'(61) 'BLACK SHIELD OF FALWORTH' (54)
  INTRADA (Koch): MAF 7054CD (CD) see COLL.309,357,
INCREDIBLE TRUE ADVENTURES OF TWO GIRLS IN LOVE (1996)
  M: TERRY DAME -S/T-*Milan (BMG): 74321 33743-2 (CD)*
INDEPENDENCE DAY (1996) Music sco: DAVID ARNOLD -S/T-
  RCA-20th Century Fox (BMG): 09026 68564-2 (CD)
  see COLL.49,71,199,229,249,267,310,329,371,389,
INDIANA JONES & THE LAST CRUSADE (1989) Music score:
  JOHN WILLIAMS -S/T- *WB (TEN): K925883-2(CD) -4(MC)*
  see COLL.175,201,403,404,
INDIANA JONES & THE TEMPLE OF DOOM (1984) Music: JOHN
  WILLIAMS *see COLL.175,201,*
INDIFFERENT The (1988) Music score: ENNIO MORRICONE
  ENNIO MORRICONE *sel: RCA (BMG): 74321 31552-2 (CD)*
INFERNO (1980) Music score: KEITH EMERSON -S/T- reiss
  CINEVOX (Koch/Silva Screen): CDMF 3060 (CD)
INFINITY (1996) Music score: BRUCE BROUGHTON -S/T- on
  INTRADA Import (Silva Screen): MAF 7072 (CD)
INFORMER The (1935) *see* 'STREETCAR NAMED DESIRE'

INN OF THE SIXTH HAPPINESS The (1958) Mus sco: MALCOLM
  ARNOLD Suite on 'Film Music' London Symphony Orch
  (R.Hicox) *CHANDOS: CHAN 9100 (CD)*
INNOCENT The (L' Innocente) (1976) Music score: FRANCO
  MANNINO -S/T- score includes 'THE STRANGER'
  DRG (Pinn): DRGCD 3292-2 (CD)

INNOCENT SLEEP The (1995) Music sco: MARK AYRES cond.by
Nic Raine / vocalist LESLEY GARRETT -S/T-
SILVA SCREEN (Koch): FILMCD 167 (CD)
INSIDE OUT (USA MUSICAL) Songs: ADRYAN RUSS / O.CAST
RECORDING on *DRG (Pinn): DRGCD 19007 (CD)*
INSIDE THE LORDS (BBC2 03/01/1999) music by RON DE JONG
unavailable
INSPECTOR GADGET (USA TV) *see COLL.347,*
INSPECTOR MORSE (ITV 1987-93) theme:BARRINGTON PHELOUNG
Collection reissue: 'INSPECTOR MORSE III' theme and
incidental classical music selection on
VIRGIN (EMI): CDVIP 178 (CD) TCVIP 178 (MC)
'PASSION OF MORSE' BARRINGTON PHELOUNG compilat. +
'Politician's Wife'/'Truly Madly Deeply'/'Saint-Ex'
TRING Int (Tring): TRING 003 (CD) MCTRING 003 (MC)
'ESSENTIAL INSPECTOR MORSE COLLECTION' *VIRGIN
(EMI): VTCD 62 (CD) VTMC 62 (MC)*
see COLL.109,110,149,262,356,390,
INSPECTOR PITT MYSTERIES (ITV 23/9/1998) Orig.music
comp.& conduct.by CHRISTOPHER GUNNING *unavailable*
INSPECTOR WEXFORD - *see* 'RUTH RENDELL MYSTERIES The'
INSTINCT (1999) Music score by DANNY ELFMAN -S/T- on
VARESE (Pinn): VSD 6041 (CD)
INTERNATIONAL ATHLETICS - *see* ATHLETICS
INTERNATIONAL DETECTIVE *see COLL.6,*
INTERNATIONAL SHOWJUMPING *see* HORSE OF THE YEAR
INTERNATIONAL TENNIS (BBC Maj.Competitions) "Brave New
World" from 'War Of The Worlds' (JEFF WAYNE)
SONY CDX (40)96000 (MC/CD) see also WIMBLEDON
INTERVIEW WITH THE VAMPIRE (1994) M: ELLIOT GOLDENTHAL
-S/T- *GEFFEN (BMG): GED 24719 (CD)*
INTO THE WOODS (MUSICAL) Songs by STEPHEN SONDHEIM
Orig.London Cast 1990 *feat:* IMELDA STAUNTON-JULIA
McKENZIE-JACQUELINE DANKWORTH-ANN HOWARD-RICHARD
DEMPSEY-NICHOLAS PARSONS-CLIVE CARTER and Company
RCA Victor (BMG): RD 60752 (CD)
INTOLERANCE (Film Silent 1916 D.W.Griffiths) New Score
by CARL DAVIS played by Luxembourg Symphony Orch
(Carl Davis): *PROMETHEUS (S.Screen): PCD 105 (CD)*
INVADERS The (USA 66) theme music: DOMINIC FRONTIERE
(USA TV) *see COLL.310,349,*
INVADERS FROM MARS (1986) *see COLL.264,*
INVASION: EARTH (BBC1 8/5/1998) Music score and theme
compsed and performed by RICHARD G.MITCHELL
-S/T- *BBC-MCI (DISC-Pinn): MPRCD 009 (CD)*
INVENTING THE ABBOTT (1997) Music sco: MICHAEL KAMEN
-S/T- *COLOSSEUM (Pinn): CST 348062 (CD)*
INVESTIGATION OF A CITIZEN ABOVE SUSPICION (1970) Mus
score ENNIO MORRICONE -S/T- with IL GIOCATTOLO Imp
CINEVOX ITALY (S.Screen): CDMDF 311 (CD)
INVISIBLE MAN RETURNS (1940) Music score: HANS SALTER
FRANK SKINNER *new recording* MOSCOW SYMPHONY ORCHEST
(Stromberg) on *MARCO POLO (Select): 8.223748 (CD)*
also includes THE WOLF MAN and SON OF FRANKENSTEIN

IOLANTHE (operetta) songs by Gilbert and Sullivan
  1.D'OYLY CARTE OPERA COMPANY New S.Orch Of London
    (I.Godrey) *LONDON (Univ): 414 145-2 (2CD) -4 (MC)*
  2.PRO-ARTE ORCHEST (Malcolm Sargent) & GLYNDEBOURNE
    FESTIVAL CHOIR Soloists: George Baker-Ian Wallace-
    Alex.Young-Owen Brannigan *EMI: CMS 764400-2 (2CDs)*
  3.D'OYLE CARTE OPERA (JOHN PRYCE JONES, musical dir)
    feat: JILL PERT-RICHARD STUART-ELIZABETH WOOLLETT-
    PHILIP BLAKE-JONES *TER (Koch): CDTER2 1188 (2CD)*
IRISH AND HOW THEY GOT AWAY WITH IT, The (1997 USA)
  based on FRANK McCOURT'S biogr. 'Angela's Ashes'
  O.CAST RECORDING *VARESE (Pinn):VSD 5916 (CD)*
IRISH JOURNEYS (BBC2 02/01/1999) music by JOHN REA and
  Irish instruments perf.by PAUL BRENNAN *unavailable*
IRMA LA DOUCE (1963) Mus: MARGUERITE MONNOT, md: ANDRE
  PREVIN -S/T- *RYKODISC (Vital): RCD 10729 (CD)*
IRON AND SILK (1991) Music score: MICHAEL GIBBS -S/T-
  IONIC (RTM/Pinn): IONIC 7C (MC) IONIC 7CD (CD)
IRON GIANT The (1999) Music score: MICHAEL KAMEN
  -S/T- (score): *VARESE (Pinn): VSD 6062 (CD)*
  -S/T- (songs): *WARNER (Ten): 8122 75943-2 (CD)*
IRON WILL (1993) -S/T- Music score: JOEL McNEELY -S/T-
  VARESE (Pinn): VSD 5467 (CD)
IRONCLADS (1991) Music score: ALLYN FERGUSON suite on
  Coll 'FILM MUSIC OF ALLYN FERGUSON III' also incl:
  'APRIL MORNING' *PROMETHEUS (S.Scr): PCD 141 (CD)*
IRONSIDE *see COLL.2,121,270,281,344,345,377,*
ISLAND OF GHOSTS: *see* MADAGASCAR
IT HAPPENED AT THE WORLD'S FAIR *see* ELVIS PRESLEY FILM
  INDEX p.360
IT HAPPENED IN BROOKLYN (1946) FRANK SINATRA -S/T-
  SELECTIONS with 'VARIETY GIRL' -S/T- selection on
  GREAT MOVIE THEMES (BMG): CD 60034 (CD)
IT TAKES A THIEF (USA TV) *see COLL.349,*
IT'S A KNOCKOUT! (revival) (C5 03/09/1999) theme music
  "Bean Bag" HERB ALPERT & TIJUANA BRASS *A.& M.delet*
  see COLL.337,
IT'S A MAD MAD MAD MAD WORLD (1963) Music: ERNEST GOLD
  -S/T- *reiss+addit. RYKODISC (Vit): RCD 10704 (CD)*
IT'S A WONDERFUL LIFE (1946, Frank Capra) music score:
  DIMITRI TIOMKIN / Coll of songs inspired by movie
  DEBUTANTE (Univ): 555 346-2 (CD) -4 (MC)
IT'S ABOUT TIME (USA TV) *see COLL.346,*
IT'S ALIVE 2 'It Lives Again' (1978) Music sc: BERNARD
  HERRMANN -S/T- *SILVA SCREEN (Koch): FILMCD 074 CD*
IT'S GARRY SHANDLING SHOW (USA TV) *see COLL.351,*
IT'S MY PARTY (1995) Music sco: BASIL POLEDOURIS -S/T-
  VARESE (Pinn): VSD 5701 (CD)
IT'S ONLY TV BUT I LIKE IT (BBC1 03/06/1999) title mus
  by PETE BAIKIE *unavailable*
ITALIAN JOB The (1960) Music score by QUINCY JONES inc
  "Self Preservation Society" by PETER KING and
  "On Days Like These" sung by MATT MONRO
  -S/T- *currently unavailable*

ITN NEWS (Orig 60's-70 theme) 'Non Stop' JOHN MALCOLM
   see COLL.172, see also NEWS AT TEN
IVAN THE TERRIBLE (1943) Music by PROKOFIEV *new vers:*
   FRANKFURT RADIO SYMPHONY ORCH (Dmitri Kitoenko)
   RCA VICTOR Red Seal (BMG): 09026 61954-2 (CD)
   other recordings: Philharmonia Orch (Neeme Jarvi)
   Linda Finnie (mez-sop) Nikita Storojev (bass-bar)
   CHANDOS (Chandos): CHAN 8977 (CD)
   Philharmonic Orch (Riccardo Muti) Ambrosian Chorus
   (J.McCarthy) Irina Arkhipova-Boris Morgunov-Anatoly
   Mokrenko *EMI: CDM 769584-2 (CD) EG 769584-4 (MC)*
IVANHOE (1951) Music sco: MIKLOS ROZSA *new digital rec
   featur:* Sinfonia of London (Bruce Broughton)
   INTRADA (Silva Screen): MAF 7055CD (CD)
   -S/T- sel. incl.music from MADAME BOVARY/QUO VADIS
   PLYMOUTH ADVENTURE *IMPORT (S.Screen): TT 3001 (CD)*
IVOR THE ENGINE (BBC1 77) theme: VERN ELLIOTT Stories
   and music from the series on *BBC: ZCM 517 (MC)*

JACK (1996) Music: MICHAEL KAMEN song "Star" sung by
   BRYAN ADAMS -S/T- *EDEL-HOLLY.(Pinn): 012063-2 (CD)*
JACK FROST (1998) Music score: TREVOR RABIN -S/T- on
   MERCURY (Univ): 538 598-2 (CD)
JACK OF HEARTS (BBC1 04/08/1999) Music by: MARK THOMAS
   title theme sung by BONNIE TYLER *unavailable*
JACKAL The (1997) Music score: CARTER BURWELL -S/T-
   *(music from and inspired by the film) VAR.ARTISTS
   MCA (BMG): MCD 11688 (CD)*
JACKIE BROWN (1998) Various Artists -S/T-
   W.BROS (TEN): 9362 46841-2 (CD) -4 (MC)
JACKIE GLEASON SHOW (USA TV) *see COLL.346,378,*

JACOB'S LADDER (1990) Music sco: MAURICE JARRE -S/T-
   VARESE (Pinn): VSD 5291 (CD)
JACQUES BREL IS ALIVE AND WELL AND LIVING IN PARIS
   ORIGINAL LONDON CAST with VARIOUS ARTISTS
   see COLLECTIONS FOR TRACK DETAILS
   TER (Koch): CDTEM2 1231 (2CD)
JAILHOUSE ROCK (1957) ELVIS PRESLEY remastered -S/T-
   RCA (BMG): 07863 67453-2 (CD)
   see also ELVIS PRESLEY INDEX p.360
JAKE'S PROGRESS (C4 12/10/95) music by RICHARD HARVEY
   & ELVIS COSTELLO -S/T- *DEMON (Pinn): DSCD 14 (CD)*
JAMAICA INN (ITV 9/5/83) Music score: FRANCIS SHAW
   see COLL.7,
JAMES AND THE GIANT PEACH (1995) M/Songs: RANDY NEWMAN
   -S/T- *W.DISNEY (B.Vista): WD 68120-2 (CD) -4 (MC)*
JAMES BOND (theme) (MONTY NORMAN)
   *see COLL.28,32,34,41,52,53,54,108,118,314,330,356,
   359,360, see also* JAMES BOND FILM INDEX p.358
JANE EYRE (1995) Music score ALLESANDRO VLAD-CLAUDIO
   CAPONI -S/T- *DRG (N.Note-Pinn): DRGCD 12619 (CD)*
JANE EYRE (1971) Music score by JOHN WILLIAMS
   SILVA SCREEN (Koch): FILMCD 204 (CD)

JANE EYRE (1943) Music sco: BERNARD HERRMANN new 1994
  recording by The SLOVAK RADIO SYMPHONY ORCHESTRA
  MARCO POLO (Select): 8.223535 (CD) also available
  +'LAURA' (D.RAKSIN) Fox-Arista (BMG):07822 11006-2
JASON AND THE ARGONAUTS (1963) Music: BERNARD HERRMANN
  New Studio Recording BRUCE BROUGHTON conduct.the
  LONDON SINFONIA *INTRADA (S.Screen): MAF 7083 (CD)*
  see COLL.188,192,385,
JASON KING (ITC 15/7/71-72) theme LAURIE JOHNSON
  see COLL.121,215,217,360,
JAWBREAKER (1999) Music score: STEPHEN ENDELMAN -S/T-
  VARESE (Pinn): VSD 6013 (CD)
JAWS (1975) Music score: JOHN WILLIAMS -S/T- *re-iss:*
  MCA MASTERS (BMG): MCLD 19281 (CD)
  see COLL.70,175,201,204,310,403,404,
JAWS 2 (1978) Music score: JOHN WILLIAMS -S/T-
  VARESE (Pinn): VSD 5328 (CD)
JAZZ AGE (BBC 1969) mus: RON GRAINER *see COLL.8,*
JAZZ ON A SUMMER'S DAY (1959) NEWPORT JAZZ FESTIVAL
  sel. *GREAT MOVIE THEMES (BMG): CD 60039 (CD)*
JAZZ SINGER The (1980) NEIL DIAMOND -S/T- *reiss:*
  COLUMBIA (Ten): 483 927-2 (CD) -4 (MC)
JEAN DE FLORETTE (1987) Music score: JEAN-CLAUDE PETIT
  main theme ad.from "La Forza Del Destino" (Verdi)
  Orchestra De Paris w.Toots Thieleman *plus* 'CYRANO
  DE BERGERAC' (90) *PLAYTIME (Discov): 302330 (CD)*
  see COLL.69,71,74,83,275,
JEEVES AND WOOSTER (Granada 22/4/90) mus: ANNE DUDLEY
  vers.by GRAHAM DALBY & THE GRAHAMOPHONES on Coll
  'Transatlantique' *PRESIDENT: PCOM 1128 (CD)*
  see also BY JEEVES (Musical)
JEFFERSONS The (USA TV) *see COLL.347,*

JEFFREY (1995) Music score: STEPHEN ENDELMAN -S/T-
  VARESE (Pinn): VSD 5649 (CD)
JEKYLL AND HYDE (ORIGINAL BROADWAY CAST RECORDING)
  Music by FRANK WILDHORN, lyr.by LESLEY BRICUSSE
  FIRST NIGHT (Pinn): CASTCD 71 (CD)
JELLIKINS (ITV/GMTV 1999) Music & songs by DAVID LOWE
  featuring voice of RIK MAYALL.14 song soundtrack
  JELLISTAR (Univ): 153 709-2 (CD) -4 (MC)
JELLO IS ALWAYS RED The (Songs: CLARK GESTNER)
  ORIGINAL CAST with The Original Cabaret Songs of
  CLARK GESTNER *HARBINGER (Pinn): HCD 1502 (CD)*
JELLY'S LAST JAM (ORIG BROADWAY CAST 1993) GREGORY
  HINES as Jelly Roll Morton / Import on
  POLYDOR (IMS-Polyg): AA 314 510 846-2 (CD)
JEOPARDY (USA TV) *see COLL.256,346,*

JERRY McGUIRE (1996) Music score: DANNY BRAMSON -S/T-
  Epic (Ten): 486 981-2 (CD)
JERRY'S GIRLS (O.BROADWAY C.1984) Songs: Jerry Herman
  CAROL CHANNING-LESLIE UGGAMS *TER: CDTER2 1093 2CD*

JESUS CHRIST SUPERSTAR - songs by Tim Rice and Andrew
LLoyd Webber
  1. ORIG LONDON CAST 1996 *feat:* STEVE BALSALMO-ZUBIN
     VARTA-JOANNA AMPILL and Company
     REALLY USEFUL-Polydor: 533 735-2 (CD) -4 (MC)
     Highlights *REALLY USEFUL: 537 686-2 (CD) -4 (MC)*
  2. FILM MUSICAL 1973 *w:* YVONNE ELLIMAN-TED NEELY-CARL
     ANDERSON-BARRY DENNEN *MCA deleted*
  3. ORIG LONDON CAST 1972 PAUL NICHOLAS-DANA GILLESPIE
     IE-PAUL JABARA & Comp *MCA (BMG): MCFC 2503 (MC)*
  4. STUDIO RECORD 1972 MURRAY HEAD-IAN GILLAN-YVONNE
     ELLIMAN *MCA (BMG): DMCX 501 (CD)*
  5. HIGHLIGHTS FROM 20TH ANNIVERSARY (1992)
     with: PAUL NICHOLAS-CLAIRE MOORE-KEITH BURNS & Com
     FIRST NIGHT (Pinn): OCRCD 6031 (CD)
  6. CARLTON SHOWS COLL 1994 *with* GODSPELL Various Arts
     CARLTON Shows Collect: PWKS(PWKMC) 4220 (CD/MC)
  7. STUDIO RECORD 1995 DAVE WILLETTS-CLIVE ROWE-ISSY
     VAN RANDWYCK-BILLY HARTMAN-ETHAN FREEMAN-ANDREW
     NEWEY-CHRIS.BIGGINS-ANDREW HALLIDAY-JAY MARCUS...
     SHOWTIME (THE-Disc): SHOW(CD)(MC) 026 (CD/MC)
  8. CLASSIC MUSICALS SERIES *feat:* DAVE WILLETS-CLIVE
     ROWE-ISSY VAN RANDWYCK-CHRISTOPER BIGGINS and Co.
     + songs 'ASPECTS OF LOVE' *KOCH Int: 34083-2 (CD)*
  9. ORIG MASTERWORKS EDIT. DAVE WILLETTS-CLIVE ROWE
     ISSY VAN RANDWYCK-ETHAN FREEMAN-CHRIS.BIGGINS
     TER (Koch): CDTER 9026 (2CD)
JETSONS The (USA TV 62) - *see COLL.256,345,373,*
JEWEL IN THE CROWN (C4 1/6/97 orig: ITV/Gran 9/1/84)
     music score by GEORGE FENTON *see COLL.270,*
JFK - *see COLL.3,404,*
JIM DAVIDSON'S GENERATION GAME (BBC1 1998/99 series)
     title music by EMERSON LAKE & PALMER *unavailable*
JIM'LL FIX IT (BBC1 1975) - *see COLL.186,*
JO WHILEY (C4 05/05/1999) title music by DAMIAN HARRIS
     V.ARTIST COLL 'The Incredible Sound Of Jo Whiley'
     incl: CHEMICAL BROTHERS/UNDERWORLD/GOMEZ/ELASTICA
     FATBOY SLIM/ORBITAL/FUN LOVIN' CRIMMINALS/COCTEAU
     TWINS/MANIC STREET PREACHERS/BOMB THE BASS etc.
     INCREDIBLE (Ten): INC7CD (2CD) INC7MC (2MC)
JOAN AND LESLIE (BBC 1950s) theme "Miss Melanie"
     RONALD BINGE *see COLL.50,*
JOAN OF ARC - *see MESSENGER*
JOE 90 (ATV/ITC 29/9/68-69) theme music BARRY GRAY
     see COLL.23,38,122,171,267,270,359,360,367,369,
JOHN PEEL'S SOUNDS OF THE SUBURBS (C4 27/02/1999)
     Collect.from TV ser.on influential British music
     SHIFTY (Pinn-Disc): SHIFTY 9901 (2CD)
JOHNNY COOL (1963) Music score: BILLY MAY -S/T- *reiss*
     RYKODISC (Vital): RCD 10744 (CD)
JOHNNY STACCATO (USA 1959) theme mus: ELMER BERNSTEIN
     see COLL.2,
JOHNS (1996) music score by CHARLES BROWN -S/T- on
     VARESE (Pinn): VSD 5778

JOLSON STORY The (1946) V.ORIG -S/T- Film songs on
    GREAT MOVIE THEMES: (Targ-BMG): CD 60021 (CD)
JOLSON: THE MUSICAL (1995) Victoria Palace London
    BRIAN CONLEY and Company - ORIG CAST RECORDING on
    FIRST NIGHT (Pinn): CASTCD 56 (CD) CASTC 56 (MC)
JONATHAN CREEK (BBC1 10/5/97) theme music "Variations
    On A Theme" 'Danse Macabre' (Saint-Saens) arrang:
    JULIAN STEWART LINDSAY *unavailable see COLL.68,*
JONATHAN LIVINGSTON SEAGULL (1973) Music: NEIL DIAMOND
    -S/T- *re-iss SONY: 467607-2 (CD)* with 'BEAUTIFUL
    NOISE'/'JAZZ SINGER' *SONY (Ten): 488676-2 (3CD)*
JONATHON ROSS - *see* FILM 99 with JONATHON ROSS
JONNY QUEST (USA TV) *see COLL.346,*
JOSEPH and THE AMAZING TECHNICOLOR DREAMCOAT - songs
    by Tim Rice and Andrew Lloyd Webber
  1.ORIG LONDON REVIVAL CAST 1991 *with:* JASON DONOVAN
    POLYDOR-REALLY USEFUL (Univ):511 130-2(CD) -4(MC)
    (Jason Donovan & Comp) *also* "Any Dream Will Do"
    "Close Every Door To Me"/"Pharaoh's Story"
    Phillip Schofield *POLY: RUR(CD)(CS)11(7"/CDs/MC)*
  2.ORIG LONDON CAST 1973 GARY BOND-PAUL BROOKE-IAN
    CHARLESON-JOAN HEAL-JEREMY JAMES TAYLOR-GAVIN REED
    MCA (BMG): MCLD 19023 (CD)
  3.CARLTON SHOWS COLL with ROBIN COUSINS-JACQUI SCOTT
    NICK CURTIS-STEVE BUTKER-BOBBY CRUSH and Company
    CARLTON: PWKS 4163 (CD) PWKMC 4163 (MC)
  4.STUDIO RECORD. PAUL JONES-TIM RICE-GORDON WALLER
    MIKE SAMMES SINGERS and GEOFF LOVE & HIS ORCHESTRA
    CFP (EMI): CC 242 (CD) HR 8200 (MC)
  5.STUDIO RECORD. DONNY OSMOND-MARIA FRIEDMAN-RICHARD
    ATTENBOROUGH-JOAN COLLINS-CHRISTOPHER BIGGINS & Co
    REALLY USEFUL: CDRUG 1000 (CD) MCRUG 1000 (MC)
JOSHUA JONES (BBC TV) *see COLL.67,186,*
JOSIE AND THE PUSSYCATS *see COLL.347,373,*
JOUR DE FETE (Jacques Tati 1948) Music sc: JEAN YATOVE
    -S/T- selection on 'Orig Music From His Films' on
    POLY (Discov): 836 983-2 (CD) see also MON ONCLE
    see COLL.343,
JOURNEY TO THE CENTRE OF THE EARTH (1999) Music score:
    BRUCE ROWLAND *VARESE Pinn): VSD 6069 (CD)*
JOURNEY TO THE CENTRE OF THE EARTH (1959) Music score:
    BERNARD HERRMANN + 4 songs sung by PAT BOONE
    VARESE (Pinn): VSD 5849 (CD) see COLL.1,
JOY LUCK CLUB The (1993) Music s: RACHEL PORTMAN -S/T-
    Songs -S/T- *ARISTA (BMG): 74321 18456-2(CD) -4(MC)*
    Score -S/T- *HOLLYWOOD (S.Screen): HR 61561-2 (CD)*
JUBILEE (1978) *V.A.* BRIAN ENO-ADAM & ANTS-WAYNE COUNTY
    & THE ELECTRIC CHAIRS-CHELSEA-SUZI PINNS-MANEATERS
    AMILCAR -S/T- *reissued EG-POLYG: EGCD 34 (CD)*
    also CAROLINE (Vital/Cargo/Greyhound): 1112 (CD)
JUDE (1996) Music score: ADRIAN JOHNSTON -S/T-
    IMAGINARY ROAD/Philips (Univ): 534 116-2 (CD)
JUDGEMENT AT NUREMBERG (1961) Music score: ERNEST GOLD
    -S/T- *RYKODISK (Vital): RCD 10723 (CD)*

JUDICIAL CONSENT (1995) Music sco: CHRISTOPHER YOUNG
-S/T- *INTRADA (Silva Screen): MAF 7062D (CD)*

JUDITH (1965) Music score: SOL KAPLAN with score from
'Exodus' (E.GOLD) *TSUNAMI (Silva S): TSU 0115 (CD)*

JUICE (1992) Music sco HANK SHOCKLEE & The Bomb Squad
-S/T- Naughty By Nature-Erik B.& Rakim-Big Daddy
Kane-Salt'n'Pepa *reis: MCA (BMG): MCLD 19308 (CD)*

JUKE BOX JURY 1959 (BBC1) theme "Hit and Miss" JOHN
BARRY 7 + 4 *see COLL.5,28,32,270,407,*

JULES ET JIM (1961) Music score: GEORGES DELERUE -S/T-
PROMETHEUS (S.Screen): PCD 103 (CD) see COLL.124,

JULIE AND THE CADILLACS (FILM MUSICAL 1999) -S/T-
RED BALL (Recognition/Universal): BALLCD 114 (CD)

JULIET BRAVO (UKGo 5/11/92 orig 30/8/80) theme: DEREK
GOOM arr.of BACH melody *see COLL.46,110,270,390,*

JULIUS CAESAR (1953) Music sco: MIKLOS ROZSA *new dig.
record* SINFONIA OF LONDON cond: Bruce Broughton
INTRADA (Silva Screen): MAF 7056D (CD)

JUMANJI (1995) Music score: JAMES HORNER -S/T-
SONY 481 561-2(CD) -4(MC) deleted 97 see COLL.49,

JUMPIN'JACK FLASH (1986) Music score: THOMAS NEWMAN
-S/T- *reissued on SPECTRUM (Univ): 551 138-2 (CD)*

JUNGLE BOOK The (1940) Music score: MIKLOS ROZSA
-S/T- with 'THIEF OF BAGHDAD' *COLOSSEUM (Pinn):
CST 348044 (CD)* also -S/T- mus from 'SPELLBOUND'
(Miklos Rozsa) *FLAPPER (Pinn): PASTCD 7093 (CD)*

JUNGLE BOOK (1967) *Sgs:* RICHARD & ROBERT SHERMAN sung
by LOUIS PRIMA-PHIL HARRIS-STERLING HOLLOWAY etc.
-S/T- *W.DISNEY (Technic): WD 70400-2 (CD) -4 (MC)
see also* WALT DISNEY INDEX p.362

JUNGLE BOOK (1994) Music sco: BASIL POLEDOURIS -S/T-
MILAN (BMG): 74321 24861-2 (CD)

JURASSIC PARK (1993) Music score: JOHN WILLIAMS -S/T-
MCA (BMG): MCD 10859(CD) see COLL

JURASSIC PARK (Sony Playstation) by MICHAEL GIACCHINO
SONY IMP (Silva Screen): SCI 8803 (CD)

JUST CAUSE (1994) Music sc: JAMES NEWTON HOWARD -S/T-
VARESE (Pinn): VSD 5596 (CD)

JUST GOOD FRIENDS (BBC1 22/9/83) theme (John Sullivan)
PAUL NICHOLAS *FIRST NIGHT (Pinn): CAST(C)(CD) 43*

JUST WILLIAM (Talisman/BBC1 13/11/94 music composed &
directed by NIGEL HESS *see COLL.6,193,*

JUSTICE GAME The (BBC1 7/4/89) "Waterfront" (Jim Kerr)
SIMPLE MINDS 'Sparkle In The Rain' *VIRGIN (EMI)
CDV 2300 (CD) V 2300 (LP) TCV 2300 (MC)*

JUSTINE (1969) Music score: JERRY GOLDSMITH -S/T- *Imp
TSUNAMI (Silva Screen): TSU 0119 (CD)*

K 2 (1991) Music score: HANS ZIMMER -S/T-
VARESE (Pinn): VSD 5354 (CD)

KAMA SUTRA (1997) Mus sco: MYCHAEL DANNA / the Sarangi
played by ARUNA NARYAN KALLE -S/T- issued on
COLOSSEUM (Pinn): CST 348063 (CD)

KANSAS CITY (1997) VAR.JAZZ ARTS Collection (inspired
by the film) *GIANTS OF JAZZ/DELTA (BMG): CD 53300*

KARAOKE (BBC1 28/4/96) Music sco: CHRISTOPHER GUNNING
-S/T- includes music from 'COLD LAZARUS' + tracks
by BING CROSBY-HANK WILLIAMS-CRAIG DOUGLAS etc.
SILVA SCREEN (Koch): FILM(CD)(C) 181 (CD/MC)

KAT AND THE KINGS (MUSICAL) Songs: DAVID KRAMER
O.CAST (STUDIO) *FIRST NIGHT (Pinn): CASTCD 64 (CD)*
O.CAST LIVE REC *FIRST NIGHT (Pinn): CASTCD 67 (CD)*

KAVANAGH QC (ITV 3/1/95) music by ANNE DUDLEY and JOHN
KEANE -S/T- *VIRGIN (EMI): VTCD(VTMC) 134 (CD/MC)*

KAZAAM (1996) Music sco: CHRISTOPHER TYNG -S/T- V.Arts
A.& M.(IMS-Poly): E.549 027-2 (CD)

KEEP THE ASIPIDISTRA FLYING (1997) Music by MIKE BATT
EMI CLASSICS: CCD 556 613-2 (CD)

KEEPER OF THE CITY (1991) Music sco: LEONARD ROSENMAN
Utah Symph Orc -S/T- *INTRADA (S.Scr) MAFCD 7024*

KEEPING UP APPEARANCES (BBC1 from 29/10/90-95) title
theme music by NICK INGMAN *unavailable*

KENTUCKIAN The (1955) Music score: BERNARD HERRMANN
PREAMBLE (SILVA SCREEN): PRCD 1777 (CD)

KERN GOES TO HOLLYWOOD (ORIG LONDON CAST 85) Songs by
Jerome Kern-Dorothy Fields etc. *feat* ELAINE DELMAR
DAVID KERNAN-ELISABETH WELCH-LIZ ROBERTSON & Comp.
FIRST NIGHT (Pinn): OCRCD 6014 (CD)

KEY LARGO (1948) Music by MAX STEINER *see COLL.65,*

KEY TO REBECCA The (USATV mini-ser 85) mus sco: J.A.C.
REDFORD -S/T- *PROMETHEUS (Silva S): PCD 123 (CD)*

KEYS OF THE KINGDOM (1944) Music score: ALFRED NEWMAN
re-recorded *TSUNAMI IMPT (S.Scr): TSU 0134 (CD)*

KICKBOXER (1989) Music score: PAUL HERTZOG + songs/mus
from 'BLOODSPORT'(87) 'CYBORG'(89-Kevin Bassinson)
'DEATH WARRANT' (90) 'DOUBLE IMPACT' (91-A.Kempel)
SILVA SCREEN (Koch): FILMCD 103 (CD)

KID The (1921) Music sco: CHARLES CHAPLIN *see Coll.66,*

KID GALAHAD *see* ELVIS PRESLEY INDEX p.360

KIDNAPPED (1971) Music score by ROY BUDD -S/T- on
CINEPHILE (Pinn): CINCD 015 (CD)

KIDS ARE ALRIGHT The (Document.Film Of THE WHO) Mus:
(Pete Townshend & others) *BMG Vid: 74321 20087-30*

KIDS IN THE HALL BRAIN CANDY (1996) Mus: CRAIG NORTHEY
DOUG ELLIOTT-PAT STEWARD -S/T- *MATADOR (Vital):
OLE 1832(CD) OLE 1831(LP) see COLL.351,*

KIDS SAY THE FUNNIEST THINGS (ITV 31/10/1999) series
theme music by MCASSO *unavailable*

KIKA (1993) music of various artists -S/T- *Import on
IMPORT MUSIC SERVICES (IMS-Pol): E.517 572-2 (CD)*

KILLER TONGUE The (1996) Music and songs by FANGORIA
-S/T- on *EDEL-CINERAMA (Pinn): 002269-2CIN (CD)*

KILLERS The (1946) Music sco: MIKLOS ROZSA selection
'LUST FOR LIFE' *VARESE (Pinn): VSD 5405 (CD)*
Coll 'FILM NOIR CLASSICS' *see* 'DOUBLE INDEMNITY'

KILLING FIELDS The (1984) Music sco: MICHAEL OLDFIELD
-S/T- *VIRGIN (EMI): OVEDC 183 (MC) CDV 2328 (CD)*
see COLL.74,

KILLING ZOE (1994) Music score (TOMandANDY) -S/T- on
   MILAN (BMG): 232 102 (CD)
KILROY (BBC1 12/10/87-1999) theme music composed and
   arranged by ROBERT HOWES *unavailable*
KIND HEARTS AND CORONETS (1949) *see COLL.86,223,*

KINDERGARTEN COP (1990) Music sc: RANDY EDELMAN -S/T-
   VARESE (Pinn): VSD(VSC) 5305 (CD/MC)
KING AND I The (1999, Animated Musical) -S/T- on
   SONY CLASSICS: SK 63386 (CD) ST 63386 (MC)
KING AND I The - songs by R.Rodgers & O.Hammerstein II
   1.FILM MUSICAL 1956 YUL BRYNNER-DEBORAH KERR *(sung
   by* MARNI NIXON) RITA MORENO-TERRY SAUNDERS -S/T-
   reissue *EMI Broadway Classics: ZDM 764 693-2 (CD)*
   2.ORIGINAL 1996 BROADWAY CAST)
   TER (Koch): CDTER2 1214 (2CD)
   3.ORIG BROADWAY CAST 1951 YUL BRYNNER-GERTRUDE
   LAWRENCE-DORETTA MORROW-LARRY DOUGLAS & Company
   MCA (BMG): MCLD 19156 (CD)
   4.STUDIO RECORDING 1992 JULIE ANDREWS-BEN KINGSLEY-
   LEA SALONGA-PEABO BRYSON-MARILYN HORNE-ROGER MOORE
   MARTIN SHEEN-HOLLYWOOD BOWL SO.cond: JOHN MAUCERI
   PHILIPS: 438 007-2 (CD) -4(MC) -5 (DCC) -1 (LP)
   5.STUDIO RECORD.1994 VALERIE MASTERSON-CHRISTOPHER
   LEE-JASON HOWARD-HARRY WILLIAMS-TINUKE OLAFIMIHAN
   SALLY BURGESS-BEA JULAKASIUN and Company
   SHOWTIME (MCI-THE): SHOW(CD)(MC) 024
   6.CLASSIC MUSICALS SERIES *feat:* VALERIE MASTERSON
   THOMAS ALLEN-MURIEL DICKINSON & MUNICH SYMPH.ORCH.
   + *songs from* 'OKLAHOMA!' *KOCH Int: 34077-2 (CD)*
   7.SHOWS COLLECTION VARIOUS ARTISTS
   CARLTON SHOWS Collect: 30362 0041-2 (CD) -4 (MC)
KING CREOLE (1958) ELVIS PRESLEY remastered -S/T-
   RCA (BMG): 07863 67454-2 (CD) 07863 67454-4 (MC)
   see also ELVIS PRESLEY FILM INDEX p.360
KING KONG (1933) Music score by MAX STEINER
   (1) *RESTORED MAX STEINER SCORE BY JOHN MORGAN*
   MOSCOW SYMPHONY ORCHESTRA (WILLIAM J.STROMBERG)
   MARCO POLO (Select): 8.223763 (CD)
   (2) NATIONAL PHILHARM ORCH (FRED STEINER) *New Rec.*
   LEGEND-5TH CONTINENT (Silva Screen): LXCD 10
   (3) *COLLECTION* 'THIS IS CINERAMA' (1955) 'DEATH OF
   A SCOUNDREL' (1956) *LABEL X (Hot): ATMCD 2005 (CD)*
   see COLL.71,248,327,
KING KONG (1976) Music score: JOHN BARRY -S/T-
   IMP (S.Screen): MK 702 (CD) see COLL.35,248,
KING MACKEREL / THE BLUES ARE RUNNING (USA MUSICALS)
   COASTAL COHORTS: DON DIXON-BLAND SIMPSON-JIM WANN
   SUGARHILL USA (Koch): SHCD 8503 (CD) SH 8503 (MC)
KING OF KINGS (1961) Music: MIKLOS ROZSA *see COLL.302,*
KING OF THE HILL (USA/C4 01/08/1997) main theme mus by
   The REFRESHMENTS. score: JOHN O'CONNOR *unavailable*
KING SOLOMON'S MINES (1985) Music sco: JERRY GOLDSMITH
   -S/T- *INTRADA USA (S.Screen): FMT 8005D (CD)*

KINGS GO FORTH (1958) Music sco: ELMER BERNSTEIN also
+ -S/T- to SOME CAME RUNNING (58-Elmer Bernstein)
CLOUD NINE/SILVA PROD: CNS 5004 (CD)

KING'S ROW (1942) Music score: ERICH WOLFGANG KORNGOLD
theme on 'WB Years' *EMI ODEON: CDODEON 13 (CD)*

KING'S THIEF (1955) Music sc: MIKLOS ROZSA new record:
BRANDENBURG S.O. *MARCO POLO (Sel): 8.223607 (CD)*

KING'S THIEF (1955) Music score by MIKLOS ROZSA
complete score *Impt. (Silva Screen): TT 3012 (CD)*

KINSEY (BBC1 2/4/91) mus: DAVE GREENSLADE *see COLL.7,*

KISMET - songs by Robert Wright and George Forrest
adapted from the music of Alexander Borodin
1. ORIG -S/T- 1955 *reissue EMI ODEON: CDODEON 23 (CD)*
2. STUDIO 1964 *reissue LONDON (Univ): 452 488-2 (CD)*
3. ORIG BROADWAY CAST 1953 *with:* ALFRED DRAKE & Comp
COLUMBIA (S.Screen): CK 32605 (CD) JST 32605 (MC)
4. STUDIO REC.1990 VALERIE MASTERSON-DONALD MAXWELL
DAVID RENDALL-ROSEMARY ASHE-BONAVENTURA BOTTONE-
RICHARD VAN ALLAN Philharmonia Orch:John O.Edwards
<u>Highlights:</u> *SHOWTIME (MCI-THE): SHOW(CD)(MC) 014*
<u>Complete:</u>   *TER: CDTER2-1170 (2CD)*
5. STUDIO REC.1992 *with:* SAMUEL RAMEY-JULIA MIGENES-
JERRY HADLEY-MANDY PATINKIN-DOM DE LUISE-RUTH ANN
SWENSON *SONY BROADWAY: SK 46438 (CD)*

KISS ME KATE - songs by Cole Porter
1. ORIG FILM -S/T- 1953 KATHRYN GRAYSON-HOWARD KEEL
ANN MILER etc. *EMI ODEON (EMI): CDODEON 25 (CD)*
2. ORIG BROADWAY CAST 1948 *with:* LISA KIRK-PATRICIA
MORISON-ALFRED DRAKE-HARRY CLARK-HAROLD LANG & Com
COLUMB (Ten): SK 60536(CD) / EMI: ZDM 764760-2(CD)
3. ORIG LONDON CAST 1987 *w:* FIONA HENDLEY-PAUL JONES-
EARLENE BENTLEY-JOHN BARDEN-TIM FLAVIN-PETER
LEDBURY-NICHOLA McAULIFFE-CYRIL NRI-EMIL WOLK Comp
reissued on FIRST NIGHT (Pinn): OCRCD 6020 (CD)
4. STUDIO RECORD.1991 *with:* JOSEPHINE BARSTOW-THOMAS
HAMPSON-KIM CRISWELL-GEORGE DVORSKY & Company.
EMI: CDS 754 033-2 (2CDs) EX 754 033-4 (2 MC)
5. STUDIO RECORD.1995 THOMAS ALLEN-DIANA MONTAGUE
GRAHAM BICKLEY *SHOWTIME (MCI): SHOW(CD)(MC) 032*
<u>Complete:</u> *TER (Koch): CDTER2 1212 (2CD)*
6. STUDIO RECORDING 1996 *with* EDMUND HOCKRIDGE
JANINE ROEBUCK-JACKIE JEFFERSON *prd: GORDON LORENZ*
CARLTON SHOWS Coll (CHE): 30362 00332 (CD) -4(MC)

KISS OF DEATH (1995) Music score: TREVOR JONES -S/T-
MILAN (BMG): 28020-2 (CD)

KISS OF THE SPIDER WOMAN (ORIG LONDON CAST 1992) *feat:*
CHITA RIVERA-BRENT CARVER-ANTHONY CRIVELLO & Comp:
reissued on FIRST NIGHT (Pinn): OCRCD 6030 (CD)

KISS OF THE VAMPIRE (1964) Music sco: JAMES BERNARD
see COLL.180,

KISSIN' COUSINS *see* ELVIS PRESLEY INDEX p.360

KISSING A FOOL (1997) Music score: JOSEPH VITARELLI
"At Last" sung by ETTA JAMES others songs by the
MIGHTY BLUES KINGS -S/T- *VARESE (Pinn): VSD 5922*

KNACK The (65) Music score: JOHN BARRY -S/T- *reissue*
  RYKODISC (Vital): RCD 10718 (CD) / theme also by
  KEN MACKINTOSH ORCH 'Mac's Back' *Presid: PLCD 532*
KNIFE IN THE WATER (1962) Mus sc: KRZYSZTOF KOMEDA +
  'CRAZY GIRL' *POWER BROS (Harm.Mundi): PB 00145 (CD)*
KNIGHT RIDER (USA 1982 ITV 1983/C5 1997) theme (Glen
  Larson-S.Phillips) *see COLL.17,38,270,311,350,*
  new vers: 1998 RAP-MIX "Turn It Up" BUSTER RHYMES
  ELEKTRA (TEN): E.3847(CD)(C)
KNOTS LANDING (USA BBC1 79) theme mus: JERROLD IMMEL
  see COLL.270,347,
KOJAK (USA 73) theme music: BILLY GOLDENBERG
  see COLL.2,52,109,110,121,122,169,270,281,363,390,
KOLCHAK THE NIGHT STALKER (USA TV) *see COLL*
KOLYA (1997) Music score: ODREJ SOUKUP inc.Classical
  -S/T- *PHILIPS (Univ): 456 432-2 (CD)*
KONGA - *see COLL.209,*
KOYAANISQATSI (1982) Music score: PHILIP GLASS -S/T-
  NONESUCH (TEN): 7559 795192-9 (2CD) / previously
  ANTILLES (Island-Poly): IMCD 98 or ANCD 8707 (CD)
KRAMER V KRAMER (1979) Mus:.'Concerto in G.Maj' for 2
  mandolins,strings & organ (VIVALDI) + 'Concerto in
  C.Maj'for mandolins, strings,harpsichord (VIVALDI)
  'Sonata D.Maj'trumpet,strings & continuo (PURCELL)
  -S/T- *SONY FR.(Discov): SK 73945(CD) ST 73945 (MC)*
KREMMEN THE MOVIE featuring KENNY EVERETT *reissued on*
  EMI GOLD-LFP (EMI): LFPS 1554 (MC)
KULL THE CONQUEROR (1997) Music score: JOEL GOLDSMITH
  -S/T- *VARESE (Pinn): VSD 5862 (CD)*
KUNDUN (1997) Music score: PHILIP GLASS -S/T- on
  Nonesuch (TEN): 7559 79460-2 (CD) -4 (MC)

L'AMANT *see* 'LOVER The'
L.A.CONFIDENTIAL (1997) Music score: JERRY GOLDSMITH
  -S/T- score *VARESE (Pinn): VSD 5885 (CD)*
  -S/T- songs *RESTLESS (BMG): 74321 52596-2 (CD)*
L.A.LAW (USA)(ITV 7/9/88) theme music: MIKE POST
  see COLL.17,283,347,390,
LA BAMBA (1987) Music: MILES GOODMAN-CARLOS SANTANA
  featuring Los Lobos -S/T- *reissue:*
  SLASH-LONDON (Ten): 3984 28226-2 (CD)
  Orig Ritchie Valens songs on ACE: CDCHD 953 (CD)
LA CAGE AUX FOLLES (MUSICAL 1983) Songs: Jerry Herman
  Orig Broadway Cast *feat:* GEORGE HEARN-GENE BARRY-
  JAY GARNER-JOHN WEINER-ELIZABETH PARRISH & Company
  RCA VICTOR (BMG): BD 84824 (CD)
LA DERNIER METRO *see* LAST METRO The
LA DOLCE VITA (1960) *see COLL.70,301,*
LA FEMME D'A COTE *see* 'WOMAN NEXT DOOR The'
LA FEMME NIKITA (USA/C5 12/9/1997) theme m: MARK SNOW
  -S/T- includ.songs *TVT Import (Cargo-Silva Scr):*
  TVT 8170-2 (CD)
LA FETE SAUVAGE (TV Sountrack) Music by VANGELIS -S/T-
  Polydor Impt (Discovery): 841 198-2 (CD)

LA FLEUR DE MON SECRET - see FLOWER OF MY SECRET
LA FOLIE, A (1994) Music: MICHAEL NYMAN feat MICHAEL
   NYMAN BAND -S/T- *Imprt (DISCOVERY): 839949-2 (CD)*
LA GLOIRE DE MON PERE - see 'GLORY OF MY FATHER'
LA HAINE (Hate)(1995) m: ISAAC HAYES-BOB MARLEY-GAP
   BAND + -S/T- 'Metisse' *MILAN (BMG): 31966-2 (CD)*
LA PASSIONE (1996) Music by CHRIS REA -S/T- on
   EAST WEST (TEN): 0630 16695-2 (CD) -4 (MC)
LA REINE MARGOT - see QUEEN MARGOT
LA REVOLUTION FRANCAISE 1789-1794 (SHOW 1990) Songs:
   Alain Boublil and Claude Michel Schonberg / Orig
   PARIS Cast on *FIRST NIGHT (Pinn): OCRCD 6006 (CD)*
LA SCORTA (The Escort) (1993) Mus: ENNIO MORRICONE
   -S/T- *EPIC Italian Impt (Discov): 474187-2 (CD)*
LA VITA E BELLA see 'LIFE IS BEAUTIFUL'
LABYRINTH (1986) Music score: TREVOR JONES-DAVID BOWIE
   -S/T- *re-issue FAME-MFP (EMI): CDFA 3322 (CD)*
LADY AND THE HIGHWAYMAN (1988) Music by LAURIE JOHNSON
   see COLL.215,217,
LADY AND THE TRAMP The (1956) Songs: PEGGY LEE-J.BURKE
   Music: OLIVER WALLACE sung by **Peggy Lee** -S/T-
   WALT DISNEY (Technicolor): WD 6021328 (CD)
   Spoken Word & Songs Walt Disney: PDC 301 (MC)
   WALT DISNEY INDEX p.362
LADY BE GOOD (1941) -S/T- ELEANOR POWELL-ANN MILLER-
   JIMMY DORSEY ORCH + *m.from* 'Four Jills In A Jeep'
   GREAT MOVIE THEMES (Target-BMG): CD 60029 (CD)
LADY BE GOOD (ORIG BROADWAY CAST) Songs (George & Ira
   Gershwin) *ELEKTRA NONESUCH (TEN):7559 79308-2 (CD)*
LADY IN THE DARK (SHOW) Songs: KURT WEILL-IRA GERSHWIN
   1997 STUDIO RECORDING *with* MARIA FRIEDMAN-ADRIAN
   DUNBAR-STEVEN E.MOOORE *TER (Koch): CDTER 1244 (CD)*
LADY SINGS THE BLUES The (1972) Music: MICHEL LEGRAND
   Songs of Billie Holiday sung by DIANA ROSS -S/T-
   re-issued MOTOWN-POLYDOR (Univ): 530 135-2 (2CD)
LADYHAWKE (1985) Mus sc: ANDREW POWELL -S/T-
   GNP (ZYX): GNPD 8042 (CD)
LADYKILLERS The (1955) Music: TRISTRAM CARY other mus
   'Minuet No.5 In E.String Quint.Op.11'(BOCCHERINI)
   see COLL.83,223,
LAGOS AIRPORT (C4 18/11/1999) orig.series music by
   MALCOLM LAWS and NAINITA DESAI *unavailable*
LAKE PLACID (1999) Music score by JOHN OTTMAN -S/T-
   VARESE (Pinn): VSD 6055 (CD)
LAKES The (2) (BBC1 10/01/1999) music: NINA HUMPHREYS
   "You've Got A Lot To Answer For" by CATATONIA on
   BLANCO Y NEGRO (TEN): 0630 16305-2 (CD)
LAKES The (1) (BBC1 14/9/97) mus score: SIMON BOSWELL
   -S/T- inc "Walk Away" by CAST and other V.ARTISTS
   TELSTAR TV (TEN): TTVCD 2923 (CD) TTVMC 2923 (MC)
LAND AND FREEDOM (1994) Music score: GEORGE FENTON
   -S/T- *DEBONAIR (Pinn): CDDEB 1001 (CD)*
LAND BEFORE TIME The (1988) Music score: JAMES HORNER
   & Diana Ross -S/T- *MCA (S.Screen) MCAD 6266 (CD)*

LAND GIRLS The (1998) Music score: BRIAN LOCK
　　-S/T- *SILVA SCREEN (Koch): FILMCD 300 (CD)*
　　see COLL.3,
LAND OF SMILES (*Operetta* by FRANZ LEHAR-LUDWIG HERZER
　　FRITZ LOHNER) *feat:* RICHARD TAUBER-MARGIT SUCHY-
　　HELLER KURTY-WILLY STETTNER *KOCH: 31373-2 (CD)*
　　*French Highlights + 'MERRY WIDOW' etc. EMI BELLE
　　EPOQUE: CZS 767 872-2 (2CD)*
LAND OF THE GIANTS (USA 68 / C4 10/1/93) theme music:
　　JOHN WILLIAMS *see COLL.38,122,308,349*
LAND OF THE PHAROAHS (1955) Music sco: DIMITRI TIOMKIN
　　-S/T- *TSUNAMI (Silva Screen): TCI 0608 (CD)*
LAND OF THE TIGER (BBC2 17/11/97) orig music specially
　　composed & performed by NICHOLAS HOOPER
　　BBC WORLDWIDE MUSIC (Pinn): WMSF 6005-2 (CD)
LAND RAIDERS (69) Music score: BRUNO NICOLAI -S/T- on
　　PROMETHEUS (Silva Screen): PCD 128 (CD)
LAND WITHOUT MUSIC (FILM OPERETTA 1936) Music: Oscar
　　STRAUSS and featuring songs sung by Richard Tauber
　　-S/T- excerpts on *PEARL (H.Mundi): GEMM 263 (LP)*
LARKRISE TO CANDLEFORD (NAT.THEATRE STAGE PROD.1978)
　　Mus: ALBION BAND *CHARISMA/VIRGIN: CDSCD 4020 (CD)*
LASSIE (USA TV) *see COLL.348,*
LAST COMMAND The (1955) Music sco: MAX STEINER / song
　　"Jim Bowie" (Steiner-Clare) sung by GORDON MacRAE
　　TARAN (Silver Sounds): W 9109 (CD)
LAST DAYS OF CHEZ NOUS (1992) Music sc: PAUL GRABOWSKY
　　-S/T- *DRG USA (Pinn): DRGCD 12607 (CD)*
LAST DAYS OF DISCO The (1998) Music score: MARK SUOZZO
　　-S/T- *WORK-COLUMBIA Sony: 49213-2 (CD) -4 (MC)*
LAST EMPEROR (1988) Mus: DAVID BYRNE-RYUICHI SAKAMOTO
　　CONG SU -S/T- *VIRGIN: CDV 2485 (CD) OVEDC 366*
LAST EXIT TO BROOKLYN (1989) Music sco: MARK KNOPFLER
　　-S/T- *VERTIGO (Univ): 838 725-2(CD) -4(MC)*
LAST MAN STANDING (1996) Music score/songs: RY COODER
　　-S/T- *VERVE-POLYDOR (Univ): 533 415-2 (CD)*
LAST METRO The (1980)+ 'THE WOMAN NEXT DOOR' (1981) M:
　　GEORGES DELERUE *on COLL* 'TRUFFAUT & DELERUE ON
　　THE SCREEN' *DRG (Pinn): 32902 (CD)*
LAST NIGHT (1998) Music score -S/T- on
　　SONY CLASSICS: SK 60830 (CD)
LAST NIGHT OF THE PROMS 1994 (BBC1 10/9/94)100th Seas.
　　BBC Symphony Orchestra (Andrew Davis) BRYN TERFEL-
　　EVELYN GLENNIE-MICHAEL DAVIS-BBC Singers & Chorus
　　TELDEC (TEN): 4509 97868-2 (CD) -4 (MC)
LAST OF ENGLAND The (1987) Music: SIMON FISHER TURNER
　　Song "Skye Boat Song" sung by Marianne Faithfull
　　-S/T- *MUTE: IONIC 1 (LP) CDIONIC 1 (CD)*
LAST OF THE HIGH KINGS The (1996) Music by MICHAEL
　　CONVERTINO -S/T- (V/A) *EMI PREMIER: PRMDCD 26 (CD)*
LAST OF THE MOHICANS (1992) Music: TREVOR JONES-RANDY
　　EDELMAN -S/T- *MORGAN CREEK (Pinn):002241-2MCM (CD)*
　　see COLL.3,49,71,91,144,401,

LAST OF THE SUMMER WINE The (BBC1 12/11/1973-1999)
theme music by RONNIE HAZLEHURST *see COLL.270,*
LAST STAND AT SABRE RIVER (1998) Music: DAVID SHIRE
-S/T- *INTRADA (Koch/S.Screen): MAF 7078CD (CD)*
LAST STARFIGHTER The (1984) Music s: CRAIG SAFAN -S/T-
reissue *INTRADA (Silva Screen): MAF 7066 (CD)*
LAST TANGO IN PARIS (1972) Music score: GATO BARBIERI
-S/T- *RYKODISC (Vital): RCD 10724 (CD)*
LAST TEMPTATION OF CHRIST (1988) Music: PETER GABRIEL
-S/T-'Passion' *R.WORLD-VIRG: RW(CD)(MC)(LP)(MD) 1*
LAST TIME I COMMITTED SUICIDE The (1997) Jazz -S/T-
BLUE NOTE (EMI): CDP 836 736-2 (CD)
LAST VALLEY The (1970) Music score: JOHN BARRY -S/T-
Import (Silva Screen): TT 3003 (CD)
LATE SHOW The (1976) Music score: KEN WANNBERG -S/T-
selection with 'THE AMATEUR'/'OF UNKNOWN ORIGIN'
PROMETHEUS (Silva Screen): PCD 137 (CD)
LATE SHOW WITH DAVID LETTERMAN (USA TV) *see COLL.351,*
LATER (WITH JOOLS HOLLAND) (BBC2) Compilation featur
BLUE/OASIS/PAUL WELLER/SUPERGRASS/ELASTICA etc.
ISLAND (Univ): CID 8053 (CD)
LAURA (1944) Music score: DAVID RAKSIN -S/T- re-issue
with 'JANE EYRE' (1943) *FOX-ARISTA (BMG): 07822
11006-2(CD) see COLL.71,90,214,318,*
LAUREL & HARDY 'Legends Of The 20th Century' (Coll)
EMI: 522 816-2 (CD) - see COLL.226,348,
LAUTREC (1998)-S/T- *XIII BIS (Discov): LBSA 98009-2 CD*
LAVERNE AND SHIRLEY (USA TV) *see COLL.347,*
LAW AND ORDER (USA TV) *see COLL.283,351,390,*
LAWMAN (USA TV) *see COLL.248,*
LAWNMOWER MAN 2: BEYOND CYBERSPACE (95) Music score:
ROBERT FOLK -S/T- *VARESE (Pinn): VSD 5698 (CD)*
LAWRENCE OF ARABIA (1962) Music score: MAURICE JARRE
-S/T- LONDON PHILHARMONIC ORCH conduct by MAURICE
JARRE *CINEPHILE-CASTLE (Pinn): CINCD 008 (CD)
VARESE (Pinn): VSD 5263 (CD) VSC 5263 (MC)
see COLL.70,204,213,298,*
LE BOSSU (1998) Music score: PHILIPPE SARDE -S/T- on
VIRGIN (EMI): 845 348-2 (CD)
LE CHATEAU DE MA MERE - *see under* 'GLORY OF MY FATHER'
LE COLONEL CHABERT (1994) *SELECTION OF CLASSICAL MUSIC
AUVIDIS (Harmonia Mundi): K.1003 (CD)*
LE JOUR ET LA NUIT (1997) Music score: MAURICE JARRE
-S/T- *imp WEA FRANCE (Discovery): 0630 18006-2 (CD)*
LEAP OF FAITH (1992) Music score: CLIFF EIDELMAN -S/T-
MCA (BMG): MCD 10671 (CD) MCC 10671 (MC)
LEAVE HER TO HEAVEN *see COLL.1,*
LEAVE IT TO BEAVER (1997) Music s: RANDY EDELMAN -S/T-
VARESE (Pinn): VSD 5838 (CD) see COLL.345,
LEAVING HOME (C4 29/9/96) 20th Century Orchestral mus
CITY OF BIRMINGHAM SYMPH.ORCH cond: SIMON RATTLE
-S/T- *EMI CDM 566 136-2 (2CDs) CDM 566 137-2 (2CD)*
LEAVING LAS VEGAS (1994) Music sc: MIKE FIGGIS + V/A
-S/T- *IRS-A.& M.(Univ): 540 476-2 (CD)*

LEAVING OF LIVERPOOL The (Austr/BBC BBC1 15/7/93)
   music score: PETER BEST -S/T- *ONE M ONE Australia*
   (Silva Screen): IMICD 1019 (CD)
LEGEND (1986) *note: this film has two -S/T-*
   Mus *(1)* JERRY GOLDSMITH Lyrics (John Bettis)
   SILVA SCREEN (Koch): FILMCD 045 (CD) / Mus *(2)*
   TANGERINE DREAM *and also feat* "Is Your Love Strong
   Enough" by BRYAN FERRY / "Loved By The Sun" by JON
   ANDERSON -S/T- *reiss: VARESE (Pinn): VSD 5645 (CD)*
LEGEND OF THE GLASS MOUNTAIN *see* GLASS MOUNTAIN
LEGEND OF JESSE JAMES (USA TV) *see COLL.348,*
LEGEND OF WYATT EARP *see* LIFE AND LEGEND OF WYATT EARP
LEGENDS OF THE FALL (1994) Music s: JAMES HORNER -S/T-
   EPIC (Ten): 478 511-2 (CD)
LENNY (1974) including music by MILES DAVIS -S/T-
   RYKODISC (Vital): RCD 10707 (CD)
LEON (The Professional) (1994) Music score: ERIC SERRA
   -S/T- *COLUMBIA (Ten): 478 323-2 (CD) -4 (MC)*
LES ENFANTS DU PARADIS (1945) Var.Music selections on
   AUVIDIS (Harmonia Mundi): K.1502 (CD)
LES MISERABLES (FILM 1997) Music sco: BASIL POLEDOURIS
   -S/T- *EDEL-HOLLYWOOD (Pinn): 012 147-2HWR (CD)*
LES MISERABLES – songs by Alain Boublil-Claude Michel
   Schonberg with English lyrics by Herbert Kretzmer
  1.ORIG LONDON CAST 1985 *with:* PATTI LuPONE and Comp
   ENCORE CD1 (CD) ENCORE C1 (2MC)
  2.O.FRENCH CAST *FIRST NIGHT (Pinn): DOCRCD 1 (2CD)*
   COMPLETE SYMPHONIC RECORD LONDON PO.+ UK/USA Casts
   FIRST NIGHT (Pinn): MIZCD1 (3CDs) MIZC1 (3MC)
  3.FIVE OUTSTANDING PERFORMANCES From Les Miserables:
   FIRST NIGHT (Pinn): SCORCD 17 (CD) Highlights from
   Int.Cast *FIRST NIGHT (Pinn):CAST(C)(CD)20 (MC/CD)*
  4.MANCHESTER 1992 CAST RECORDING *FIRST NIGHT (Pinn):*
   SCORECD 34 (CDep)
  5.CARLTON SHOWS COLLECTION 1993 STUDIO RECORD *with:*
   DAVE WILLETTS-CLAIRE MOORE & West End Concert Orch
   CARLTON SHOWS: PWKS 4175 (CD) PWKMC 4175 (MC)
  6.ROYAL PHILHARMONIC ORCHESTRA *PLAY SUITES from*
   Miss Saigon and Les Miserables
   CARLTON Shows: PWKS(PWKMC) 4079 (CD/MC)
  7.10TH ANNIVERARY LONDON STAGE SHOW 1995
   FIRST NIGHT (Pinn):ENCORECD 8 (2CD) ENCOREC 8(2MC)
LES SILENCES DU PALAIS – *see* 'SILENCES OF THE PALACE'
LES VALSEUSES (1974 Fra) Music sco: STEPHANE GRAPPELLI
   -S/T- *MUSIDISC (Discovery): 10870-2 (CD)*
LESLEY GARRETT TONIGHT (BBC2 14/11/1998) 20 SONGS on
   BBC-BMG Conifer (BMG): 75605 51338-2 (CD) -4 (MC)
LET IT BE (1970) Songs: JOHN LENNON-PAUL McCARTNEY
   PARLOPHONE: CDP 746 447-2(CD) (TC)PCS 7096 (MC/LP)
LET'S DO IT! (Chichester Festival Prod 1994) Songs by
   (Noel Coward and Cole Porter) DAVID KERNAN-LOUISE
   GOLD-LIZ ROBERTSON-ROBIN RAY-PETER GREENWELL-PAT
   KIRKWOOD *SILVA SCREEN (Koch): SONG(C)(CD) 910*
LETHAL WEAPON – *see COLL 165,*

LETHAL WEAPON 4 (1998) music score: MICHAEL KAMEN-ERIC
CLAPTON-DAVID SANDBORN. music inspired by the film
BGRM (Silver Sounds): 1096 34010-2 (CD)
LEVIATHAN (1989) Music score: JERRY GOLDSMITH -S/T-
VARESE (Pinn): VSD 5226 (CD)
LEXX: THE DARK ZONE STORIES (SKY1 8/97) Music score by
MARTY SIMON -S/T- *COLOSS (Pinn): CST 348064 (CD)*
LIBERTY THE AMERICAN WAR OF INDEPENDENCE (C4 19/9/1998)
orig music by RICHARD EINHORN-MARK O'CONNOR with
DAVID & GINGER HILDEBRAND + JAMES TAYLOR & others
-S/T- *SONY CLASSICS: SK 63216 (CD)*
LICENCE TO KILL - see *COLL.54,55,203,*
see also JAMES BOND FILM INDEX p.358
LIDO LADY (O.LONDON CAST 1926) Songs (Rodgers- Hart)
feat: CICELY COURTNEIDGE-BOBBY COMBER-PHYLLIS DARE
JACK HULBERT *PEARL (Pavilion): GEMMCD 9105 (CD)*
LIEBESTRAUM (1991) Music score: MIKE FIGGIS and tracks
by Earl Bostic & His Orch and Bennie Moiseiwitsch
-S/T- *VIRGIN (EMI): CDV 2682 (CD) TCV 2682 (MC)*
LIFE (1999) V.ARTS -S/T- (music inspired by the film)
INTERSCOPE (Uni): 490 314-2 (CD)
LIFE AND DEATH OF RICHARD III (originally 1912,silent)
'Symphony For Richard III' comp.by ENNIO MORRICONE
SONY Classics: SK 60086 (CD)
LIFE AND LEGEND OF WYATT EARP (USA TV)
see *COLL.178,348,*
LIFE AND TIMES OF DAVID LLOYD GEORGE (BBC2 4/3/81)
theme music 'Chi Mai' ENNIO MORRICONE
see *COLL.250,251,262,270,*
LIFE AND TIMES OF GRIZZLY ADAMS (USA 78) theme "Maybe"
THOM PACE) instrumental version ('The Man From The
Mountains') see *COLL.349,*
LIFE IS BEAUTIFUL (La Vita E Bella) (1997) Music score
NICOLA PIOVANI -S/T- *VIRGIN (EMI): CDVIR 81 (CD)*
LIFE OF BIRDS The (BBC1 21/10/1998) Music score by
IAN BUTCHER and STEVEN FAUX -S/T-
BBC WORLD (Pinn): WMSF 60032 (CD)
LIFE OF GRIME, A (BBC1 20/04/1999) theme music "What A
Wonderful World" (Weiss-Douglas) from the album
'The Genius of LOUIS ARMSTRONG' on
LIFE LESS ORDINARY, A (1997) Music score: DAVID ARNOLD
-S/T-BECK-UNDERWORLD-REM-ELVIS PRESLEY-PRODIGY-ASH
DUSTED-BOBBY DARIN-CARDIGANS-FAITHLESS & others
A.& M.(Univ): 540 837-2 (CD) -4 (MC) and LIFECD 1
LIFE SUPPORT (BBC1 19/07/1999) Music by PAUL CONROY &
ADRIAN CORKER. theme "Let The Feeling Wash Over
You" (-) *uncredited vocalist*
LIFE WITH FRED (BBC2 10/3/94) theme music "Carnival Of
Venice" (Briccialdi) version by JAMES GALWAY on
RCA (BMG): PD 70260 (CD) PK 70260 (MC)
LIFEFORCE see *COLL.328,*
LIFESTYLES OF THE RICH & FAMOUS (USA TV) see *COLL.350,*
LIGHT OF EXPERIENCE The (BBC2 76-87) theme "Doina De
Jale" GHEORGE ZAMFIR *MCI (THE-DISC) MCCD 202 (CD)*

LIKE SOLDIERS DO (BBC1 03/08/1999) title song composed
and sung by BILLY BRAGG from 'Back To Basics'
COOKING VINYL (Vital): COOKCD 060(CD)
LIKE WATER FOR CHOCOLATE (93) Music score: LEO BROWER
-S/T- *Milan (BMG): 887 797 (CD)*
LILAC TIME (O.LONDON CAST 1922) Mus (Franz SCHUBERT)
Lyr (Adrian ROSS) *feat:* CLARA BUTTERWORTH-DOROTHY
CLAYTON-EDMUND GWENN + *RIO RITA (1930) SOUTHERN
MAID (1920) PEARL (Pavilion): GEMMCD 9115 (CD)*
LILIES OF THE FIELD (1963) Music sco: JERRY GOLDSMITH
-S/T- *TSUNAMI Imp (Silva Screen): TSU 0101 (CD)*
LILIES (1997) Music score: MYCHAEL DANNA -S/T- on
VARESE (Pinn): VSD 5868 (CD)
LILLIPUT IN ANTARCTICA (Cousteau Society/BBC1 2/8/93)
"Antarctica" VANGELIS *POLYD: 839 518-2(CD) -4(MC)*
LILY WAS HERE *see COLL.262,*
LIMELIGHT (1937) 4 songs on Coll 'LOUIS LEVY-MUSIC
FROM T.MOVIES' *EMPRESS (Koch): RAJCD 884*
LIMELIGHT (1952) Music score: CHARLES CHAPLIN
see COLL.170,228,
LIMEY The (1999) Music score by CLIFF MARTINEZ -S/T-
feat various 1960's/70's rock tracks
FLASH CUT-ARTISAN (Pinn-Sil.Sounds): 543 522 (CD)
LINGUINI INCIDENT The (1992) Music sco: THOMAS NEWMAN
-S/T- *VARESE (Pinn): VSD 5372 (CD)*
LION KING The (Original Broadway Cast Recording 1997)
Music and lyrics by ELTON JOHN and TIM RICE with
addit.music by LEBO M-MARK MANCINA-JAY RIFKIN-
JULIE TAYMOR and HANS ZIMMER
DISNEY-EDEL (Pinn): 010 455-2DNY (CD)
LION KING The (Original London Cast 1999) CORNELL JOHN
ROGER WRIGHT-LUKE YOUNGBLOOD-JOSETTE BUSHELL MINGO
ROB EDWARDS-SIMON GREGOR-MARTYN ELLIS and Company
ORIG LONDON CAST RECORDING CURRENTLY UNAVAILABLE
LION KING The (FILM 1994) Music score by HANS ZIMMER
Disney's Sounds & Stories *DISNEY WD 60802-2 (CD)*
LION KING 2 - *see* **SIMBA'S PRIDE** *see also p.362*
LION OF THE DESERT (1981) Music score: MAURICE JARRE
L.Symph Orch *SILVA SCREEN (Koch): FILMCD 060 (CD)*
also inc music from 'THE MESSAGE' (1977) (JARRE)
LIONHEART (1987) Music score: JERRY GOLDSMITH -S/T-
VARESE (Pinn): VCD 47282 (CD-V1) VCD 47288 (CD-V2)
LIPSTICK ON YOUR COLLAR (C4 21/2/93) opening t.song
sung by CONNIE FRANCIS, closing mus "The Man With
The Golden Arm" BILLY MAY ORCH. -S/T- selection
SPECTRUM (Univ): 552 901-2 (CD) -4 (MC)
see also 'PENNIES FROM HEAVEN'/'SINGING DETECTIVE'
LIQUID TELEVISION (USA TV) *see COLL.351,*
LISTEN TO THE WIND (MUSICAL 1996) songs: VIVIAN ELLIS
feat: PAULA WILCOX-NAOMI BELL-CAMERON BLAKELY & Co
TER (Koch): CDTER 1251 (CD)
LITTLE BOY BLUE (1998) Music score: STEWART COPELAND
-S/T- *Sonic Images (Cargo-Silver Sounds-Greyhound)
7828 278810-2 (CD)*

LITTLE BY LITTLE (OFF BROADWAY CAST PRODUCTION)
  VARESE (Pinn): VSD 6024 (CD)
LITTLE FAUSS AND BIG HALSY (1970) Music by JOHNNY CASH
  BOB DYLAN-CARL PERKINS -S/T- w 'I WALK THE LINE'
  BEAR FAMILY (Rollercoaster): BCD 16130 (2CD)
LITTLE GIRL WHO FELL OFF A TREE (Ein Todliches
  Verhaltnis) -S/T- *COLOSS (Pinn): CST 348074 (CD)*
LITTLE HOUSE ON THE PRAIRIE (USA 74 rpt C4-13/10/91)
  theme: DAVID ROSE *see COLL.17,347,*
LITTLE MARY SUNSHINE (ORIGINAL LONDON CAST 1962)
  Songs: RICK BESOYAN *DRG (Pinn): CDSBL 13108 CD*
LITTLE ME - songs by Cy Coleman and Carolyn Leigh
  1.ORIG BROADWAY CAST 1962 w Sid Caesar-Virginia Mart
    in-Nancy Andrews-Mort Marshall-Peter Turgeon-Micky
    Deems-Joey Faye *RCA Vict (BMG): 09026 61482-2 (CD)*
  2.ORIG LONDON CAST 1964 BRUCE FORSYTH-AVRIL ANGERS-
    JACK FRANCOIS-EILEEN GOURLAY-DAVID HENDERSON TATE-
    BERNARD SPEAR-SVEN SVENSON *DRG (Pin): CDSBL 13111*
  3.USA MUSICAL REVIVAL 1988 Songs: CY COLEMAN
    NEW BROADWAY CAST *VARESE (Pinn): VSD 6011 (CD)*
LITTLE MERMAID The (1998) Disney's Sounds & Stories
  DISNEY (Technic) WD 60628-2 (CD) WD 60628-4 (MC)
  DISNEY (Technic) WD 60946-2 (CD) WD 60946-4)
  see also WALT DISNEY FILM INDEX p.362
LITTLE NIGHT MUSIC, A - songs by Stephen Sondheim
  1.NATIONAL THEATRE PROD 1996 JUDI DENCH-PATRICIA
    HODGE-SIAN PHILLIPS-SEAN MATHIAS & Com ORIG.CAST
    TRING Int (THE): TRING 001 (CD) MCTRING 001 (MC)
  2.ORIG BROADWAY CAST 1973 w: GLYNIS JOHNS-LEN CARIOU
    H.GINGOLD-VICTORIA MALLORY-LAURENCE GUITTARD & Co.
    COLUMBIA (Ten): SMK 65284 (CD)
  3.ORIG LONDON CAST 1975 *with:* JEAN SIMMONS-HERMOINE
    GINGOLD-JOSS ACKLAND & Co *RCA (BMG) GD 5090 (CD)*
  4.STUDIO RECORDING w: SIAN PHILLIPS-SUSAN HAMPSHIRE
    ELISABETH WELCH arrang.& cond.by JOHN OWEN EDWARDS
    TER (Koch): CDTER 1179 (CD)
  5.STUDIO RECORDING *feat* TERRY TROTTER (solo piano)
    VARESE (Pinn): VSD 5819 (CD)
LITTLE PRINCESS, A (1995) Music score: PATRICK DOYLE
  -S/T- *VARESE (Pinn): VSD 5628 (CD)*
LITTLE RASCALS (USA TV) *see COLL.345,*

LITTLE SHOP OF HORRORS (FILM MUSICAL 1987) Songs (Alan
  Menkin-Howard Ashman) Orig Film sco: MILES GOODMAN
  -S/T- *GEFFEN-MCA (BMG): GFLD 19289 (CD)*
LITTLE VOICE (1998) Music sc: JOHN ALTMAN -S/T- JANE
  HORROCKS-JUDY GARLAND-BILLIE HOLIDAY-TOM JONES-
  SHIRLEY BASSEY-ETHEL MERMAN-MARILYN MONROE on
  EMI: 498 071-2 (CD)
LITTLEST HOBO The (USA 1979) series theme music "Maybe
  Tomorrow" composed & sung by TERRY BUSH *(also used
  for 'NAT.WEST' TV ad. unavailable*
LIVE A LITTLE LOVE A LITTLE (1968)
  see ELVIS PRESLEY FILM INDEX p.360

LIVE AND LET DIE (1993) Music sco: GEORGE MARTIN title
   song (Paul & Linda McCartney) by PAUL McCARTNEY
   -S/T- *reissue EMI PREMIER (EMI): CZ 553 (CD)*
   see JAMES BOND FILM INDEX p.358
   see COLL.54,314,365,
LIVE FLESH (1998) Music score: ALBERTO IGLESIAS -S/T-
   RCA VICTOR (BMG): 74321 54273-2 (CD)
LIVE FOR LIFE 'Vivre Pour Vivre' (1967) Music score:
   FRANCIS LAI incl: 'A Man And A Woman' (1966) -S/T-
   DRG (New Note-Pinn): DRGCD 12612 (CD)
LIVE FROM A QUARRY (1998) Music score: PAUL K.JOYCE
   -S/T- *PKJ (Else): PKJCD 002 (CD)*
LIVER BIRDS The (BBC1 6/5/96) theme mus re-recorded by
   MIKE McCARTNEY & Fuzzy "On A Mountain Stands A
   Lady" (trad.) performed by SCAFFOLD / orig BBC1
   series (BBC1 14/4/69-5/1/79) *see COLL.2,5,407,*
LIVERPOOL 1 (ITV 7/9/1998) o.music by JERRY FREEDMAN
   unavailable. also used 'IRIS' by The GOO GOO DOLLS
   on 'CITY OF ANGELS' *WB (Ten): 9362 46867-2 (CD)*
LIVING BRITAIN (BBC2 31/10/1999) series music by
   BRIAN BENNETT *unavailable*
LIVING DAYLIGHTS (1987) Title song "Living Daylights"
   (John Barry-A.HA) "If There Was A Man" sung by The
   PRETENDERS -S/T- *RYKODISC (Vital): RCD 10725 (CD)*
   BOND FILM INDEX p.358 *also see COLL.55,88,286,*
LIVING OUT LOUD (1998) Music score by GEORGE FENTON
   -S/T- *feat:* QUEEN LATIFAH-MEL TORME-DEAN MARTIN-
   ETTA JAMES-SLY & FAMILY STONE-CLARK ANDERSON etc.
   RCA VICTOR (BMG): 09026 63363-2 (CD)
LIZA WITH A 'Z' (USA TV Concert 1972) -S/T- feat LIZA
   MINNELLI reissue *SONY Coll: 982994-2 (CD) -4 (MC)*
LOADED (1994) Music score: SIMON FISHER TURNER -S/T-
   OCEAN DEEP (Grapev/Polyg): OCD 001 (CD)
LOCAL HERO (1982) Music: MARK KNOPFLER -S/T- *Vertigo*
   (Univ): 811038-2 (CD)
LOCK STOCK AND TWO SMOKING BARRELS (1998) Music score:
   DAVID A.HUGHES-JOHN MURPHY -S/T- feat VARIOUS ARTS
   -S/T- *ISLAND (Univ): CID 8077 (CD) also on*
   SIMPLY VINYL (Telstar): SVLP 89 (LP)
LODGER The (1944) Music score: HUGO FRIEDHOFER / Suite
   on Coll *with* 'RAINS OF RANCHIPUR'/'SEVEN CITIES OF
   GOLD'/'ADV.OF MARCO POLO' The MOSCOW SYMPHONY ORCH
   (W.T.Stromberg) *MARCO POLO (Select): 8.223857 (CD)*
LODOSS WAR 1/2/3 (Japan 95) Animated MANGA Film -S/T-
   Animanga-New Note (Pinn): AM 3 / 4 / 8 (CDs)
LOIS AND CLARK see 'NEW ADVENTURES OF SUPERMAN'
LOLA RENNT - see 'RUN LOLA RUN'
LOLITA (1998) Music score: ENNIO MORRICONE conducting
   the ACCADEMIA MUSICALE ITALIANA -S/T- on
   MILAN (BMG): 74321 52318-2 (CD, 05.1998)
LOLITA (1961) Music sc: BOB HARRIS *feat:* NELSON RIDDLE
   complete -S/T- EMI SOUNDTRACKS: 821 978-2 (CD)
LONDON MARATHON The (BBC1 13/5/84-98) theme "The Trap"
   by RON GOODWIN *see COLL.168,169,170,176,*

LONDON'S BURNING (LWT 20/2/1988) theme "Blue Watch"
SIMON BRINT-RODDY MATTHEWS on 'LONDON'S BURNING'
-S/T- *SOUNDTRACKS EMI GOLD: 521 944-2 (CD)*
see COLL.149,270,

LONE RANGER The (USA 1949 re-run C4 88) theme "William
Tell Overture" (ROSSINI) *see COLL.273,345,*

LONE STAR (1996) Music score: MASON DARING -S/T-
Daring (Direct): DARINGCD 3023 (CD)

LONELY ARE THE BRAVE (1962) Music sco: JERRY GOLDSMITH
Tsunami-Delphi (Greyhound): NR 9104 (CD)

LONELY PLANET (C4 from 28/9/94) theme mus: IAN RITCHIE
MICHAEL CONN sel.of World Music on 'Music For The
Lonely Planet' *KAZ (BMG): KAZ(CD)(MC) 223 (CD/MCs)*
new:'MORE MUSIC FROM THE LONELY PLANET' *KAZ-Castle
Comm (Pinn): KAZCD 224 (2CD) KAZMC 224 (2MC)*
also available 'LISTEN TO THE PLANET' Var.Artists
MILAN (BMG): 74321 37243-2 (CD)

LONER The (USA TV 1965) themes by JERRY GOLDSMITH on
Coll 'Stagecoach' (Limited edition impt.) includes
score from 'STAGECOACH' (1966, J.GOLDSMITH) on
RETROGRADE (Silva Screen/MFTM): FSMCD 1 (CD)

LONESOME DOVE (USA TV/BBC1 30/8/93) music score: BASIL
POLEDOURIS -S/T- *SONIC IMAGES: SID 8816 (CD)*

LONG GOOD FRIDAY The (1980) Music sco: FRANCIS MONKMAN
feat KEVIN PEEK-TRISTRAM FRY-HERBIE FLOWERS (SKY)
-S/T- *SILVA SCREEN (Koch): FILMCD 020 (CD)*
see COLL.359,

LONG KISS GOODNIGHT The (1996) Music: ALAN SILVESTRI
-S/T- *MCA (BMG): MCD 11526 (CD)*

LONG WAY HOME The (1997) Music score: LEE HOLDRIDGE
-S/T- *PROMETHEUS (Silva Screen): PCD 145 (CD)*

LONGEST DAY The (1962) Music score: PAUL ANKA
see COLL.71,383,384,

LONGITUDE (Time Season) (BBC2 04/01/1999) music by
DAN JONES *unavailable*

LOONEY TUNES (USA TV) *see COLL.346,*

LOOSE WOMEN (ITV 06/09/1999) t.music by PATRICK DUFFIN
unavailable

LORD JIM (1964) Music score: BRONISLAU KAPER
TARAN (Silver Sounds): W 9108 (CD)

LORD OF ILLUSIONS (1995) Music sc: SIMON BOSWELL -S/T-
IONIC/MUTE/RTM (Disc): IONIC 13CD (CD)

LORD OF THE DANCE 1996 SHOW Music: RONAN HARDIMAN feat
MICHAEL FLATLEY and Comp / Music cond and orch by
ANNE DUDLEY *POLYGRAM TV: 533 757-2 (CD) -4 (MC)*

LORD OF THE FLIES (1990) Music score: PHILIPPE SARDE
London Symphony Orch & The Trinity Boys Choir
-S/T- *SILVA SCREEN (Koch): FILMCD 067 (CD)*

LORD OF THE RINGS The (1978) Music: LEONARD ROSENMAN
-S/T- *FANTASY/INTRADA (S.Screen): FMTCD 8003 (CD)*

LORENZO'S OIL (1992) Classical music - *see COLL.83,*

LORNA (1964,RUSS MEYER) V.ARTS -S/T- *with* 'VIXEN'/
'FASTER PUSSYCAT' *NORMAL/QDK (Pinn/Greyh/Dir):
QDKCD 008 (CD) QDKLP 008 (LP)*

LOST BOYS The (1987) Music score: THOMAS NEWMAN -S/T-
  ATLANTIC (TEN): 781767-2 (CD) -4(MC)
LOST CHILD (BBC2 29/6/97) Violin Sonatas (FREDERICK
  DELIUS) performed by TASMIN LITTLE and BOURNEMOUTH
  SO (R.Hickox) *CON.CLASS (BMG): 75605 51315-2 (CD)*
LOST CONTINENT The *see* 'HORRORS OF THE BLACK MUSEUM'
LOST EMPIRES (Granada 24/10/86) music: DEREK HILTON
  TER (Koch): CDTER 1119 (CD)
LOST HIGHWAY (1996) Music score: ANGELO BADALAMENTI
  V.Arts -S/T- *INTERSCOPE-MCA (BMG): IND 90090 (CD)*
  also on SIMPLY VINYL (Vital): SVLP 119 (2LP)
LOST HORIZON (1937) Mus sco: DIMITRI TIOMKIN cond.by
  MAX STEINER -S/T- *TSUNAMI (S.Scr): TSU 0135 (CD)*
LOST IN SPACE (1998) Music score: BRUCE BROUGHTON
  SINFONIA OF LONDON conducted by BRUCE BROUGHTON
  *INTRADA (Silva Screen): MAF 7086 (CD) also on
  TVT SOUNDTRAX: TVT 8180-2 (CD)* also on
  EPIC Soundtracks: 491 303-2 (CD) -4(MC) -8(MD)
  2nd theme vers.by APOLLO 440 *EPIC: SSR9CD (CDs)*
LOST IN SPACE (USA TV)
  see COLL.38,122,267,270,308,345,349,362,
LOST PATROL The (1934) Music: MAX STEINER *new record*
  MOSCOW SO (Stromberg) + 'BEAST WITH 5 FINGERS'/
  'VIRGINIA CITY' *MARCO POLO (Select): 8.223870 (CD)*
LOST WEEKEND The (1945) Music sc: MIKLOS ROZSA / Suite
  on Coll FILM NOIR CLASSICS *see* 'DOUBLE INDEMNITY'
LOST WORLD: Jurassic Park 2 (1997) Mus: JOHN WILLIAMS
  -S/T- *MCA (BMG): MCAD 11628 (CD)*
LOTUS EATERS The (UKGO 12/9/93 orig BBC 71) theme "Ta
  "Ta Trena Pou Fyghan" STAVROS XARAHAKOS
  see COLL.281,
LOU GRANT (USA 77/C4 84) theme mus: PATRICK WILLIAMS
  see COLL.17,
LOUIS L'ENFANT ROI (1993) Music by JEAN PIERRE FOUQUEY
  AUVIDIS (Harmonia Mundi): K.1001 (CD)
LOUISIANA PURCHASE (USA CAST RECORDING 1996) on
  DRG-NEW NOTE (Pinn): DRGCD 94766 (CD)
LOVE AND DEATH (1975) *see COLL.86,105,*
LOVE AND DEATH ON LONG ISLAND (1997) Music: INSECTS
  -S/T- *OCEAN DEEP (Univ): OCD 014 (CD)*
LOVE BOAT (USA TV) *see COLL.347,*
LOVE IN THE 21ST CENTURY (C4 21/07/1999) series title
  music by MURRAY GOLD *unavailable*
LOVE IS A MANY SPLENDORED THING - *see COLL.1,*
LOVE IS THE DEVIL (1997) Music sco: RYUICHI SAKAMOTO
  ASPHODEL (Pinn): ASP 0987CD (CD)
LOVE JONES (1996) -S/T- featuring Various Artists on
  COLUMBIA (Ten): 487 230-2 (CD) -4 (MC)
LOVE LETTER The (1999) Music score: LUIS BACALOV -S/T-
  RCA VICTOR (BMG): 09026 63521-2 (CD)
LOVE ME TENDER (56) - *see* ELVIS PRESLEY INDEX p.360

LOVE STORY (1944) Music score: HUBERT BATH
  see COLL.170,386,

LOVE STORY (1970) Music score: FRANCIS LAI -S/T-
   MCA (BMG) MCLD 19157 (CD)
      see COLL.37,41,52,106,204,224,238,239,
LOVE STORY (TV 1970's) theme music: TONY HATCH
      see COLL.23,184,
LOVE VALOUR COMPASSION (1997) Music sc: HAROLD WHEELER
   -S/T- *DECCA (Univ): 455 644-2 (CD)*
LOVE YOU 'TIL TUESDAY (1969) C4 14/2/88 Music by
   DAVID BOWIE -S/T- *CARLTON: PWKS 4131P(CD)*
LOVED UP (BBC2 23/9/95) Rave mus BANCO DE GAIA-ORBITAL
   PRODIGY-LEFTFIELD -S/T- on *PRIMAVERA (Vital):*
   PRIMACD 002 (CD) PRIMAMC 002(MC) PRIMALP 002 (LP)
LOVEJOY (BBC1 10/1/86-1994) theme music: DENIS KING
      see COLL.6,19,
LOVERS The (L'Amant) (1991) Music score: GABRIEL YARED
   -S/T- *CIRCA / VIRGIN (EMI): CDVMM 9 (CD)*
LOVING YOU (1957) feat ELVIS PRESLEY remastered -S/T-
   RCA (BMG): 07863 67452-2 (CD) 07863 67452-4 (MC)
      see also ELVIS PRESLEY INDEX p.360
LOW DOWN DIRTY SHAME (1994) Music: V.Arts -S/T- *JIVE*
   (BMG): CHIPCD 156 (CD) HIPC 156 (MC) HIP 156 (LP)
LOYALISTS (BBC2 21/01/1999) music by DAVID FERGUSON
   unavailable
LUCY SULLIVAN IS GETTING MARRIED (ITV 08/11/1999)
   music score & theme "Stargazing" by ROGER JACKSON
   sung by HANNAH *unavailable*
LULLABY OF BROADWAY (1950)*see COLL.174,237,255,272,396*
LUST FOR LIFE (1956) Music score: MIKLOS ROZSA -S/T-
   VARESE (Pinn): VSD 5405 (CD)
LUV (BBC1 9/3/93) theme m. 'Intermezzo from Cavalleria
   Rusticana' MASCAGNI *see COLL.79,92,95,99,100,106,*
   144,158,274,275,317,

M .BUTTERFLY (1993) Music score: HOWARD SHORE -S/T- on
   VARESE (Pinn): VSD 5435 (CD)
M.SQUAD (USA TV 1957-60) theme mus: COUNT BASIE (ser.
   2/3) STANLEY WILSON (1) 'Music From M.SQUAD' on
   RCA (BMG): 74321 43397-2 (CD)   see COLL.348,375,
McCALLUM (ITV 28/12/95) mus: DAEMION BARRY *unavailable*
   "Cry Me A River" (A.Hamilton) sung by MARI WILSON
   MANTRA (Import through Discovery): MANTRA 058 (CD)
   original version by JULIE LONDON *(Capitol-EMI)*
McCLOUD - *see COLL.2,*
MacGYVER (USA88)(BBC1 8/4/89) theme mus: RANDY EDELMAN
      see COLL.17,350,
McHALE'S NAVY (USA TV) *see COLL.345,*
McVICAR (1980) Music score: JEFF WAYNE featuring ROGER
   DALTREY-JEFF WAYNE-PETE TOWNSHEND -S/T- *re-issue:*
   POLYDOR (Univ.): 527 341-2 (CD)
MACK AND MABEL - songs by Jerry Herman
   1.ORIG BROADWAY CAST 1974 ROBERT PRESTON-BERNADETTE
      PETERS *MCA (BMG): MCLD 19089 (CD)*
   2.LIVE IN CONCERT RECORDING UK 1988 Various Artists
      First Night (Pinn): OCRCD 6015 (CD)

MACKENNA'S GOLD (69) Music score: QUINCY JONES title song sung by JOSE FELICIANO -S/T- *TSUNAMI Import (Silva Screen): TSU 0123 (CD)*

MACROSS PLUS 2 (Japanese Animated MANGA video) -S/T- *DEMON (Pinn): DSCD 13 (CD)*

MAD CITY (1997) Music score: THOMAS NEWMAN -S/T- *VARESE (Pinn): VSD 5887 (CD)*

MAD COWS (1998) Music score by MARK THOMAS -S/T- on *EAST WEST (Ten): 8573 80314-2 (CD)*

MAD DOG AND GLORY (1992) Music score: ELMER BERNSTEIN -S/T- *VARESE (Pinn): VSD 5415 (CD)*

MAD LOVE (1995) Music sco: ANDY ROBERTS -S/T- inc V/A: 7YEAR BITCH-THRONEBERRY-GRANT LEE BUFFALO-FLUORESC EIN-ROCKET FROM THE CRYPT-HEAD CANDY-MADDER ROSE & KIRSTY MacCOLL *DEDICATED (RTM/DISC):DEDCD 022 (CD)*

MAD MAX (1979) Music score: BRIAN MAY -S/T- Import on *VARESE (Pinn): VCD 47144 (CD) see COLL.165,*

MAD MAX 2 (1981) Music score: BRIAN MAY -S/T- *VARESE (Pinn) VCD 47262 (CD) see COLL.165,264,*

MAD MAX 3 'Beyond Thunderdome' (1985) M: MAURICE JARRE -S/T- *GNP (ZYX): GNPD 8037 (CD)* see COLL.36,121,202,330,

MAD MONSTER PARTY (1966) Music by MAURY LAWS songs by MAURY LAWS & JULES BASS.t.song sung by ETHEL ENNIS *RETROGRADE (Hot/Silver Sounds): FSM 80125-2 (CD)*

MADAGASCAR:ISLAND OF GHOSTS (SURVIVAL) Anglia 13/11/91 Original music by ROSSY on 'Island Of Ghosts' on *REAL WORLD (Virgin): CDRW 19 (CD) RWMC 19 (MC)*

MADAME BOVARY (1949) Music score by MIKLOS ROSZA -S/T- sel.inc.music from IVANHOE/MADAME BOVARY/QUO VADIS PLYMOUTH ADVENTURE *IMPT (Silva Scr): TT 3001 (CD)*

MADAME SOUSATZKA (1988) Music score: GERALD GOURIET -S/T- *VARESE (Pinn): VSD 5204 (CD)* see COLL.83,85,313,

MADDIE ORIG LONDON CAST 1997 Songs by STEPHEN KEELING-SHAUN McKENNA. O.L.C. *feat:* SUMMER ROGNLIE-GRAHAM BICKLEY-KEVIN COLSON-LYNDA BARON *recording on DRESS CIRCLE (Silver Sounds): DRESSCD 003 (CD)*

MADELINE (1998) Music score: MICHEL LEGRAND -S/T- *SONY WONDER: 493 409-2 (CD) -4 (MC)*

MADNESS OF KING GEORGE The (94) Mus sco: GEORGE FENTON adapting music of G.F.HANDEL) with BAROQUE ORCH see COLL.73,144,

MAGDALENE (1988) Music score: CLIFF EIDELMAN -S/T- on *INTRADA (Koch/S.Screen): MFCD 7029 (CD)*

MAGIC ROUNDABOUT The (BBC1 64) theme: ALAIN LEGRAND VID: *BBC: BBCV 4278, 4494 see COLL.186,360,*

MAGIC SWORD The 2: The Quest For Camelot (1998) feat: vocals of ANDREA CARR and BRYAN WHITE -S/T- on *W.BROS (TEN): 7567 83112-2 (CD) -4 (MC)*

MAGICAL MYSTERY TOUR (1967) Feat music by The BEATLES -S/T- *PARLOPHONE (EMI): PCTC 255 (LP) TC-PCS 3077 (MC) CD-PCTC 255 (CD) SMMT 1 (2 x 7" singles)*

MAGICIAN The (USA TV) see COLL.349,

MAGICIAN'S HOUSE The (BBC1 31/10/1999) music score by
    KEN WILLIAMS *unavailable*
MAGILLA GORILLA (USA TV) *see COLL.345,*
MAGNIFICENT AMBERSONS The (1942) Mus: BERNARD HERRMANN
    -S/T- *5TH CONTINENT (Silva Screen): PRCD 1783 (CD)*
MAGNIFICENT SEVEN The (1960) Music sc: ELMER BERNSTEIN
    -S/T- also containing music from sequel 'RETURN OF
    THE M...' *RYKODISC (Vital): RCD 10741 (CD)*
    New recording by ROYAL SCOTTISH NATIONAL ORCHESTRA
    conducted and produced by ELMER BERNSTEIN on
    RCA VICTOR (BMG): 09026 63240-2 (CD)
    see COLL.41,70,358,400,401,
MAGNUM; P.I. (USA1980) theme: MIKE POST-PETE CARPENTER
    see COLL.17,109,110,270,283,347,363,390,
MAHABARAHTA (C4 9/12/90 Music composed & performed by
    TOSHI TCHUCHITORI -S/T- *REAL WORLD-VIRGIN (EMI):*
    CDRW 9 (CD) RWLP 9 (LP) RWMC 9 (MC)
MAHOGANY (1975) Music sc: MICHAEL MASSER theme "Do You
    Know Where You're Going To" (M.Masser-G.Goffin) by
    DIANA ROSS -S/T- *MOTOWN (Univ): E.530 277-2(CD)*
    see COLL.278,
MAHONEY'S LAST STAND (1975) *feat music by* RONNIE LANE
    and RON WOOD *produced by* GLYN JOHNS -S/T- reissue
    NEW MILLENNIUM (Pinn): PILOT 29 (CD)
MAIGRET (BBC1 1961) theme music: RON GRAINER
    see COLL.4,8,23,109,110,270,377,
MAIGRET (Granada 9/2/1991) theme music by NIGEL HESS
    vocal by OLIVE SIMPSON   *see COLL.7,193,*
MAJOR BARBARA (1941) Music score by Sir WILLIAM WALTON
    New Recording: Academy Of St.Martin-In-The Fields
    (Sir Neville Marriner) *CHANDOS: CHAN 8841 (CD)*
    + Music from 'Richard III' & 'Macbeth'
MAJOR DAD (USA TV) *see COLL.351,*

MAJOR DUNDEE (1965) Music score: DANIELE AMFITHEATROF
    -S/T- *TSUNAMI Germany (S.Screen): TSU 0111 (CD)*
MAJOR YEARS The (BBC1 11/10/1999) series music by
    HOWARD DAVIDSON *unavailable*
MAKING THE GRADES - *see* ALLAN QUARTERMAIN
MALCOLM (1986) Mus: SIMON JEFFES PENGUIN CAFE ORCH.
    Penguin Cafe Orch *EG-VIRG: EGED 11(CD)* Music From
     The PCO' *EGED 27* 'Broadcasting From Home' *EGED 38*
MALICE (1993) Music score: JERRY GOLDSMITH -S/T-
    VARESE (Pinn): VSD 5442 (CD)
MALICE AFORETHOUGHT (BBC2 15/3/79) music: RON GRAINER
    see COLL.8,
MAMBO KINGS The (1992) Music by various artists -S/T-
    ELEKTRA (TEN): 7559 61240-2 (CD) -4 (MC)
MAME - songs by Jerry Herman
  1.ORIG BROADWAY CAST 1966) *with* ANGELA LANSBURY & Co
    CBS USA (Sil.Screen) CK 03000 (CD) JST 03000 (MC)
MAMMA MIA (SHOW 1999) Songs of ABBA (Benny ANDERSSON
    Bjorn ULVAEUS & others) ORIGINAL LONDON CAST 1999
    POLYDOR (Univ): 543 115-2 (CD) -4 (MC)

MAN ABOUT THE HOUSE (UKGO 7/2/94 orig Thames 73) theme
"Up To Date" (JOHNNY HAWKESWORTH)
see *COLL.5,179,363,*

MAN ALIVE (BBC2 1960's) theme music: TONY HATCH
see *COLL.4,23,377,*

MAN AND A WOMAN A 'Un Homme Et Une Femme' (1966) Music
by FRANCIS LAI incl: 'Live For Life' (67) -S/T-
DRG (N.Note-Pinn): DRGCD 12612 (CD)
see *COLL.69,211,224,*

MAN CALLED HORSE, A (1970) Mus score: LEONARD ROSENMAN
-S/T- reissue *(Silva Screen): TT 3004 (CD)*

MAN CALLED IRONSIDE, A (USA) theme music: QUINCY JONES
see *COLL.2,121,270,281,344,345,377,*

MAN CALLED PETER, A see *COLL.1,*

MAN FROM U.N.C.L.E. The (1966) music: HUGO MONTENEGRO
(theme by JERRY GOLDSMITH) *imports via DISCOVERY*
MAN FROM UNCLE *RCA VICT.EUROPE 74321 63819-2 (CD)*
MORE MUSIC FROM T.MAN FROM UNCLE *74321 63706-2 CD*
also on *SIMPLY VIYNL (Telstar): SVLP 74 (2LP)*
ORIG TV -S/T- *RAZOR & TIE (Koch): RE 2133 (CD)*
HUGO MONTENEGRO -S/T-*RCA (BMG):74321 24179-2(CD)*
see *COLL.17,109,110,150,185,270,345,360,378,382,*

MAN IN A SUITCASE (ITC 27/9/67-68) theme: RON GRAINER
see *COLL.4,8,23,360,365,*

MAN IN THE GREY FLANNEL SUIT see *COLL.1,*

MAN IN THE IRON MASK The (1997) Music s: NICK GLENNIE-
SMITH -S/T- *MILAN (BMG): 74321 56495-2 (CD)*

MAN IN THE IRON MASK The (1976) Music: ALLYN FERGUSON
-S/T- incl: 'COUNT OF MONTE CRISTO' music (Allyn
Ferguson) *PROMETHEUS (Sil.Screen): PCD 130 (CD)*

MAN IN THE NEWS (LWT 69) mus: RON GRAINER see *COLL.8,*

MAN OF LA MANCHA - songs by Mitch Leigh and Joe Darion
1. FILM (1972) -S/T- *RYKODISC (Vital): RCD 10730 (CD)*
2. COMPLETE STUDIO RECORDING 1996 PLACIDO DOMINGO-
MANDY PATINKIN-SAMUEL RAMEY-JERRY HADLEY-CAROLANN
PAGE-ROBERT WHITE-ROSALIND ELIAS and Orchestra
SONY Classical (Ten): SK 46436 (CD) ST 46436 (MC)
3. ORIG BROADWAY CAST 1965 RICHARD KILEY-JOAN DIENER
IRVING JACOBSON-RAY MIDDLETON-ROBERT ROUNSEVILE-
JON CYPHER *MCA USA (S.Screen): MCAD 31065 (CD)*
4. ORIG FRENCH CAST "L'Homme De La Mancha" w: JACQUES
BREL-JOAN DIENER & Comp *(S.Screen): 839 586-2 (CD)*

MAN ON THE MOON (1999) featuring music by REM
-S/T- *WARNER (TEN): 9362 47483-2 (CD) -4 (MC)*

MAN TROUBLE (1992) see *COLL.84,86,*

MAN WHO KNEW TOO LITTLE The (1997) Music: CHRISTOPHER
YOUNG -S/T- *VARESE (Pinn): VSD 5886 (CD)*

MAN WITH THE GOLDEN GUN The (1974) Music: JOHN BARRY
title song (John Barry-Don Black) sung by LULU
-S/T- *reissue EMI PREMIER: CZ 552 (CD)*
see JAMES BOND FILM INDEX p.358   see *COLL.54,55,*

MAN'S TRAGEDY, A (1981) Music score ENNIO MORRICONE on
'BERNARDO BERTOLUCCI DOUBLE FEATURE' Collection on
DRG (Pinn): DRGCD 32910 (CD)

MANCHURIAN CANDIDATE The (1962) Music sco: DAVID AMRAM
 -S/T- *PREAMBLE (Silver Sounds): PRCD 1059 (CD)*
MANDELA (1996) -S/T- featuring VARIOUS ARTISTS on
 MANGO-ISLAND (Univ): CIDM(MCT) 1116
MANGALA THE INDIAN GIRL Film Soundtrack -S/T-
 Club Du Disques Arabe (HARMONIA MUNDI): AAA121(CD)
MANHATTAN (1979) Music score: GEORGE GERSHWIN -S/T-
 SONY: MK 36020(CD) see COLL.74,79,105,106,
MANNIX (USA/1967-74) theme music: LALO SCHIFRIN
 -S/T- SCORE *ALEPH (Koch): ALEP 014 (CD)*
 see *COLL.195,345,378,*
MANON DES SOURCES (1987) Music sco: JEAN CLAUDE PETIT
 see *COLL 74,*
MAP OF THE WORLD, A (1999) Music score by PAT METHENY
 -S/T- *WARNER USA: WB 47366 (CD)*
MARCUS WELBY, MD (USA TV) see *COLL.243,347,*
MARIUS (1931) MARCEL PAGNOL'S TRILOGY (1)/ music by
 FRANCIS GROMON on Coll 'Films Of Marcel Pagnol' on
 EMI FRA.(Discov): 855 883-2 (CD) see also 'FANNY'
MARK OF THE VAMPIRE (1957) - see 'RETURN OF DRACULA'
MARK OF ZORRO (1940) see *COLL.71,338,*
MARK TWAIN (MUSICAL) songs by WILLIAM PERRY
 ORIG CAST *PREAMBLE (Silver Sounds) PRCD 1012 (CD)*
MARLENE: A TRIBUTE TO DIETRICH (ORIG CAST RECORD 1997)
 PLAYBACK (Pinn): PBMARCD 1 (CD) PBMART 01 (MC)
MARNIE (1964) Music by BERNARD HERRMANN
 see *COLL.108,190,191,195,196,197,*
MARRYING MAN The - see 'TOO HOT TO HANDLE'
MARS ATTACKS! (1996) Mus score by DANNY ELFMAN -S/T-
 W.BROS (TEN): 7567 82992-2 (CD)
MARSEILLE CONTRACT (1974) Music sco: ROY BUDD -S/T-
 CINEPHILE (Pinn): CINCD 015
MARTHA MEET FRANK DANIEL AND LAURENCE (1998) Mus score
 by ED SHEARMUR -S/T- feat Various Artists on
 MERCURY (Univ): 558 396-2 (CD) -4 (MC)
MARTIN GUERRE songs: Alain Boublil-CLaude Michel
 Schonberg-Edward Hardy ORIGINAL LONDON CAST 1998
 FIRST NIGHT (Pinn): CASTCD 70 (CD)
 O.L.CAST 1996: FIRST NIGHT (Pinn): CAST(CD)(C) 59
MARVIN'S ROOM (1996) Music sco: RACHEL PORTMAN -S/T-
 with V.Arts *EDEL-HOLLYWOOD (Pinn): 012062-3 (CD)*
MARY HARTMAN, MARY HARTMAN (USA TV) see *COLL.349,*
MARY POPPINS (1964) Songs: RICHARD & ROBERT SHERMAN
 DISNEY'S MUSIC AND STORIES *DISNEY (Technicolor):*
 WD 77572-2 (CD) -4(MC) see WALT DISNEY INDEX p.362
MARY QUEEN OF SCOTS (1971) Music score: JOHN BARRY
 see *COLL.27,30,*
MARY TYLER MOORE SHOW (USA TV) see *COLL.256,346,*
M*A*S*H (FILM 1970) Mus sco: JOHNNY MANDEL-MIKE ALTMAN
 -S/T- *reissue: Columbia (Ten): CK 66804 (CD)*
 see *COLL.52,122,*
M*A*S*H (TVUSA 71-84 BBC2: 20/5/73) theme "Suicide Is
 Painless" (J.Mandel-M.Altman) *SONY: 983380-2(CD)*
 see *COLL.243,255,256,270,281,347,364,382,*

MASK OF ZORRO The (1998) Music score: JAMES HORNER
 song: "I Want To Spend My Lifetime Loving You"
 performed by TINA ARENA and MARC ANTHONY -S/T-
 SONY CLASSICS : SK 60627 (CD) ST 60627 (MC)
MASTER OF BALLANTRAE The (1984) Music: BRUCE BROUGHTON
 featuring The SINFONIA OF LONDON (Bruce Broughton)
 -S/T- on *PROMETHEUS (Silva Screen): PCR 501 (CD)*
MASTERMIND (BBC 1972-97 theme mus "Approaching Menace"
 NEIL RICHARDSON *see COLL.7,270,*
MATCH The Coca-Cola Cup theme "You Are The Number One"
 (Charlie Skarbek) UNION feat Paul Young *JIVE (BMG)*
 JIVECD 309 (CDs) see COLL.149,
MATCH OF THE DAY (BBC1 1970-99) theme mus "Offside" by
 BARRY STOLLER *see COLL.148,176,270,281,*
MATCH OF THE DAY (BBC1 1960's) theme "Drum Majorette"
 see COLL,147,176,
MATCH OF THE DAY 'Goal Of The Month' (BBC1 1999)
 "Sequence 3" GIAN PIERO REVERBERI-FRANCO REVERBERI
 from 'EROTICA ITALIA' *RCA (BMG):74321 54193-2 (CD)*
MATEWAN (1987) Music score: MASON DARING -S/T- Import
 DARING (Topic/Proj/DIR/CMD): DARINGCD 1011 (CD)
MATRIX The (1999) Music score by DON DAVIS
 -S/T- score: *VARESE (Pinn): VSD 6026 (CD)*
 -S/T- songs: *MAVERICK (Ten):9362 47419-2(CD)-4(MC)*
MATT HOUSTON (USA TV) *see COLL.350,*
MAVERICK (FILM 1994) *see COLL.165,*
MAVERICK (TV USA 57) title theme: PAUL FRANCIS WEBSTER
 and DAVID BUTTOLPH *see COLL.346,367,401,*
MAX HEADROOM (TV) *see COLL.311,323,351,*
MAYERLING (1935) Music score: ARTHUR HONEGGER Suite on
 MARCO POLO (Select): 8.223467 (CD)
ME AND MY GIRL - songs by Noel Gay and Douglas Furber
 1.ORIG LONDON CAST 1985 ROBERT LINDSAY-EMMA THOMPSON
 FRANK THORNTON and Company *EMI: CDP 746393-2 (CD)*
 2.ORIG BROADWAY CAST 1987 w ROBERT LINDSAY-MARYANN
 PLUNKETT *TER: CDTER 1145 (CD) DELETED 98*
 3.CARLTON SHOWS COLL STUDIO *with:* DAVID KERNAN-JACQUI
 SCOTT-TRACEY COLLIER-JOHN HOWARD-MASTER SINGERS
 CARLTON: PWKS(PWKMC) 4143 (CD/MC)
 4.CLASSIC MUSICALS SERIES *feat:* ROBERT LINDSAY
 MARYANN PLUNKETT-JANE SUMMERHAYS-GEORGE S.IRVING
 +songs from 'THE BOYFRIEND' *KOCH Int: 34080-2 (CD)*
MEDIC (USA 1955)"Blue Star" VICTOR YOUNG *see COLL.348,*
MEDICAL CENTER (USA TV) *see COLL.346,382,*

MEET JOE BLACK (1999) Music score: THOMAS NEWMAN -S/T-
 UNIVERSAL (BMG): UND 53229 (CD)
MEET ME IN ST.LOUIS (FILM 1944) *featuring JUDY GARLAND*
 -S/T- *reissue EMI PREMIER: CDODEON 2 (CD)*
MEET ME IN ST.LOUIS (O.BROADWAY CAST 1990) Songs (Hugh
 Martin-Ralph Blane) at Gershwin Theatre)
 DRG USA (Pinn): CDSBL 19002 (CD) SBLC 19002 (MC)
MEET THE FEEBLES (1991) Music sco: PETER DASENT + V/A
 -S/T- *NORMAL (Topic-Project-Dir): QDKCD 003 (CD)*

MEETING VENUS (1991) Mus (WAGNER) incid.score: RACHEL PORTMAN -S/T- *feat* KIRI TE KANAWA-RENE KOLLO with 'Tannhauser' *TELDEC: 229246336-2 -S/T- deleted see COLL.84,87,*

MELODY FOR TWO (1937) Film Musical - VARIOUS ARTISTS -S/T- includ.songs from 'GO INTO YOUR DANCE'/'YOU CAN'T HAVE EVERYTHING'/'YOU'LL NEVER GET RICH' on *GREAT MOVIE THEMES (Target-BMG): CD 60014 (CD)*

MELROSE PLACE (USA TV/SKY1 94) TV Soundtrack feat Var. Artists on *GIANT (BMG): 74321 22608-2(CD) -4(MC) see COLL.17,351,376,*

MEMORIES (Japan 95) Animated MANGA Film -S/T- *ANIMANGA-New Note (Pinn): AM 7 (CD)*

MEMPHIS BELLE (1990) Music score: GEORGE FENTON -S/T- *VARESE (Pinn): VSD(VSC) 5293 (CD/MC)* "Danny Boy" by Mark Williamson on: *VS 52937 (7"s)*

MEN BEHAVING BADLY (BBC1 1/7/94) theme music by ALAN LISK on COLL 'MEN BEHAVING BADLY' *REMEDIA (Pinn): REP 001CD (CD) see COLL.270,*

MEN FROM SHILOH (USA TV) *see COLL.349,*

MEN IN BLACK The (1996) M.sco: DANNY ELFMAN -S/T- V/A "Men In Black" composed and sung by WILL SMITH -S/T- *COLUMBIA (SM): 488 122-2 (CD) -04 (MC)*

MEN OF TWO WORLDS (1946) Music sco: Sir ARTHUR BLISS *new recording by* SLOVAK RADIO S.O. (Adriano) on *MARCO POLO (Select): 8.223315 (CD)*

MEN WITH GUNS (1998) Music sco: MASON DARING -S/T- VARIOUS ARTS *RYKODISC (Vital): RCD 10437 (CD)*

MEPHISTO WALTZ The (1971) Music sco: JERRY GOLDSMITH + score 'The OTHER' *VARESE (Pinn): VSD 5851 (CD)*

MERCURY RISING (1998) Music score: JOHN BARRY -S/T- *VARESE (Pinn): VSD 5925 (CD)*

MERLIN (1997,USA TV) Music score by TREVOR JONES with LONDON SYMPHONY ORCHESTRA *VARESE (Pinn): VSD 5929 (CD)*

MERRIE MELODIES (USA TV) *see COLL.332,346,*

MERRILY WE ROLL ALONG (CAST RECORDING) Songs: STEPHEN SONDHEIM Highlights: *TER (Koch): CDTER 1225*

MERRY CHRISTMAS MR.LAWRENCE (1983) M: RYUICHI SAKAMOTO *reiss: MILAN (BMG): 74321 22048-2 (CD) also on VIRGIN: CDV 2276 (CD) OVEDC 237 see COLL.122,262,*

MERRY WIDOW The (operetta) - songs by Franz Lehar

1. Studio Recording 1994 COMPLETE Operetta in German wit dialogue *feat:* BARBARA BONNEY-BRYN TERFEL-BOJE SKOVHUS-CHERYL STUDER-RAINER TROST-KARL MAGNUS FREDRIKSSON with Vienna Philh.Orch (Gardiner) *DG (Univers.): 439 911-2 (CD) -4 (MC)*
2. Studio Recording 1995 HIGHLIGHTS in English by SCOTTISH OPERA CHORUS & SCOTTISH NAT.ORCHESTRA (A.Gibson) *CFP (EMI): CDCFPSD 4742 (2CD)*
3. NEW SADLERS WELLS 1986 CAST (2 versions) Highlights 1: *SHOWTIME (THE-Disc): SHOWCD 037 (CD)*

<u>Highlights</u> 2: *TER (Koch): CDTEO 1003 (CD)*
<u>Complete</u>: *TER (Koch): CDTER 1111 (CD)*
  4.Studio Recording HIGHLIGHTS + songs from 'Land Of
    Smiles' on *EMI BELLE EPOQUE: CZS 767 872-2 (2CD)*
MERSEY BLUES (BBC2 14/01/1999) music by NEIL BARCLAY
  unavailable
MESSAGE The (MOHAMMED MESSENGER OF GOD)(1977) Music
  score: MAURICE JARRE Royal P.Orch on *SILVA SCREEN*
  (Koch): FILMCD 060 (CD) + mus 'Lion Of The Desert'
MESSAGE IN A BOTTLE (1999) Music score: GABRIEL YARED
  -S/T- (V.ARTISTS) *ELEKTRA (TEN) 7567 83163-2 (CD)*
MESSAGE TO LOVE: THE ISLE OF WIGHT FESTIVAL 1970 (BBC2
  26/8/95) *feat:* JIMI HENDRIX-FREE-BOB DYLAN-EMERSON
  LAKE & PALMER-JETHRO TULL-MILES DAVIS-THE DOORS-
  THE WHO-TINY TIM *ESSENTIAL (BMG): EDFCD 327 (CD)*
MESSENGER The: THE STORY OF JOAN OF ARC (1999) Music
  score by ERIC SERRA -S/T- on
  COLUMBIA (Ten): SK 66537 (CD)
METROLAND (1997) Music score: MARK KNOPFLER -S/T- on
  MERCURY (Univ): 536 912-2 (CD) -4 (MC)
METROPOLIS (O.LONDON CAST 1988) Music (Joe BROOKS) Lyr
  ics (Joe BROOKS-Dusty HUGHES) *with* BRIAN BLESSED-
  JUDY KUHN-GRAHAM BICKLEY-JONATHAN ADAMS & Company
  TER (Koch): CDTER2 1168 (CDx2)
MIAMI 7 (BBC1 08/04/1999) music by PAUL HARDCASTLE and
  KEN BOLAM *unavailable* / featuring music by S CLUB 7
  "Bring It All Back" *POLYD: 561 085-2 (CDs) -4 (MCs)*
  "S Club Party" *POLYDOR: 561 417-2 (CDs)*
   S CLUB 7 ALBUM *POLYDOR: 543 103-2 (CD) -4 (MC)*
MIAMI VICE (USA orig BBC1 4/2/85) theme: JAN HAMMER
  'Best Of Miami Vice' *MCA: 241 746-2/-4/-1(CD/MC)*
  'MIAMI VICE 1' *MCA (BMG): MCLD 19024 (CD)*
  see COLL.109,110,122,270,339,347,356,
MICHAEL (1997) Mus score by RANDY NEWMAN -S/T- V.Arts
  REVOLUTION (BMG): 74321 41880-2 (CD)
MICHAEL COLLINS (1996) Music score: ELLIOT GOLDENTHAL
  -S/T- *Atlantic (TEN): 7567 82960-2 (CD) -4 (MC)*
MICHAEL PALIN'S HEMINGWAY ADVENTURE (BBC1 17/10/1999)
  Series music score by HOWARD DAVIDSON *unavailable*
MICHURIN (FILM Score) Suite Op.78 (Shostakovich) USSR
  RADIO & TV ORCH *Melodiya (BMG): 74321 32041-2 CD*
MICKEY BLUE EYES (1999) Music score: BASIL POLEDOURIS
  -S/T- *MILAN (BMG): 73421 69991-2 (CD)*
MICKEY'S CHRISTMAS CAROL *see* WALT DISNEY INDEX p.362
MICROCOSMOS (1996) Music score by BRUNO COULAIS and
  featuring mezzo-soprano MARIE KOBAYASHI -S/T-
  AUVIDIS (Harmonia Mundi): K.1028 (CD)
MIDNIGHT CALLER (USA)(BBC 28/1/89) theme: BRAD FIEDEL
  see COLL.17,351,
MIDNIGHT COWBOY (1969) Music score: JOHN BARRY t.song
  "Everybody's Talkin'" (Fred Neil) by NILSSON -S/T-
  EMI PREMIER: PRMCD 6 (CDP 748409-2) (CD)
  SIMPLY VINYL (Vital): SVLP 150 (LP)
  see COLL.27,28,29,30,31,34,35,52,238,239,359,

MIDNIGHT EXPRESS (1978) Music: GIORGIO MORODER -S/T-
    CASABLANCA (Univ): 824 206-2 (CD)
    see *COLL.122,*
MIDNIGHT IN THE GARDEN OF GOOD AND EVIL (1997) Music
    score: LENNIE NIEHAUS inc.songs by Various Arts
    -S/T- *MALPASO-WARNER (TEN): 9362 46829-2 (CD)*
MIDSOMER MURDERS (ITVN 23/3/1997) Music by JIM PARKER
    -S/T- *OCEAN DEEP (Grapevine/Poly): OCD 013 (CD)*
MIDSUMMER NIGHT'S DREAM, A (1999) Music: SIMON BOSWELL
    -S/T- *DECCA (Univ): 466 098-2 (CD)*
MIDSUMMER NIGHT'S SEX COMEDY (1982) music MENDELSSOHN
    see *COLL.82,84,*
MIDWAY (1976) Music sco: JOHN WILLIAMS / new record
    VARESE (Pinn): VSD 5940 (CD)
MIDWEEK see *COLL.6,*
MIGHTY APHRODITE (1996) Music arr/cond: DICK HYMAN
    -S/T- on *SONY Classics (SM): SK 62253 (CD)*
MIGHTY JOE YOUNG (1998) Music sco: JAMES HORNER -S/T-
    EDEL-Hollywood (Pinn): 010090-2HWR (CD)
MIGHTY MOUSE (USA TV) see *COLL.346,*
MIKADO The (operetta) - songs by Gilbert and Sullivan
    1.D'OYLY CARTE OPERA COMPANY 1989 (Jonathan Miller)
      featuring LESLIE GARRETT-ERIC IDLE-FELICITY PALMER
      Highlights: *SHOWTIME (MCI-THE): SHOW(CD)(MC) 005*
      Complete: *TER: CDTER2 1178 (2CD) ZCTED 1178 (2MC)*
    2.SADLER'S WELLS OPERA ORCH & CHORUS (A.FARIS) JOHN
      HOLMES-JOHN WAKEFIELD-CLIVE REVILL-DENIS DOWLING
      JOHN HEDDLE NASH-MARION STUDHOLME-PATRICIA KERN-
      CFP (EMI): CDCFPD(TCCPFD)4730 (2CDs/2MC)
    3.PRO-ARTE ORCHEST (Malcolm Sargent) GLYNDEBOURNE
      FESTIVAL CHOIR Solo: OWEN BRANNIGAN-RICHARD LEWIS
      GERAINT EVANS-IAN WALLACE *EMI:CMS 764403-2 (2CD)*
    4.HIGHLIGHTS feat National Opera Company
      TER (Koch): CDTER 1121 (CD)
    5.D'OYLY CARTE OPERA COMPANY - Royal Philharm Orch
      (R.Nash) - *LONDON (Univ): 425 190-2 (CDx2)*
MIKE AND ANGELO (ITV 05/01/1999) music by ALAN COATES
    and KIM GOODY *unavailable*
MIKE HAMMER (USA 83 revival) theme "Harlem Nocturne"
    (Earle Hagen) KEN MACKINTOSH ORCH on 'Mac's Back'
    President: PLCD 532 (CD) see COLL
MILL ON THE FLOSS The (BBC1 1/1/1997) Music score by
    JOHN SCOTT -S/T- *JOS (Silva Screen): JSCD 124 (CD)*
MILLENNIUM (BBC2 UK/Canada Co-Prod 3/1/93) music score
    HANS ZIMMER arranged & performed by MARK MANCINA
    -S/T- *NARADA Cinema (Pinn): ND 66001 (CD)*
MILLENNIUM: A 1000 YEARS OF HISTORY (BBC2 18/10/1999)
    Music score by RICHARD BLACKFORD and GLENN KEILES
    performed by The BBC CONCERT ORCHESTRA with The
    BOURNEMOUTH SYMPHONY CHORUS
    -S/T- *POINT (Pinn): MM 8969CD (CD) MM 8969MC (MC)*
MILLION TO JUAN, A (1993) Music: STEVEN JAE JOHNSON &
    JEFFREY DEAN JOHNSON and Various Artists -S/T-
    RMM (N.Note-Pinn/Silver Sounds): RMD 81305-2 (CD)

MIMIC (1997) Music score: MARCO BELTRAMI -S/T- on
  VARESE (Pinn): VSD 5863 (CD)
MINDER (Thames 11/9/80) "I Could Be So Good For You"
  (Gerard Kenny-Pat Waterman) by DENNIS WATERMAN
  see COLL.363,
MINTY (ITV Children 08/11/1998) MINTY TV series songs
  VIRGIN: VTCD 233 (CD) VTMC 233 (MC) VSCDT 1728 CDs
MINUS MAN (1999) Music score by CHRIS COVERT -S/T-
  VARESE (Pinn): VSD 6043 (CD)
MIRACLE ON 34TH STREET (1994) Music s: BRUCE BROUGHTON
  -S/T- NATALIE COLE-DIONNE WARWICK-ELVIS PRESLEY
  ARISTA (BMG): 07822 11022-2 (CD) -4 (MC)
MIRROR HAS TWO FACES The (96) Mus sco: MARVIN HAMLISCH
  -S/T- *feat:* BARBRA STREISAND-RICHARD MARX-LUCIANO
  PAVAROTTI *COLUMBIA (Ten): 485 395-2 (CD) -4 (MC)*
MISFITS The (1961) Music score: ALEX NORTH -S/T- reis
  RYKODISC (Vital): RCD 10735 (CD, 1998)
  TSUNAMI (Silva Screen): TCI 0609 (CD)
MISHIMA 'A Life In Four Chapters' (1985) Music: PHILIP
  GLASS -S/T- *ELEKTRA Nonesuch (TEN): 7559 79113-2*
MISS MARPLE (BBC1 from 26/12/84) theme: ALAN BLAIKLEY-
  KEN HOWARD *see COLL.46,109,110,170,390,*
MISS SAIGON - songs by Alain Boublil - Claude Michel
  Schonberg and Richard Maltby Jnr.
  1.ORIG LONDON CAST 1989   LEA SALONGA-JONATHAN PRYCE
  SIMON BOWMAN-PETER POLYCARPOU & Company
  2.HIGHLIGHTS: *FIRST NIGHT (Pinn): CAST(C)(CD) 38*
  3.SYMPHONIC SUITES: *KIMCD1 (2CD) KIMC1 (MC) also on*
  CASTCD 39 (CD) CASTC 39 (MC)
  4.ROYAL PHILHARMONIC ORCHESTRA *PLAY SUITES from*
  Miss Saigon and Les Miserables
  CARLTON INT: PWKS(PWKMC) 4079 (CD/MC)
  5.INTERNATIONAL CAST RECORDING (HIGHLIGHTS)
  FIRST NIGHT (Pinn): CASTCD 60 (CD) CASTMC 60 (MC)
  6.SHOWS COLLECT *CARLTON: PWKS(PWKMC) 4229 (CD/MC)*
MISSA LUBA (AFRICAN MASS) KENYAN FOLK MELODIES By The
  MUUNGANO NATIONAL CHOIR, Boniface MGANGA (M.dir)
  PHILIPS (Univ): 426 836-2 (CD) -4 (MC)
MISSING (1982) Music score: VANGELIS available vers:
  VANGELIS on 'Themes' *POLYDOR: 839518-2 (CD) -4(MC)*
  SHADOWS on 'Diamonds' *CARLTON: PWKS 4018P (CD)*
  see COLL.278,380,
MISSION IMPOSSIBLE (ORIG TV ser) theme: LALO SCHIFRIN
  TV -S/T- *reissue:* MCA (BMG): MCLD 19320 (CD)
  see COLL.3,110,118,121,229,360,365,366,
MISSION IMPOSSIBLE (1996) Music sco: DANNY ELFMAN orig
  theme (Lalo Schifrin) version by Larry Mullen and
  Adam Clayton (U2) -S/T- *feat* PULP-GARBAGE-BJORK-
  MASSIVE ATTACK-CAST-GAVIN FRIDAY-MULLEN & CLAYTON
  MOTHER-ISLAND (Univ): MUMCD 9603 (CD)
  see COLL.13,49,52,195,199,372,
MISSION IMPOSSIBLE (USA 60s re-r BBC2 87) theme: LALO
  SCHIFRIN plus NEW 91 series music: JOHN E.DAVIS
  -S/T- *GNP (ZYX): GNPD(GNP-5) 8029 (CD-MC)*

MISSION The (1986) Music sco ENNIO MORRICONE -S/T-
  Virgin (EMI): TCV 2402 (MC) CDV 2402 (CD) MDV
  2402 (MiniD) see COLL.43,144,239,250,251,262,331,
MISSOURI BREAKS (1976) Music sco: JOHN WILLIAMS -S/T-
  reissue RYKODISC (Vital): RCD 10748 (CD)
MISSISSIPPI: RIVER OF SONG (USA TV SERIES 1999)
  FOLK MUSIC HISTORY OF AMERICA - VARIOUS ARTISTS
  SMITHSONIAN FOLKWAYS (Koch): SFW 40086 (2CD)
MISSISSIPPI BURNING (1988) Music sco: TREVOR JONES
  -S/T- *re-iss.on Spectrum (Univ): 551 100-2 (CD)*
MISTER - *see under 'MR.'*
MOBO AWARDS 1999 (C4   07/10/1999) VARIOUS ARTISTS COLL
  UNIVERSAL MUSIC: 545 143-2 (2CD) 545 143-4 (2MC)
MOBY DICK (USA TV mini-s.1998) Music sco: CHRISTOPHER
  GORDON -S/T- *VARESE (Pinn): VSD 5921 (CD)*
MOBY DICK (O.LONDON CAST 1992) Songs (Robert Longdon-
  Hereward Kaye) *w.* TONY MONOPOLY-HOPE AUGUSTUS-THE
  RESA KARTEL & Co *FIRST NIGHT (Pinn): DICKCD 1 (CD)*
MOD SQUAD The (1999) Music score: B.C.SMITH -S/T- V/A
  ELEKTRA (TEN): 7559 62364-2 (CD) -4 (MC)
MOD SQUAD (USA TV) *see COLL.345,378,*
MODERN TIMES (1936) Music by CHARLES CHAPLIN
  see COLL.66,90,211,
MODERNS The (1988) Music score: MARK ISHAM Songs by
  Charles Couture -S/T- *VIRGIN (EMI): CDV 2530 (CD)*
MOJO (1997) Music sco: MURRAY GOLD -S/T- V.ARTISTS
  EMI Premier -S/T- 821 718-2 (CD)
MOLL FLANDERS (ITV 1/12/1996) Original music composed
  and directed by JIM PARKER *unavailable*
MOLL FLANDERS (FILM 1996) Music score: MARK MANCINA
  -S/T- *Import LONDON (Univ): 452 485-2 (CD)*
MOLL FLANDERS (O.LONDON CAST 1993) Songs (Geo.Stiles-
  -Paul Leigh) *feat* JOSIE LAWRENCE-ANGELA RICHARDS
  FIRST NIGHT (Pinn): OCRCD 6036 (CD)
MON ONCLE (Jacques Tati 1956) Music sco: ALAIN ROMAINS
  -S/T- + 'JOUR DE FETE'/'MONSIEUR HULOT'S HOLIDAY'
  POLY (Discov): 836 983-2 (CD)   see COLL.343,
MONA LISA (1986) *see COLL.77,238,*
MONDO TOPLESS - *see* 'CHERRY HARRY AND RAQUEL'
MONEY PROGRAMME (BBC2 4/1966-88 & 1995-99) 'theme from
  Carpetbaggers' (ELMER BERNSTEIN) by JIMMY SMITH on
  'The Cat' *VERVE (Univ): 810 046-2 (CD)*
MONEY TALKS (1997) V/A *inc:* BARRY WHITE & FAITH EVANS-
  LISA STANSFIELD-MARY J.BLIGE-SWV-ANGIE STONE-DEVOX
  -S/T- *RCA (BMG): 07822 18975-2 (CD) -4 (MC) -1(LP)*
MONK DAWSON (1998) Music score: MARK JENSEN -S/T- V/A
  De WARRENNE PICTURES (Koch): DWPCD 01 (CD)
MONKEES The (USA 1966) theme (Boyce-Hart) THE MONKEES
  ARISTA: 257874 (CD)   see COLL.346,364, (Head)
MONOCLED MUTINEER (BBC1 31/8/86) *see COLL.19,*
MONSIEUR HULOT'S HOLIDAY (Jacques Tati 1953) Mus score
  (A.ROMAINS-Franck BARCELLINI) Music from His Films
  POLYG (Discov): 836 983-2 (CD) see COLL 343,
MONTH IN THE COUNTRY, A (1987) *see COLL.86,*

MONTY PYTHON AND THE HOLY GRAIL (1975) Mus: NEIL INNES
-S/T- *VIRGIN (EMI): VCCCD 004 (CD) VCCMC 004 (MC)*
MONTY PYTHON'S FLYING CIRCUS (BBC2 5/10/69-1974) theme
music "Liberty Bell March" (John Phillip SOUSA)
"INSTANT MONTY PYTHON CD COLLECTION" (6CD Box set)
VIRGIN: CDBOX 3 (CDx6) "Ultimate MONTY PYTHON Rip
Off" *VIRGIN (EMI): CDV(TCV) 2748 (CD/MC)*
see COLL.104,122,270,346,
MONTY PYTHON'S LIFE OF BRIAN (1979) Music score by
GEOFFREY BURGON, Songs by ERIC IDLE
VIRGIN (EMI): VCCCD 009 (CD) VCCMC 009 (MC)
MONTY PYTHON'S MEANING OF LIFE (1983) M: JOHN DU PREZ
ERIC IDLE *VIRGIN EMI: VCCD 010(CD) VCCMC 010(MC)*
see COLL.338,
MOON AND SON (BBC1 4/6/92) Mus:DENIS KING see COLL.19,
MOON OVER MIAMI (1941) -S/T- featur: BETTY GRABLE-DON
AMECHE incl.mus.from 'Broadway Melody Of 1938'
GREAT MOVIE THEMES (Target-BMG): CD 60030 (CD)
MOONLIGHTING (USA BBC2 29/5/86) t.theme (Al Jarreau-
Lee Holdridge) by AL JARREAU see COLL.350,
MOONRAKER (1979) Music score: JOHN BARRY title song
(John Barry-Hal David) sung by SHIRLEY BASSEY
-S/T- *EMI PREM: CZ 551 (CD)* see COLL.54,273,314,
see also JAMES BOND FILM INDEX p.358
MOONSTRUCK (1987) see COLL.80,81,159,271,273,274,275,
MOONWALKER (1988) Music sco: BRUCE BROUGHTON Songs by
Michael Jackson "Bad" *EPIC: 450290-2(CD) -4(MC)*
'Moonwalker Suite' (Bruce BROUGHTON) "Fantastic
Journey" *TELARC (BMG-Con): CD 80231 (CD)*
MORE (1969) Music score comp/performed by PINK FLOYD
-S/T- reiss: *EMI: CDEMD 1084 (CD) TCEMD 1084 (MC)*
MORE THAN A MIRACLE (1967) Music score: PIERO PICCIONE
-S/T- Import *(SILVA SCREEN): CDST 304 (CD)*
MORECAMBE & WISE SHOW The (BBC1 1966-84) Var.themes:
"Bring Me Sunshine"/"Positive Thinkin'"/"We Get
Along So Easily Don't You Agree" sung by MORECAMBE
& WISE on 'Get Out Of That' *EMI: ECC 29 (MC only)*
'Bring Me Sunshine' see COLL.281,407,
MORK AND MINDY (USA 78 / C4 16/3/93) theme music by
PERRY BOTKIN JNR see COLL.17,350,362,
MORTAL KOMBAT (1995) Music sco: GEORGE S.CLINTON -S/T-
+ V.Arts *LONDON (Univ.): 828 715-2 (CD) -4 (MC)*
'MORE KOMBAT' on *EDEL (Pinn): 0022672CIN (CD)*
MORTAL KOMBAT: ANNIHILATION (1997) VARIOUS ARTS -S/T-
LONDON (Univ): 828 999-2 (CD) -4 (MC)
MOST HAPPY FELLA The - songs by Frank Loesser
 1.NEW BROADWAY CAST 1991 SPIRO MALAS-SOPHIE HAYDEN
CLAUDIA CATTANIA *RCA (BMG):09026 61294-2 CD* del.95
MOTOR RACING see GRAND PRIX (BBC) 'F1'(FORMULA 1 (ITV)
MOTORWAY LIFE (ITV 05/9/1998) theme "2-4-6-8 Motorway"
by TOM ROBINSON BAND on 'Rising Free: The Best Of
Tom Robinson' *EMI GOLD (EMI): CDGOLD 1098 (CD)*
MOUSE HUNT (1997) Music score: ALAN SILVESTRI -S/T-
VARESE (Pinn): VSD 5892 (CD)

MR.& MRS.(Border 18/1/84) theme music "Be Nice To Each
Other" TONY HATCH & JACKIE TRENT *see COLL.184,*
MR.BEAN (ITV 1/1/1990) theme "Ecce Homo Qui Est Faba"
(Behold The Man Who Is A Bean) by HOWARD GOODALL
on collection 'HOWARD GOODALL'S CHOIR WORKS'
ASV (Select): CDDCA 1028 (CD)
MR.CINDERS (REV.LONDON CAST 1983) Songs (Vivian Ellis
Richard Myers-Clifford Grey-Leo Robin)
TER (Koch): CDTER 1069 (CD)
MR.ED (USA 60s) *see COLL.256,345,*
MR.HOLLAND'S OPUS (1995) Mus sco: MICHAEL KAMEN + V/A:
-S/T-(songs) *POLYDOR (Univ): 529 508-2 (CD)*
-S/T-(score) *POLYDOR (Univ): 452 062-2 (CD) -4(MC)*
MR.LUCKY (USA) theme: HENRY MANCINI *see COLL.238,378,*
MR.MAGOO (USA TV) *see COLL.347,*
MR.MEN & LITTLE MISSES (BBC1 76) Arthur LOWE-Pauline
COLLINS-J.ALDERTON *MSD: KIDM 9002/3 (MC)* also
'BEST MR.MEN ALBUM IN THE WORLD..EVER' inc: THEME
VIRGIN (EMI): VTCD 166 (CD) VTMC 166 (MC)
MR.ROSE (Granada 17/2/67-5/12/68) theme music "Mr.Rose
Investigates" (Snow) *see COLL.23,60,185,*
MR.SKEFFINGTON (1944) Music by FRANZ WAXMAN. *NEW REC:*
MOSCOW SYMPHONY ORCH. (William T.Stromberg,cond.)
MARCO POLO (Select(: 8225037 (CD) see COLL.393,
MR.WONDERFUL (O.BROADWAY CAST 1956) Songs (Jerry Bock-
George Weiss-Larry Holfencor) *with* Sammy Davis Jnr
MCA USA (S.Screen): MCAD 10303(CD) MCAC 10303(MC)
MR.WRONG (1996) Music score by CRAIG SAFAN -S/T- on
EDEL-HOLLYWOOD (Pinn): 012 041-2 (CD)
MRS.BRADLEY MYSTERIES (BBC1 31/8/1998) mus.arranged by
GRAHAM DALBY, perf.by GRAHAM DALBY & GRAHAMOPHONES
on 'MAD DOGS AND ENGLISHMEN' *PRESIDENT: PCOM 1097
(CD)* 'TRANSATLANTIQUE' *PRESIDENT: PCOM 1128 (CD)*
MRS.BROWN (1997) Music score: STEPHEN WARBECK -S/T- on
MILAN (BMG): 74321 51072-2 (CD)
MRS.DALLOWAY (1997) Music score: ILONA SEKACZ -S/T- on
MILAN (BMG): 74321 57231-2 (CD)
MRS.DOUBTFIRE (1993) Music score: HOWARD SHORE -S/T-
ARISTA (BMG): 07822 11015-2 (CD) -4 (MC)
see COLL.74,105,273,
MRS.MERTON AND MALCOLM (BBC1 22/02/1999) music by
JONATHAN WHITEHEAD *unavailable*
MRS.PARKER AND THE VICIOUS CIRCLE (1994) Music: MARK
ISHAM -S/T- *VARESE (Pinn): VSD 5471 (CD)*
MRS.WINTERBOURNE (1996) Music sco: PATRICK DOYLE -S/T-
VARESE (Pinn): VSD 5720 (CD)
MULAN (1998) Music: JERRY GOLDSMITH -S/T- *DISNEY-EDEL
(Pinn): 010 631-2 (CD) -4 (MC) see also p.362*
MULHOLLAND FALLS (1996) Music score: DAVE GRUSIN -S/T-
EDEL-Cinerama (Pinn): 002259-2CIN (CD)
MUMMY The (1959) Music score by FRANZ REIZENSTEIN
GDI (ABM): GDICD 006 (CD)
MUMMY The (1997) Music score by JERRY GOLDSMITH -S/T-
DECCA (Univ): 466 458-2 (CD)

MUNSTERS The (USA 63) title theme: JACK MARSHALL
    see COLL.17,345,378,
MUPPET SHOW The (ITV 76/BBC1 86) theme: SAM POTTLE
    see COLL.270,347,
MUPPET MOVIE The (1979) Music and songs: PAUL WILLIAMS
    KENNY ASCHER feat: JIM HENSON-FRANK OZ-DAVE GOELZ
    reiss: ARISTA (BMG): 74321 18247-2 (CD) -4 (MC)
MUPPETS FROM SPACE (1999) Music sco: JAMSHIED SHARIFI
    VARESE (Pinn): VSD 6060 (CD)
MURDER ON THE ORIENT EXPRESS see COLL.387,
MURDER SHE WROTE (USA) theme music by JOHN ADDISON
    see COLL.17,270,
MURDER WAS THE CASE (1994) Mus by SNOOP DOGGY DOGG+ VA
    -S/T- INTERSCOPE-MCA (BMG): IND 92484 (CD) also on
MURIEL'S WEDDING (1994) Music score: PETER BEST -S/T-
    POLYDOR (Univ): 527 493-2 (CD) 527 493-4 (MC)
MURPHY BROWN (USA TV) see COLL.351,
MURPHY'S LAW (1986) - see DEATH WISH
MUSE The (1999) Music score by ELTON JOHN -S/T- on
    IMS MERCURY (Univ): AA 3145 46517-2 (CD)
MUSIC AND THE MIND (C4 5/5/96) feat The MEDICI STRING
    QUARTET / PAUL ROBERTSON (speaker) music to accomp
    any the series KOCH SCHWANN (Koch): 36437-2 (CD)
MUSIC IN MINIATURE (BBC) theme "Elizabethan Serenade"
    RONALD BINGE see COLL.50,56,138,142,147,170,
MUSIC MAN The - Songs by Meredith Willson
    1.FILM MUSICAL 1962 ROBERT PRESTON-SHIRLEY JONES
    -S/T- WB USA (S.Screen): 1459-2 (CD) M5 1459 (MC)
    2.ORIG LONDON CAST 1961 with VAN JOHNSON-PATRICIA
    LAMBERT-RUTH KETTLEWELL-MICHAEL MALNICK and Comp
    LASERLIGHT POP-TARGET (BMG): 12447 (CD)
MUSIC TEACHER The (1990) -S/T- Operatic Classical Mus
    PRESIDENT (BMG): PCOM(PTLC) 1109 (CD/MC)
MUTINY ON THE BOUNTY (1984) - see BOUNTY
MY BEST FRIEND'S WEDDING (1997) Music sco:JAMES NEWTON
    HOWARD -S/T- (V.Arts) SONY: 488 115-2 (CD) -4(MC)
MY COUSIN RACHEL (1952) see COLL.394,
MY COUSIN VINNY (1991) Music sco: RANDY EDELMAN -S/T-
    VARESE (Pinn): VSD 5364 (CD)
MY DINNER WITH ANDRE (1981) see COLL.74,84,
MY FAIR LADY - songs Alan Jay Lerner & Frederick Loewe
    1.FILM MUSICAL 1964 REX HARRISON-AUDREY HEPBURN
    sung by MARNI NIXON -S/T- SONY: CD 70000 (CD) and
    also SK(ST) 66711 (CD/MC)
    2.O.BROADWAY CAST 1956 REX HARRISON-JULIE ANDREWS-
    STANLEY HOLLOWAY-ROBERT COOTE-ZENA DARE-AL.DUDLEY
    COLUMBIA (Ten): SMK 60539 (CD)
    3.O.LONDON CAST 1958 REX HARRISON-JULIE ANDREWS-STAN
    LEY HOLLOWAY COL (S.Scr): CK 02105(CD) 02105 (MC)
    4.STUDIO RECORD 1987 w: KIRI TE KANAWA-JEREMY IRONS-
    WARREN MITCHELL-JOHN GIELGUD DECCA: 421 200-2 CD
    5.CARLTON SHOWS COLLECT.STUDIO 1994 DENNIS QUILLEY
    LIZ ROBERTSON-IAN WALLACE-NICK CURTIS and Company
    CARLTON SHOWS: PWKS(PWKMC) 4174 (CD/MC)

6.CLASSIC MUSICALS SERIES *w:* ALEC McCOWEN and TINUKE OLAFIMIHAN-RON MOODY-HENRY WICKMAN & others + *songs from* 'CAMELOT' *KOCH INT: 34079-2 (CD)*

7.ORIG MASTERWORKS EDIT. *w:* ALEC McCOWEN-BOB HOSKINS TINUKE OLAFIMIHAN-DUCLIE GRAY-HENRY WICKHAM-MICHAEL DENISON *TER (Koch): CDTER2 1211 (2CD)*

MY FAVORITE MARTIAN (USA TV) *see COLL.346,*

MY FELLOW AMERICANS (1996) -S/T- with VARIOUS ARTISTS -S/T- *SNAPPER (Pinn): SMACD 807 (CD)*

MY GEISHA (1962) *see COLL.81,394,*

MY LEFT FOOT (1989) *see COLL.81,88,274,*

MY MOTHER THE CAR (USA TV) *see COLL.346,*

MY NAME IS JOE (1998) Music score: GEORGE FENTON -S/T- + "Down The Dustpipe" (STATUS QUO) "Spirit In The Sky" (NORMAN GREENBAUM) Violin Con.Op.61 BEETHOVEN *DEBONAIR (Pinn): CDDEB 1008 (CD, 10.1998)*

MY NAME IS NOBODY (1973) Music score ENNIO MORRICONE ENNIO MORRICONE ORCH on Coll 'An Ennio Morricone Quintet' *DRG USA (Pinn): DRGCD 32907 (CD)* *see COLL.250,358,*

MY SO CALLED LIFE (C4 26/7/95) mus: W.G.SNUFFY WALDEN -S/T- *WEA: 7567 82721-2 (CD)* -4 *(MC) see COLL.351,*

MY SON THE FANATIC (1998) Music score: STEPHEN WARBECK -S/T- (Var.Arts) *MCI (Pinn-Disc): MPRCD 010 (CD)*

MY THREE SONS (USA TV) *see COLL.345,378,*

MY TWO DADS (USA C4 from 10/5/90) theme "You Can Count On Me" (GREG EVIGAN-Lenny Macallso-Michael Jacobs) *see COLL.351,*

MY WILDERNESS REPRIEVED (BBC2 8/4/93) theme mus "Minuet" from 'A Downland Suite' (John Ireland) ENGLISH CHAMBER ORCH, David Garforth *CHANDOS: CHAN 8390 CD*

MYSTERIES OF EDGAR WALLACE The (ITV 60s) Theme "Man Of Mystery" (Michael Carr) THE SHADOWS 'In The 60s' *MFP (EMI): CDMFP 6076 (CD) (TC)MFP 5873 (MC/LP)*

MYSTERIOUS ISLAND (1961) Music: BERNARD HERRMANN -S/T- *see COLL.188,192,248,*

MYSTERIOUS UNIVERSE - *see* ARTHUR C.CLARKE'S...

MYSTERY MOVIE (USA TV) *see COLL.346,*

MYSTERY OF MEN (BBC1 30/08/1999) incidental music by COLIN TOWNS *unavailable.* theme music "HI HO SILVER LINING" by JEFF BECK on 'Best Of of Jeff Beck' *MFP (EMI): CDMFP 6202 (CD) TCMFP 6202 (MC)*

MYTH OF FINGERPRINTS (1997) Music score: DAVID BRIDIE- and JOHN PHILLIPS -S/T- *featuring* VARIOUS ARTISTS *VELVET (Pinn): VEL 797052 (CD)*

N AKED (BBC2 25/11/1998) Mus: ANDY COWTON *unavailable*

NAKED BOYS SINGING (CELEBRATION THEATRE CAST 1998) *DUCY LEE (Silver Sounds): 7042 771210-2 (CD)*

NAKED CAGE The (1985) - *see* CRY IN THE DARK

NAKED CHEF The (BBC2 14/04/1999) ser.title music by LUKE GORDON *unavailable*

NAKED CITY The (1948) Music sco: MIKLOS ROZSA select. on 'LUST FOR LIFE' *VARESE (Pinn): VSD 5405 (CD)*

NAKED CITY The (USA 1958-63) theme music by BILLY MAY
   versions by KEN MACKINTOSH 'Mac's Back' *PRESIDENT:*
   PLCD 532 (CD) see COLL.23,184,377,378,
NAKED NASHVILLE (C4 11/7/1998) ser.title music "Good
   Luck'n'Good Truckin' Tonite" DALE WATSON -S/T- inc
   MINDY McCREADY-GEORGE STRAIT-REBA McENTIRE-TRISHA
   YEARWOOD-RICKY SKAGGS-PATSY CLINE-TAMMY WYNETTE
   RCA NASHVILLE/C4 (BMG): 74321 58757-2 (CD) -4 (MC)
NAME OF THE ROSE (1986) Music sco: JAMES HORNER -S/T-
   VIRGIN France (Discovery): 88085-2 (CD)
NAPOLEON (1927) 1982 Score composed and conducted by
   CARL DAVIS *SILVA SCREEN (Koch): FILMCD 149 (CD)*
   also with S.C.Orchestra *CFP (EMI): CDCFP 4542 (CD)*
NATIONAL LAMPOON'S ANIMAL HOUSE (1978) Music: ELMER
   BERNSTEIN -S/T- *re-iss MCA (BMG): MCLD 19086 (CD)*
NATIONAL LOTTERY (BBC1 19/11/94) theme composed and
   arranged by ED WELCH *unavailable*
NATIONWIDE (BBC 70's) theme music "The Good Word" by
   JOHN SCOTT *see COLL.2,6,104,*
NATURAL The (1984) Music sco: RANDY NEWMAN -S/T- Imp
   W.BROS USA (Silva Screen) 925116-2 -4 (CD/MC)
NATURAL BORN KILLERS (1994) music by VARIOUS ARTISTS
   INTERSCOPE (MCA/BMG): IND 92460-2 (CD)
   SIMPLY VINYL (Vital): SVLP 118 (2LP)
NAZIS: A WARNING FROM HISTORY (BBC2 10/9/97) open.mus:
   'German Requiem' Op.45 (BRAHMS) *version by* VIENNA
   PHIL.ORCH (Haitink) *Philips (Univ): 446 681-2 (CD)*
   also used: "Kline Dreigschenmusik" (arrangement of
   'Moritat'("Mack The Knife" 'The Threepenny Opera')
   (Weill-Brecht-Blitzstein) *BBC ARCHIVE unavailable*
NEAR DARK (1988) Music score: TANGERINE DREAM -S/T-
   SILVA SCREEN (Koch): FILMCD 026 (CD) see COLL.51,
NED KELLY (1970) Music score: SHEL SILVERSTEIN *feat*
   WAYLON JENNINGS "She Moved Through The Fair" -S/T-
   RYKODISC (Vital): RCD 10708 (CD)
NEEDFUL THINGS (1993) Music score: PATRICK DOYLE -S/T-
   VARESE (Pinn): VSD 5438 (CD)
NEIGHBOURS (Austr.85/BBC1 27/10/86-98) *theme* by JACKIE
   TRENT-TONY HATCH) *orig vers.*sung by BARRY CROCKER
   see COLL.150,270,376,
NELL (1994) Music: MARK ISHAM. solo flute (Jim Walker)
   -S/T- *LONDON (IMS-Poly): E.444 818-2 (CD)*
NET The (1995) Music score: MARK ISHAM -S/T- on
   VARESE (Pinn): VSD 5662 (CD)
NETWORK FIRST (THE VISIT) (Man Alive Prod for Carlton)
   (7/12/94) theme music "Caribbean Blue" by ENYA
   'Shepherd Moons' *WEA: 9031 75572-2 (CD) -4 (MC)*
NEVADA SMITH (1966) Music score: ALFRED NEWMAN
   -S/T- *TSUNAMI Germ (Silva Screen): TSU 0113 (CD)*
NEVER BEEN KISSED (1999) Music score by DAVID NEWMAN
   -S/T- *feat:* BEACH BOYS/CARDIGANS/REM/JOHN LENNON
   and YOKO ONO/SMITHS/SEMISONIC/WILLIS etc.
   EMI SOUNDTRACKS: 498 505-2 (CD)
NEVER CRY WOLF (1983) Mus: MARK ISHAM *see* MRS.SOFFEL

NEVER MIND THE BUZZCOCKS (BBC2 12/11/96) title music:
   SWITCH AND THE GINGER GP *unavailable*
NEVER ON SUNDAY (1959) Music score: MANOS HADJIDAKIS
      -S/T- *RYKODISC (Vital): RCD 10722 (CD)*
NEVER SAY NEVER AGAIN - *see* JAMES BOND INDEX p.358
NEW ADVENTURES OF BLACK BEAUTY (Pro Films Australia/
   BBC1 11/4/94) theme "Galloping Home" by DENIS KING
   see COLL.149,
NEW ADVENTURES OF SUPERMAN (USA/BBC1 8/1/1994) orig
   music: JAY GRUSKA *SONIC IMAGES (Cargo-Greyhound):
   SI 8703 (CD) see COLL.311,351,*
NEW AVENGERS The (ITV 22/10/76-78) theme mus: LAURIE
   JOHNSON *see COLL.5,215,360,*
NEW BRAIN, A (ORIG USA CAST RECORDING)
   RCA (BMG): 09026 63298-2 (CD)
NEW JACK CITY (91) Music score: MICHEL COLOMBIER -S/T-
   reiss feat V.ARTS: *GIANT (BMG): 74321 15104-2 (CD)*
NEW JERSEY DRIVE (1994) *feat:* Var.RAP & R.& B. -S/T-
   TOMMY BOY (Pinn): TB(CD)(C)(V) 1114 (CD/MC/2LP)
   TOMMY BOY (Pinn): (Volume 2) - 1130 (CD/MC/2LP)
NEW MOON - songs by Sigmund Romberg-Oscar Hammerstein
   1.ORIG LONDON CAST 1929   EVELYN LAYE-GENE GERRARD
      PEARL (Pavil): GEMMCD 9100(CD)
   2.STUDIO RECORDING   GORDON MacRAE-DOROTHY KIRSTEN
      see under 'DESERT SONG'
NEW ORLEANS (1947) *featur* LOUIS ARMSTRONG & ALL STARS
   BILLIE HOLIDAY-WOODY HERMAN ORCHESTRA and others
   -S/T- *JASMINE (BMG-Con): GOJCD 1025 (CD)*
   DEFINITIVE (Discovery): SFCD 33506 (CD)
NEW ROCKY HORROR SHOW (SHOW 1999 Victoria Palace)
   Songs by RICHARD O'BRIEN featuring JASON DONOVAN
   DAMN IT JANET! (Pinn): DAMJAM 2 (CD)
   see also ROCKY HORROR SHOW
NEW SCOOBY DOO MOVIES *see COLL.373,*
NEW SWISS FAMILY ROBINSON: see SWISS FAMILY ROBINSON 2
NEW YEARS DAY CONCERT 1998 (Austria) BBC2 1/1/1998
   VIENNA PHILHARMONIC ORCHESTRA cond: ZUBIN MEHTA
   and the VIENNA BOYS CHOIR with various artists
   RCA VICTOR (BMG): 09026 63144-2
NEW YORK NEW YORK - songs by John Kander and Fred Ebb
   1.FILM MUSICAL 1977 *with:* LIZA MINNELLI -S/T-
      LIBERTY EMI Eur (Disc): 746 090-2 (CD)
NEW YORK ROCK (O.NEW YORK CAST RECORDING) *featuring*
   YOKO ONO *CAPITOL (EMI): CDP 829 843-2 (CD)*
NEW YORK UNDERCOVER (1995) Various Artists -S/T-
   MCA (BMG): MCD 11342 (CD) MCC 11342 (MC)
NEWCOMERS The (BBC 1960's) - *see COLL.6,*
NEWS AT TEN (ITN 3/7/67-98) theme "The Awakening" from
   '20th Century Portrait' by JOHNNY PEARSON orig ver
   Coll 'SOUNDS VISUAL' *deleted see also* 'ITN NEWS'
NEWSNIGHT (BBC2 28/1/80-98) theme music composed by
   GEORGE FENTON *unavailable*
NIAGARA NIAGARA (1997) Music score: MICHAEL TIMMINS &
   JEFF BIRD -S/T- import on *VTW (Silver Sounds):
   6381 27014-2 (CD)*

NICHOLAS NICKLEBY Life & Advent. ORIG LONDON CAST 1982
    Songs: STEPHEN OLIVER *with* Royal Shakespeare Comp
    TER (Koch): CDTER 1029 (CD)
NICK & NORA (ORIG.BROADWAY CAST 1991) Music: CHARLES
    STROUSE Lyrics: RICHARD MALTBY JNR. ORIG CAST on
    TER (Koch): CDTER 1191 (CD)
NIGHT AT THE OPERA (1935) *featuring* MARX BROTHERS
    selection DEFINITIVE (Discovery): SFCD 33502 (CD)
    see COLL CINEMA CLASSICS 9 / 'OPERA AT THE MOVIES'
NIGHT COURT (USA/ITV 91) theme music: JACK ELLIOTT
    see COLL.17,350,
NIGHT DIGGER The (1971) *see* BATTLE OF NERETVA
NIGHT GALLERY (USA TV) *see COLL.309,349,*
NIGHT MAIL (1936 Post Office) Mus s: BENJAMIN BRITTEN
    score select.*HYPERION (Select): CDA 66845 (CD)*
NIGHT OF THE HUNTER MUSICAL Music
    VARESE (Pinn): VSD 5876 (CD)
NIGHT PASSAGE (1957) Music sco: DIMITRI TIOMKIN theme
    see COLL.368,
NIGHTMARE ON ELM STREET 1 (1984) Mus:CHARLES BERNSTEIN
NIGHTMARE ON ELM STREET 2: Freddy's Revenge (1985) Mus
    CHRISTOPHER YOUNG *both Soundtracks VARESE (Pinn)*
    VSD 47255 (CD)
NIGHTMARE ON ELM STREET 3: Dream Warriors (1987) Mus:
    ANGELO BADALAMENTI -S/T- *VARESE: VCD 47293 (CD)*
NIGHTMARE ON ELM STREET 4: Dream Master (1988) Music
    CRAIG SAFAN -S/T- *VARESE (Pinn): VSD 5203 (CD)*
NIGHTMARE ON ELM STREET 5: Dream Child (1989) Music:
    JAY FERGUSON -S/T- *VARESE (Pinn): VSD 5238 (CD)*
NIGHTMARE ON ELM STREET 6: Freddie's Dead (1991) Mus:
    BRIAN MAY -S/T- *VARESE (Pinn): VSD 5333 (CD)*
    see also 'FREDDIE'S DEAD - THE FINAL NIGHTMARE'
NIKITA (1989) Music score: ERIC SERRA -S/T-
    VIRGIN (EMI): CDVMM 2 (CD) TCVMM 2 (MC)
NIKITA (TV series) - see 'LA FEMME NIKITA'
NIL BY MOUTH (1997) Music score: ERIC CLAPTON
    -S/T- *unavailable.* song "PANDORA" by FRANCE on
    SUPER VILLAIN WRECKUDS (Arabesque): SVP 001CDs
NINE - songs by Maury Yeston
    ORIG LONDON CONCERT CAST 1992 *with:* JONATHAN PRYCE
    ELAINE PAIGE   *TER (Koch): CDTER2 1193 (2CD)*
NINE MONTHS (1995) Music sco HANS ZIMMER *feat* "Time Of
    Your Life" by LITTLE STEVEN + tracks from MARVIN
    GAYE-TYRONE DAVIS -S/T- *MILAN (BMG): 30110-2 (CD)*
NINTH GATE The (1999) Music score by WOJCIEK KILAR
    performed by CITY OF PRAGUE PHILHARMONIC & CHORUS
    and featuring Soprano SUMI JO. -S/T-
    SILVA SCREEN (Koch): FILMCD 321 (CD)
NO BANANAS (BBC1 5/3/96) mus: JOHN ALTMAN -S/T- V.Arts
    VIRGIN (EMI): CDVIP 176(CD) TCVIP 176(MC)
NO HIDING PLACE (ITV 16/9/59-67) theme: LAURIE JOHNSON
    see COLL.4,23,109,110,216,270,
NO HONESTLY (ITV 4/10/84) theme by LYNSEY DE PAUL
    see COLL.2,

NO NO NANETTE - songs by Vincent Youmans-Otto Harbach
and Irving Caesar
  1.REVIVAL CAST 1971 *with* RUBY KEELER *COLUMBIA Imp*
    (Silva Screen): CK 30563 (CD) JST 30563 (MC)
  2.ORIG LONDON REVIVAL CAST 1973 *w:* ANNA NEAGLE-TONY
    BRITTON-ANNE ROGERS.*SONY West End: SMK 66173 (CD)*
NO RETREAT NO SURRENDER (1985) Music sc: PAUL GILREATH
   -S/T- *SILVA SCREEN (Koch): FILMCD 150 (CD)*
NO WAY HOME (1997) Mus score: RICK GIOVINAZZO -S/T-
   OCEAN DEEP (Grapev/Polyg): OCD 005 (CD)
NO WAY TO TREAT A LADY (ORIG USA CAST) songs: (DOUGLAS
   J.COHEN) *VARESE (Pinn): VSD 5815 (CD)*
NOAH'S ARK (1998) Music score by PAUL GRABOWSKY -S/T-
   VARESE (Pinn): VSD 6027 (CD)
NODDY BBC1 17/9/92) music: PAUL K.JOYCE *see COLL.67,*
NOEL AND GERTIE (O.LONDON CAST 1986) Songs NOEL COWARD
   with Lewis FIANDER-Patricia HODGE and Company
   TER (Koch): CDTER 1117 (CD)
NOMADS OF THE WIND (BBC2 9/1/94) mus: BRIAN BENNETT
   TV -S/T- *Karussell (Univ): IMS E.513 931-2 (CD)*
NORMA JEAN AND MARILYN (TVM 1996) Music: CHRISTOPHER
   YOUNG -S/T- *INTRADA (S.Screen): MAF 7070 (CD)*
NORTH AND SOUTH (USA TV) *see COLL.17,*
NORTH BY NORTHWEST (1959) Music sco: BERNARD HERRMANN
   -S/T- *re-issue EMI PREMIER (EMI): CDODEON 6 (CD)*
   see COLL.24,70,188,190,191,194,196,197,363,366,
NORTH STAR (1996) Music score: JOHN SCOTT -S/T- on
   JOHN SCOTT Records (Silva Screen): JSCD 120 (CD)
NORTHERN EXPOSURE (USA/C4 16/3/92)theme:DAVID SCHWARTZ
   -S/T- *with Var.Arts MCA (BMG): MCD 10685 (CD)*
   -S/T- 'More Music' *MCA (BMG): MCLD 19350 (CD)*
   see COLL.270,364,
NOSFERATU (1922) *RESTORED 1996 VERSION.* NEW SCORE BY
   JAMES BERNARD. PRAGUE CITY PHILHARMONIC ORCH.cond:
   NIC RAINE *SILVA SCREEN (Koch): FILMCD 192 (CD)*
NOSFERATU (1922) Music sco: HANS ERDMANN orchestral
   version on *RCA (BMG): 09026 68143-2 (CD)*
NOT ONLY...BUT ALSO... (BBC2 4/11/90 orig 1965) theme
   "Goodbyee" (P.Cook-Dudley Moore) PETE & DUD 'The
   Clean Tapes' on *RIO (AMT): RDC 1206 (MC)*
NOT SINCE CASANOVA Mus: JOHN DEBNEY -S/T- incl 'EYE OF
   THE PANTHER' *PROMETHEUS (S.Screen): PCD 140 (CD)*
NOT THE NINE O'CLOCK NEWS (BBC2 16/10/79) theme mus:
   NIC ROWLEY *TV Cast Rec BBC (Tech): ZBBC 1009 2MC*
NOT WITHOUT MY DAUGHTER (1991) Music: JERRY GOLDSMITH
   -S/T- *SILVA SCREEN (Koch): FILM(C)(CD) 091*
NOTTING HILL (1999) -S/T- inc: ELVIS COSTELLO/ANOTHER
   LEVEL/RONAN KEATING/LIGHTHOUSE FAMILY/SHANIA TWAIN
   ISLAND (Univ): 546 207-2 (CD) -4 (MC)
NOUVELLE VAGUE (1990) Mus: DINO SALUZZI-DAVID DARLING
   ECM (New Note-Pinn): 449 891-2 (2CD)
NOW AND THEN (95) Music sco: CLIFF EIDELMAN -S/T- (2)
   score: *VARESE (Pinn): VSD 5675 (CD)*
   songs: *COLUMBIA (Ten): 481 606-2 (CD) -4 (MC)*

NOW VOYAGER! (1942) *see COLL.90,336,*

NOWHERE (1997) Various Arts -S/T- including RADIOHEAD-
   ELASTICA-CHEMICAL BROTHERS-MASSICE ATTACK etc.
   MERCURY (Univ): 534 522-2 (CD)

NUNSENSE - songs by Dan Goggin
   1. ORIG LONDON CAST 1987 HONOR BLACKMAN-ANNA SHARKEY
      LOUISE GOLD   *TER (Koch): CDTER 1132 (CD)*
   2. ORIG OFF-BROADWAY CAST 1986 *w:* CHRISTINE ANDERSON
      SEMINA de LAURENTIS *DRG (Pinn): CDSBL 12589 (CD)*

NUNSENSE 2: The Second Coming ORIG CAST RECORDING
   DRG USA (Pinn): DRGMC 12608 (MC)

NUTTY PROFESSOR The (1995) Music score: DAVID NEWMAN
      Rap Songs *(INSPIRED BY THE FILM) inc:* CASE-MONTELL
      JORDAN-TRIGGER THE GAMBLER-AZ YET-LL COOL J-MONICA
      DEF SQUAD *MERCURY-Def Jam (Univ): 531 911-2 /-4*

NYPD BLUE (USA1993) Music theme by MIKE POST on Coll
   'NYPD BLUE THE BEST OF MIKE POST'
   SILVA TREASURY (Koch/S.Screen): SILVAD 3511 (CD)
   see COLL.270,283,390,

O LUCKY MAN (1973) Music sco: ALAN PRICE -S/T- *reiss:*
   WARNER BROS (TEN): 9362 46137-2 (CD)

O PIONEERS! (1991) Music score: BRUCE BROUGHTON -S/T-
   INTRADA USA (Silva Screen) MAFCD 7023 (CD)

OAKIE DOKE (BBC1 11/9/95) theme music by ERNIE WOOD
   see COLL.67,

OBJECT OF MY AFFECTION (1998) Music sco: GEORGE FENTON
   -S/T- *ARK 21 (Grapev/Poly): 61868 10027-2 (CD)*

OBJECTIVE BURMA! (1944) Music score: FRANZ WAXMAN
   see COLL.391,

OBSESSION (1976) Music sco: BERNARD HERRMANN conduct:
   NAT.PHILHARMONIC ORCHESTRA
   UNICORN KANCHANA (Harmonia Mundi): UKCD 2065 (CD)

OCTOBER SKY (1999) Music score by MARK ISHAM -S/T- on
   SONY CLASSICS: SK 61696 (CD)

OCTOPUSSY (1983) Music score: JOHN BARRY / theme song:
   "All Time High" sung by RITA COOLIDGE -S/T- *reiss*
   + addit.items RYKODISC (Vital): RCD 10705 (CD)
   see JAMES BOND FILM INDEX p.358
   see COLL.55,189,314,

ODD COUPLE The (USA 70 BBC rerun 89) theme: NEAL HEFTI
   see COLL.185,281,346,281,346,377,378,

ODD MAN OUT (1946) Music score by WILLIAM ALWYN
   Suite LSO (Richard Hickox) *CHANDOS: CHAN 9243 (CD)*

OF LOVE AND SHADOWS (1994) Music score: JOSE NIETO
   JOSE NIETO with Middle Slovak Philharmonic Orchest
   -S/T- *CUBE-FLY (FLY Direct): FLYCD 107 (CD)*

OF UNKNOWN ORIGIN (1983) Music sc: KEN WANNBERG -S/T-
   selection with 'LATE SHOW'/'THE AMATEUR' on Imprt
   PROMETHEUS (Silva Screen): PCD 137 (CD)

OH DOCTOR BEECHING (BBC1 1/7/96) theme song sung by SU
   POLLARD & CAST *(unavailable)* based on song 'Oh Mr.
   Porter' (George & Thomas Le Brun) *version (1931)*
   NORAH BLANEY on 'Glory Of The Music Hall Vol.3' on
   PEARL (Pavillion): GEMMCD 9477 (CD)

OH KAY! (MUSICAL) songs by GEORGE and IRA GERSHWIN
   COLUMBIA (Ten): SMK 60703 (CD)
OKLAHOMA! songs: Richard Rodgers-Oscar Hammerstein II
  1.FILM MUSICAL 1955 GORDON MacRAE-SHIRLEY JONES-
    GLORIA GRAHAM-ROD STEIGER-GENE NELSON- and Company
    -S/T- *EMI: ZDM 764 691-2 (CD)*
  2.ORIG LONDON CAST 1998/99 HUGH JACKMAN-MAUREEN
    LIPMAN-PETER POLYCARPOU-JOSEFINA GABRIELLE-VICKY
    MON-JIMMY JOHNSTON-SHULER HENSLEY and Company
    FIRST NIGHT (Pinn): CASTCD 69 (CD) CASTC 69 (MC)
  3.ORIG LONDON CAST 1980 *with:* JOHN DIEDRICH-ROSAMUND
    SHELLEY-MADGE RYAN-MARK WHITE-ALFRED MOLINA-
    JILLIAN MACK-LINAL HAFT and Co.
    Highlights: *SHOWTIME (MCI-THE): SHOW(CD)(MC) 001*
    Complete: *TER (Koch): (CD)(ZC)TEM 1208 (CD/MC)*
    FOR OTHER RECORDINGS SEE TELE-TUNES 1998 p.175/176
  4.ORIG LONDON CAST 1947 *with:* HOWARD KEEL-BETTY JANE
    WATSON-WALTER DONAHUE-ISABEL BIGLEY-HENRY CLARKE
    LASERLIGHT (Target/BMG): 12 450 (CD)
  5.STUDIO RECORD USA 1952 NELSON EDDY-KAYE BALLARD-
    VIRGINIA HASKINS-PORTIA NELSON-LEE CASS-DAVID
    ATKINSON-DAVID MORRIS *SONY Broadway: SK 53326 (CD)*
  6.BROADWAY CAST RECORDING 1979 LAURENCE GUTTARD-
    CHRISTINE ANDREAS-MARY WICKES *RCA: RD 83572 (CD)*
  7.CLASSIC MUSICALS SERIES *feat:* JOHN DIEDRICH-MADGE
    RYAN-ROSAMUND SHELLEY-MARK WHITE-ALFRED MOLINA
    + *songs from* 'THE KING & I' *KOCH INT: 34077-2 (CD)*
OLD GRINGO (89) Music score: LEE HOLDRIDGE Suite on
   'LONESOME DOVE' *SILVA SCREEN (Koch): FILMCD 176 CD*
OLD MAN AND THE SEA The (Yorkshire / 90) music: BRUCE
   BROUGHTON -S/T- *INTRADA (S.Screen): RVF 6008D (CD)*
OLIVER! - songs by Lionel Bart
  1.FILM MUSICAL 1968 *w:* HARRY SECOMBE-RON MOODY-SHANI
    WALLIS-JACK WILD -S/T- *RCA: ND(NK) 90311 (CD/MC)*
  2.NEW LONDON CAST 1994 JONATHAN PRYCE-SALLY DEXTER
    FIRST NIGHT (Pinn): CASTCD 47 (CD) CASTC 47 (MC)
  3.CARLTON SHOWS COLLECTION Studio 1994 *w* IAN WALLACE
    BONNIE LANGFORD-GARETH STRINGER-VICTOR SPINETTI &
    West End Concert Orch & Chorus (Matthew Freeman)
    CARLTON SHOWS: PWKS(PWKMC) 4194 (CD/MC)
  4.STUDIO RECORD 1991 JOSEPHINE BARSTOW-JULIAN FORS
    YTHE-SHEILA HANCOCK-STUART KALE-RICHARD VAN ALLAN
    National Symphony Orchestra (JOHN OWEN EDWARDS)
    <u>Highlights</u>: *SHOWTIME (MCI-THE): SHOW(CD)(MC) 004*
    <u>Complete</u>: *TER (Koch): CDTER 1184 (CD)*
  5.LONDON STUDIO RECORD 1966 *w:* JON PERTWEE-JIM DALE
    NICOLETTE ROEG-BLANCHE MOORE-TOMMY MANN-FRED LUCAS
    CHARLES GRANVILLE and GEOFF LOVE & HIS ORCHESTRA
    MFP (EMI):CC 8253 (CD) HR 8253 (MC)
  6.ORIG BROADWAY CAST 1963 CLIVE REVILL-GEORGIA BROWN
    RCA (BMG): GD 84113 (CD) GK 84113 (MC)
  7.ORIG LONDON CAST 1960 *w:* RON MOODY-GEORGIA BROWN-
    PAUL WHITSUN JONES-HOPE JACKMAN-DANNY SEWELL & Co
    DERAM (Univ): 820 590-2 (CD)

OLIVER AND COMPANY (1989) Music score: J.A.C.REDFORD
  -S/T- *DISNEY-EDEL (Pinn): 010 890-2 (CD) -4 (MC)*
OLIVER TWIST (1948) Music score by ARNOLD BAX
  see COLL.70,173,
OLIVER TWIST (BBC 1962) music: RON GRAINER peformed by
  The EAGLES *see COLL.8,*
OLIVIER OLIVIER (1991) Music: ZBIGNIEW PREISNER incl
  'EUROPA EUROPA' -S/T- *DRG (Pinn): DRGCD 12606 (CD)*
OLYMPIC GAMES 1996 (JULY) (themes and trailer music)
  (BBC1) "Tara's Theme" from 'Gone With The Wind'
  MAX STEINER) *TV:* SPIRO & WIX *EMI Premier: PRESCD 4
  (CDs) PRESTC 4 (MC) PRES 4 (7"s)* also on 'MOTION'
  EMI Premier: PRMDCD 8 (CD) PRMDTC 8 (MC)
  (SKYTV) Trailer "Yeha Noha" (Wishes Of Happiness)
  from SACRED SPIRIT *VIRGIN (EMI):CDV(TCV) 2753*
  (USA: SUMMON THE HEROES: Official Olympic Theme)
  JOHN WILLIAMS on 'Summon The Heroes' *Sony Class
  SK(ST) 62622 (CD/MC)*
OLYMPIC GRANDSTAND Lillehammer Norway 1994 BBC2 12/2/94
  theme "Pop Looks Bach" SAM FONTEYN *see* 'SKI SUNDAY'
OLYMPIC WINTER GAMES *see* 'WINTER OLYMPIC GAMES'
OMEN The (1976) M: JERRY GOLDSMITH -S/T- *VARESE (Pinn)
  VSD 5281 (CD) VSC 5281 (MC)* 'O Fortuna' "Carmina
  Burana" (CARL ORFF) *see COLL.72,121,167,208,309,*
OMEN II 'Damien' (1978) Music score: JERRY GOLDSMITH
  -S/T- *SILVA SCREEN: FILMCD 002 (CD)*
OMEN III 'Final Conflict' (1981) Mus: JERRY GOLDSMITH
  -S/T- *VARESE (Pinn): VCD 47242 (CD)*
OMEN IV The Awakening' (1991) Music: JONATHAN SHEFFER
  -S/T- *VARESE (Pinn): VSD(VSC) 5318 (CD/MC)*
ON BORROWED TIME (39) *see COLL.394,*
ON DANGEROUS GROUND (1951) Music: BERNARD HERRMANN
  -S/T- with 'HANGOVER SQUARE'/'A HATFUL OF RAIN'
  TSUNAMI Imp (Silva Screen): TCI 0610 (CD)
ON DEADLY GROUND (1993) Music score: BASIL POLEDOURIS
  -S/T- *VARESE (Pinn): VSD 5468 (CD)*
ON HER MAJESTY'S SECRET SERVICE (1969) Music sco: JOHN
  BARRY title song (J.Barry-Hal David) sung by LOUIS
  ARMSTRONG -S/T- *reissue EMI PREMIER: CZ 549 (CD)*
  see also JAMES BOND INDEX p.358
  see COLL.27,30,31,34,53,54,55,106,314,359,
ON MY OWN (1992) Music: FRANCO PIERSANTI -S/T- *Imp
  (Sil.Screen): OST 117(CD)* with 'CHILDREN'S THIEF'
ON THE AVENUE (FILM CAST 1937) -S/T- *with* DICK POWELL-
  incl. -S/T- to 'THANKS A MILLION'
  SANDY HOOK (Silver Sounds): CDSH(CSH) 2012 (CD/MC)
ON THE BUSES (ITV 28/2/69) theme music: TONY RUSSELL
  see COLL.7,179,363,
ON THE LINE *see COLL.149,*
ON THE RECORD (BBC1 1988-96) theme "Allegro" (Divertis
  mento No.5 in C, K187)(MOZART) *vers:* Philharmonia
  Orchestra (Wright) *NIMBUS: NI 5121 (CD)*
ON THE TOWN (FILM 1949) -S/T- *Imp* + 'ANCHORS AWEIGH'
  BLUE MOON (Discovery): BMCD 7007 (CD)

ON THE TOWN (MUSICAL 1945) Music: LEONARD BERSTEIN and lyr: ADOLPH GREEN-BETTY COMDEN. *ORIG BROADWAY CAST COLUMBIA (Ten): SMK 60538 (CD)*

ON THE TOWN - songs by Leonard Bernstein-Betty Comden and Adolph Green
  1. STUDIO RECORD ST.LOUIS SYMPHONY ORCH Felix Slatkin *inc:* CANDIDE/FANCY FREE. *EMI Eminence:CDEMX 2242 CD*
  2. ORIG BROADWAY CAST 1944 VARIOUS ARTISTS *Columbia Masterworks (Ten): SK 60538 (CD)*
  3. ORIG LONDON CAST 1963 CAROL ARTHUR-ELLIOTT GOULD-ROSAMUND GREENWOOD.. *SONY BROADWAY:SMK 53497 (CD)*
  4. ORIG MASTERWORKS EDIT (First Complete R) GREGG EDELMAN-TIM FLAVIN-ETHAN FREEMAN-KIM CRISWELL-JUDY KAYE-VALERIE MASTERSON *TER Koch:CDTER2 1217 (2CD)*

ON THE UP (BBC1 from 4/9/90) Open mus "Concerto Grossi in A.op.6 no.11" 1st m/m (Handel) by GUILDHALL STRING ENSEMBLE - *RCA (BMG): RD(RK) 87921 (CD/MC)* Closing theme comp & sung by DENNIS WATERMAN *unav.*

ON YOUR TOES (REVIV.BROADWAY CAST 1983) Mus R.RODGERS L.HART *TER (Koch): CDTER 1063 (CD)*

ON YOUR TOES (CLASSIC MUSICALS SERIES) *feat:* EUGENE J. ANTHONY-BETTY ANN GROVE-MARY C.ROBARE-LARA TEETER *+ songs from* 'PAL JOEY' *KOCH INT: 34082-2 (CD)*

ONCE ON THIS ISLAND *sgs:* Lynn AHRENS-Stephen FLAHERTY
  1. ORIG LONDON CAST 1994 VARIOUS ARTISTS *TER (Koch): CDTER 1224 (CD)*
  2. ORIG BROADWAY CAST 1990 VARIOUS ARTS *RCA IMPORT (Silva Screen) 60595-2 (CD) 60595-4 (MC)*

ONCE UPON A MATTRESS (Musical Comedy by MARY RODGERS & MARSHALL BAREN) NEW BROADWAY CAST featuring SARAH JESSICA PARKER *RCA Vict (BMG): 09026 68728-2 (CD)*

ONCE UPON A TIME IN AMERICA (1984) Music score compos. and conducted by ENNIO MORRICONE - *special edition RESTLESS (BMG): 74321 61976-2 (CD) see COLL.70,144,239,250,251,363,*

ONCE UPON A TIME IN THE WEST (1968) Music score by ENNIO MORRICONE -S/T- complete with 'A FISTFUL OF DOLLARS' (1964) /'FOR A FEW DOLLARS MORE' (1965) *RCA VICTOR (BMG): 74321 66040-2 (CD) see COLL.70,71,203,211,250,251,358,400,401,*

ONCE WERE WARRIORS (1994) Music sco: MURRAY GRINDLEY and MURRAY McNABB -S/T- feat Various Artists on *MILAN (BMG): 74321 24902-2 (CD)*

ONE AGAINST THE WIND (1992) Music sco: LEE HOLDRIDGE -S/T- *INTRADA (S.Screen): MAF 7039D (CD)*

ONE EYED JACKS (1961) Music score: HUGO FRIEDHOFER -S/T- *TSUNAMI Germ (Silva Screen): TSU 0114 (CD)*

ONE FINE DAY (1996) Mus sco: JAMES NEWTON HOWARD -S/T- *COLUMBIA (Ten): 486 910-2 (CD)*

ONE FLEW OVER THE CUCKOO'S NEST (1975) Music sco: JACK NITZSCHE -S/T- *FANTASY Imp FCD 4531 (CD) deleted MOVING IMAGE (Cargo): MIE 001 (LP)*

ONE FOOT IN THE GRAVE (BBC1 4/1/90-1995) theme song by ERIC IDLE *VICTA-Total (BMG):CDVICTA 1 deleted*

ONE FROM THE HEART (1982) Mus/Songs: TOM WAITS-CRYSTAL
GAYLE -S/T- re-iss *SONY MUSIC (SM):467 609-2 (CD)*

ONE GAME The (Central 4/6/88) theme mus "Saylon Dola"
NIGEL HESS sung CHAMELEON *see COLL.6,149,193,*

ONE MAN AND HIS DOG (BBC2 1976-1999) title theme music
composed by ALAN BENSON *unavailable*

ONE MILLION YEARS BC (1966) Music sc: MARIO NASCIMBENE
+ 'WHEN DINOSAURS RULED THE EARTH'/'CREATURES THE
WORLD FORGOT' *LEGEND (S.Screen): LEGEND CD13 (CD)*

ONE NIGHT STAND (1997) Music score: MIKE FIGGIS -S/T-
VERVE (Univ): 539 025-2 (CD)

ONE TOUGH COP (1997) Music sco: BRUCE BROUGHTON -S/T-
INTRADA (S.Screen/Koch): MAF 7084CD (CD) also on
HOLA (Silver Sounds): 6119 341035-2 (CD)

ONE TRICK PONY (1980) Music score: PAUL SIMON -S/T-
WB (TEN): K4-56846 (MC) K2-56846 (CD)

ONE TRUE THING (1998) Music sco: CLIFF EIDELMAN -S/T-
VARESE (Pinn): VSD 5972

ONEDIN LINE The (BBC1 15/10/71) theme music 'Adagio'
from 'Spartacus' Ballet (KHACHATURIAN)
see COLL.2,46,270,271,281,

ONLY FOOLS AND HORSES (BBC1 8/9/81-96) theme composed
& sung by JOHN SULLIVAN *unavailable see COLL.270,*

ONLY THE LONELY: Roy Orbison Story (O.LONDON CAST 1995)
LARRY BRANSON *FIRST NIGHT (Pinn): ORCD 6054 (CD)*

ONLY WHEN I LARF (1968) *see COLL.8,*

OPERA (1987,Italy) - *see COLL.319,*

OPERA (Terror At The Opera) (87) Music: ROGER & BRIAN
ENO-BILL WYMAN & extracts from var.Operas -S/T-
CINEVOX Italy Import (Silva Screen): CIA 5074 (CD)

OPERA SAUVAGE FRENCH TV Music score: VANGELIS -S/T- on
import: *POLYDOR (IMS-Poly): E.829 663.2 (CD)*

OPERATION DUMBO DROP (1995) Music by DAVID NEWMAN
-S/T- *EDEL-Hollywood (Pinn): 012 032-2HWR (CD)*

OPPOSITE OF SEX The (1998) Music score: MASON DARING
-S/T- *DARING (Direct): DARINGCD 3034 (CD)*

OPRAH WINFREY SHOW The (USA/BBC2 96/97) end theme song
"Ten Years" composed/sung by PAUL SIMON on Coll:
'CARNIVAL!' *RCA Vict (BMG): 74321 44769-2 (CD)*

ORANGES ARE NOT THE ONLY FRUIT (BBC2 10/1/90) music by
RACHEL PORTMAN - *2 Story MC BBC (Tech): ZBBC 1151*

ORCA - KILLER WHALE (1977) Music score ENNIO MORRICONE
-S/T- *LEGEND IMPT (Silva Screen): CD 10 (CD)*

ORCHESTRA! (C4 6/1/91) Sir GEORG SOLTI & DUDLEY MOORE
Orchestral Music -S/T- *DECCA:430 838-2(CD) -4(MC)*

ORCHESTRA WIVES (1942 MUSICAL) *with* GLENN MILLER BAND
RAY EBERLE *includ.songs from* 'SUN VALLEY SERENADE'
TARGET (BMG): CD 60002 (CD)

ORDINARY PEOPLE (1980) Theme 'Canon In D' (PACHELBEL)
on COLL.78,106,271,

ORGAZMO (1997) -S/T- *NICKELBAG (Cargo): NB 009LP (LP)*

ORIENT EXPRESS (1979) Music score: ENNIO MORRICONE
ENNIO MORRICONE -S/T- selection on 'TV FILM MUSIC'
RCA (BMG): 74321 31552-2 (CD)

ORIGIN UNKNOWN (Gran 19/01/1999) music: DAVID KESTER
  unavailable
ORIGINAL GANGSTAS (1996) RAP FILM -S/T- LUNIZ-ICE T-
  SMOOTH-JUNIOR MAFIA *VIRGIN (EMI): CDVUS 104 (CD)*
ORLANDO (1992) Music: SALLY POTTER-DAVID MOTION-JIMMY
  SOMERVILLE -S/T- *VARESE (Pinn): VSD 5413 (CD)*
ORPHEUS IN THE UNDERWORLD (MUSICAL OPERETTA) Music by
  Jacques OFFENBACH / English text by S.Wilson- D.
  Pountney - *English National Opera* (Mark Elder) on
  TER (Koch):CDTER 1134 HIGHLIGHTS: *CDTEO 1008 (CD)*
OSCAR AND LUCINDA (1998) Mus score: THOMAS NEWMAN
  feat PAULIST BOY CHORISTERS OF CALIFORNIA -S/T-
  SONY Classics: SK 60088 (CD)
OSCAR'S ORCHESTRA (ITV 12/9/95) var.classical music
  Mozart-Glinka-Chopin-Tchaikovsky-Rimsky Korsakov-
  JS Bach-Beethoven-Holst-Grieg etc. -S/T- *available*
  ERATO (WEA Classics): 0630 11865-2 (CD) -4 (MC)
OSTERMAN WEEKEND The (1983) Music score: LALO SCHIFRIN
  ALEPH (Koch): ALEP 010 (CD)
OTHELLO (1995-O.Parker) Music: CHARLIE MOLE -S/T-
  VARESE (Pinn): VSD 5689 (CD)
OTHELLO Music score: ELLIOT GOLDENTHAL
  VARESE (Pinn): VSD 5942 (CD)
OTHER The (1972) Music score: JERRY GOLDSMITH score w:
  'MEPHISTO WALTZ' *VARESE (Pinn): VSD 5851 (CD)*
OUR FRIENDS IN THE NORTH (BBC2 15/1/96 and 19/7/97)
  theme/incidental score by COLIN TOWNS *unavailable*
  -S/T- *(V.ARTS) TELSTAR TV (TEN): TTV(CD)(MC) 2922*
OUR HOUSE (ITV 1960 series) theme music (Maxim-Hudis)
  see COLL.23,369,
OUR MAN FLINT (1965) Music score: JERRY GOLDSMITH also
  includes music from 'IN LIKE FLINT'
  VARESE (Pinn): VSD 5935 (CD)
OUR TUNE (SIMON BATES, R1) "Romeo & Juliet Love Theme"
  (NINO ROTA) *SILVA SCREEN (Koch): FILMCD 200 (CD)*
OUT FOR JUSTICE (1991) Music sco: DAVID MICHAEL FRANK
  -S/T- *VARESE (Pinn): VSD 5317 (CD)*
OUT OF AFRICA (1986) Music JOHN BARRY + Melissa Manche
  ster-Al Jarreau -S/T- *MCA (BMG): MCLD(MCLC) 19092*
  new recording by ROYAL SCOTTISH NATIONAL ORCHESTRA
  (Joel McNeely,cond) *VARESE (Pinn): VSD 5816 (CD)*
  see COLL.29,30,77,89,100,105,106,202,204,271,
OUT OF IRELAND (1995) *feat* SEAMUS EGAN-MICK MOLONEY-
  EILEEN IVOR *SHANACHIE (Direct/Koch):*
  SHANCD 79092 (CD) SHANMC 79092 (MC)
OUT OF SIGHT (1997) Music score: DAVID HOLMES -S/T-
  MCA (BMG): MCD 11799 (CD)
OUT OF THIS WORLD (1) songs: Cole Porter
  1.ORIG NEW YORK CAST 1995 *featur:* ANDREA MARTIN-MARY
    ANN LAMB *DRG (New Note-Pinn): DRGCD 94764 (CD)*
  2.ORIG BROADWAY CAST 1950 *feat:* CHARLOTTE GREENWOOD-
    WILLIAM REDFIELD-WILLIAM EYTHE-PRISCILLA GILLETTE-
    BARBARA ASHLEY-DAVID BURNS *SONY: SK 48223 (CD)*
OUT OF THIS WORLD (2) (ITV 24/6/62) *see COLL.23,184,*

OUT OF TOWNERS (1999) Music score by MARC SHAIMAN
     -S/T- *RCA (BMG): 74321 67193-2 (CD)*
OUTBREAK (1995) Music score: JAMES NEWTON HOWARD -S/T-
     VARESE (Pinn): VSD 5599 (CD)
OUTER LIMITS 1 (USA TV 1963) Music: DOMINIC FRONTIERE
     see COLL.38,122,270,309,346,362,
OUTER LIMITS 2 (USA TV 1995) Music: MARK MANCINA-JOHN
     VAN TONGREN *SONIC IMAGES (Greyhound): SI 8604 (CD)*
OUTLAND (1981) Music sc: JERRY GOLDSMITH -S/T- (also
     containing music from 'CAPRICORN ONE') on *GNP USA
     (ZYX): GNPD 8035 (CD) GNP-5 8035 (MC)*
OUTSIDE EDGE (Central 24/3/94) music: FIACHRA TRENCH
     -S/T- *ECHO (Pinn): LBWCD 1 (CD) LBWMC 1 (MC)*
OUTSIDER The (1983) Music score by ENNIO MORRICONE
     DRG (Pinn): DRGCD 32927 (2CD)
OVER THE TOP - *see COLL.51,*
OVERLANDERS The (1946) Music sco: DIMITRI TIOMKIN West
     Australian S.O.(David MEASHAM) *UNICORN KANCHANA
     (Harmonia Mundi): UKCD 2062 (CD)*
OWEN MD (BBC1 1970) theme mus: "Sleepy Shores" by
     JOHNNY PEARSON *see COLL.2,5,243,281,*
OZ FILM -S/T- *Animanga-New Note (Pinn): AM 2 (CD)*

P.D.JAMES Thrillers (Anglia TV various dates) theme
     music "Elegy" by RICHARD HARVEY *unavailable*
PACIFIC BLUE (USA) Music by CHRISTOPHER FRANKE -S/T-
     SONIC IMAGES (Silva Screen): SI 8700 (CD)
PACIFIC OVERTURES - songs by Stephen Sondheim
     1.ORIG BROADWAY CAST 1976 *w:* MAKO-SOON TECK OH-YUKI
       SHIMODA *RCA (S.Screen) RCD14407(CD) CBK14407(MC)*
     2.ENGLISH NATIONAL OPERA CAST *TER (Koch): CDTER
       1151 (CD Highlights) CDTER2 1152 (2CD Complete)*
PADDINGTON (BBC1 74) theme "Size Ten Shuffle" HERBERT
     CHAPPELL Spoken word MC *BBC (Tech): YBBC 1481 (MC)*
PADDINGTON GREEN (BBC1 28/12/1998) music by GUY DAGUL
     unavailable
PAGEMASTER The (1994) Music: JAMES HORNER. Song "Dream
     Away" perf.by BABYFACE and LISA STANSFIELD -S/T-
     ARISTA (BMG): 07822 11019-2(CD) 07822 11019-4(MC)
PAINT YOUR WAGON *sgs:* Alan Jay Lerner-Frederick Loewe
     1. Film Soundtrack 1969 *w:* LEE MARVIN-CLINT EASTWOOD
       -S/T- *reissued on MCA (BMG): MCLD 19310 (CD)*
     2. Orig Broadway Cast 1951 JAMES BARTON-OLGA ST.JOHN
       -TONY BAVAAR *RCA (BMG): GD 60243 (CD)*
PAJAMA GAME The - Songs by RICHARD ADLER-JERRY ROSS
     1.HIGHLIGHTS STUDIO RECORDING 1998
       NATIONAL SYMPHONY ORCH (JOHN OWEN EDWARDS) *feat:*
       JUDY KAYE-RON RAINES-KIM CRISWELL-AVERY SALTZMAN
       TER (Koch): CDTEH 6004 (CD)
     2.First Complete Recording JUDY KAYE-RON RAINES-KIM
       CRISWELL-AVERY SALTZMAN-BROOKE ALMY-DAVID GREEN-
       NATIONAL SYMPHONY ORCH. cond: JOHN OWEN EDWARDS
       TER (Koch): CDTER2 1232 (2CD)

3.FILM MUSICAL 1957 *with:* DORIS DAY -S/T- songs
  SONY 467610-2 (CD) + 'CALAMITY JANE' (1953) **also**
  on *ENTERTAINERS (BMG): CD 343 (CD)*
4.ORIG BROADWAY CAST 1954 *w:* John Raitt-JANIS PAIGE-
  EDDIE FOY JNR-CAROL HANEY-RETA SHAW-RALPH DUNN
  COLUMBIA (S.Screen): CK 32606 (CD) JST 32606 (MC)
PAL JOEY - songs by Richard Rodgers and Lorenz Hart
  1.REVIVAL LONDON CAST 1980 *with:* SIAN PHILLIPS-DENIS
    LAWSON and Company
    Highlights: *SHOWTIME (MCI-THE): SHOW(CD)(MC) 008*
    Complete: *TER (Koch): (CD)(ZC)TER 1005 (CD/MC)*
  2.ORIG BROADWAY CAST 1940 GENE KELLY-VIVIENNE SEGAL
    CBS USA (Sil.Screen) CK 04364 (CD) JST 04364 (MC)
  3.BROADWAY CAST OF 1952 HAROLD LANG-VIVIENNE SEGAL
    HELEN GALLAGHER-LIONEL STANDER-PATRICIA NORTHROP-
    ELAINE STRITCH *EMI ANGEL ZDM 764696-2 (CD)*
  4.STUDIO RECORDING 1995 NEW YORK'S CITY CENTRE MUS
    ICALS IN CONCERT PROD *DRG (Pinn): DRGCD 94763(CD)*
  5.CLASSIC MUSICALS SERIES *feat:* DENIS LAWSON-
    SIAN PHILLIPS-DANIELLE CARSON-DARLENE JOHNSON etc
    + *songs from* 'ON YOUR TOES' *KOCH INT: 34082-2 (CD)*
PALLISERS The (BBC1 19/1/74) music: HERBERT CHAPPELL
  see COLL.2,46,
PANAMA HATTIE (1942) inc.songs by COLE PORTER
  recording also incl.extracts from 'ANYTHING GOES'
  SANDY HOOK (Silver Sounds): CDSH 2043 (CD)
PANORAMA (BBC1 11/11/53-1997) Various Themes includ:
  1980-2000 Theme "Aujourd Hui C'est Toi" from
  'A MAN AND A WOMAN' (66-FRANCIS LAI) available
  -S/T- MUSIDISC (Pinn): 10129-2 (CD) -4 (MC)
PAPER CHASE (1973) Music score: JOHN WILLIAMS on
  'POSEIDON ADVENTURE' (Ltd edition import) on
  RETROGRADE (S.Screen/MFTM): FSMCD 2 (CD)
PAPER CHASE (USA TV) *see COLL.350,*
PAPER TIGER (1974) Music score: ROY BUDD -S/T- on
  CINEPHILE-CASTLE (Pinn): CINCD 012 (CD)
PAPILLON (1973) Music score: JERRY GOLDSMITH -S/T-
  SILVA SCREEN (Koch): FILMCD 029 (CD) see COLL.71,
PARADE (ORIGINAL BROADWAY CAST 1998)
  Songs by JASON ROBERT BROWN / ORIG CAST RECORDING
  RCA VICTOR (BMG): 09026 633780-2 (CD)
PARADINE CASE The (1947) Music score: FRANZ WAXMAN sel
  'Hollywood Piano Concertos' *Koch Int: 37225-2 (CD)*
PARADISE HAWAIIAN STYLE *see* PRESLEY FILM INDEX p.360
PARADISE ROAD (1996) Music: DVORAK and other classics
  -S/T- SONY CLASSICS: SK 63026 (CD)
PARENT TRAP The (1998) Music sco: ALAN SILVESTRI -S/T-
  NAT KING COLE-LOVIN'SPOONFUL-LA'S-GEORGE THOROGOOD
  -BOB GELDOF-DJ JAZZY JEFF-YOUNG HOLT UNLTD
  -S/T- (songs) *HOLLYWOOD (Univ): 162 167-2 (CD)*
PARIS BLUES (1961) Music by DUKE ELLINGTON and others
  -S/T- *re-issue RYKODISC (Vital): RCD 10713 (CD)*
PARIS TEXAS (1984) Original Songs by RY COODER -S/T-
  W.BROS (TEN): 925 270-2 (CD) 925 270-4 (MC)

PARK IS MINE The (1991) Music score: TANGERINE DREAM
   -S/T- *S.SCREEN (Koch): FILMCD 080 (CD) see COLL*
PARKING WARS (ITV 19/02/1999) music by DEBBIE WISEMAN
   unavailable
PARKINSON (BBC1 1970-81 & 1997/98) *see COLL.407,*
PARTRIDGE FAMILY The (USA TV 70s) *see COLL.346,*
PARTY The (1968) Music sco: HENRY MANCINI -S/T- reis:
   RCA (BMG): 74321 61056-2 (CD)
PARTY OF 5 (1997) Music sco: STEVEN CAHILL -S/T- V/A
   WEA: 9362 46431-2(CD) -S/T- EMI UK: PRMDCD 32(CD)
PARTY PARTY (1983) Music by Various Arts -S/T- *reiss:*
   SPECTRUM (Univ): 551 440-2 (CD)
PASSAGE TO INDIA, A (1985) Music score: MAURICE JARRE
   see COLL.70,213,
PASSION - Songs by STEPHEN SONDHEIM
   (1) O.LONDON CAST 1996-MICHAEL BALL-MARIA FRIEDMAN
   FIRST NIGHT (Pinn): CASTCD 61 (CD) CASTC 61 (MC)
   (2) O.BROADWAY CAST 1994 *w:* DONNA MURPHY & Company
   EMI CLASSICS: CDQ 555 251-2 (CD)
PASSION The (BBC1 01/05/1999) o.music by SIMON LACEY
   songs by SUPERGRASS from CD 'IN IT FOR THE MONEY'
   PARLOPHONE (EMI): CD(TC)PCS 7388 (CD/MC/LP)
PASSION FISH (1993) Music score: MASON DARING -S/T-
   DARING (Project-CMD-ADA):DRCD 3008 (CD)
PASSPORT TO PIMLICO (1949)
   see COLL.22,223,
PAT GARRETT & BILLY THE KID (1973) Songs: BOB DYLAN
   -S/T- reiss *SONY M: CD 32098 (CD) 40-32098 (MC)*
PATCH ADAMS (1998) Music score: MARC SHAIMAN -S/T- on
   UNIVERSAL (BMG): UND 53245 (CD)
PATCH OF BLUE, A (1965) Music score: JERRY GOLDSMITH
   -S/T- *INTRADA (Koch/Silva Screen): MAF 7076CD (CD)*
   Imp + 'PATTON' *TSUNAMI (S.Screen): TCI 0606 (CD)*
PATIENCE (operetta) - songs by Gilbert and Sullivan
   1.D'OYLE CARTE OPERA CHORUS AND ORCHESTRA 1994
   TER (Koch): CDTER2 1213 (2CD)
   2.D'OYLY CARTE OPERA COMPANY New Symph.Or.Of London
   (Is.Godfrey) *LONDON (Univ): 425 193-2 (CDx2)*
PATLABOR 2 (95 MANGA VIDEO) Music:(-)
   -S/T- *DEMON (Pinn): DSCD 15 (CD)*
PATTON (70) Music by JERRY GOLDSMITH + *music* 'TORA
   TORA TORA' *VARESE (Pinn): VSD 5796 (CD) also*
   'A PATCH OF BLUE' *Tsunami (S.Scre): TCI 0606 (CD)*
   see COLL.1,167,198,384,
PATTY DUKE SHOW (USA TV) *see COLL.345,*
PAUL CRONE'S TV TIMES (ITV 13/05/1999) title music by
   ROB & ALLAN FENNAH additional mus.by ADRIAN BURCH
   unavailable
PAUL TEMPLE (BBC1 23/11/69) theme music: RON GRAINER
   see COLL.8,104,147,172,
PAULIE: A PARROT'S TALE (1998) Music sco: JOHN DEBNEY
   feat LOS LOBOS -S/T- *VARESE (Pinn): VSD 5936 (CD)*
PAYBACK (1998) Music score: CHRIS BOARDMAN -S/T- on
   VARESE (Pinn): VSD 6003 (CD)

PEACEMAKER The (1997) Music score: HANS ZIMMER
-S/T- *DREAMWORKS (BMG): DRD 50027 (CD)*
PEAK PRACTICE (ITV 10/5/1993) orig music: JOHN ALTMAN
-S/T- *SOUNDTRACKS EMI GOLD: 521 943-2 (CD)*
see COLL.243,
PEANUTS (USA TV) *see COLL.346,*

PEANUTS BANK FOOTS THE BILL (1995) -S/T- Import on
COLOSSEUM (Pinn): CST 348053 (CD)
PEAU D'ANE (FILM Jacques Demy) Music s: MICHEL LEGRAND
-S/T- *PLAYTIME (Discovery): 302542-2 (CD)*
PECKER (1998) Music score by STEWART COPELAND -S/T- on
RCA VICTOR (BMG): 09026 63339-2 (CD)
PEG (O.LONDON CAST 1984) Songs: DAVID HENEKER *featur:*
SIAN PHILLIPS *TER (Koch): CDTER 1024 (CD)*
PENNIES FROM HEAVEN (BBC2 7/2/90 prev.shown 1/12/1978)
1930's music re-recorded from orig 78's / 65 songs
CONNOISS (Pinn): POTTCD 300 (2CD) POTTMC 300 (2MC)
see also entry 'SINGING DETECTIVE'
PEOPLE: A MUSICAL CELEBRATION OF DIVERSITY (1995)
PEABO BRYSON-LEA SALONGA-AL JARREAU-CHAKA KHAN-
VANESSA WILLIAMS *LIGHTYEAR (Pinn): 54150-2 (CD)*
PEOPLE IN LONDON (ITV 1964) theme mus "Spanish Armada"
LES REED *see COLL.7,*
PEOPLE'S CENTURY (BBC2 13/9/95) t.music by ZBIGNIEW
PRIESNER other mus by ORLANDO GOUGH-FIACHRA TRENCH
DEBBIE WISEMAN -S/T- *VIRGIN (EMI): CD(TC)VIP 177*
PEOPLE'S COURT (USA TV) *see COLL.350,*
PEOPLE'S VETS (ITV 02/06/1999) music by PHIL BINDING &
SIMON MOORE *unavailable*
PERCY (1971) Music: RAY DAVIES Songs sung by The KINKS
-S/T- *CASTLE Classics (Pinn): CLACD 164 (CD)*
PERDITA DURANGO (1998) Music score by SIMON BOSWELL
-S/T- (Var.Arts) *ARISTA (BMG): 74321 54116-2 (CD)*
PERFECT MURDER,A (1997) Music sco: JAMES NEWTON HOWARD
-S/T- *VARESE (Pinn): VSD 5946 (CD)*
PERFECT SCOUNDRELS (TVS from 22/4/90) mus (2nd ser) by
NIGEL HESS *see COLL.193,*
PERFECT STRANGERS (USA TV) *see COLL.350,*
PERFORMANCE (1970) Music score: JACK NITZSCHE Songs by
RANDY NEWMAN-RY COODER-MERRY CLAYTON-BUFFY SAINTE
MARIE-LAST POETS -S/T- *WB (TEN): 7599 26400-2 (CD)*
PERILS OF PENELOPE PITSTOP *see COLL.373,*
PERRY MASON (USA TV) Music theme by FRED STEINER
see COLL.23,109,110,121,270,345,363,375,377,
PERSONAL SERVICES (C4 12/11/1998) theme "Typewriter"
LEROY ANDERSON *RCA (BMG): 09026 68048-2 (CD)*
PERSONALS ORIG.LONDON CAST (1998) *feat* DAVID BARDSLEY-
MARTIN CALLAGHAN-MARCUS ALLEN COOPER-CHRISTINA FRY
RIA JONES-SUMMER ROGNLIE *TER (Koch): CDTER 1254 CD*
PERSUADERS The (ITV 17/9/71-72) theme mus: JOHN BARRY
see COLL.2,5,29,34,121,270,281,344,360,
PERVIRELLA (1997) Music score: FRANCOIS EVANS -S/T-
DIONYSUS (Cargo): ID 123369CD (CD) ID 123369 (LP)

PETE KELLY'S BLUES (USA TV) *see COLL.348,*
PETE'S DRAGON - *see* WALT DISNEY INDEX p.362

PETER AND THE WOLF (1996) SERGEI PROKOFIEV *feat.voices*
KIRSTIE ALLEY-ROSS MALINDER-LLOYD BRIDGES *with the*
RCA SYMPHONY ORCHESTRA (cond;Daughterty)
RCA VICTOR Gold Seal (BMG): 74321 31869-2 (CD)
PETER GUNN (USA TV 1959) Music score by HENRY MANCINI
TV -S/T- *BUDDAH-RCA (BMG): 74321 69203-2 (CD)*
also on FRESH SOUNDS (Disc): FSCD 2009 (CD)
'MORE MUSIC FROM PETER GUNN' Henry Mancini on *RCA
(BMG): 74321 29857-2 (CD)*
see COLL.118,238,344,346,356,375,
PETER PAN (FILM 1953) Music: OLIVER WALLACE-PAUL SMITH
DISNEY-EDEL (Pinn): 017 582-2 (CD) -4 (MC)
DISNEY'S MUSIC & STORIES *DISNEY (Technicol):
WD 77583-2 (CD) WD 77583-4 (MC) see also p.362*
PETER PAN - songs by MOOSE CHARLAP and CAROLYN LEIGH +
add.material: JULE STYNE-BETTY COMDEN-ADOLPH GREEN
1.*TER* STUDIO REC.1998 CATHY RIGBY-PAUL SCHOEFFLER-
JENNY AGUTTER-HELEN HOBSON-LISA SAGARDIA
TER (Koch): CDTER 1252 (CD)
2.ORIG LONDON CAST 1994 *featuring:* RON MOODY-NICOLA
STAPLETON & Company
FIRST NIGHT (Pinn): CASTCD 46 (CD) CASTC 46 (MC)
3.THE BRITISH MUSICAL / ORIG CAST RECORDING
EMI: CDEMC 3696 (CD)
PETER'S FRIENDS (1992) The Album (Various Artists)
EPIC (Ten): MOODCD 27 (CD) see COLL
PETTICOAT JUNCTION (USA TV) *see COLL.345,*
PEYTON PLACE (USA TV)
see COLL.23,270,349,367,376,391,
PHAEDRA (1961) Music score: MIKIS THEODORAKIS -S/T-
Sakkaris Imprt (Pinn): SR 50060 (CD)
PHANTOM: The American Musical Sensation (O.CAST 1993)
Songs (Maury YESTON) *feat:* Glory Crampton-Richard
White-Paul Schoeffler-Jack Dabdoub and Company
RCA Victor (BMG): 09026 61660-2 (CD)
PHANTOM OF THE OPERA (1) songs by Andrew Lloyd Webber
Charles Hart and Richard Stilgoe
1.ORIG LONDON CAST 1986 *with:* MICHAEL CRAWFORD-SARAH
BRIGHTMAN & Company *POLYDOR: 831 273-2 (2CD) also*
2.HIGHLIGHTS *831563-2(CD) -5(DCC) POLH(C) 33(MC/LP)*
3.STUDIO RECORD 1993 *w:*GRAHAM BICKLEY-JOHN BARROWMAN
CLAIRE BURT Munich Symph Orch (John Owen Edwards)
<u>Highlights:</u> *SHOWTIME (MCI-THE): SHOW(CD)(MC) 002*
<u>Complete:</u> *TER (Koch): CDTEM 1207 (CD)*
4.CARLTON SHOWS COLL.1993 Studio Record *w:*PAUL JONES
STEPHANIE LAWRENCE-CARL WAYNE-FIONA HENDLEY & Comp
CARLTON: PWKS 4164 (CD) PWKMC 4164 (MC)
also contains songs from 'ASPECTS OF LOVE'
5.CLASSIC MUSICALS SERIES *feat:*GRAHAM BICKLEY-CLAIRE
MOORE-JOHN BARROWMAN-MUNICH SYMPH.ORCH+ *songs from*
'CATS' *KOCH Int: 34078-2 (CD)*

PHANTOM OF THE OPERA (2) (1925 FILM *featur.*LON CHANEY)
  1.(1996 restoration) Music by Carl Davis conducting
   The CITY of PRAGUE PHILHARMONIC, organ: JOHN BIRCH
   SILVA SCREEN (Koch): FILMCD 193 (CD)
  2.(Studio Recording 1995) music by Rick Wakeman on
   'Phantom Power' *AMBIENT (AMT): A10M2 (CD)*
  3.(1977 version) Music: Gaylord Carter organ 'Mighty
   Wurlitzer' *NEW WORLD (Conifer): NW 227 (LP) delet.*
PHANTOM OF THE OPERA (1998) Music sco: ENNIO MORRICONE
  DRG IMPRT (Pinn): DRGCD 12620 (CD)
PHANTOM OF THE OPERA (1989) FILM feat: Robert Englund)
  Symphonic music score by Mischa Segal -S/T- on
  SILVA SCREEN (Koch): FILMCD 069 (CD)
PHANTOM OF THE OPERA ON ICE (1996) Mus: ROBERTO DANOVA
  -S/T- *Roberto Danova-PLAZA (Pinn): PZA 008(CD(MC)*
PHAT BEACH (1996) -S/T- *EDEL (Pinn): 0022622CIN (CD)*

PHENOMENA aka CREEPERS (1984) Music by IRON MAIDEN
  SIMON BOSWELL TURNER-BILL WYMAN-GOBLIN-MOTORHEAD
  CINEVOX ITALY (Silva Screen): CDCIA 5062 (CD)
  also DCMDF 303 (CD) see COLL.319,
PHENOMENON (1996) Music score: THOMAS NEWMAN -S/T-
  REPRISE (TEN): 9362 46360-2 (CD) see COLL.199,
PHILADELPHIA (1994) Music score: HOWARD SHORE opening
  song by BRUCE SPRINGSTEEN 2 Soundtracks available
  -S/T- Songs *EPIC (SM): 474998-2(CD) -4(MC) -8(MD)*
  -S/T- Score *EPIC (SM): 475800-2(CD) -4(MC) delet*
  see COLL.3,87,274,
PHILADELPHIA EXPERIMENT The (1984) Mus: KEN WANNBERG
  -S/T- *also contains score from* 'MOTHER LODE' on
  PROMETHEUS (S.Screen): PCD 121(CD)
  see COLL.264,
PHILADELPHIA STORY The (1940) Music sco: FRANZ WAXMAN
  see COLL.395,
PI THE MOVIE (1998) Music score: CLINT MANSELL -S/T-
  incl.songs by MASSIVE ATTACK-APHEX TWIN-ORBITAL-
  GUSGUS-AUTOCHRE-RONI SIZE-DAVID HOLMES
  SILVA SCREEN (Koch): FILMCD 312 (CD)
PIAF (ORIG LONDON CAST 1994) *featuring* ELAINE PAIGE
  WB (TEN): 4509 94641-2 (CD) -4 (MC)
PIANO The (1993) Music score: MICHAEL NYMAN -S/T- on
  VENTURE-VIRGIN (EMI): CD(TC)VE 919 (CD/MC)
  see COLL.100,106,144,262,331,
PICKING UP THE PIECES (ITV 29/10/1998) ser.theme mus
  comp.& performed by KIRSTY MacCOLL *unavailable*
PICKWICK THE MUSICAL CHICHESTER FESTIVAL THEATRE 1993
  Songs (Cyril ORNADEL-Leslie BRICUSSE) *featuring:*
  HARRY SECOMBE-ALEXANDRA BASTEDO-ROY CASTLE-RUTH
  MADOC-GLYN HOUSTON-DAVID CARDY-MICHAEL HOWE & Comp
  <u>Highlights</u>: *SHOWTIME (MCI-THE): SHOW(CD(MC) 023*
  <u>Complete</u>: *TER (Koch): CDTER 1205 (CD)*
  <u>Classic Musicals series</u> *feat:* HARRY SECOMBE
  RUTH MADOC-ROY CASTLE-DAVID CARDY-ROBERT MEADMORE
  + *songs from* 'SCROOGE' *KOCH INT: 34081-2 (CD)*

PICNIC (1956) Music sco: GEORGE DUNING -S/T- *MCA USA
    Import (Silva Screen): MCAD 31357 (CD)
    see COLL.240,*
PICNIC AT HANGING ROCK *see COLL.85,*
PILLOW BOOK The (1996) Music score: BRIAN ENO -S/T-
    XIII BIS (Discovery): LBS 197101 (CD)
PILLOW TALK (1959) Mus sco: FRANK DE VOL -S/T- feat
    DORIS DAY *Bear Family (Topic/Proj): BCD 15913 2CD*
PINGU (BBC1 27/9/91) theme music *see COLL.67,*
PINK PANTHER The (1963) Music score by HENRY MANCINI
    -S/T- complete with 'RETURN OF THE PINK PANTHER'
    RCA CAMDEN (BMG): 74321 66047-2 (CD)
    see COLL.121,238,281,286,337,346,356,
PINK PANTHER The (FILM 1963) Mus: HENRY MANCINI *-S/T-
    (SPECIAL AUDIO LP EDITION) Import (VIVANTI dist)
    AUDIOLP LSP 2795 (LP Audio Quality) -S/T- also on
    RCA: ND(NK) 80832 (CD/MC)*
PINK PANTHER The (TV-USA Cartoon) song "Panther Pink
    From Head To Toes" by DOUG GOODWIN *unavailable*
PINK PANTHER STRIKES AGAIN (1976) Music: HENRY MANCINI
    "Come To Me" sung by TOM JONES -S/T- on
    RYKODISC (Vital): RCD 10739 (CD)
PINKY AND PERKY (BBC 60's) Song compilation on *EMI:
    CD(TC)EMS 1470 (CD/MC)*
PINOCCHIO (1939) M: LEIGH HARLINE-P.SMITH-N.WASHINGTON
    -S/T- *DISNEY (B.Vista): WD 75430-2 (CD) -4 (MC)*
    see also WALT DISNEY INDEX p.362
PINOCCHIO (1996) Music sco: RACHEL PORTMAN -S/T- *feat:*
    STEVIE WONDER-JERRY HADLEY & SISSEL and BRIAN MAY
    DECCA (Univ.): 452 740-2 (CD) -4 (MC)
PIRATES OF PENZANCE (operetta) songs by W.S.Gilbert
    and A.Sullivan
    1. D'OYLY CARTE OPERA COMPANY 1989 STUDIO RECORDING
      with: MARILYN HILL SMITH and Company
      <u>Highlights</u>: *SHOWTIME (MCI-THE): SHOW(CD)(MC) 010*
      <u>Complete</u>:*TER (Koch): CDTER2 1177 (2CD)*
    2. ORIGINAL BROADWAY CAST 1983
      feat: KEVIN KLINE-LINDA RONSTADT and Company on
      IMPRT (Silva Screen): WA 601 (CD)
    3. PRO-ARTE ORCHEST (Malcolm Sargent) GLYNDEBOURNE
      FESTIVAL CHOIR Solo: George Baker-James Milligan-
      John Cameron-Richard Lewis *EMI: CMS 764409-2 (2CD)*
    4. D'OYLY CARTE OPERA COMP with RPO cond: I.Godfrey
      LONDON (Univ): 425 196-2 (CDx2) 425 196-4 (MC)
PISTOL FOR RINGO, A - *see* DEATH RIDES A HORSE
PJ'S The (USA) -S/T- from and inspired by TV series
    EDEL-HOLLYWOOD (Pinn): 010 089-2HWR
PLAGUE AND THE MOONFLOWER The (BBC2 31/12/1994) Music
    by RICHARD HARVEY lyrics by RALPH STEADMAN *featur:*
    JOHN WILLIAMS-KYM AMPS-RICHARD STUDT-ROGER CHASE-
    and BEN KINGSLEY-IAN HOLM-PENELOPE WILTON
    ALTUS RECORDS: ALU 0001 (CD)
PLAN 9 FROM OUTER SPACE (1956) mus.sup: GORDON ZAHLER
    -S/T- *Impt. PERFORMANCE (Greyhound): PERF 391 (LP)*

PLANET OF THE APES (1968) Music score: JERRY GOLDSMITH
score on *VARESE (Pinn): VSD 5848 (CD)*
see COLL.264,308,362,

PLANET SHOWBIZ (C4 30/4/97) title mus: DAVID BALL and
INGO VAUK incid. music by SIMON BRINT *unavailable*

PLANETS The (BBC) Orig music score by JIM MEACOCK and
music from 'The Planets' (Gustav HOLST) -S/T- on
BBC (Pinn): WMSF 60102 (CD)

PLATOON 1.(1986) Mus: GEORGES DELERUE (rejected orig
score) *PROMETHEUS (Silva Screen): PCD 136 (CD)*
also contains complete score 'SALVADOR'
see COLL.77,100,105,125,286,364,

PLATOON 2. (1986) Music: GEORGES DELERUE Main theme
'Adagio For Strings' (Samuel BARBER) Vancouver SO
-S/T- *ATLANTIC (TEN): 781 742-2 (CD) WX 95 (MC)*

PLATOON LEADER (1988) Music score: GEORGE S.CLINTON
-S/T- *GNP CRESCENDO (ZYX): GNPD 8013 (CD)*

PLAY AWAY / PLAY SCHOOL (BBC1-2 / 1964-88)
MFP:TC-DL 1114 (2MC) see COLL.186,

PLAY ON! (ORIG BROADWAY CAST RECORDING) featuring the
songs of DUKE ELLINGTON in 'TWELFTH NIGHT' setting
ORIG BROADWAY CAST *VARESE (Pinn): VSD 5837 (CD)*

PLAYING BY HEART (1998) Music by JOHN BARRY with CHET
BAKER-CHRIS BOTTI -S/T- MOBY/NENEH CHERRY/GOMEZ
-S/T- score: *DECCA (Univ): 466 275-2 (CD) -4 (MC)*
-S/T- songs: *EMI: 520 510-2 (CD)*

PLAYING THE FIELD (BBC1 8/3/1998) title song (A.Moyet-
P.Glenister) sung by ALISON MOYET *unavailable*

PLAYDAYS: Lizzie Singalong (BBC) *BBC (Tech): YBBC 1490*
*theme on Coll 'TV TUNES FOR KIDS' see Coll / also
avail:* 'PLAYDAYS LIVE ON STAGE' *BMG Kidz: 74321
24486-4 (MC)* PLAYDAYS (BBC2) CHRISTMAS SONGS AND
STORIES *LFP (EMI): LFPK 2019 (MC) see COLL.67,*

PLAYER The (1991) Music score: THOMAS NEWMAN -S/T-
VARESE USA (Pinn): VSD 5366 (CD)

PLEASANTVILLE (1998) Music score by RANDY NEWMAN
-S/T- score: *VARESE (Pinn): VSD 5988 (CD)*
-S/T- songs: *COLUMBIA (Ten): 492 594-2 (CD)*

PLEASE SAVE MY EARTH (Japan 1995) Animated MANGA Film
-S/T- *ANIMAMGA-New Note (Pinn): AM 6 (CD)*

PLEASE SIR (LWT 68) theme music: SAM FONTEYN
see COLL.4,363,

PLUNKETT & MACLEANE (1997) Music sco: CRAIG ARMSTRONG
"Houses In Motion" sung by LEWIS PARKER-HELEN
WHITE -S/T- *MELANKOLIC-VIRGIN: CDSAD 7 (CD)*

PLYMOUTH ADVENTURE (1952) Mus.sco by MIKLOS ROSZA -S/T
selection incl.music from MADAME BOVARY/QUO VADIS
IVANHOE on *IMPORT (Silva Screen): TT 3001 (CD)*

POCAHONTAS (1995) Music score: ALAN MENKEN Songs (Alan
MENKEN-Stephen SCHWARTZ) including "Colours Of The
Wind" sung: VANESSA WILLIAMS -S/T- *DISNEY Records*
-S/T- *DISNEY-EDEL (Pinn): 015462-2 (CD)*
*Sing-A-Long: Walt Disney: DISCD(MC) 481 (CD/MC) /
Story & Songs: Disney: PDC 316 (CD) see also p.362*

POINT BREAK (1991) Music: MARK ISHAM + JIMI HENDRIX
  PIL-RATT-LA GUNS-WESTWORLD-LIQUID JESUS-WIRETRAIN
  re-iss: MCA GEFFEN (BMG): MCLD 19327 (CD)
POINT OF NO RETURN - *see under* 'ASSASSIN, The'
POIROT *see* 'AGATHA CHRISTIE'S POIROT' *see COLL.6,390,*
POKEMON (SKY1/GMTV 1999) TV -S/T- 'POKEMON 2BA MASTER'
  MUSIC FROM THE HIT TV SERIES inc.theme "PokeRap"
  KOCH INT: 33362-2 (CD) -4 (MC)
POKEMON THE FIRST MOVIE (1999) Theme by BILLY CRAWFORD
  -S/T- *ATLANTIC (Ten): 7567 83261-2 (CD) -4 (MC)*
POLDARK (BBC1 5/10/75) theme mus: KENYON EMRYS-ROBERTS
  see COLL.2,46,
POLICE SQUAD (USA) *see COLL.122,350,*
POLICE STORY (USA) *see COLL.17,349,382,*
POLICE WOMAN (USA) *see COLL.109,110,270,349,382,*
POLITICIAN'S WIFE The (C4 16/5/95|) music: BARRINGTON
  PHELOUNG compilation 'PASSION OF MORSE' also inc
  'Inspector Morse'/'Truly Madly Deeply'/'Saint-Ex'
  TRING INT (Tring): TRING 003 (CD) MCTRING 003 (MC)
POLTERGEIST (1982) Music score: JERRY GOLDSMITH -S/T-
  EMI SOUNDTRACKS (EMI): 821 957-2 (CD) DELETED
  see COLL.68,175,309,
POLTERGEIST: THE LEGACY (1997) mus: MARK MANCINA-JOHN
  VAN TONGREN sco: JOHN VAN TONGREN-CHRISTOPHER WARD
  SONIC IMAGES (Greyhound-Cargo): SI 8701 (CD)
POPEYE (USACart.40s) theme "I'm Popeye The Sailor Man"
  (Sammy Lerner) *see COLL.270,345,*
POPPIE NON GENA (MUSICAL 83) JOE BOYD / ORIG S.AFRICAN
  CAST *reissued May 96 HANNIBAL-RYKODISK (Vital):*
  HNCD 1351 (CD) HNBC 1351 (MC)
PORGY AND BESS - songs by George and Ira Gershwin
                                     with DuBose Heyward
  1.FILM MUSICAL 1959 DOROTHY DANDRIDGE-SIDNEY POITIER
   -S/T- *SONY Europe (Discovery): CD 70007 (CD)*
  2.Studio HIGHLIGHTS LEONTYNE PRICE-WILLIAM WARFIELD
   JOHN W.BUBBLES-McHENRY BOATWRIGHT+Symphonic Dances
   to WEST SIDE STORY *RCA (BMG): 74321 24218-2 (CD)*
  3.ORIG BROADWAY CAST 1942 *w:* Todd Duncan-Anne Brown-
   Edward Matthews-Helen Dowdy *MCA (BMG):MCLD 19158*
  4.GLYNDEBOURNE FESTIVAL OPERA 1988 WILLARD WHITE-
   CYNTHIA HAYMON-DAMON EVANS-BRUCE HUBBARD-LPO(Simon
   Rattle) *EMI ANGEL: CDS 556 220-2 (3CDs-Compl) orig*
   LDB 491 131-2 (2CDs) or CDC 754 325-2 Highlights
  5.Houston Grand Opera: DONNIE RAY ALBERT-CLAMMA DALE
   ANDREW SMITH-WILMA SHAKESNIDER-BETTY LANE and Comp
   Complete Rec: *RCA Red Seal (BMG): RD 82109 (3 CDs)*
   Highlights Only: *RCA Red Seal (BMG): RD 84680 (CD)*
  6.STUDIO HIGHLIGHTS (1975) WILLARD WHITE-BARBARA
   HENDRICKS & Comp with CLEVELAND ORCH & CHOIR cond
   LORIN MAAZEL *DECCA (Univ): 436 306-2DH (CD)*
  7.STUDIO RECORDING 'Great Scenes From PORGY & BESS'
   LEONTYNE PRICE/WILLIAM WARFIELD/RCA VICTOR ORCHEST
   McHENRY BOATWRIGHT/JOHN W.BUBBLES/BARBARA WEBB etc
   RCA HIGH PERFORMANCE (BMG): 09026 63312-2 (CD)

PORTERHOUSE BLUE (C4 3/6/87) Title theme by Rick Lloyd sung by FLYING PICKETTS *see COLL.7,*

PORTRAIT OF A LADY (1996) Music score: WOJCIECH KILAR plus additional music by FRANZ SCHUBERT -S/T- on *DECCA (Univ): 455 011-2 (CD) -4 (MC)*

PORTRAIT OF TERROR (1998) Music score: JOHN OTTMAN -S/T- *VARESE (Pinn): VSD 5986 (CD)*

POSEIDON ADVENTURE The (1972) Music sco: JOHN WILLIAMS complete score (Ltd edit.imp) with 'PAPER CHASE' *RETROGRADE (S.Screen/MFTM): FSMCD 2 (CD)*

POSTMAN The (1997) Music score: JAMES NEWTON HOWARD theme song sung by KEVIN COSTNER -S/T- on *WARNER SUNSET (TEN) 9362 46842-2 (CD)*

POSTMAN The (Il Postino) (1994) Music sc: LUIS BACALOV *EDEL-HOLLYWOOD (Pinn): 012 029-2HWR (CD)*

POSTMAN PAT (BBC1 from 5/7/82-1996) music: BRYAN DALY narrated and sung by KEN BARRIE *POST MUSIC (Pinn): PPCD 101 (CD) PMC 101 (MC)* also available with KEN BARRIE-CAROL BOYD *BBC (Tech): YBBC 1491 (MC)* also available '100 RHYMES AND SONGS' *REDROCK (Univ): RKCD 27 (CD)* see COLL.67,186,

POSTMAN PAT (MUSICAL VERSION OF ANIMATED TV SERIES) *EPIC (Ten): 480 686-4 (MC)*

POSTMAN The (Il Postino) (95) Mus sco: LUIS E.BACALOV -S/T- *MILAN (Pinn): 162 209-2 (CD)* also available -S/T- *HOLLYWOOD (Silva Screen): HW 62029-2 (CD)*

POT BLACK/JUNIOR P.BLACK (BBC2 1972-86) "Black & White Rag" (George Botsford) WINIFRED ATWELL *PRESIDENT: PLCD 531 (CD) (TC)PLE 531* see COLL.148,

POTTER'S WHEEL (BBC 1950's) *see COLL.147,172,*

POWAQQATSI (1988) Music score: PHILIP GLASS -S/T- on *ELEKTRA NONESUCH (TEN): 7559 79192-2 (CD) -4(MC)*

POWDER (1995) Music score: JERRY GOLDSMITH -S/T- *Import (Silva Screen): HW 20384-2 (CD)*

POWER The (1967) Music score: MIKLOS ROZSA Suite + music from 'BEN HUR'/'KING OF KINGS' 12 choral pieces *PROMETHEUS (Silva Screen): PCD 122 (CD)*

POWER GAME The (ITV 65) theme music: CYRIL STAPLETON *see COLL.23,*

PRACTICAL MAGIC (1998) Music sco: ALAN SILVESTRI -S/T- VARIOUS ARTISTS *WARNER: 9362 47253-2 (CD)*

PRAYER FOR THE DYING, A (1988) Orig score: JOHN SCOTT *(replaced by BILL CONTI score)* - John Scott vers available on *JOS (Silva Screen): JSCD 102 (CD)* inc John Scott's score 'WINTER PEOPLE' (1989)

PREACHER'S WIFE The (1996) Music sc: HANS ZIMMER songs comp/produced by Annie LENNOX/David FOSTER/Trevor HORN/BABYFACE and performed by WHITNEY HOUSTON -S/T- *ARISTA (BMG): 74321 44125-2 (CD) -4 (MC)* -S/T- special ltd ed: *07822 18951-2 (CD) -4 (MC)*

PREACHING TO THE PEVERTED (1997) Various Arts -S/T- on *NAKED (Pinn): PERVCDLP 001 (CD) PERVMCLP 001 (MC)*

PREDATOR 2 (1990) Music score: ALAN SILVESTRI -S/T- on *VARESE (Pinn): VSD 5302 (CD)*

PRELUDE TO A KISS (1992) Music sco: HOWARD SHORE -S/T-
    MILAN (BMG): 11125-2 (CD) 11125-4 (MC)
PRESIDENT'S LADY The see *COLL.1,*
PRESTON FRONT (BBC1 16/7/95) theme song "Here I Stand"
    sung by The MILLTOWN BROTHERS on album 'Slinky'
    A.& M. (Univ): 395 346-2 (CD) 395 346-4 (MC)
PRESUMED INNOCENT (1990) Music score: JOHN WILLIAMS
    -S/T- *VARESE (Pinn): VSD 5280 (CD)*
PRET-A-PORTER (1994) INA KAMOZE-TERENCE TRENT D'ARBY-
    CRANBERRIES-M.PEOPLE *COLUMB (Ten): 478 226-2 (CD)*
PRETTY WOMAN (1989) Music by JAMES NEWTON HOWARD -S/T-
    EMI USA (EMI): CDP 793492-2 (CD) TCMTL 1052 (MC)
    see *COLL.13,36,83,105,*
PRICKLY HEAT (SKY1 11/10/1998) theme mus "Oooie Oooie
    Oooie" PRICKLY HEAT *VIRGIN (EMI):VSCDT 1727(CDs)*
PRIDE AND PREJUDICE (BBC1 24/9/95) orig mus.composed
    and conducted by CARL DAVIS -S/T- *featuring*
    MELVYN TAN (fortepiano) on *EMI: CDEMC 3726 (CD)*
PRIDE AND THE PASSION The (1957) Music: GEORGE ANTHEIL
    with 'AGONY & THE ECSTASY' (ALEX NORTH) 75m
    CLOUD NINE (BMG-Con): CNS 5001 (CD)
PRIMAL FEAR (1996) Music sco: JAMES NEWTON HOWARD
    -S/T- *MILAN (BMG): 74321 35545-2 (CD)*
PRIMARY COLORS (1998) Music score: RY COODER -S/T- on
    MCA (BMG): MCD 11775 (CD)
PRIME SUSPECT (Gran 7/4/91) (2) 15/12/92 (3) 19/12/93)
    theme by STEPHEN WARBECK *currently unavailable*
PRINCE AMONG ISLANDS, A (ITV 10/5/92) mus CAPERCAILLIE
    "Coisich A Ruin" featuring KAREN MATHIESON -*S/T*-
    selection on SURVIVAL (BMG): ZT 45394 (MC)
PRINCE AND THE PAUPER (1937) Music sco: ERICH WOLFGANG
    KORNGOLD perform.by BRANDENBURG PHILHARMONIC ORCH
    (William T.Stromberg) *with* 'ADVENTURES OF MARK
    TWAIN' (MAX STEINER) *RCA (BMG): 09026 62660-2 (CD)*
    also on VARESE (Pinn): VSD 5207 (CD)
PRINCE AND THE SHOWGIRL 1957 see *COLL.9,*
PRINCE OF DARKNESS (1988) Music: JOHN CARPENTER & ALAN
    HOWARTH -S/T- *COLOSSEUM (Pinn): CST348031 (CD)*
    VARESE (Pinn): VCD 47310 (CD)
PRINCE OF EGYPT (1996) Music score: HANS ZIMMER
    -S/T- (music sco) *DREAMWORKS (BMG): DRD 50041 (CD)*
    -S/T- (nashville) *DREAMWORKS (BMG): DRD 50045 (CD)*
    -S/T- (inspirational)   "   *(BMG): DRD 50050 (CD)*
    see *COLL.3,*
PRINCE OF PLAYERS (1955) Music score: BERNARD HERRMANN
    new recording: MOSCOW SYMPHONY ORCH. (W.Stromberg)
    also features music from 'GARDEN OF EVIL' (1954)
    MARCO POLO (Select): 8.223841 (CD) see COLL.1,
PRINCE VALIANT (1954) Music sco: FRANZ WAXMAN
    see *COLL.1,*
PRINCESS BRIDE The (1987) Music score: MARK KNOPFLER
    -S/T- *VERTIGO: VERH 53C (MC) 832864-2 (CD)*
PRINCESS MONONOKE (1999) Music score by JOE HISAISHI
    -S/T- *MILAN (BMG): 74321 35864-2 (CD)*

PRISCILLA: QUEEN OF THE DESERT (1994) Mus: GUY CROSS
   -S/T- *MOTHER (Univ): 516 937-2 (CD) -4 (MC)*
PRISONER The (ITV 29/9/1967) Theme music: RON GRAINER
   score by RON GRAINER-ALBERT ELMS etc.*SILVA SCREEN
   (Koch): FILMCD 042* (V1) *FILMCD 084* (V2) *FILMCD 126*
   (Vol.3)   see *COLL.8,38,121,270,278,309,344,360,*
PRISONER CELL BLOCK H (Australia 79-87)(UK 84) theme
   "On The Inside" (Alan Caswell) sung LYNNE HAMILTON
   see *COLL.150,270,376,*
PRISONERS OF CONSCIENCE (BBC2 27/11/89) theme music
   "Fragile" (G.Sumner) STING 'Nothing Like The Sun'
   A.& M. CDA 6402 (CD) AMA 6402 (LP) AMC 6402 (MC)
PRIVATE LIVES OF ELIZABETH AND ESSEX (1939) Music sco
   ERICH WOLFGANG KORNGOLD. *NEW COMPLETE RECORDING on
   VARESE (Pinn): VSD 5696 (CD). Selections available
   on SILVA SCREEN: FILMXCD 188 and EMI: CDODEON 13*
   see *COLL.221,338,*
PRIVATE PARTS (1996) Score: VAN DYKE PARKS -S/T- V.Art
   W.BROS (TEN): 9362 46477-2 (CD)
PRIZZI'S HONOR (1987) Music score: ALEX NORTH
      see *COLL.81,273,275,*
PRODUCERS The (1968,Mel Brooks) music sco: JOHN MORRIS
   -S/T- + dialogue *RAZOR & TIE (Koch): RE 2147 (CD)*
PROFESSIONAL The - see 'LEON'
PROFESSIONAL The (1981) Music score by ENNIO MORRICONE
   DRG (Pinn): DRGCD 32927 (2CD)
PROFESSIONALS The (LWT 30/12/77-1983/Granada+ 15/2/97)
   theme: LAURIE JOHNSON. LAURIE JOHNSON'S LONDON BIG
   BAND *VIRGIN (EMI): VSCDT 1643* (CDs) *VST 1643* (12")
   see *COLL.6,149,203,215,217,360,363,401,*
PROFESSIONALS The (1966) Music sc: MAURICE JARRE -S/T-
   SILVA TREASURY (Koch): SSD 5002 (CD)
PROFUNDO ROSSO (Horror Film) Music score: GOBLIN -S/T-
   CINEVOX (S.Screen) CIAK 75005 (MC) CIA 5005 (LP)
PROMENADE (MUSICAL) Music by AL CARMINES Lyrics by
   MARIA IRENE FORNES. *ORIG 1969 OFF BROADWAY CAST
   RCA (BMG): 09026 63333-2 (CD)*
PROMISES PROMISES songs: Burt Bacharach-Hal David
   O.BROADWAY CAST 1968 *feat* JERRY ORBACH-JILL O'HARA
   EDWARD WINTER *RYKODISC (Vital): RCD 10750 (CD)*
PROPOSITION The (1998) Music score by STEPHEN ENDELMAN
   -S/T- *PHILIPS (Univ): 462 504-2 (CD)*
PROSPERO'S BOOKS (1991) Music: MICHAEL NYMAN -S/T-
   PHILIPS (Univ): 425 224-2 (CD) -4 (MC)
PROTECTORS The (ITC orig 29/9/72) theme music "Avenues
   & Alleyways" (Mitch Murray-Pete Callander) sung by
   TONY CHRISTIE *MCA (BMG): MCLD(MCLC) 19204 (CD/MC)*
   see *COLL.2,360,*
PSYCHO (1960) Music score by BERNARD HERRMANN
   NAT.PHILHARMONIC ORCH (B.Herrmann) Studio Record
   UNICORN KANCHANA (H.Mundi): UKCD 2021 (CD)
   new record.by ROYAL SCOTTISH NATIONAL ORCH cond,
   Joel McNEELY *VARESE (Pinn): VSD 5765 (CD)*
   see *COLL.68,70,188,190,191,192,194,195,196,197,*

PSYCHODERELICT (Rock Opera 93) Songs: PETER TOWNSHEND
ATLANTIC/EAST WEST (TEN): 7567 82494-2(CD) -4(MC)

PSYCHOS (C4 06/05/1999) recordings used included
"Pearl's Girls" and "Cherry Pie" by UNDERWORLD on
JUNIOR-TVT (Cargo-Greyhound): TVT 87482 (CD)

PUBLIC EYE (1992) Music score: MARK ISHAM -S/T-
VARESE (Pinn): VSD 5374 (CD)

PULP FICTION (1993) Music by Various Artists -S/T-
*MCA (BMG): MCD 11103 (CD) MCC 11103 (MC) also on
SIMPLY VINYL (Telstar): SVLP 27 (LP)
see COLL.36,143,145,364,*

PUMP UP THE VOLUME (1990) -S/T- feat VARIOUS ARTISTS
MCA (BMG): MCD 06121 (CD)

PURE COUNTRY (1992) Music comp/perf. by GEORGE STRAIT
-S/T- MCA (BMG): MCD 10651 (CD) MCC 10651 (MC)

PURE WICKEDNESS (BBC1 14/09/1999) Music by JOHN KEANE
Songs included "Sexy Boy" by AIR on 'MOON SAFARI'
*SOURCE-VIRGIN (EMI): CDV(TCV)(MDV) 2848 (CD/MC/md)
also VSCDT 1672 (CDs) VSC 1672 (MC) VST 1672 (12")
end song* "Blood Red River" BETH ORTON on 'Central
Reservation' *HEAVENLY (BMG): HVNLP 22 (CD)*

PURPLE RAIN (1984) Music: PRINCE & REVOLUTION -S/T-
WB (TEN): 759 925 110-2 (CD) -4 (MC) -5 (DCC)

PURSUIT (USA) *see COLL.17,*

PUSHER (1997) Music score: PETER PETER-POVI KRISTIAN
-S/T- VARIOUS ARTISTS MCA (BMG): MCD 85013 (CD)

PUSHING TIN (1999) Music score by ANNE DUDLEY -S/T-
RESTLESS (BMG): 73421 67253-2 (CD)

PUTTING IT TOGETHER (O.USA CAST 1993) Songs (Stephen
SONDHEIM) *featuring* JULIE ANDREWS-STEPHEN COLLINS
RCA (BMG): 09026 61729-2 (CD) -4 (MC) see COLL

PYROMANIAC'S LOVE STORY, A (1994) Music score: RACHEL
PORTMAN -S/T- *VARESE (Pinn): VSD 5620 (CD)*

Q MILLIGAN (BBC2 5/9/93) "Q Theme": SPIKE MILLIGAN on
'BRITISH COMEDY CLASSICS' *EMI: ECC 7 (2MC)*

Q THE WINGED SERPENT (1982) Music sc: ROBERT O.RAGLAND
-S/T- reiss: CAM (SSD): CSE 800128 (CD)

QB VII (74 Mini-series) Music by JERRY GOLDSMITH -S/T-
INTRADA (S.Screen): MAF 7061D (CD)

QUADROPHENIA (1979) Songs: PETE TOWNSHEND feat WHO
*POLYDOR (Univ): 531 971-2 (Complete 2CDs) also on
813 074-2 (2CD's) also: 519 999-2 (CD)*

QUANTUM LEAP (USA 89)(BBC2 13/2/90) theme: MIKE POST
*-S/T- GNP (ZYX) GNPD 8036(CD) GNP-5 8036(MC)
see COLL.17,38,270,283,311,351,*

QUATERMASS - *see COLL.7,*

QUATERMASS II(1957) M: JAMES BERNARD *see COLL.181,293,*

QUATERMASS AND THE PIT *see COLL.180,292,293,*

QUATERMASS EXPERIMENT The (1955) Music: JAMES BERNARD
see COLL.293,
BBC TV Main theme "Mars" 'Planets Suite' (G.HOLST)

QUEEN MARGOT (La Reine Margot) (1994) Music sco: GORAN
BREGOVICH "Elohi" performed by OFRA HAZA -S/T- Imp
(SILVA SCREEN): 522 655-2 (CD)

QUEER AS FOLK (C4 23/02/1999) score mus.by MURRAY GOLD
unavailable / 32 trk.V.ARTS.select.incl: BLONDIE/
RUFF DRIVERZS/ALEXIA/ULTRA NATE/WEATHER GIRLS etc.
ALMIGHTY (BMG): ALMYCD 28 (2CD)
QUEST (1996) Music score: RANDY EDELMAN -S/T- on
VARESE (Pinn): VSD 5716 (CD)
QUESTION OF SPORT, A (BBC1 1970-98) current theme by
RICHIE CLOSE *see COLL.148,*
Competition Music "There Are More Questions Than
Answers" JOHNNY NASH 'Gr.Hits' *EPIC 465306-2 (CD)*
QUESTION TIME (BBC1 25/9/79-1999) theme music composed
by STANLEY MYERS *unavailable*
QUICK AND THE DEAD The (1994) Mus sco: ALAN SILVESTRI
-S/T- *VARESE (Pinn): VSD 5595 (CD)*
QUICK DRAW McGRAW (USA TV) *see COLL.348,373,*
QUICKSILVER (1986) Music sco: TONY BANKS + 'Lorca
& The Outlaws' *Charisma (VIRGIN): CASCD 1173 (CD)*
QUIEN SABE - *see under* 'BULLET FOR THE GENERAL'
QUIET AMERICAN The (1958) Music sco: MARIO NASCIMBENE
-S/T- *'ROOM AT THE TOP'/'BAREFOOT CONTESSA'*
DRG (Pinn): DRGCD 32961 (CD) see COLL.261,
QUIET DAYS IN CLICHY (1989)
-S/T- *VANGUARD (Pinn-ADA): VMD 79303 (CD)*
QUIET MAN The (1952) Music sco: VICTOR YOUNG *complete
orig score* DUBLIN SCREEN ORCH (K.Alwyn) *SCANNAN
(Koch): SFC 1501 (CD) also inc* 'SAMSON & DELILAH'
VARESE (Pinn): VSD 5497 (CD) see COLL.90,409,
QUIGLEY DOWN UNDER (1990) Music sco: BASIL POLEDOURIS
-S/T- *INTRADA (S.Screen): MAF 7006(D)(C) (CD/MC)*
QUINCY (USA 76) theme mus: GLEN A.LARSON-STU PHILLIPS
see COLL.243,347,
QUIZ SHOW (1994) Music score: MARK ISHAM -S/T- *reissue
EDEL-HOLLYWOOD (Pinn): 012000-2HWR (CD)*
QUO VADIS (1951) Music by MIKLOS ROSZA -S/T- selection
inc: MADAME BOVARY/IVANHOE/PLYMOUTH ADVENTURE
(Silva Screen): TT 3001 (CD) see COLL.70,302,
RAB C.NESBITT (BBC2 27/9/90) series theme music by
DAVID McNIVEN *unavailable*
RACE FOR THE YANKEE ZEPHYR (1981) / SURVIVOR (1980)
Mus: BRIAN MAY *ONEMONE (S.Screen):1MI 1008 (CD)*
RAD (C5 06/02/1999) theme music "Get Up 52" by KANE
RAD (Pinn): LJCD 012 (CD)
RAGE OF THE HEART (ORIG CONCEPT ALBUM) Songs (Enrico
Garzilli) *feat* MICHAEL BALL and JANET MOONEY
FIRST NIGHT (Pinn): OCRCD 6025 (CD)
RAGING BULL (1980) "Intermezzo" 'Cavalleria Rusticana'
(MASCAGNI) *see COLL.79,100,144,271,274,*
RAGTIME (BBC TV 1970s) *see COLL.186,*
RAGTIME (MUSICAL: ORIGINAL BROADWAY CAST RECORDING)
RCA VICTOR (BMG): 09026 63167-2 (2CDs)
RAIDERS OF THE LOST ARK (1981) Music: JOHN WILLIAMS
*SILVA SCREEN (Koch): RAIDERS 001 (CD) -S/T- Imp
(S.Screen): 821 583-4 (MC)*
see COLL.70,175,198,201,202,404,

RAILWAY CHILDREN The (1970) Music sco: JOHNNY DOUGLAS
   also feat LIONEL JEFFRIES *-S/T- reiss: MFP (EMI):*
   CDMFP 6373 (CD and 7243 857005-2) TCMFP 6383 (MC)
   also 'On Screen' *DULCIMA: DLCD 110* 'Dancing Feet'
   Andy ROSS ORCH *PRESIDENT: PCOM 1107 (CD)*
RAIN MAN (1989) Music sco: HANS ZIMMER + Belle Stars-
   Delta R.Boys-Etta James-Ian Gillan-Roger Glover
   -S/T-CAPITOL EMI: CDP 791 866-2 (CD)
RAINBOW The (1989) Music score by CARL DAVIS with
   Philharmonia & Graunke Orchestra of Munich *-S/T-*
   SILVA SCREEN (Koch): FILMCD 040 (CD)
RAINMAKER The (1997) Music sco: ELMER BERNSTEIN *-S/T-*
   HOLLYWOOD-PHILIPS CLASS (Univ): 162 141-2PH (CD)
RAINS OF RANCHIPUR (1955) Music score: HUGO FRIEDHOFER
   Suite on Coll *inc* 'ADV.OF MARCO POLO'/'THE LODGER'
   'SEVEN CITIES OF GOLD' by MOSCOW SYMPHONY ORCH.
   (W.Stromberg) *MARCO POLO (Select): 8.223857 (CD)*
   see COLL.1,
RAISE THE TITANIC (1980) Music score by JOHN BARRY
   WORLD PREMIERE REC.OF COMPLETE SCORE conducted by
   NIC RAINE *SILVA SCREEN (Koch): FILMCD 319 (CD)*
   see COLL.29,129,
RAISING THE ROOF (BBC2 18/01/1999) music by MICHAEL
   PORTMAN and VINCENT BROWETT *unavailable*
RAKE'S PROGRESS (48) Music: WILLIAM ALWYN 'Calypso'
   from film played by LONDON Symphony Orch (Richard
   Hickox) on *CHANDOS: CHAN 9243 (CD)*
RALLY REPORT (BBC2 22/11/96) theme "Duel" - PROPAGANDA
   from 'Secret Wish' *ZTT (Pinn): ZTT 118CD (CD)*
RAMBLING ROSE (1991) Music sco: ELMER BERNSTEIN *-S/T-*
   VIRGIN Movie Music (EMI): CDVMM 5(CD) TCVMM 5(MC)
RAMBO 'FIRST BLOOD PART 1' (1982) Mus: JERRY GOLDSMITH
   IMPORT (Silva Screen): FMT 8001D (CD)
RAMBO 'FIRST BLOOD PART 2' (1985) Mus: JERRY GOLDSMITH
   -S/T- SILVA SCREEN (Koch): FILMCD 307 (CD) also
   COLOSS.(Pinn):CST 348005 (CD)   *see COLL.167,*
RAMBO III (1988) Music sco: GIORGIO MORODER
   Orch Score: Imp *INTRADA (Silva Sc): RVF 6006D (CD)*
RANCHO DE LUXE (1974) Music score: JIMMY BUFFETT *-S/T-*
   RYKODISC (Vital): RCD 10709 (CD)
RANDALL AND HOPKIRK (DECEASED) (ITV 26/9/69) theme mus
   EDWIN ASTLEY *see COLL.7,121,360,*
RANDOM HEARTS (1999) Music score by DAVE GRUSIN *-S/T-*
   SONY CLASSICAL (TEN): SK 51336-2 (CD)
RANSOM (1996) Music score: JAMES HORNER *-S/T-*
   EDEL-HOLLYWOOD (Pinn): 012 086-2HWR (CD)
RANSOM (aka The Terrorists) (1975) Music: JERRY GOLDS
   MITH *-S/T-* includes 'The Chairman' (69) reissued
   SILVA SCREEN (Koch): FILMCD 081 (CD)
RAPA NUI: The Centre Of The World (1993) Mus: STEWART
   COPELAND *-S/T- MILAN (BMG): 214 402 (CD)*
RAPID FIRE (1992) Music score: CHRISTOPHER YOUNG
   -S/T- VARESE (Pinn): VSD 5388 (CD)
RAT PATROL (USA TV) *see COLL.346,*

RAT RACE The (1960) Music score by ELMER BERNSTEIN
   feat SAM BUTERA & THE WITNESSES -S/T-
   JASMINE (Koch): JASCD 356 (CD)
RATTLE AND HUM (1988) Music by U2 -S/T- *ISLAND (Univ):
   U 27 (Dbl LP) UC 27 (MC) CID U27 (CD)*
RAUMPATROUILLE (Euro TV Sci-Fi series 1960s) Music by
   PETER THOMAS SOUND ORCHESTRA -S/T- *BUNGALOW-CITY
   (Vital): BUNGCD 009 (CD) BUNGLP 009 (LP)* also on
RAVENOUS (1998) Music by MICHAEL NYMAN-DAMON ALBARN &
   WILLIAM ORBIT -S/T- *EMI SOUNDTRACK: 522 370-2 (CD)*
RAWHIDE (USA 57) title song (D.Tiomkin-Ned Washington)
   FRANKIE LAINE *vers.on* 'Round-Up' *TELARC (BMG-Con):
   CD 80141 (CD)* see Coll 'MY RIFLE MY PONY & ME'
   see COLL.2,137,260,346,
RAZOR'S EDGE - *see COLL.1,*
RE-ANIMATOR / BRIDE OF THE RE-ANIMATOR (1985/86) Music
   RICHARD BAND -S/T- *S.SCREEN (BMG) FILMCD 082 (CD)*
REACH THE ROCK (1997) Music score: JOHN McENTIRE -S/T-
   HEFTY (Pinn-Greyh): HEFTY 005 (CD)
READY STEADY COOK (BBC2 24/10/94) theme music by
   KEN BOLAM *unavailable*
REAL McCOY (1993) Music score: BRAD FIEDEL -S/T-
   VARESE (Pinn): VSD 5450 (CD)
REAL McCOYS (USA TV) *see COLL.348,*
REAL WOMEN (BBC1 26/2/1998) Music (98 ser.) CARL DAVIS
   ROBERT LOCKHART (99 ser) song "She's A Good Girl"
   composed and sung by EDDI READER *unavailable*
REALITY BITES (1993) -S/T- incl LENNY KRAVITZ & V.Arts
   -S/T- *RCA (BMG): 07863 66364-2 (CD) -4 (MC)*
REBECCA (1940) Music score: FRANZ WAXMAN
   see COLL.194,195,197,395,
REBECCA (BBC2 17/1/79) music: DEBUSSY *see COLL.8,*
REBEL (USA TV) *see COLL.260,346,401,*
REBEL WITHOUT A CAUSE (1955) Music: LEONARD ROSENMAN
   new Recording LONDON SINFONIETTA (J.ADAMS) *with*
   'EAST OF EDEN' (1954 Leonard Rosenman) *NONESUCH
   (TEN): 7559 79402-2 (CD)* + 'GIANT'/'EAST OF EDEN'
   CINERAMA-EDEL (Pinn): CIN 2206-2 (CD) -4 (MC)
RECORD BREAKERS (BBC TV) *see COLL.186,*
RED CORNER (1998) Music score: THOMAS NEWMAN -S/T-
   EDEL-CINERAMA (Pinn): 0022882CIN (CD)
RED DAWN (1984) Music sco: BASIL POLEDOURIS -S/T- IMPT
   INTRADA USA (Silva Screen): RVF 6001D (CD)
RED DWARF (BBC2 15/2/88-1997) music and theme song by
   HOWARD GOODALL *see COLL.38,121,267,270,362,*
RED HEAT (1988) Music score: JAMES HORNER -S/T-
   VIRGIN (EMI): CDV 2558 (CD)
RED KNIGHT WHITE KNIGHT (1989) Mus: JOHN SCOTT -S/T-
   INTRADA (Koch/Silva Screen): MAF 7016D (CD)
RED RIVER (1948) Music score: DIMITRI TIOMKIN
   see COLL.368,
RED SHOE DIARIES (Films) Music (George Clinton) GEORGE
   CLINTON on 'Music Of The RED SHOE DIARIES' on
   WIENERWORLD/GRAPEVINE (Discov): WNRCD 6001 (CD)

RED SHOES The (1948) Music score: BRIAN EASDALE *see COLL* 'CLASSIC BRITISH FILM MUSIC' *(SILVA SCREEN)*

RED TENT The (1970) Music score ENNIO MORRICONE -S/T- *LEGEND IMPT (Silva Screen): LEGEND CD 5 (CD)*

RED VIOLIN The (1997) Music sco: JOHN CORIGLIANO -S/T- *SONY CLASSICS: SK 63010 (CD) SM 63010 (MC)*

REDS (1981) Music: STEPHEN SONDHEIM-DAVE GRUSIN -S/T- *RAZOR & TIE (Koch): RE 82203-2 (CD)*

REF The (1998) Music: DAVID A.STEWART -S/T- on *IMAGO (Direct): 7278 723014-2 (CD)*

REGENERATION (1998) Music score by MYCHAEL DANNA -S/T- *VARESE (Pinn): VSD 6005 (CD)*

REILLY-ACE OF SPIES (Thames 9/83) theme from 'Romance' (Shostakovich) arr Harry Rabinowitz

REMINGTON STEELE (USA)(BBC1 3/9/83) *see COLL.17,*

REN AND STIMPY SHOW The (USA/BBC1 10/1/94) theme song "Dog Pound Hop" *see COLL.351,*

RENAISSANCE (BBC2 21/11/1999) (various period CHORAL WORKS) -S/T- *BBC RECORDS: number to be confirmed*

RENAISSANCE MAN (1993) Music score HANS ZIMMER -S/T- *VARESE (Pinn): VSD 5502 (CD)*

RENT - songs: Jonathan Larson / Orig 1996 Broadway Cast *DREAMWORKS-MCA (BMG): DRD 50003 (CD)*

REPLACEMENT KILLERS The (1997) Music sc: HARRY GREGSON WILLIAMS -S/T- *VARESE (Pinn): VSD 5915 (CD)*

REQUIEM (ROCK REQUIEM 1985) Music: ANDREW LLOYD WEBBER Placido DOMINGO-Sarah BRIGHTMAN-Paul M.KINGSTON ENGLISH CHAMBER ORCH *EMI: EL 270 242-2 (CD)*

RESCUERS The / RESCUERS DOWN UNDER - see DISNEY p.362

RESERVOIR DOGS (1992) -S/T- featuring VARIOUS ARTISTS *reissue: MCA (BMG): MCD 10793 (CD) MCC 10793 (MC) S.VINYL (Telstar): SVLP 28 (LP) see COLL.143,359,*

RESORT TO MURDER (BBC1 27/7/95) Music sco: BILL CONNOR -S/T- *Debonair (Pinn): CDDEB 1002 see COLL.7,19,*

RESPECTABLE TRADE, A (BBC1 19/4/1998) Music score by JULIAN NOTT with the CITY OF PRAGUE PHILHARMONIC *WARNER ESP (TEN): 3984 23248-2 (CD) -4 (MC)*

RESTORATION (1995) Music score: JAMES NEWTON HOWARD + selections from the works of HENRY PURCELL -S/T- *MILAN (BMG): 74321 35522-2 (CD)*

RETURN OF DRACULA The (1958) Music score: GERALD FRIED on Ltd Ed.Import COLL incl: 'MARK OF THE VAMPIRE', 'I BURY THE LIVING' and 'THE CABINET OF CALIGARI' *RETROGRADE (Silva Scren/MFTM): FSMCD 4 (CD)*

RETURN OF THE JEDI (Star Wars 3) Music: JOHN WILLIAMS Special-Edition ORIG SOUNDTRACK Recording (1997) *RCA (BMG): 09026 68748-2 (Deluxe 2CD)* *RCA (BMG): 09026 68774-2 (Slimline 2CD) -4 (2MC)* *see COLL.198,264,267,306,307,308,334,335,404,*

RETURN OF THE PINK PANTHER The (1974) Music score by HENRY MANCINI -S/T- complete + 'THE PINK PANTHER' *RCA CAMDEN (BMG): 74321 66047-2 (CD)*

RETURN OF THE SAINT The (ITV 78) theme: IRVING MARTIN-BRIAN DEE *see COLL.4,281,363,369,*

RETURN OF THE SEVEN (1966) Music sco: ELMER BERNSTEIN
   -S/T- *reissue RYKODISC (Vital): RCD 10714 (CD)*
   see COLL.47,358,
RETURN TO PARADISE (1998) Music sc: MARK MANCINA -S/T-
   VARESE (Pinn): VSD 5964 (CD)
RETURN TO THE FORBIDDEN PLANET (ORIG LONDON CAST 1989)
   Bob CARLTON'S Sci-Fi Musical *VIRGIN: CDV(TCV) 2631*
REVENGE (1990) Music score: JACK NITZSCHE -S/T- on
   SILVA SCREEN (Koch): FILMCD 065 (CD)
   see COLL.51,111,
REX (MUSICAL 1976) Songs: RICHARD RODGERS and SHELDON
   HARNICK *feat:* NICOL WILLIAMSON and Company
   Broadway Cast Rec. *RCA (BMG): 09026 68933-2 (CD)*
RHAPSODY IN BLUE (1945) VARIOUS -S/T- SELECTIONS on
   GREAT MOVIE THEMES: (Targ-BMG): CD 60028 (CD)
RHYTHM ON THE RIVER (1940) VARIOUS -S/T- SELECTIONS on
   GREAT MOVIE THEMES: (Targ-BMG): CD 60025 (CD)
RICHARD III (1955) Music: WILLIAM WALTON / Academy Of
   St.Martin-In-The-Fields,Neville MARRINER with Sir
   John GIELGUD *CHANDOS: CHAN 8841 (CD)*
RICHARD BOONE SHOW (USA) *see COLL.23,*
RICHIE RICH (1994) Music score: ALAN SILVESTRI -S/T-
   VARESE (Pinn): VSD 5582 (CD)
RICK STEIN'S SEAFOOD ODYSSEY (BBC2 05/01/1999) music:
   CROCODILE *see COLL.342.*
RICK STEIN'S TASTE OF THE SEA (BBC2 12/9/95) music by
   CROCODILE MUSIC *see COLL.342,*
RIDDLE OF THE SKIES (C4 01.02/1999) original music by
   GUY PRATT *unavailable*
RIDE WITH THE DEVIL (1999) Music score: MYCHAEL DANNA
   -S/T- *ATLANTIC (TEN): 7567 83262-2 (CD) -4 (MC)*
RIDICULE (1996) Music sco: ANTOINE DUHAMEL -S/T-
   DECCA (Univ): 452 990-2 (CD) Poly: 452 697-2 (CD)
RIFLEMAN The (USA TV 60s) *see COLL.345,*
RIGHT STUFF The (1983) Music sco: BILL CONTI+ mus from
   'NORTH & SOUTH' -S/T- *VARESE Pinn: VCD 47250 (CD)*
   see COLL.71,328,
RIN TIN TIN (USA TV) *see COLL.345,*
RING The (Danielle Steel's) (96 TV mini-s) Music score
   MICHEL LEGRAND cond: CITY OF PRAGUE PHILHARM.ORCH.
   -S/T- *SILVA AMERICA (Koch): SSD 1072 (CD)*
RINK The - songs by John Kander and Fred Ebb
   1.ORIG LONDON CAST 1987/88) DIANE LANGTON-JOSEPHINE
   BLAKE & COMP *TER (Koch): CDTERS 1155 (CD)*
   2.ORIG BROADWAY CAST 1983 *with* LIZA MINNELLI and CO
   TER (Koch): CDTER 1091 (CD)
RIO BRAVO (1959) Music score: DIMITRI TIOMKIN
   Title theme (D.Tiomkin-P.F.Webster) by DEAN MARTIN
   MFP EMI: CDMFP 6032 (CD) see COLL.260,358,368,
RIO CONCHOS (1964) Music score: JERRY GOLDSMITH -S/T-
   INTRADA (Sil.Screen): RVF 6007D(CD) inc.'prelude'
   from 65 film 'The Agony & The Ecstasy' *see COLL.1,*
RIO GRANDE (1950) Music score: VICTOR YOUNG -S/T-
   VARESE (Pinn): VSD 5378 (CD)

RIO RITA (ORIG LONDON CAST 1930) Songs (Harry Tierney-Joseph McCarthy) *feat:* EDITH DAY-MARIA DE PIETRO-*PEARL (Pavilion): GEMMCD 9115 (CD)*

RISING DAMP (ITV orig 1974) ORIG TV CAST RECORDING on *MAGMASTERS (Koch): MSE 011 (MC) see COLL.179,*

RISING SUN (1993) Music sco: TORU TAKEMITSU + Various Artists -S/T- *ARISTA (BMG): 07822 11003-2 (CD)*

RISKY BUSINESS (1983) Mus: TANGERINE DREAM-BOB SEGER -S/T- *VIRGIN (EMI): CDV 2302 (CD) OVEDC 240 (MC)*

RIVER OF SOUND, A (BBC2 27/12/95) featur: MICHEAL O' SUILLEABHAIN + various artists -S/T- *VIRGIN (EMI): CDV 2776 (CD) TCV 2776 (MC)*

RIVERDANCE SHOW The (1995) music by BILL WHELAN *reis CELTIC HEARTBEAT (BMG): UND(UMC) 53076 / 53106* New Version (Oct 95) *WEA 7567 82816-2(CD) -4(MC) see COLL.155,262,* RIVERDANCE (TRIBUTE TO) 'THIS LAND' Various Arts *MFP (EMI): CDMFP 6237 (CD) TCMFP 6237 (MC)*

RIVERDANCE / LORD OF THE DANCE (Highlights from both) VOICES OF IRELAND *K-TEL: ECD 3396 (CD)*

RIVIERA POLICE (TV 1960's) *see COLL.23,*

ROAD HOUSE (1989) Music: MICHAEL KAMEN + JEFF HEALEY BAND-BOB SEGER-OTIS REDDING-LITTLE FEAT-PATRICK SW AYZEE-KRIS McKAY -S/T- *ARISTA (BMG): 259.948 (CD)*

ROAD RUNNER (USA TV) *see COLL.346,*

ROAD TO MOROCCO (1942) *feat* BING CROSBY-BOB HOPE and DOROTHY LAMOUR + 'TWO FOR TONIGHT' & 'HOLIDAY INN' *GREAT MOVIE THEMES (Target-BMG): CD 60027 (CD)*

ROAD TO WELLVILLE The (1994) Music sco: RACHEL PORTMAN -S/T- *VARESE (Pinn): VSD 5512 (CD)*

ROB ROY (1995) Music: CARTER BURWELL Songs performed by CAPERCAILLIE feat KAREN MATHIESON -S/T- on *VIRGIN: CDVMM 18 (CD) TCVMM 18 (MC) see COLL.3,*

ROBE The (1953) Mus: ALFRED NEWMAN -S/T- *FOX-ARISTA (BMG): 07822 11011-2 (CD) and Import version on VARESE (Pinn): VARESE: VSD 5295 (CD)*

ROBERT AND ELIZABETH songs: Ron Grainer-Ronald Miller 1.ORIG CHICHESTER THEATRE CAST 1987 MARK WYNTER-GAYNOR MILES-JOHN SAVIDENT and Company *FIRST NIGHT (Pinn): OCRCD 6032 (CD)*

ROBIN AND MARIAN (1976) *see COLL.29,202,338,*

ROBIN HOOD (1973 Cartoon) *see* WALT DISNEY INDEX p.362

ROBIN HOOD (1991) (w: Patrick Bergin) Music: GEOFFREY BURGON -S/T- *SILVA SCREEN (Koch): FILMCD 083 CD*

ROBIN HOOD 'The Adventures Of' *see* ADVENTURES OF ROBIN

ROBIN HOOD: PRINCE OF THIEVES (1991) Music sc: MICHAEL KAMEN song "(Everything I Do) I Do It For You" (B. Adams-R.Lange-M.K.) BRYAN ADAMS *(A.& M): AMCD 789* -S/T- *reiss MORGAN CREEK (Univ): 002249-2 MCM (CD) see COLL.106,111,218,*

ROBIN OF SHERWOOD (HTV 28/4/84) theme music "Robin The Hooded Man)" CLANNAD *RCA (BMG): 74321 48674-2 (CD)*

ROBINSON CRUSOE (Adventures of) (BBC1 12/10/65) Music
score: ROBERT MELLIN-GIAN PIERO REVERBERI Original
TV S/TRACK *reissued w.ADDITIONAL unreleased music
SILVA SCREEN (Koch): FILMCD 705 (CD)*

ROBINSON CRUSOE & MAN FRIDAY (Filmed TV Mini ser.88)
music score: MAURICE JARRE -S/T- *PROMETHEUS Imp
(Silva Screen): PST 501 (LP)*

ROBOCOP (1987) Music score: BASIL POLEDOURIS -S/T-
*VARESE: (Pinn) VSD 47298 (CD) reissue / also on
ESSENTIAL (BMG):ESSCD 285(CD) ESSMC 285(MC)*
also -S/T- *TER (Koch): CDTER 1146 (CD)*
see COLL.307,311,

ROBOCOP: THE TV SERIES (ITV 7/9/96) Soundtrack feat
JOE WALSH-LITA FORD-THE BAND-DAVE EDMUNDS-TODD
RUNDGREN *ESSENTIAL-CASTLE (Pinn): ESMCD 491 (CD)*
see COLL.311,

ROBOCOP 2 (1990) Music score: LEONARD ROSENMAN -S/T-
VARESE USA (Pinn): VSD 5271 (CD)

ROBOCOP 3 (1993) Music score: BASIL POLEDOURIS -S/T-
VARESE USA (Pinn): VSD 5416 (CD)

ROCCO & HIS BROTHERS *on COLL* 'FILM MUSIC OF NINO ROTA'
Italian Import (Silva Screen): VCDS 7001 (CD)
see COLL.32,300,

ROCK The (1996) Music score by NICK GLENNIE SMITH and
HANS ZIMMER -S/T- with VARIOUS ARTISTS *-REISSUE-
EDEL-HOLLYWOOD (Pinn): 010 262-2HWR (CD)*

ROCKERS (1978) Music score (Reggae) featur PETER TOSH
GREGORY ISAACS-THE MIGHTY DIAMONDS & others -S/T-
REGGAE REFRESHERS-ISLAND (Univ): RRCD 45 (CD)

ROCKETEER The (1991) Music score: JAMES HORNER -S/T-
HOLLYWOOD Imp (S.Screen): HWD 161117 (CD)
see COLL.121,205,206,

ROCKFORD FILES (USA75) theme: MIKE POST-PETE CARPENTER
see COLL.17,109,110,270,283,347,

ROCKY 1 (1976) Music: BILL CONTI Song "Gonna Fly Now"
(B.Conti-C.Connors-A.Robbins) Frank Stallone -S/T-
*re-issue EMI EUROPE (Discovery): 746081-2 (CD) &
LIBERTY (Silva Screen) 46081-2 (CD) 46081-4 (MC)*
see COLL.41,70,204,

ROCKY 2 (1979) Music sco: BILL CONTI -S/T- *LIBERTY
USA (Silva Screen): 46082-2 (CD) 46082-4 (MC)*
see COLL.203,

ROCKY 3 (1982) Music sco: BILL CONTI song "Eye Of The
Tiger" by SURVIVOR -S/T- *EMI EUROPE (Discovery):
746561-2 (CD) also (S.Screen): 46561-2(CD) -4(MC)*
see COLL

ROCKY 4 (1985) Music score: VINCE DI COLA Songs V.Arts
-S/T- *Imp (SILVA SCREEN):75240-2(CD) -4(MC)*

ROCKY HORROR SHOW The - songs by Richard O'Brien
  1.FILM MUSICAL 1975 (Rocky Horror Picture Show) *with*
    TIM CURRY-LITTLE NELL-MEATLOAF-SUSAN SARANDON
    Castle Comm (Pinn): ROCKY1 (4CD inc.O.LONDON Cast)
  2.ORIG LONDON CAST 1973 TIM CURRY-RICHARD O'BRIEN-
    LITTLE NELL- *First Night (Pinn): OCRCD 6040 (CD)*

3. CARLTON SHOWS COLLECTION 1995 CHERYL BAKER-ROBIN
   COUSINS-TRACEY MILLER-NICK CURTIS *pr* Gordon Lorenz
   CARLTON SHOWS Collect: 30362 0016-2 (CD) -4 (MC)
4. STUDIO R.1995 ANITA DOBSON-TIM FLAVIN-KIM CRISWELL
   HOWARD SAMUELS-AIDAN BELL-ISSY VAN RANDWYCK-
   CHRISTOPHER LEE <u>Complete:</u> *TER (Koch): CDTER 1221*
   <u>Highlights:</u> *SHOWTIME (MCI-THE):SHOW(CD)(MC) 025*
5. REVIVAL LONDON CAST 1990 TIM McINNERNY-ADRIAN
   EDMONDSON-GINA BELLMAN and Company / *reissued on*
   MFP (EMI): CD(TC)MFP 5977 (CD/MC)
   see also NEW ROCKY HORROR SHOW

ROGUE TRADER (1999) Music score by IAIN JAMES -S/T-
   COLUMBIA (Ten): 495 051-2 (CD)
ROLLERBALL (1975) *see COLL.81,88,105,362,*
ROMA (1972) Music score: NINO ROTA cond: CARLO SAVINA
   -S/T- *Screen Trax (Silv.Sounds): CDST 311 (CD)*
ROMANCE ROMANCE (O.BROADWAY CAST 1988) Songs: KEITH
   HERRMANN-BARRY HARMON *TER (Koch): CDTER 1161 (CD)*
ROMEO AND JULIET (1996) Music score: CLIFF EIDELMAN
   -S/T- songs (vol.1) *CAPITOL EMI: PRMDCD 28 (CD)*
   -S/T- songs (vol.2) *CAPITOL EMI: PRMDCD 34 (CD)*
ROMEO AND JULIET (1968) Music score by NINO ROTA
   SILVA SCREEN (Koch): FILMCD 200 (CD)
   see COLL.71,204,238,239,299,
ROMPER STOMPER (1992) Music score: JOHN CLIFFORD WHITE
   "Pearl Fishers Duet" (Bizet) ERNEST BLANC-NICOLAI
   GEDDA -S/T- *PICTURE THIS (Greyhound): PTR 002 (CD)*
ROMY AND MICHELE'S HIGH SCHOOL REUNION (1997) -S/T-
   HOLLYWOOD (Univ): 162 098-2 (CD)
RONIN (1998) Music score: ELIA CMIRAL -S/T- on
   VARESE (Pinn): VSD 5977
ROOBARB (BBC1 70's) music: JOHNNY HAWKSWORTH
   orig theme see COLL.186,363,
ROOM AT THE TOP (1958) Music score: MARIO NASCIMBENE
   -S/T- inc.'BAREFOOT CONTESSA'/'THE QUIET AMERICAN'
   DRG (Pinn): DRGCD 32961 (CD)
ROOM WITH A VIEW, A (1986) Music sco: RICHARD ROBBINS
   -S/T- *DRG (Pinn): CDSBL 12588 (CD)*
   see COLL.70,77,80,82,113,115,116,117,159,271,274,
   275,286,
ROOTS (USA TV) *see COLL.350,*
ROSE The (1979) *featuring* BETTE MIDLER -S/T- on
   ATLANTIC (TEN): K2 50681 (CD) K4 50681 (MC)
ROSE GARDEN The (1989) *see under* 'CRY IN THE DARK, A'
ROSE OF WASHINGTON SQUARE (1939 MUSICAL) ALICE FAYE-
   AL JOLSON-TYRONE POWER *inc.songs* 'DOLLY SISTERS'
   'GOLD DIGGERS OF 1933' *TARGET (BMG): CD 60009*
ROSE OF WASHINGTON SQUARE
   VARESE (Pinn): VSD 6089 (CD)
ROSEANNA'S GRAVE (1996) Music score by TREVOR JONES
   London Symphony Orch (Nick ingman) 'For Roseanna'
   RCA VICTOR (BMG): 09026 68836-2 (CD)
ROSEANNE (USA C4 from 27/1/89) theme mus: DAN FOLIART
   HOWARD PEARL *see COLL.17,270,351,*

ROSEMARY'S BABY (1968) Music score: CHRISTOPHER KOMEDA
  reiss *POLONIA (Silva Screen): POLONIA CD 160 (CD)*
  also includes music of 'FEARLESS VAMPIRE KILLERS'
  DISCMEDI (Silver Sounds): PIG 02 (CD)
ROSIE (-) *SWARF FINGER (Cargo): SF 034CD (CD)*
ROTHSCHILD'S VIOLIN (Film Score) Music: FLEISCHMANN m
  comleted & orches. by SHOSTAKOVICH. The ROTTERDAM
  PHILHARMONIC ORCH *RCA V (BMG): 09026 68434-2 (CD)*
ROTTENTROLLS The (ITV 23/09/1998) theme ROTTENTROLLS
  HIT LABEL (Univ): HLC 14 (CDs)
ROUGH RIDERS (1997 USA Mini-series) Music score by
  PETER BERNSTEIN."G.Troop" theme by ELMER BERNSTEIN
  -S/T- *INTRADA (USA): MAF 7079 (CD)*
ROULA: HIDDEN SECRETS (1996) Music sco: DIETER SCHLEIP
  -S/T- *COLOSSEUM (Pinn): CST 34 8056 (CD)*
ROUND MIDNIGHT (1986) Mus sc: HERBIE HANCOCK w: DEXTER
  GORDON -S/T- reiss *(SM): 486799-2 (CD)* also 'OTHER
  SIDE OF ROUND MIDNIGHT' *BLUENOTE: CDP 746386-2 CD*
ROUNDERS (1998) Music score: CHRISTOPHER YOUNG -S/T-
  VARESE (Pinn): VSD 5980 (CD)
ROUSTABOUT see ELVIS PRESLEY INDEX p.360
ROUTE 66 (USA) see COLL.346,
ROWAN AND MARTIN'S LAUGH-IN (USA TV) see COLL.349,
ROYAL ASCOT (BBC1 20/6/95) theme "Odissea" (Reverberi-
  Farina) by RONDO VENEZIANO on 'Odissea' *BMG Italy
  (Select): 610 529 (CD)* also used 'Regata Dei Dogi'
  RONDO VENEZIANO *BMG ITALY (Select): 610 535 (CD)*
ROYAL WEDDING: EDWARD & SOPHIE RHYS-JONES (19/07/1999)
  Music Select: *BBC (Pinn): WMEF 0042-2 (CD) -4 (MC)*
ROYLE FAMILY The (BBC2 14/9/1998) theme mus "Half The
  World Away" composed and sung by OASIS (b side of
  "Whatever") *CREATION (Vital): CRESCD 195 (CDs)*
RUDDIGORE (operetta) W.S.Gilbert & A.Sullivan
  1.NEW SADLERS WELLS OPERA COMPANY *KOCH Int (Koch):
  340342 (CD) 240344 (MC)* also on *TER: CDTER2 1128
  (2CD) ZCTED 1128 (2MC)*
RUGBY SPECIAL (BBC2 78-90) "Holy Mackerel" by BRIAN
  BENNETT see COLL.5,148,176,
RUGBY UNION 5 NATIONS CUP (BBC1 20/1/96) trailer music
  "Adiemus" (KARL JENKINS) from 'Songs Of Sanctuary'
  VIRGIN (EMI): CD(TC)VE 925 (CD/MC)
RUGBY WORLD CUP 1999 (ITV 01/10/1999) ser.theme music
  "World in Union" (C.Skarbek-G.Holst) BRYN TERFEL &
  SHIRLEY BASSEY *DECCA (Univ): 466 940-2 (CDs)*
  WORLD CUP 99 ALBUM *'LAND OF MY FATHERS'* feat: BRYN
  TERFEL-SHIRLEY BASSEY-MICHAEL BALL-BLACK MOUNTAIN
  CHORUS-THE LADYSMITH BLACK MAMBAZO-RUSSELL WATSON
  DECCA (Univ): 466 567-2 (CD)
RUGBY WORLD CUP 1995 (ITV 25/5/95) Anthems: "World In
  Union"/"Sakura" with LADYSMITH BLACK MAMBAZO & PJ
  POWERS *POLYGRAM TV: 527 807-2 (CD) -4 (MC)
  RUGBY 2 (CDs) RUGBY 4 (MC) RUGBY 7 (7")* also:-
  "Swing Low Sweet Chariot" by CHINA BLACK
  POLYGRAM: SWLOW 2 (CDs) SWLOW 4 (MC) SWLOW 7 (7"s)

RUGRATS The (1998) Music score: MARK MOTHERSBAUGH -S/T-
   INTERSCOPE (BMG): IND 90181 (CD) INTC 90181 (MC)
RUMBLE FISH (1983) Music score: STEWART COPELAND -S/T-
   A.& M. (IMS-Polyg): AA 750 214983-2 (CD) reissue
RUN LOLA RUN (LOLA RENNT) (1999) Music score by TOM
   TYKWER-JOHNNY KLIMEK-REINHOLD HEIL. -S/T- includes
   songs by FRANKA POTENTE & MORITZ BLEIBTREU -S/T-
   BMG SOUNDTRACKS: 74321 60477-2 (CD)
RUNAWAY BRIDE (1999) Music score by
   -S/T- *COLUMBIA (Ten): 494 873-2 (CD) -4 (MC)*
RUNNING MAN The (1988) Music score: HAROLD FALTERMEYER
   -S/T- reissue *COLOSSEUM (Pinn): CST 348032 (CD)*
RUSH HOUR (1998) Music score by LALO SCHIFRIN
   -S/T- score: *ALEPH (Koch): ALEP 005 (CD)*
   -S/T- songs: *MERCURY-DEFJAM (Univ): 558 663-2 (CD)*
                              558 663-1 (2LP)
RUSHMORE (1998) Music score: MARK MOTHERSBAUGH -S/T-
   -S/T- (score) *LONDON (Univ): 556 074-2 (CD)*
   -S/T- (songs) *LONDON (Ten): 3984 263691-2 (CD)*
RUSSIA HOUSE The (1990) Music score: JERRY GOLDSMITH
   -S/T- *MCA USA (S.Screen): MCAD(MCAC) 10136 (CD/MC)*
RUTH RENDELL MYSTERIES The (TVS 19/6/1988) theme music
   and incidental score by BRIAN BENNETT -S/T- on
   SOUNDTRACKS EMI GOLD: 520 687-2 (CD)
   see COLL.6,149,270,390,
RUTLES The (1978 'All You Need Is Cash' seq) 'ARCHAE
   OLOGY' *VIRGIN (EMI): CDVUS 119 (CD) VUSMC 119 (MC)*

S.W.A.T. (USA) see COLL.347,382,
SAFE (1994) Music score: ED TOMNEY -S/T- issued on
   MUTE-Fine Line (RTM-Pinn): IONIC 14CD (CD)
SAIL AWAY MUSICAL by NOEL COWARD
   NOEL COWARD SINGS SONGS FROM SAIL AWAY
   EMI Catalogue: 520 726-2 (CD)
SAIL THE WORLD WHITBREAD ROUND THE WORLD YACHT RACE 94
   (ITV 19/3/94) music score: ANTHONY PHILLIPS -S/T-
   RESURGENCE-BLUEPRINT (Pinn): RES 102CD (CD)
SAINT The (1997) Music score: GRAEME REVELL -S/T-
   V.Arts: ORBITAL-CHEMICAL BROTHERS-UNDERWORLD-
   DAVID BOWIE-DAFT PUNK *VIRGIN (EMI): CDVUS 126 (CD)*
   VUSMC 126 (MC) ORBITAL *Fffr (Univ): FCD 296 (CDs)*
SAINT The (ITC 4/10/62-69) theme music: EDWIN ASTLEY
   TV -S/T- *RAZOR & TIE (Koch): RE 21562 (CD)*
   see COLL.2,4,74,121,143,150,344,346,360,365,367,
   369,377,
SAINT ELMO'S FIRE (1985) Music sco: DAVID FOSTER *feat*
   JOHN PARR -S/T- *ATLANTIC (TEN): 7567 81261-2 (CD)*
   see COLL.145,
SAINT ELSEWHERE (USA) theme music by DAVE GRUSIN
   see COLL.17,347,
SAINT-EX (BBC2 25/12/96) music: BARRINGTON PHELOUNG on
   compilation 'PASSION OF MORSE' also includes 'The
   Politician's Wife'/'Truly Madly Deeply'/'Saint-Ex'
   TRING INT (Tring): TRING 003 (CD) MCTRING 003 (MC)

SAINT SHE AIN'T, A! (MUSICAL SHOW) Music by DENIS KING
Lyrics & book by DICK VOSBURGH / ORIG LONDON CAST
FIRST NIGHT (Pinn): CASTCD 73 (CD)
SALAAM BOMBAY! (1988) Music score: L.SUBRAMANIAM -S/T-
DRG (Pinn): CDSBL 12595 (CD)
SALAD DAYS songs by Julian Slade and Dorothy Reynolds
  1.REVIVAL LONDON CAST *with:* ELIZABETH SEAL-SHEILA
   STEAFEL-CHRISTIINA MATTHEWS-ADAM BAREHAM & Company
   <u>Highlights</u>: *SHOWTIME (MCI-THE): SHOW(CD)(MC) 009*
   <u>Complete</u>: *TER (Koch): CDTER 1018 (CD)*
  2.40th Anniv.STUDIO Record 1994 SIMON GREEN-JANIE
   DEE-TIMOTHY WEST-JOSEPHINE TEWSON-PRUNELLA SCALES-
   VALERIE MASTERSON-JOHN WARNER-TONY SLATTERY *and Co*
   EMI: CDC 555200-2 (CD) EL 555200-4 (MC)
  3.5TH ANNIVERSARY PROD *FIRST NIGHT: SCORECD 43 (CD)*
SALTIMBANCO (1996) Music by RENE DUPERE performed by
CIRQUE DU SOLEIL (Circus Of The Sun) ORIG CAST REC
RCA VICTOR (BMG): 74321 25707-2 (CD) -4 (MC)
SALVADOR (1986) Music score: GEORGES DELERUE -S/T- and
'WALL STREET' *TER (Koch): CDTER 1154 (CD)*
SAM BENEDICT *see COLL.23,*
SAMMY GOING SOUTH *see COLL.292,*
SAMSON AND DELILAH (1949) Music: VICTOR YOUNG -S/T-
incl. 'THE QUIET MAN' *VARESE (Pinn): VSD 5497 (CD)*
SAN FRANCISCO (1936) *COLLECTION with* 'DAMES'/'SUZY' on
GREAT MOVIE THEMES (Targ-BMG): CD 60022 (CD)
SAND PEBBLES The (1966) Music score: JERRY GOLDSMITH
new recording incl.previously unreleased material
VARESE (Pinn): VSD 5795 (CD)
SANDPIPER The (1965) Music sc: JOHNNY MANDEL song "The
Shadow Of Your Smile"(J.Mandel-P.F.Webster) *-S/T-*
VERVE (Univ): 531 229-2 (CD) see COLL.52,71,
SANTA CLAUSE The (1995) Music sco: MICHAEL CONVERTINO
"Jingle Bells" YELLO *-S/T-Milan (BMG):32364-2 (CD)*
SANTA SANGRE (1990) Mus: SIMON BOSWELL + Circus Orgo
Silver Hombre-Concha Y Fenix *PRESID: PCOM 1104 CD*
SAPPHIRE AND STEEL (ITV 10/7/79) theme music: CYRIL
ORNADEL *see COLL.360,*
SARAFINA: THE SOUND OF FREEDOM (1992) Mus: STANLEY
MYERS -S/T- V.Ars *WB (TEN) 9362 45060-2 (CD)*
SATURDAY NIGHT Songs by STEPHEN SONDHEIM - V.ARTISTS
FIRST NIGHT (Pinn): CASTCD 65 (CD)
SATURDAY NIGHT FEVER (ORIGINAL LONDON CAST 1998) *feat:*
ADAM GARCIA-TARA WILKINSON-ANITA LOUISE COMBE-
SIMON GRIEFF *O.CAST REC. POLYDOR: 557 932-2 (CD)*
SATURDAY NIGHT FEVER (1978) Music by BEE GEES -S/T-
RSO (Univ): 825 389-2 (CD)
SATURDAY NIGHT LIVE (USA TV) *see COLL.347,*
SAVED BY THE BELL (NBC USA/C4 1/1/95) theme music by
SCOTT GALE and RICH EAMES *see COLL.351,*
SAVING PRIVATE RYAN (1997) Music score: JOHN WILLIAMS
-S/T- *DREAMWORKS (BMG): DRD 50046 (CD, 07.1998)*
song "Tu Es Partout" by EDITH PIAF *(not on -S/T-)*
ON FLAPPER (Pinn): PASTCD 7820 (CD)

SAYONARA (1957) Music sco: FRANZ WAXMAN orch.suite
RCA Red Seal (BMG): 09026 62657-2 (CD)
SCANNERS (1980) - *see* DEAD RINGERS / *see* COLL 309,
SCARAMOUCHE (1952) Music: VICTOR YOUNG new recording
BRANDENBURG S.ORCH.(KAUFMAN) with other items on
MARCO POLO (Select): 8.223607 (CD)
SCARFACE (1983) Music sco: GIORGIO MORODER / songs V/A
-S/T- *reissue MCA (BMG): MCD 06126 (CD)*
SCARLET PIMPERNEL The (BBC1 24/01/1999) Music score by
MICHAL PAVLICEK conducted by MARIO &d ADAM KLEMENS
and performed by PRAGUE PHILHARMONICS
-S/T- *BBC WORLDWIDE (Pinn): WMSF 60022 (CD)*
SCARLET PIMPERNEL The (ORIG.BROADWAY CAST RECORDING)
FIRST NIGHT (Pinn): 61CASTCD 72 (CD)
SCARLET TUNIC The (1997) Music score: JOHN SCOTT -S/T-
JOHN SCOTT Records (Silva Screen): JSCD 125 (CD)
SCARS OF DRACULA (1970) Music score: JAMES BERNARD
see COLL.180,
SCHINDLER'S LIST (1993) Music: JOHN WILLIAMS / Violin
Itzhak PERLMAN -S/T- *MCA (BMG): MCD 10969 (CD) see*
COLL.3,43,70,89,120,175,201,211,262,286,403,404
SCOOBY DOO (USA TV) *see COLL.347,373,*
SCREAM (1997) Music sco: MARCO BELTRAMI -S/T- **V.Arts**
EDEL (Pinn): 0022822CIN (CD)
SCREAM / SCREAM 2 (1997/1998) Music sc: MARCO BELTRAMI
scores only *VARESE (Pinn): VSD 5959*
SCREAM 2 (1998) -S/T- Music score: MARCO BELTRAMI
EMI PREMIER: 821 911-2 (CD) -4 (MC)
SCROOGE (O.LONDON CAST 1992) Songs: LESLIE BRICUSSE *w:*
ALBERT FINNEY *TER (Koch): CDTER 1194 (CD)*
SCROOGE (Classic Musicals series) *feat:* ANTHONY NEWLEY
TOM WATT-GEORGE ASPREY-TANYA COOKE-JON PERTWEE etc
+ *songs from* 'PICKWICK' *KOCH INT: 34081-2 (CD)*
SEA HAWK The (1940) Music sco: ERICH WOLFGANG KORNGOLD
NEW RECORDING with OREGON SYMPHONY ORCH (James De
Priest) *DELOS (Nimbus): DE 3234 (CD) also availab:*
VARESE (Pinn): VSD 47304 (CD)
see COLL.71,221,338,
SEA HUNT (USA TV) Theme music by RAY LLEWELLYN
see COLL.346,
SEA OF LOVE (1989) Music score: TREVOR JONES -S/T-
SPECTRUM (Univers.): 550130-2 (CD) -4 (MC)
SEA WOLVES The (1980) Music score by ROY BUDD with the
NATIONAL PHILHARMONIC ORCHESTRA
CINEPHILE (Pinn): CINCD 023 (CD)
SEAFORTH (BBC1 9/10/94) Music sco: JEAN-CLAUDE PETIT
-S/T- *D.SHARP-JADEAN (Pinn): DSCHCD(DSHMC) 7016*
SEAQUEST DSV (USA/ITV 16/10/93) Mus: JOHN DEBNEY -S/T-
VARESE (Pinn): VSD 5565 (CD) see COLL.38,121,312,
SEARCHERS The (1956) Music score by MAX STEINER
see COLL.70,260,401,
SEASON IN HELL, A (1971) Musc sco: MAURICE JARRE -S/T-
Imp (Silva Screen): CDST 310 (CD) 'MAURICE JARRE
TRILOGY' *DRG (Pinn): DRGCD 32906 (2CD)*

SECOND JUNGLE BOOK The (1997) Music score: JOHN SCOTT
-S/T- *JOHN SCOTT Rec (Silva Screen): JSCD 123 (CD)*
SECRET AGENT - *see* DANGER MAN
SECRET GARDEN The (1992) Music sco: ZBIGNIEW PREISNER
"Winter Light" (Z.Preisner-L.Ronstadt-E.Kaz) by
LINDA RONSTADT -S/T- *VARESE (Pinn):VSD 5443 (CD)*
SECRET GARDEN The (BBC1 75 & 85) theme "The Watermill"
see COLL.50,56,
SECRET HISTORY (C4 DOCUMENTARY SERIES)
individual programme music details on request from
MIKE PRESTON MUSIC
SECRET LIFE OF MACHINES The (Artifax/C4 from 15/11/88)
theme "The Russians Are Coming" based on 'Take 5'
(Paul Desmond) by VAL BENNETT Coll 'Rebel Music'
Trojan (Pinn): CDTRD 403 (2CD) TRLD 403 (2LP)
SECRET LIVES (C4 BIOGRAPHICAL DOC.SERIES)
individual programme music details on request from
MIKE PRESTON MUSIC
SECRET OF NIMH The (1982) Mus: JERRY GOLDSMITH Songs:
PAUL WILLIAMS -S/T- *VARESE (Pinn): VSD 5541 (CD)*
also on TER (Koch): CDTER 1026 (CD)
SECRET OF NIMH 2: Timmy To The Rescue (1998) Music sc:
LEE HOLDRIDGE, lyrics by RICHARD SPARKS -S/T- on
SONIC IMAGES (Cargo): SID 8820 (CD)
SECRET OF THE ICE CAVE (1989) *see* FIELD OF HONOR
SECRET OF THE SAHARA (RAI/ZDF/TFI Co.Prod ITV 12/9/93)
music score: ENNIO MORRICONE vocal by AMII STEWART
-S/T- *RCA (BMG): 74321 34226-2 (CD) also on COLL*
TV FILM MUSIC (COLL) RCA (BMG): 74321 31552-2 (CD)
SECRET SQUIRREL (USA TV) *see* COLL.349,373,
SECRETS OF THE ANCIENTS (BBC2 01/11/1999) series music
by DEBORAH MOLLISON *unavailable*
SECRETS OF THE MOORS (C4 HTV/Forum 23/7/92) theme and
incid.music from 'The Wasps' (VAUGHAN WiLLIAMS)
LONDON PHILHARMONIC ORCH (Sir Adrian Boult)
EMI: CDM 764020-2 (CD) EG 764020-4 (MC)
SEE HOW THEY RUN (BBC1 05/01/1999) music: MARIO MILLO
unavailable
SEESAW (ITV 12/3/1998) Music by CARL DAVIS *unavailable*
SEESAW (Musical 1973) Songs: CY COLEMAN-DOROTHY FIELDS
Orig BROADWAY Cast *DRG USA (Pinn): CDRG 6108 (CD)*
SEINFELD (USA 90)(BBC2 6/10/93) mus: JONATHAN WOLFF
see COLL.351,
SELFISH GIANT The (O.CAST RECORD 1993) Songs: MICHAEL
JENKINS-NIGEL WILLIAMS *featur:* GRAHAM TREW-ALISON
CAIN-RICHARD TILEY *TER (Koch): CDTER 1206 (CD)*
SENSE AND SENSIBILITY (1996) Music sco: PATRICK DOYLE
-S/T- *SONY CLASSICS: SK 62258 (CD) ST 62258 (MC)*
SENSELESS (1997) Music by VARIOUS ARTISTS -S/T- on
GEE STREET (V2-Pinn): GEE 100136-2 (CD)
SENTINEL The (USA DRAMA SERIES) theme m: JAMES NEWTON
HOWARD. incidental score by JOHN KEANE, songs by
STEVE POCORO (Toto). -S/T- on import
SONIC IMAGES (Cargo-Grehound): SI 8802 (CD)
SENZA PELLE - *see* NO SKIN

SERIAL MOM (1993) Music score: BASIL POLEDOURIS -S/T-
MCA Imp (SIlva Screen): MCAD(MCAC) 11052 (CD/MC)
SERPICO (1973) Mus score: MIKIS THEODARAKIS
see COLL.87,203,
SESAME STREET (USA 70's) theme: JOE RAPOSO-Stone-Hart)
see COLL.270,281,347,
SEVEN (1994) Music score: HOWARD SHORE -S/T- VAR.ARTS.
CINERAMA/TVT/EDEL UK (Pinn): 002243-2(CD)
SEVEN BRIDES FOR SEVEN BROTHERS - songs: Johnny Mercer
Gene De Paul + additional music by Adolph Deutsch
  1.ORIG FILM -S/T- 1954 with HOWARD KEEL-JANE POWELL-
JEFF RICHARDS-RUSS TAMBLYN-TOMMY RALL -S/T- 27trks
EMI PREMIER (EMI): CDODEON 17 (CD)
  2.ORIG LONDON CAST 1986 with new songs by Al Kasha-
Joel Hirschhorn w: RONI PAGE-STEVE DEVEREAUX-GEOFF
STEER-PETER BISHOP-JACKIE CRAWFORD and Company
FIRST NIGHT (Pinn): OCRCD 6008 (CD)
  3.CARLTON SHOWS COLLECTION (STUDIO RECORDING 1994)
EDMUND HOCKRIDGE-BONNIE LANGFORD-MASTERSINGERS
CARLTON SHOWS Coll (Carlton): PWKS(PWKMC) 4209
SEVEN CITIES OF GOLD (1955) Mus score: HUGO FRIEDHOFER
Suite on Coll with 'THE RAINS OF RANCHIPUR' + 'THE
LODGER' by The MOSCOW SYPHONY ORCH (W.T.Stromberg)
MARCO POLO (Select): 8.223857 (CD)
SEVEN DEADLY SINS (SHOW) / SONGS by KURT WEILL sung by
MARIANNE FAITHFULL and conducted by RUSSELL DAVIS
RCA VICTOR (BMG): 74321 60119-2 (CD, 10.1998)
SEVEN FACES OF WOMAN see COLL.2,149,281,
SEVEN MOONS (Sieben Monde)
-S/T- COLOSSEUM (Pinn): CST 348072 (CD)
SEVEN WAVES AWAY (1956) Music score: Sir ARTHUR BLISS
new recording by SLOVAK RADIO S.O. (Adriano) on
MARCO POLO (Select): 8.223315 (CD)
see also under 'CHRISTOPHER COLUMBUS'
SEVEN YEAR ITCH The (1955) see COLL.1,78,388,
SEVEN YEARS IN TIBET (1997) Music score: JOHN WILLIAMS
-S/T- SONY CLASSICS: SK 60271 (CD)
SEVENTH VOYAGE OF SINBAD The (1958) Music sco: BERNARD
HERRMANN. Re-mastered edition feat ROYAL SCOTTISH
NATIONAL ORCHESTRA (John Debney, cond) on
VARESE (Pinn): VSD 5961 (CD) see COLLS
SEVENTY GIRLS 70 - songs by John Kander and Fred Ebb
  1.ORIG LONDON CAST 1991 with DORA BRYAN and Company
TER (Koch): CDTER 1186 (CD)
SEX CENSORSHIP & T.SILVER SCREEN(USA/BBC2 16/04/1999)
main title theme by STEVE GOLDSTEIN, music score
by LAURA KARPMAN unavailable
SEX CHIPS AND ROCK'N'ROLL (BBC1 05/09/1999) orig music
by MIKE MORAN,songs by MIKE MORAN-DEBBIE HORSFIELD
-S/T- feat: 'The ICE CUBES' + VAR.60's CHART HITS
VIRGIN (EMI): VTDCD 264 (2CD) VTDMC 264(2MC) other
music: "Rhapsody in G.minor Op.79,No.2" (J.BRAHMS)
SEX LIES & VIDEOTAPE (1989) Music sco: CLIFF MARTINEZ
-S/T- VIRGIN (EMI): CDV 2604 (CD)

SEXTON BLAKE (BBC 1967) theme music: FRANK CHACKSFIELD
 see COLL.6,
SHADOW The (1993) Music score: JERRY GOLDSMITH -S/T-
 ARISTA (BMG): 0782218763-2 (CD) 0782218763-4 (MC)
SHADOW CONSPIRACY (1996) Mus sco: BRUCE BROUGHTON
 -S/T- *INTRADA Import (Silva Screen): MAF 7073 (CD)*
SHADOW OF THE NOOSE (BBC2 1/3/89) *see COLL.7,19,*
SHADOWLANDS (1993) Music score: GEORGE FENTON -S/T-
 EMI: CDQ 555093-2 (CD) -4 (MC) see COLL.100,
SHAFT (1971) Music by ISAAC HAYES / theme on Coll
 'THIS IS CULT FICTION' *VIRGIN (EMI) VTCD 59 (CD)*
 MOVING IMAGE ENT (Silver Sounds): MIE 0022 (2LP)
 see COLL.185,359,
SHAKA ZULU *featuring* LADYSMITH BLACK MAMBEZO -S/T- on
 WB (TEN): 7599 25582-2 (CD) WX 94C (MC)
SHAKA ZULU (ITV 22/6/91) music composed & performed by
 DAVE POLLECUTT TV-S/T- *Imp: CDC 1002 (CD) deleted*
SHAKEDOWN (1994) Doctor Who *Video* Spin-off / Music
 Sco: MARK AYRES *SILVA SCREEN Koch: FILMCD 718(CD)*
SHAKESPEARE IN LOVE (1998) Music sco: STEPHEN WARBECK
 -S/T- *SONY CLASSICS: SK 63387 (CD)*
SHAKESPEARE REVUE (CHRISTOPHER LUSCOMBE-MALCOLM McKEE)
 feat: SUSIE BLAKE-MARTIN CONNOR-JANIE DEE-C.LUS
 COMBE-MALCOLM McKEE *TER (Koch): CDTEM2 1237 (CD)*
SHALL WE DANCE (1937) FILM MUSICAL *feat* FRED ASTAIRE &
 GINGER ROGERS -S/T- *inc.songs from* 'SWINGTIME'
 SANDY HOOK (Silver Sounds): CSH 2028 (MC)
 also with 'TOP HAT' excerpts on
 GREAT MOVIE THEMES (Target-BMG): CD 60042 (CD)
SHAMPOO (ITV 12/11/1999) theme music by ADRIAN BURCH &
 DAVID WHITAKER *unavailable*
SHANE (Film 1953/TV 1966) "Call Of The Faraway Hills"
 (Victor YOUNG-Mac DAVID) *see COLL.409,*
SHANGHAI TRIAD (1995) Music score: ZHANG GUANGTIAN
 -S/T- *VIRGIN (EMI): CDVIR 44 (CD)*
SHANGHAI VICE (C4 28/02/1999) Music sco: GEORGE FENTON
 -S/T- *DEBONAIR (Pinn): CDDEB 1009 see COLL.19,*
SHARPE (ITV 05/5/93-96) Music: JOHN TAMS and DOMINIC
 MULDOWNEY *Collection* 'Music from Sharpe' (Various)
 VIRGIN (EMI): VTCD 81 (CD) VTMC 81 (MC)
SHE (1965) Music score: JAMES BERNARD *see Coll.180,*
SHE WORE A YELLOW RIBBON (1949) Music score: RICHARD
 HAGEMAN and others *see COLL.401,*
SHE'S THE ONE (1995) Music by TOM PETTY -S/T- on
 WEA (TEN): 9362 46285-2 (CD) -4 (MC)
SHELTERING SKY The (1990) Music sco: RYIUCHI SAKAMOTO
 -S/T- *VIRGIN (EMI): CDV 2652 (CD)*
SHERLOCK HOLMES (Granada) 'Adventures'/'Return'/'Sign'
 music: PATRICK GOWERS St.Paul's Cathedral Choir &
 Gabrieli String Quartet and The Wren Orchestra
 TER (Koch): CDTER 1136
SHERLOCK HOLMES The Musical (O.LONDON CAST 92) Songs
 (L.BRICUSSE) *feat:* ROBERT POWELL-ROY BARRACLOUGH-
 LOUISE ENGLISH *TER (Koch):CDTER 1198 (CD)*

SHETLAND SESSIONS The (BBC2 2/9/92) VARIOUS ARTISTS on
'Shetland Sessions V.1-2' *LISMOR (Gordon Duncan)*
LCOM 7021/7022 (CD) LICS 7021/7022 (MC) Themes:
"The Constitution" / "Scalloway Lasses" (ALY BAIN)

SHILOH (1997) Music score: JOEL GOLDSMITH. song "Are
There Angels" sung by SHEENA EASTON -S/T- on
VARESE (Pinn): VSD 5893 (CD)

SHINE (1996) Mus score: DAVID HIRSCHFELDER *piano music
p:* DAVID HIRSCHFELDER-DAVID HELFGOTT-RICKY EDWARDS
WILHELM KEMPF -S/T- *PHILIPS (Univ): 454 710-2 CD
454 710-4 (MC)* / also : 'BRILLIANTISSIMO' feat
DAVID HELFGOTT *RCA: 74321 46725-2 (CD) -4(MC)*
see COLL.74,76,100,

SHIRLEY VALENTINE (1989) Music: WILLY RUSSELL-GEORGE
HATZINASSIOS "The Girl Who Used To Be Me" (Marvin
HAMLISCH) sung by PATTI AUSTIN -S/T- on
Silva Screen (Koch): FILMCD 062 (CD)

SHIRLEY'S WORLD (ATV 1971) "Shirley's Theme"/"Rickshaw
Ride" by LAURIE JOHNSON *see COLL.215,217,*

SHOESTRING (UKGold 2/11/92 / BBC1 30/9/79) theme music
GEORGE FENTON *see COLL.6,46,*

SHOOT LOUD LOUDER..I DON'T UNDERSTAND (1966) Music:
NINO ROTA score on *DRG (Pinn): DRGCD 32914 (CD)*

SHOOTING FISH (1997) Mus score: STANISLAS SYREWICZ
-S/T- *EMI: PRMDCD 35 (CD) PRMDTC 35 (MC)*

SHOOTING PARTY The (1985) Music sco: JOHN SCOTT Royal
Phil Orch (J.Scott) *JS (limited ed) JSCD 113 (CD)*

SHOOTING THE PAST (BBC2 10/01/1999) music score by
ADRIAN JOHNSTON *unavailable*

SHOOTIST The (1976) Music sco: ELMER BERNSTEIN suite
VARESE (Pinn): VCD 47264 (CD)

SHORT CUTS (1993) VARIOUS ARTISTS -S/T- (Import) on
IMAGO (Direct): IMACD 23013 (CD)

SHORT EYES (1977) Music by CURTIS MAYFIELD -S/T-
with 'SUPERFLY' on *SEQUEL (BMG): NEMCD 964 (2CD)*
song "BreakIt Down" performed by FREDDY FENDER
-S/T- also on *CHARLY (Koch): CPCD 8183 (CD)*

SHORTLAND STREET (ITV 6/12/93) theme by GRAEME BOLLARD
sung by TINA CROSS *unavailable*   *see COLL.243,*

SHORTY THE PIMP *feat* DON JULIAN AND THE LARKS
SOUTHBOUND (Pinn): CDSEWD 122 (CD)

SHOW BOAT - songs by Jerome Kern-Oscar Hammerstein II
  1.FILM SOUNDTRACK 1951 *feat:* HOWARD KEEL-AVA GARDNER
    KATHRYN GRAYSON -S/T- *29tks EMI PREM.CDODEON 5*
  2.STUDIO RECORDING 1993 National Symphony Orchestra
    (John Owen Edwards) *w:* BRIAN GREENE-FRAN LANDESMAN
    JASON HOWARD-JANIS KELLY-WILLARD WHITE-SALLY BURGE
    SS-SHEZWAE POWELL-CAROLINE O'CONONOR-SIMON GREEN-
    JAMES BULLER-GARETH SNOOK and Company
    <u>Highlights:</u> *SHOWTIME (MCI-THE): SHOW(CD)(MC) 011*
    <u>Complete:</u> *TER (Koch): CDTER2 1199 (2CD)*
  3.CARLTON SHOWS COLL Studio Record 1993 *with* GEMMMA
    CRAVEN-DENIS QUILLEY-DAVID KERNAN-TRACEY MILLER
    CARLTON Shows Coll: PWKS 4161(CD) PWKMC 4161(MC)

SHOW BOAT *Continued...*

   4. REVIVAL USA CAST 1991 LINCOLN CENTER THEATRE
     RCA (BMG): 09026 61182-23 (CD)
   5. STUDIO RECORDING 1988 *1st complete* FREDERICA VON
     STADE-JERRY HADLEY-TERESA STRATAS-BRUCE HUBBARD-
     KARLA BURNS-DAVID GARRISON-PAIGE O'HARA-ROBERT
     NICHOLS-NANCY KULP-LILLIAN GISH with the AMBROSIAN
     CHORUS and LONDON SINFONIETTA (John McGlinn)
     EMI HMV: TCRIVER 1 (3MC) CDRIVER 1 (3CD)
     HIGHLIGHTS: *EMI CDC 749847-2(CD) EL 749847-4(MC)*
   6. ORIG BROADWAY REVIVAL CAST 1946 *with:* JAN CLAYTON-
     Carol Bruce-Charles Fredericks-Kenneth Spencer-Col
     ette Lyons *SONY BROADWAY: SK 53330 (CD)*
   7. O.LONDON CAST 1928 MARIE BURKE-COLIN CLIVE-VIOLA
     COMPTON-EDITH DAY-CEDRIC HARDWICKE-PAUL ROBESON
     LESLIE SARONY-HOWETT WORSTER *+ mus 'LIDO LADY' &*
     'SUNNY' (1926) PEARL (Pavilion): GEMMCD 9105 (CD)
   8. ORIG LONDON CAST 1971 *with* CLEO LAINE-ANDRE
     JOBIN-LORFNA DALLAS-THOMAS CAREY-ENA CABAYO & Comp
     LASERLIGHT POP-TARGET (BMG): 12446 (CD)
SHOW GOES ON The (ORIGINAL CAST RECORDING)
   DRG USA (New Note-Pinn): DRGCD 19008 (CD)
SHOW JUMPING - *see* HORSE OF THE YEAR SHOW
SIEGE (1998) Music score: GRAEME REVELL -S/T- on
   VARESE (Pinn): VSD 5989 (CD)
SIESTA (1988) Music sco: MARCUS MILLER-MILES DAVIS
   -S/T- *WB (TEN) K925655-4 (MC) -2 (CD)*
SILENCE OF THE LAMBS The (1991) Music: HOWARD SHORE
   -S/T- *MCA IMP: MCAD 10194 (CD) deleted*
   see COLL.74,105,144,
SILENCES OF THE PALACE (Les Silence Du Palais) (1994)
   Music sc: ANOUR BRAHEM -S/T- *VIRGIN: CDVIR 35 (CD)*
SILENT FALL (1995) Music score: STEWART COPELAND -S/T-
   MORGAN CREEK (Pinn): 002250-2 MCM (CD)
SILENT WITNESS (BBC1 21/2/96) theme mus (series 2 & 3)
   by JOHN HARLE on 'SILENCIUM' *see COLL.182,*
   orig.series theme by GEOFFREY BURGON *unavailable*
SILK ROAD The (ITV 23/6/87) 'Silk Road Suite' KITARO
   + LSO 'Silk Road 1' *Domo (Pinn): DOMO 71050-2 (CD)*
   -4 (MC) 'Silk Road 2' *Domo: 71051-2 (CD) -4 (MC)*
SILKWOOD (1983) Music sco: GEORGES DELERUE -S/T- *reiss*
   DRG (Pinn): DRGCD 6107 (CD)
SILVER LAKE The (Der Silbersee) MUSICAL PLAY IN 3 ACTS
   Music: KURT WEILL. Libr: GEORG KAISER *with* HEINZ
   KRUSE-HK.GRUBER-JUANITA LASCARRO-GRAHAM CLARK-
   HELGA DERNESCH-HEINZ ZEDNIK-PAUL WHELAN-GIDON SAKS
   -STEPHEN ADLER-ANDREW WEALE-CATRIN WYN DAVIES
   RCA RED SEAL: 09026 63447 (2CDs)
SIMBA'S PRIDE (LION KING 2)(1998) Music: MARK MANCINA
   song "He Lives In You" vocal by TINA TURNER. other
   sgs: LEBO M./LADYSMITH BLACK MAMBAZO/KENNY LATTIM
   ORE-HEATHER HEADLEY-ANGELIQUE KIDJO *'THE LION KING*
   COLL' EDEL-DISNEY (Pinn): 010150-2DNY (CD) -4(MC)

SIMON BATES OUR TUNE - *see* OUR TUNE
SIMON BIRCH (1999) Music score by MARC SHAIMAN -S/T-
  EPIC (Ten): 491 826-2 (CD) -4 (MC)
SIMPLE MAN, A (BBC2 1987) Music by CARL DAVIS (Ballet)
  about L.S.LOWRY *FIRST NIGHT (Pinn): OCRCD 6039 CD*
SIMPLE PLAN, A (1998) Music score: DANNY ELFMAN -S/T-
  SILVA SCREEN (Koch): FILMCD 310 (CD) also on imp:
  CMP USA (Silva Screen-Koch): 6676 03015-2 (CD)
SIMPLE TWIST OF FATE, A (1994) Music: CLIFF EIDELMAN
  -S/T- *VARESE (Pinn): VSD 5538 (CD)*
SIMPLY BARBRA ORIG.CAST REC. *feat:* STEVEN BRINBERG as
  BARBRA STREISAND.RECORDED 'LIVE' ABBEY RD STUDIOS
  TER (Koch): CDTER 1256 (CD)
SIMPSONS The (Sky90/BBC1 23/11/96) theme: DANNY ELFMAN
  score: RICHARD GIBBS /'Simpsons Sing The Blues' +
  "Do The Bartman" *GEFFEN (BMG): GED 24308 (CD)*
  'SIMPSONS-THE YELLOW ALBUM' *GEFFEN: GED 24480 (CD)*
  'SONGS IN THE KEY OF SPRINGFIELD' Various Artists
  RHINO (TEN): 8122 72723-2 (CD)
  'GO SIMPSONIC WITH THE SIMPSONS' *WEA ESP (TEN):*
  8122 75480-2 (CD) *see* COLL.270,351,
SINBAD AND THE EYE OF THE TIGER (1977) Music: ROY BUDD
  -S/T- *CINEPHILE-CASTLE (Pinn): CINCD 005 (CD)*
SINCE YOU WENT AWAY (1944) Music sc: MAX STEINER -S/T-
  reissue TSUNAMI IMPT (Silva Screen): TSU 0133 (CD)
  see also STREETCAR NAMED DESIRE A
SINGAPORE SLING (Australian TV 1993) series score by
  MARIO MILLO *unavailable*
SINGIN' IN THE RAIN (FILM 1952) Songs: ARTHUR FREED-
  NACIO HERB BROWN *-S/T- reiss EMI ODEON: CDODEON 14*
  (CD) also: Impt.sco.+ -S/T- 'AN AMERICAN IN PARIS'
  BLUE MOON (Discovery): BMCD 7008 (CD)
SINGIN' IN THE RAIN (NEW DIGITAL RECORDING 1998) *feat:*
  MICHAEL GRUBER-NANCY RINGHAM-RANDY ROGEL-CHRISTINA
  SAFFRAN & NATIONAL SYMPHONY ORCHEST (CRAIG BARNA)
  TER (Koch): CDTER 1240 (CD)
SINGIN' IN THE RAIN (O.LONDON CAST 1983) TOMMY STEELE-
  ROY CASTLE-SARAH PAYNE-DANIELLE CARSON & Company
  MD:Michael Reed *FIRST NIGHT (Pinn):OCRCD 6013 (CD)*
SINGING DETECTIVE The (BBC1 16/11/86 + 6/88 + 11/7/94)
  theme m "Peg O' My Heart" Max Harris Novelty Trio
  -S/T- *CONNOISSEUR (Pinn): POTT(CD)(MC)200 (2CD/MC)*
SINGING FOOL The (1928 FILM CAST *feat:* AL JOLSON)
  SANDY HOOK (Silver Sounds): CDSH 2107 (CD)
SINGLES (1992) -S/T- feat Various Artists
  EPIC (Ten): 471 438-2 (CD)
SIR FRANCIS DRAKE (ABC/ATV 12/11/61-29/4/62) theme m:
  (Ventura) *see COLL.23,*
SIR HENRY AT RAWLINSON END (1980) M: VIVIAN STANSHALL
  featur: TREVOR HOWARD-PATRICK MAGEE-DENISE COFFEY-
  J.G.DEVLIN and VIVIAN STANSHALL -S/T- *re-issued on*
  VIRGIN (EMI): VCCCD 18 (CD) VCCMC 18 (MC)
SISTER ACT (1992) Music sco: MARC SHAIMAN -S/T- *reiss:*
  EDEL-HOLLYWOOD (Pinn): 011334-2 (CD)

SISTER ACT 2: BACK IN THE HABIT (1993) Music score by
MILES GOODMAN -S/T- with VARIOUS ARTISTS - *REISSUE*
EDEL-HOLLYWOOD (Pinn): 011 562-2HWR (CD)

SISTERS (1973) - *see* BATTLE OF NERETVA

SIX DAYS SEVEN NIGHTS (1998) Music sco: RANDY EDELMAN
-S/T- *HOLLYWOOD (Univ): 162 163-2 (CD)*

SIX DEGREES OF SEPARATION (1993) Mus: JERRY GOLDSMITH
-S/T- *Imp (SILVA SCREEN) EA 61623-2 (CD) -4(MC)*

SIX MILLION $ MAN (USA 1970's) *see* COLL.311,349,363,

SIX WEEKS (1982) Music score by DUDLEY MOORE on
GRP (BMG): GRP 96612 (CD) GRP 96614 (MC)

SIXTH SENSE (1999) Music score by JAMES NEWTON HOWARD
-S/T- *VARESE (Pinn): VSD 6061 (CD)*

SKELETON COAST (BBC2 7/1/97) title mus: JON ATTARD and
additional music by WENTWORTH NORMAN *unavailable*

SKI SUNDAY (BBC2 72-93) theme mus "Pop Goes Bach" SAM
FONTEYN *see* COLL.6,176,363,

SKIN The (LA PELLE/LA PEAU)(81) Mus sco: LALO SCHIFRIN
-S/T- *CINEVOX Ita (Silva Screen): CDCIA 5095 (CD)*

SKIPPY THE BUSH KANGAROO (Austral.TV 1966-68) theme by
ERIC JUPP *see* COLL.349,

SKY AT NIGHT The (BBC1 24/4/57-99)theme "At The Castle
Gate" from 'Pelleas et Melisande' Op.46 (SIBELIUS)

SKY'S THE LIMIT (1943 MUSICAL) *feat:* FRED ASTAIRE and
JOAN LESLIE *inc.songs from* 'DUBARRY WAS A LADY' +
'42ND STREET' *TARGET (BMG):CD 60010 (CD)*

SLAB BOYS The (1997) Mus.arr.by JACK BRUCE *feat:* EDWYN
COLLINS-PAT KANE-PROCLAIMERS-LULU-EDDI READER
-S/T- *OCEAN DEEP (Grapevine-Poly): OCD 006 (CD)*

SLAM (1998) *EPIC (Ten): 492 607-2 (CD) -4 (MC) -1 (LP)*

SLAUGHTERHOUSE 5 (1972) *see* COLL.82,

SLAUGHTER'S BIG RIP-OFF (1973) Music by JAMES BROWN
-S/T- *POLYDOR: 517 136-2 (CD)*

SLEDGEHAMMER (ITV 12/1/89)m: DANNY ELFMAN *see* COLL.17,

SLEEPING BEAUTY (1959) Mus d: GEORGE BRUNS -S/T- songs
EDEL-DISNEY (Pinn): WDR 75622 (CD) see p.362

SLEEPING WITH THE ENEMY *see* COLL.74,80,

SLEEPLESS IN SEATTLE (1993) Music: MARC SHAIMAN -S/T-
J.DURANTE-L.ARMSTRONG-N.KING COLE-DR.JOHN-GENE
AUTRY-HARRY CONNICK JNR *EPIC (Ten): 473 594-2 (CD)*
-4 (MC) -8 (MD) see COLL.36,120,255,

SLEEPY HOLLOW (1999) Music score by DANNY ELFMAN -S/T-
HOLLYWOOD USA: 162 262-2 (CD)

SLICE OF SATURDAY NIGHT, A (O.LONDON CAST 1989) Arts
Theatre Club / *with* BINKY BAKER-DAVID EASTER-
CLAIRE PARKER-MITCH JOHNSON-ROY SMILES
reissue: FIRST NIGHT (Pinn): OCRCD 6041 (CD)

SLIDING DOORS (1998) Music score: DAVID HIRSCHFELDER
-S/T- *MCA (BMG): MCD 11715 (CD)*

SLIVER (1993) Music score: HOWARD SHORE var.arts inc:
-S/T- *VIRGIN Movie M (EMI): CD(TC)VMMX 11 (CD/MC)*

SLOW DRAG The (SHOW 1997) by CARSON KREITZER *featur:*
KIM CRISWELL-LIZA SADOVY-CHRISTOPHER COLQUHOUN
1940's Jazz Standards *TER (Koch): CDTER 1249 (CD)*

SLUMS OF BEVERLY HILLS (1998) Music sco: ROLFE KENT
  -S/T- with VAR.ARTS *RCA (BMG): 09026 63269-2 (CD)*
SMACK THE PONY (C4 19/02/1999) mus: JONATHAN WHITEHEAD
  theme "In The Middle Of Nowhere" (Kaye-Verdi) sung
  by JACKIE CLUNE *unavailable*.orig DUSTY SPRINGFIELD
  on 'Goin' Back' *PHILIPS: 848 789-2 (CD) -4 (MC)*
SMALL SOLDIERS (1998) Music sco: JERRY GOLDSMITH
  -S/T- (score) *VARESE (Pinn): VSD 5963*
  -S/T- (songs) *Dreamworks (BMG): DRD 50051 (CD)*
SMILLA'S FEELING FOR SNOW (1997) Music by HANS ZIMMER-
  HARRY GREGSON WILLIAMS + "Stabat Mater"(PERGOLESI)
  -S/T- *TELDEC (TEN): 0630 17872-2 (CD)*
SMOKEY JOE'S CAFE (Songs JERRY LEIBER & MIKE STOLLER)
  O.LONDON CAST *FIRST NIGHT (Pinn): ENCORECD10 (2CD)*
  O.BROADWAY CAST *ATLANTIC (TEN): 7567 82765-2 (CD)*
SMURFS The (1974) *see COLL.347,*
SNAGGLEPUSS - *see COLL.373,*
SNAKE EYES (1998) Music score: RYUICHI SAKAMOTO -S/T-
  EDEL-HOLLYWOOD (Pinn): 012 155-2HWR (CD)
SNAPPER The (BBC2 4/4/93) theme "Can't Help Falling In
  Love With You" (George Weiss-Hugo & Luigi) perf.by
  LICK THE TINS *MOONCREST (BMG): CRESTCD 012 (CD)*
SNOOKER (BBC Sport) theme music "Drag Racer" by the
  DOUGLAS WOOD GROUP *see COLL.148,176,*
  see also WORLD SNOOKER
SNOOKER Liverpool Victoria Champ.Cup (ITV 28/08/99)
  theme music "All That Glitters" from 'Dead Elvis'
  by DEATH IN VEGAS *CONCRETE (BMG): HARD22LPCD (CD)*
SNOOPY THE MUSICAL (ORIG USA CAST RECORDING 1981) on
  DRG USA (Pinn): CDRG 6103 (CD)
SNOW WHITE & T.SEVEN DWARFS (1937) S: FRANK CHURCHILL-
  LEIGH HARLINE-PAUL SMITH feat: ADRIANA CASELOTTI
  -S/T-*DISNEY-EDEL (Pinn): WD 74540-2 (CD) see p.362*
SNOW WHITE: A TALE OF TERROR (1996) Music score by
  JOHN OTTMAN -S/T- *CITADEL (import): STC 77116 (CD)*
SNOWMAN The (C4 Cartoon 24/12/85) music: HOWARD BLAKE
  Narr: Bernard Cribbins with The Sinfonia Of LONDON
  Song *"Walking In The Air"* sung by PETER AUTY -S/T-
  COLUMBIA (Ten) CDX 71116 (CD) 40-71116 (MC)
SNOWS OF KILIMANJARO The (1952) Mus: BERNARD HERRMANN
  score select *SILVA SCREEN (Koch): FILMCD 162 (CD)*
  also on 'Citizen Kane' *DECCA 417852-2 (CD)-4 (MC)*
SO YOU THINK YOU'RE A GOOD DRIVER (BBC1 04/06/1999)
  theme adapted from "Oh Yeah!" by YELLO *MERCURY*
SOAP (USA 1980's) *see COLL.281,350,*
SOFTLY SOFTLY (BBC1 1970-80s) - *see COLL.2,270,*

SOLDIER BLUE (1970) Music score: ROY BUDD -S/T-Collect
  also feat 'CATLOW' (1971) and 'ZEPPELIN' (1971) on
  CINEPHILE (Pinn): CINCD 022 (CD)
SOLDIER SOLDIER (ITV from 10/6/1991) music: JIM PARKER
  -S/T- *SOUNDTRACK EMI GOLD: 520 686-2 (CD)*
SOLDIER TOWN (C4 03/06/1999) Music by ALEX LEE and
  NICK PWELL *unavailable*

SOLDIER'S DAUGHTER NEVER CRIES, A (1998) Music score:
RICHARD ROBBINS -S/T- *also featuring:* DAVID BOWIE/
DEEP PURPLE/10CC/TITO PUENTE and RICHARD ROBBINS
EMI PREMIER: 497 060-2 (CD)

SOLOMON AND SHEBA (1959) Music score: MARIO NASCIMBENE
new recording of score with 'The Vikings' music on
DRG-New Note (Pinn): DRGCD 32963 (CD)

SOME KIND OF WONDERFUL (1987) Music by Var.Arts -S/T-
Beat Goes On (Pinn): BGO(CD)(MC) 178 (CD/MC) also
MCA USA (S.Screen): MCAD 6200 (CD) MCAC 6200 (MC)

SOME LIKE IT HOT (1959) Music score: ADOLPH DEUTSCH
songs "I Wanna Be Loved By You" / "I'm Thru' With
Love" performed by MARILYN MONROE -S/T- *CD de-luxe*
RYKODISC (Vital): RCD 10715 (CD)

SOME LIKE IT HOT (O.LONDON CAST 1992) Songs Jule STYNE
BoB MERRILL w.TOMMY STEELE-BILLY BOYCE-ROYCE MILLS
MANDY PERRYMENT *First Night (Pinn): OCRCD 6028 CD*

SOME PEOPLE music: RON GRAINER *see COLL.8,*

SOMEONE TO WATCH OVER ME (1987)
see COLL.87,104,162,274,320,

SOMETHING TO BELEIVE IN (1997) Music sc: LALO SCHIFRIN
-S/T- *ALEPH (Koch): ALEP 008 or 6517 926329-2 (CD)*

SOMEWHERE IN TIME (1980) Music: JOHN BARRY -S/T- on
BEAT GOES ON (Pinn): BGO(CD)(MC) 222.new recording
ROYAL SCOTTISH NATIONAL ORCHEST (John Debney,cond)
VARESE (Pinn): VSD 5911 (CD)
see COLL.29,74,80,100,121,

SOMMERSBY (1993) Music score: DANNY ELFMAN -S/T-
ELEKTRA (TEN): 7559 61491-2 (CD) -4 (MC)

SON OF FRANKENSTEIN (1939) Music score: FRANK SKINNER
new record MOSCOW SYMPHONY ORCHESTRA (Stromberg)
on *MARCO POLO (Select): 8.223748 (CD) also includ:*
INVISIBLE MAN RETURNS-THE WOLF MAN

SONDHEIM: A MUSICAL TRIBUTE ORIG BROADWAY CAST *with*
DOROTHY COLLINS-CHITA RIVERA-ANGELA LANSBURY etc.
RCA Vict: RD 60515 (2CDs)

SONG AND DANCE - songs: Andrew Lloyd Webber-Don Black
1.ORIG LONDON CAST 1982 *with:* MARTI WEBB & Company
POLYDOR: 843 619-2 (CD) PODVC 4 (2Cas)
2.SONG AND DANCE / TELL ME ON A SUNDAY (STUDIO 1984)
with SARAH BRIGHTMAN and WAYNE SLEEP and Company
RCA (BMG) BD 70480 (CD) BK 70480 (MC)
see also EUROVISION SONG CONTEST

SONG OF BERNADETTE The (1943) Music sco: ALFRED NEWMAN
NEW RECORDING: VARESE (Pinn): VSD 26025 (2CD)
-S/T- IMPORT TSUNAMI (Silva Screen): TSI 0617 (CD)
see COLL.1,

SONG OF NORWAY (STUDIO RECORDED MUSICAL) Songs (Robert
Wright-George Forrest adapt.from music by Edvard
GRIEG) *feat:* VALERIE MASTERSON-DONALD MAXWELL-
DIANA MONTAGUE *TER (Koch) CDTER2 1173 (2CD)*

SONG OF THE SOUTH - *see also* WALT DISNEY INDEX p.362
see COLL.42,130,

SONGBOOK (ORIG LONDON CAST 1979) Songs by Monty Norman
   & Julian More *feat:* GEMMA CRAVEN-DAVID HEALY-DIANE
   LANGTON-ANTON RODGERS-ANDREW C.WADSWORTH *reissue:*
   DRG (New Note-Pinn): DRGCD 13117 (CD)
SONGS FOR A NEW WORLD (1996) Songs: JASON ROBERT BROWN
   ORIG BROADWAY CAST   *RCA (BMG): 09026 68631-2 (CD)*
SONGS OF PRAISE (BBC1 12/9/93) Organ theme by ROBERT
   PRIZEMAN recorded by STEPHEN CLEOBURY on Coll
   'Splendour Of Kings' *COLLINS (Koch): 14012 (CD)*
   Collection of hymns recorded at Old Trafford (BBC)
   EMI ALLIANCE (EMI): ALD 026 (CD) ALC 026 (MC)
   'CHRISTMAS SONGS OF PRAISE' *BBC WORLDWIDE (Pinn):*
   WMEF 0049-2 (CD) WMEF 0049-4 (MC)
SONS AND DAUGHTERS (Australia ITV 19/10/83) title song
   (Peter Pinne-D.Battye) KERRI & MICK *see COLL.376,*
SONS AND LOVERS (1960) Music: MARIO NASCIMBENE -S/T- +
   'A FAREWELL TO ARMS' *DRG (Pinn): DRGCSD 32962 (CD)*
SONS OF KATIE ELDER The (1965) Music: ELMER BERNSTEIN
   -S/T- *TSUNAMI Imp (Silva Screen): TSU 0104 (CD)*
SOOTY SHOW The (ITV 5/1/83-98) theme: MATTHEW CORBETT
   'SOOTY & CO.' *MFP (EMI): TCMFP 6103 (MC)*
SOPHIE'S CHOICE (1983) Orig mus: MARVIN HAMLISCH -S/T-
   SOUTHERN CROSS (Hot/S.Screen) SCCD 902 (CD)
SOPRANOS The (USA 1998/C4 15/07/1999) ser.theme music
   "Woke Up This Morning" by ALABAMA 3 on *ELM 41CDS1*
   SOPRANOS -S/T- *COLUMB (Ten): 497 403-2 (CD) -4(MC)*
SORCERER The - *see under* 'Wages Of Fear' (1978)
SOUL FOOD (1997) -S/T- featuring VARIOUS ARTISTS on
   LaFACE-RCA (BMG): 73008 26041-2 (CD) -4 (MC)
   also on (BMG): 74321 52307-2 (CD)
SOUL IN THE HOLE (1997) Basketball Drama-Documentary
   ORIG.MUSIC FROM AND INSPIRED BY MOTION PICTURE
   -S/T- (V.ARTISTS) *CLOUD (BMG): 07863 67531-2 (CD)*
SOUL MAN (1986) Music sco: TOM SCOTT + V.Arts -S/T-
   re-issued on SPECTRUM (Univ): 551 431-2 (CD)
SOUL MUSIC (TERRY PRATCHETT'S) - *see* DISCWORLD
SOUND BARRIER The (1952) M: MALCOLM ARNOLD "Rhapsody"
   'Film Music' LSO (R.Hickox) *CHANDOS: CHAN 9100 CD*
   see COLL.173,
SOUND OF MUSIC The - songs by Richard Rodgers and
   Oscar Hammerstein II
   1.FILM MUSICAL 1965 *with:* JULIE ANDREWS-CHRISTOPER
     PLUMMER -S/T- *collector's 30th anniversary edition*
     on *RCA (BMG): 077850 66587-2 (CD) -4 (MC)*
   2.CARLTON SHOWS COLLECT STUDIO 1993 *w:* DENIS QUILLEY
     LIZ ROBERTSON-LINDA HIBBERD-MASTER SINGERS & Comp
     CARLTON SHOWS: PWKS 4145(CD) PWKMC 4145 (MC)
   3.ORIG BROADWAY CAST 1959 MARY MARTIN-THEODORE BIKEL
     PATRICIA NEWAY-KURT KASZNAR-MARION MARLOWE-LAURIE
     PETERS-BRIAN DAVIES *SONY BROADWAY: SK 60583 (CD)*
   4.ORIG LONDON CAST 1961 *with* JEAN BAYLESS-CONSTANCE
     SHACKLOCK-OLIVE GILBERT-SYLVIA BEAMISH-LYNN KENNIN
     GTON *LASERLIGHT (BMG): 12448 (CD) also on*
     FIRST NIGHT (Pinn): OCRC 2 (MC)

SOUNDS OF THE SUBURBS - *see* John Peel's Sounds Of...
SOUTH BANK SHOW The (LWT 1978-99) theme "Caprice In A.
  Minor No.24" 'Themes & Variations 1-4' (PAGANINI)
  ANDREW & JULIAN LLOYD WEBBER *MCA: MCLD 19126 (CD)*
SOUTH PACIFIC - songs by Richard Rodgers and Oscar
  Hammerstein II
  1. FILM MUSICAL 1958 MITZI GAYNOR-ROSSANO BRAZZI-
     (sung by Giorgio Tozzi*)* JOHN KERR-JUANITA HALL
     (by Muriel Smith*)* -S/T- *RCA (BMG): (ND)(NK) 83681*
  2. REVIVAL LONDON CAST 1988 *w:* GEMMA CRAVEN-BEATRICE
     READING *FIRST NIGHT (Pinn): OCRCD 6023 (CD)*
  3. STUDIO RECORDING 1986 KIRI TE KANAWA-JOSE CARRERAS
     Sarah Vaughan-Mandy Patinkin-Ambrosia Singers
     L.S.O.(Jonathan Tunick) *SONY: CBSCD 42205 (CD)*
  4. CARLTON SHOWS COLLECTION *with:* GEMMA CRAVEN-DAVID
     KERNAN-LINDA HIBBERD-MASTER SINGERS-NIC CURTIS etc
     CARLTON SHOWS Coll: PWKS 4162(CD) PWKMC 4162(MC)
  5. ORIG BROADWAY CAST 1949 MARY MARTIN-EZIO PINZA-
     JUANITA HALL-BARBARA LUNA-MICHAEL DeLEON-MYRON
     McCORMICK-WILLIAM TABBERT-BETTA St.JOHN and Comp
     COLUMBIA (Ten): SMK 60722 (CD)
  6. STUDIO RECORDING 1996) *feat* PAIGE O'HARA
     JUSTINO DIAZ-SHEZWAE POWELL-SEAN McDERMOTT with
     NATIONAL SYPHONY ORCH conductor: JOHN OWEN EDWARDS
     TER (Koch): CDTER 1242 (2CD)
SOUTH PARK - **Bigger Longer and Uncut** / VARIOUS ARTISTS
  ATLANTIC (TEN): 7567 83199-2 (CD) -4 (MC)
SOUTH PARK (USA 97/C4 10/7/1998) "South Park Theme" by
  PRIMUS. 'SOUTH PARK CHEF AID' V.Arts compilation
  COLUMBIA (Ten): 491 700-2 (CD) 491 700-4 (MC)
  see **COLL** 'HIT TV' on **VARESE (Pinn): VSD 5957 (CD)**
SOUTH RIDING (ITV 16/9/74) music by RON GRAINER
  see COLL.8,
SOUTHERN MAID (O.LONDON CAST 1920) Songs: H.FRASER
  SIMPSON-DION CLAYTON CALTHROP-HARRY GRAHAM with
  addit.songs by IVOR NOVELLO-DOUGLAS FURBER *feat:*
  GWENDOLINE BROGDEN-ERNEST BERTRAM-JOSE COLLINS
  Pearl (Pavilion): GEMMCD 9115 (CD)
SOUVENIR DE VOYAGE Music score: BERNARD HERRMANN
  VARESE (Pinn): VSD 5559 (CD)
SPACE 1999 (ITC 4/9/75-77) music by BARRY GRAY
  see COLL.38,122,308,333,360,362,
SPACE...ABOVE AND BEYOND (USA) *see COLL.308,*
SPACE IS THE PLACE featuring music by SU RA -S/T- on
  EVIDENCE (Harmonia Mundi): ECD 22070-2 (CD)
SPACE JAM (1996) Music score: JAMES NEWTON HOWARD
  -S/T-songs: *ATLANTIC (TEN): 7567 82961-2(CD)-4(MC)*
  -S/T-score: *ATLANTIC (TEN): 7567 82979-2(CD)*
SPACED (C4 24/09/1999) theme by GUY PRATT *unavailable*
SPARTACUS (USA-60/renovated 91) Music sco: ALEX NORTH
  -S/T- *MCA (S.Screen): MCAD 10256 (CD)* addit.mus.
  Imp TSUNAMI (S.Screen): TSI 0603 (CD)
SPARTACUS (Jeff Wayne's Musical Version 1992)
  Columbia (Ten): 472030-4 (2 MC) 472030-2 (2CD)

SPAWN (1997) Music score: GRAEME REVELL -S/T- (V.Arts)
   SONY: 488 188-2 (CD) -4 (MC) 488 118-0 (3LP's)
SPECIES (1994) Music sco: CHRISTOPHER YOUNG
   Symphonic suite *see COLL.328,389,*
SPEED (94) Music score: MARK MANCINA V.Arts -S/T-
   Songs: *ARISTA (BMG): 07822 11018-2 (CD)*
   Score: *MILAN (BMG): 234 652 (CD)*
SPEED 2: CRUISE CONTROL (1997) Music sco: MARK MANCINA
   VIRGIN (EMI): CDVUS 129 (CD)
SPEEDWAY *see* ELVIS PRESLEY INDEX p.360
SPELLBOUND (1945) Music score: MIKLOS ROSZA -S/T- with
   music from 'JUNGLE BOOK' (Miklos ROSZA) on *FLAPPER*
   (Pinn): PASTCD 7093 (CD) see COLL.197,386,387,
SPENSER FOR HIRE (USA 85)(BBC1 12/9/89) theme: STEVE
   DORFF-LARRY HERBSTRITT *see COLL.17,*
SPHERE (1997) Music score: ELLIOT GOLDENTHAL -S/T- on
   VARESE (Pinn): VSD 5913 (CD)
SPIDERMAN (USA TV) *see COLL.346,*
SPIES *see COLL.23,377,*
SPINAL TAP - *see* THIS IS SPINAL TAP
SPINOUT *see* ELVIS PRESLEY INDEX p.360
SPIRITS GHOSTS AND DEMONS (C4 27/9/94) orig music by
   GEORGE FENTON - *see* 'BEYOND THE CLOUDS' entry
SPITFIRE GRILL The (1996) Music sco: JAMES HORNER
   -S/T- *SONY CLASSICS USA: SK 62776 (CD)*
SPITTING IMAGE (Central 6/86) 'Spit In Your Ear' V/A
   VIRGIN (EMI) CDVIP 110 (CD) TCVIP 110 (MC)
SPORTSMASTER *see COLL.147,176,*
SPORTSNIGHT (BBC1 70-97) title theme: TONY HATCH
   see COLL.4,176,184,270,281,
SPORTSVIEW (BBC 1954-68) theme music "Saturday Sports"
   by WILFRED BURNS *see COLL.7,176,*
SPOT (BBC Children's TV) *see COLL.67,*
SPRINGTIME IN THE ROCKIES (1942 FILM CAST) *feat:* BETTY
   GRABLE-CARMEN MIRANDA inc.sel.from 'SWEET ROSIE O'
   GRADY' *SANDY HOOK (Silver Sounds): CDSH 2090 (CD)*
SPRUNG (1997) Various Artists -S/T- on
   WEA (TEN): 9362 46557-2 (CD) -4 (MC)
SPY WHO LOVED ME The (1977) Music sco: MARVIN HAMLISCH
   title song (M.Hamlisch-Carole Bayer Sager) sung by
   CARLY SIMON -S/T- *reissue EMI PREMIER: CZ 555 (CD)*
   JAMES BOND FILM INDEX p.358
   see COLL.55,87,314,
SPYSHIP (BBC1 9/11/83) theme "A Cold Wind" by RICHARD
   HARVEY vocal by JUNE TABOR *K-TEL: ONCD 3435 (CD)*
ST. - *see under* 'SAINT...'

STAGE DOOR CANTEEN (1943) ORIGINAL FILM CAST RECORDING
   SANDY HOOK (Silver Sounds): CDSH 2093 (CD)
STAGECOACH (1965) Music score: JERRY GOLDSMITH -S/T-
   inc music to 'THE LONER' Ltd Edition Import on
   RETROGRADE (S.Screen/MFTM): FSMCD 1 (CD)
STAND The (1993) Music score: W.G.SNUFFY WALDEN -S/T-
   VARESE (Pinn): VSD 5496 (CD)

STAND BY ME (1987) Mus sco: JACK NITZSCHE -S/T- V.ARTS
 ATLANTIC (TEN): CD 7567 81677-2 (CD) WX 92C (MC)
STAND BY YOUR MAN (MUSICAL) *feat* HELEN HOBSON & Comp.
 SILVA SCREEN (Koch): SONGCD 913 (CD) SONGC 913(MC)
STAR! (1968) feat JULIE ANDREWS as Gertrude Lawrence
 -S/T- *FOX-ARISTA (BMG): 07822 11009-2 (CD)*
STAR DUST (1940) VARIOUS -S/T- SELECTIONS on
 GREAT MOVIE THEMES: (Targ-BMG): CD 60032 (CD)
STAR IS BORN,A (54) JUDY GARLAND-JAMES MASON -S/T-
 CBS USA (S.Screen): CK 44389 (CD) JST 44389 (MC)
STAR IS BORN,A (76)BARBRA STREISAND-KRIS KRISTOFFERSON
 -S/T- *COLUMBIA Sony: 474905-2 (CD) -4 (MC)*
STAR KID (1997) Music score: NICHOLAS PIKE -S/T- on
 SONIC IMAGES (Cargo-Greyhound): SCI 8800 (CD)
STAR SPANGLED RHYTHM (1942 MUSICAL) *feat:* BETTY HUTTON
 BING CROSBY-DICK POWELL *incl.songs from* 'FOOTLIGHT
 PARADE' *TARGET (BMG): CD 60013 (CD)*
STAR TREK (TV) (USA 66) theme: ALEXANDER COURAGE *note*
 30TH BIRTHDAY EDITION (Coll) Music taken from best
 STAR TREK 1966-1968 ROYAL PHILHARMONIC ORCHESTRA
 orch: FRED STEINER *VARESE (Pinn): VSD 25762 (2CD)*
 also VOLS 1/2 *VARESE (Pinn): VSD 47235 / 457240*
 25TH ANNIVERSARY (The Astral Symphony) Feat music
 inc theme *Milan (BMG): 262 832 (CD) DELETED 99*
 CLASSIC SERIES V.1 *GNPD 8006 (CD) GNP-5 8006 (MC)*
 CLASSIC SERIES V.2 *GNPD 8025 (CD) GNP-5 8025 (MC)*
 CLASSIC SERIES V.3 *GNPD 8030 (CD) GNP-5 8030 (MC)*
 SOUND EFFECTS (60) *GNPD 8010 (CD) GNP-5 8010 (MC)*
 STAR TREK *GNP (Vivanti): GNP 8006 (LP Audio Qual)*
 TV SCORES 1/2 (R.P.Orch) *CBS USA: LXE 703/704 (CD)*
 see COLL.2,38,52,711,121,150,166,167,169,219,229,
 264,267,270,307,308,329,333,345,362,382,
STAR TREK (TV): THE NEXT GENERATION (88)(BBC2-26/9/90)
 New theme: JERRY GOLDSMITH-ALEXANDER COURAGE plus
 music by DENNIS McCARTHY *all distributed by ZYX*
 Volume 1 - *GNPD 8012 (CD) GNP-5 8012 (MC)*
 Volume 2 - *GNPD 8026 (CD) GNP-5 8026 (MC)*
 Volume 3 - *GNPD 8031 (CD) GNP-5 8031 (MC)*
 see COLL.17,264,267,270,307,308,334,351,
STAR TREK (TV): DEEP SPACE NINE (BBC2 28/9/95) music:
 DENNIS McCARTHY-JAY CHATTAWAY -S/T- *GNP (ZYX)*
 GNPD 8034 (CD) GNP-5 8034 (MC)
 see COLL.264,270,306,307,
STAR TREK (TV): VOYAGER (USA 94/BBC 6/95) theme JERRY
 GOLDSMITH score: JAY CHATTAWAY -S/T- *GNPD 8041*
 (CD) GNP-5 8041 (MC) see COLL.166,167,256,267,270,
STAR TREK: THE MOTION PICTURE (1979) Music score JERRY
 GOLDSMITH. *reiss:* GENE RODDENBERRY'S 'INSIDE STAR
 TREK' *SONY: SK 66134 (2CD) / 489 929-2 (CD) -4(MC)*
STAR TREK (2) The Wrath Of Khan (1982) Mus sco: JAMES
 HORNER) -S/T- *GNP USA IMPT (ZYX): GNPD 8022*
 (CD) GNP-5 8022 (MC) with orig Alex.Courage theme
STAR TREK (3) Search For Spock (1984) M: JAMES HORNER
 -S/T- *GNP-58023 (MC)*

STAR TREK (4) The Voyage Home (1987) Mus sco: LEONARD
ROSENMAN -S/T- *MCA (BMG): MCLD 19349 (CD deleted)*
STAR TREK (5) The Final Frontier (1989) Mus sc: JERRY
GOLDSMITH -S/T- *EPIC: 465925-2(CD) -4(MC) deleted*
STAR TREK (6) The Undiscovered Country (1991) Mus sco
CLIFF EIDELMAN -S/T- *MCA (BMG): MCLD 19348 (CD)*
STAR TREK (7) Generations (1994) Mus sc: DENNIS McCAR
THY -S/T- *GNP (ZYX): GNPD(GNP5) 8040 (CD/MC)*
STAR TREK (8) First Contact (Generations 2) (1996) Mus
JERRY GOLDSMITH *GNP (ZYX): GNPD 8052 (CD)*
STAR TREK (9) Insurrection (1998) Mus: JERRY GOLDMITH
-S/T- *GNP CRESCENDO (ZYX): GNPD 8059 (CD)*

STAR WARS EPISODE 1: THE PHANTOM MENACE (1998) Music:
JOHN WILLIAMS conducting LONDON SYMPHONY ORCHESTRA
*SONY CLASSICAL: SK 61816 (CD) ST 61816 (MC) also
VARESE (Pinn): VSD 6086 (CD)*
other version available by SPACE GALAXY ORCHESTRA
HALLMARK (CHE): 31175-2 (CD) -4 (MC)
STAR WARS (1) (1977) Music score: JOHN WILLIAMS -S/T-
*RSO 2679 092 (LP) 800 096-2 (CD) also available
on RCA RCD 13650 (CD) c/w 'Close Encounters..'*
see COLL.41,70,106,229,264,267,298,306,307,308,
327,328,333,334,335,362,403,404,
STAR WARS (2) The Empire Strikes Back (1981) Mus sco
JOHN WILLIAMS -S/T-*Imp (S.Screen): 827580-4 (MC)*
Special Edit: *RCA (BMG): 09026 68773-2 (CD) -4(MC)*
STAR WARS (3) Return Of The Jedi (1983) Music score:
JOHN WILLIAMS - National Philharmonic Orchestra
(Charles Gerhardt) *-RCA Vict (BMG): GD 60767 (CD)*
-S/T- *RCA: RK 14748 (MC) RCD 14748 (CD)*
Special Edit. *RCA (BMG): 09026 68774-2 (CD) -4(MC)*
STAR WARS (A NEW HOPE) Music score: JOHN WILLIAMS
Special Edition ORIG SOUNDTRACK RECORDING (1997)
RCA (BMG): 09026 68746-2 (Deluxe 2CD)
Special Ed: *RCA (BMG): 09026 68772-2 (2CD) -4(2MC)*
also available -S/T- VARESE (Pinn): VSD 5794 (CD)
STAR WARS: SHADOWS OF THE EMPIRE Music by JOEL McNEELY
VARESE (Pinn): VSDE 5700 (CD)
STAR WARS TRILOGY - The ORIGINAL SOUNDTRACK ANTHOLOGY
Music score by JOHN WILLIAMS / also containing the
20th Cent.Fox Fanfare with Cinemascope Extention
(Alfred Newman) *this collect. contains previously
UNRELEASED m. FOX-Arista (BMG): 07822 11012-2 4CDs*
STAR WARS TRILOGY Sel.mus.from 3 films + 'Close Encou
nters' UTAH SYMPH OR *VARESE (Pinn): VCD 47201(CD)*
STARCRASH - *see* UNTIL SEPTEMBER
STARGATE (1994) Music score: DAVID ARNOLD -S/T- reiss:
MILAN BMG: 74321 24901-2(CD) see COLL 49,308,329,
STARLIGHT EXPRESS - songs by Andrew Lloyd Webber and
Richard Stilgoe
1.ORIG LONDON CAST 1993 *Apollo Victoria Cast*
POLYDOR 519 041-2 (CD) 4 (MC) -1 (LP) -5 (Mini-D)
2.SHOWS COLLECTION *CARLTON: PWKS(PWKMC) 4192 (CD/MC)*

STARMAN (1985) Music score: JACK NITZSCHE -S/T-
   VARESE (Pinn):VCD 47220 (CD) see COLL.306,310,329,
STARS FELL ON HENRIETTA (1995) Music sco: DAVID BENOIT
   -S/T- VARESE (Pinn): VSD 5667 (CD)
STARSHIP TROOPERS (1997) Music score: BASIL POLEDOURIS
   -S/T- VARESE (Pinn): VSD 5877 (CD)
STARSKY & HUTCH (USA 75) theme "Gotcha" TOM SCOTT
   'The Theme' Various VIRGIN (EMI): VSCDT 1708 (CDs)
   see COLL.347,363,382,390,
STARTING HERE STARTING NOW songs: David Shire-Richard
   Maltby Jr O.LONDON CAST TER (Koch): CDTER 1200
STATE FAIR songs: Richard Rodgers-Oscar Hammerstein II
   BROADWAY CAST 1996 JOHN DAVIDSON-DONNA McKECHNIE
   DRG (Pinn): DRG(CD)(MC) 94765 (CD/MC)
STATE FAIR 2 VARESE (Pinn): VSD 6090 (CD)
STAY AWAY JOE see ELVIS PRESLEY INDEX p.360
STAY TUNED (1992) Music sc: BRUCE BROUGHTON + Various
   Arts -S/T- MORGAN CREEK (Pinn): 002251-2 MCM (CD)
STAYING ALIVE (1983) Music score: JOHNNY MANDEL feat:
   BEE GEES reissued -S/T- RSO (Univ): 813269-2 (CD)
STAYING ALIVE (ITV 1/11/96)theme "Coming Around Again"
   (C.Simon) sung by JESSICA STEVENSON unavailable
STEALING HEAVEN (1989) Music score: NICK BICAT -S/T-
   TER (Koch): CDTER 1166 (CD)
STEEL PIER (ORIG BROADWAY CAST RECORDING)
   RCA Victor (BMG): 09026 68878-2 (CD)
STENDHAL SYNDROME The (1996) Music sc: ENNIO MORRICONE
   -S/T- DRG (Pinn): DRGCD 12621 (CD)
STEP LIVELY (1944 MUSICAL) feat FRANK SINATRA-ADOLPHE
   MENJOU-GLORIA DE HAVEN inc.songs from 'HIGHER AND
   HIGHER' TARGET (BMG): CD 60004 (CD)
STEPPING OUT (ORIGINAL LONDON CAST 1997)
   FIRST NIGHT (Pinn): SCENECD 24 (CD)
STEPTOE & SON (BBC 5/1/62) theme "Old Ned" RON GRAINER
   Orig Cast Rec BBC: ZBBC 1145 (MC)
   see COLL.8,23,270,367,377,
STEVEN BRINBERG IS SIMPLY BARBARA (ORIG LONDON CAST)
   TER (Koch): CDTER 1256 (CD)
STEVEN SPIELBERG'S AMAZING STORIES see AMAZING STORIES
STIFF UPPER LIPS (1998) VARIOUS CLASSICAL MUSIC -S/T-
   EMI PREMIER Soundtracks: 495 529-2 (CD)
STIGMATA (1999) Music score by ELIA CMIRAL -S/T- on
   VIRGIN (EMI): CDVUS 161 (CD)
STILL BREATHING (1998) -S/T- on
   WILL (Silver Sands): 7801 633649-2 (CD)
STILL CRAZY (1998) Music: CLIVE LANGER-ALAN WINSTANLEY
   feat JIMMY NAIL and STRANGE FRUIT & BILLY CONNOLLY
   -S/T- (10/1999) LONDON (Ten): 3984 28235-2 (CD)
   -S/T- (10/1998) LONDON (Univ): 556 055-2 (CD)
STING The (1973) Music: MARVIN HAMLISCH-SCOTT JOPLIN
   -S/T-MCA (BMG): MCLD 19027(CD) see COLL.41,
STINGRAY (ATV/ITC 6/10/64 reshown BBC2 11/9/92) music
   BARRY GRAY (vocal: GARRY MILLER)
   see COLL.4,23,38,122,171,349,360,367,

STIR OF ECHOES (1999) Music score: JAMES NEWTON HOWARD
-S/T- *(USA IMPORT) NETTWERK 30145 (CD)*

STOLEN HEARTS (1996) Mus: NICK GLENNIE SMITH-PADDY MOL
ONEY (CHIEFTAINS) "Haunted" perf: SHANE MacGOWAN-
SINEAD O'CONNOR -S/T- *M.CREEK (Pinn) 002253-2 MCM*

STONE KILLER The (1973) Music score: ROY BUDD -S/T-
(Silva Screen Import): LEGEND CD6 (CD)

STOP IN THE NAME OF LOVE (ORIG LONDON CAST 1990) *with*
Fabulous Singlettes Live From The Piccadilly on
FIRST NIGHT (Pinn): OCRCD 6017 (CD)

STOP MAKING SENSE (LIVE CONCERT FILM 1984) Music by
DAVID BYRNE and TALKING HEADS *remixed, remastered,
re-edited by* DAVID BYRNE and containing 7 extra
tracks not on original *EMI: 522 453-2 (CD) -4 (MC)*

STOP THE WORLD I WANT TO GET OFF (ORIG LONDON CAST 61)
1.*with* MIKE HOLOWAY-LOUISE GOLD and The NSO ENSEMBLE
(Martin Yates, MD) *TER (Koch): CDTER 1226 (CD)*

STOREFRONT HITCHCOCK (1998) Music sco: ROBYN HITCHCOCK
-S/T- *WARNER: 9362 46848-2 (CD)*

STORMY MONDAY (1988) Music sco: MIKE FIGGIS also music
by B.B.KING -S/T- *VIRGIN (EMI): CDV 2537 (CD)*

STORMY WEATHER (1943 FILM CAST) *feat* LENA HORNE-BENNY
CARTER-CAB CALLOWAY AND HIS BAND-FATS WALLER etc.
*SANDY HOOK (Silver Sounds): CDSH 2037 (CD) also on
DEFINITIVE (Discovery): SFCD 33505 (CD) and*

STORY OF JOAN OF ARC - see MESSENGER

STORY OF THREE LOVES The (1953) 'Rhapsody On A Theme
Of Paganini' (RACHMANINOV) on 'CLASSIC EXPERIENCE'
EMI PREMIER (EMI): CDCLEXP 1 (2CD) TCLEXP 1 (2MC)

STRADIVARI (1989) -S/T- Class Mus: TELEMANN-H.PURCELL
VIVALDI-PACHELBEL-HANDEL -S/T- *PHIL: 422849-2 (CD)*

STRAIGHT STORY The (1999) Music sc: ANGELO BADALAMENTI
-S/T- *RCA (BMG): 01934 11513-2 (CD)*

STRAIGHT TO HELL (1987) Mus: POGUES-JOE STRUMMER-ELVIS
COSTELLO-PRAY FOR RAIN-ZANDER SCHLOSS -S/T- on
RERERTOIRE (Pinn): REP 4224WY (CD)

STRANGE DAYS (1995) Music sco: GRAEME REVELL -S/T- inc
"While The Earth Sleeps" PETER GABRIEL-DEEP FOREST
EPIC (Ten): 480 984-2 (CD) -4 (MC)

STRANGE REPORT (ITV 21/9/68) theme music by ROGER WEBB
see COLL.360,

STRANGER The (Lo Straniero) (1967) Music score: PIERO
PICCIONE -S/T- score includes 'THE INNOCENT'
DRG (Pinn): DRGCD 3292-2 (CD)

STRANGER THAN PARADISE (1986) + 'The Resurrection of
Albert Ayler' Music sco: JOHN LURIE -S/T- score
MADE TO MEASURE (New Note-Pinn): MTM 7 (CD)

STREET SCENE (SHOW 1989) Songs: KURT WEILL-LANGSTON
HUGHES / O.LONDON CAST *feat* KRISTINE CIESINSKI-
JANIS KELLY-RICHARD VAN ALLAN-CATHERINE ZETA JONES
BONAVENTURA BOTTONE *TER (Koch): CDTER2 1185 (2CD)*

STREETCAR NAMED DESIRE A (1951) Music sco: ALEX NORTH
Orchestral score: NATIONAL PHILHARMONIC ORCH cond.
by JERRY GOLDSMITH *VARESE (Pinn): VSD 5500 (CD)*

STREETCAR NAMED DESIRE A (1951) Music sco: ALEX NORTH
Orchestral score: NATIONAL PHILHARMONIC ORCH cond.
by JERRY GOLDSMITH *VARESE (Pinn): VSD 5500 (CD)*
also avail.on CLOUD NINE (S.Screen): CNS 5003 (CD)
with symphonic suites from 'The INFORMER' (35-Max
Steiner) 'NOW VOYAGER' (42-Max STEINER) & 'SINCE
YOU WENT AWAY' (44-Max STEINER) *Archive Series*

STREETFIGHTER (1994) Music sco: GRAEME REVELL 2 -S/T-
Songs: *VIRGIN: CDPTY(PTYMC)(PTYLP) 114 (CD/MC/LP)*
Score: *VARESE (Pinn): VSD 5560 (CD)*

STREETHAWK (USA84 ITV) m: TANGERINE DREAM *see COLL.17,*

STREETS APART (BBC1 1988) mus:DAVE MACKAY *see COLL.19,*

STREETS OF FIRE (1984) Songs: JIM STEINMAN -S/T- *reiss*
Beat Goes On (Pinn): BGO(CD)(MC) 220 (CD/MC) also
Import: MCA USA (Silva Screen) MCAD 5492 (CD)

STREETS OF SAN FRANCISCO (USA) Music by PAT WILLIAMS
see COLL.122,270,347,359,382,

STRICTLY BALLROOM (1992) Music sco: DAVID HIRSCHFELDER
-S/T- reissue *COLUMBIA (Ten): 472300-2*

STRIKE UP THE BAND (40) Songs: GEORGE & IRA GERSHWIN
new recording on *VIRGIN (EMI): VM 561247-2 (CD)*
ORIG USA CAST Brent Barrett-Rebecca Luker-Don Chas
tain-J.Mauceri *ELEKTRA-Nones: 7559 79273-2(CD) -4*

STRIPPER The (1963) Music score: JERRY GOLDSMITH -S/T-
-S/T- *TSUNAMI Imp (Silva Screen): TCI 0613 (CD) +*
-S/T- to 'The TRAVELLING EXCECUTIONER' (GOLDSMITH)
see COLL.1,

STUDENT PRINCE The - songs by Sigmund Romberg
1.FILM MUSICAL 1954 *with:* MARIO LANZA *RCA Red Seal*
(BMG): GD(GK) 60048 (CD/MC) with: The DESERT SONG
2.STUDIO REC.1990 *with:* NORMAN BAILEY-MARILYN HILL
SMITH-DIANA MONTAGUE-DAVID RENDALL-ROSEMARY ASHE
Highlights: *TER (Koch): CDTEO 1005 (CD)*
Complete: *TER (Koch): CDTER2 1172 (2CDs)*
3.STUDIO RECORDING *with:* GORDON MacRAE and Company
see under 'DESERT SONG The'

STUFF THE WHITE RABBIT (Granada 3/6/96)theme "I Put A
Spell On You" (Jay Hawkins) NINA SIMONE on Coll
'The 60's Vol.1' *MERCURY (Univ): 838 543-2 (CD)*

STUPIDS The (1996) Music sco: CHRISTOPHER STONE -S/T-
INTRADA USA (Silva Screen) MAF 7071 (CD)

SUCH A LONG JOURNEY (1999) Music by JONATHAN GOLDSMITH
-S/T- *NETTWERK (Pinn): 6242 840008-2 (CD)*

SUDDEN DEATH (1995) Music score: JOHN DEBNEY -S/T- on
VARESE (Pinn): VSD 5663 (CD)

SUGAR (songs: Jule Styne-Bob Merrill)
ORIG BROADWAY CAST (1972) *feat:* ROBERT MORSE-TONY
ROBERTS-CYRIL RITCHARD-ELAINE JOYCE-SHEILA SMITH
RYKODISC (Vital): RCD 10760 (CD)

SUGARFOOT (aka TENDERFOOT) (USA 1960's) theme music
by MAX STEINER & RAY HEINDORF *see COLL.178,*

SUMMER HOLIDAY (FILM MUSIC.1963) CLIFF RICHARD-Shadows
-S/T- *MFP (EMI): TCMFP 5824 (MC) CDMFP 6021 (CD)*
see COLL.296,

SUMMER HOLIDAY (MUSICAL 96 Opera House Blackpool 1996)
  w:DARREN DAY-CLARE BUCKFIELD-ROSS KING-FAITH BROWN
  RCA (BMG): 74321 45616-2 (CD) -4 (MC)
  DARREN DAY *MEDLEY: RCA (BMG): 74321 38447-2 (CDs)*
SUMMER MAGIC - *see* WALT DISNEY INDEX p.362
SUMMER OF LOVE (umbrella title for C4 series beginning
  14 AUG 1999) Collection of music (inspired by the
  series) on *EMI-VIRGIN-C4: VTDCD 280 (2CD)*
SUMMER OF SAM (1999) Music sc: TERENCE BLANCHARD -S/T-
  V/A MARVIN GAYE/ABBA/WHO/ROY AYERS/GRACE JONES etc
  EDEL-HOLLYWOOD (Pinn): 012 190-2HWR (CD)
SUMMER'S LEASE (BBC2 1/11/89) theme "Carmina Valles"
  NIGEL HESS sung CHAMELEON *see COLL.149,193,*
SUN VALLEY SERENADE (1941 MUSICAL) *w* GLENN MILLER BAND
  and TEX BENEKE *includ.songs from* 'ORCHESTRA WIVES'
  TARGET (BMG): CD 60002 (CD)
SUNBURN (BBC1 16/01/1999) mus: JULIAN NOTT *unavailable*
  songs: "Sunburn" sung by MICHELLE COLLINS on
  BBC AUDIO INT (Pinn): WMSS 6008-2 (CDs) -4 (MC)
  "Can't Smile Without You" sung by JAMES BULLER on
  BBC AUDIO INT (Pinn): WMSS 6009-2 (CDs) -4 (MC)
SUNDAY BLOODY SUNDAY (71) *see COLL.273,274,*
SUNDAY IN THE PARK WITH GEORGE (O.BROADWAY CAST 1984)
  Songs: STEPHEN SONDHEIM Mandy PATINKIN-Bernadette
  PETERS *RCA (BMG):RD 85042 (CD) RK 85042 (MC)*
SUNDOWN: THE VAMPIRE IN RETREAT (1990) Music: RICHARD
  STONE -S/T- *SILVA SCREEN (Koch): FILMCD 044 (CD)*
SUNNY (ORIG LONDON CAST 1926) Songs (Jerome Kern-Oscar
  Hammerstein II) *feat:* JACK BUCHANAN-BINNIE HALE-
  PEARL (Pavilion): GEMMCD 9105 (CD)
SUNSET (O.OFF-BROADWAY CAST 1984) Music: GARY WILLIAM
  FRIEDMAN Words: WILL HOLT *feat* TAMMY GRIMES-RONEE
  BLAKELY-KIM MILFORD   *TER (Koch): CDTER 1180 (CD)*
SUNSET BOULEVARD - songs by Andrew Lloyd Webber
 1a ORIG LONDON CAST 1993 PATTI LuPONE-KEVIN ANDERSON
  REALLY USEFUL (Univ): 519 767-2 (2CD) -4 (2MC)
 1b Highlights *POLYDOR (Univ): 527 241-2 (CD) -4 (MC)*
 2. USA STAGE CAST 1994 *with:* GLENN CLOSE and Company
  REALLY USEFUL (Univ): 523 507-2 (2CD) -4 (2MC)
SUNSET BOULEVARD (1950) Music sco: FRANZ WAXMAN on Col
  'Sunset Boulevard' *RCA (BMG): RD 87017 (CD only)*
SUPER MARIO BROS. (1993) Music of Various Arts -S/T-
  CAPITOL: CDESTU 2201 (CD)
SUPERCAR (ITV 9/61) music: BARRY GRAY *see COLL.5,360,*
SUPERFLY (1972) Music by CURTIS MAYFIELD -S/T- reiss.
  with 'SHORT EYES' *SEQUEL (BMG): NEMCD 964 (2CD) +
  NEMLP 964 (LP) / also on CHARLY: CDNEW 1302 (2CDs)*
SUPERGIRL (1984) Music score: JERRY GOLDSMITH -S/T-
  SILVA SCREEN (Koch): FILMCD 132 (CD)
SUPERMAN THE MOVIE (1978) Music score: JOHN WILLIAMS
  new recording by SCOTTISH NATIONAL ORCHESTRA cond.
  JOHN WILLIAMS *VARESE (Pinn): VSD 25981 (2CD)*
  see COLL.120,121,122,198,203,229,264,267,307,311,
                              334,345,403,404,

SUPERMAN (LOIS AND CLARK) - see 'New Adventures of Superman' *see COLL.351,*
SUPERMAN THE ULTIMATE COLLECTION VARIOUS ARTISTS *VARESE (Pinn): VSD 5998 (CD)*
SUPERNATURAL (BBC1 30/03/1999) Music sco: WILL GREGORY *unavailable*
SUPERSTARS (BBC 80s) *see COLL.176,*
SUPERTED! - *see COLL.186,*
SURVIVAL: THE MUSIC OF NATURE (Anglia TV) Various Arts *VIRGIN (EMI): VTCD 148 (CD) see also* 'MADAGASCAR' and 'DESERT SONG' *music by various composers*
SURVIVAL GUIDE (BBC2 14/6/1998) series theme music by NIGEL BEAHAM POWELL and BELLA RUSSELL *unavailable*
SURVIVAL OF THE ILLEST VARIOUS HIP-HOP ARTISTS *DEF JAM (Univ): 538 176-2 (CD) -4 (MC) -1 (LP)*
SURVIVING PICASSO (1996) Mus: RICHARD ROBBINS -S/T- V.Arts *EPIC Soundtrax (SM): 486 820-2 (CD)*
SUSPIRIA (1976) Music score: DARIO ARGENTO by GOBLIN -S/T- *CINEVOX Ita (Silva Screen): CDCIA 5005 (CD) CIAK 75005 (MC) see also COLL* 'SIMONETTI PROJECT'
SUTHERLAND'S LAW (UKGO 18/2/95 orig BBC1 6/6/73) theme music (Hamish MacCunn) SCOTTISH NATIONAL ORCHESTRA conduct: Alexander Gibson *CHANDOS: CHAN 8379 (CD)*
SUZY (1936) *COLLECTION with* 'SAN FRANCISCO'/'DAMES' on *GREAT MOVIE THEMES (Targ-BMG): CD 60022 (CD)*
SWAN PRINCESS The (1994) Songs: LEX DE AVEZEDO & DAVID ZIPPEL *feat* LIZ CALLOWAY *SONY WOND: 483772-2 (CD)*
SWAP SHOP - *see COLL.186,*
S.W.A.T. (USA TV) *see COLL.347,382,*
SWEENEY The (Thames 2/1/75) theme music: HARRY SOUTH *see COLL.2,6,109,110,270,359,360,390,*
SWEENEY TODD (O.BROADWAY CAST 1979) Songs: STEPHEN SONDHEIM *feat:* ANGELA LANSBURY-LEN CARIOU *RCA Imp (S.Screen): 3379-2 (2CD)* HIGHLIGHTS *RCD1 5033 (CD)*
SWEET CHARITY - songs by Cy Coleman and Dorothy Fields
  1.FILM MUSICAL 1969 *SHIRLEY MacLAINE-SAMMY DAVIS JR. CHITA RIVERA -S/T- EMI AMERICA: ZDM 746562-2 (CD)*
  2.STUDIO RECORD 1995 JACQUELINE DANKWORTH-GREGG EDELMAN-JOSPEHINE BLAKE-SHEZWAE POWELL-DAVID HEALEY *TER (Koch): CDTER2 1222 (2CD, 09.1998)*
  3.ORIG BROADWAY CAST 1966 *with:* GWEN VERDON & Comp. *CBS USA (S.Screen): CK 02900 (CD) JST 02900 (MC)*
  4.ORIG LONDON CAST 1967 JULIET PROWSE-ROD MacLENNAN JOSEPHINE BLAKE-ROGER FINCH-PAULA KELLY-JOHN KESTON etc.*SONY WEST END (TEN): SMK 66172 (CD)*
SWEET HEREAFTER The (1997) Music score: MYCHAEL DANNA -S/T- (VAR.ARTS) *VIRGIN (EMI): CDVIR 68 (CD)*
SWEET ROSIE O'GRADY (1943 FILM CAST) *feat* BETTY GRABLE inc.selection from 'SPRINGTIME IN THE ROCKIES' *SANDY HOOK (Silver Sounds): CDSH 2090 (CD)*
SWEET SMELL OF SUCCESS The (1957) Music score: ELMER BERNSTEIN with songs by CHICO HAMILTON & FRED KATZ -S/T- incl. 'WALK ON THE WILD SIDE' (1962 -S/T-) *Import (Silva Screen): TT 3002 (CD)*

SWEPT FROM THE SEA (1998) Music sco: JOHN BARRY -S/T-
   DECCA (Univ): 458 793-2 (CD)
SWING (1998) VARIOUS ARTISTS inc LISA STANSFIELD -S/T-
   BMG SOUNDTRACKS: 74321 66923-2 (CD)
SWING KIDS (1993) Music score: JAMES HORNER -S/T-
   MILAN (BMG): 14210-2 (CD) 14210-4 (MC) see also
SWING TIME (1936) *with* FRED ASTAIRE-GINGER ROGERS
   -S/T- *selection on* 'Let's Swing and Dance' + songs
   from 'FOLLOW THE FLEET'/'TOP HAT'/'CAREFREE'
   GREAT MOVIE THEMES (Target-BMG): CD 60015 (CD)
   +'FOLLOW THE FLEET'*IRIS Mus-Chansons Cin (Discov):*
   CIN 006 (CD)   see COLL.21,128,228,255,
SWINGERS (1996) Music score: JUSTIN REINHARDT -S/T-
   Various Artists *POLYDOR (Univ): 162 091-2 (CD)*
SWISS FAMILY ROBINSON 2 (1999) Music score: JOHN SCOTT
   -S/T- *JOHN SCOTT REC (Silva Screen): JSCD 126 (CD)*
SWITCH (USA TV) *see COLL.349,*
SWORD IN THE STONE - *see* WALT DISNEY INDEX p.362
SWORDSMAN OF SIENNA (1962) *see COLL.338,*

TAFFETAS The (O.OFF-BROADWAY CAST 1988) by RICK LEWIS
   with Jody ABRAHAMS-Karen CURLEE-Melanie MITCHELL-
   Tia SPEROS *TER (Koch): CDTER 1167 (CD)*
TAGGART (Scottish TV began 2/7/85) music: MIKE MORAN
   theme song "No Mean City" sung by MAGGIE BELL
   -S/T- *SOUNDTRACKS EMI GOLD: 521 942-2 (CD)*
   see COLL.270,390,
TAKE ME HIGH (1973) songs TONY COLE *feat* CLIFF RICHARD
   EMI: CDEMC 3641 (CD) with 'HELP IT ALONG' album
   see COLL 'CLIFF RICHARD: AT THE MOVIES'
TAKE ME HOME (BBC1 2/5/89) theme "The Very Thing" from
   'Raintown' DEACON BLUE *SONY: 450549-2 (CD) -4 (MC)*
TAKE THREE GIRLS (BBC2 1971) theme "Light Flight" by
   PENTANGLE from 'Basket Of Light' *Transatlantic-*
   Essential (BMG): ESMCD 406 (CD) see COLL.23,
TAKING OF PELHAM 1,2,3 (1974) Music score: DAVID SHIRE
   -S/T- *RETROGRADE (Hot/Sil.Sounds) FSM 80123-2 (CD)*
TALE OF TWO CITIES, A (1958) *see COLL.9,*
TALENT TO AMUSE, A (SHOW 1995) Songs: NOEL COWARD *feat*
   PETER GREENWELL *rec.Swan Theatre STRATFORD-UPON-*
   AVON SIL.SCREEN (Koch): SILVAD(SILKC) 3009 (CD/MC)
TALES FROM THE CRYPT (USA TV) *see COLL.351,*
TALES FROM THE DARKSIDE-THE MOVIE (90) Music (Donald B
   Rubinstein-Pat Regan-Jim Manzie-Chaz Jankel) -S/T-
   GNP (ZYX): GNPD 8021(CD) GNP-5 8021 (MC)
TALES OF BEATRIX POTTER (1971) Music: JOHN LANCHBERRY
   ROYAL OPERA HOUSE ORCHESTRA (John Lanchbery) -S/T-
   re-issued on *CFP (EMI): CDCFP 6074   (CD)*
   see also (TT1998)'WORLD OF PETER RABBIT & FRIENDS'
TALES OF THE UNEXPECTED (Ang.79-87) theme: RON GRAINER
   see COLL.8,149,270,360,363,
TALL MEN The - *see COLL.1,*
TAMING OF THE SHREW The (1967) Music score: NINO ROTA
   NEW RECORDING *DRG (Pinn): DRGCD 32928 (CD)*

TANGO (1997) Music score by LALO SCHIFRIN -S/T- on
   DG (Universal): 459 145-2 (CD)
TARAS BULBA (1962) Music score: FRANZ WAXMAN -S/T-
   *RYKODISC (Vital): RCD 10736 (CD) / also on Import
   TARAN (Silver Sounds): W 9107 (CD)*
   see COLL.203,330,385,395,
TARZAN (1999) Music score by MARK MANCINA
   "You'll Be In My Heart" and other songs composed
   and sung by PHIL COLLINS -S/T- on
   DISNEY-EDEL (Pinn): 010247-2DNY (CD) -4DNY (MC)
   DISNEY-EDEL: 010248-2DNY (CD) 010249-4DNY (MC)
   see COLL.346, see also WALT DISNEY INDEX p.362
TASTE THE BLOOD OF DRACULA see *COLL.180,208,*
TATIE DANIELLE (France 1990) - *see* AUNTIE DANIELLE

TAXI (USA1979/BBC1 17/4/80) Mus: BOB JAMES 'The Genie:
   Themes & Variations from TV Series TAXI'+ "Angela"
   (theme m) *ESSENTIAL-CASTLE (Pinn): ESMCD 465 (CD)*
   see COLL.17,256,281,347,363,
TAXI (1999) Music score: IAM -S/T- + VARIOUS ARTISTS
   COLUMBIA (TEN/Sony Eur-Discovery): 489990-2 (CD)
TAXI DRIVER (1976) Music score BERNARD HERRMANN
   SIMPLY VINYL (Telstar): SVLP 60 (LP)
   also ARISTA (BMG): 78221 9005-1 (LP)
   previously unreleased tracks and new dialogue on
   ARISTA (BMG): 07822 19005-2 (CD) also 258 774 (CD)
   see COLL.70,121,188,190,192,359,
TEA WITH MUSSOLINI (1998) Music score composed by
   ALESSIO VLAD and STEFANO ARNALDI -S/T- on
   *FIRST NIGHT (Pinn): REELCD 101 (CD) / also import
   DRG (New Note/Pinn): DRGCD 12618 (CD)*
TEACHING MRS.TINGLE (1999) Music score: JOHN FRIZZELL
   -S/T- *VARESE (Pinn): VSD 6064 ()CD)*
TEENAGE OPERA, A (1967 musical) songs by MARK WIRTZ
   feat KEITH WEST & others. *RPM (Pinn): RPM 165 (CD)*
TELETUBBIES (BBC1 31/3/97) m.dir: ANDREW McCRORY-SHAND
   'TELETUBBIES' *BBC (BMG): WMXU 0014-2 (CD) -4 (MC)*
   'Fun With The TELETUBBIES' *BBC: YBBC 2063 (MC)*
TELEVISION NEWSREEL (BBC 1950's) theme "Girls in Grey"
   CHARLES WILLIAMS see *COLL.57,172,*
TELL ME ON A SUNDAY (STUDIO RECORDING 1979) Songs by
   DON BLACK-ANDREW LLOYD WEBBER *with* MARTI WEBB
   POLY: 833 447-2 (CD) see *COLL.231,232,233,234,397,*
TEN COMMANDMENTS The (1956) Music sco: ELMER BERNSTEIN
   -S/T- *TSUNAMI Imp (Sil.Screen): TSU 0123 (CD) and*
   -S/T- *MCA USA (Silva Screen): MCAD 42320 (CD)*
TEN THINGS I HATE ABOUT YOU (1998) Mus: RICHARD GIBBS
   -S/T- *HOLLYWOOD-EDEL (Pinn): 010254-2HWR (CD)*
TEN TO MIDNIGHT (1983) - *see under* 'DEATH WISH'

TENANT OF WILDFELL HALL The (BBC1 17/11/96)
   Music score: RICHARD G.MITCHELL -S/T- on
   Trident-New Mill. (Pinn): KCCD 4 (CD) KCMC 4 (MC)
TENDERFOOT (aka SUGARFOOT) (USA) see *COLL.178,*

TENDERLOIN (ORIG BROADWAY CAST 1960) Songs: JERRY BOCK
    SHELDON HARNICK *feat:* MAURICE EVANS and Company
    EMI Angel: ZDM 565 022-2 (CD)

TENEBRAE (1982) Music score composed and performed by
    GOBLIN -S/T- *CINEVOX (S.Screen): CDCIA 5035 (CD)*
    inc 'Zombie' *see COLL.319,*

TERMINATOR The (1984) Music sc: BRAD FIEDEL definitive
    edition *EDEL-CINERAMA (Pinn): 0022082CIN (CD) also*
    SILVA SCREEN (Koch): FILM(C)(CD) 101 (LP/MC/CD)
    see COLL.70,203,264,304,305,311,362,

TERMINATOR 2 (1991) Music sco: BRAD FIEDEL -S/T- score
    VARESE (Pinn): VSD(VSC) 5335 (CD/MC)
    special edition *VARESE (Pinn): VSD 5861 (CD)*
    see COLL.200,229,304,305,306,

TERMS OF ENDEARMENT (1983) Music by MICHAEL GORE -S/T-
    CAPITOL (S.Screen): 46076-2 (CD)   *see COLL.204,*

TERRORISTS The - *see* RANSOM

TERRY PRATCHETT'S DISCWORLD *see* DISCWORLD / SOUL MUSIC

TEST CRICKET (C4 22/07/1999) "Mambo No.5" (P.Prado) by
    LOU BEGA *RCA: 74321 69672-2 (CDs) -4 (MC) -1 (12")*
    'A LITTLE BIT OF MAMBO' *RCA: 74321 68861-2 (CD)*

TEST CRICKET (BBC 'til 1998) "Soul Limbo" by BOOKER T.
    & The MG's.'Great Sporting Experience' Collection
    EMI: CDGOAL 1 (2CD) see COLL.148,257,

TESTAMENT (C4 6/11/88) theme: NIGEL HESS *see COLL.193,*

TESTAMENT OF YOUTH (BBC2 4/11/79 also BBC2 3/10/92)
    theme music: GEOFFREY BURGON *see COLL.61,*

TESTAMENT: THE BIBLE IN ANIMATION (BBC2 16/10/96)
    mus "Adiemus" by KARL JENKINS from 'ADIEMUS-SONGS
    OF SANCTUARY' *VIRGIN (EMI): CD(TC)VE 925 (CD/MC)*
    see COLL.12,

TESTED TO DESTRUCTION (ITV 26/07/1999) title music by
    DAVID ARNOLD *unavailable*

TFI FRIDAY (Ginger Pr/C4 9/2/96) opening mus "Man In A
    Suitcase" by RON GRAINER *see* 'MAN IN A SUITCASE'
    see COLL.4,8,23,185,360,365,

THANK YOUR LUCKY STARS (1943 FILM CAST) -S/T- select:
    SANDY HOOK (Silver Sounds): CDSH 2012 (CD)

THANK YOUR LUCKY STARS (ATV 1960's) theme music: PETER
    KNIGHT *see COLL.4,23,377,*

THANKS A MILLION (FILM CAST 1935) -S/T- w: DICK POWELL
    PAUL WHITEMAN BAND incl. -S/T- to 'ON THE AVENUE'
    SANDY HOOK (Silver Sounds): CDSH(CSH) 2012 (CD/MC)

THAT'S ENTERTAINMENT (1974) VARIOUS ART.COMPILATION
    -S/T- *16 tracks EMI SOUNDTRACK: CDODEON 21 (CD)*

THAT'S ENTERTAINMENT 3 (1994) Mus: MARC SHAIMAN -S/T-
    EMI: CDQ 555215-2 (CD) -4 (MC)

THAT'S THE WAY IT IS *see* ELVIS PRESLEY INDEX p.360

THELMA & LOUISE (1991) Music score: HANS ZIMMER -S/T-
    reissue MCA (BMG): MCLD 19313 (CD)

THERE'S NO BUSINESS LIKE SHOW BUSINESS (1954) Songs by
    IRVING BERLIN *feat* MARILYN MONROE-ETHEL MERMAN-DAN
    DAILEY-DONALD O'CONNOR. *DIGITALLY RE-MIXED -S/T-*
    FOX CLASSICS-VARESE (Pinn): VSD 5912 (CD)

THERE'S SOMETHING ABOUT MARY (1998) music VAR.ARTISTS
  -S/T- *EMI PREMIER: 495 737-2 (CD)*
THEY CALL ME MR.TIBBS! (1970) Music sco: QUINCY JONES
  -S/T- inc.mus.from 'IN THE HEAT OF THE NIGHT (67)
  RYKODISC (Vital): RCD 10712 (CD)
THEY DIED WITH THEIR BOOTS ON (1941) Music score: MAX
  STEINER orchestrated by HUGO FRIEDHOFER.*new record*
  MOSCOW SYMPHONY ORCH conductor: Willam T.STROMBERG
  MARCO POLO Select: 8225079 (CD)
THEY THINK IT'S ALL OVER (BBC1 14/9/95) theme music by
  STEVE BROWN *unavailable*
THEY'RE PLAYING OUR SONG – songs by Marvin Hamlisch
  and Carole Bayer Sager
  1. ORIG LONDON CAST 1980 *with:* GEMMA CRAVEN-TOM CONTI
     <u>Complete</u>: *TER (Koch): CDTER 1035 (CD)*
  2. ORIG BROADWAY CAST 1979 *with:* LUCIE ARNAZ-ROBERT
     KLEIN *CASABLANCA (IMS-Poly):AA826 240-2 (CD)*
THIEF (aka Violent Streets)(1981) Mus: TANGERINE DREAM
  -S/T- TANGERINE DREAM *VIRGIN (EMI): TAND 12 (CD)*
THIEF OF BAGHDAD The (1940) Music: MIKLOS ROZSA -S/T-
  with 'JUNGLE BOOK' *COLOSS (Pinn):CST 348044 (CD)*
THIN BLUE LINE The (1989) Music score: PHILIP GLASS
  -S/T- *ELEKTRA NONESUCH (TEN): 7559 79209-2 (CD)*
THIN LINE BETWEEN LOVE AND HATE, A (1995) V.Arts inc:
  LBC CREW-TEVIN CAMPBELL-R.KELLY-ADINA HOWARD etc.
  -S/T- *WB (TEN): 9362 46134-2 (CD) -4 (MC)*
THIN RED LINE The (1997) Music score: HANS ZIMMER
  -S/T- score: *RCA VICTOR (BMG): 09026 63382-2 (CD)*
  chants: Melanesian Choirs *RCA: 09026 63470-2 (CD)*
THING The (1982) Music score ENNIO MORRICONE -S/T-
  VARESE (Pinn): VSD 5278 (CD) VSC 5278 (MC)
THING CALLED LOVE (1993) -S/T- Var.COUNTRY Artists
  GIANT (BMG): 74321 15793-2 (CD)
THINGS TO COME *see COLL.333,*
THINNER (1996) Music score: DANIEL LICHT -S/T- on
  VARESE (Pinn): VSD 5761 (CD)
THIRD MAN The (1949) *see COLL.270,367,*
THIRTEENTH FLOOR The (1999) Music score: HARALD KLOSER
  -S/T- *MILAN (BMG): 73138 35882-2 (CD)*
THIRTEENTH WARRIOR The (1999) Music by JERRY GOLDSMITH
  -S/T- *VARESE (Pinn): VSD 6038 (CD)*
THIRTYSOMETHING (USA)(C4 18/1/89) theme: W.G.SNUFFY
  WALDEN-STEWART LEVIN *see COLL.351,*
THIS EARTH IS MINE (1959) Music score: HUGO FRIEDHOFER
  w 'THE YOUNG LIONS' *VARESE (Pinn): VSD 25403 (2CD)*
THIS GUN FOR HIRE (1942) MUSICAL *feat* VERONICA LAKE-
  ALAN LADD *incl.*songs from 'BATHING BEAUTY' & 'HERE
  COMES THE WAVES' *TARGET (BMG): CD 60001 (CD)*
THIS IS MODERN ART (C4 06/06/1999) theme "Cassette" by
  FRIDGE from 'Semaphore' *OUTPUT (SRD): OPR12CD (CD)*
THIS IS SPINAL TAP (1984) Music comp/sung by SPINAL
  TAP -S/T- *RAZOR-Castle (Pinn): LUSLP(MC)2 (LP/MC)*
THIS IS THE ARMY (1943 FILM CAST) -S/T- selection on
  SANDY HOOK (Silver Sounds): CDSH 2035 (CD)

THIS IS YOUR LIFE (BBC1 1994-99/ITV 1968-93) series
  theme music "Gala Performance" by LAURIE JOHNSON
  see COLL.6,215,270,
THIS MORNING (ITV 3/10/88-2000) theme music by DAVID
  PRINGLE and RAY MONK *unavailable*
THIS WEEK (ITV) theme "Alla Marcia 3 -Karelia Suite"
  (Sibelius) Academy of Saint Martin-in-the-Fields
  (Neville Marriner) *PHILIPS (Univ): 412727-2 (CD)*
THIS WORLD THEN THE FIREWORKS (1997) Orig.Jazz score
  PETE RUGOLO / *songs* "The Thrill Is Gone" and "You
  Don't Know" performed by CHET BAKER -S/T- on
  VARESE (Pinn): VSD 5860 (CD)
THIS YEARS LOVE (1998) Music score: SIMON BOSWELL
  -S/T- *V2 (3MV-Pinn): VVR 100636-2 (CD)*
THOMAS AND THE KING Songs: John Williams-James Harbert
  O.LONDON CAST 1975: JAMES SMILLIE-DILYS HAMLETT-
  LEWIS FIANDER-RICHARD JOHNSON-CAROLINE VILLIERS
  TER (Koch): CDTER 1009 (CD, reiss 09.1998)
THOMAS CROWN AFFAIR The (1999) Music score: BILL CONTI
  "Windmills Of Your Mind" (Legrand-Bergman) STING
  -S/T- *(USA IMPORT) PANGEA 810049 (CD)*
THOMAS CROWN AFFAIR The (1968) Music by MICHEL LEGRAND
  Song "Windmills Of Your Mind" (Lyr: Alan & Marilyn
  Bergman) sung by NOEL HARRISON -S/T- *reissued on*
  RYKODISC (Vital): RCD 10719 (CD)   see COLL.71,128,
THOMAS THE TANK ENGINE & FRIENDS (ITV 25/2/92) theme m
  JUNIOR CAMPBELL-MIKE O'DONNELL *MFP (EMI): TCMFP*
  6104 (MC) theme also on Coll 'TV TUNES FOR KIDS'
THORN BIRDS The (USA BBC1 8/1/84) music: HENRY MANCINI
  see COLL.155,
THORN BIRDS 2: Missing Years (1995) M: GARRY MacDONALD
  LAURIE STONE -S/T- *VARESE (Pinn): VSD 5712 (CD)*
THOUSAND ACRES, A (1997) Music score: RICHARD HARTLEY
  -S/T- *VARESE (Pinn): VSD 5870 (CD)*
THREE COINS IN THE FOUNTAIN (1954) t.song (Sammy CAHN-
  Jule STYNE) sung by FRANK SINATRA 'Screen Sinatra'
  MFP (EMI): CD(TC)MFP 6052 (CD/MC) see COLL
THREE COLEURS: BLEU-BLANC-ROUGE (1993-94) M: ZBIGNIEW
  PREISNER *VIRGIN Fra (EMI): CDVMM 15 (3 CDbox set)*
THREE COLOURS: BLUE (1993) Music sc: ZBIGNIEW PREISNER
  VIRGIN France (EMI): CDVMM 12 (CD)
THREE COLOURS: RED (1994) Music sc: ZBIGNIEW PREISNER
  VIRGIN Fra (EMI): CDVMM 14 (CD) or 839 784-2 (CD)
THREE COLOURS: WHITE (1993) Music s: ZBIGNIEW PREISNER
  VIRGIN France (EMI): 839 472-2 (CD)
THREE DAYS OF THE CONDOR (1975) Music sco: DAVE GRUSIN
  -S/T- *LEGEND Impt.(Silva Screen): LEGENDCD 27 (CD)*
THREE MUSKETEERS The (1935) Music sco: MAX STEINER **new**
  record BRANDENBURG S.ORCH. (Kaufman) + other items
  MARCO POLO (Select): 8.223607 (CD)
THREE MUSKETEERS The (1993) Music score: MICHAEL KAMEN
  -S/T- *A.& M. (IMS-Poly): E.540 190-2 (CD)*
THREE O'CLOCK HIGH (1987) Music score: TANGERINE DREAM
  -S/T- *VARESE (Pinn): VCD 47307 (CD)*

THREE SISTERS (1970) Music sco: Sir WILLIAM WALTON New
  Recording by Academy of St.Martin-in-the-Fields
  (Neville Marriner) *CHANDOS: CHAN 8870 (CD)*
THREE STOOGES The (USA) *see COLL.346,*
THREE TENORS CONCERT 1998 Paris LUCIANO PAVAROTTI-
  PLACIDO DOMINGO-JOSE CARRERAS; JAMES LEVINE (cond)
  DECCA: 460 500-2 (CD) -4 (MC) / 056 212-3 (VHS)
THREE TENORS CONCERT 1994 (BBC1 17/7/94) JOSE CARRERAS
  PLACIDO DOMINGO-LUCIANO PAVAROTTI and ZUBIN MEHTA
  (cond) *TELDEC (TEN): 4509 96200-2 (CD) -4 (MC)
  -5 (MD) 4509 962013 (VHS Video)*
THREE TENORS CONCERT 1990 (C4 7/9/90) JOSE CARRERAS
  PLACIDO DOMINGO-LUCIANO PAVAROTTI and ZUBIN MEHTA
  (cond) *DECCA (Univ): 430 433-2 (CD) -4 (MC)*
THREE TOUGH GUYS - *see* TRUCK TURNER
THREE WORLDS OF GULLIVER (1959) Music score by
  BERNARD HERRMANN *see COLL.188,192,*
THREEPENNY OPERA 1.(ORIG DONMAR WAREHOUSE CAST 1994/5)
  Songs: KURT WEILL-MARC BLITZSTEIN *w:* TARA HUGO-TOM
  MANNION-SHARON SMALL-TOM HOLLANDER-SIMON DORMANDY
  TER (Koch): CDTER 1227 (CD)
THREEPENNY OPERA 2.(ORIG BROADWAY CAST 1954) Songs by:
  KURT WEILL-MARC BLITZSTEIN *feat* LOTTE LENYA & Comp
  TER (Koch): CDTER 1101 (CD)
THUNDERBALL (1965) Music sco: JOHN BARRY title song by
  John Barry-Don Black) sung by TOM JONES -S/T-
  EMI: CZ 556 (CD) see COLL.27,34,41,53,54,55,314,
  see also JAMES BOND FILM INDEX p.358
THUNDERBIRDS! (ATV/ITC 30/9/1965-66 / BBC2 20/9/1991)
  theme music by BARRY GRAY
  see COLL.2,18,23,38,122,150,171,267,270,296,307,
                    311,349,360,362,367,369,377,
TICKLE ME *see* ELVIS PRESLEY INDEX p.360
TIGER BAY (1959) Music by LAURIE JOHNSON
  see COLL.215,217,
TIGHTROPE (USA TV) *see COLL.348,*

TILL THE CLOUDS ROLL BY (FILM MUS.1946,JEROME KERN)
  FRANK SINATRA-JUDY GARLAND-TONY MARTIN-LENA HORNE
  SANDY HOOK (Silver Sounds): CDSH 2080 (CD)
TILLY TROTTER (Catherine Cookson's) (ITV 08/01/1999)
  music by COLIN TOWNS *unavailable*
TIME AFTER TIME (1979) Music score by MIKLOS ROZSA
  -S/T- *SOUTHERN CROSS Import (HOT): SCCD 1014 (CD)*
TIME MACHINE The (1960) Music (Russell Garcia) -S/T-
  GNP (ZYX): GNPD (GNP5) 8008 (CD/MC)
TIME OF THE GYPSIES (1989) Music by GORAN BREGOVICH
  -S/T- *Imp.(VIRGIN Imports): 842 764-2 (CD)*
TIME REGAINED (Le Temps Retrouve) (1999) Music score:
  JORGE ARRIAGADA -S/T- *VIRGIN FRANCE: 45355-2 (CD)*
TIME TUNNEL (USA 66) theme music: JOHN WILLIAMS
  see COLL.38,122,267,308,
TIMECOP (1993) Music score: MARK ISHAM -S/T- on
  VARESE (Pinn): VSD 5532 (CD)

TIMEWATCH (BBC2 6/11/94) opening t.music "In Trutina" from 'Carmina Burana' CARL ORFF *vers.by* LUCIA POPP *EMI Studio Plus: CDM 764328-2 (CD)*

TINA: WHAT'S LOVE GOT TO DO WITH IT (1993) Music score STANLEY CLARKE. Songs sung by TINA TURNER -S/T- on *EMI Parlophone: CDP 789 486-2 (CD) TCPCSD 128 (MC)*

TINKER TAILOR SOLDIER SPY (BBC1 10/9/79) theme "Nunc Dimittis" GEOFFREY BURGON Seaford Col.Chapel Choir *see COLL.7,61,157,*

TIP ON A DEAD JOCKEY (19557) Music score: MIKLOS ROZSA -S/T- *Import (Silva Screen): TT 3011 (CD)*

TISWAS (ATV 1970s) *see COLL.360,*

TITANIC (FILM 1997) Music score: JAMES HORNER "Love Theme" from 'The TITANIC' performed by CELINE DION -S/T- *SONY CLASSICS: SK(ST)(SM) 63213 (CD/MC/MD)* + 'Back To Titanic' *SONY CLASS: SK(ST) 60691 (CD/MC)*

  a) 'THE LAST DANCE: MUSIC FOR A VANISHING ERA' by I SALONISTI *CONIFER (BMG): 05472 77377-2 (CD)*

  b) 'TITANTIC: MELODIES FROM THE WHITE STAR MUSIC book on The TITANIC' *FLAPPER (Pinn): PASTCD 7822 (CD)*

  c) HITS AND THEMES FROM THE TITANIC AND EARLY CENTURY *DELTA MUSIC (Target-BMG): CD 6135 (CD) MC 7135(MC)* V.ARTS songs inc: MY HEART WILL GO ON-ENTERTAINER

  d) 'TITANIC: THE ULTIMATE COLLECTION' (from 5 'TITANIC' productions) 1.CURRENT 1997 film 2.The 1953 version. 3.1958 'A Night To Remember' 4.The 1996 Mini-series 5. The BROADWAY Musical. V.Arts *VARESE (Pinn): VSD 5926 (CD)*

  e) 'MUSIC INSPIRED BY THE TITANIC' (Jigs, Reels,and Palm Court Themes) and other music from the movie *HALLMARK (CHE): 30938-2 (CD) 30938-4 (MC)*

  f) 'TITANIC' The NEW WORLD ORCHESTRA plays music from the movie *EMI GOLD: 497 138-2 (CD) -4 (MC)*

  g) 'TITANIC & Other Film Scores' by JAMES HORNER *VARESE (Pinn): VSD 5943 (CD)*

  h) 'TITANIC TUNES' by The MUSICAL MURRAYS *VARESE (Pinn): VSD 5965 (CD)*

  i) 'SONGS FROM THE TITANIC ERA' NEW WHITE STAR ORCH. *VARESE (Pinn): VSD 5966 (CD)*

TITANIC THE MUSICAL (MUSICAL 1997) Songs: MAURY YESTON ORIG.BROADWAY CAST *RCA (BMG): 09026 68834-2 (CD)*

TITANIC TOWN (1998) Music score by TREVOR JONES -S/T- *ISLAND (Univ) CID 8081 (CD)*

TITFIELD THUNDERBOLT The (1952) *see COLL.22,223,*

TJ HOOKER (USA) *see COLL.350,*

TO DIE FOR (1989) Music score: CLIFF EIDELMAN / also

TO HAVE AND HAVE NOT (1945) Music score: FRANZ WAXMAN also VARIOUS -S/T- SELECTIONS *GREAT MOVIE THEMES: (Targ-BMG): CD 60032 (CD) see also* CASABLANCA

TO HAVE AND TO HOLD (1995) M: NICK CAVE-BLIXA BARGOED MICK HARVEY-S/T- *MUTE-RTM (Vit): IONIC 015CD (CD)*

TO KILL A MOCKINGBIRD (1962) Music sc: ELMER BERNSTEIN
rec.by ROYAL SCOTTISH NATIONAL ORCH (E.Bernstein)
VARESE (Pinn): VSD 5754 (CD)

TO LIVE AND DIE IN L.A. (1986) Music: WANG CHUNG -S/T-
GEFFEN-MCA Goldline (BMG): GED 24081 (CD)

TO SIR WITH LOVE (1967) Music: RON GRAINER / t.song
by LULU -S/T- also featuring The MINDBENDERS
-S/T- *RETROACTIVE (Greyhound): RECD 9004 (CD)*

TO WONG FOO (1995) var.artists inc SALT.N.PEPA-CRYSTAL
WATERS-TOM JONES-CYNDI LAUPER-LABELLE -S/T- on
MCA (BMG): MCD 11231 (CD)

TOM BROWN'S SCHOOLDAYS (1950) *see COLL.9,*

TOM JONES (BBC1 9/11/97) Music score: JIM PARKER -S/T-
OCEAN DEEP (Univ): OCD 012 (CD)

TOMBSTONE (1993) Music score: BRUCE BROUGHTON -S/T- on
INTRADA USA (Silva Screen): MAF 7038D (CD)

TOMMY (FILM ROCK OPERA 1975) Music by PETE TOWNSHEND
The WHO-ELTON JOHN etc.-S/T- *POLYD 841 121-2 (CD)*
RE-MASTERED VERSION 1996 on POLYD 531 043-2 (CD)

TOMMY (ROCK OPERA) LONDON SYMPH ORCH / PETE TOWNSHEND
Roger DALTREY-Maggie BELL-Rod STEWART-Sandy DENNY-
Ringo STARR-John ENTWISTLE-Steve WINWOOD-R.HAVENS
ESSENTIAL-CASTLE (Pinn): ESMCD 404 CD)

TOMMY (ORIG BROADWAY CAST 1993) Songs: PETE TOWNSHEND
RCA VICTOR (BMG): 09026 6187402 (CD)

TOMORROW NEVER DIES (1997) Music score: DAVID ARNOLD
title song by SHERYL CROW with end song by k.d.lang
-S/T- *A.& M: 540 830-2 (CD) -4 (MC) see COLL.3,54,*
see also JAMES BOND FILM INDEX p.358

TOMORROW PEOPLE The (Thames 30/4/73-79) music: DUDLEY
SIMPSON and BRIAN HODSON *see COLL.362,*

TOMORROW'S WORLD (BBC2 1997/1999 s) theme "In Pursuit
of Happiness" (Neil Hannon) DIVINE COMEDY 'Short
Album About Love" *SETANTA (Vital): SET(CD)(MC) 036*
and on 'SHOOTING FISH' -S/T- EMI: 7243 821495-2 CD

TONIGHT WITH TREVOR McDONALD (ITV 08/04/1999) theme m
MIKE WOOLMANS *unavailable*

TONITE LET'S ALL MAKE LOVE IN LONDON (FILM MUSIC.1967)
SEE FOR MILES (Pinn): SEECD 258 (CD)

TOP CAT (USA 62/BBC UKtitle 'Boss Cat') md HOYT CURTIN
"Top Cat" theme *see COLL.373,*

TOP GEAR (BBC2 70's-99) *Opening theme* "Jessica" ALLMAN
BROTHERS BAND on 'Brothers and Sisters' album
CAPRICORN (Univ.): 825 092-2 (CD)

TOP GEAR RALLY REPORT (BBC2 22/11/96) theme "Duel" by
PROPAGANDA from the album 'Secret Wish' on
ZTT (Pinn): ZTT 118CD (CD)

TOP GUN (1986) Music score by HAROLD FALTERMEYER
"Take My Breath Away" by BERLIN -S/T- on
COLUMBIA (Ten): CD 70296 (CD) see COLL.106,

TOP HAT (1935) FILM MUSICAL *feat* FRED ASTAIRE-GINGER
ROGERS -S/T- *sel.on* 'Let's Swing and Dance'+ songs
from 'FOLLOW THE FLEET'/'SWING TIME'/'CAREFREE'
GREAT MOVIE THEMES (Target-BMG): CD 60015 (CD)

also available a recording with 'THE GAY DIVORCEE'
IRIS-Mus-Chansons Cinema (Discovery): CIN 005 (CD)
also available with 'SHALL WE DANCE'
GREAT MOVIE THEMES (Target-BMG): CD 600423 (CD)
TOP HAT with Yehudi Menuhin (v) Stephane Grappelli
(violin/pno) + N.Riddle *CFP (EMI):CDCFP 4509 (CD)*
see COLL.21,174,

TOP OF THE FORM (BBC2 1960's) theme "Marching Strings"
(Ross) *see COLL.407,*

TOP OF THE POPS (BBC1 1/1/64-1999) various theme mus:
(from 1/5/98) "Whole Lotta Love" *re-arrangement by*
BAD MAN BAD and LED ZEPPELIN *unavailable*
(from 2/2/95) theme: VINCE CLARKE *unavailable*
(from 3/10/91) "Get Out Of That" by TONY GIBBER
(from 1986-91) "The Wizard" PAUL HARDCASTLE *delet.*
(from 1981-85) "Yellow Pearl" (M.URE-PHIL LYNOTT)
VERTIGO (Univ): PRICE(PRIMC) 88 (LP/MC)
(from 1974-80) "Whole Lotta Love" CCS *see COLL*
(orig by *LED ZEPPELIN ATLANTIC (TEN): K(2)(4)40037*
(from 1969-74) theme arrangement by JOHNNY PEARSON
(from 1965-69 o.theme: JOHNNIE STEWART-HARRY RABIN
OWITZ version by BOBBY MIDGLEY (2 versions)

TOP OF THE POPS 2 (BBC2 17/9/94) series theme music by
BILL PADLEY *unavailable*

TOP SECRET (ITV 11/8/61-62) "Sucu Sucu" LAURIE JOHNSON
see COLL.4,23,216,377,

TOPLESS WOMEN TALK ABOUT THEIR LIVES (1998) Music by
FLYING NUN -S/T- *CURVEBALL (3M-Pin): FNCD 402 (CD)*

TORA! TORA! TORA! (1970) music score: JERRY GOLDSMITH
score + 'PATTON' new rec: ROYAL SCOTTISH NAT.ORCH.
(Jerry Goldsmith) *VARESE (Pinn): VSD 5796 (CD)*

TORN CURTAIN (1966) *original score:* JOHN ADDISON
VARESE (Pinn): VSD 5817 (CD)

TORN CURTAIN (1966) *rejected score:* BERNARD HERRMANN
SILVA SCREEN (Koch): FILMCD 162 (CD) -S/T- reissue
see COLL.188,190,191,192,197,202,

TOTAL ECLIPSE (1995) Music: JAN A.P.KACZMAREK -S/T-
Var.Arts *SONY Classics (SM): SK 62037 (CD)*

TOTAL RECALL (1989) Music score: JERRY GOLDSMITH -S/T-
VARESE (Pinn): VSD 5267 (CD) VSC 5267 (MC)
see COLL.166,167,264,304,305,306,308,330,334,

TOTO THE HERO (1991) Music score by PIERRE VAN DORMAEL
"Boum" (Char.Trenet-Roma Campbell Hunter) sung by
CHARLES TRENET *EMI: CDP 794 464-2 (CD)*

TOTS TV (Ragdoll/Central 4/1/93) theme "I'm A Tot"
ANDREW McCRORIE SHAND TV -S/T- *MFP (EMI): TCMFP
6148 (MC)* theme also on 'TV TUNES FOR KIDS 2'*BMG*
-S/T- 'Tilly's Disco' *MFP (EMI): (CD)(TC) 6154*

TOUCH (1998) Music score: DAVID GROHL (FOO FIGHTERS)
-S/T- *CAPITOL-ROSWELL (EMI): 855 632-2 (CD)*

TOUCH OF CLASS, A (1973) Music score by JOHN CAMERON
"All That Love Went To Waste" (Sammy Cahn-George
Barrie) sung by MADELINE BELL -S/T- *reissue on*
DRG-NEW NOTE (Pinn): DRGCD 13115 (CD)

TOUCH OF EVIL, A (1958) Music score by HENRY MANCINI
UNIVERSAL INTERNATIONAL ORCH (Joseph Gershenson)
-S/T- *BLUE MOON (Discovery): BMCD 7050 (CD)*
VARESE (Pinn): VSD 5414 (CD) + DISCOVERY: MSCD 401

TOUCH OF FROST,A (YTV 6/12/92) music composed/perform
by BARBARA THOMPSON and JON HISEMAN *see COLL*

TOUCHE TURTLE - *see COLL.373,*

TOUCHED BY AN ANGEL (USA/BBC1 22/2/1998) theme & music
(MARC LICHTMAN) "Walk With Me" sung by DELLA REESE
-S/T- *EPIC (Ten): 491 828-3 (CD)*

TOUGH GUYS DON'T DANCE (1987) - *see* DEATH WISH

TOUR DE FRANCE (TSL/C4 1991-98) theme music composed &
peformed by PETER SHELLEY *(p.Virgin) unavailable*
note: earlier theme *see COLL.176,*

TOUS LE MATINS DU MONDE (France 1992) Music sco: JORDI
SAVALL -S/T- *AUVIDIS Valoir (H.Mundi): AUV 4640 CD*
AUV 54640 (MC)   see COLL.82,

TOWERING INFERNO The (1974) Music score: JOHN WILLIAMS
see COLL.129,371,403,

TOY STORY (1996) Mus.songs: RANDY NEWMAN "You've Got A
Friend In Me" (Newman) sung by RANDY NEWMAN -S/T-
DISNEY (Technicolor): WD 77130-2(CD) WD 771304(MC)

TOY STORY 2 (1999) Music score and songs: RANDY NEWMAN
-S/T- *DISNEY USA Impt: 60647 (CD) see also p.362*

TOYTOWN (BBC TV) *see COLL.186,*

TRACEY ULLMAN SHOW The (USA TV) *see COLL.351,*

TRACKS (BBC2 18/5/94) music 'DREAMCATCHER' composed
and performed by DAVID LOWE *unavailable*

TRADING PLACES (1983) *see COLL.85,274,*

TRAFFIK (C4 22/6/89) theme arr.FIACHRA TRENCH part of
Chamber Symph.For Strings Op.110A (SHOSTAKOVICH)
CHANDOS: CHAN 8357 (CD)

TRAGICALLY HIP (1995) -S/T- *MCA (BMG): MCLD 19314 (CD)*

TRAIL OF GUILT (BBC1 19/07/1999) mus by DEBBIE WISEMAN
unavailable

TRAINSPOTTING (1995) -S/T- VARIOUS ARTISTS
EMI:CDEMC 3739 (CD) TCEMC 3739 (MC) EMC 3739 (2LP)
VOL.2 EMI SOUNDTRACK: PRMDCD 36 (CD) PRMDTC 36(MC)

TRAP The (1966) Music sco: RON GOODWIN *theme also used
for* BBCTV 'LONDON MARATHON' coverage / Film -S/T-
(S.Screen): LXE 708 (CD) see COLL.168,169,170,176,

TRAPPER JOHN, MD (USA TV) *see COLL.350,*

TRAVELLER (1997) -S/T- VARIOUS ARTISTS
WB (TEN): 7559 62030-2 (CD)

TRAVELLING MAN (Granada 3/9/85) theme: DUNCAN BROWNE &
SEBASTION GRAHAM JONES *see COLL.7,19,*

TREAD SOFTLY STRANGER *see COLL.292,*

TREASURE ISLAND (ORIG LONDON CAST 1973)
Music: CYRIL ORNADEL Lyrics: HAL SHAPER
PRESTIGE (THE-DISC): CDSGP 9801 (CD)

TREASURE OF THE SIERRA MADRE (1948) Music score: MAX
STEINER *new rec* SLOVAK STATE PHILHARMONIC (Barry
COLEMAN, cond) + 'CHARGE OF THE LIGHT BRIGADE
CENTAUR (Comp/Pinn): CRC 2367 (CD) see COLL.65,71,

TREATY The (Thames/RTE/ABC 15/1/92) music sco: MICHEAL
   O'SUILLEABHAIN from the album 'Oilean' on
   VIRGIN Venture: CDVE 40(CD) TCVE 40(MC) VE 40(LP)
TRIAL BY JURY (Operetta) *D'Oyly Carte Opera Company*
   (GILBERT & SULLIVAN) also 'Yeomen Of The Guard'
   London (Univ): 417 358-2CD
TRIALS OF LIFE (BBC1 3/10/1990) mus sco: GEORGE FENTON
   PRESTIGE (BMG): CDSGP 030 (CD)   see COLL.6,19,
TRIBE The (C5 24/04/1999) theme "The Dream Must Stay
   Alive" sung by MERYL CASSIE / Music by SIMON MAY
   -S/T- *TO BE CONFIRMED*
TRIBUTE TO THE BLUES BROTHERS (ORIG.LONDON CAST 1991)
   feat Con O'Neill-Warwick Evans & Company
   FIRST NIGHT (Pinn): CASTCD 25 (CD) CASTC 25 (MC)
TRIP The (1967) Music score by THE ELECTRIC FLAG -S/T-
   CURB USA (Greyhound/Silver Sounds): D.277836 (CD)
TRIPODS The (BBC1 15/9/1984) theme and incidental mus:
   KEN FREEMAN -S/T- *G.R.FORRESTER (Pin):GERCD 1(CD)*
TRIPPIN' (1999) VARIOUS ARTISTS -S/T-
   EPIC (Ten): 494 391-2 (CD) -4 (MC)
TRIUMPH OF LOVE (ORIGINAL BROADWAY CAST 1997) *Songs by*
   JEFFREY STOCK-SUSAN BIRKHENHEAD *O.BROADWAY CAST:*
   BETTY BUCKLEY-CHRIS.SIEBER-ROGER BART-F.MURRAY
   ABRAHAM-SUSAN EGAN *TER (Koch): CDTER 1253 (CD)*
TROMEO AND JULIET (1996) Music score: WILLIE WISELY
   -S/T- *TROMA (Greyhound): 42907 (CD)*
TROUBLE MAN (1972) Music & songs by MARVIN GAYE -S/T-
   MOTOWN (Univ): 530 884-2 (CD)
TROUBLE WITH GIRLS The see ELVIS PRESLEY INDEX p.360
TROUBLE WITH HARRY The (1955) Music: BERNARD HERRMANN
   VARESE: VSD 5971 (CD)   see COLL.188,191,196,197,
TROUBLESHOOTERS (BBC TV) "Mogul" by TOM SPRINGFIELD
   see COLL.337,
TROUBLESOME CREEK: A MID-WESTERN (1995) Music score
   by SHELDON MIROWITZ and DUKE LEVENE -S/T-
   Daring Rec.(Pinn/Topic): DARINGCD 3024 (CD)
TRUCK TURNER (1974) Music sco: ISAAC HAYES -S/T-
   reissue STAX (Pinn): SXD 129 (LP) also with
   'THREE TOUGH GUYS' (1974) *STAX: CDSXE 2095 (2CD)*
TRUE BLUE (1996) Music: STANISLAS SYREWICZ -S/T- V/A
   DECCA (Univers.): 455 012-2 (CD) -4 (MC)
TRUE GRIT (1969) Music sco: ELMER BERNSTEIN title song
   (Bernstein-Black) GLEN CAMPBELL on 'Country Boy'
   MFP EMI:CDMFP 6034 (CD)   see COLL.178,358,400,401,
TRUE LIES (1994) Mus: BRAD FIEDEL *see COLL.89,304,305,*
TRUE ROMANCE (1993) Music: HANS ZIMMER & MARK MANCINA
   -S/T- *reiss: MORGAN CREEK (Univ): 002242-2MCM (CD)*
TRUE STORIES (1986) Music: DAVID BYRNE / TALKING HEADS
   -S/T- *EMI: TC-EMC 3520 (MC) CDP 746345-2 (CD)*
TRUE WOMEN (TVM) Music score: BRUCE BROUGHTON -S/T- on
   INTRADA (Koch): MAFD 7077 (CD)
TRULY MADLY DEEPLY (BBC2 1/3/92) m:BARRINGTON PHELOUNG
   on 'PASSION OF MORSE' + 'Politician's Wife'/'Insp.
   Morse'/'Saint-Ex' *TRING INT (Tring): TRING 003CD*

TRUMAN SHOW The (1998) Music score: BURKHARD DALLWITZ
-S/T- VAR.ARTISTS *RCA (BMG): 74321 60822-2 (CD)*
TRUMPTON (BBC 1967) Music & songs by FREDDIE PHILLIPS
sung by BRIAN CANT *see COLL.186,*
TRUST (ITV 04/05/1999) original music score by
ROBERT LOCKHART *unavailable*
TRUSTING BEATRICE (Film) Music score: STANLEY MYERS
with Suite from 'COLD HEAVEN' (Stanley MYERS) on
INTRADA Imprt (Silva Screen): MAF 7048D (CD)
TUBE The (C4 Tyne Tees 82-84) theme "Star Cycle" (JEFF
BECK) 'Best Of Beckology' *EPIC: 471348-2 (CD) -4MC*
TURKISH BATH (Il Bagno Turco) (1997) Music: HAMAM
TRANSCENDENTAL (PIVIO, ALDO DE SCALZI)
-S/T- *CNI (Discovery): MDL 978 (CD)*
TURTLE BEACH (1991) Music sco: CHRIS NEAL theme *on*
'BLADE RUNNER' *SIL.SCREEN (Koch): SILVAD 3008(CD)*
TV NEWSREEL (BBC 50's) Theme "Girls In Grey" CHARLES
WILLIAMS *see COLL.57,172,*
TWEENIES (BBC1 06/09/1999) Music and songs by
LIZ KITCHEN and GRAHAM PIKE *unavailable*
TWELFTH NIGHT (1996) Music sc: SHAUN DAVEY recorded by
IRISH NATIONAL FILM ORCHESTRA cond: FIACHRA TRENCH
SILVA SCREEN (Koch): FILMCD 186 (CD)
TWILIGHT (1998) Music score: ELMER BERNSTEIN -S/T- on
EDEL-CINERAMA (Pinn): 0022902CIN (CD)
TWILIGHT ZONE The (TV USA 60's) theme: BERNARD HERRMANN
BEST OF TWILIGHT ZONE *VARESE (Pinn): VCD 47233 (CD)*
V.2' *VCD 47247 (CD) + VSD 26087 (CD)*'TWILIGHT ZONE'
/ 1986 *theme by* GRATEFUL DEAD &
MERL SAUNDERS *SILVA SCREEN (Koch): FILMCD 203 (CD)*
40th ANNIVERSARY COLL *SILVA SCREEN (Koch) STD 2000*
TWILIGHT'S LAST GLEAMING (1977) Music: JERRY GOLDSMITH
-S/T- *SILVA SCREEN (Koch): FILMCD 111 (CD)*
TWIN PEAKS (USA 90)(BBC2-23/10/90) music score: ANGELO
BADALMENTI) songs (David Lynch-Angelo Badalamenti)
"Falling" v: JULEE CRUISE 'Music From Twin Peaks'
WEA: 7599 26316-2 (CD) -4 (MC) / for theme see
COLL.17,38,143,144,262,270,331,340,351,359,360,
TWIN PEAKS: FIRE WALK WITH ME (1992) Music: ANGELO
BADALAMENTI) -S/T- *WB (TEN): 9362 45019-2 (CD) -4*
TWIN TOWN (1997) Music sco MARK THOMAS / Var.Artists
-S/T- on *A.& M. (Univ): 540 718-2 (CD)*
TWIST OF SAND, A *see COLL.292,*
TWISTER (1996) Music score: MARK MANCINA -S/T-
WEA: 9362 46265-2 (CD) -4 (MC)
TWO (USA/C5 05/01/1999) music by CHRISTOPHE BECK
unavailable
TWO DAYS IN THE VALLEY (1996) Music: ANTHONY MARINELLI
-S/T- *EDEL (Pinn): 0029772EDL (CD)*
TWO FAT LADIES (BBC2 9/10/96) theme music: PETE BAIKIE
JENNIFER PATERSON & CLARISSA DICKSON-WRIGHT vocals
unavailable
TWO FOR THE ROAD (1966) Music score: HENRY MANCINI
-S/T- reissue *RCA (BMG): 74321 62997-2 (CD)*

TWO FOR TONIGHT (1935) *feat* BING CROSBY-JOAN BENNETT
  with 'HOLIDAY INN' & 'ROAD TO MOROCCO'
  GREAT MOVIE THEMES (Target-BMG): CD 60027 (CD)
TWO GIRLS AND A SAILOR (1944) -S/T- JUNE ALLYSON-JIMMY
  DURANTE-GLORIA DE HAVEN-VAN JOHNSON-TOM DRAKE
  GREAT MOVIE THEMES (Target-BMG): CD 60023 (CD)
TWO MOON JUNCTION (1988) Music: JONATHAN ELIAS -S/T-
  VARESE (Pinn): VSD 5518 (CD)
TWO RONNIES The (BBC1 70s-80s)(The DETECTIVES 'Charley
  Farley and Piggy Malone') *see COLL.326,363,*
TWO THOUSAND YEARS (ITV 18/04/1999) title music by
  ROBERT HARTSHORNE -S/T- *feat Various Classics on*
  CONIFER CLASSICS (BMG): 75605 51353-2 (2CD)
U.F.O. (ATV/ITC 16/9/70-73) music: BARRY GRAY
  see COLL.122,270,310,360,362,
U.S.MARSHALLS (1997) Music sco: JERRY GOLDSMITH -S/T-
  VARESE (Pinn): VSD 5914 (CD)
U.TURN (1997) Music score: ENNIO MORRICONE -S/T-
  SONY MUSIC: 489 003-2 (CD) -4 (MC)
UK OK! (BBC2 22/2/1998) t.mus: NIAL BROWN *unavailable*
ULEE'S GOLD (1997) Music score: CHARLES ENGSTROM -S/T-
  RYKODISC (Vital): RCD 10731 (CD)
ULYSSES GAZE (1995) Music sco: ELENI KARAINDROU -S/T-
  ECM NEW NOTE (Pinn): 449 153-2 (CD) -4 (MC)
UMBRELLAS OF CHERBOURG (1964) Music sc: MICHEL LEGRAND
  -S/T- *ACCORD (Discovery): 10326-2 (CD) also*
  SILVA SCREEN: 834 139-2 (CD) see COLL.89,337,
UN COEUR EN HIVER - *see* HEART IN WINTER, A
UN HOMME ET UNE FEMME - *see* MAN AND A WOMAN, A
UNCLE TOM'S CABIN - Music composed by PETER THOMAS
  BEAR FAMILY (Rollercoaster): BCD 16238(CD)
UNDER SIEGE (1992) Music score: GARY CHANG -S/T-
  VARESE (Pinn): VSD 5409 (CD) VSC 5409 (MC)
UNDER THE CHERRY MOON (1986) Music: PRINCE -S/T- on
  WB (TEN): 925 395-2 (CD)
UNDERCOVER HEART (BBC1 01/10/1998) Music score by NIC
  BICAT *unavailable* / also "Dance The Night Away" by
  The MAVERICKS *MCA (BMG): MCSTD 48081 (CDs)*
UNDERGROUND (IL ETAIT UNE FOIS UN PAYS) (1995) Music:
  GORAN BREGOVICH -S/T- *POLY (IMS): E.528 910-2 (CD)*
  POLYGRAM France (Discovery): 528 910-2 (CD)
UNDERNEATH THE ARCHES (O.LONDON CAST 1982) Songs of
  FLANAGAN & ALLEN *feat* ROY HUDD-CHRISTOPHER TIMOTHY
  TER (Koch): CDTER 1015 (CD)
UNE FEMME FRANCAISE (1995) Music score: PATRICK DOYLE
  -S/T- *WEA France: 4509 99630-2 (CD)*
UNFORGIVEN (1992) Music score: LENNIE NIEHAUS -S/T-
  VARESE (Pinn): VSD 5380 (CD)
UNINVITED The (FILM 1944) Music score by VICTOR YOUNG
  NEW RECORDING by MOSCOW SYMPHONY ORCHESTRA *+suites*
  from 'GULLIVER'S TRAVELS'/'GREATEST SHOW ON EARTH'
  MARCO POLO (Select): 8225063 (CD)
UNINVITED The (ITV 25/9/97) Music score: MARTIN KISZKO
  -S/T- *OCEAN DEEP (Univ): OCD 007 (CD)*

UNION GAME: A RUGBY HISTORY (BBC2 22/08/1999) series
    theme music by ANDY PRICE *see COLL.19,*
UNIVERSAL SOLDIER (1992) Music sco: CHRISTOPHER FRANKE
    -S/T- *VARESE (Pinn): VSD 5373 (CD*
UNIVERSAL SOLDIER 2:THE RETURN (1999) Music: DON DAVIS
    -S/T- *VARESE (Pinn): VSD 6068 (CD)*
UNIVERSITY CHALLENGE (BBC2 21/9/94) theme music
    "College Boy" DEREK NEW (new arr.) *unavailable*
UNLAWFUL ENTRY (1992) Music score: JAMES HORNER -S/T-
    INTRADA (S.Screen): MAFCD 7031 (CD)
UNTAMED (1955) - *see COLL.394,*
UNTAMED HEART (1992) Music score: CLIFF EIDELMAN -S/T-
    VARESE (Pinn): VSD 5404 (CD) VSC 5404 (MC)
UNTOUCHABLES The (1987) Music score ENNIO MORRICONE
    -S/T- *A.& M.(IMS-Poly): E.393 909-2 (CD)*
    see COLL.111,118,239,251,274,275,348,366,
UP - *see* BENEATH THE VALLEY OF THE ULTRA VIXENS
UP 'N' UNDER (1997) Music score: MARK THOMAS -S/T- V/A
    EDEL UK (Pinn): 0022872CIN (CD)
UP CLOSE AND PERSONAL (1995) Music sco: THOMAS NEWMAN
    V/A -S/T- *EDEL-HOLLYWOOD (Pinn): 012 053-2HWR (CD)*
UP ON THE ROOF (1997) Music score: ALAN PARKER -S/T-
    OCEAN DEEP (Univ): OCD 009 (CD)
UP THE JUNCTION (1967) Music by MIKE HUGG-MANFRED MANN
    -S/T- reissued on *RPM (Pinn): RPM 189 (CD)*
UPSTAIRS DOWNSTAIRS (LWT 70 rep C4-13/11/82) theme mus
    "The Edwardians" by ALEXANDER FARIS
    see COLL.2,5,149,270,281,
URBAN LEGEND (1998) Music score: CHRISTOPHER YOUNG
    -S/T- *RCA (BMG): 74321 63477-2 (CD)*
URGA (1990) Music score: EDWARD ARTEYMEV -S/T- *Import*
    PHILIPS (Discovery): 510 608-2 (CD)
US GIRLS (BBC1 27/2/92) theme music: NIGEL HESS
    see COLL.193,
USUAL SUSPECTS The (1995) Music score: JOHN OTTMAN
    -S/T- *MILAN (BMG): 30107-2 (CD)*
UTILIZER The (USA TV Sci-fi) Music sc: DENNIS McCARTHY
    -S/T- *INTRADA (Silva Screen): MAF 7067 (CD)*

V : THE SERIES (USA 84 ITV 2/1/89) theme music: DENNIS
    McCARTHY Orchestral score JOE HARNELL *see COLL.17,*
VALIANT YEARS The (USA TV) *see COLL.383,*

VALLEY OF THE DOLLS (1967) Music score: ANDRE PREVIN
    PHILIPS (Univ.): 3145 36876-2 (CD) / title song by
    Andre & Dory PREVIN voc.by DIONNE WARWICK on 'Love
    Songs Coll' *PICKWICK: PWKS 525 (CD) HSC 3258 (MC)*
VALLEY OF THE KINGS (1954) Music score: MIKLOS ROZSA
    -S/T- *Imprt (Silva Screen): TT 3010 (CD)*
VALMOUTH (O.LONDON CAST 1958) Songs: SANDY WILSON *feat*
    MARCIA ASHTON-CLEO LAINE-FENELLA FIELDING-PETER
    GILMORE-IAN BURFORD *DRG (Pinn): CDSBL 13109 (CD)*
VALMOUTH (O.CHICHESTER CAST) BERTICE READING-FENELLA
    FIELDING-DORIS HARE *TER (Koch): CDTER 1019 (CD)*

VALOUR AND THE HORROR The (Galafilms Can.-C4 31/8/94)
"Requiem Op.48" (Gabriel FAURE) performed by ROYAL
PHILHARMONIC ORCH (R.Hickox) with ALED JONES (sop)
RPO-PICKWICK (Pickw-Koch): CD(ZC)RPO 8004 (CD/MC)
VAMPIRES (John Carpenter's) (1998) Music score by
JOHN CARPENTER -S/T- *MILAN (USA)*
VAN DER VALK (ITV 73) theme "Eye Level" (JACK TROMBEY)
SIMON PARK ORCHESTRA *see COLL.2,5,270,281,360,*
VANITY FAIR (BBC1 01/11/1998) Music score: MURRAY GOLD
-S/T- *BBC AUDIO INT (Pinn): WMSF 60042 (CD)*
VANITY FAIR (BBC1 6/09/1987) music by NIGEL HESS
see COLL.56,138,142,193,
VARIETY GIRL (1947) -S/T- + 'IT HAPPENED IN BROOKLYN'
selections *GREAT MOVIE THEMES (BMG): CD 60034 (CD)*
VARSITY BLUES (1998) Music score: MARK ISHAM -S/T- inc
FOO FIGHTERS/THIRD EYE BLIND/LOUDMOUTH/VAN HALEN
EDEL-Hollywood (Pinn): 010 205-2HWR (CD)
VELVET GOLDMINE (1998) Music score: CARTER BURWELL
VARIOUS ARTS -S/T- *LONDON (Univ): 556 035-2 (CD)*
VERSACE MURDER The (1999) Music sco: CLAUDIO SIMONETTI
-S/T- *TSUNAMI (Discovery): TOS 0308 (CD)*
VERTIGO (1958) Mus sc: BERNARD HERRMANN -S/T- original
restored 1958 score conducted by Muir Mathieson
VARESE (Pinn): VSD 5759 (CD) / ALSO AVAILABLE:
new 1995 recording by Royal Scottish National Orch
(Joel NcNeely) on *VARESE (Pinn): VSD 5600 (CD)*
see COLL.144,188,190,191,192,194,195,196,197,327,
VERY GOOD EDDIE (REV.BROADWAY CAST 1975) Songs: JEROME
KERN-SCHUYLER GREENE *DRG (Pinn): CDRG 6100 (CD)*
VETS IN PRACTICE (BBC1 26/8/97) and VET'S SCHOOL (BBC1
14/10/96) orig mus.by DEBBIE WISEMAN *unavailable*
VETS IN THE WILD (BBC2 00/00/2000) Music score:-
-S/T- *BBC WORLDWIDE (Pinn): WMSF 6018-2 (CD)*
VETS TO THE RESCUE (BBC1 18/10/1999) s.theme music by
DAVE GALE and ANDY BUSH *unavailable*
VICAR OF DIBLEY The (BBC1 10/11/1994) theme m. (Psalm
23) on collection 'HOWARD GOODALL'S CHOIR WORKS'
ASV (Select): CDDCA 1028 (CD)
ORIG TV CAST -S/T- *BBC (Techn): ZBBC 2113 (2MC)*
VICE The (ITV 04/01/1999) series music by JULIAN NOTT
unavailable. theme song "Sour Times" by PORTISHEAD
from 'Dummy' *GO DISCS (Univ): 828 522-2(CD) -4(MC)*
VICTOR VICTORIA O.BROADWAY CAST RECORDING *with* JULIE
ANDREWS-TONY ROBERTS-MICHAEL NOURI-RACHEL YORK
PHILIPS (Univ): 446 919-2 (CD) 446 919-4(MC)
VICTOR VICTORIA (1982) Music: HENRY MANCINI Lyrics by
LESLIE BRICUSSE *feat* JULIE ANDREWS-ROBERT PRESTON
-S/T- *GNP CRESCENDO (ZYX): GNPD 8038 (CD)*
VICTORIA WOOD AS SEEN ON TV (BBC2 1986) mus: VICTORIA
WOOD on 'BBC RADIO COLLECTION' sketches & songs on
BBC (Techn): ZBBC 1263 (2MC)
VICTORIAN KITCHEN GARDEN The (BBC2 8/5/1998 orig 1987)
theme by PAUL READE perf.by EMMA JOHNSON (flute)
'ENCORES' *ASV (Select): CDDCA 800 (CD)*

VICTORY AT SEA (USA 50's) music score: RICHARD RODGERS
arr/cond: Robert Russell BENNETT *version on*
TELARC USA (BMG): CD 80175 see COLL.170,383,
VIDEO GIRL -S/T- *Animanga-New Note (Pinn): AM 2 (CD)*
VIDEO GIRL A1 2ND *Animanga-New Note (Pinn): AM 9 (CD)*
VIDEODROME (1982) Music score by HOWARD SHORE -S/T- on
VARESE (Pinn): VSD 5975 (CD)
VIETNAM A TV HISTORY (USA TV) *see COLL.350,*
VIEW TO A KILL A - *see* JAMES BOND FILM INDEX p.358
see COLL.54,55,
VIKINGS The (1958) Music score: MARIO NASCIMBENE new
recording of score with 'Solomon and Sheba' music
DRG-NEW NOTE (Pinn): DRGCD 32963 (CD)
see COLL.71,72,261,385,
VILLAGE OF THE DAMNED (1994) Music sco: JOHN CARPENTER
VARESE (Pinn): VSD 5629 (CD)
VIOLENT SATURDAY - *see COLL.1,*
VIOLENT STREETS ('THIEF') (1981) Mus: TANGERINE DREAM
VIRGIN (EMI): CDV 2198 (CD)
VIRGIN GARDENS (C5 10/5/1998)m: ANDY COLES *unavailable*
VIRGINIA CITY (1940) Mus sco: MAX STEINER *new record:*
MOSCOW SO (Stromberg) *inc:* 'BEAST WITH 5 FINGERS'
'LOST PATROL' *MARCO POLO (Select) 8.223870 (CD)*
VIRGINIAN The (USATV)(rpt.BBC2 128/4/1998) theme music
PERCY FAITH on 'TELEVISION'S GREATEST HITS VOL.2'
EDEL-CINERAMA (Pinn): 0022712CIN (CD)
see COLL.2,346,
VIRTUAL SEXUALITY (1999) M: POCKET SIZE/BASEMENT JAXX-
IMOGEN HEAP/TOUCH & GO/JUSTINE/MANDALAY-GUTTER
BROS/K7/MOA/BERTINE ZETLITZ/NARCISSUS/ALL SAINTS
& RUPERT GREGSON WILLIAMS -S/T- on
EMI SOUNDTRACKS: 521 821-2 (CD)
VISION ON (BBC1 1964-76) pict.gallery "Left Bank Two"
(WAYNE HILL) The NOVELTONES *see COLL.5,363,*
VISITOR The (USA 1997/ITV 25/4/1998) Main theme by
DAVID ARNOLD / score by KEVIN KINER *unavailable*
VIVA LAS VEGAS *see* ELVIS PRESLEY INDEX p.360
VIVA ZAPATA! (1952) Music sco: ALEX NORTH. new record
ing by SCOTTISH NATIONAL ORCHESTRA conducted by
JERRY GOLDSMITH on *VARESE (Pinn): VSD 5900 (CD)*
see COLL.1,
VIVRE POUR VIVRE - *see* 'LIVE FOR LIFE' + 'UN HOMME ET
UNE FEMME' (MAN AND A WOMAN, A) *see COLL.294,*
VIXEN (1968,RUSS MEYER) Mus: WILLIAM LOOSE -S/T- *reiss*
LASERLIGHT (Greyhound): 12922 (CD) ALSO ON QD with
'LORNA'/'FASTER PUSSYCAT' - *NORMAL/QDK MEDIA*
(Pinn/Greyhound/Direct) QDK(CD)(LP) 008
VOLCANO (1997) Music score: ALAN SILVESTRI -S/T- score
VARESE (Pinn): VSD 5833 (CD)
VON RYAN'S EXPRESS (1965) Music score: JERRY GOLDSMITH
score includ.music from 'OUR MAN FLINT'/'IN LIKE
FLINT' *TSUNAMI IMPT (S.Screen): TCI 0602 (CD)*
VOYAGE TO THE BOTTOM OF THE SEA (USA TV)
see COLL.38,122,308,346,

W **ACKY RACES** (USA68/BBC 70's) theme music (Hoyt Curtin
    W.Hanna-J.Barbera) (USA TV) *see COLL.349,373,*
WAG THE DOG (1997) Music score: MARK KNOPFLER -S/T-
    MERCURY (Univ): 536 864-2 (CD) -4 (MC)
WAGES OF FEAR (1978)'The Sorcerer' M: TANGERINE DREAM
    MCA Imp (Silva Screen): MCAD 10842 (CD)
WAGON TRAIN (USA1957) Theme 1 "Roll Along Wagon Train"
    (Fain-Brooks) *vocal version by* ROBERT HORTON on
    'TV CLASSICS 4' *CASTLE (Pinn): MBSCD 412 (4CDset)*
    Theme 2 "Wagons Ho!"JEROME MOROSS *MFP: HR418109-4*
    Theme 3 "Wagon Train" (Rene-Russell)
    see COLL.2,178,346,367,369,401,
WAITING FOR GOD (BBC1 28/6/90) theme 'Piano Quintet in
    A'("Trout") D.667 (SCHUBERT) *HMV: CDC 747 448-2
    (CD) -4 (MC) TV vers unavailable see COLL.104,*
WAITING TO EXHALE (1995) *featuring* WHITNEY HOUSTON
    -S/T- *ARISTA (BMG): 07822 18796-2(CD) -4(MC)*
WAKING NED (1998) Music score by SHAUN DAVEY -S/T-
    featuring "Fisherman's Blues" by The WATERBOYS
    LONDON (Univ): 460 939-2 (CD)
WALDEN ON HEROES (BBC2 6/1/1998) t.music "Brandenburg
    Concerto No.5 in D.Major" (BACH) recording used:
    NAXOS (Select): 8.550048 (CD)
WALK IN THE CLOUDS, A (1995) Music sco: MAURICE JARRE
    -S/T- *MILAN (BMG): 28666-2 (CD)*
WALK ON THE MOON, A (1999) Music score: MASON DARING
    -S/T- (VARIOUS ARTS) *SIRE (TEN): 4344 31041-2 (CD)*
WALK ON THE WILD SIDE (1962) Music sc: ELMER BERNSTEIN
    -S/T- including 'SWEET SMELL OF SUCCESS' (1957)
    Import (Silva Screen): TT 3002 (CD)
WALKABOUT (1970) Music JOHN BARRY *see COLL.27,30,*
WALKING THUNDER (1996) Music sco: JOHN SCOTT -S/T- on
    JS (Silva Screen): JSCD 117 (CD)
WALKING WITH DINOSAURS (BBC1 10/1999) Music score by
    BEN BARTLETT -S/T- *BBC (Pinn): WMSF 6013-2 (CD)*
WALL The (1981) Music: PINK FLOYD -S/T-
    Harvest (EMI): CDS 746036-8(2CD) TC2SHDW 411(2MC)
WALL STREET (1988) Music sc: STEWART COPELAND
    see COLL.79,410,
WALLACE AND GROMIT - see under 'GRAND DAY OUT'/'WRONG
    TROUSERS'/'CLOSE SHAVE'
WALLY GATOR (USA TV) *see COLL.348,373,*
WALTONS The (USA 1972-81) theme mus: JERRY GOLDSMITH
    see COLL.17,347,
WANDERERS The (1979) Songs by V.Artists -S/T- reissue
    SEQUEL (BMG): NEMCD 765 (CD)
WAR AND PEACE (1956) *COLL* 'FILM MUSIC OF NINO ROTA'
    Ital.IMPT (Silva Screen): VCDS 7001 (CD)
WAR AND PISTE (BBC1 18/11/1998) theme music "Lust For
    Life" by IGGY POP on *VIRGIN (EMI): CDOVD 278 (CD)*
WAR AND REMEMBRANCE (ITV (USA) 3/9/89) music sco: BOB
    COBERT spin-off 'Winds Of War' *see COLL.383,*
WAR LORD The (1965) Music: JEROME MOROSS -S/T- + 'THE
    CARDINAL' *TSUNAMI (S.Scr): TSU 0117 (CD)*

WAR OF THE BUTTONS (1994) Music score: RACHEL PORTMAN
-S/T- *VARESE (Pinn): VSD 5554 (CD)*

WAR OF THE WORLDS (JEFF WAYNE'S Musical Concept Album)
COLUMBIA (Ten): CDX 96000 (2CD) 4096000 (2MC)
Highlights on SONY: CDX 32356 (CD)

WAR REQUIEM (1988) Music: BENJAMIN BRITTEN based on
'War Requiem Op.66' C.B.S.O.(Simon RATTLE) *EMI:*
CDS 747 034-8 (2CDs) LONDON SYMPH.ORCH (B.BRITTEN)
DECCA (Univ): 414 383-2DH2 (2CD) K27K22 (MC)

WARRIORS (BBC1 21/11/1999) Music by DEBBIE WISEMAN
-S/T- *BBC WORLDWIDE (Pinn): WMSF 6019-2 (CD)*

WARRIORS The (1979) Music sco: BARRY DE VORZON + V/A
-S/T- *re-iss on SPECTRUM (Univ): 551 169-2 (CD)*

WARRIORS OF VIRTUE (1997) Music score: DON DAVIS -S/T-
PROMETHEUS (Silva Screen): PCD 144 (CD) also on
KID RHINO (TEN): 8122 72640-2 (CD)

WASHINGTON SQUARE (1997) Music sco: JAN A.P.KACZMAREK
-S/T- *VARESE (Pinn): VSD 5869 (CD)*

WATERBOY The (1998) Music score: ALAN PASQUA -S/T- inc
LENNY KRAVITZ/CANDYSKINS/DOORS/RUSH/CCR/MELLENCAMP
EDEL-Hollywood (Pinn): 010 092-2HWR (CD)

WATERCOLOUR CHALLENGE (C4 14/7/1998) original music by
DAVID ARNOLD and PAUL HART *unavailable*

WATERLOO (1970) Music score: NINO ROTA -S/T- Import
LEGEND Italy (Silva Screen): LEGENDCD 20 (CD)

WATERLOO BRIDGE (1940) VARIOUS -S/T- SELECTIONS on
GREAT MOVIE THEMES: (Targ-BMG): CD 60032 (CD)

WAY OF THE LAKES (BBC1 6/8/93) incidental music "The
Watermill" RONALD BINGE *see COLL.50,56,*

WAY WE WERE The (1973) Mus: MARVIN HAMLISCH Lyr: ALAN
/MARILYN BERGMAN -S/T- feat BARBRA STREISAND on
Sony: 474911-2 (CD) 474911-4 (MC)
see COLL.25,71,255,278,

WEDDING BELL BLUES (1996) Music by Var.Artists -S/T-
VARESE (Pinn): VSD 5853 (CD)

WEDDING SINGER The (1998) -S/T- with VARIOUS ARTISTS
Volume 1 - *WBROS (TEN): 9362 46840-2 (CD) -4 (MC)*
Volume 2 - *WBROS (TEN): 9362 46984-2 (CD) -4 (MC)*

WEDLOCK - *see COLL.51* DEADLOCK

WEEKEND IN HAVANA (1941) ALICE FAYE-CARMEN MIRANDA
plus 'HOLIDAY IN MEXICO' selections on
GREAT MOVIE THEMES (BMG): CD 60036 (CD)

WEEKEND WORLD (LWT 1987) theme "Nantucket Sleighride"
(Felix Pappalardi-Les West) by MOUNTAIN 'Best Of'
BEAT GOES ON (Pinn): BGO(CD)(LP) 33 (CD/LP)

WELCOME BACK KOTTER (USA TV) *see COLL.347,*

WELCOME TO SARAJEVO (1997) Music sco: ADRIAN JOHNSTON
EMI SOUNDTRACKS: 493 014-2 (CD)

WEST The (BBC2 21/12/1998) Music: JAY UNGAR & others
-S/T- *SONY CLASSICS: SK 62727 (CD)*

WEST SIDE STORY - songs by Leonard Bernstein and
  Stephen Sondheim
  1. FILM MUSICAL 1961 NATALIE WOOD *sung:* *Marnie Nixon*
     RICHARD BEYMER *by Jim Bryant* RITA MORENO *by Betty
     Wand* CHITA RIVERA-GEORGE CHAKIRIS-RUSS TAMBLYN
     COLUMBIA (Ten): 467606-2 *(CD)* -4*(MC) and*
  2. STUDIO RECORDING 1997 *feat* PAUL MANUEL-CAROLINE O'
     CONNOR-TINUKE OLAFIMIHAN *with* NATIONAL SYMPH ORCH.
     conducted by JOHN OWEN EDWARDS
     TER-Music Theatre Hour (Koch): CDTEH 6002 (CD)
  3. STUDIO RECORD 1984 TV-BBC1 10/5/1985 *with:* KIRI TE
     KANAWA-JOSE CARRERAS-TATIANA TROYANOS-KURT OLLMAN-
     MARILYN HORN and LEONARD BERNSTEIN *DG-POLYGRAM:
     415253-2(2CD) -4(MC) Highl: 415963-2 (CD) -4 (MC)*
  4. STUDIO RECORD 1993 MICHAEL BALL-BARBARA BONNEY-
     LA VERNE WILLIAMS-CHRISTOPHER HOWERD-MARY CAREWE-
     JENNY O'GRADY-LEE GIBSON + RPO: BARRY WORDSWORTH
     CARLTON-IMG (Carlton): IMGCD(IMGMC)1801 (CD/MC)
  5. LEICESTER HAYMARKET THEATRE PROD 1993 *with* Nat.
     Symph.Orch (John Owen Edwards) PAUL MANUEL-TINUKE
     OLAFIMIHAN-CAROLINE O'CONNOR-NICK FERANTI and Comp
     <u>Complete</u>: *TER: CDTER2 1197 (2CD) ZCTER2 1197(2MC)*
  6. STUDIO RECORD 1989 *with* KATIA & MARIBELLEe LaBEQUE
     'Symphonic Dances and Songs From West Side Story'
     arr for 2 pianos by Irwin Kostal *CBSCD 45531 (CD)*
  7. ORIG BROADWAY CAST 1957 CAROL LAWRENCE-LARRY KERT
     CHITA RIVERA *COLUMBIA (Ten): SK 60724 (CD)*
  8. ORIG NEW YORK CAST 1957 *with:* CAROL LAWRENCE-LARRY
     KERT-CHITA RIVERA-ART SMITH-MICKEY CALIN-KEN LeROY
     COLUMBIA (Ten): SMK 60724 (CD)
WHAT A FEELING! (ORIG LONDON CAST 1997) Music from
  Various Musicals *feat* LUKE GOSS-SINITTA-SONIA
  MCI (THE-Disc): MCCD 287 (CD)
WHAT DREAMS MAY COME (1998) Music score: MICHAEL KAMEN
  -S/T- *DECCA (Univ.): 460 858-2 (CD)*
WHAT I HAVE WRITTEN (1996) Music: JOHN PHILLIPS-DAVID
  BRIDIE -S/T- *ICON (Pinn.Imports): ICON 19963 (CD)*
WHAT THE PAPERS SAY (BBC2 23/3/90 previous C4-Granada)
  "English Dance No.5" ('Eight English Dances')
  (Malcolm ARNOLD) Philharmonic Orch (Thompson)
  CHANDOS: CHAN 8867 (CD)
WHAT'S LOVE GOT TO DO WITH IT - *see* TINA
WHAT'S MY LINE (BBC 1951) *see COLL.172,*
WHAT'S NEW PUSSYCAT (1965) Music score: BURT BACHARACH
  title song sung by TOM JONES -S/T- on
  RYKODISC (Vital): RCD 10740 (CD)
WHAT'S UP, TIGER LILY (1966) Music: JOHN SEBASTIAN The
  LOVIN' SPOONFUL -S/T- with 'YOU'RE A BIG BOY NOW'
  RCA CAMDEN (BMG): 74321 69952-2 (CD)
  RAZOR & TIE (Koch): RE 2167-2 (CD) previously
WHATEVER (1996) -S/T- *CREATION (Pinn): CRECD 249 (CD)*
WHATEVER HAPPENED TO THE LIKELY LADS (BBC2 9/1/1973)
  theme m: "Whatever Happened To You" (Mike Hugg-Ian
  La Frenais) by HIGHLY LIKELY *see COLL.2,5,270,*

WHEN A MAN LOVES A WOMAN (94) Music: ZBIGNIEW PRIESNER
  Songs PERCY SLEDGE-LOS LOBOS-RICKIE LEE JONES etc
  -S/T- reis *EDEL-HOLLYWOOD (Pinn): 011 606-2HWR (CD)*
WHEN ANGELS FALL (1959) Music score: KRZYSZTOF KOMEDA
  -S/T- *POWER BROS (Harmonia Mundi): PB 11075 (CD)*
WHEN DINOSAURS RULED T.EARTH see ONE MILLION YEARS BC
WHEN HARRY MET SALLY (89) Music adapted & arranged by
  Marc Shaiman and performed by Harry Connick Jnr.on
  -S/T- reissue *CBS 465 753-2 (CD)* see COLL.255,
WHEN THE BOAT COMES IN (BBC1 4/1/76)
  theme mus "Dance To Your Daddy" (trad.arranged by
  David Fanshawe) sung by ALEX GLASGOW see COLL.2,6,
WHEN THE WIND BLOWS (Cartoon 1987) Music score: ROGER
  WATERS Title song sung by DAVID BOWIE / songs by
  Genesis-Hugh Cornwell-Squeeze-Paul Hardcastle
  -S/T- *VIRGIN (EMI): CDVIP 132 (CD) TCVIP 132 (MC)*
WHEN WE WERE KINGS -S/T- *MERCURY (Uni): 534 462-2 (CD)*
WHERE EAGLES DARE (1968) Music score: RON GOODWIN
  for theme only see COLL.70,137,384,
WHERE THE ACTION IS (USA TV) see COLL.349,
WHERE THE HEART IS (ITV 6/4/97) theme "Home Is Where
  The Heart Is" sung by PADDY McALOON see COLL.243,
WHICKER'S WORLD (BBC 60s) theme "West End" by LAURIE
  JOHNSON see COLL.7,23,377,
WHILE I LIVE (1947) Music score: CHARLES WILLIAMS incl
  'The Dream Of Olwen' see COLL.170,
WHILE YOU WERE SLEEPING (1995) Music: RANDY EDELMAN
  -S/T- *VARESE (Pinn): VSD 5627 (CD)*
WHISKY GALORE! (1949) see COLL.223,
WHISPERERS The (1966) Music score: JOHN BARRY -S/T- on
  RYKODISC (Vital): RCD 10720 (CD)
WHISTLE DOWN THE WIND (SHOW 1998)(ANDREW LLOYD WEBBER-
  JIM STEINMAN) title song by TINA ARENA / ORIG CAST
  Complete: *REA.USEFUL Poly: 547 261-2 (2CD) -4(2MC)*
  Highlights: *REA.USEFUL Poly: 559 441-2 (CD) -4(MC)*
WHISTLE DOWN THE WIND (1961) Music sco: MALCOLM ARNOLD
  LONDON Symphony Orchestra (Richard HICOX) on coll
  'Film Music' *CHANDOS: CHAN 9100 (CD)*
WHITBREAD ROUND T.WORLD YACHT RACE see SAIL THE WORLD
WHITE CHRISTMAS (1954) Songs by IRVING BERLIN feat:
  BING CROSBY-DANNY KAYE -S/T- *MCA: MCLD 19191 (CD)*
WHITE MISCHIEF (1988) Music score: GEORGE FENTON
  -S/T- *TER (Koch): CDTER 1153 (CD)*
WHITE NIGHTS (1985) see COLL.82,145,
WHITE ROCK (1976) Mus scored & perf. by RICK WAKEMAN
  A.& M.(Univ): RWCD 20 (CD Box Set)
WHITE ROCK 2 (1999) Music by RICK WAKEMAN
  MUSIC FUSION (Pinn): MFCD 004 (CD)
WHITE SANDS (1992) Music score: PATRICK O'HEARN -S/T-
  MORGAN CREEK (Univ): 002252-2 MCM (CD)
WHO FRAMED ROGER RABBIT (1988) see COLL.80,313,
WHO IS SYLVIA see COLL.23,
WHO PAYS THE FERRYMAN (UKGold 24/4/93 orig BBC1 1977)
  music: YANNIS MARKOPOULOS see COLL.281,

WHO PLAYS WINS (ORIG LONDON CAST 1985) comp/performed
by PETER SKELLERN-RICHARD STILGOE *re-issued on*
FIRST NIGHT (Pinn): OCRCD 6037 (CD)

WHO WANTS TO BE A MILLIONAIRE (ITV 04/09/1998-2000)
music: MATTHEW STRACHAN-KEITH STRACHAN *unavailable*

WHO'S AFRAID OF VIRGINIA WOOLF (1966) Music sco: ALEX
NORTH new recording by NAT.PHILHARMONIC ORCHESTRA
(Jerry Goldsmith) *VARESE (Pinn): VSD 5800 (CD)*

WHO'S THAT GIRL (1987) Music: STEPHEN BRAY -S/T- incl
MADONNA-SCRITTI POLITTI-CLUB NOUVEAU-COATI MUNDI
-S/T- *SIRE (TEN): WX 102C (MC) 7599 25611-2 (CD)*

WHO'S THE BOSS (USA TV) *see COLL.350,*

WHODUNNIT *see COLL.360,*

WHOSE LINE IS IT ANYWAY (C4/Hat Trick 23/9/88-1999)
theme music: PHILIP POPE *unavailable*

WHY DO FOOLS FALL IN LOVE (1998) Music: STEPHEN JAMES
TAYLOR -S/T- with VARIOUS ARTISTS on
ELEKTRA (TEN): 7559 62265-2 (CD) -4 (MC)

WICKER MAN The (1973) Music by PAUL GIOVANNI & MAGNET
-S/T- *TRUNK (SRD): BARKED 4CD (CD) BARKED 4 (LP)*

WIGGLES The (ITV 02/01/1999) Music & songs The WIGGLES
-S/T- 'GET READY TO WIGGLE' on
EDEL-DISNEY (Pinn): 010246-2DNY (CD)

WILD AMERICA (1997) Music score: JOEL McNEELY -S/T-
PROMETHEUS (Silva Screen): PCD 147 (CD)

WILD AT HEART (1990) Music score: ANGELO BADALAMENTI
V.Arts + CHRIS ISAAK 'Wicked Game' -S/T- *SPECTRUM
(Univ): 551 318-2 (CD) see COLL.364,*

WILD BUNCH The (1969) Music sco: JERRY FIELDING -S/T-
WEA France (Import, Discovery): 9362 46295-2 (CD)
also on *RETROGRADE (Impt): FSMCD 1 (CD)*

WILD GEESE The (1978) Music score by ROY BUDD -S/T- on
CINEPHILE (Pinn): CINCD 014 (CD) see COLL.155,

WILD IN THE COUNTRY *see* ELVIS PRESLEY FILM INDEX p.360

WILD IS THE WIND (1957) Music score by DIMITRI TIOMKIN
-S/T- *TSUNAMI Germ (Silva Screen): TSU 0110 (CD)*
see COLL.370,

WILD ROVERS (1) & 'THE FIRST GREAT TRAIN ROBBERY' 1978
Music scores: JERRY GOLDSMITH 2 -S/T-
MEMOIR-Castle (Pinn): CDMOIR 601 (CD)

WILD THINGS (1997) Music sco: GEORGE S.CLINTON. songs
by MORPHINE -S/T- *VARESE (Pinn): VSD 5924 (CD)*

WILD WEST The (USA/C4 14/5/95) original music: BRIAN
KEANE -S/T- *SHANACHIE (Koch): SHCD 6013 (2CD)*

WILD WILD WEST (1998) Music sco: ELMER BERNSTEIN -S/T-
score: *VARESE (Pinn): VSD 6042 (CD)*
songs: *INTERSCOPE (Univ): IND 90344 (CD) INC 90344*

WILD WILD WEST (USA TV) *see COLL.122,401,*

WILDE (1997) Music score: DEBBIE WISEMAN -S/T- on
MCI (THE-DISC-Pinn): MPRCD 001 (CD)

WILDLIFE ON ONE / TWO (BBC1/2 WILDLIFE SERIES)
*individual programme music details on request from
MIKE PRESTON MUSIC*

WILL SUCCESS SPOIL ROCK HUNTER - *see COLL.1,*

WILLIAM TELL (The Adventures Of)(ITV-1958) title theme
sung by DAVID WHITFIELD on 'Sings Stage And Screen
Favourites' *CARLTON: PWK 096 (CD) SDTO 2004*
WILLIAM'S WISH WELLINGTONS (BBC1 25/10/94) KICK PROD
see COLL.67,
WILLO THE WISP (BBC TV) *see COLL.147,186,*

WILLOW (1988) Music score: JAMES HORNER -S/T-
VIRGIN (EMI): CDV 2538 (CD) see COLL.205,338,
WIMBLEDON (BBC1/2 1972-1999)
opening theme 1974-98 "Light & Tuneful" by KEITH
MANSFIELD *see COLL.7,148,176,*
Closing theme "Sporting Occasion" by ARNOLD STECK
see COLL.176,
WIND AND THE LION The (1975) Music sc: JERRY GOLDSMITH
-S/T- *INTRADA (Silva Screen): MAF 7005D (CD)*
WINDS OF WAR The (ITV 9/1983 & 5/1985) Mus: BOB COBERT
-S/T- Nurnberg S.O.*TER Koch: ZCTER 1070 (MC) delet*
see WAR AND REMEMBRANCE *see COLL.270,383,*
WING AND A PRAYER, A (C5 13/01/1999) music by ROB LANE
unavailable
WING COMMANDER (1998) Mus.sc: DAVID ARNOLD-KEVIN KINER
-S/T- *SONIC IMAGES (Grey-Cargo):7828 278905-2 (CD)*
WINGS OF COURAGE (1995) Music sco: GABRIEL YARED -S/T-
Imprt COLUMBIA (Silva Screen): SK 68350 (CD)
WINGS OF THE DOVE (1998) Music score: EDWARD SHEARMUR
-S/T- *CONIFER (BMG): 74321 55881-2 (CD)*
WINNER The (1997) Music score: DANIEL LICHT -S/T- on
RYKODISC (Vital-ADA): RCD 10392 (CD)
WINNIE THE POOH 'The Many Songs of WINNIE THE POOH'
DISNEY (Carlton-Polyg): WD 11564-2 (CD) -4 (MC)
see also WALT DISNEY FILM INDEX p.362
WINTER GUEST The (1997) Music sco: MICHAEL KAMEN -S/T-
VARESE (Pinn): VSD 5895 (CD)
WINTER OLYMPIC GAMES 1992 (BBC1 1992) theme "Pop Looks
Bach" (Sam FONTEYN) also "Chorus Of Hebrew Slaves"
from 'Nabucco' (VERDI) *see COLL.93,97,273,*
WISH ME LUCK (LWT 8/1/89) theme music: JIM PARKER
see COLL.6,149,
WISH YOU WERE HERE (Thames/Cent) theme 'Carnival" by
GORDON GILTRAP *MUNCHKIN GRCD 1 deleted* link music
"The Long Road" by MARK KNOPFLER -S/T- 'CAL'
VERTIGO Poly: 822 769-2 (CD) VERHC 17 (MC)
WITCHCRAFT (BBC 1992) Music score: JOHN SCOTT -S/T- on
JOHN SCOTT Rec. (Silva Screen): JSCD 121 (CD)
WITCHES OF EASTWICK The (1987) Music sc: JOHN WILLIAMS
see COLL.79,274,275,
WITHNAIL AND I (1986) Music score: DAVID DUNDAS-RICK
WENTWORTH -S/T- VARIOUS ARTISTS *reissue*
DRG USA (Pinn): DRGCD 12590 (CD)
see COLL.122,144,
WITNESS (1985) Music score: MAURICE JARRE -S/T-
VARESE (Pinn): VCD 47227 (CD) +
TER (Koch): CDTER 1098 (CD) see COLL.70,213,366,

WIZARD OF OZ The- songs: Harold Arlen & E.Yip Harburg
1. FILM MUSICAL 1939 *with:* JUDY GARLAND-RAY BOLGER-
   JACK HALEY-BERT LAHR-FRANK MORGAN -S/T- *reissue*
   EMI PREMIER (EMI): CDODEON 7 (CD)
2. ROYAL SHAKESPEARE COMPANY CAST 1988 (Barbican)
   <u>Highlights:</u> *SHOWTIME (MCI-THE): SHOW(CD)(MC) 003*
   <u>Complete:</u> *TER (Koch): CDTER 1165 (CD)*

WKRP IN CINCINNATI (USA TV) *see COLL.347,*

WOGAN'S ISLAND (BBC1 28/6/95) theme mus "The Celts" by
   ENYA on *WEA (TEN): 4509 91167-2 (CD) WX 498C (MC)*
   see COLL.141,

WOLF MAN The (1940) Music: HANS SALTER-FRANK SKINNER
   new recording MOSCOW SYMPHONY ORCHEST (STROMBERG)
   MARCO POLO (Select): 8.223748 (CD) also includes
   INVISIBLE MAN RETURNS-SON OF FRANKENSTEIN

WOLVES OF WILLOUGHBY CHASE (1989) Music: COLIN TOWNS
   -S/T- *TER (Koch): CDTER 1162 (CD)*

WOMAN IN RED The (1984) Songs: STEVIE WONDER featur:
   STEVIE WONDER-DIONNE WARWICK -S/T-
   MOTOWN (Univ): 530 030-2 (CD) 530 030-4 (MC)

WOMAN IN WHITE The (BBC1 28/12/1997) Music score by
   DAVID FERGUSON *see COLL.151,*

WOMAN OF SUBSTANCE, A (C4 2/1/85) theme: NIGEL HESS
   see COLL.149,

WOMAN OF THE YEAR songs: John Kander and Fred Ebb
   ORIG BROADWAY CAST 1981 with LAUREN BACALL
   RAZOR & TIE (Koch): RE 21462 (CD)

WOMBLES The (BBC1 73) theme and songs: MIKE BATT all
   on 'Wombling Hits' THE WOMBLES (prod by Mike BATT)
   CBS SONY: 466118-2 (CD) -4(MC)

WOMBLES The (ITV 4/3/1998) "Remember You're A Womble"
   (Mike BATT) WOMBLES *SONY: 665 620-2 (CDs) -4 (MC)*

WONDER WOMAN (USA TV) *see COLL.347,*

WONDERFUL TOWN - songs: Leonard Bernstein-Betty Comden
   and Adolph Green
1. *TER* STUDIO RECORD.1998   KAREN MASON-REBECCA LUKER-
   RON RAINES-GREG EDELMAN-DON STEPHENSON & Company
   NAT.SYMPHONY ORCH.*conductor:* JOHN OWEN EDWARDS
   TER (Koch): CDTER2 1223 (2CD, 11.1998)
2. ORIG LONDON CAST 1986 MAUREEN LIPMAN-JOHN CASSADY-
   NICHOLAS COLICOS-DANIEL COLL-ROY DURBIN-RAY LONNEN
   FIRST NIGHT (Pinn) OCRCD 6011 (CD)
3. ORIG BROADWAY CAST 1953 *w:* ROSALIND RUSSELL-SYDNEY
   CHAPLIN *SONY BROADWAY: SK 48021 (CD)*
4. STUDIO RECORDING, conducted by SIMON RATTLE
   EMI CLASSICS: CDC 556 753-2 (CD)

WONDERWALL (1968) Music score: GEORGE HARRISON *Re-iss:*
   EMI-APPLE: CDSAPCOR 1 (CD) (TC)SAPCOR 1 (MC/LP)

WOO (1998) VARIOUS ARTISTS -S/T-
   EPIC (Ten): 491 121-2 (CD) -4 (MC)

WOOD The (1998) VARIOUS ARTISTS -S/T-
   JIVE (Pinn): 052 371-2 (CD) 523 711 (2LP)

WOODLANDERS The (1996) Mus score: GEORGE FENTON -S/T-
   DEBONAIR (Pinn): CDDEB 1007 (CD)

WOODSTOCK 1969 Woodstock Music Festival *with* JOAN BAEZ
JOE COCKER-RICHIE HAVENS-COUNTRY JOE & FISH-CROSBY
NASH & NEIL YOUNG-ARLO GUTHRIE-JIMI HENDRIX-
SANTANA-ShaNaNa-JOHN SEBASTIAN-SLY & FAMILY STONE-
TEN YEARS AFTER-WHO -S/T- 'BEST OF WOODSTOCK'
WEA: 7567 82618-2 (CD) -4 (MC) -S/T- reissue
WEA: (1) 7567 80593-2 (2CD) (2) 7567 80594-2 (2CD)
WOODSTOCK II (1970) Woodstock festival 69 feat V.Arts
-S/T- re-issue: *ATLANTIC (TEN): 7567 81991-2 (CD)*
WOODY WOODPECKER (USA) ORIGINAL CARTOON CAST RECORDING
DRIVE ARCHIVE (SIlver Sounds): 7806 747112-2 (CD)
song also by DANNY KAYE *(MCA) / see COLL.345,*
WOOF! (Carlton 18/2/89) theme: PAUL LEWIS *see COLL.6,*
WORKERS AT WAR (BBC2 09/02/1999) series title music by
JULIAN STEWART LINDSAY *unavailable*
WORKING GIRL (1988) Music score: ROB MOUNCEY songs by
CARLY SIMON -S/T- *feat:* CARLY SIMON-SONNY ROLLINS
POINTER SISTERS *reiss: ARISTA (BMG): 259 767 (CD)*
WORLD AT WAR The (BBC2 5/9/94 orig ITV 31/10/73) theme
music by CARL DAVIS *see COLL.184,281,*
WORLD CHESS CHAMPIONSHIPS (The Times) 1993 from 7/9/93
BBC theme music: 'Symphony No.12 in D.min.Op.112'
(SHOSTAKOVICH) THE ROYAL CONCERTGEBOUW ORCHESTRA
(Bernard Haitink) *DECCA (Univ): 417 392-2 (2CDs)*
C4 theme music: o.music by PAUL MARDLE *unavailable*
WORLD CHESS (BBC2 8/1986) theme "Montagues & Capulets"
'Suite No.2 Romeo & Juliet' (Sergei PROKOFIEV)
WORLD CUP 1998 (France, 10 June 1998 - 12 July 1998)

1. BBC TV theme (arrangement of "Pavane" (FAURE) by
   ELIZABETH PARKER with WIMBLEDON CHORAL SOCIETY
   BBC-TELSTAR (TEN): CDSTAS(CASTAS) 2979 (CDs/MC)
2. ITV TV theme "Rendezvous" by JEAN MICHEL JARRE
   with APOLLO 440 *EPIC (Ten): EPC 666110-2 (CDs)*
3. England World Cup Song "(How Does It Feel) To Be
   On Top Of The World" (Ian McCulloch-Johnny Marr)
   ENGLAND UNITED *LONDON (Univ): LON(CD)(CS) 414*
4. Scotland "Don't Come Home Too Soon" by DEL AMITRI
   A.& M.(Univ): 582 705-2 (CDs) -4 (M C)
   FOR ALL OTHER 1998 ITEMS *see TELE-TUNES 1998*
WORLD CUP 1994 (BBC trailer & theme) "America" by
L.BERNSTEIN-S.SONDHEIM from 'West Side Story'
POLY (Univ) USACD 1 (CDsingle USAMC 1 (MC) deleted
WORLD CUP 1994 (ITV trail.& theme) "Gloryland"(Charlie
Skarbek-Rick Blacksey) SOUNDS OF BLACKNESS & DARYL
HALL *MERCURY (Univ): 522 384-2(CD) -4(MC) deleted*
WORLD CUP 1990 *see COLL.271,273,*
WORLD CUP CRICKET 1999 (BBC/Sky 15/05-20/06/1999)
1. "Soul Limbo" BOOKER T.& THE MG's *STAX (CD)*
2. "All Over The World" by DAVE STEWART
   RCA (BMG): 74321 66374-2 (CDs)
3. "Come On England" by BARMY ARMY *WILDSTAR (CDs)*
4. "Starsky & Hutch re-mix" JAMES TAYLOR QUARTET
   URBAN: URB(X) 24 (7"s/12"s) del.

5. "Summertime" sung by LUCY TREGEAR *unavailable*
6. "Laudate Dominum" (MOZART) from the 'Inspector
   Morse' album *VIRGIN (EMI): VTCDX 2 (2CD)*
WORLD CUP RUGBY 1999 /1995 - see RUGBY WORLD CUP
WORLD CUP RUGBY 1991 - *see COLL.148,406,*

WORLD DARTS (BBC) Theme music "Cranes" by DOUGLAS WOOD
   see COLL 176,
WORLD FIGURE SKATING CHAMPIONSHIPS (BBC) theme music
   "Mornings At Seven" (J.Last) JAMES LAST ORCH on
   'By Request' *POLYDOR (Univ): 831 786-2 (CD)*
WORLD IS NOT ENOUGH The (1999, JAMES BOND) Music score
   by DAVID ARNOLD. title song (D.Arnold-Don Black)
   sung by GARBAGE -S/T- *UNIVERSAL: 112 161-2 (CD)*
WORLD OF PETER RABBIT AND FRIENDS (BBC1 9/4/93) music
   COLIN TOWNS theme "Perfect Day" sung by MIRIAM
   STOCKLEY on *Carlton: PWKS 4200 (CD)*
WORLD OF SPORT (ITV) *see COLL.6,148,176,270,363,*
WORLD SNOOKER (BBC Embassy World Championship) theme
   "Drag Racer" DOUGLAS WOOD GROUP *see COLL.148,176,*
   Shot Of The Championship "Wicked Game" CHRIS ISAAK
   Lond: LON(X)(CD)(MC)279 see COLL.148,176,
WORLD OF TIM FRAZER The (BBC 1960) theme music" Willow
   Waltz" by CYRIL WATTERS *see COLL.7,23,184,*
WORLD WRESTLING - see WWF
WRAPPERS (BBC2 17/11/1998) theme music "Sentimental
   Journey" (Les Brown-Ben Homer-Bud Green) *TV vers.:*
   ESQUIVEL on 'This is Easy' *VIRGIN: VTDCD 80 (2CD)*
WRESTLING - see WWF
WRONG TROUSERS,The (Wallace & Gromit)(1993) M: JULIAN
   NOTT v/o PETER SALLIS -S/T- *inc:* 'A Grand Day Out'
   BBC (Techn): ZBBC 1947 (MC) / BBC Video: BBCV 5201
   (Wrong Trousers) *BBCV 5155* (A Grand Day Out) *(VHS)*
WUTHERING HEIGHTS (ITVN 05/4/1998) Music score by
   WARREN BENNETT -S/T- *WEEKEND (BMG): CDWEEK 108 CD*
WUTHERING HEIGHTS (STUDIO REC.1991) Songs: BERNARD J.
   TAYLOR *with* DAVE WILLETTS-LESLEY GARRETT & Company
   SILVA SCREEN (Koch): SONG(CD)(C) 904 (CD/MC)
WUTHERING HEIGHTS (FILM 1991) Music: RYUICHI SAKAMOTO
   VIRGIN Classics (EMI): VC 759276-2 (CD)
WWF (WORLD WRESTLING FEDERATION) (SKY SPORTS VARIOUS)
   VARIOUS ARTIST COMPILATIONS / THE WRESTLING ALBUM
   WWF: THE MUSIC VOLUME 1   - *KOCH: 37994-2 (CD)*
   WWF: THE MUSIC VOLUME 2   - *KOCH: 38709-2 (CD)*
   WWF: THE MUSIC VOLUME 3   - *KOCH: 38803-2 (CD)*
   WWF: THE MUSIC VOLUME 4   - *KOCH: 33361-2 (CD)*
WYATT EARP (Life and Legend of) (USA TV/ITV 1955-61)
   see COLL.111,178,330,348,401,
WYATT EARP (1993) Music score: JAMES NEWTON HOWARD
   -S/T- *WB (TEN): 9362 445660-2 (CD) -4 (MC)*
WYCLIFFE (ITV 7/8/93) theme music by NIGEL HESS
   see COLL.6,193,
WYRD SISTERS (C4 18/5/97) m: KEITH HOPWOOD-PHIL BUSH
   see under 'SOUL MUSIC' *and* 'DISCWORLD'

X-FILES (BBC2 96) theme: MARK SNOW -S/T-"Songs In The
Key Of X" with MARK SNOW-SHERYL CROW-FOO FIGHTERS-
NICK CAVE-ELVIS COSTELLO & BRIAN ENO and others on
WEA: 9362 46079-2 (CD) "The Truth And The Light"
X files theme song MARK SNOW on *WEA: 9362 46279-2
(CD) -4 (MC)*
see *COLL.38,121,229,249,256,262,267,307,309,323,*
                                 331,344,362,389,
X-FILES: FIGHT THE FUTURE (FILM 1998) Music: MARK SNOW
   music score: *WARNER BROS: 7559 62217-2 (CD) -4(MC)*
   songs by VA: *WARNER BROS: 7599 62266-2 (CD) -4(MC)*
X-RAY (1980) - see DEATH WISH
X-THE UNKNOWN (1956) Music score by JAMES BERNARD
   'DEVIL RIDES OUT' *S SCREEN: FILMCD 174 (CD) DELET.*
XANADU (1980) Music score: BARRY DE VORZON -S/T- *feat:*
   OLIVIA NEWTON JOHN-ELECTRIC LIGHT ORCHESTRA-CLIFF
   RICHARD -S/T- *re-issue EPIC (Ten): 486 620-2 (CD)*
XENA: WARRIOR PRINCESS (SKY2 8/9/96) mus.theme & score
   JOSEPH LoDUCA / song "Burial" sung by LUCY LAWLESS
   -S/T- *VARESE (Pinn): VSD 5750 (CD)* (Volume 1)
   -S/T- *VARESE (Pinn): VSD 5883 (CD)* (Volume 2)
   -S/T- *VARESE (Pinn): VSD 6031 (CD)* (Volume 3)
   -S/T- *VARESE (Pinn): VSD 6032 (CD)* (Volume 4)
   see *COLL.38,122,312,*
XENA: WARRIOR PRINCESS (THE BITTER SUITE, all musical
   episode) feat music by JOSEPH LoDUCA and includes
   vocals by LUCY 'XENA' LAWLESS, MICHELLE NICASTRO,
   KEVIN SMITH and the cast of XENA: WARRIOR PRINCESS
   VARESE (Pinn): VSD 5918 (CD)
YAKSA (1985) *Music by* Nancy Wilson-Toots Thielmans-
   Masahiko Satoh -S/T- *DENON: C38-7556 (CD)*
YEAR OF LIVING DANGEROUSLY (1981) Music: MAURICE JARRE
   see *COLL.165,*
YEAR WITH FRED (BBC2 9/2/87) mus "Carnival Of Venice"
   (Briccialdi) JAMES GALWAY *RCA: (PD)(PK)PL 70260*
YELLOW SUBMARINE (1967) Music score: GEORGE MARTIN
   songs by JOHN LENNON and PAUL McCARTNEY
   digitally remastered/remixed (1999) 'songtrack' on
   APPLE-PARL.(EMI): 521 481-2 (CD) -4 (MC) -1 (LP)
   orig -S/T- (George Martin score and 6 songs) on
   APPLE EMI: CDP 746 445-2(CD) & (TC)PCS7070 (MC/LP)
YENTL (1983) Music: MICHEL LEGRAND Songs (M.LEGRAND-
   Alan & Marilyn BERGMAN) *sung by* BARBRA STREISAND
   -S/T- *SONY EUROPE (Discovery): CD 86302 (CD)*
YEOMAN OF THE GUARD (operetta) songs by W.S.Gilbert &
   A.Sullivan
   1.PRO-ARTE ORCHEST (Malcolm Sargent) GLYNDEBOURNE
     FESTIVAL CHOIR Soloists: ALEX YOUNG-DENIS DOWLING
     RICHARD LEWIS-JOHN CAMERON *EMI:CMS 764415-2 (2CDs)*
   2.D'OYLY CARTE OPERA COMPANY *incl* 'TRIAL BY JURY'
     LONDON (Univ): 417 358-2 (2CD)
   3.D'OYLY CARTE OPERA COMPANY *feat:* DAVID FIELDSEND-
     FENTON GRAY-DONALD MAXWELL / MD: JOHN OWEN EDWARDS
     TER (Koch): CDTER2 1195 (2CD)

YOLANDA AND THE THIEF (1945) *feat* FRED ASTAIRE
plus 'THE FLEET'S IN' -S/T- selections on
GREAT MOVIE THEMES (BMG): CD 60033 (CD)

YO-YO MA: INSPIRED BY BACH (BBC2 7/2/1998) 'Suites For
Cello Solo' (J.S.Bach) YO-YO MA 'The Cello Suites
Inspired by BACH' *SONY CLASSICS: S2K 63203 (2CD)*

YOGI BEAR (USA TV) *see COLL.345,373,*

YOU CAN'T HAVE EVERYTHING 1937 ALICE FAY-DON AMECHE
-S/T- select.including songs from 'MELODY FOR TWO'
'GO INTO YOUR DANCE'/'YOU'LL NEVER GET RICH' on
GREAT MOVIE THEMES (Target-BMG): CD 60014 (CD)

YOU GOTTA WALK IT LIKE YOU TALK IT (1971) Music score:
Walter BECKER-Donald FAGEN (from STEELY DAN) -S/T-
SEE FOR MILES (Pinn): SEECD 357 (CD)

YOU MUST REMEMBER THIS (BBC1 8/5/95) VE Day Special
Various Wartime Artists (original recordings) on
HAPPY DAYS (BMG-Con): UCD 252 (CD)

YOU ONLY LIVE TWICE (1967) Music score: JOHN BARRY
t.song (John BARRY-L.BRICUSSE) by NANCY SINATRA
-S/T- *reissue EMI PREMIER: CZ 559 (CD)*
JAMES BOND FILM INDEX p.358
see COLL.34,53,54,55,286,314,

YOU'LL NEVER GET RICH (1941) Film Musical: COLE PORTER
feat: FRED ASTAIRE-RITA HAYWORTH -S/T- including
songs from 'MELODY FOR TWO'/'YOU CAN'T HAVE
EVERYTHING'/'GO INTO YOUR DANCE'
GREAT MOVIE THEMES (Target-BMG): CD 60014 (CD)

YOUNG AMERICANS The (1993) Music: DAVID ARNOLD songs:
-S/T- *ISLAND MAST (Univ): IMCD 220 (CD) ICT 8019*

YOUNG AND THE RESTLESS The (US soap 73)'Nadia's theme'
(H.MANCINI) JAMES GALWAY *RCA (BMG): 09026 61178-2
(CD) -4 (MC) - see COLL.382,*

YOUNG BESS (1953) Music score: MIKLOS ROZSA -S/T-
Import PROMETHEUS (Silva Screen): PCD 133 (CD)

YOUNG DOCTORS The (Australian TV/ITV 80's) theme mus
(King-Ollman) *see COLL.376,*

YOUNG EINSTEIN (1988) Music sco: WILLIAM MOTZING -S/T-
IMS (Univ): E.393 929-2 (CD)

YOUNG GIRLS OF ROCHEFORT The (1968) Music sco: MICHEL
LEGRAND -S/T- *POLYGRAM FRANCE (Discov): 558 408-2
(CD) also on 834 140-2 (CD)*

YOUNG GUARD (1948) Music: D.SHOSTAKOVICH *see* ZOYA

YOUNG GUNS (BBC2 01/01/1999) title song by WHAM! on
'Fantastic' *EPIC (Ten): 450 090-2 (CD)*

YOUNG HERCULES (USA TV) Music score: JOSEPH LoDUCA
-S/T- *VARESE (Pinn): VSD 5983 (CD)*
see also HERCULES

YOUNG INDIANA JONES CHRONICLES (BBC1 20/11/94) mus:
LAURENCE ROSENTHAL -S/T- *VARESE (Pinn): VSD 5381
Vol.1 VSD 5391 (2) VSD 5401 (3) VSD 5421 (4) CDs*

YOUNG LIONS The (1958) Music sc: HUGO FRIEDHOFER -S/T-
+THIS EARTH IS MINE *VARESE (Pinn): VSD 25403 (2CD)*

YOUNG MAN OLDER WOMAN (O.CAST ALBUM) *feat* REYNALDO REY
ICHIBAN (Koch): ICHO 1159-2 (CD) -4 (MC)

YOUNG ONES The (1962) CLIFF RICHARD & SHADOWS -S/T-
MFP (EMI): CDMFP 6020 (CD) see COLL.296,350,
YOUNG PERSON'S GUIDE TO BECOMING A ROCK STAR The
(C4 10/11/1998) Music score: GUY PRATT -S/T- with
V/A *VIRGIN (EMI): VTDCD 231 (2CD) VTDMC 231 (MC)*
YOUNG RIDERS The (USA 90/ITV 5/91) theme: JOHN DEBNEY
see COLL.17,
YOU'RE A BIG BOY NOW (1967) Music: JOHN SEBASTIAN The
LOVIN' SPOONFUL -S/T- with 'WHAT'S UP, TIGER LILY'
RCA CAMDEN (BMG): 74321 69952-2 (CD)
RAZOR & TIE (Koch): RE 2167-2 (CD)
YOU'VE GOT MAIL (1998) Music score: GEORGE FENTON
-S/T- (score) *VARESE (Pinn): VSD 6015 (CD)*
-S/T- (songs) *ATLANTIC (TEN): 7567 83153-2 (CD)*
Z (1969) Mus: MIKIS THEODORAKIS Suite on
DRG (Pinn): 32901-4 (2MC)
Z CARS (BBC1 began 2/1/62) theme "Johnny Todd" (Trad.)
see COLL.2,4,270,
ZABRISKIE POINT (1969) Music: PINK FLOYD-KALEIDOSCOPE
GRATEFUL DEAD-PATTI PAGE-YOUNGBLOODS-JERRY GARCIA-
-S/T- *reissue EMI S/TRACKS: 823 364-2 (2CD)*
ZACHARIAH (1971) V.Arts: COUNTRY JOE & FISH-JAMES GANG
ELVIN JONES -S/T- *SEE FOR MILES: SEEK 91 (MC)*
ZED AND TWO NOUGHTS, A (1985) Music sco: MICHAEL NYMAN
-S/T- *VIRGIN (EMI): CDVE 54 (CD) TCVE 54 (MC)*
ZEPPELIN (1971) Music score: ROY BUDD -S/T- Coll.also
feat 'SOLDIER BLUE' (1970) & 'CATLOW' (1971) on
CINEPHILE (Pinn): CINCD 022 (CD)
ZERO PATIENCE (1993) Music sc: GLEN SCHELLENBERG *feat:*
POISON-SWOON + oth -S/T- *MILAN (BMG): 287971 (CD)*
ZIEGFELD FOLLIES (1944) *featur* FRED ASTAIRE-GENE KELLY
LUCILLE BALL -S/T- *reiss EMI PREM: CDODEON 3 (CD)*
ZIEGFELD GIRL (1941) *feat* JUDY GARLAND-TONY MARTIN
plus 'EVERY SUNDAY' -S/T- selections on
GREAT MOVIE THEMES (BMG): CD 60026 (CD)
ZIGGY STARDUST (THE MOTION PICTURE) (1982) *featuring*
DAVID BOWIE -S/T- *EMI: CDP 780 411-2 (CD)*
ZOMBIE PROM (1997) ORIGINAL BROADWAY CAST RECORDING
FIRST NIGHT (Pinn): CASTCD 66 (CD)
ZOO (BBC1 07/07/1999) theme music by DEBBIE WISEMAN
performed by BBC CONCERT ORCHESTRA *unavailable*
ZORBA THE GREEK (1964) Music composed and performed by
MIKIS THEODORAKIS *INTUITION (Pinn): INT 31032 (CD)*
see COLL.70,211,
ZOYA (1944) Music score: DIMITRI SHOSTAKOVICH + 'THE
YOUNG GUARD' *RUSSIAN DISC (Koch): RDCD 10002 (CD)*
ZULU! (1963) Music score by JOHN BARRY
ORIG -S/T- *reissue with* 'FOUR IN THE MORNING' on
RPM (Pinn): RPM 195 (CD)
New Record: CITY OF PRAGUE PHILHARMONIC & CROUCH
END FESTIVAL CHORUS conducted by NIC RAINE + other
tracks* *SILVA SCREEN (Koch): FILMXCD 305 (2CD)*
SILVA SCREEN (Koch): FILMCD 022 (CD)
see COLL.29,33,35,70,140,202,

FOR SUBSCRIPTION INFORMATION SEE p.357

FOR TELE-TUNES HISTORY SEE p.368

SEE ALSO INTRODUCTION NOTES p.4

LAYOUT

THE FOLLOWING 104 PAGES ARE DEVOTED TO COLLECTIONS OF

TELEVISION, FILM AND SHOW MUSIC COMPLETE WITH TRACK

DETAILS. *ENTRIES ARE CROSS-REFERENCED AGAINST THE MAIN*

TEXT OF THE BOOK. FOR EXAMPLE 'ZULU'

```
ZULU! (1963) Music score by JOHN BARRY
  ORIG -S/T- reissue with 'FOUR IN THE MORNING' on
  RPM (Pinn): RPM 195 (CD)
  New Recording CITY OF PRAGUE PHILHARMONIC & CROUCH
  END FESTIVAL CHORUS cond: NIC RAINE + other tracks
  SILVA SCREEN (Koch): FILMXCD 305 (2CD)

...see COLL.29,33,35,70,140,202,
```

ZULU IS LISTED ON SIX SEPARATE COLLECTIONS. THE FIRST

NUMBER IS *29,* SO LOOK ALONG THE PAGE HEADERS FOR

COLLECTION *29, (page 261: COLLECTIONS 25-30,)* AND YOU

WILL SEE ENTRY *29,* WITH FULL TRACK DETAILS

```
29.BARRY John - CLASSIC JOHN BARRY - City Of Prague
   Symphony Orch (Nicholas Raine) Suites and Themes
   SILVA SCREEN (Koch): FILMCD 141 (CD)        1993
   ZULU-OUT OF AFRICA-BODY HEAT-MIDNIGHT COWBOY-THE
   LAST VALLEY-BORN FREE-CHAPLIN-ELEANOR & FRANKLIN
   DANCES WITH WOLVES-INDECENT PROPOSAL-PERSUADERS
   ROBIN AND MARIAN-SOMEWHERE IN TIME-THE LION IN
   WINTER-HANOVER STREET-RAISE THE TITANIC
```

IF THIS PARTICULAR COLLECTION IS NOT TO YOUR TASTE THEN

PROCEED TO CHECK OUT THE REMAINDER *33,35,70,140,202,*

*1.***20TH CENTURY FOX: MUSIC FROM THE GOLDEN AGE** V.Arts.
Orig Soundtrack Recordings by Orig Composers
VARESE (Pinn): VSD 5937 (CD)   *1998*
Alfred Newman: 20TH CENTURY FOX FANFARE/SEVEN YEAR
ITCH/RAZOR'S EDGE/CAPTAIN FROM CASTILE/LEAVE HER TO
HEAVEN/ALL ABOUT EVE/THE SONG OF BERNADETTE/BEST OF
EVERYTHING/THE PRESIDENT'S LADY/A MAN CALLED PETER
Franz Waxman: PRINCE VALIANT
Bernard Herrmann: ANNA AND THE KING/BENEATH THE 12
MILE REEF/THE GHOST AND MRS.MUIR/PRINCE OF PLAYERS/
THE MAN IN THE GREY FLANNEL SUIT-THE GARDEN OF EVIL
JOURNEY TO THE CENTRE OF THE EARTH Alex North VIVA
ZAPATA/DADDY LONG LEGS Victor Young THE TALL MEN
Sammy Fain: LOVE IS A MANY SPLENDORED THING Hugo
Friedhofer: THE RAINS OF RANCHIPUR/VIOLENT SATURDAY
Cyril Mockridge: WILL SUCCESS SPOIL ROCK HUNTER
Jerry Goldsmith: THE STRIPPER/RIO CONCHOS/PATTON

*2.***50 CLASSIC TV THEMES** - Bruce Baxter Orchestra
CARLTON SOUNDS: 33043-2 (2CD) (orig 2LP 1977)   *1998*
IRONSIDE-KOJAK-COLUMBO-ONEDIN LINE-POLDARK-LIVER
BIRDS (On A Mountain Stands A Lady)-PALLISERS-NO HO
NESTLY-WHATEVER HAPPENED TO THE LIKELY LADS-SEVEN
FACES OF WOMAN (She)-BROTHERS-PROTECTORS (Avenues &
Alleyways)-COLDITZ-DAD'S ARMY (Who Do You Think You
Are Kidding Mr.Hitler)-BONANZA-WAGON TRAIN-MISSION
IMPOSSIBLE-ALIAS SMITH&JONES-ANGELS-JOHNNY STACCATO
EMERGENCY WARD 10-THE SAINT-PERSUADERS-DEPARTMENT S
VIRGINIAN-DEPUTY-RAWHIDE-HAWAII FIVE O-McCLOUD-
CORONATION ST.-CROSSROADS-DR.KILDARE (3 Stars Will
Shine Tonight)-OWEN MD (Sleepy Shores)-DR.FINLAY'S
CASEBOOK (A Little Suite No.2)-TODAY (Windy)-ON THE
MOVE-NATIONWIDE(Good Word)-THE SWEENEY-THUNDERBIRDS
STAR TREK-SOFTLY SOFTLY-DIXON OF DOCK GREEN-Z CARS-
UPSTAIRS DOWNSTAIRS (Edwardians)-DUCHESS OF DUKE
STREET-WHEN THE BOAT COMES IN (Dance To Your Daddy)
THE AVENGERS-CALLAN-VAN DER VALK (Eye Level)

*3.***90's MOVIES THEMES** The New World Orchestra
EMI GOLD: 522 311-2 (CD)   *1999*
1.SURRENDER *(TOMORROW NEVER DIES)* 2.BRAVEHEART 3.
SCHINDLER'S LIST 4.BELOVED 5.KISSING YOU *(ROMEO &
JULIET)* 6.AS GOOD AS IT GETS 7.LAST OF THE MOHICANS
8.LAND GIRLS 9.WHEN YOU BELIEVE *(PRINCE OF EGYPT)*
10.MISSION IMPOSSIBLE 11.ROBERT AND MARY *(ROB ROY)*
12.JFK 13.STREETS OF PHILADELPHIA *(PHILADELPHIA)* 14
AMISTAD 15.LOVE IS ALL AROUND *(4 WEDDINGS & A FUN.)*
16.THE GHOST AND THE DARKNESS 17.NEARER TO THEE MY
GOD *(TITANIC)* 18.MY HEART WILL GO ON *(TITANIC)*

*4.***A-Z OF BRITISH TV THEMES FROM THE 60's and 70's**
PLAY IT AGAIN (S.Screen-Koch): PLAY 004 (CD)   *1993*
AVENGERS-CAPTAIN SCARLET & MYSTERONS-CATWEAZLE-THE
CHAMPIONS-CROSSROADS-DAD'S ARMY-DANGER MAN-DEPT.S
DOCTOR IN THE HOUSE-DR.WHO-EMMERDALE FARM-FIREBALL
XL5-FORSYTE SAGA-HADLEIGH-HANCOCK-MAIGRET-MAN ALIVE
MAN IN A SUITCASE-NO HIDING PLACE-PLEASE SIR-POWER

GAME-RETURN OF THE SAINT-THE SAINT-SPORTSNIGHT-STEP
TOE AND SON-STINGRAY-THANK YOUR LUCKY STARS-THUNDER
BIRDS-TOP SECRET-Z CARS *incl: 21 original versions*
5.A-Z OF BRITISH TV THEMES VOLUME 2 - Various Artists
PLAY IT AGAIN (S.Screen-Koch): PLAY 006 (CD)   1994
ADVENTURES OF BLACK BEAUTY-ALL CREATURES GREAT AND
SMALL-ANGELS-ANIMAL MAGIC-AUF WIEDERSEHEN PET-BBC
CRICKET-BERGERAC-BREAD-BUDGIE-DANGER MAN-DOCTOR WHO
THE FENN STREETGANG-FOUR FEATHER FALLS-FREEWHEELERS
GRANDSTAND-HERE'S HARRY-HUMAN JUNGLE-JUKE BOX JURY-
LIVER BIRDS-MAN ABOUT THE HOUSE-THE NEW AVENGERS-
OWEN MD-THE PERSUADERS-RUGBY SPECIAL-SUPERCAR-TALES
OF THE UNEXPECTED-UPSTAIRS DOWNSTAIRS-VAN DER VALK-
VISION ON-WHATEVER HAPPENED TO THE LIKELY LADS
6.A-Z OF BRITISH TV THEMES VOLUME 3 - Various Artists
PLAY IT AGAIN (S.Screen-Koch): PLAY 010 (CD)   1996
THE BEIDERBECKE CONNECTION *(CRYIN' ALL DAY)* Frank
Ricotti All Stars BLAKE'S 7 Dudley Simpson BLOTT ON
THE LANDSCAPE Dave MacKay DANGERFIELD Nigel Hess
DEMPSEY AND MAKEPEACE South Bank Or DOCTOR FINLAY'S
CASEBOOK *(MARCH FROM A LITTLE SUITE)* Trevor Duncan
EMERGENCY WARD 10 *(SILKS AND SATINS)* Peter Yorke
HETTY WAINTHROPP INVESTIGATES Nigel Hess INTERNATIO
NAL DETECTIVE Edwin Astley JUST WILLIAM Nigel Hess
LOVEJOY Denis King MIDWEEK /NATIONWIDE *(Good Word)*
John Scott THE NEWCOMERS *(FANCY DANCE)* John Barry
THE ONE GAME *(SAYLON DOLAN)* Nigel Hess / Chameleon
POIROT Christopher Gunning THE PROFESSIONALS South
Bank Orch RUTH RENDELL MYSTERIES Brian Bennett
SEXTON BLAKE Vic Flick Snd SHOESTRING George Fenton
SKI SUNDAY *(POP LOOKS BACH)* Sam Fonteyn THE SWEENEY
Harry South TERRY & JUNE *(BELL HOP)*John Shakespeare
THIS IS YOUR LIFE *(GALA PERFORMANCE)* Laurie Johnson
TRIALS OF LIFE George Fenton WHEN THE BOAT COMES IN
(DANCE TI THI DADDY) Alex Glasgow WISH ME LUCK Jim
Parker WOOF! Paul Lewis Woof Band WORLD OF SPORT
(W.OF SPORT MARCH) Don Jackson WYCLIFFE Nigel Hess
7.A-Z OF BRITISH TV THEMES VOLUME 4 - Various Artists
PLAY IT AGAIN (S.Screen-Koch): PLAY 009 (CD)   1998
1.ADVENTURES OF NICHOLAS NICKELBY Stephen Oliver 2.
ASK THE FAMILY *SUNRIDE* John Leach 3.AUF WIEDERSEHEN
PET *BACK WITH THE BOYS* Joe Fagin 4.BBC WIMBLEDON
LIGHT & TUNEFUL Keith Mansfield 5.BIG DEAL Bobby G.
6.BIG MATCH *LA SOIREE* David Ordini 7.BIRD OF PREY
Dave Greenslade8.CAMPION Nigel Hess 9.CRIMEWATCH UK
EMERGENCY John Cameron 10.DID YOU SEE Francis Monkm
an 11.FOLLYFOOT *THE LIGHTNING TREE* The Settlers 12.
GRANDSTAND (1950's-60's) *NEWSCOOP* Len Stevens 13.
HOLIDAY *HEARTSONG* Gordon Giltrap 14.JAMAICA INN
Francis Shaw 15.KINSEY Dave Greenslade 16.MAIGRET
(1990s) Nigel Hess 17.MASTERMIND *APPROACHING MENACE*
Neil Richardson 18.ON THE BUSES Tony Russell 19.
PEOPLE IN LONDON *SPANISH ARMADA* Les Reed 20.
PORTERHOUSE BLUE Flying Picketts 21.QUATERMASS II

MARS (G.HOLST) 22.RANDALL AND HOPKIRK DECEASED
Edwin Astley 23.RESORT TO MURDER Bill Connor 24.
SHADOW OF THE NOOSE Isabel Buchanan 25.SPORTSVIEW
SATURDAY SPORTS Wilfred Burns 26.TINKER TAILOR
SOLDIER SPY *(Main title)* Geoffrey Burgon 27.TINKER
TAILOR SOLDIER SPY *(NINC DIMITIS)* Lesley Garrett 28
TRAVELLING MAN *(MAX'S THEME)* Duncan Browne 29.
WHICKER'S WORLD *(THE TRENDSETTERS)* Laurie Johnson
30.WORLD OF TIM FRAZER *(WILLOW WALTZ)* Cyril Watters

8.<u>A-Z OF BRITISH TV THEMES - THE RON GRAINER YEARS</u>
PLAY IT AGAIN (S.Screen-Koch): PLAY 008 (CD)   1994
Ron Grainer themes and recordings
A TOUCH OF VELVET A STING OF BRASS *(M.Wirtz)(Disco)*
ALONG THE BOULEVARDS *(from 'MAIGRET')*-ANDORRA *(from
'Andorra' and 'Danger Island')*-ASSASSINATION TROT
(Assassination Bureau)-BORN AND BRED-BOY MEETS GIRL
-HAPPY JOE *('Comedy Playhouse')*-DETECTIVE-DR.WHO
(orig) - DR.WHO *(disco)*- BUTTERED CRUMPET *('Fanny
Craddock')*-JAZZ AGE-JOHNNY'S TUNE *('Sunday Break' &
'Some People')* -LOVE THEME FROM 'ONLY WHEN I LARF'-
MAIGRET-MALICE AFORETHOUGHT-MAN IN A SUITCASE-ILLIC
IT CARGO *('Man In The News')*-OLIVER TWIST *performed
by The Eagles* - PAUL TEMPLE-THE PRISONER *(original)*
THE PRISONER *(orch)*- REBECCA-SOUTH RIDING-TALES OF
THE UNEXPECTED *(orig)*-TALES OF T.UNEXPECTED *(disco)*
OLD NED *('Steptoe & Son')*-TRAIN NOW STANDING *(Green
Pastures)*-TROUBLE WITH YOU LILIAN *('Counting The Co
ster')*-WHEN LOVES GROWS COLD *(Edward & Mrs.Simpson)*

--- <u>A-Z OF FANTASY TV THEMES</u> - see BATTLESTAR GALACTICA

9.<u>ADDINSELL Richard</u> - BRITISH LIGHT MUSIC BBC Concert
Orch (Kenneth Alwyn) +Philip Martin & Roderick Elms
MARCO POLO (Select): 8.223732 (CD)   1995
GOODBYE MR.CHIPS (1939) THE PRINCE AND THE SHOWGIRL
(1957) TOM BROWN'S SCHOOLDAYS (1951) A TALE OF TWO
CITIES (58) FIRE OVER ENGLAND (1937) + other music

10.<u>ADDINSELL Richard</u> - FILM MUSIC
Royal Ballet Sinfonia conducted by Kenneth Alwyn
WHITE LINE (Select): CDWHL 2115   1999
BLITHE SPIRIT-ENCORE-FIRE OVER ENGLAND-GASLIGHT
PRELUDE-PARISIENNE-PASSIONATE FRIENDS-SCROOGE-SOUTH
RIDING-SOUTHERN RHAPSODY-WALTZ OF THE TORREADORS-
WRNS MARCH

11.<u>ADDINSELL Richard</u> - WARSAW CONCERTO
Royal Ballet Sinfonia (Kenneth Alwyn) *
ASV (Select): CDWHL 2108 (CD) ZCWHL 2018 (MC)   1997
INVOCATION for Piano and Orchestra (1955)-MARCH OF
THE UNITED NATIONS (1942)-WARSAW CONCERTO (1941)
BLITHE SPIRIT (1945)-THE DAY WILL DAWN (1942)-THE
GREENGAGE SUMMER (1961)-HIGHLY DANGEROUS (1950)-
THE LION HAS WINGS (1939)-OUT OF THE CLOUDS (1954)
PASSIONATE FRIENDS (1948)-THE SEA DEVILS (1953)-
UNDER CAPRICORN (1949) * Concert recorded 1996

*12.*__ADIEMUS__ - THE JOURNEY: BEST OF ADIEMUS
   VIRGIN (EMI): (CD)(TC)(MD)VE 946 (CD/MC/MD)   *1999*
   DELTA AIRLINES AD MUSIC / CHELTENHAM & GLOUCESTER
   BUILDING SOC.AD MUSIC (Cantus Song Of Tears) / etc.
   __ADIEMUS: SONGS OF SANCTUARY__ with London Philharm.
   Orch (Karl Jenkins) with Miriam Stockley
   VIRGIN (EMI): CD(TC)VE 925   *1995*
   ADIEMUS *(DELTA AIRLINES AD / TESTAMENT:THE BIBLE IN*
   ANIMATION BBC2) + 8 all composed by KARL JENKINS
   __ADIEMUS 2: CANTATA MUNDI__ *Virg: CD(TC)VE(X) 932 1997*
   SONG OF TEARS *(CHELTENHAM & GLOUCESTER AD)* + others
   see COLL 'NEW PURE MOODS' *VIRGIN: VTDCD 158 (2CD)*
--- __ALIEN INVASION__ - see 'SPACE AND BEYOND 2'
*13.*__ALL TIME GREATEST MOVIE SONGS__ - Various Artists
   SONYMUSIC TV: MOODCD 61 (2CD) MOODC 61 (MC)   *1998*
   1.LOVE IS ALL AROUND Wet Wet Wet 2.BECAUSE YOU LOVE
   ME Celine Dion 3.HOW DEEP IS YOUR LOVE Bee Gees 4.
   OCEAN DRIVE Lighthouse Family 5.TAKE MY BREATH AWAY
   Berlin 6.STARS Simply Red 7.MY GIRL Temptations 9.
   LADY IN RED Chris DeBurgh 10.UP WHERE WE BELONG Joe
   Cocker-Jennifer Warnes 11.A WHOLE NEW WORLD Regina
   Belle-Peabo Bryson 12.DREAM A LITTLE DREAM OF ME
   Mama Cass 13.ARTHUR'S THEME Christopher Cross 14.
   THE CRYING GAME Boy George 15.SON OF A PREACHER MAN
   Dusty Springfield 16.SOMEDAY Eternal 17.TURN BACK
   TIME Aqua 18.WAITING FOR A STAR TO FALL Boy Meets
   Girl 19.SAN FRANCISCO Scott MacKenzie 20.CALFORNIA
   DREAMIN'Mamas & Papas 21.UNCHAINED MELODY Righteous
   Brothers 22.MISSION IMPOSSIBLE Adam Clayton-Larry
   Mullen 23.MEN IN BLACK Will Smith 24.DEEPER UNDERGR
   OUND Jamiroquai 25.HOLD ME THRILL ME KISS ME KILL
   U2 26.BLAZE OF GLORY Bon Jovi 27.HOT STUFF Donna
   Summer 28.GOT TO BE REAL Cheryl Lynn 29.GANGSTA'S
   PARADISE Coolio 30.SOMEDAY Lisa Stansfield 31.LET'S
   STAY TOGETHER Al Green 32.LOVETRAIN O'Jays 33.THE
   SHOOP SHOOP SONG Cher 34.A GIRL LIKE YOU Edwyn
   Collins 35.SHY GUY Diana King 36.LOVEFOOL Cardigans
   37.SHOW ME HEAVEN Maria McKee 38.PICTURE OF YOU Boy
   zone 39.WHAT A FOOL BELIEVES Doobie Brothers 40.
   BROWN EYED GIRL Van Morrison 41.EIGHTEEN WITH A BUL
   LET Pete Wingfield 42.OH PRETTY WOMAN Roy Orbison
   43.WATERLOO Abba
*14.*__ALL TIME GREATEST MOVIE SONGS__ VOLUME 2 - V.Artists
   SONYMUSIC TV: MOODCD 67 (2CD) MOODC 67 (MC)   *1999*
   1.MY HEART WILL GO ON Celine Dion 2.WHEN YOU SAY
   NOTHING AT ALL Ronan Keating 3.STREETS OF PHILADELP
   HIA Bruce Springsteen 4.AS I LAY ME DOWN Sophie B.
   Hawkins 5.I SAY A LITTLE PRAYER Diana King 6.WHOLE
   NEW WORLD P.Bryson-Regina Belle 7.I'M KISSING YOU
   Des'Ree 8.BABY CAN I HOLD YOU Boyzone 9.TOO MUCH
   Spice Girls 10.FROM THE HEART Another Level 11.
   I WANT TO SPEND MY LIFETIME LOVING YOU Tina Arena &
   Marc Anthony 12.HEART OF A HERO Luther Vandross 13.
   FOR THE FIRST TIME Kenny Loggins 14.YOU WERE THERE

Babyface 15.I FINALLY FOUND SOMEONE B.Streisand &
Bryan Adams 16.A KISS FROM A ROSE Seal 17.WILL YOU
BE THERE Michael Jackson
CD2: 1.MEN IN BLACK Will Smith 2.I DON'T WANT TO
MISS A THING Aerosmith 3.SWEETEST THING Lauryn Hill
4.KISS ME Sixpence None The Richer 5.MANEATER Hall
& Oates 6.HEAVEN'S WHAT I FEEL Gloria Estefan 7.
ARMAGEDDON Trevor Rabin 8.PLAY DEAD Bjork & David
Arnold 9.GO THE DISTANCE Michael Bolton 10.KNOCKIN'
ON HEAVEN'S DOOR Bob Dylan 11.BLAZE OF GLORY Bon
Jovi 12.MODERN WOMAN Billy Joel 13.ALL AROUND THE
WORLD Lisa Stansfield 14.SPOOKY Dusty Springfield
15.AIN'T NO SUNSHINE Bill Withers 16.IT HAD TO BE
YOU Harry Connick Jnr.17.THE WAY YOU LOOK TONIGHT
Tony Bennett 18.DANCING QUEEN Abba 19.BUILD ME UP
BUTTERCUP Foundations

*15.*__ALMODOVAR Pedro__ - **SONGS OF ALMODOVAR** (songs from
films directed by PEDRO ALMODOVAR) V.Spanish Arts
EMI: 494 674-2 (CD)   *1998*
High Heels: 1.ONE YEAR OF LOVE 2.THINKS OF ME
Labyrinth Of Passion: 3.SUCK IT TO ME 4.GREAT GANGA
Pepi Luci Bom and Other Girls: 5.IT WAS WRITTEN
Dark Habits: 6.CHAINED 7.I LEFT BECAUSE I LEFT
Matador: 8.WAIT FOR ME IN HEAVEN / Flower Of My
Secret: 9.OH MY LOVE 10.IN THE LAST SIP / Women On
The Edge Of A Nervous Breakdown: 11.I'M UNHAPPY 12.
PURE THEATRE / Tie Me Up Tie Me Down: 13.I WILL RES
IST / Law Of Desire: 14.SATANASA 15.I'M GOING TO BE
A MOTHER 16.IF YOU GO AWAY 17.SUSAN GET DOWN 18.I
DOUBT IT 19.LET ME REMEMBER / What Have I Done To
Deserve This: 20.WELL PAID ONE 21.NUR NICHTAUS LIBE
WEINEN / Kika: 22.MOONLIGHT 23.OUR LOVE WAS BROKEN

*16.*__AMERICAN LIGHT MUSIC CLASSICS__ - **New London Orchest***
HYPERION: CDA 67067 (CD) KA 67067 (MC)   *1998*
1.THE ARKANSAS TRAVELER *(DAVID GUION)* 2.WASHINGTON
POST *(J.P.SOUSA)* 3.THE MARCH OF THE TOYS *(VICTOR
HERBERT)* 4.TO A WILD ROSE *(EDWARD MACDOWELL)* 5.
NARCISSUS *(ETHEL NEVIN)* 6.THE TEDDY BEARS PICNIC
(JOHN W.BRATTON) 7.WHISTLING RUFUS *(FREDERICK ALLEN
MILLS)* 8.THE WHISTLER AND HIS DOG *(ARTHUR PRYOR)* 9.
BLAZE AWAY *(ABE HOLZMANN)* 10.CHANSON *(RUDOLF FRIML)*
11.NOLA *(FELIX ARNDT)* 12.PROMENADE*(GEORGE GERSHWIN)*
13.CAROUSEL WALTZ *(RICHARD RODGERS)* 14.BELLE OF THE
BALL/PLINK PLANK PLUNK *(LEROY ANDERSON)* 15.THE TOY
TRUMPET *(HARRY WARNOW)*16.HOLIDAY FOR STRINGS *(DAVID
ROSE)* 17.SYMPHONY NO.5 & A HALF *(DON GILLIS)* 18.
PAVANNE *(MORTON GOULD)* / * Ronald Corp (conductor)

*17.*__AMERICAN TELEVISION'S GREATEST HITS__ - Daniel Caine
SILVA SCREEN (Koch): TVPMCD 804 (2CD) 1994 A.TEAM-
AIRWOLF-BARNABY JONES-BATTLESTAR GALACTICA-BAYWATCH
BEVERLY HILLS 90210-BUCK ROGERS IN T.25TH CENTURY-
CAGNEY & LACEY-CHEERS-COSBY SHOW-DOOGIE HOWSER MD-
EERIE INDIANA-EQUALIZER-EVENING SHADE-FALCON CREST-
FREDDY'S NIGHTMARES-HARDCASTLE & McCORMICK-HILL ST.

BLUE-HIGHWAY TO HEAVEN-INCREDIBLE HULK-KNIGHT RIDER
HUNTER-L.A.LAW-LITTLE HOUSE ON T.PRAIRIE-LOU GRANT-
MacGYVER-MAGNUM-MAN FROM UNCLE-MELROSE PLACE-MORK &
MINDY-MIDNIGHT CALLER-MUNSTERS-MURDER SHE WR.-NIGHT
COURT-NORTH & SOUTH-NORTHERN EXPOSURE-POLICE STORY-
PURSUIT-QUANTUM LEAP-ROCKFORD FILES-REMINGTON STEEL
ROSEANNE-SLEDGEHAMMER-STAR TREK: NEXT GEN.-SPENSER
FOR HIRE-ST.ELSEWHERE-TAXI-TWIN PEAKS-STREETHAWK
21 JUMP STREET-V: THE SERIES-WALTONS-YOUNG RIDERS

18.ANDERSON Gerry - EVOCATION (Various Artists)
EMI SONGBOOK: 7243 496612-2 (CD)   *1999*
1.THE EVE OF WAR *JEFF WAYNE* 2.ADAGIO *(ALBINONI)* 3.
COSSACK PATROL *RED ARMY CHOIR* 4.RHAPSODY IN BLUE
(GERSHWIN) 5.PRELUDE BEN HUR *(ROSZA)* 6.THUNDERBIRDS
BAND OF ROYAL MARINES 7.CALLING ELVIS *DIRE STRAITS*
8.FOUR FEATHER FALLS *MICHAEL HOLLIDAY* 9.SINGIN' IN
THE RAIN *GENE KELLY* 10.PUPPET ON A STRING *SANDIE
SHAW*11.SHOOTING STAR *SHADOWS* 12.TAKE 5 *DAVE BRUBECK*
13.GALLEY BEN HUR *(ROSZA)*14.RITUAL FIRE DANCE *LARRY
ADLER* 15.WHO DONE IT *HARRY NILSSON* 16.FINGAL'S CAVE
(MENDELSSOHN) 17.LAVENDER CASTLE *CRISPIN MERRELL*

19.AS SEEN ON TV - *GEORGE FENTON + Various Artists
DEBONAIR (Pinn): CDDEB 1010 (CD)   *1999*
1.BEYOND THE CLOUDS* 2.SALVA ME:SHADOW OF THE NOOSE
Isobel Buchanon 3.FRIENDS IN HIBERNATION:FIRST SNOW
OF WINTER) Music Sculptors 4.TRAVELLING MAN Duncan
Browne 5.HANNAY Denis King 6.THAT'S LIVIN' ALRIGHT
Joe Fagin 7.UNION GAME Andy Price 8.BARNEY MILLER
Elliott & Ferguson 9.HOME (BREAD) Cast 10.BERGERAC*
11.LOVEJOY Denis King 12.MARCH OF THE LOBSTERS (THE
TRIALS OF LIFE* 13.SHANGHAI VICE* 14.DR.WILLOUGHBY
David Mackay 15.HENRY VIII Adrian Thomas 16.STREETS
APART Neil Lockwood 17.THIEF IN THE NIGHT:RESORT TO
MURDER) Bill Connor 18.MONOCLED MUTINEER* 19.MOON &
SON Denis King 20.BLOTT ON THE LANDSCAPE Viv Fisher

--- **ARNOLD David** - *see* SHAKEN AND STIRRED
20.ARNOLD Malcolm - Film Music Of (London Symph.Orch*)
CHANDOS (Chandos): CHAN 9100 (CD)
THE BRIDGE ON THE RIVER KWAI (Suite For Large Orch
feat 'Colonel Bogey' (Kenneth Alford)-WHISTLE DOWN
THE WIND (Small Suite For Small Orchest)-THE SOUND
BARRIER (A Rhapsody For Orchestra Op.38)-HOBSON'S
CHOICE (Orchestral Suite)-THE INN OF THE SIXTH HAPP
INESS (Orchestral Suite) *Conductor: *RICHARD HICKOX*

21.ASTAIRE Fred - Songs From The Movies (Orig Tracks)
PAST PERFECT (THE): PPCD 78115   *1994*
Top Hat (35): NO STRINGS-ISN'T THIS A LOVELY DAY-
TOP HAT WHITE TIE & TAILS-CHEEK TO CHEEK-PICCOLINO
Follow The Fleet (36): WE SAW THE SEA-LET YOURSELF
GO-I'D RATHER LEAD A BAND-I'M PUTTING ALL MY EGGS
IN ONE BASKET-LET'S FACE THE MUSIC AND DANCE
Swing Time (36): PICK YOURSELF UP-THE WAY YOU LOOK
TONIGHT-A FINE ROMANCE-BOJANGLES OF HARLEM-NEVER
GONNA DANCE / Shall We Dance (37): BEGINNER'S LUCK

SLAP THAT BASS-THEY ALL LAUGHED-LET'S CALL THE WHOLE THING OFF-THEY CAN'T TAKE THAT AWAY FROM ME SHALL WE DANCE / A Damsel In Distress (37): I CAN'T BE BOTHERED NOW-THINGS ARE LOOKING UP-A FOGGY DAY-NICE WORK IF YOU CAN GET IT

22. <u>**AURIC Georges**</u> - **Film Music of Georges Auric**
The BBC Philharmonic condicted by Rumon Gamba
CHANDOS (Chandos): CHAN 9774 (CD) *1999*
BBC Philharmonic Orchestra conducted by Rumon Gamba
1.CAESAR AND CLEOPATRA (1945) 2.THE TITFIELD THUNDERBOLT (1952) 3.DEAD OF NIGHT (1945) 4. PASSPORT TO PIMLICO (1949) 5.THE INNOCENTS (1961) 6.THE LAVENDER HILL MOB (1951) 7.MOULIN ROUGE(1952) 8.FATHER BROWN (1954) 9.IT ALWAYS RAINS ON SUNDAY (1947) 10.HUE AND CRY (1946)

23. <u>**AVENGERS AND OTHER TOP 60s TV THEMES**</u> V.Artists *1998*
SEQUEL-CASTLE (Pinn):NEMCD 976 (2CD) NELP 976 (3LP)
1.AVENGERS 2.MAN IN A SUITCASE 3.THUNDERBIRDS 4.DR. WHO 5.STEPTOE & SON 6.DAD'S ARMY 7.CAPTAIN SCARLET 8.Z-CARS 9.SAINT 10.DEPARTMENT S 11.JOE 90 12. CROSSROADS 13.THANK YOUR LUCKY STARS 14.TAKE THREE GIRLS 15.STINGRAY 16.DANGER MAN 17.THE CHAMPIONS 18 HANCOCK 19.FORSYTE SAGA 20.WORLD CUP THEME 'ON THE BALL' 21.POWER GAME 22.DOCTOR FINLAY'S CASEBOOK 23. FIREBALL XL5 24.MAIGRET 25.OUT OF THIS WORLD 26.NO HIDING PLACE 27.FUGITIVE 28.WHODUNIT 29.W.SOMERSET MAUGHAM 30.COMEDY PLAYHOUSE CD2: 1.SCARLETT HILL 2.RICHARD BOONE SHOW 3.TIM FRAZER THEME 4.MR.ROSE INVESTIGATES 5.THE DOCTORS 6.SAM BENEDICT 7.BEN CASEY 8.SIR FRANCIS DRAKE9.PERRY MASON 10.OUR HOUSE 11.WHO IS SYLVIA 12.RIVIERA POLICE 13.GHOST SQUAD 14.ECHO FOUR-TWO 15.LOVE STORY 'OUR LOVE STORY' 16. NAKED CITY 17.TOP SECRET 18.CRANE 19.(-) 20.SENTIME NTAL AGENT 21.SPIES 22.THE DEPUTY 23.MAN ALIVE 24. LOVE STORY 'MEMORIES OF SUMMER' 25.THANK YOUR LUCKY STARS 'LUNA WALK' 26.WHICKER'S WORLD 27.THREE LIVE WIRES 28.QUICK BEFORE THEY CATCH US 29.RONNIE CORBE TT'S THEME 'THAT'S ME OVER HERE' 30.PEYTON PLACE

--- <u>**AYRES Mark**</u> - *see* CINEMA CAFE

24. <u>**BACHELOR IN PARADISE**</u> - **COCKTAIL CLASSICS FROM MGM**
EMI SOUNDTRACKS (EMI) 821 963-2 (CD) Var.Arts. 1997
BACHELOR IN PARADISE *(MAIN TITLE)*-BOSSA NOVA BESSIE *(GLASS BOTTOM BOAT)*-OVER THE RAINBOW *(WIZARD OF OZ)* SUNDAY IN NEW YORK *(TITLE)*-OL'MAN RIVER *(SHOW BOAT)* HOW ABOUT YOU*(BACHELOR IN PARIS)*-LOVE IS OH SO EASY *(KALUGA)(HONEYMOON HOTEL)*-ARUBA LIBERACE *(WHEN THE BOYS MEET THE GIRLS)*-I'VE GOT YOU UNDER MY SKIN*(THE MATING GAME)*-I GOT RHYTHM *(GIRL CRAZY)*-TEMPTATION *(GOING HOLLYWOOD)*-GIRL FROM IPANEMA *(GET YOURSELF A COLLEGE GIRL)*-FASHION SHOW *(NORTH BY NORTHWEST)*-THE WONDERFUL WORLD OF THE BROTHERS GRIMM *(TITLE THEME)* APPRECIATION *(VIVA LAS VEGAS)*-DANCING IN THE DARK *(BAND WAGON)*-COFFEE TIME *(SUBTERRANEANS)*-BACHELOR IN PARADISE *(END TITLE) Various Original Artists*

25.BALL Michael - Movies   *Polyg: 559 241-2 (CD)   1998*
1.THE WIND BENEATH MY WINGS 2.LOVE ON THE ROCKS
3.WE HAVE ALL THE TIME IN THE WORLD 4.PEOPLE ARE
STRANGE 5.MY HEART WILL GO ON 6.HAVE I TOLD YOU
LATELY 7.EVERYBODY'S TALKIN' 8.HOT STUFF 9.HOW DEEP
IS YOUR LOVE 10.I BELIEVE I CAN FLY 11.WAY WE WERE
12.AGAINST ALL ODDS 13.BLUES BROS Med: SHAKE/THINK/
EVERYBODY NEEDS SOMEBODY 14.BECAUSE YOU LOVE ME

26.BACHARACH Burt - The Burt Bacharach Album / V.Arts
*VARESE (Pinn): VSD 5889 (CD) 1998 inc:*ONE LESS BELL
TO ANSWER-I'LL NEVER FALL IN LOVE-THE LOOK OF LOVE-
ANYONE WHO HAD A HEART-THAT'S WHAT FRIENDS ARE FOR-
A HOUSE IS NOT A HOME-WHAT'S NEW PUSSYCAT-MY LITTLE
RED BOOK-WHOEVER YOU ARE-ARE YOU THERE-THE BLOB etc

27.BARRY John - BEST OF JOHN BARRY (Film & TV Themes)
POLYDOR: 849 095-2 (CD) 849 095-4 (MC)   1991
GOLDFINGER-SAIL THE SUMMER WINDS *(The Dove)*-LOVE AM
ONG THE RUINS-LOLITA-A DOLL'S HOUSE-FOLLOW FOLLOW
(Follow Me)-DIAMONDS ARE FOREVER-BOOM-MIDNIGHT COWB
OY-THIS WAY MARY *(Mary Queen Of Scots)*-THE GLASS ME
NAGERIE-THUNDERBALL-007-PLAY IT AGAIN *(The Tamarind
Seed)*-ORSON WELLES GREAT MYSTERIES-WE HAVE ALL THE
TIME IN THE WORLD *(On Her Majesty's Secret Service)*
THE WHISPERERS-CURIOUSER AND CURIOUSER *(Alice's Adv
entures In Wonderland)*-BILLY-THE GOOD TIMES ARE COM
ING *(Monte Walsh)*-WALKABOUT-THE ADVENTURER

28.BARRY John - BEST OF THE EMI YEARS
EMI: 523 073-2 (CD)   1999
1.HIT AND MISS *(JUKE BOX JURY THEME)* 2.BEAT GIRL 3.
BEAT FOR BEATNIKS 4.THE CHALLENGE 5.THE AGRESSOR 6.
SPINNEREE Michael Angelo Orch 7.SATIN SMOOTH 8.THE
JAMES BOND THEME 9.HUMAN JUNGLE *alternative version*
10.ROMAN SPRING OF MRS.STONE Michael Angelo Orch 11
TEARS Michael Angelo Orch 12.THE PARTY'S OVER 13.
CUTTY SARK *(DATELINE THEME)* 14.MARCH OF T.MANDARINS
15.ONWARD CHRISTIAN SPACEMEN 16.HUMAN JUNGLE *THEME*
17.GOLDFINGER Shirley Bassey 18.OUBLIE CA 19.SEVEN
FACES 20.SEANCE ON A WET AFTERNOON 21.MR.KISS KISS
BANG BANG Shirley Bassey 22.BORN FREE Matt Monro 23
MIDNIGHT COWBOY 24.DIAMONDS ARE FOREVER Shir.Bassey

29.BARRY John - CLASSIC JOHN BARRY - City Of Prague
Symphony Orch (Nicholas Raine) Suites and Themes
SILVA SCREEN (Koch): FILMCD 141 (CD)   1993
ZULU-OUT OF AFRICA-BODY HEAT-MIDNIGHT COWBOY-THE
LAST VALLEY-BORN FREE-CHAPLIN-ELEANOR AND FRANKLIN-
DANCES WITH WOLVES-INDECENT PROPOSAL-THE PERSUADERS
ROBIN AND MARIAN-SOMEWHERE IN TIME-THE LION IN WINT
ER-HANOVER STREET-RAISE THE TITANIC

30.BARRY John - MOVIOLA
EPIC (SONY: 472490-2 (CD)   1992
OUT OF AFRICA-MIDNIGHT COWBOY-BODY HEAT-SOMEWHERE
IN TIME-MARY QUEEN OF SCOTS-BORN FREE-DANCES WITH
WOLVES-CHAPLIN-COTTON CLUB-WALKABOUT-FRANCES-ON HER
MAJESTY'S S.SERVICE (WE HAVE ALL THE TIME)-MOVIOLA

*31.*__BARRY JOHN__ - __READY WHEN YOU ARE J.B.__
PEG Reiss: PEG 043 (CD 1999) orig: CBS 63952 (1970)
MIDNIGHT COWBOY theme *(MIDNIGHT COWBOY)*-WE HAVE ALL
THE TIME IN THE WORLD *(ON HER MAJESTY'S SECRET
SERVICE)*-ROMANCE FOR GUITAR & ORCHESTRA *(DEADFALL)*-
WHO WILL BUY MY YESTERDAYS-FUN CITY *MIDNIGHT COWBOY*
THE LION IN WINTER-ON HER MAJESTY'S SECRET SERVICE-
THE APPOINTMENT-TRY *(ON HER MAJESTY'S SECR.SERVICE)*
THE MORE THINGS CHANGE-AFTERNOON-BORN FREE theme

*32.*__BARRY John__ - __THE HITS & MISSES__ / Various Artists
PLAY IT AGAIN (Koch-S.Screen): PLAY 007 (2CD) 1998
CD1 1.WHAT DO YOU WANT Adam Faith 2.CAN'T FORGET
Johnny Gavotte 3.HIT AND MISS *(JUKE BOX JURY)* John
Barry 4.BOSTON TEA PARTY The Dallas Boys 5.BIG TIME
Adam Faith6.CARVE UP Adam Faith 7.IT DOESN'T MATTER
Danny Williams 8.WALK DON'T RUN John Barry Seven 9.
GREENFINGER Adam Faith 10.PEPE Russ Conway 11.
MATADOR FROM TRINIDAD Russ Conway 12.NOT GUILTY
Johnny De Little 13.BIG WHEEL Gerry Dorsey 14.WHERE
YOU ARE Denis Lotis 15.DJANGO'S CASTLE Diz Disley &
Downbeats 16.MY LAST WISH Adam Faith 17.MY ONE AND
ONLY Anita Harris 18.I HAVEN'T GOT YOU Anita Harris
19.ROCCO'S THEME *(ROCCO AND HIS BROTHERS)* Michael
Angelo 20.LITTLE YELLOW ROSES Adam Faith 21.OVER
AND OVER Bobby Shafto22.YOU KNOW WHAT I MEAN Johnny
Worth 23.ALL THESE THINGS Johnny Worth24.CUTTY SARK
(DATELINE LONDON) J.Barry 25.STALEMATE Tony Rocco
CD2 1.YOU'RE FOLLOWING ME Peter Gordeno 2.I'VE JUST
FALLEN FOR SOMEONE Darren Young3.MY TEARS WILL TURN
TO LAUGHTER Darren Young 4.UPTOWN Peter Gordeno 5.
COFFEE GRINDER Van Doren 6.CARAVAN OF LONELY MEN
Mark Tracey 7.SOMEONE NICE LIKE YOU Billy Cotton &
Kathie Kay 8.JAMES BOND THEME John Barry 9.NO LOVE
BUT YOUR LOVE Marion Ryan 10.DOWN BY THE RIVERSIDE
Peter Gordeno11.LOVER Johnny De Little 12.AWAY IN A
MANGER Nina and Frederick 13.LONELY AVENUE Marty
Wilde 14.MAM'SELLE Dick Kallman 15.MY ROMANCE Dick
Kallman 16.GLORY OF LOVE Dick Kallman 17.DEED I DO
Dick Kallman 18.SAY IT ISN'T SO Dick Kallman 19.YOU
CAN DO IT IF YOU TRYPeter Gordeno 20.RIDE ON Johnny
De Little21.DAYS OF WINE AND ROSES Johnny De Little
22.UNCHAINED MELODY Johnny De Little23.WIND AND THE
RAIN Johnny De Little 24.DREAM MAKER Tommy Steele
25.GOLDFINGER Shirley Bassey

*33.*__BARRY John__ - __THE NAME IS BARRY...JOHN BARRY__
EMBER (TKO-Magnum-Pinn): EMBCD 001 (CD)   1999
ZULU-FROM RUSSIA WITH LOVE-007-KINKY-LONELINESS OF
AUTUMN-FANCY DANCE-TROUBADOR-FOUR IN THE MORNING-
ELIZABETH-LONDON THEME-MONKEY FEATHERS-BIG SHIELD-
JUDI COMES BACK-RIVER WALK-NORMAN LEAVES-MOMENT OF
DESCISION-ALIKI-NGENZENI-THETHA LAVANTO-FIRST
RECONCILLIATION-LOVERS TENSION-LOVERS CLASP-
FIRE OF LONDON-RIVER RIDE

34. **BARRY John** - THEMEOLOGY: THE BEST OF JOHN BARRY
SIMPLY VINYL (Vital): SVLP 29 (2LP)   *1999*
COLUMBIA (Ten): 488 582-2 (CD) -4 (MC)   *1997*
1.PERSUADERS THEME 2.MIDNIGHT COWBOY 3.IPCRESS FILE
4.THE KNACK 5.WEDNESDAY'S CHILD 6.SPACE MARCH (CAPS
ULE IN SPACE) 7.THE GIRL WITH THE SUN IN HER HAIR
(SUNSILK 70's AD) 8.VENDETTA 9.DANNY SCIPIO THEME
10.JAMES BOND THEME 11.GOLDFINGER 12.DIAMONDS ARE
FOREVER 13.FROM RUSSIA WITH LOVE 14.YOU ONLY LIVE
TWICE 15.THUNDERBALL 16.ON HER MAJESTY'S SECRET SER
VICE 17.007 18.WALK DON'T RUN 19.BEAT FOR BEATNIKS
20.HIT AND MISS 21.BORN FREE 22.I HAD A FARM IN
AFRICA 23.JOHN DUNBAR THEME (DANCES WITH WOLVES)

35. **BARRY John** - ZULU -S/T- plus other filmworks
New Recording by CITY OF PRAGUE PHILHARMONIC & The
Crouch End Festival Chorus (conducted by NIC RAINE)
SILVA SCREEN (Koch): FILMXCD 305 (2CD)   *1999*
COMPLETE 'ZULU' MUSIC + selections from: THE COTTON
CLUB-DANCES WITH WOLVES-KING KONG-THE DEEP-KING RAT
THE SPECIALIST-MERCURY RISING-FRANCES-THE TAMARIND
SEED-'SUNSILK AD'GIRL WITH THE SUN IN HER HAIR HAIR
LAST VALLEY-LOVE AMONG THE RUINS-'FLORIDA FANTASY'
(from MIDNIGHT COWBOY)-MY SISTERS KEEPER-HAMMETT-
MISTER MOSES

--- *see also* EMBER YEARS Vol.1/2 (Collections 139/140)

36. **BASSEY Shirley** - Sings The Movies (1)
POLYGRAM TV (UNIV): 529 399-2 (CD) -4 (MC)   *1995*
GOLDFINGER / CRAZY *COALMINER'S DAUGHTER* / THE BEST
THAT YOU CAN DO (ARTHUR'S THEME) *ARTHUR* / LOVE ON
THE ROCKS *JAZZ SINGER* / ELEANOR RIGBY *YELLOW SUBMA
RINE* / LET'S STAY TOGETHER *PULP FICTION* / THE ROSE
THE ROSE / DO YOU KNOW WHERE YOU'RE GOING TO *MAHOG
GANY* / WE DON'T NEED ANOTHER HERO *MAD MAX BEYOND
THUNDERDOME* / IT MUST HAVE BEEN LOVE *PRETTY WOMAN*
TRY A LITTLE TENDERNESS *COMMITTMENTS* / HOPELESSLY
DEVOTED TO YOU *GREASE* / MAKIN' WHOOPEE *SLEEPLESS
IN SEATTLE* / WHO WANTS TO LIVE FOREVER *HIGHLANDER*

37. **BASSEY Shirley** - Sings The Movies (2)
MFP (EMI): CD(TC)MFP 6205 (CD/MC)   *1995*
GOLDFINGER / WHERE DO I BEGIN *LOVE STORY* / TONIGHT
WEST SIDE STORY / BIG SPENDER *SWEET CHARITY* / AS
LONG AS HE NEED ME *OLIVER* / DIAMONDS ARE FOREVER /
LADY IS A TRAMP *PAL JOEY* / AS TIME GOES BY *CASABLAN
CA* / YOU'LL NEVER WALK ALONE *CAROUSEL* / CLIMB EVERY
MOUNTAIN *SOUND OF MUSIC* / MOON RIVER *BREAKFAST AT
TIFFANY'S* / FUNNY GIRL / JUST ONE OF THOSE THINGS
NIGHT AND DAY / S'WONDERFUL *AN AMERICAN IN PARIS* /
YOU'LL NEVER KNOW *HELLO FRISCO HELLO* / MORE *MONDO
CANE* / LIQUIDATOR / I DON'T KNOW HOW TO LOVE HIM

38. **BATTLESTAR GALACTICA** - The A-Z Of Fantasy TV Themes
The Ultimate Collection of Classic & Cult Fantasy
SILVA SCREEN: TVPMCD 806 (2CDs)   *1999*
ADDAMS FAMILY-AIRWOLF-AVENGERS-BATMAN-BLAKE'S 7-

BUCK ROGERS-CAPTAIN SCARLET-DOCTOR WHO-FIREBALL XL5
HERCULES-JOE 90-KNIGHT RIDER-LAND OF THE GIANTS-
LOST IN SPACE-THE OUTER LIMITS-THE PRISONER-QUANTUM
LEAP-RED DWARF-SEAQUEST DSV-SPACE 1999-STAR TREK-
STINGRAY-THE SURVIVORS-THUNDERBIRDS-THE TIME TUNNEL
TWLIGHT ZONE-TWIN PEAKS-V-VOYAGE TO THE BOTTOM OF
THE SEA-XENA WARRIOR PRINCESS-X.FILES *and others*

--- **BAXTER Bruce** - *see COLLECTION 2*

39. **BBC CONCERT ORCHESTRA - DISNEY MOVIE FAVOURITES**
    DELTA-TARGET (BMG): CD 11022 (CD)   *1999*
    I WANNA BE LIKE HYOU-CAN YOU FEEL THE LOVE TONIGHT-
    WHOLE NEW WORLD-SOME DAY-CRUELLA DE VILLE-COLOURS
    OF THE WIND-BEAUTY AND THE BEAST-CIRCLE OF LIFE-
    WHEN I SEE AN ELEPHANT FLY-DREAM IS A WISH YOUR
    HEART MAKES-EVERYBODY WANTS TO BE A CAT-BIBBIDI
    BOBBIDI BOO-ALICE IN WONDERLAND-YOU CAN FLY-UNDER
    THE SEA-WHEN YOU WISH UPON A STAR

40. **BBC CONCERT ORCHESTRA - PLAYS THE HITS FROM BROADWAY**
    DELTA-TARGET (BMG): CD 11242 (CD)   *1999*
    JELLICLE BALL-TONIGHT-DON'T RAIN ON MY PARADE-SEND
    IN THE THE CLOWNS-SUNSET BOULEVARD-ALL I ASK OF YOU
    CAROUSEL WALTZ-WHAT I DID FOR LOVE-WHY GOD WHY-
    COME FOLLOW THE BAND-BRING HIM HOME-GUYS AND DOLLS-
    AS IF WE NEVER SAID GOODBYE-CRAZY FOR YOU

41. **BBC CONCERT ORCHESTRA - THE MOVIES**
    DELTA-TARGET (BMG): CD 10682 (CD)   *1999*
    BIG COUNTRY-STAR WARS-CASABLANCA-DAMBUSTERS-MOON
    RIVER (BREAKFAST AT TIFFANYS)-BRIDGE OVER THE RIVER
    KWAI-CHARIOTS OF FIRE-JAMES BOND *MEDLEY:* JAMES BOND
    THEME/THUNDERBALL/FROM RUSSIA WITH LOVE/GOLDFINGER-
    DOCTOR ZHIVAGO-ROCKY-LOVE STORY-THE GREAT ESCAPE-
    THE GODFATHER-THE ENTERTAINER (THE STING)-THE ALAMO
    MAGNIFICENT 7-GONE WITH THE WIND **cond:** DAVID ARNOLD

42. **BBC CONCERT ORCHESTRA - THE MUSICALS**
    DELTA-TARGET (BMG): CD 10692 (CD)   *1999*
    THAT'S ENTERTAINMENT-SINGIN'IN THE RAIN-CAROUSEL-
    BALI HAI (SOUTH PACIFIC)-SHALL WE DANCE (KING & I)-
    DON'T CRY FOR ME ARGENTINA (EVITA)-CABARET-DISNEY
    MEDLEY: PINOCCHIO/SONG OF THE SOUTH/LADY AND THE
    TRAMP/ALICE IN WONDERLAND/SNOW WHITE & THE 7 DWARFS
    THANK HEAVEN FOR LITTLE GIRLS (GIGI)-I COULD HAVE
    DANCED ALL NIGHT(MY FAIR LADY)-IF I WERE A RICH MAN
    (FIDDLER ON THE ROOF)-76 TROMBONES (THE MUSIC MAN)-
    HELLO DOLLY-FOOD GLORIOUS FOOD (OLIVER)-BIG SPENDER
    (SWEET CHARITY)-THE SOUND OF MUSIC

43. **BEAUTIFUL HOLLYWOOD** Cincinnati Pops Orch (E.Kunzel)
    TELARC-Conifer (BMG): CD 80440 (CD)   *1997*
    FORREST GUMP-RIVER RUNS THROUGH IT-ROB ROY-JERRY
    MAGUIRE-LEGENDS OF THE FALL-EVITA-THE BRIDGES OF
    MADISON COUNTY-POCAHONTAS-THE MISSION-FREE WILLY-
    FOREVER YOUNG-CINEMA PARADISO-RUDY-CHAPLIN-GRUMPIER
    OLD MEN-BUGSY-SCHINDLER'S LIST-GETTYSBURG

44. **BERGMAN SUITES:** Classic Film Music of ERIK NORDGREN
    Slovak Radio Symphony Orch.conducted by Adriano

MARCO POLO (Select): 8.22368-2 (CD)   *1998*
Suites from scores for INGMAR BERGMAN films: SMILES
OF A SUMMER NIGHT (1955) WAITING WOMEN (1952) THE
FACE (1958) WILD STRAWBERRIES (1957) GARDEN OF EDEN
--- **BERKELEY Busby** - *see* LULLABY OF BROADWAY
45.**BERNSTEIN Leonard** - **Unforgettable Classics**
CLASSICS FOR PLEASURE (EMI): CDCFP 6062 (CD)   *1998*
CANDIDE OVERTURE-CHICHESTER PSALMS-SIMPLE SONG from
ON THE TOWN-SEENA (1600 PENNSYLVANIA AVENUE)- WEST
SIDE STORY SYMPHONIC DANCES-PRELUDE FUGUE AND RIFFS
46.**BEST OF BRITISH TV MUSIC Orig.Music From Hit TV Ser**
Various Artists *(orig issued 1993)*
SOUNDTRACKS EMI GOLD: 520 688-2 (CD)   *1999*
CASUALTY-THE BILL-DALLAS-DYNASTY-EASTENDERS-BREAD-
JULIET BRAVO-MISS MARPLE-BERGERAC-DUCHESS OF DUKE
STREET-DOCTOR WHO-THE PALLISERS-TO SERVE THEM ALL
MY DAYS-POLDARK-SHOESTRING-THE BROTHERS-ONEDIN LINE
--- **BEST OF JAMES BOND** - *see* BOND James
47.**BEST OF THE WEST: GREAT MGM WESTERN MOVIE THEMES**
RYKODISC (Vital): RCD 10721 (CD)   *1998*
ORIGINAL SOUNDTRACK RECORDING EXTRACTS FROM:-
1.BIG COUNTRY *(J.MOROSS)* 2.UNFORGIVEN *(D.TIOMKIN)* 3
WONDERFUL COUNTRY *(A.NORTH)* 4.SCALPHUNTERS *(E.BERNS
TEIN)* 5.RETURN OF A MAN CALLED HORSE *(L.ROSENTHAL)*
6.HALLELUJAH TRAIL *(E.BERNSTEIN)* 7.HOUR OF THE GUN
(J.GOLDSMITH) 8.YOUNG BILLY YOUNG *(S.MANNE)* 9.HANG
EM HIGH *(D.FRONTIERE)* 10.HORSE SOLDIERS *D.BUTTOLPH)*
11.RETURN OF THE SEVEN *(E.BERNSTEIN)*
48.**BICKLEY Graham** - **Does The Moment Ever Come**
National Symphony Orchestra,conductor Martin Yates
TER (Koch): CDVIR 8335 (CD)   *1999*
1.DOES THE MOMENT EVER COME *(from JUST SO)*
2.SUNSET BOULEVARD 3.EMPTY CHAIRS *MISS SAIGON* 4.
IT IT'S ONLY LOVE / BRING ON THE NIGHT *METROPOLIS*
5.LAST NIGHT OF THE WORLD *MISS SAIGON* 6.WHERE DO I
GO *HAIR* 7.ANTHEM *CHESS* 8.ALL I ASK OF YOU *PHANTOM*
9.STARLIGHT EXPRESS 10.SUN AND MOON *MISS SAIGON* 11
HEY THERE *PAJAMA GAME* 12.WHY GOD WHY *MISS SAIGON*
13.ROLLING STOCK *STARLIGHT EXPRESS* 14.TOO MUCH IN
LOVE TO CARE *SUNSET BOULEVARD* 15.TRY TO REMEMBER
FANTASTICKS also *feat* Joanna Ampil (tracks 4,5,10)
Catherine Porter (14,15) Katrina Murphy (8)
49.**BIG PICTURE The** - **Cincinnati Pops Orch Erich Kunzel**
TELARC (Con-BMG): CD 80437 (CD)   *1997*
SYMPHONIC SUITES & THEMES from: MISSION IMPOSSIBLE-
BATMAN FOREVER-APOLLO 13-CRIMSON TIDE-FIGHTER SQUAD
RON-INDEPENDENCE DAY-BRAVEHEART-CUTTHROAT ISLAND-
TWISTER-LAST OF THE MOHICANS-DRAGONHEART-EXECUTIVE
DECISION-STARGATE-GETTYSBURG-JUMANJI-SPEED
50.**BINGE Ronald** - **BRITISH LIGHT MUSIC** with the Slovak
Radio Symphony Orchestra (Ernest Tomlinson)
MARCO POLO (Select): 8.223515 (CD)   *1994*
ELIZABETHAN SERENADE *(BBC: MUSIC TAPESTRY Theme)*
SCOTTISH RHAPSODY-MISS MELANIE *(ITV:JOAN AND LESLIE*

Theme) LAS CASTANUELAS-MADRUGADU (DAYBREAK)-THE RED
SOMBRERO-TRADE WINDS-FAIRE FROU FOU-STRING SONG *BBC
STRING SONG Theme)* CONCERTO FOR SAXOPHONE (3 M/M)
THE WATERMILL *(BBC THE SECRET GARDEN Theme)* SCHERZO
THE DANCE OF THE SNOWFLAKES-HIGH STEPPER *(ITV: THE
ADVENTURES OF AGGIE Theme)* PRELUDE: THE WHISPERING
VALLEY-VENETIAN CARNIVAL-SAILING BY *(DOCUMENTARY:
INTERNAT.BALLOON RACE & BBC RADIO4 CLOSEDOWN THEME)*

51.BLADE RUNNER: Synthesizer Soundtracks Various Arts
SILVA SCREEN (Koch): SILVAD 3008 (CD)   *1994*
THE HITCHER: HEADLIGHTS *(Mark Isham)* HEART OF MIDNI
GHT: OVERTURE CAROL'S THEME *(Yanni)* BIG TROUBLE IN
LITTLE CHINA: MAIN TITLE *(John Carpenter)* HAUNTED
SUMMER: NIGHT WAS MADE FOR LOVING *Christopher Young*
DAS BOOT The Boat: THEME *(Klaus Doldinger)* REVENGE:
LOVE THEME *(Jack Nitzsche)* LOCK UP: BREAKING POINT
(Bill Conti) TURTLE BEACH: HOMECOMING *(Chris Neal)*
THE PARK IS MINE: HELICOPTER ATTACK *Tangerine Dream*
I LOVE YOU PERFECT: OPENING CREDITS *Yanni* HALLOWEEN
MAIN TITLE *(John Carpenter)* NEAR DARK: BUS STATION
(Tangerine Dream) DEADLOCK: WE KNOW YOU'RE IN THERE
(Richard Gibbs) OVER THE TOP: THE FIGHT *(Giorgio Mo
roder)* BLADE RUNNER: END TITLES *(Vangelis)*
*tracks 3,11 performed by Daniel Caine tracks 5,7,14
15 Mark Ayres all others performed by the composer*

52.BLUE MOVIES: SCORING FOR THE STUDIOS - Various Arts
BLUE NOTE (EMI): CDP 857748-2 (CD)   *1997*
1.I WISH I KNEW *(FILM 97)* Billy Taylor 2.JAMES BOND
THEME Leroy Holmes 3.KOJAK Willie Bobo 4.BULLITT
Wilton Felder 5.FROM RUSSIA WITH LOVE Count Basie 6
SHADOW OF YOUR SMITH *(SANDPIPER)* Lou Donaldson 7.
DOWN HERE ON THE GROUND *(COOL HAND LUKE)*Grant Green
Dianne Reeves 8.BLOW UP Bobby Hutherson 9.STAR TREK
The Three Sounds 10.MISSION IMPOSSIBLE Billy May 11
ALFIE John Patton 12.MIDNIGHT COWBOY Lee Morgan 13.
LAST TANGO IN PARIS Marlena Shaw 14.MOON RIVER *BREA
KFAST AT TIFFANY'S* Nancy Wilson 15.LOVE STORY THEME
Richard Groove Holmes 16.MASH Bobby Hutcherson 17.
WINDMILLS OF YOUR MIND *THOM.CROWN AFFAIR* Bud Shank

--- BOGART Humphrey - *see* **CASABLANCA**

53.BOND James: BACK IN ACTION! - Various Artists
SILVA SCREEN (Koch): FILMCD 317 (CD)   *1999*
New Digital Recordings of Suites from the first 7
James Bond films inc.previously unreleased material
DR.NO-FROM RUSSIA WITH LOVE-GOLDFINGER-THUNDERBALL-
YOU ONLY LIVE TWICE-ON HER MAJESTY'S SECRET SERVICE
DIAMONDS ARE FOREVER

54.BOND James: BEST OF JAMES BOND - 30th Anniversary
EMI: 523 294-2 (CD) -4 (MC)   *1999*
1.JAMES BOND THEME Monty Norman Orch 2.GOLDFINGER
Shirley Bassey 3.NOBODY DOES IT BETTER Carly Simon
4.A VIEW TO A KILL Duran Duran 5.FOR YOUR EYES ONLY
Sheena Easton 6.WE HAVE ALL THE TIME IN THE WORLD
Louis Armstrong 7.LIVE AND LET DIE Paul McCartney &

Wings 8.ALL TIME HIGH Rita Coolidge 9.THE LIVING
DAYLIGHTS A-Ha 10.LICENCE TO KILL Gladys Knight 11.
FROM RUSSIA WITH LOVE Matt Monro 12.THUNDERBALL Tom
Jones 13.YOU ONLY LIVE TWICE Nancy Sinatra 14.
MOONRAKER Shirley Bassey 15.ON HER MAJESTY'S SECRET
SERVICE John Barry Orch 16.MAN WITH THE GOLDEN GUN
Lulu 17.DIAMONDS ARE FOREVER S.Bassey 18.GOLDENEYE
Tina Turner 19.TOMORROW NEVER DIES Sheryl Crow

55.**BOND James: THE ESSENTIAL** City Of Prague Symph.Orch
cond: Nicholas Raine   *(1993, revised reissue 1998)
S.Screen (Koch): FILMCD 007 (CD)* DR.NO-FROM RUSSIA
WITH LOVE-007-GOLDFINGER-THUNDERBALL-YOU ONLY LIVE
TWICE-ON HER MAJESTY'S SECRET SERVICE-DIAMONDS ARE
FOREVER-MAN WITH T.GOLDEN GUN-SPY WHO LOVED ME-MOON
RAKER-FOR YOUR EYES ONLY-OCTOPUSSY-LIVING DAYLIGHTS
A VIEW TO A KILL-LICENCE TO KILL-GOLDENEYE

--- BRELL Jacques *see* JACQUES BELL IS ALIVE AND WELL...
--- **BRIDESHEAD REVISITED** - *see* BURGON Geoffrey

--- **BRITISH LIGHT MUSIC**   - *see* ADDINSELL Geoffrey
--- **BRITISH LIGHT MUSIC**   - *see* BINGE Ronald
--- **BRITISH LIGHT MUSIC**   - *see* DUNCAN Trevor
--- **BRITISH LIGHT MUSIC**   - *see* ELIZABETHAN SERENADE
--- **BRITISH LIGHT MUSIC**   - *see* ESSENTIAL BRITISH LIGHT
--- **BRITISH LIGHT MUSIC**   - *see* GOODWIN Ron

56.**BRITISH LIGHT MUSIC CLASSICS - NEW LONDON ORCHEST** *
HYPERION Records (Select): CDA 66868 (CD)   1996
1.CALLING ALL WORKERS *(Eric Coates/BBC:MUSIC WHILE
YOU WORK)* 2.HAUNTED BALLROOM *(Geoffrey Toye/BALLET)*
3.VANITY FAIR *(Anthony Collins)* 4.JUMPING BEAN *(Rob
ert Farnon)* 5.DESTINY *(Sydney Baynes/WALTZ)* 6.THE
BOULEVARDIER *(Frederic Curzon)* 7.PAS DE QUATRE *(W.
Meyer Lutz/FAUST UP TO DATE)* 8.THE WATERMILL*(Ronald
Binge/BBC:THE SECRET GARDEN)* 9.THE DEVIL'S GALLOP
(Charles Williams/BBC:DICK BARTON) 10.DUSK *(Armstro
ng Gibbs/FANCY DRESS)* 11.PUFFIN'BILLY*(Edward White/
BBC:CHILDREN'S FAVOURIT.)*12.BELLS ACROSS THE MEADOW
(Albert Ketelby) 13.THE OLD CLOCKMAKER *(Charles Wil
liams/BBC:JENNING'S AT SCHOOL)* 14.DREAMING *(Archiba
ld Joyce/WALTZ)* 15.ELIZABETHAN SERENADE *(Ronald Bin
ge/BBC)* 16.CORONATION SCOTT *(Vivian Ellis/BBC: PAUL
TEMPLE)* 17.NIGHTS OF GLADNESS *(Charles Ancliffe/WAL
TZ)* * NEW LONDON ORCHESTRA conducted by RONALD CORP
57.**BRITISH LIGHT MUSIC CLASSICS 2 - NEW LONDON ORCHES***
HYPERION (Select): CDA 66968 (CD) *Ronald Corp 1997
1.KNIGHTSBRIDGE *(Eric Coates/BBC:IN TOWN TONIGHT)*
2.BAL MASQUE *(Percy Fletcher/WALTZ)* 3.GRASSHOPPER'S
DANCE *(Ernest Bucalossi/MILK TV AD)* 4.BARWICK GREEN
(Arthur Wood/ARCHERS THEME) 5.ROUGE ET NOIR *(Fred
Hartley)* 6.PEANUT POLKA *(Robert Farnon)* 7.CARRIAGE
AND PAIR *(Benjamin Frankel/SO LONG AT THE FAIR)* 8.
HORSE GUARDS WHITEHALL *(Haydn Wood/BBC:DOWN YOUR
WAY)* 9.MARCH FROM A LITTLE SUITE *(Trevor Duncan/BBC*

DR.FINLAY'S CASEBOOK) 10.SAILING BY *(Ronald Binge/ BBC: RADIO 4 CLOSING MUSIC)* 11.PORTUGESE PARTY *(Gil bert Vinter)* 12.BEACHCOMBER *(Clive Richardson)* 13. IN THE SHADOWS *(Herman Finck)* 14.TABARINAGE *(Robert Docker)* 15.SANCTUARY OF THE HEART *(Albert Ketelbey)* 16.WESTMINSTER WALTZ *(Robert Farnon/BBC:IN TOWN TON IGHT PROGAMME LINK MUS)* 17.CARISSIMA *(Edward Elgar)* 18.GIRLS IN GREY *(Charles Willliams/BBC: TELEVISION NEWSREEL)* 19.RUNAWAY ROCKING HORSE *(Edward White)* 20.MARCH OF THE BOWMEN *(Fr.Curzon/ROBIN HOOD SUITE)*

--- **BRITISH TV MUSIC** - *see* **BEST OF BRITISH TV MUSIC**
58. **BROADWAY...THE GREAT ORIGINAL CAST RECORDINGS** - **V/A**
SONY MUSIC: J2K 65910-2 (2CD) *1999*
CD1: BILL *SHOW BOAT* Helen Morgan 1.CAN'T HELP LOVIN DAT MAN *SHOW BOAT* 2.HOW ARE THINGS IN GLOCCA MORRA *FINIAN'S RAINBOW*Ella Logan 3.WUNDERBAR *KISS ME KATE* Alfred Drake & Patricia Morison 4.SOME ENCHANTED EVENING *SOUTH PACIFIC* Enzio Pinza 5.WONDERFUL GUY *SOUTH PACIFIC* Mary Martin 6.DIAMONDS ARE A GIRL'S BEST FRIEND *GENTLEMEN PREFER BLONDES* Carol Channing 7.BEWITCHED BOTHERED AND BEWILDERED *PAL JOEY* Vivien Segal 8.STRANGER IN PARADISE *KISMET* Doreta Morow & Richard Kiley 9.HEY THERE *PAJAMA GAME* John Raitt 10 HERNANDO'S HIDEAWAY *PAJAMA GAME* Carol Haney 11.THE RAIN IN SPAIN *MY FAIR LADY* 12.I COULD HAVE DANCED ALL NIGHT *MY FAIR LADY* Julie Andrews 13.I'VE GROWN ACCUSTOMED TO HER FACE *MY FAIR LADY* Rex Harrison 14 STANDING ON THE CORNER *MOST HAPPY FELLA* 15.PARTY'S OVER *BELLS ARE RINGING* Judy Holliday 16.TONIGHT *WEST SIDE STORY* Larry Kert-Carol Lawrence 17. AMERICA *WEST SIDE STORY* Chita Rivera 18.SOMEWHERE *WEST SIDE STORY* 19.CONGA *WONDERFUL TOWN* Rosalind Russell 20.I ENJOY BEING A GIRL *FLOWER DRUM SONG* Pat Suzuki 21.EVERYTHING'S COMING UP ROSES *GYPSY* Ethel Merman CD2: 1.MY FAVOURITE THINGS *SOUND OF MUSIC* Mary Martin 2.DO RE MI *SOUND OF MUSIC* Mary Martin 3.PUT ON A HAPPY FACE *BYE BYE BIRDIE* Dick Van Dyke 4.CAMELOT Richard Burton 5.ANYONE CAN WHISTLE Lee Remick 6.DO I HEAR A WALTZ Elizabeth Allen 7.BIG SPENDER *SWEET CHARITY* Helen Gallagher Thelma Oliver 8.MAME Charles Braswell 9.WILLKOMMEN *CABARET* Joel Grey 10.CABARET Jill Haworth 11.LADIES WHO LUNCH *COMPANY* Elaine Stritch 12.I WANT TO BE HAPPY *NO NO NANETTE* Jack Gilford-Susan Watson 13. SEND IN THE CLOWNS *LITTLE NIGHT MUSIC* Glynis Johns 14.WHAT I DID FOR LOVE *CHORUS LINE* Priscilla Lopez 15.ONE *A CHORUS LINE* Company 16.TOMORROW *ANNIE* Andrea McArdle 17.FOLLIES BERGERES *NINE* Lilane Montevecchi & Stephanie Cotsirilos 18.NEVER MET A MAN I DIDN'T LIKE *WILL ROGERS FOLL.* Keith Carradine 19.MY FRIEND *THE LIFE* Pamela Isaacs-Lilias White
59. **BROADWAY'S BIGGEST '97/'98** - Various Artists
VARESE (Pinn): VSD 5923 (CD) *1998*
CIRCLE OF LIFE *(LION KING)* WHO WILL LOVE ME AS I AM

(SIDE SHOW) GOODBYE MY LOVE *(RAGTIME)* SATIN SUMMER NIGHTS *(THE CAPEMAN)* HOME AGAIN *(SCARLET PIMPERNEL)* HAKUNA MATATA *(LION KING)* THIS IS THE MOMENT *(JEKYLL & HYDE)* I JUST CAN'T WAIT TO BE KING *(LION KING)* BORN IN PUERTO RICO *(THE CAPEMAN)* ANYHTING FOR YOUR LOVE *(TRIUMPH OF LOVE)* EDELWEISS *(SOUND OF MUSIC)* WE'LL MEET TOMORROW *(TITANIC)*

--- <u>**BROADWAY HITS**</u> - *see* BBC CONCERT ORCHESTRA

--- <u>**BROOKS Paul**</u> - *see* 'COPS'

60.<u>**BUDD Roy**</u> - **Rebirth Of The Budd**
SEQUEL-Castle (Pinn): NEMCD 927 (CD)   *1997*
1.FEAR IS THE KEY 2.BIRTH OF THE BUDD 3.GET CARTER 4.SOLDIER BLUE 5.THEME TO MR.ROSE 6.ARANJUEZ MON AMOR 7.JESUS CHRIST SUPERSTAR 8.WHIZZ BALL 9.IN MY HOLE 10.TOO MUCH ATTENTION 11.LEAD ON 12.ZEPPELIN 13.THE CAREY TREATMENT 14.ENVY GREED AND GLUTTONY 15.GIRL TALK 16.PAVANE 17.CALL ME 18.PLAYTHING 19. BARQUINHO (LITTLE BOAT) 20.SO NICE 21.HOW WONDERFUL LIFE IS 22.FIELDS OF GREEN SKY OF BLUE 23.LUST 24. HURRY TO ME 25.THE HOSTAGE ESCAPES

--- <u>**BUGS BUNNY ON BROADWAY**</u> - **Warner Bros Symphony Orch**
WARNER USA (Silv.Screen): 926494-2(CD)-4(MC)   *1991*
Music by Carl Stalling and Milt Franklyn feat the voice talents of Mel Blanc *see also* 'STALLING Carl'

61.<u>**BURGON Geoffrey**</u> - **BRIDESHEAD REVISITED: TV Scores**
SILVA SCREEN (Koch): FILMCD 117 (CD)   *1992*
THE CHRONICLES OF NARNIA-BLEAK HOUSE-TESTAMENT OF YOUTH-BRIDESHEAD REVISITED (Suite)-NUNC DIMITTIS fr om TINKER TAILOR SOLDIER SPY sung by *LESLEY GARRETT Philharmonia Orchestra conducted by Geoffrey Burgon*

--- <u>**BY GEORGE!**</u> - *see* GERSHWIN George

--- <u>**CAREY Tristram**</u> - *see* QUATERMASS AND THE PIT

--- <u>**CARL STALLING PROJECT**</u> - *see* STALLING Carl

62.<u>**CARPENTER John**</u> - The Best Of Volume 1
VARESE (Pinn): VSD 5266 (CD)
music composed by John Carpenter and Alan Howarth tracks include: DARK STAR / ESCAPE FROM NEW YORK / THE FOG / PRINCE OF DARKNESS / HALLOWEEN etc. music composed by John Carpenter and Alan Howarth

63.<u>**CARPENTER John**</u> - The Best Of Volume 2
VARESE (Pinn): VSD 5336 (CD)
music composed by John Carpenter and Alan Howarth tracks include: ESCAPE FROM NEW YORK / PRINCE OF DARKNESS / HALLOWEEN 4 and 5 / CHRISTINE etc

64.<u>**CARRY ON ALBUM**</u> Bruce Montgomery & Eric Rogers Music City Of Prague Philharmonic.cond: Gavin Sutherland James Hughes (harmoncia) Vladimir Pilar (violin)
WHITE LINE-ASV (Select): CDWHL 2119 (CD)   *1999*
ANGLO-AMALGAMATED FANFARES + music from CARRY ON.. AT YOUR CONVENIENCE / BEHIND / CABBY / CAMPING / CLEO / DOCTOR/DOCTOR AGAIN / JACK / CARRY ON SUITE CARRY ON THEME / UP THE KHYBER / RAISING THE WIND

65.<u>**CASABLANCA**</u>   **Classic Film Scores For HUMPHREY BOGART**
RCA VICTOR (BMG): GD 80422 (CD)   *1990*

CASABLANCA-PASSAGE TO MARSEILLE-TREASURE OF THE SIE
RRA MADRE-BIG SLEEP-CAINE MUTINY-TO HAVE & HAVE NOT
TWO MRS.CARROLLS-SABRINA-LEFT HAND OF GOD-SAHARA-VI
VIRGINIA CITY-KEY LARGO *N.Phil.Or.Charles Gerhardt*

--- **CENTRAL BAND OF THE R.A.F.** - *see* **HEROES OF THE AIR**

66.**CHAPLIN Charles** - **Film Music Of CHARLES CHAPLIN**
Brandenburg Symph.Orch, Berlin conduct: CARL DAVIS
RCA (BMG): 09026 68271-2 (CD) *1996*
Music scores: THE KID / THE GOLD RUSH / THE CIRCUS
CITY LIGHTS / MODERN TIMES

67.**CHILDREN'S BBC THEME TUNES** - Various Artists
BBC (Technicolor): BBC 1761 (MC) *1995*
NODDY-POSTMAN PAT-SPOT-FUNNY BONES-PINGU-FIREMAN
SAM-WILLIAM'S WISH WELLINGTONS-ANIMALS OF FARTHING
WOOD-LIZZIE'S SONG from PLAYDAYS-JOSHUA JONES from
PLAYDAYS-JESS THE CAT from POSTMAN PAT-OAKIE DOKE-
THE WORLD OF BEATRIX POTTER-NODDY SAYS GOODNIGHT

68.**CHILLER** - **Cincinnati Pops Orchestra** - **Erich Kunzel**
TELARC USA (BMG-Conif): CD 80189 (CD) *1989*
PHANTOM OF THE OPERA-NIGHT ON BALD MOUNTAIN-DANSF M
ACABRE-MARCH TO THE SCAFFOLD-PANDEMONIUM DAMNATION
OF FAUST-IN THE HALL OF THEMOUNTAIN KING-Theme From
TWILIGHT ZONE-BRIDE OF FRANKENSTEIN-THE DEVIL & DAN
IEL WEBSTER-PSYCHO-SLEUTH-POLTERGEIST-WITHOUTA CLUE
FUNERAL MARCH OF A MARIONETTE:Alfred Hitchock Theme

--- <u>**CINCINNATI POPS ORCHESTRA**</u> - *see* **BEAUTIFUL HOLLYWOOD**
--- <u>**CINCINNATI POPS ORCHESTRA**</u> - *see* **BIG PICTURE**
--- <u>**CINCINNATI POPS ORCHESTRA**</u> - *see* **CHILLER**
--- <u>**CINCINNATI POPS ORCHESTRA**</u> - *see* **GREAT MOVIE SCORES**
--- <u>**CINCINNATI POPS ORCHESTRA**</u> - *see* **HOLLYWOOD'S GREATEST**
--- <u>**CINCINNATI POPS ORCHESTRA**</u> - *see* **LLOYD WEBBER Andrew**
--- <u>**CINCINNATI POPS ORCHESTRA**</u> - *see* **VICTORY AT SEA**

69.**CINEMA CAFE: EUROPEAN FILM MUSIC ALBUM** - **Mark Ayres**
SILVA SCREEN (Koch/S.Scr): FILMXCD 302 (2CD) *1998*
37 Tracks including: JEAN DE FLORETTE-A MAN AND A
WOMAN-BILITIS-DIVA-BETTY BLUE-THE TIN DRUM-OPERA
SAUVAGE-SUBWAY-LA FEMME NIKITA-ATLANTIS-LE GRAND
BLUE (THE BIG BLUE)-THE DOUBLE LIFE OF VERONIQUE
EMMANUELLE-LAST TANGO IN PARIS-PLAYTIME-MON ONCLE-
IL POSTINO-CINEMA PARADISO-CYRANO DE BERGERAC-THE
HAIRDRESSER'S HUSBAND etc.

70.**CINEMA CENTURY** - Various Artists and Orchestras
SILVA SCREEN (Koch): FILMCD 180 (3CDs) *1996*
20TH CENTURY FOX FANFARE *(A.NEWMAN)* CITY LIGHTS *(C.*
CHAPLIN) BRIDE OF FRANKENSTEIN *(F.WAXMAN)* GONE WITH
THE WIND *(M.STEINER)* STAGECOACH *(R.HAGEMAN +others)*
CITIZEN KANE *(B.HERRMANN)* CASABLANCA *(M.STEINER)*
OLIVER TWIST *(A.BAX)* QUO VADIS *(M.ROZSA)* THE QUIET
MAN *(V.YOUNG)* THE HIGH AND THE MIGHTY *(D.TIOMKIN)*
THE SEARCHERS *(M.STEINER)* BRIDGE ON THE RIVER KWAI
(K.J.ALFORD) THE BIG COUNTRY *(J.MOROSS)* NORTH BY NO

RTHWEST *(B.HERRMANN)* BEN HUR *(M.ROZSA)* PSYCHO *(B. HERRMANN)* LA DOLCE VITA *(N.ROTA)* MAGNIFICENT SEVEN *(E.BERNSTEIN)* Disc 2 THE ALAMO *(D.TIOMKIN)* THE PINK PANTHER *(H.MANCINI)* LAWRENCE OF ARABIA*(M.JARRE)* THE GREAT ESCAPE *(E.BERNSTEIN)* 633 SQUADRON *(R.GOODWIN)* ZULU *(J.BARRY)* ZORBA THE GREEK *(M.THEODORAKIS)* DOCT OR ZHIVAGO *(M.JARRE)* BORN FREE *(J.BARRY)*THE LION IN WINTER *(J.BARRY)* ONCE UPON A TIME IN THE WEST *(E. MORRICONE)* WHERE EAGLES DARE *(R.GOODWIN)* MIDNIGHT COWBOY *(J.BARRY)* THE WILD BUNCH *(J.FIELDING)* THE GODFATHER *(N.ROTA)* JAWS *(J.WILLIAMS)* ROCKY*(B.CONT/)* TAXI DRIVER *(B.HERRMANN)* STAR WARS*(J.WILLIAMS)* DIVA 'La Wally' sung by Lesley Garrett *(CATALINI)* Disc 3 RAIDERS OF T.LOST ARK *(J.WILLIAMS)* CHARIOTS OF FIRE *(VANGELIS)* CONAN THE BARBARIAN *(B.POLEDOURIS)* E.T. *(J.WILLIAMS)* ONCE UPON A TIME IN AMERICA *(E.MORRICO NE)* THE TERMINATOR *(B.FIEDEL)* WITNESS *(M.JARRE)* OUT OF AFRICA *(J.BARRY)* A PASSAGE TO INDIA*(M.JARRE)* THE MISSION *(E.MORRICONE)* A ROOM WITH A VIEW 'O Mio Bab bino Caro' *(PUCCINI)* sung by Lesley Garrett CINEMA PARADISO *(E.MORRICONE)* GHOST *(M.JARRE)* DANCES WITH WOLVES *(J.BARRY)* 1492:CONQUEST OF PARADISE *VANGELIS* UNFORGIVEN *(L.NIEHAUS-CLINT EASTWOOD)* THE FUGITIVE *JN.HOWARD* JURASSIC PARK-SCHINDLER'S LIST *J.WILLIAMS*

71.**CINEMA CENTURY 2000** - **Various Artists**
   SILVA SCREEN (Koch): FILMXCD 318 (2CDs)   *1999*
   56 Classic Themes: KING KONG-WUTHERING HEIGHTS-THE
   SEA HAWK-LAURA-THE VIKINGS-BREAKFAST AT TIFFANY'S-
   EL CID-THE LONGEST DAY-HATARI-THE SANDPIPER-RYAN'S
   DAUGHTER-THE THOMAS CROWN AFFAIR-THE WAY WE WERE-
   DEER HUNTER-PAPILLON-JEAN DE FLORETTE-BATMAN-THE
   MASK OF ZORRO-ADVENTURES OF ROBIN HOOD-ALEXANDER
   NEVSKY-THIEF OF BAGDAD-TREASURE OF THE SIERRA MADRE
   WAR OF THE WORLDS-PRINCE VALIANT-THE CAINE MUTINY-
   TO CATCH A THIEF-GUNS OF NAVARONE-DOCTOR NO-HOW THE
   WEST WAS WON-DR.STRANGELOVE-ROMEO AND JULIET-2001 A
   SPACE ODYSSEY-ONCE UPON A TIME IN THE WEST-SUMMER
   OF 42-LAST TANGO IN PARIS-GODFATHER-STAR TREK-BODY
   HEAT-EXCALIBUR-RIGHT STUFF-COTTON CLUB-GHOST-LETHAL
   WEAPON-BASIC INSTINCT-PRINCE OF TIDES-LAST OF THE
   MOHICANS-BODYGUARD-IL POSTINO-BRAVEHEART-APOLLO 13-
   INDEPENDENCE DAY-EBGLISH PATIENT-TITANIC-SAVING
   PRIVATE RYAN-MARK OF ZORRO

72.**CINEMA CHORAL CLASSICS** - **City Of Prague Philh.Orch***
   SILVA SCREEN (Koch): SILK(D)(C) 6015 (CD/MC)   *1997*
   EXCALIBUR-SCARLET LETTER-JESUS OF NAZARETH-KING OF
   KINGS-LION IN WINTER-MISSION-CONAN THE BARBARIAN-
   ABYSS-FIRST KNIGHT-1492 CONQUEST OF PARADISE-HENRY
   V-OMEN-VIKINGS *Nic Raine conducting The* Crouch End
   Festival Chorus *(David Temple)*

73.**CINEMA CHORAL CLASSICS 2** - **City Of Prague Phil.Orch**
   (Paul Bateman) and Crouch End Festival Chorus
   SILVA SCREEN (Koch-S.Scr): SILK(D)(C) 6017 (CD/MC)
   THE MADNESS OF KING GEORGE-DOUBLE LIFE OF VERONIQUE

HOW THE WEST WAS WON-IF-EMPIRE OF THE SUN-ALEXANDER NEVSKY-MUCH ADO ABOUT NOTHING-SENSE AND SENSIBILITY EDWARD SCISSORHANDS-PARADISE ROAD-TH.ALAMO-THE ROBE THE GREATEST STORY EVER TOLD-TRADITION OF THE GAMES

74.**CINEMA CLASSICS (EMI) 2** Collection - Var.Artists
EMI Classics: CMS 566647-2 (2CD)   *1997*
CD1: 1.SHINE: *1st m/m PIANO CON.NO.3 Rachmaninov* 3. ENGLISH PATIENT: *I'LL ALWAYS GO BACK TO THAT CHURCH Yared* 3.BABE: *PIZZICATO from SYLVIA Delibes* 4.ROMEO & JULIET: *OST VOL.2* 5.HEAVENLY CREATURES: *E LUCEVAN LE STELLE Puccini* 6.COURAGE UNDER FIRE *Horner* 7. SEVEN: *AIR ON THE G STRING FROM SUITE 3 Bach* 8.LAST ACTION HERO: *LE NOZZE DI FIGARO OVERTURE Mozart* 9. HOWARDS END: *MOCK MORRIS Grainger* 10.THE FRENCH LIEUTENANT'S WOMAN: *PIANO SONATA IN D.K576 Mozart* 11.SHAWSHANK REDEMPTION: *SULL'ARIA: FIGARO Mozart* 12.PRINCE OF TIDES: *SYMPHONY NO.104 'LONDON' Haydn* 13.PORTRAIT OF A LADY: *IMPROMPTU A.FLAT NO.4 D899 Schubert* 14.DANGEROUS LIAISONS:*CUCKOO & NIGHTINGALE ORGAN CONCERTO Handel* 15.MRS.DOUBTFIRE: *LARGO AL FA FACTOTUM:BARBER OF SEVILLE Rossini* 16.FOUR WEDDINGS AND A FUNERAL: *THE WEDDING MARCH Mendelssohn* 17. SLEEPING WITH THE ENEMY: *WITCHES'SABBATH Berlioz.*
CD2 MANHATTAN: *RHAPSODY IN BLUE Gershwin* 2.FANTASIA SORCERER'S APPRENTICE Dukas* 3.BRIDGES OF MADISON COUNTY: *MON COEUR S'OUVRE A TA VOIX: Saint Saens* 4. EVENING STAR: *-S/T- Ross* 5.UN COUER EN HIVER: *PIANO TRIO Ravel* 6.HANNAH AND HER SISTERS: *HARPSICHORD CONC.NO.5 Bach* 7.THE SAINT: *LOVE THEME Revell* 8.THE FIFTH ELEMENT: *LUCIA DI LAMMERMOOR Donizetti* 9.JFK: *HORN CON.NO.2 Mozart* 10.SOMEWHERE IN TIME: *18th VAR IATION ON THEME OF PAGANINI Rachmaninov* 11.LOOKING FOR RICHARD: *-S/T- Shore* 12.HENRY V *-S/T- Doyle* 13. KILLING FIELDS: *NESSUN DORMA Puccini* 14.MY DINNER WITH ANDRE: *GYMNOPEDIE NO.1 Satie* 15.SILENCE OF THE LAMBS: *GOLDBERG VAR.ARIA Bach* 16.AMADEUS: *EINE KLEI KLEINE NACHT MUSIK Mozart* 17.JEAN DE FLORETTE/MANON DES SOURCES: *LA FORZA DEL DESTINO OVERTURE Verdi*

75.**CINEMA CLASSICS** (NAXOS) 1998 - Various Artists
NAXOS (Select): 8.551182 (CD)   *1998*
1.BRASSED OFF *WILLIAM TELL OVERTURE (ROSSINI)* 2.THE DEVIL'S OWN *FRUHLINGSSTIMMEN (JOHANN STRAUSS II)* 3. FACE OFF *PAMIN'A ARIA from The MAGIC FLUTE (MOZART)* 4.FIFTH ELEMENT *MAD SCENE from LUCIA DI LAMMERMOOR (DONIZETTI)* 5.G.I.JANE *O MIO BABBINO CARO (PUCCINI)* 6.JURASSIC PARK 2 *ADAGIO CANTABILE from PATHETIQUE SONATA (BEETHOVEN)* 7.L.A.CONFIDENTIAL *HEBRIDES OVER TURE (MENDELSSOHN)* 8.ONE NIGHT STAND *AIR (J.S.BACH)* 9.PARADISE ROAD *MARCH fr.PIANO SONATA NO.2 (CHOPIN)* 10.THE PEACEMAKER *NOCTURNE IN F.MINOR (CHOPIN)* 11. TITANIC *THE BLUE DANUBE (J.STRAUSS II)*

76.**CINEMA CLASSICS** (NAXOS) 1997 - Various Artists
NAXOS (Select): 8.551181 (CD)   *1997*
1.THE PEOPLE VS.LARRY FLYNT *POLONAISE FROM RUSALKA*

(DVORAK) 2.THE PEOPLE VS.LARRY FLYNT *MAZURKA NO.47 IN A.MINOR OP.68 NO.2 (CHOPIN)* 3.BREAKING THE WAVES *SONATA IN E.FLAT MAJOR BWV 1031.SICILIANA (BACH)* 4. THE ENGLISH PATIENT *ARIA FROM 'GOLDBERG VARIATIONS' BWV 988 (BACH)* 5.TIN CUP *WINTER FROM FOUR SEASONS SUITE Allegro Non Molto(VIVALDI)* 6.ROMEO AND JULIET *SYMPHONY NO.25 IN G.MINOR K.183 Allegro Con Brio (MOZART)* 7.THE PORTRAIT OF A LADY *STRING QUARTET NO 14 IN D.MINOR D.810 Death and The Maiden (SCHUBERT)* 8.PRIMAL FEAR *REQUIEM: LACRYMOSA (MOZART)* 9.SHINE *POLONAISE 6 A.FLAT MAJ.OP53 (CHOPIN)* 10.SHINE *PIANO CONC.3 IN D.MIN.OP30 Allegro Ma Non..(RACHMANINOV)*

77.**CINEMA CLASSICS (NAXOS) 1** - Various Artists
NAXOS (Select): 8.551151 (CD)   *1992*
1.2001 A SPACE ODYSSEY: *ALSO SPRACH ZARATHUSTRA (R. Strauss)* 2.A ROOM WITH A VIEW: *O MIO BABBINO CARO-GIANNI SCHICCHI (Puccini)* 3.DEATH IN VENICE: *ADAGIE TTO FROM SYMPHONY NO.5 (Mahler)* 4.MONA LISA: *LOVE DUET FR.MADAME BUTTERFLY-VOGLIATEMI BENE (Puccini)* 5.PLATOON / THE ELEPHANT MAN: *ADAGIO FOR STRINGS (Barber)* 6.HANNAH AND HER SISTERS: *LARGO FROM PIANO CONCERTO NO.5 (J.S.Bach)* 7.HEAT AND DUST:*TALES FROM THE VIENNA WOODS (J.Strauss)* 8.OUT OF AFRICA:*ADAGIO CLARINET CONCERTO IN A.MAJOR (Mozart)* 9.APOCALYPSE NOW: *RIDE OF THE VALKYRIES-DIE WALKURE (Wagner)*

78.**CINEMA CLASSICS (NAXOS) 2** - Various Artists
NAXOS (Select): 8.551152 (CD)   *1992*
1.CLOCKWORK ORANGE: *WILLIAM TELL OVERTURE (Rossini)* 2.DIVA: *EBBEN NE ANDRO MONTANA LA WALLY (Catalini)* 3.ORDINARY PEOPLE: *CANON (Pachelbel)* 4.AMADEUS: *SYM PHONY NO.25-ALLEGRO CON BRIO (Mozart)* 5.SEVEN YEAR ITCH / BRIEF ENCOUNTER: *PIANO CONCERTO NO.2 (Rachma ninov)* 6.GALLIPOLI: *ADAGIO IN G (Albinoni)* 7.SUNDAY BLOODY SUNDAY: *SOAVE SIA IL VENTO FROM COSI FAN TUTTE (Mozart)* 8.DIE HARD 2: *FINLANDIA (Sibelius)*

79.**CINEMA CLASSICS (NAXOS) 3** - Various Artists
NAXOS (Select): 8.551153 (CD)   *1992*
1.AMADEUS: *EINE KLEINE NACHT MUSIK ALLEGRO (Mozart)* 2.HOT TO TROT:*PREMIERE SUITE DE SYMPHONIES (Mouret)* 3.WITCHES OF EASTWICK: *NESSUN DORMA FROM TURANDOT (Puccini)* 4.MANHATTAN: *RHAPSODY IN BLUE (Gershwin)* 5.RAGING BULL / GODFATHER III: *CAVALLERIA RUSTICANA INTERMEZZO (Mascagni)* 6.BARRY LYNDON: *SARABANDE-SUI TE NO.11 IN D.MIN(Handel)* 7.EXCALIBUR: *EXCERPT FROM CARMINA BURANA (Orff)* 8.ELVIRA MADIGAN: *PIANO CONCE RTO NO.21-ANDANTE K.467 (Mozart)* 9.WALL STREET: *QUE STA O QUELLA-RIGOLETTO (Verdi)* 10.CLOCKWORK ORANGE *ODE TO JOY FROM SYMPHONY NO.9 (Beethoven)*

80.**CINEMA CLASSICS (NAXOS) 4** - Various Artists
NAXOS (Select): 8.551154 (CD)   *1992*
1.CLOCKWORK ORANGE:*POMP AND CIRCUMSTANCE MARCH No.1 (Elgar)* 2.AMADEUS: *SYMPHONY No.29 ALLEGRO MODERATO (Mozart)* 3.A ROOM WITH A VIEW: *IL SOGNO DI DORETTA from LA RONDINE (Puccini)* 4.SLEEPING WITH THE ENEMY

SYMPHONIE FANTASIQUE (Berlioz) 5.SOMEWHERE IN TIME:
18TH PAGANINI VARIATION (Rachmaninov) 6.WHO FRAMED
ROGER RABBIT:HUNGARIAN RHAPSODY NO 2.IN D.m (Listz)
7.MOONSTRUCK: CHE GELIDA MANINA-LA BOHEME (Puccini)
8.FRENCH LIEUTENANT'S WOMAN: PIANO SON.No.17 K.576
(Mozart) 9.10: BOLERO (Ravel)

81.**CINEMA CLASSICS (NAXOS) 5** - Various Artists
NAXOS (Select): 8.551155 (CD)   1992
1.MY GEISHA: UN BEL DI VEDREMO 'MADAME BUTTERFLY'
(Puccini) 2.PRIZZI'S HONOR: OVERTURE TO BARBER OF
SEVILLE (Rossini) 3-6.AMADEUS: 4 EXCERPTS FROM THE
REQUIEM 7.PIANO CONCERTO No.20 K.466 (Mozart) 8.
ROLLERBALL: TOCCATA AND FUGUE IN D.MINOR BWV 565
(Bach) 9.MOONSTRUCK: O SOAVE FANCIULLA 'LA BOHEME'
(Puccini) 10.THE UNRTOUCHABLES: RECITAR VESTI LA
GIUBBA'I PAGLIACCI' (Leoncavallo) 11.HANNAH AND HER
SISTERS: SOLA PERDUTA ABBANDONATA 'MANON LESCAUT'
(Puccini) 12.CHILDREN OF A LESSER GOD: DOUBLE CONCE
RTO D.MIN,LARGO MA NAN TANTO (Bach) 13.MY LEFT FOOT
UN AURA AMAROSA FROM 'COSI FAN TUTTE' (Verdi) 14.
BREAKING AWAY:'ITALIAN SYMPHONY' (Mendelssohn)

82.**CINEMA CLASSICS (NAXOS) 6** - Various Artists
NAXOS (Select): 8.551156 (CD)   1994
1.EXCALIBUR: PRELUDE TO TRISTAN AND ISOLDE (Wagner)
2.AMADEUS:SERENADE NO.10 B.FLAT.K361 ADAGIO(Mozart)
3.MIDSUMMER NIGHT'S SEX COMEDY: SCHERZO 'MIDSUMMER
NIGHTS DREAM' OP.61 (Mendelssohn) 4.TOUS LE MATINS
DU MONDE TOMBEAU "LES REGRETS" (Sainte-Colombe) 5.
FIVE EASY PIECES: PRELUDE NO.4 OP.28 (Chopin) 6.
WHITE NIGHTS: PASSCAGLIA IN C.MINTO FROM BWV 582
(Bach) 7.ROOM WITH A VIEW: FIRENZE E COME UN ALBERO
FIORITO 'GIANNI SCHICCHI' (Puccini) 8.GOODBYE AGAIN
SYMPHONY NO.3 IN F.MAJ.OP.90 POCO ALLEGRETO(Brahms)
9.SLAUGHTERHOUSE FIVE: BRANDENBURG CONCERTO NO.4 IN
G.MAJOR BWV 1049 PRESTO (Bach) 10.THE MUSIC LOVERS:
1812 OVERTURE OP.49 (Tchaikovsky)

83.**CINEMA CLASSICS (NAXOS) 7** - Various Artists
NAXOS (Select): 8.551157 (CD)   1994
JEAN DE FLORETTE: OVERTURE-FORCE OF DESTINY (Verdi)
FANTASIA: WALTZ OF THE FLOWERS - 'NUTCRACKER SUITE'
(Tchaikovsky) MADAME SOUSATZKA: ALLEGRO VIVACE FROM
PIANO CONCERTO IN A.MINOR OP.54 (Schumann) ANONIMO
VENEZIANO: ADAGIO FROM OBOE CONCERTO IN D.MINOR (A.
arcello) EXPOSED:ADAGIO VIVACISSIMO-VIOLIN CONCERTO
IN D.MAJ.OP.35 (Tchaikovsky) PRETTY WOMAN: DAMMI TU
FORZA-LA TRAVIATA (Verdi) THE LADYKILLERS: MINUETTO
FROM STRING QUARTET IN E.MAJOR G.275 (Boccherini)
LORENZO'S OIL: AVE VERUM CORPUS K.618 (Mozart)
SWING KIDS: ALLEGRO MODERATO-PIANO TRIO IN B.FLAT
MAJOR 'ARCHDUKE' OP.97 (Beethoven)

84.**CINEMA CLASSICS (NAXOS) 8** - Various Artists
NAXOS (Select): 8.551158 (CD)   1994
MEETING VENUS: OVERTURE TO TANNHAUSER (Wagner)
MAN TROUBLE: NOCTURNE NO.2,E.FLAT MAJ.OP.9 (Chopin)

DANGEROUS LIAISONS: *LARGO FROM SERSE (Handel)*
MY DINNER WITH ANDRE: *GYMNOPEDIE NO.1 (Erik Satie)*
SNEAKERS: *ALLEGRO VIVO-APPASSIONATO FROM STRING QUA
RTET NO.1 IN E.MIN.(Smetana)* AU REVOIR LES ENFANTS:
MOMENT MUSICAL NO.2 (Schubert) CHARIOTS OF FIRE:
MISERE (Allegri) A MIDSUMMER NIGHT'S SEX COMEDY:
ADAGIO FR.PIANO CONC.NO.2,D.MIN.OP.40 (Mendelssohn)
FANTASIA: *SORCERER'S APPRECTICE (Dukas)*

85. <u>**CINEMA CLASSICS (NAXOS)**</u> 9 - Various Artists
NAXOS (Select): 8.551159 (CD)   *1994*
TRADING PLACES: *OVERTURE:- MARRIAGE OF FIGARO K.492
(Mozart)* SNEAKERS: *WALTZ NO.15 IN E.MINOR (Chopin)*
MUSIC LOVERS: *ANDANTINO SEMPLICE-PRESTISSIMO PIANO
CONCERTO NO.1 IN B.FLAT MIN.OP.23 (Tchaikovsky)*
EXCALIBUR: *SIEGFRIED'S DEATH AND FUNERAL MARCH FROM
GOTTERDAMMERUNG (Wagner)* NIGHT AT THE OPERA: *ANVIL
CHORUS FROM IL TROVATORE (Verdi)* MADAME SOUSATZSKA:
*ALLEGRO ASSAI - PIANO SONATA NO.23 IN F.MINOR OP.57
(APPASSIONATA) (Beethoven)* DEAD POETS SOCIETY: *ALLE
GRO-ANDANTE: WATER MUSIC (Handel)* UN COEUR EN HIVER
BLUES (MODERATO) FROM VIOLIN SONATA (Ravel) EXPOSED
COURANTE FROM PARTITA NO.4 IN D.MAJ.BWV 828 (Bach)
PICNIC AT HANGING ROCK:*ANDANTE UN POCO MOSSO (PIANO
CONC.NO.5 IN E.FLAT MAJ OP.73 (EMPEROR) (Beethoven)*
FANTASIA:*DANCE OF THE HOURS LA GIOCONDA(Ponchielli)*

86. <u>**CINEMA CLASSICS (NAXOS)**</u> 10 - Various Artists
NAXOS (Select): 8.551160 (CD)   *1994*
HEARTBURN: *ARRIVAL OF THE QUEEN OF SHEBA (SOLOMON)
(Handel)* BARRY LYNDON: *ANDANTE CON MOTO FROM PIANO
TRIO NO.2 IN E.FLAT MAJOR D.929 (Schubert)* A MONTH
IN THE COUNTRY: *ANDANTE ALLEGRO NON TROPPO FROM VIO
LIN CONCERTO IN E.MINOR OP.64 (Mendelssohn)* TOUS LE
MATINS DU MONDE: *SONNERIE DE SAINTE GENEVIEVE DU
MONT DE PARIS (Marais)* DANEROUS LIAISONS: *ALLEGRO
FROM ORGAN CONC.NO.13 IN F.MAJ (Handel)* GREYSTOKE:
THE LEGEND OF TARZAN, LORD OF THE APES: *ANDANTE NOB
ILMENTE E SEMPLICE FROM SYMPHONY NO.1 IN A.FLAT MAJ
(Elgar)* AUTUMN SONATA: *PRELUDE NO.2 IN A.MIN.OP.28
(Chopin)* MAN TROUBLE: *ET RESURREXIT (MASS IN B.MIN)
BWV 232 (Bach)* LOVE AND DEATH: *TROIKA FROM LIEUTENA
NT KIJE (Prokofiev)* KIND HEARTS AND CORONETS:*IL MIO
TESORO FROM DON GIOVANNI K.527 (Mozart)* FANTASIA:
NIGHT ON BARE MOUNTAIN (Mussorgsky)

87. <u>**CINEMA CLASSICS (NAXOS)**</u> 11 - Various Artists
NAXOS (Select): 8.551171 (CD)   *1995*
PETER'S FRIENDS: *CAN-CAN FROM ORPHEUS IN THE UNDERW
ORLD (Offenbach)* SPY WHO LOVED ME: *AIR FROM SUITE
3 IN D BWV 1068 (Bach)* JFK: *RONDO ALLEGRO FROM HORN
CONCERTO NO.2 IN E.FLAT MAJ.K.417 (Mozart)* SERPICO:
E LUCEVAN LE STELLE FROM TOSCA (Pucchini) FORBIDDEN
GAMES: *ROMANCE D'AMOUR (Anon)* SOMEONE TO WATCH OVER
ME:*VIENS MALLIKA..DOME EPAIS LA JASMIN (FLOWER DUET
FROM LAKME)(Delibes)* HARD TARGET: *FINALE FROM PIANO
SONATA 23 IN F.M.OP.57 (Beethoven)* HENRY V: *BAILERO*

FROM CHANTS D'AUVERGNE (Canteloube) FOUR WEDDINGS &
A FUNERAL: *WEDDING MARCH FROM A MID-SUMMER NIGHTS
DREAM(Mendelssohn)* PHILADELPHIA:*LA MAMMA MORTA FROM
ANDREA CHENIER (Giordano)* AUTUMN SONATA: *SARABANDE
FROM CELLO SUITE NO.4 IN E.FLAT MAJ.BWV 1010 (Bach)*
MEETING VENUS: *PILGRIMS' CHORUS-TANNHAUSER (Wagner)*

88.**CINEMA CLASSICS (NAXOS) 12** - Various Artists
NAXOS (Select): 8.551172 (CD)   1995
LIVING DAYLIGHTS: *MOLTO ALLEGRO FROM SYMPHONY NO.40
IN G.MINOR K.550 (Mozart)* ACE VENTURA PET DETECTIVE
ROMANCE FROM EINE KLEINE NACHT MUSIK K.525 (Mozart)
FANTASIA:*AVE MARIA D.839 (Schubert)* ROSEMARY'S BABY
BAGATELLE IN A M. (Beethoven) DEER HUNTER
CAVATINA (Myers) THE GREY FOX: *M'APPARI TUTT' AMOR
FROM MARTHA (Flotow)* AGE OF INNOCENCE: *ADAGIO CANTA
BILE FROM PIANO SONATA NO 8 IN C MINOR, OP.13 'PATH
ETIQUE' (Beethoven)* MY LEFT FOOT: *ANDANTINO THEME
FROM PIANO QUINTET IN A.MAJ,D.667 (TROUT)(Schubert)*
DRIVING MISS DAISY: *SONG TO THE MOON FROM RUSALKA
OP.114 (Dvorak)* CRIES AND WHISPERS: *SARABANDE FROM
CELLO SUITE NO.5 IN C.MIN, BWV 1011 (Bach)* TURNING
POINT:*BALCONY SCENE FROM ROMEO & JULIET (Prokofiev)*
ROLLERBALL:*SYMPH NO.5 IN D.MINOR OP.47 Shostakovich*

89.**CINEMA SERENADE** - Pittsburgh Symphony Orchestra *
SONY CLASSICS: SK 63005 (CD)   1998
Excerpts: THE COLOR PURPLE *(composer: QUINCY JONES)*
TRUE LIES (Por Una Cabeza) *(CARLOS GARDEL)* / YENTL
(MICHEL LEGRAND) / IL POSTINO *(LUIS BACALOV)* / THE
AGE OF INNOCENCE *(ELMER BERNSTEIN)* / FAR AND AWAY
(JOHN WILLIAMS) /UMBRELLAS OF CHERBOURG *(M.LEGRAND)*
FOUR HORSEMEN OF THE APOCALYPSE *(ANDRE PREVIN)* /
SABRINA *(JOHN WILLIAMS)* /OUT OF AFRICA *(JOHN BARRY)*
BLACK ORPHEUS *(LUIS BONFA)* / SCHINDLER'S LIST *(JOHN
WILLIAMS)* / CINEMA PARADISO *(ENNIO MORRICONE)*
* conducted by John T.Williams with I.Perlman (vln)

90.**CINEMA SERENADE 2: The Golden Age** - Various Artists
SONY CLASSICS: SK 60773 (CD) SM 60773 (MC)   1999
1.LAURA *(DAVID RASKIN)* 2.NOW VOYAGER *(MAX STEINER)*
3.MODERN TIMES *(CHARLES CHAPLIN)* 4.LOST WEEKEND
(MIKLOS ROZSA) 5.THE QUIET MAN *(VICTOR YOUNG)* 6.THE
ADVENTURES OF ROBIN HOOD *(ERICH WOLFGANG KORNGOLD)*
7.AS TIME GOES BY (from CASABLANCA)*(HERMAN HUPFELD)*
8.HENRY V *(WILLIAM WALTON)* 9.THE UNINVITED *V.YOUNG*
10.GONE WITH THE WIND *(MAX STEINER)* 11.WUTHERING
HEIGHTS *(ALFRED NEWMAN)* 12.MY FOOLISH HEART *(VICTOR
YOUNG)* extracts from film suites played by Isaac
Perlman *(vln)* Boston Pops Orchestra (J.T.Williams)

91.**CINEMA'S CLASSIC ROMANCES** - City Of Prague Philharm
conducted by Kenneth Alwyn
SILVA SCREEN (Koch-S.Screen): SILKD 6018 (CD) 1998
THE ENGLISH PATIENT *(YARED)* MUCH ADO ABOUT NOTHING
and HAMLET *(DOYLE)* HAMLET *(MORRICONE)* EMMA*(PORTMAN)*
WUTHERING HEIGHTS *(NEWMAN)* ROMEO & JULIET *(ROTA)*
LAST OF THE MOHICANS *(JONES)* MRS.DALLOWAY *(SEKACZ)*

TWELFTH NIGHT*(DAVEY)* SENSE AND SENSIBILITY *(DOYLE)*
TESS *(SARDE)* PRIDE AND PREJUDICE *(DAVIS)* LITTLE
WOMEN *(NEWMAN)* FAR FROM THE MADDING CROWD *(BENNETT)*
92.**CLASSIC ADS** - Various Artists and Orchestras
   EMI: CDZ 568116-2 (CD)   *1994*
   Citroen ZX: OVERTURE (Marriage Of Figaro) *(Mozart)*
   Philips DCC: Sorcerer's Apprentice *(Dukas)* *Nescafe:*
   ADAGIO (Spartacus)*(Khachaturuan)* *Tixylix:* DANCE OF
   THE SUGAR PLUM FAIRY (Nutcracker Suite)*Tchaikovsky)*
   British Airways: FLOWER DUET(Lakme)*(Delibes)* *Maxell*
   Tapes: A NIGHT ON BARE MOUNTAIN *(Mussorgsky)* *Bio Sp*
   eed Weed: CAN CAN (Orpheus) *(Offenbach)* *Philips DCC*
   O MIO BABBINO CARO (Gianni Schicci) *(Puccini)* *Hovis*
   LARGO (New World Symph.No.9) *(Dvorak)* *TSB:* MORNING
   PAPERS WALTZ *(J.Strauss II)* *Ragu Pasta Sauce:* ANVIL
   CHORUS (Il Trovatore) *(Verdi)* *AEG:* MORNING (Peer Gy
   nt Suite)*(Grieg)* *Woolworths:*ARRIVAL OF THE QUEEN OF
   SHEBA (Solomon) *(Handel)* *Ragu Pasta S:* LA DONNA E.
   MOBILE (Rigoletto)*(Verdi)* *Jus-Rol:* WALTZ (Coppelia)
   (Delibes) *Alton Towers:* IN THE HALL OF THE MOUNTAIN
   KING (Peer Gynt) *(Grieg)* *Stella Artois:* OVERTURE La
   Forza Del Destino *(Verdi)* *Comfort Fabric Softener:*
   WHAT IS LIFE TO ME WITHOUT THEE (Orpheo & Eurydice)
   (Gluck) *Baci Choc:* INTERMEZZO Cavalleria Rusticana)
   (Mascagni) *Peugeot 605:* The Moldau (Ma Vlast) *(Smet
   ana)* *Thresher Wines:* CANON IN D *(Pachelbel)* *Lloyds*
   Bank: SLEEPERS AWAKE (Cantata No.140) *(J.S.Bach)*
93.**CLASSIC ADS Volume 2** - Various Artists & Orchs
   EMI: CDM 565721-2 (CD) EG 565721-4 (MC)   *1995*
   Baileys Irish Cream: BARCAROLLE (Tales Of Hoffman)
   (Offenbach) *British Airways:* VA PENSIERO (Chorus Of
   The Hebrew Slaves from Nabucco) *(Verdi)* *Kingsmill*
   Bread: SPRING (1st m/m Four Seasons Suite)*(Vivaldi)*
   Batchelor Slimmer Soups: DANCE OF THE LITTLE SWANS
   (Swan Lake) *(Tchaikovsky)* *Lurpak:* FLIGHT OF THE BUM
   BLEBEE (Tsar Sultan) *(Rimsky Korsakov)* *Panasonic:*
   RONDO (Eine Kleine Nacht Musik) *(Mozart)* *Cadbury's*
   Choc Break: TRAUMERI (Kinderszenen) *(Schumann)* *Save*
   & Prosper Building S: MINUET *(Boccherini)* *Cadbury's*
   Fruit & Nut: DANCE OF THE MIRLITONS (Nutcracker Su)
   (Tchaikovsky) *Timex Indiglo:* DANCE OF THE HOURS (La
   Gioconda) *(Ponchielli)* *Hamlet Cigars:* AIR (Suite No
   3) *(Bach)* *Boursin Cheese:* CLAIR DE LUNE *(Debussy)*
   Terry's Nutcracker: CHINESE DANCE(Nutcracker Suite)
   (Tchaikovsky) *Old Spice:* O FORTUNA (Carmina Burana)
   (Orff) *Tesco:* FOSSILES (Carnival Of The Animals)
   (Saint-Saens) *IBM Computers:* FUR ELISE *(Beethoven)*
   Royal Bank Of Scotland: PLAYFUL PIZZICATO (Silly Sy
   mph.)*(Britten)* *ST.Bruno:* NIMROD (Enigma Variations)
   (Elgar) *Today Newspaper:* DIES IRAE (Requiem)*(Verdi)*
   Buxton Mineral Water: ADAGIO (1st mm Cello Concerto
   in E.Min) *(Elgar)* *Clark's Shoes:* PETER AND THE WOLF
   (Prokofiev) *Chanel L'Egoiste:* DANCE OF THE KNIGHTS
   (Romeo & Juliet)*(Prokofiev)* *Dulux* JUPITER *(Holst)*

94.CLASSIC BRITISH FILM MUSIC   Philharmonia Orch* 1990
*SILVA SCREEN (Koch): FILMCD 713 (CD) *Kenneth Alwyn*
COASTAL COMMAND (42-R.V.Williams)-Conquest Of The
Air (38-Arthur Bliss)-Red Shoes (48-Brian Easdale)

95.CLASSIC EXPERIENCE - Various Artists & Orchestras
EMI PREMIER: CD(TC)CLEXP 1(2CD/2MC) 1988 reiss 1996
Collect of Popular Classics used extensively in TV
Commercials, Films and Television Programmes
ARRIVAL OF QUEEN OF SHEBA *(Handel)*-INTERMEZZO KAREL
IA SUITE *(Sibelius)*-BOLERO *(Ravel)*-AIR *(J.S.Bach)*-
ADAGIO from SPARTACUS *(Khachaturian)*-RHAPSODY IN BL
UE *(Gershwin)*-DANCE OF THE REED FLUTE-*(Tchaikovsky)*
SUGAR PLUM FAIRY Coda & Pas De Deux *(Tchaikovsky)*-
MORNING (PEER GYNT)*(Grieg)*-SPRING (FOUR SEASONS) *Vi
valdi)*-RHAPSODY ON A THEME OF PAGANINI*(Rachmaninov)*
LARGO (NEW WORLD SYMPH) *(Dvorak)*-NIMROD from ENIGMA
VARIATIONS *(Elgar)* MEDITATION from THAIS *(Massenet)*
FANTASIA GREENSLEEVES *(V.Williams)*-Canon in D *(Pach
elbel)*-FANFARE FOR COMMON MAN*(Copland)*-WILLIAM TELL
OVFRTURE *(Rossini)*-RIDE OF THE VALKYRIES *(Wagner)*-
MONTAGUES & CAPULETS *(Prokofiev)*-NIGHT ON THE BARE
MOUNTAIN *(Mussorgsky)*-MARS from THE PLANEIS *(Holst)*
RADETZKY MARCH *(Strauss)*-1812 OVERTURE*(Tchaikovsky)*
TROIKA *(Prokofiev)*-BLUE DANUBE *(Strauss)*-MINUET by
(Boccherini)-TURKISH RONDO *(Mozart)*-BARCAROLLE from
The TALES OF HOFFMANN *(Offenbach)*-SLEEPING BEAUTY
WALTZ and DANCE OF THE LITTLE SWANS *(Tchaikovsky)*
INTERMEZZO from CAVALLERIA RUSTICANA *(Mascagni)*-
POMP and CIRCUMSTANCE MARCH NO.1 *(Elgar)*

96.CLASSIC EXPERIENCE 2 - Various Artists & Orchestras
EMI PREMIER: CD(TC)CLEXP 2(2CD/2MC) 1990 reiss 1996
O FORTUNA (CARMINA BURANA) *(Orff)*-SWAN LAKE ACT 2
(Tchaikovsky)-FLOWER DUET (LAKME) *(Delibes)*-IN THE
HALL OF THE MOUNTAIN KING (PEER GYNT) *(Greig)*-OVERT
URE (CARMEN)/CHANSON BOHEME (CARMEN Act 2) *(Bizet)*-
RONDO SERENADE NO.13 IN GM (EINE KLEINE NACHTMUSIK)
(Mozart)-LARGO AL FACTOTEM DELLA CITTA (BARBER OF
SEVILLE)*(Rossini)*-RONDO (HORN CONCERTO NO.4 K.495)-
(Mozart)-ADAGIO IN G.MINOR *(Albinoni)*-WALTZ OF THE
FLOWERS (NUTCRACKER SUITE) *(Tchaikovsky)*-FUR ELISE
(BAGATELLE IN A.MINOR OP.173) *(Beethoven)*-CELLO CON
CERTO IN E.MINOR OP.85 *(Elgar)*-PAVANE Op.50 *(Faure)*
PIZZICATI (SYLVIA) *(Delibes)*-GYMNOPEDIE N.1 *(Satie)*
NESSUN DORMA (TURANDOT)*(Puccini)*-ADAGIO FOR STRINGS
(Barber)-O MIO BABBINO CARO (GIANNI SCHICCHI) *(Pucc
ini)*-ADAGIO FOR STRINGS *(Barber)*-WATER MUSIC *Handel*
SUMMER (FOUR SEASONS SUITE)*(Vivaldi)*-SLEEPERS AWAKE
(CANTATA 140)*(Bach)*-SHERPHERD'S HYMN PASTORAL SYMPH
(Beethoven)-SKATER'S WALTZ *(Waldteufel)*-BADINERIE
(SUITE NO.2) *(Bach)*-LA DONNA E MOBILE (RIGOLETTO)
(Verdi)-RONDO (A MUSICAL JOKE *(Mozart)*-DAYBREAK fr.
DAPHNIS & CHLOE *(Ravel)*-1ST M/M SYMPH.NO.6 *(Vaughan
Williams)*-SUNRISE(ALSO SPRACH ZARATHUSTRA)*(Strauss)*
PRELUDE ACT III (LOHENGRIN) *(R.Wagner)*-JUPITER (PLA

NET'S SUITE) *(Holst)*-ROMEO AND JULIET *(Tchaikovsky)*
THIEVING MAGPIE *(Rossini)*-EXCERPTS from MANFRED and
PATHETIQUE SYMPH.*(Tchaikovsky)*-FINLANDIA *(Sibelius)*
97.CLASSIC EXPERIENCE 3 - Various Artists & Orchestras
EMI PREMIER: CD(TC)CLEXP 3(2CD/2MC) 1991 reiss 1996
SYMPH.NO.9 *(Dvorak)*-MY COUNTRY *(Smetana)*-BARBER OF
SEVILLE *(Rossini)*-BRINDISI from LA TRAVIATA *(Verdi)*
OVERTURE to DIE FLEDERMAUS *(Strauss)* SYMPHONY NO.4
ITALIAN *(Mendelssohn)*-CHINESE DANCE from NUTCRACKER
(Tchaikovsky)-WALTZ NO 6.(MINUTE WALTZ *(Chopin)*-
SYMPHONY NO.40 IN G.MAJOR *(Mozart)*-CHANSON DE MATIN
Op.15 NO.2 *(Elgar)*-ADAGIO GUITAR CONCER.DE ARANJUEZ
(Rodrigo)-SYMPHONY NO.1 IN A.FLAT MAJ.Op.55 *(Elgar)*
ARIA CANTILENA-BACHIANAS BRASILEIROS *(Villa-Lobos)*-
IN THE DEPTHS OF THE TEMPLE (PEARL FISHERS)*(Bizet)*-
CLAIR DE LUNE *(Debussy)*-VESTI LA GIUBBA I PAGLIACCI
(Leoncavallo)-VA PEINSERO CHORUS OF HEBREW SLAVES
NABUCCO *(Verdi)*-SHEEP MAY SAFELY GRAZE *(BACH)*-PIANO
CONCERTO NO.5 EMPEROR *(Beethoven)*-OVERTURE HEBRIDES
(Mendelssohn)-SCHEHERAZADE YOUNG PRINCE & PRINCESS
Rimsky-Korsakov)-FARANDOLE *Bizet*-PETER AND THE WOLF
Tchaikovsky-RUSSIAN DANCE (NUTCRACKER)*(Tchaikovsky)*
BALLET EGYPTIEN *(Luigeni)*-FLIGHT OF THE BUMBLEBEE
(Rimsky-Korsakov)-DANCE OF THE HOURS *(Ponchielli)*-
SABRE DANCE *(Khachaturian)*-SORCERER'S APPRENTICE
Dukas-RITE OF SPRING *(Stravinsky)*-ESPANA *(Chabrier)*
ITALIAN CAPRICE/SYMPHONY NO.9 (CHORAL) *(Beethoven)*
98.CLASSIC EXPERIENCE 4 - Various Artists & Ocrhestras
EMI PREMIER: CD(TC)CLEXP 4(2CD/2MC) 1993 reiss 1996
RUSSLAN & LUDMILLA *(Glinka)*-HOLBERG SUITE *(Grieg)*-
O SOLE MIO *(DiCapua)*-AQUARIUM from CARNIVAL OF THE
ANIMALS (Saint-Saens)-DANSE MACABRE *(Saint-Saens)*-
TRIUMPHAL MARCH AIDA *(Verdi)*-LULLABY from DOLLY *(Fa
ure)*-FANTASIA ON A THEME OF THOMAS TALLIS *(Vaughan
Williams)*-LIGHT CAVALRY OVERTURE *(Suppe)*-THE SWAN
CARNIVAL OF THE ANIMALS *(Saint-Saens)*-NOCTURNE from
SPRING QUARTET No.2 *(Borodin)*-MOONLIGHT SONATA *(Bee
thoven)*-BAILERO from SONGS OF THE AUVERGNE *(Cantelo
ube)*-THE STARS SHINE BRIGHTLY from TOSCA *(Puccini)*-
MEMORIES OF THE ALHAMBRA *(Tarrega)*-STRING QUARTET
(Ravel)-RECUERDOS DE LA ALHAMBRA*(Tarrega)*-YOUR TINY
HAND IS FROZEN:LA BOHEME *(Puccini)*-NEPTUNE from the
PLANETS SUITE *(Holst)*-VIOLIN CONCERTO IN D.MAJ.Op35
(Tchaikovsky)-MARCH from KARELIA SUITE *(Sibelius)*-
ANVIL CHORUS: IL TROVATORE *(Verdi)*-HUNGARIAN MARCH
DAMNATION OF FAUST *(Berlioz)*-CLASSICAL SYMPHONY FIN
ALE *(Prokofiev)*-WALTZ:COPPELIA *(Delibes)*-I SHALL GO
FAR AWAY:LA WALLY *(Catalani)*-HUNGARIAN RHAPSODY NO.
2 *(Liszt)*-PIANO CONCERTO IN A.MINOR *(Greig)*-TURKISH
MARCH: RUINS OF ATHENS *(Beethoven)*-FLYING DUTCHMAN
OVERTURE *(Wagner)*-DANCE OF THE COMEDIANS: BARTERED
BRIDE *(Smetana)*-FORCE OF DESTINY *(Verdi)* YOUNG PERS
ONS GUIDE TO T.ORCHESTRA *(Britten)*- PROMENADE/GREAT
GATE OF KIEV:PICTURES AT AN EXHIBITION *(Mussorgsky)*

99.<u>**CLASSIC FM: RELAX..**</u> **- Var.Artists & Orchestras 1999**
BMG-CONIFER (BMG): CFMCD 30 (3CDs) CFMMC 30 (2MC)
CD1: PIANO CONC.NO.2 IN C.MIN (2nd m/m) *RACHMANINOV*
2.THE LARK ASCENDING *VAUGHAN WILLIAMS* 3.CANON IN D.
PACHELBEL 4.CONCIERTO DE ARANJUEZ (2nd m/m) *RODRIGO*
5.NULLA IN MUNDO PAX SINCERA *VIVALDI* 6.SYMPH.NO 5
IN C.SHARP MIN. (4th m/m) *MAHLER* 7.THE WALK TO THE
PARADISE GARDEN *DELIUS* CD2: MEDITATION from THAIS
MASSENET 2.VIOLIN CON.NO.1 IN G.MIN.(2nd m/m) *BRUCH*
3.RHAPSODY ON A THEME OF PAGANINI (18th Variation)
RACHMANINOV 4.AIR ON THE G.STRING *BACH* 5.RECUERDOS
DE LA ALHAMBRA *TARREGA* 6.SYMPH.6 IN B.MIN (2nd m/m)
TCHAIKOVSKY 7.SPARTACUS (Adagio) *KHACHATURIAN* 8.
CAVALLERIA RUSTICANA *(MASCAGNI)* 9.CELLO SUITE NO.1
IN G (1st m/m) *J.S.BACH* 10.FANTASIA ON A THEME OF
THOMAS TALLIS *V.WILLIAMS* 11.THE GADFLY *SHOSTAKOVICH*
CD3: ADAGIO FOR STRINGS *S.BARBER* 2.PAVAVE *FAURE* 3.
PIANO CONC.IN A.MINOR (2nd m/m) *GRIEG* 4.ADAGIO IN G
MINOR *ALBINONI* 5.ON HEARING THE FIRST CUCKOO IN
SPRING *DELIUS* 6.GYMNOPEDI NO.1 *SATIE* 7.PRELUDE A
L'APRES-MIDI D'UN FAUNE *DFBUSSY* 8.CHANSON DE MATIN
ELGAR 9.MISERERE MEI, DEUS *ALLEGRI*

99a.<u>**CLASSIC LOVE AT THE MOVIES**</u> **- Various Artists**
DECCA (Univ): 466 563-2 (2CDs)   *1999*
33 Track 2CD set *including* BRIEF ENCOUNTER-OUT OF
AFRICA-CASABLANCA etc. *full details in next edition*

100.<u>**CLASSIC MOODS: LOVE**</u> **- Various Artists**   *1998*
EMI CLASSICS: CDM 566758-2 (CD) EG 566758-4 (MC)
1.PIANO CONCERTO NO.3 1st m/m *(RACHMANINOV)* Shine /
Shadowlands 2.CLARINET CONCERTO IN A.2nd m/m *MOZART*
Out Of Africa 3.THE PIANO excerpt *(NYMAN)* The Piano
4.INTERMEZZO FROM CAVALLERIA RUSTICANA *(MASCAGNI)*
Raging Bull 5.PIANO CONCERTO NO.2 IN C.MINOR
(RACHMANINOV) Brief Encounter 6.E.LUCEVAN LE STELLE
FROM TOSCA *PUCCINI* Heavenly Creatures 7.ADAGIO FOR
STRINGS *(BARBER)* Platoon/Elephant Man 8.LOVE THEME
FROM THE SAINT *(REVELL)* The Saint 9.KISSING YOU
(WEEKES & ATACK) Romeo and Juliet 10.RHAPSODY ON A
THEME OF PAGANINI 18th variation *(RACHMANINOV)*
Somewhere In Time 11.EVENING SONG The Evening Song

101.<u>**CLASSIC ITALIAN SPAGHETTI WESTERNS VOL.1**</u> **- Var.Arts**
DRG (Pinn): DRGCD 32905 (2CD)   *1995*
COMPOSERS: Ennio Morricone-Pino Donaggio-Riz Ortola
ni-Francesco De Masi-Carlo Rusticelli-Angelo France
sco Lavagnina-Franco Bixia VOCALS: Katina Ranieri-
Vittorio Bezzi and others
67 SELECTIONS FROM 28 SPAGHETTI WESTERNS (1966-81)

102.<u>**CLASSIC ITALIAN SPAGHETTI WESTERNS VOL.2**</u> **- Var.Arts**
DRG (Pinn): DRGCD 32909 (2CD)   *1995*
COMPOSERS: Ennio Morricone-Bruno Nicolai-Carlo Savi
na-Francesco De Masi-Luis Bacalov-Piero Piccioni-
Riz Ortolani-Armando Trovaioli and others
SPAGHETTI WESTERN MUSIC FROM THE LIBRARY OF ITALY'S
GENERAL MUSIC / MAIN TITLES-VOCALS-RARE TRACKS etc.

103.CLASSIC PAN PIPES - Classical Music from TV ADS
CARLTON SOUNDS (CHE): 30360 00682 (CD) -4 (MC) 1996
1.FLOWER DUET, LAKME *(DELIBES)* Br.Airways 2.MORNING
PEER GYNT *(GRIEG)* AEG 3.SPRING, 4 SEASONS *(VIVALDI)*
Kingsmill Bread 5.CHINESE DANCE, NUTCRACKER SUITE
(TCHAIKOVSKY) Terry's Choc 6.RONDO, EINE KLEINE NAC
HT MUSIK *(MOZART)* Panasonic 7.FUR ELISE *(BEETHOVEN)*
IBM 8.AIR ON A G.STRING *(BACH)* Hamlet 9.IN THE HALL
OF THE MOUNTAIN KING,PEER GYNT *(GREIG)* Alton Towers
10.LA DONNA E MOBILE. RIGOLETTO *(VERDI)* Ragu 11.THE
MOLDAU, MA VLAST *(SMETANA)* Peugeot 605 12.LARGO,NEW
WORLD SYMPHONY *(DVORAK)* Hovis 13.PETER AND THE WOLF
(PRKOFIEV) Clark's 14.KANON IN D *(PACHELBEL)* Thresh
er Wines 15.BARCAROLLE,TALES OF HOFFMAN *(OFFENBACH)*
Bailey's 16.DANCE OF THE SUGAR PLUM FAIRY, NUTCRACK
ER *(TCHAIKOVSKY)* Tixylix 17.DANCE OF THE HOURS from
LA GIOCONDA*(PONCHIELLI)*Timex 18.DANCE OF THE LITTLE
SWANS, SWAN LAKE *(TCHAIKOVSKY)* Batchelor Soups 19.O
MIO BABBINO CARO, GIANNI SCHICCHI *(PUCCINI)* Philips
20.ADAGIO, SPARTACUS BALLET *(KHACHATURIAN)* Nescafe
21.CLAIR DE LUNE *(DEBUSSY)* Boursin Cheese

--- **CLASSIC SCI-FI/SPACE THEMES** *see* **LIVE LONG & PROSPER**

104.CLASSIC THEMES FROM TV AND RADIO - Var.Artists *1996*
HAPPY DAYS (Conif-BMG): 75605 52271-2 (CD) -4 (MC)
1.BARWICK GREEN *(THE ARCHERS)* New Concert Orchestra
2.WON'T YOU GET OFF IT PLEASE *(Tate & Lyle Sugar)*
Fats Waller 3.BY A SLEEPY LAGOON *(DESERT ISLAND DIS
CS)* Eric Coates Symphony Orchestra 4.DEVIL'S GALLOP
(DICK BARTON) Charles Williams Queens Hall Light Or
5.NESSUN DORMA fr.Turandot (Puccini) Jussi Bjorling
6.TROUT QUINTET(Schubert)*(WAITING FOR GOD)* Pro-Arte
Quart.Artur Schnabel 7.CORONATION SCOT *(PAUL TEMPLE
DULUX AD)* Queen's Hall Light Orch 8.AS TIME GOES BY
Turner Layton 9.AIR ON A G.STRING (Bach)*(HAMLET CIG
ARS AD)* L.S.O.10.GRASSHOPPER'S DANCE *(MILK AD)* Jack
Hylton Orch 11.SOMEONE TO WATCH OVER ME *(PPP HEALTH
CARE)* Frances Langford 12.DANCE OF THE FLUTES from
'NUTCRACKER SUITE' Tchaikovsky *(CADBURY'S FRUIT AND
NUT)* Philadelphia Orch. 13.I WANNA BE LOVED BY YOU
(CHANEL NO.5) Helen Kane 14.RONDO ALLA TURCA Mozart
(FORD MOTORS) Symph.Orch 15.OH WHAT A BEAUTIFUL MOR
NIN'*(KELLOGG'S CORNFLAKES)* Glenn Miller Army Air Fo
rces Training Command Orch. 16.ORIENTAL SHUFFLE *(RA
DIO TIMES AD)* Django Reinhardt & Hot Club Of France
17.ITMA SIGNATURE TUNE BBC Variety Orch 18.MY SHIP
(GALAXY AD) Gertrude Lawrence 19.TEA FOR TWO *(NEXT
OF KIN)* Raie Da Costa 20.MAKIN' WHOOPEE *(NATIONWIDE
BUILDING SOC)* Eddie Cantor 21.LIBERTY BELL MARCH
(MONTY PYTHON'S FLYING CIRCUS) Famous Cresswell Col
liery Band 22.LARGO (NEW WORLD SYMPHONY (Dvorak)
(HOVIS) Czech Harmonic Orch 23.ROSES FROM THE SOUTH
(J.Strauss II)*(GRAND HOTEL/YARDLEY LIPSTICK)* Albert
Sandler Palm Court Orch.24.LET'S FALL IN LOVE *(HALI
FAX BUILDING SOC)* Annette Hanshaw 25.WITH A SONG IN
MY HEART *(TWO-WAY FAMILY FAVOURITES)* Andre Kostelan

etz Orch 26.GOODNIGHT SWEETHEART *(GOODNIGHT SWEETHE ART)* Al Bowlly & New Mayfair Dance Orch (Ray Noble)

105.<u>**CLASSICAL FILM THEMES**</u> - Various Artists
RCA INT (BMG): RCA(CD)(MC) 221 (2CD/2MC)   *1997*
2001 A SPACE ODYSSEY 2:INDECENT PROPOSAL 3:AMADEUS
4:GROUNDHOG DAY 5:HOWARDS END 6:ELVIRA MADIGAN 7:
APOCALYPSE NOW 8:DIVA 9:SILENCE OF THE LAMBS 10:
BRIEF ENCOUNTER 11:DIE HARD 2 12:WAYNE'S WORLD 13:
MANHATTAN 14:PLATOON 15:PRETTY WOMAN <u>CD</u> <u>2:</u> 1:DOORS
2:10 3:GODFATHER III 4:FATHER OF THE BRIDE 5:FIRM
6:DIE HARD 7:THE LAST EMPEROR 8:DEATH IN VENICE (1)
9:ROLLERBALL 10:HONEYMOON IN VEGAS 11:CROSSING DELA
NCEY 12:DEATH IN VENCICE (2) 13:OUT OF AFRICA 14:
LOVE AND DEATH 15:MRS.DOUBTFIRE

106.<u>**CLASSIC LOVE AT THE MOVIES**</u> - **Various Artists**
Greatest Movie Love Themes (Instrumentals)
DECCA (Universal): 466 563-2 (2CD) -4 (2MC)   *1999*
1.MY HEART WILL GO ON *(TITANIC)* 2.I WILL ALWAYS
LOVE YOU *(BODYGUARD)* 3.LOVE THEME *(ROMEO & JULIET)*
4.WE HAVE ALL THE TIME IN T.WORLD *(ON HER MAJESTY'S
SECRET SERVICE)* 5.UP WHERE WE BELONG *(AN OFFICER &
A GENTLEMAN)* 6.JOHN DUNBAR THEME *DANCES WITH WOLVES*
7.FOR THE LOVE OF A PRINCESS *(BRAVEHEART)* 8.AS TIME
GOES BY *(CASABLANCA)* 9.OUT OF AFRICA 10.TAKE MY
BREATH AWAY *(TOP GUN)* 11.CAN YOU FEEL THE LOVE
TONIGHT *(LION KING)* 12.UNCHAINED MELODY *(GHOST)* 13.
LOVE IS ALL AROUND *(FOUR WEDDINGS & A FUNERAL)* 14.
EVERYTHING I DO I DO IT FOR YOU *(ROBIN HOOD PRINCE
OF THIEVES)* 15.PIANO CONCERTO No.2 (RACHMANINOV)
(BRIEF ENCOUNTER) 16.CINEMA PARADISO 17.CAVALLERIA
RUSTICANA *(GODFATHER 3)* 18.GABRIEL'S OBOE *(MISSION)*
19.TRY A LITTLE TENDERNESS *COMMITMENTS* 20.EVERGREEN
(A STAR IS BORN) 21.MOON RIVER *(BREAKFAST AT TIFF.)*
22.WHERE DO I BEGIN *LOVE STORY* 23.WHEN A MAN LOVES
A WOMAN 24.LEIA'S THEME *(STAR WARS)* 25.CLARINET
CONCERTO (MOZART) *(OUT OF AFRICA)* 26.CANON IN D.
(PACHELBEL)*(ORDINARY PEOPLE)* 27.CELLO SONATA (BACH)
(TRULY MADLY DEEPLY) 28.RHAPSODY IN BLUE *MANHATTAN)*
29.BOLERO*(10)* 30.THE PIANO 31.SOMEWHERE IN MY HEART
DR.ZHIVAGO 32.HOW DEEP IS YOUR LOVE *SATURDAY NIGHT*

--- <u>**CLOSE ENCOUNTERS**</u> - *see* **WILLIAMS John**
--- <u>**COASTAL COMMAND**</u> - *see* **CLASSIC BRITISH FILM MUSIC**
---.<u>**COMMERCIAL BREAK**</u> - **Old Tunes From New Ads** *see p.41*

107.<u>**COODER Ry**</u> - **Ry Cooder Film Soundtrack Music**
WB (TEN): 9362 45987-2 (CD x 2)   *1995*
Long Riders (1980) Southern Comfort (1981) Border
(1982) Paris Texas (1984) Streets Of Fire (1984)
Alamo Bay (1985) Blue City (1986) Crossroads (1986)
Johnny Handsome (1989) Trespass (92) Geronimo (93)

108.<u>**CONNERY Sean**</u> - **Music From The Films Of** / *featuring*
City Of Prague Philharmonic Orch (Nic Raine-Paul
Bateman, conducting) MARK AYRES (additional synths)
SILVA SCREEN (Koch): FILMCD 189 (CD)   *1998*
THE FIRST GREAT TRAIN ROBBERY-THE ROCK-THE RUSSIA
HOUSE-THE NAKE OF THE ROSE-THE HUNT FOR RED OCTOBER
MEDICINE MAN-MARNIE and The JAMES BOND films

109.<u>COPS</u> - PAUL BROOKS
    K-TEL (K-Tel): ECD 3369 (CD) EMC 2369 (MC)   *1997*
    Medley: HAWAII 5-O/CAGNEY & LACEY/HILL STREET BLUES
    Z.CARS/DRAGNET/MIAMI VICE - INSPECTOR MORSE-MISSION
    IMPOSSIBLE-AVENGERS-MISS MARPLE-KOJAK-THE SWEENEY-
    A.TEAM-ROCKFORD FILES-CHARLIE'S ANGELS-MAGNUM P.I;-
    PERRY MASON-MAN FROM UNCLE. Medley: THE BILL/JULIET
    BRAVO/BERGERAC/NO HIDING PLACE/POLICE WOMAN/STREETS
    OF SAN FRANCISCO/MAIGRET/HEARTBEAT
110.<u>COPS ON THE BOX</u> - 26 Great Cop Themes / V.Artists
    CASTLE COMM (Pinn): MACCD 367 (CD)   *1998*
    1.Medley:HAWAII FIVE-O/CAGNEY AND LACEY/HILL STREET
    BLUES/Z.CARS/DRAGNET/MIAMI VICE 2.INSPECTOR MORSE
    3.MISSION IMPOSSIBLE 4.THE AVENGERS 5.MISS MARPLE
    6.KOJAK 7.THE SWEENEY 8.THE A.TEAM 9.ROCKFORD FILES
    10.CHARLIE'S ANGELS 11.MAGNUM P.I. 12.PERRY MASON
    13.MAN FROM UNCLE 14.Medley: THE BILL/JULIET BRAVO/
    BERGERAC/NO HIDING PLACE/POLICE WOMAN/STREETS OF
    SAN FRANCISCO/MAIGRET/HEARTBEAT
111.<u>COSTNER Kevin</u> - Music From The Films Of / *featuring*
    City Of Prague Philharmonic Orch (Nic Raine-Paul
    Bateman, conducting) MARK AYRES (additional synths)
    SILVA SCREEN (Koch): FILMCD 194 (CD)   *1998*
    WYATT EARP-DANCES WITH WOLVES-NO WAY OUT-REVENGE-
    THE UNTOUCHABLES-THE BODYGUARD-FIELD OF DREAMS-JFK-
    WATERWORLD-TIN CUP-SILVERADO-ROBIN HOOD PRINCE OF T
--- <u>COULTER Phil</u> - *see* <u>GALWAY James 'Legends'</u>
112.<u>COWARD Noel</u> - 20TH CENTURY BLUES: Words & Music of
    Noel Coward (BBC2 11/4/1998) *contemporary artists*
    EMI: 494 631-2 (CD) 494 631-2 (MC) featuring:-
    SHOLA AMA with CRAIG ARMSTRONG/DAMON ALBARN with
    MICHAEL NYMAN/THE DIVINE COMEDY/MARIANNE FAITHFULL
    BRYAN FERRY/ELTON JOHN/PAUL McCARTNEY/PET SHOP BOYS
    VIC REEVES/SPACE/STING/SUEDE featuring RAISSA-TEXAS
    ROBBIE WILLIAMS
113.<u>COWARD Noel</u> - MARVELLOUS PARTY Songs of Noel Coward
    & Friends. PICCADILLY DANCE ORCH (Michael Law) *with*
    Janice Day-Julia Shore-Alison Williams-Michael Law
    TER (Koch): CDVIR 8333 (CD)   *1999*
    1.DANCE LITTLE LADY 2.ROOM WITH A VIEW 3.I WENT TO
    A MARVELLOUS PARTY 4.CHANGE PARTNERS 5.BEGIN THE
    BEGUINE 6.NINA 7.NEVER GONNA DANCE 8.MAD ABOUT THE
    BOY 9.I'VE GOT YOU UNDER MY SKIN 10.LONDON PRIDE 11
    HALF-CASTE WOMAN 12.LADY IS A TRAMP 13.POOR LITTLE
    RICH GIRL 14.DEAREST LOVE 15.MAD DOGS & ENGLISHMEN
    16THE PARTY'S OVER NOW
114.<u>COWARD Noel</u> - THE GREAT SHOWS
    EMI CATALOGUE: 521 808-2 (2CDs) CD1:-
    I'LL SEE YOU AGAIN-IF LOVE WERE ALL-ZIGEUNER-
    DEAR LITTLE CAFE-LOVER OF MY DREAMS-20TH CENTURY
    BLUES-TOAST TO ENGLAND-I'LL FOLLOW MY SECRET HEART-
    REGENCY RAKES-CHARMING CHARMING-ENGILSH LESSON-DEAR
    DEAR LITTLE SOLDIERS-THERE'S ALWAYS SOMETHING FISHY
    ABOUT THE FRENCH-MELANIE'S ARIA-NEVERMORE

CD2:-COUNTESS MITZI-DEAREST LOVE-GYPSEY MELODY-
STATELY HOMES OF ENGLAND-WHERE ARE THE SONGS WE
SUNG-OPERETTE-NOTHING CAN LAST FOREVER-I'D NEVER
KNOW-SOMETHING ABOUT A SOLDIER-MY KIND OF MAN-THIS
COULD BE TRUE-JOSEPHINE-SAIL AWAY-WHY DOES LOVE GET
IN THE WAY-IN A BOAT ON THE LAKE WITH MY DARLING-
CHASE ME CHARLIE-EVENING IN SUMMER-I LIKE AMERICA-
THREE JUVENILE DELINQUENTS-JOSEPHINE-WHY DOES LOVE
GET IN THE WAY-I LIKE AMERICA

115. COWARD Noel - THE REVUES
EMI CATALOGUE: 520 729-2 (2CDs) (37 tracks) CD1:
PARISIEN PIERROT-THERE'S LIFE IN THE OLD GIRL YET-
WHAT LOVE MEANS TO GIRLS LIKE ME-POOR LITTLE RICH
GIRL-A ROOM WITH A VIEW-DANCE LITTLE LADY DANCE-
MARY MAKE BELIEVE-TRY TO LEARN TO LOVE-LORELEI-A
DREAM OF YOUTH (THE DREAM IS OVER)-HALF CASTE WOMAN
ANY LITTLE FISH-LET'S SAY GOODBYE-SOMETHING TO DO
WITH SPRING-THE PARTY'S OVER NOW CD2: MAD DOGS AND
ENGLISHMEN-THREE WHITE FEATHERS-WORLD WEARY-MRS.
WORTHINGTON-LONDON PRIDE-IM WONDER WHAT HAPPENED TO
HIM-SIGH NO MORE-MATELOT-NINA-NEVER AGAIN-THERE ARE
BAD TIMERS JUST AROUND THE CORNER-WAIT A BIT JOE-
DON'T MAKE FUN OF THE FESTIVAL-TIME AND TIME AGAIN-
MEDLEY:- PARISIEN PIERROT/POOR LITTLE RICH GIRL/A
ROOM WITH A VIEW/DANCE LITTLE LADY DANCE-*MEDLEY:-*
SOMEDAY I'LL FIND YOU-ANY LITTLE FISH-IF YOU COULD
ONLY COME WITH ME-I'LL SEE YOU AGAIN

116. COWARD Noel - THE SONGS OF NOEL COWARD
FLAPPER-PAVILION (Pinn): PASTCD 7080 1996
1. MRS.WORTHINGTON 2. PARISIAN PIERROT 3. THERE'S LIFE
IN THE OLD GIRL YET 4. POOR LITTLE RICH GIRL 5. I'LL
SEE YOU AGAIN 6. IF LOVE WERE ALL 7. ZIEGUENER 8. A
ROOM WITH A VIEW 9. DANCE LITTLE LADY 10. I'LL FOLLOW
MY SECRET HEART 11. REGENCY RAKES 12. THERE'S ALWAYS
SOMETHING FISHY ABOUT THE FRENCH13. HAS ANYBODY SEEN
OUR SHIP 14. YOU WERE THERE 15. SOMEDAY I'LL FIND YOU
16. DEAREST LOVE 17. THE STATELY HOMES OF ENGLAND 18.
LONDON PRIDE19. ANY LITTLE FISH 20. MAD ABOUT THE BOY
21. MAD DOGS AND ENGLISHMEN 22. THE PARTY'S OVER NOW

117. COWARD Noel - THE WORDS AND MUSIC OF NOEL COWARD
EMI CATALOGUE: 520 727-2 (CD) *reiss.1999*
OVERTURE-DEAREST LOVE-MAD DOGS AND ENGLISHMEN-A
ROOM WITH A VIEW-MAD DOGS AND ENGLISHMEN-IF LOVE
WERE ALL-I'LL SEE YOU AGAIN-SIMEDAY I'LL FIND YOU-
MRS.WORTHINGTON-MATELOT-STATELY HOMES OF ENGLAND-
YOU WERE THERE-NINA-THE PARTY'S OVER NOW-FINALE

118. CRIME SCENE The - Var.Artists (Ultra Lounge series)
CAPITOL-EMI Premier (EMI): CDEMS 1594 (CD) 1996
1. DRAGNET/ROOM 43 Ray Anthony 2. I-SPY Earle Hagen 3
THINKING OF BABY Elmer Bernstein 4. FROM RUSSIA WITH
LOVE Count Basie 5. BIG TOWN Laurindo Almeida 6. THE
MAN WITH THE GOLDEN ARMBilly May 7. THE UNTOUCHABLES
Nelson Riddle 8. JAMES BOND THEME Leroy Holmes 9.
MISSION IMPOSSIBLE Billy May 10. HARLEM NOCTURNE Spi

ke Jones New Band 11.WALK ON THE WILD SIDE Si Zentn
er 12.MISTER KISS KISS BANG BANG Elliott Fisher 13.
WILD ONES Lou Busch 14.STACCATO'S THEME Elmer Berns
tein 15.SEARCH FOR VULCANLeroy Holmes 16.PETER GUNN
SUITE Ray Anthony 17.SILENCERS Vicki Carr 18.MUSIC
TO BE MURDERED BY Jeff Alexander w.Alfred Hitchcock

119.CRISWELL Kim - Back To Before
TER (Koch): CDVIR 8332 (CD)   *1999*
1.BROADWAY BABY *FOLLIES* 2.ON MY OWN *LES MISERABLES*
3.NOTHING *A CHORUS LINE* 4.UNEXPECTED SONG *SONG AND
DANCE* 5.AS LONG AS HE NEEDS ME *OLIVER* 6.WHAT DOES
HE WANT OF ME*MAN OF LA MANCHA* 7.MR.MONOTONY *JEROME
ROBBINS BROADWAY* 8.UNUSUAL WAY *NINE* 9.DON'T RAIN ON
MY PARADE *FUNNY GIRL* 10.I DON'T KNOW HOW TO LOVE
HIM *JESUS CHRIST SUPERSTAR* 11.RAINBOW HIGH *EVITA* 12
MEMORY *CATS* 13.WHO WILL LOVE ME AS I AM *SIDE SHOW*
14.COUNT YOUR BLESSINGS *WHITE CHRISTMAS* 15. BACK TO
BEFORE *RAGTIME* 16.TOMORROW *ANNIE*

120.CRUSH Bobby - Melodies From The Movies
HALLMARK (CHE-Technicolor): 30955-2 (CD)   *1998*
1.SCHINDLER'S LIST 2.A WHOLE NEW WORLD *ALADDIN* 3. I
ONLY HAVE EYES FOR YOU *MIAMI RHAPSODY* 4.I'VE NEVER
BEEN TO ME *PRISCILLA QUEEN OF THE DESERT* 5.CAN YOU
FEEL THE LOVE TONIGHT *LION KING* 6.SHAKING THE BLUES
AWAY *THAT'S ENTERTAINMENT* 7.CAN YOU READ MY MIND
(SUPERMAN love theme) 8.FORREST GUMP 9.LOVE IS ALL
AROUND *FOUR WEDDINGS AND A FUNERAL* 10.TWO FOR THE
ROAD 11.LET ME BE YOUR WINGS *THUMBELINA* 12.ENDLESS
LOVE 13.WHEN I FALL IN LOVE *SLEEPLESS IN SEATTLE*
14. AS TIME GOES BY *CASABLANCA*

--- CULT FICTION - see THIS IS CULT FICTION

121.CULT FILES The - Royal Philharm.Concert Orch (Mike
Townsend) + City Of Prague Philharmonic (Nic Raine)
SILVA SCREEN (Koch): FILMX(CD)(C)184 (2CD/2MC) 1996
CD1: THE X.FILES-THE PRISONER-THE SAINT-DANGERMAN-
RANDALL & HOPKIRK DECEASED-THE AVENGERS-JASON KING-
THE PERSUADERS-BLAKE'S 7-RED DWARF-DOCTOR WHO-THE
ADVENT.OF ROBINSON CRUSOE-ALFRED HITCHCOCK PRESENTS
HAWAII 5.0.-PERRY MASON-A MAN CALLED IRONSIDE-KOJAK
MISSION IMOSSIBLE-STAR TREK-SEAQUEST DSV-BABYLON 5
CD2:2001-EXCALIBUR-ALIEN-MAD MAX:BEYOND THUNDERDOME
BODY HEAT-THE OMEN-HALLOWEEN-ASSAULT ON PRECINCT 13
BLADERUNNER-BATMAN-SUPERMAN-THE SHADOW-ROCKETEER
HEAVEN'S GATE-LEGEND-SOMEWHERE IN TIME-TAXI DRIVER-
PINK PANTHER-THE BLUES BROTHERS

122.CULT FILES: RE-OPENED Royal Phil.Concert Orch (Mike
Townsend) + City Of Prague Philharmonic (Nic Raine)
Silv.Screen (Koch): FILMX(CD)(C)191 (2CD/2MC) 1997
CD1: XENA THE WARRIOR PRINCESS-BATTLESTAR GALACTICA
HITCHHIKERS GUIDE TO THE GALAXY-SPACE: ABOVE AND
BEYOND-TWILIGHT ZONE-THE OUTER LIMITS-THUNDERBIRDS-
FIREBALL XL5:ZERO G-FIREBALL XL5:FIREBALL-STINGRAY
vocal-STINGRAY:MARCH OF THE OYSTERS-CAPTAIN SCARLET
JOE 90-UFO-SPACE 1999:1st series-SPACE 1999:2nd ser

BATMAN-THE TIME TUNNEL-LOST IN SPACE-VOYAGE TO THE
BOTTOM OF THE SEA-LAND OF THE GIANTS-HERCULES-
STINGRAY:Orch.version **CD2**: POLICE SQUAD-BURKE'S LAW
FUGITIVE-KOJAK-MIAMI VICE-STREETS OF SAN FRANCISCO-
BEAUTY & THE BEAST TV-SUPERMAN-EDWARD SCISSORHANDS-
BEETLEJUICE-YOUNG FRANKENSTEIN-MIDNIGHT EXPRESS-
SUSPIRIA-MERRY CHRISTMAS MR.LAWRENCE-WITHNAIL AND I
A CLOCKWORK ORANGE-THE WILD WILD WEST-ADDAMS FAMILY
MASH-MONTY PYTHON'S FLYING CIRCUS

--- <u>**CURSE OF THE CAT PEOPLE**</u> - *see* WEBB Roy
123.<u>DAY Doris</u> - THE MAGIC OF THE MOVIES
SONY MUSIC (Ten): SONYTV79(CD)(MC) (2CD/MC)   *1999*
1.IT'S MAGIC 2.MOVE OVER DARLING 3.SECRET LOVE 4.
TUNNEL OF LOVE 5.LET'S FACE THE MUSIC AND DANCE 6.
THREE COINS IN THE FOUNTAIN 7.NIGHT AND DAY 8.ON
THE STREET WHERE YOU LIVE 9.I'VE GROWN ACCUSTOMED
TO HIS FACE 10.THEY SAY IT'S WONDERFUL 11.LOVER
COME BACK 12.SINGIN' IN THE RAIN 13.A WONDERFUL GUY
14.SOMETHING WONDERFUL 15.AS LONG AS HEE NEEDS ME
16.PILLOW TALK 17.I'LL NEVER STOP LOVING YOU 18.THE
BLACK HILLS OF DAKOTA 19.TEACHER'S PET 20.DEADWOOD
STAGE **CD2** QUE QUE SERA SERA 2.HOLD ME IN YOUR ARMS
3.CHEEK TO CHEEK 4.OVER THE RAINBOW 5.I SPEAK TO
THE STARS 6.PRETTY BABY 7.VERY THOUGHT OF YOU 8.
I WANT TO BE HAPPY 9.MAKIN' WHOOPEE 10.I KNOW A
PLACE 11.NO TWO PEOPLE 12.LOVE YOU DEARLY 13.APRIL
IN PARIS 14.WHITE CHRISTMAS 15.THIS CAN'T BE LOVE
16.SWINGING ON A STAR 17.HIGH HOPES 18.TILL WE MEET
AGAIN 19.WHEN I FALL IN LOVE 20.THE PARTY'S OVER
124.<u>DELERUE Georges</u> - Francois Truffaut Film Music
London Sinfonietta conducted by Hugo WOLFF
NONESUCH (TEN): 7559 79405-2 (CD)   *1997*
JULES ET JIM-LE DERNIER METRO-LA VALSE DE FRANCOIS
T-SHOOT THE PIANO PLAYER and others
125.<u>DELERUE Georges</u> - The London Sessions (1)
VARESE USA (Pinn): VSD 5241 (CD)   *1990*
Music (Suites and Themes) by Georges Delerue from
his scores for PLATOON-RICH AND FAMOUS-HER ALIBI-
BEACHES-EXPOSED-BILOXI BLUES-CRIMES OF THE HEART
126.<u>DELERUE Georges</u> - The London Sessions (2)
VARESE USA (Pinn): VSD 5245 (CD)   *1990*
Music (Suites and Themes) by Georges Delerue from
his scores for STEEL MAGNOLIAS-INTERLUDE-THE ESCAPE
ARTIST-SALVADOR and 'HOMMAGE TO FRANCOIS TRUFFAUT'
127.<u>DELERUE Georges</u> - The London Sessions (3)
VARESE USA (Pinn): VSD 5256 (CD)   *1992*
SOMETHING WICKED THIS WAY COMES-THE HOUSE ON CAROLL
STREET-A LITTLE SEX-MAID TO ORDER-MAN WOMAN AND CHI
LD-MEMORIES OF ME-AGNES OF GOD-TRUE CONFESSIONS
--- <u>**DIAL M FOR MURDER**</u> - *see* HITCHCOCK Alfred
128.<u>DIAMOND Neil</u> - As Time Goes By
COLUMB (Ten): 491 655-2 (2CD) -4 (MC) -8 (md) 1998
1.AS TIME GOES BY *CASABLANCA* 2.SECRET LOVE *CALAMITY*
JANE 3.UNCHAINED MELODY *UNCHAINED/GHOST* 4.CAN YOU

FEEL THE LOVE TONIGHT *LION KING* 5.THE WAY YOU LOOK
TONIGHT *SWING TIME* 6.LOVE WITH THE PROPER STRANGER
7.PUTTIN' ON THE RITZ 8.WHEN YOU WISH UPON A STAR
PINOCCHIO 9.WINDMILLS OF YOUR MIND *THOMAS CROWN AFF
AIR* 10.EBB TIDE *SWEET BIRD OF YOUTH* 11.TRUE LOVE
HIGH SOCIETY 12.MY HEART WILL GO ON *TITANIC* 13.THE
LOOK OF LOVE *CASINO ROYALE* 14.CAN'T HELP FALLING IN
LOVE *BLUE HAWAII* 15.RUBY *RUBY GENTRY* 16.I'VE GOT
YOU UNDER MY SKIN *BORN TO DANCE* 17.ONE FOR MY BABY
SKY'S THE LIMIT 18.AND I LOVE HER *HARD DAY'S NIGHT*
19.MOON RIVER *BREAKFAST AT TIFFANY'S* 20.IN THE STILL
OF THE NIGHT *NIGHT AND DAY* 21.AS TIME GOES BY...

129. <u>**DISASTER MOVIE MUSIC ALBUM**</u> - Various Artists
SILVA SCREEN (Koch): FILMCD 301 (CD)   *1998*
THE TOWERING INFERNO-TYE POSEIDON ADVENTURE-TITANIC
A NIGHT TO REMEMBER-RAISE THE TITANIC-DAYLIGHT-THE
SWARM-AIRPLANE-TWISTER-VOLCANO-DANTE'S PEAK-THE
HINDENBERG-DEEP IMPACT-THE ABYSS-THE HIGH AND THE
MIGHTY-EARTHQUAKE

--- <u>**DISNEY MOVIE FAVOURITES**</u> - see **BBC CONCERT ORCHESTRA**

130. <u>**DISNEY'S HIT SINGLES & MORE**</u> - Var.Orig Arts
WALT DISNEY (Pinn): WD 11563-2 (CD) -4 (MC)   *1997*
1.CIRCLE OF LIFE *(LION KING)* Elton John 2.SHOOTING
STAR *(HERCULES)* Boyzone 3.SOMEDAY *(HUNCHBACK OF NOT
RE DAME)* Eternal 4.BEAUTY AND THE BEAST Celine Dion
& Peabo Bryson 5.COLOURS OF THE WIND *(POCAHONTAS)*
Vanessa Williams 6.YOU'VE GOT A FRIEND IN ME *(TOY
STORY)* Randy Newman 7.CRUELLA DE VILLE *(101 DALMAT
IONS)* Dr.John 8.HE'S A TRAMP *(LADY AND THE TRAMP)*
Peggy Lee 9.BIBBIDI BOBBIDI BOO *(CINDERELLA)* Louis
Armstrong 10.EVERYBODY WANTS TO BE A CAT *ARISTOCATS*
O.Cast 11.ZIP A DEE DOO DAH *(SONG OF THE SOUTH)* Or.
Cast 12.CHIM CHIM CHEREE *(MARY POPPINS)* O.Cast 13.
JUNGLE BOOK GROOVE: I WANNA BE LIKE YOU + BARE NECE
SSITIES Master Upbeat Mix 14.WHISTLE WHILE YOU WORK
(SNOW WHITE) O.Cast 15.HAKUNA MATATA *(LION KING)* OC
16.A STAR IS BORN *HERCULES* Jocelyn Brown 17.PART OF
YOUR WORLD *LITTLE MERMAID* Olivia Newton John 18.A
WHOLE NEW WORLD *(ALADDIN)* P.Bryson-Regina Belle 19.
CAN YOU FEEL THE LOVE TONIGHT *LION KING* Elton John
20.WHEN YOU WISH UPON A STAR *PINOCCHIO* L.Armstrong

131. <u>**DR.SRANGELOVE**</u> MUSIC FROM STANLEY KUBRICK FILMS
SILVA SCREEN (Koch): FILMCDC 303 (CD)   *1999*
City Of Prague Philharmonic Orchest (Paul Bateman)
Electronic music produced by Mark Ayres
including LOLITA-2001 A SPACE ODYSSEY-BARRY LYNDON-
A CLOCKWORK ORANGE-DOCTOR STRANGELOVE-FULL METAL
JACKET-DAY OF THE FIGHT-THE KILLING-FEAR AND DESIRE
PATHS OF GLORY-KILLER'S KISS-THE SHINING-SPARTACUS
includes orig songs by Al Bowlly-Vera Lynn-Trashmen

--- <u>**DR.ZHIVAGO**</u> *see* JARRE Maurice (Classic Film Music
132. <u>**DUNCAN Trevor**</u> - BRITISH LIGHT MUSIC
with Slovak Radio Symphony Orchestra (Andrew Penny)

MARCO POLO (Select): 8.223517 (CD)   *1997*
1.20TH CENTURY EXPRESS 2-5.LITTLE SUITE: MARCH/LULL
ABY/JOGTROT/HIGH HEELS 6-8 CHILDREN IN THE PARK:
DANCING FOR JOY/AT THE POOL/HIDE AND SEEK 9.MAESTRO
VARIATIONS 10.THE GIRL FROM CORSICA 11.MEADOW MIST
12.VALSE MIGNONETTE 13.WINE FESTIVAL 14.SIXPENNY
RIDE 15.ENCHANTED APRIL 16.ST.BONIFACE DOWN 17.LA
TORRIDA 18.VISIONARIES GRAND MARCH 20.LITTLE DEBBIE

133.<u>DURBIN Deanna</u> - **Can't Help Singing**
     LIVING ERA-ASV (Select): CDAJA 5149 (CD)   *1995*
ANNIE LAURIE-AVE MARIA (Bach-Gounod)-IL BACHIO (The
Kiss)-BECAUSE-BENEATH THE LIGHTS OF HOME-CAN'T HELP
SINGING (with Robert Paige)-ESTRELLITA (Ponce)-GOD
BLESS AMERICA-HOME SWEET HOME-IT'S RAINING SUNBEAMS
IT'S FOOLISH BUT IT'S FUN-KISS ME AGAIN-LAST ROSE
OF SUMMER-LOCH LOMOND-LOVE IS ALL-LOVE'S OLD SWEET
SONG-MAIDS OF CADIZ-MUSETTA'S WALTZ SONG(La Boheme)
MY HERO MY OWN-ONE FINE DAY (from Madame Butterfly)
PERHAPS-POOR BUTTERFLY-SPRING IN MY HEART-WALTZING
IN THF CLOUDS-WHEN APRIL SINGS

134.<u>DURBIN Deanna</u> - **Sensational Songbird**
     PRESIDENT (BMG): PLCD 567 (CD)   *1998*
1.THE TURNTABLE SONG 2.MORE AND MORE 3.SPRING WILL
BE A LITTLE LATE THIS YEAR 4.UN BEL DI VEDREMO (ONE
FINE DAY 5.ALWAYS 6.BENEATH THE LIGHTS OF HOME 7.
ANY MOMENT NOW 8.CALIFORN-I-AY 9.CAN'T HELP SINGING
10.LOVE IS ALL 11.AVE MARIA 12.OLD FOLKS AT HOME 13
SOMEONE TO CARE FOR ME 14.IL BACIO (THE KISS) 15.
ALLELUJAH 16.IT'S FOOLISH BUT IT'S FUN 17.WHEN THE
ROSES BLOOM AGAIN 18.LOVE'S OLD SWEET SONG 19.
AMAPOLA 20.LES FILLES DE CADIZ (MAIDS OF CADIZ) 21.
AVE MARIA 22.SAY A PRAYER FOR THE BOYS OVER THERE

135.<u>DURBIN Deanna</u> - **The Fan Club**
     FLAPPER-PAVILION (Pinn): PASTCD 9781 (CD)   *1992*
AMAPOLA-BECAUSE-WHEN APRIL SINGS-WALTZING IN THE CL
OUDS-MY OWN-BRINDISI-BENEATH THE LIGHTS OF HOME-SPR
ING IN MY HEART-IT'S RAINING SUNBEAMS-MUSETTA'S WAL
TZ SONG-LOVE IS ALL-PERHAPS-ONE FINE DAY-HOME SWEET
HOME-LAST ROSE OF SUMMER-IL BACIO-AVE MARIA-LOCH LO
MONS-ALLELULIA-AVE MARIA   *DEANNA DURBIN Film Songs*

136.<u>DURBIN Deanna</u> - **The Golden Voice Of**
     HALLMARK (Carlton): 30818-2 (CD) -4 (MC)   *1997*
CAN'T HELP SINGING-MORE AND MORE-SPRING IN MY HEART
CALIFORN...-ALWAYS-ONE FINE DAY-LE FILLES DE CADIZ-
AVE MARIA-LOVE IS ALL-HOME SWEET HOME-BENEATH THE
LIGHTS OF HOME-ANY MOMENT NOW-MY OWN-LAST ROSE OF
SUMMER-SPRING WILL BE A LITTLE LATE THIS...-SOMEONE
TO CARE FOR ME-IT'S FOOLISH BUT IT'S FUN-WALTZING
IN THE CLOUDS-ANNIE LAURIE-LOVE'S OLD SWEET SONG

137.<u>EASTWOOD Clint</u> - **Music From His Films:** City Of
     Prague Symphony Orchestra (cond: Derek Wadsworth)
     SILVA SCREEN (Koch): FILMCD 138 (CD)   *1993*
THE UNFORGIVEN-THE GOOD THE BAD AND THE UGLY-A FIST
FUL OF DOLLARS-FOR A FEW DOLLARS MORE-HANG 'EM HIGH

WHERE EAGLES DARE-PLAY MISTY FOR ME-OUTLAW JOSEY WA
LES-RAWHIDE-DIRTY HARRY-SUDDEN IMPACT-MAGNUM FORCE-
TWO MULES FOR SISTER SARA-IN THE LINE OF FIRE

138.<u>ELIZABETHAN SERENADE</u> - Best Of BRITISH Light Music
NAXOS (Select): 8.553515 (CD)   *1996*
1.BY THE SLEEPY LAGOON *(E.COATES)* 2.MARCH OF THE BO
WMAN 'Robin Hood Suite' *(F.CURZON)* 3.BELLS ACROSS
THE MEADOWS *(A.KETELBEY)* 4.CORONATION SCOT *V.ELLIS)*
5.SKETCH OF A DANDY *(H.WOOD)* 6.WESTMINSTER WALTZ
(R.FARNON) 7.MARCH FROM A LITTLE SUITE *(T.DUNCAN)*
8.SAILING BY *(R.BINGE)* 9.JAMAICAN RHUMBA *A.BENJAMIN*
10.KNIGHTSBRIDGE MARCH from 'London Suite' *E.COATES*
11.IN A MONASTERY GARDEN *(A.KETELBEY)* 12.LITTLE SER
ENADE *(E.TOMLINSON)* 13.ROSES OF PICARDY *(H.WOOD)* 14
PUFFIN' BILLY *(E.WHITE)* 15.ELIZABETHAN SERENADE *(R.*
BINGE) 16.TOM JONES WALTZ *(E.GERMAN)* 17.VANITY FAIR
(A.COLLINS) 18.MARIGOLD *(B.MAYERL)* 19.IN A PERSIAN
MARKET *(A.KETELBEY)* 20.DAM BUSTERS MARCH *(E.COATES)*

139.<u>EMBER YEARS 1</u>:JOHN BARRY/ELIZABETH TAYLOR In London
PLAY IT AGAIN (S.Screen-Koch): PLAY 002 (CD)   *1992*
JOHN BARRY: -S/T- to 'Four In The Morning' (65) and
ELIZABETH TAYLOR IN LONDON (63) Music by JOHN BARRY

140.<u>EMBER YEARS 2</u>: JOHN BARRY / ANNIE ROSS
PLAY IT AGAIN (S.Screen-Koch): PLAY 003 (CD)   *1992*
JOHN BARRY: FROM RUSSIA WITH LOVE-HIGH GRASS-KINKY-
ZULU STAMP-LONELINESS OF AUTUMN-NGENZENI-BIG SHIELD
ALIKI-TETHA LEYANTO-TROUBADOR-MONKEY FEATHERS-007
ANNIE ROSS:RHYTHM OF THE WORLD-A LOT OF LIVIN'TO DO
LET ME LOVE YOU-ALL THE THINGS YOU ARE-I'M GONNA GO
FISHIN-LIKE SOMEONE IN LOVE-LIMEHOUSE BLUES-HANDFUL
OF SONGS-ALL OF YOU-NATURE BOY-WHAT'S NEW & others

141.<u>ENYA</u>   *VARIOUS MUSIC USED IN FILM AND TV taken from*
'The Celts' *WEA: 4509 91167-2(CD) WX 498C(MC)* 1987
'Watermark' *WEA: 243875-2 (CD) -4 (MC)*   1988
'Shepherd Moons' *WEA: 9031 75572-2(CD) -4(MC)* 1991
'Memory Of Trees' *WEA: 06301287-2 (CD) -4(MC)* 1995
'Paint The Sky With Stars' *WEA: 3984 20895-2* 1997

--- <u>ESSENTIAL ALFRED HITCHCOCK</u> - *see* PSYCHO

142.<u>ESSENTIAL BRITISH LIGHT MUSIC COLLECT.</u> - Classic FM
BBC Concert Orchestra conducted by Vernon Handley
BMG-CLASSIC FM (BMG): 75605 57003-2 (CD)   *1997*
1.633 SQUADRON *(RON GOODWIN)* 2.CORONATION SCOTT
(V.ELLIS) 3.WESTMINSTER WALTZ *(R.FARNON)* 4/5.LONDON
SUITE: KNIGHTSBRIDGE MARCH/COVENT GARDEN *(E.COATES)*
6.NIGHTS OF GLADNESS *(C.ANCLIFFE)* 7.MEXICAN HAT
DANCE *(P.HOPE)* 8.SAILING BY *(R.BINGE)* 9.HORSEGUARDS
WHITEHALL *(H.WOOD)* 10.ELIZABETHAN SERENADE *(BINGE)*
11.MARCH FROM A LITTLE SUITE *(T.DUNCAN)* 12.JAMAICAN
RUMBA *(A.BENJAMIN)* 13.CONCERT JIG *(E.TOMLINSON)* 14.
BY THE SLEEPY LAGOON *(E.COATES)* 15.PUFFIN' BILLY*(E.*
WHITE) 16.VANITY FAIR *(A.COLLINS)* 17.JUMPING BEAN
(R.FARNON) 18.GRASSHOPPER'S DANCE *(E.BUCALOSSI)* 19.
BARWICK GREEN*(H.WOOD)* 20.DAM BUSTERS MARCH *(COATES)*

--- <u>ESSENTIAL JAMES BOND The</u> - *see* BOND James

143. <u>**ESSENTIAL SOUNDTRACKS**</u> - FILM FOUR / Var.Orig.Arts.
TELSTAR: TTVCD 3038 (2CD) TTVMC 3038 (2MC) 1999
1.LUST FOR LIFE Iggy Pop *TRAINSPOTTING* 2.MISIRLOU
Dick Dale & Deltones *PULP FICTION* 3.PAYBACK James
Brown *LOCK STOCK & 2 SMOKING BARRELS* 4.THERE SHE
GOES La's *FEVER PITCH* 5.JUST LOOKIN' Stereophonics
THIS YEAR'S LOVE 6.SHALLOW GRAVE Leftfield *S.GRAVE*
7.BIG SPENDER Shirley Bassey *LITTLE VOICE* 8.LET'S
STAY TOGETHER Al Green *PULP FICTION* 9.STUCK IN THE
MIDDLE WITH YOU Stealers Wheel *RESERVOIR DOGS* 10.
PLAY DEAD Bjork & David Arnold *YOUNG AMERICANS*
11.FOR WHAT YOU DREAM OF Bedrock feat KYO *TRAIN
SPOTTING* 12.SAINT Orbital *THE SAINT* 13.FOOL'S GOLD
Stone Roses *LOCK STOCK..*14.A LIFE LESS ORDINARY
Ash *A LIFE LESS ORDINARY* 15.HUNDRED MILE HIGH CITY
Ocean Colour Scene *LOCK STOCK..*16.HEROIN The Doors
THE DOORS 17.OYE COMO VA Santana *CARLITO'S WAY* 18.
JUNGLE BOOGIE Kool & The Gang *PULP FICTION* 19.
MACHINE GUN Commodores *BOOGIE NIGHTS* 20.ACROSS
110TH STREET Bobby Womack *JACKIE BROWN* CD2: 1.BORN
SLIPPY Underworld *TRAINSPOTTING* 2.LITTLE GREEN BAG
George Baker Selection *RESERVOIR DOGS* 3.SON OF A
PREACHER MAN Dusty Springfield *PULP FICTION* 4.
DON'T BLOW YOUR MIND THIS TIME Delfonics *JACKIE
BROWN* 5.TROUBLE MAN Marvin Gaye *SEVEN* 6.BULLITT
Lalo Schifrin *BULLITT* 7.BLUE VELVET Bobby Vinton
BLUE VELVET 8.AC-CENT-CHU-ATE THE POSITIVE Johnny
Mercer *L.A.CONFIDENTIAL* 9.KING OF THE ROAD Roger
Miller *SWINGERS* 10.SOUL ON FIRE LaVern Baker *ANGEL
HEART* 11.YOU'RE THE FIRST THE LAST MY EVERYTHING
Barry White *FOUR WEDDINGS AND A FUNERAL* 12.HOT
STUFF Donna Summer *FULL MONTY* 13.BEST OF MY LOVE
Emotions *BOOGIE NIGHTS* 14.GOT TO BE REAL Cheryl
Lynn *LAST DAYS OF DISCO* 15.I'LL TAKE YOU THERE
Staple Singers *CASINO* 16.MAKE ME SMILE Steve Harley
Cockney Rebel *VELVET GOLDMINE* 17.BORN TO BE WILD
Steppenwolf *EASY RIDER* 18.GREEN ONIONS Booker T.&
MG's *GET SHORTY* 19.LAURA'S THEME Angelo Badalemnti
TWIN PEAKS 20.PERFECT DAY Lou Reed *TRAINSPOTTING*
144. <u>**ESSENTIAL SOUNDTRACKS**</u> - **THE CLASSIC COLLECTION**
TELSTAR: TTVCD 3082 (2CD) TTVMC 3082 (2MC) 1999
CD1: 1.HEART ASKS PLEASURE FIRST/THE PROMISE *PIANO*
2.ZADOK THE PRIEST *THE MADNESS OF KING GEORGE* 3.
ELIZABETH OVERTURE *ELIZABETH* 4.DUETTINO SULL'ARIA
from MARRIAGE OF FIGARO *SHAWSHANK REDEPTION* 5.CHE
GELIDA MANINA from LA BOHEME *MIDSUMMER NIGHTS DREAM*
6.INTERMEZZO CAVALLERIA RUSTICANA *RAGING BULL* 7.
CHASING SHEEP IS BEST LEFT TO SHEPHERDS
DRAUGHTSMAN'S CONTRACT 8.CONCERTO IN A.MINOR for 4
HARPSICHORDS *DANGEROUS LIAISONS* 9.SILENCE OF THE
LAMBS MAIN TITLE 10.ON EARTH AS IT IS IN HEAVEN
THE MISSION 11.LAST OF THE MOHICANS MAIN TITLE
12.THE ENGLISH PATIENT 13.EN ARANJUEZ CON TU AMOR
BRASSED OFF CD2: 1.WALTZ TWO from THE JAZZ SUITE

EYES WIDE SHUT 2.MATTHAUS PASSION *CASINO* 3.DRAMATIC
DEPARTURE *DAMAGE* 4.AIR ON A G.STRING *SEVEN* 5.THEME
FROM TWIN PEAKS 'FIRE WALK WITH ME' 6.ONCE UPON A
TIME IN AMERICA 7.PRELUDE AND ROOFTOP *VERTIGO* 8.
WAR ZONE THEME 9.MONTY REMEMBERS *WITHNAIL AND I*
10.LOVE THEME FROM BLADERUNNER 11.NUOVO CINEMA
PARADISO *CINEMA PARADISO* 12.BILITIS 13.4TH M/M 9TH
SYMPHONY (ABRIDGED) *CLOCKWORK ORANGE*

145.ESSEX David - A NIGHT AT THE MOVIES
POLYGRAM TV: 537 608-2 (CD) -4 (MC)   1997
1.GIRL YOU'LL BE A WOMAN SOON *(PULP FICTION)* 2.CAN
YOU FEEL THE LOVE TONIGHT *(LION KING)* 3.CRYING GAME
4.THE WIND BENEATH MY WINGS *(BEACHES)* 5.STARDUST 6.
TOGETHER IN ELECTRIC DREAMS 7.OH WHAT A CIRCUS *(EVI
TA)* 8.SEPERATE LIVES *WHITE NIGHTS* 9.ST.ELMO'S FIRE
10.KISS FROM A ROSE *BATMAN FOREVER* 11.SOMEWHERE OUT
THERE *AN AMERICAN TALE)* 12.SILVER DREAM MACHINE 13.
SEA OF LOVE 14.IF I HAD WORDS (ANTHEM) *(CHESS)*

146.EUROPEAN LIGHT MUSIC CLASSICS - New London Orch *
HYPERION: CDA 66998 (CD)   1998
1.PARADE OF THE TIN SOLDIERS *(L.JESSEL)* 2.GOLD AND
SILVER *(LEHAR)* 3.MARCH OF THE LITTLE LEAD SOLDIERS
(G.PIERNE) 4.TRITSCH TRATSCH POLKA *(J.STRAUSS II)*
5.GLOW WORM IDYLL *(P.LINKE)* 6.SWEDISH POLKA *(HUGO
ALFVEN)* 7.FUNERAL MARCH OF A MARIONETTE *(C.GOUNOD)*
8.THE SKATERS (LES PATINEURES) *(E.WALDTEUFEL)* 9.
SERENADE *(J.HEYKENS)* 10.EL RELICARIO *(J.PADILLA)*
11.TESORO MIO MY TREASURE*(E.BECUCCI)* 12.BALL SCENE
(J.HELLMESBERGER) 13.POLKA (SCHWANDA THE BAGPIPER)
(J.WEINBERGER) 14.MOONLIGHT ON THE ALSTER *O.FETRAS*
15.THE ENTRY OF THE BOYARS *(J.HALVORSEN)*
* *Ronald Corp (conductor) David Juritz (leader)*

147.FAMOUS THEMES (1): Remember These ? - Var.Artists
GRASMERE (BMG): GRCD 10 (CD) GRTC 10 (MC)   1986
PUFFIN' BILLY (Childrens Fav)-MUSIC EVERYWHERE (Red
iffusion)-CORONATION SCOT (Paul Temple)-ON A SPRING
NOTE (Pathe Gazette)-RHYTHM ON RAILS Morning Mus-BY
THE SLEEPY LAGOON(Desert Island Discs) HORSE GUARDS
WHITEHALL (Down Your Way)-DEVIL'S GALLOP (Dick Bart
on)-DESTRUCTION BY FIRE (Pathe News)-ALL SPORTS MAR
CH (Pathe News)-SPORTSMASTER (Peter Styvestant)-ALP
INE PASTURES (My Word)-CAVALCADE OF YOUTH (Barlowes
Of Beddington)-DRUM MAJORETTE (Match Of The Day)
ELIZABETHAN SERENADE (Music in Miniature)-MELDOY ON
THE MOVE/YOUNG BALLERINA (The Potter's Wheel)-GIRLS
IN GREY (BBC TV News)-WILLO THE WISP/PORTRAIT OF A
FLIRT/JUMPING BEAN (In Town Tonight)-HORSE FEATHERS
Meet The Huggetts)-JOURNEY INTO MELODY/SAPPHIRES &
SABLES/INVITATION WALTZ (Ring Around The Moon)

148.FAVOURITE SPORT THEMES - Various Artists
HALLMARK (CHE): 31113-2 (CD)   1999
ABC WIDE WORLD OF SPORTS-MATCH OF THE DAY-HORSE OF
THE YEAR SHOW-GARY LINEKER'S GOLDEN BOYS (How Does
It Feel To Be On Top Of The World)-POT BLACK (Black

& White Rag)-RADIO 5 LIVE SPORTS REPORT (Out Of The
Blue)-GRANDSTAND-WORLD OF SPORT (Sporty Type)-BBC
SNOOKER (Drag Racer)-WIMBLEDON (Light and Tuneful)-
SPORTNIGHT-SPORTS ARENA MARCH-RUGBY SPECIAL (Holy
Mackerel)-RUGBY WORLD CUP (World in Union)-BBC
CRICKET (Soul Limbo)-BBC GRAND PRIX (The Chain)-
A QUESTION OF SPORT-EURO 96 THEME (Three Lions)

--- **FAVOURITE THEMES FROM BBC TV** *see* WORLD OF SOUND
149.**FAVOURITE TV THEMES** - Various Artists
MCI (Disc-THE): MCCD 069 (CD) MCTC 069 (MC)   1992
INSPECTOR MORSE-RUTH RENDELL MYSTERIES-SEVEN FACES
OF WOMAN-UPSTAIRS DOWNSTAIRS-AGATHA CHRISTIE'S POIR
OT-A WOMAN OF SUBSTANCE-TALES OF THE UNEXPECTED-THE
PROFESSIONALS-THE MATCH-THE AVENGERS-FOREVER GREEN-
NEW ADVENTURES OF BLACK BEAUTY-CHIMERA-LONDON'S BUR
NING-DR.WHO-THE ONE GAME-WORLD CUP 90-ON THE LINE-
A HUNDRED ACRES-WISH ME LUCK-SUMMER'S LEASE-ITV ATH
LETICS-THE GOOD GUYS-CLASSIC ADVENTURE

150.**FAVOURITE TV THEMES** - Various Artists
MUSIC DIGITAL (Target-BMG): CD 6112 / MC 7112 1998
CORONATION STREET-EASTENDERS-PRISONER CELL BLOCK-H
DALLAS-DYNASTY-BROOKSIDE-DR.WHO-STAR TREK-BATMAN-
THE MAN FROM U.N.C.L.E.-THE AVENGERS-THE FUGITIVE-
THE SAINT-DOCTOR KILDARE-THUNDERBIRDS-CROSSROADS-
EMMERDALE-NEIGHBOURS-HOME AND AWAY-COUNTRY PRACTICE

--- **FELLINI Federico** - *see* **ROTA Nino**
151.**FERGUSON David** - **The View From Now (TV Soundtracks)**
CHANDOS RECORDS: CHAN 9679 (CD)   1998
1.WILDERNESS AND WEST *(AMERICAN VISIONS)* 2.FLOWERS
ON THE ROAD *(SOME KIND OF LIFE)* 3.TO BE A SOMEBODY
(CRACKER) 4.ME OR THE SCULPTURE *(ICE HOUSE)* 5.LA
PESTE *(ALBERT CAMUS COMBAT CONTRE L'ABSURDE)* 6.LONG
RUN *(BRAVO 2 ZERO)* 7.GRAVEYARD SUITE*(THE WOMAN IN
WHITE)* 8.I DIDN'T ASK YOU TO FIGHT*(LIFE AFTER LIFE)*
9.LUMINISTYS AND RAILWAYS *(AMERICAN VISIONS)* 10.BIG
CRUNCH *(CRACKER)* 11.TWO WELCOMES *(HOSTILE WATERS)*
12.RABBIT'S FOOT *(BREAKOUT)* 13.GENTLE KIDNAP *(DARK
ADAPTED EYE)* 14.OBJECTS TROUVEES *(AMERICAN VISIONS)*
15.MAGGIE'S BABY *(BAD GIRL)* 16.NOT WAVING *(DISASTER
AT VALDEZ)* 17.MARILYN/EDEN'S DEBT*(DARK ADAPTED EYE)*

--- **FILM MUSIC** - *see* I.SALONISTI
152.**FORMBY George** - **At The Flicks**
PRESIDENT (BMG): PLCD 554 (CD)   1996
1.I COULD MAKE A GOOD LIVING AT THAT 2.BABY *(BOOTS
BOOTS)* 3.IT'S IN THE AIR 4.THEY CAN'T FOOL ME *(IT'S
IN THE AIR)* 5.GOODNIGHT LITTLE FELLOW GOODNIGHT 6.
PARDON ME 7.I'M MAKING HEADWAY NOW 8.I COULDN'T LET
THE STABLE DOWN *(COME ON GEORGE)* 9.I WISH I WAS
BACK ON THE FARM *(SPARE A COPPER)* 10.COUNT YOUR
BLESSINGS AND SMILE 11.OH DON'T THE WIND BLOW COLD
(LET GEORGE DO IT) 12.THE EMPEROR OF LANCASHIRE 13.
YOU'RE EVERYTHING TO ME 14.YOU CAN'TGO WRONG IN
THESE *(TURNED OUT NICE AGAIN)* 15.I PLAYED ON MY SPA
NISH GUITAR 16.I'D DO IT WITH A SMILE 17.BARMAID AT

THE ROSE AND CROWN *(SOUTH AMERICAN GEORGE)* 18.WHEN
THE LADS OF THE VILLAGE GET CRACKIN' 19.HOME GUARD
BLUES *(GET CRACKIN')* 20.BELL BOTTOM GEORGE 21.IT
SERVES YOU RIGHT *(BELL BOTTOM GEORGE)* 22.GOT TO GET
YOUR PHOTO IN THE PRESS 23.HILL BILLY WILLY 24.
UNCONDITIONAL SURRENDER *(SHE SNOOPS TO CONQUER)*

153.<u>FORMBY George</u> - **Very Best Of George FORMBY**
SOUND WAVES (BMG): SWNCD 017 (CD) SWN 017 (MC) 1997
LEANING ON A LAMP POST-RIDING IN THE TT RACES-
AUNTIE MAGGIE'S REMEDY-WHEN I'M CLEANING WINDOWS-
WITH MY LITTLE STICK OF BLACKPOOL ROCK-WINDOW CLEAN
ER-I'M THE UKELELE MAN-THE LANCASHIRE TOREADOR-
SITTING ON THE TOP OF BLACKPOOL TOWER-I DON'T LIKE-
BLESS 'EM ALL-MOTHER WHAT'LL I DO NOW-IT'S TURNED
OUT NICE AGAIN-FRIGID AIR FANNY-GRANDAD'S FLANELETT
NIGHTSHIRT-HI TIDDLEY HI TI ISLAND-MR WU'S A WINDOW
CLEANER NOW-WINDOW CLEANER NO.2-OH DON'T THE WIND
BLOW COLD-THE EMPEROR OF LANCASHIRE-IN MY LITTLE
SNAPSHOT ALBUM-HOME GUARD BLUES

154.<u>FORMBY George</u> - **When I'm Cleaning Windows**
PRESIDENT (BMG): PLCD 538 (CD)   *1995*
SITTING ON THE ICE IN THE ICE RINK -WHY DON'T WOMEN
LIKE ME *(from BOOTS BOOTS)* / DO DE OH DOH-CHINESE
LAUNDRY BLUES-YOU CAN'T STOP ME FROM DREAMING /
PLEASURE CRUISE *(ZIP GOES A MILLION)* / KEEP FIT
(KEEP FIT) / RIDING IN THE TT RACES *(NO LIMIT)* /
HINDOO MAN-IT AIN'T NOBODY'S BIZ'NESS WHAT I DO/
GOODY GOODY/I LIKE BANANAS-THE LANCASHIRE TOREADOR
A FARMER'S BOY-YOU CAN'T KEEP A GROWING LAD DOWN
YOU'RE A LI-A-TY/ WITH MY LITTLE STICK OF BLACKPOOL
ROCK-TRAILING AROUND IN A TRAILER-DARE DEVIL DICK-
SOMEBODY'S WEDDING DAY-SITTING ON THE SANDS ALL NIG
HT-MADAME MOSCOVITCH/WITH MY LITTLE UKELELE IN MY
HAND *(OFF THE DOLE)* FANLIGHT FANNY*(TROUBLE BREWING)*
WHEN I'M CLEANING WINDOWS *(KEEP YOUR SEATS PLEASE)*
LEANING ON A LAMP POST *(FEATHER YOUR NEST)*

155.<u>GALWAY James</u> and **PHIL COULTER** - **Legends**
RCA Victor (BMG): 09026 68776-2 (2CD) -4 (2MC) 1997
RIVERDANCE-HARRY'S GAME-BELIEVE ME IF ALL THOSE END
EARING YOUNG CHARMS-THE GENTLE MAIDEN-WOMEN OF IREL
AND (Mna Na Ehireann)-THE BATTLE OF KINSDALE (THE
VALLEY OF TEARS)-THE THORNBIRDS-LANNIGAN'S BALL-
KERRY DANCES-DANNY BOY-MUSIC FOR A FOUND HARMONIUM-
LAMENT FOR THE WILD GEESE-MY LAGAN LOVE-NATASHA (An
Cailin Fionn)-ASHOKAN FAREWELL (theme from the TV
series 'The CIVIL WAR')-HOEDOWN

156.<u>GARLAND Judy</u> - **Collector's Gems From The MGM Films**
EMI ODEON: CDODEON 22 (7243 854533-2) (CD)   *1997*
WALTZ WITH A SWING/AMERICANA-OPERA V.JAZZ-EVERYBODY
SING-YOURS AND MINE-YOUR BROADWAY AND MY BROADWAY-
GOT A PAIR OF NEW SHOES-SUN SHOWERS-DOWN ON MELODY
FARM-WHY BECAUSE-EVER SINCE THE WORLD BEGAN/SHALL I
SING A MELODY-IN BETWEEN-IT NEVER RAINS BUT WHAT IT
POURS-BEI MIR BIST DU SCHOEN-MEET THE BEAT OF MY HE

ART-ZING WENT THE STRINGS OF MY HEART-ON THE BUMPY
ROAD TO LOVE-TEN PINS IN THE SKY-I'M NOBODY'S BABY-
ALL I DO IS DREAM OF YOU-ALONE-IT'S A GREAT DAY FOR
THE IRISH-DANNY BOY-A PRETTY GIRL MILKING HER COW-
SINGIN' IN THE RAIN-EASY TO LOVE-WE MUST HAVE MUSIC
I'M ALWAYS CHASING RAINBOWS-MINNIE FROM TRINIDAD-
EVERY LITTLE MOMENT HAS A MEANING OF IT'S OWN-TOM
TOM THE PIPER'S SON-WHEN I LOOK AT YOU-PAGING MR.GR
EENBACK-WHERE THERE'S MUSIC-JOINT IS REALLY JUMPIN'
DOWN AT CARNEGIE HALL-D'YA LOVE ME-MACK THE BLACK-
LOVE OF MY LIFE-VOODOO-YOU CAN'T GET A MAN WITH A
GUN-THERE'S NO BUSINESS LIKE SHOW BUSINESS-THEY SAY
IT'S WONDERFUL-THE GIRL THAT I MARRY-I'VE GOT THE
SUN IN THE MORNING-LET'S GO WEST AGAIN-ANYTHING YOU
CAN DO-THERE'S NO BUSINESS LIKE SHOW BUSINESS

157.GARRETT Lesley - A Soprano In Love
SILVA SCREEN (Koch): SILKTVCD 4 (CD)   *1998*
CARMEN JONES *(HAMMERSTEIN)* NEW MOON *(ROMBERG)* LOVE
ME TONIGHT *(RODGERS)* KISSING BANDIT *(BROWN)* KISS ME
KATE *(PORTER)* CHANCE D'AUVERGNE *(CANTELOUBE)* DIE
FLEDERMAUS *(STRAUSS)* MIKADO *(SULLIVAN)* GUIDITTA
(LEHAR) LUSTIGE WITWE *(LEHAR)* ONLY GIRL *(HERBERT)*
ENCHANTRESS ENCHATRESS *(HERBERT)* KISMET *(FORREST)*
STREET SCENE *(WEILL)* BITTER SWEET *COWARD)* WUTHERING
HEIGHTS *(TAYLOR)* TINKER TAILOR *(BURGON)* INNOCENT
SLEEP *(AYRES)* PHANTOM OF THE OPERA *(LLOYD WEBBER)*
CATS *(LLOYD WEBBER)* REQUIEM *(LLOYD WEBBER)* SIMPLE
GIFTS *(TRAD.)*

158.GARRETT Lesley - A Soprano Inspired
Conifer Class (BMG): 75605 51329-2 (CD) -4(MC) 1997
1.ALLELUIA (Exsultate Jubilate)*(MOZART)* 2.AVE MARIA
*(CACCINI)*3.THE LORD'S PRAYER *(MALOTTE)*4.LAUDAMUS TE
(Mass In C.Min) *MOZART* 5.BLESS THIS HOUSE *(BRAHE)* 6
LA VERGINE DEGLI ANGELI(La Forza Del Destino)*VERDI*
7.NULLA IN MUNDO PAX SINCERA (1st m/m) *(VIVALDI)* 8.
ZUEIGNUNG *R.STRAUSS)* 9.I KNOW THAT MY REDEEMER LIVE
TH (Messiah) *(HANDEL)* 10.AVE MARIA *(SCHUBERT)* 11.BY
AND BY (A Child Of Our Time)*(TIPPETT)* 12.CLIMB EVERY
MOUNTAIN (Sound Of Music) *(RODGERS-HAMMERSTEIN)* 13.
PANIS ANGELICUS *(FRANCK)* 14.THE HOLY CITY *(ADAMS)* 15
PIE JESU (Requiem)*(FAURE)* 16.PRAYER(Hansel & Gretel)
(HUMPERDINCK) 17.BECAUSE *(D'HARDELOT)* 18.EASTER HYMN
(Cavalleria Rusicana) *(MASCAGNI)*

159.GARRETT Lesley - DIVA! - A Soprano At The Movies
SILVA SCREEN (Koch): SONG(CD)(C)903 (CD/MC)   *1991*
La Boheme (MOONSTRUCK)-Gianni Schicchi (A ROOM WITH
A VIEW)-Rusalka(DRIVING MISS DAISY)-The Marriage Of
Figaro (THE MODERNS)-Carmen (CARMEN JONES)-La Wally
(DIVA)-Lakme Flower Duet (THE HUNGER) *PHILHARMONIA*
ORCHESTA (Andrew Greenwood) LESLEY GARRETT Soprano

160.GARRETT Lesley - Soprano In Hollywood / BBC Concert
Orch conducted/orchestrated by PAUL BATEMAN   *1996*
SILVA SCREEN (Koch): SILKTVCD 2 (CD) SILKTVC 2 (MC)
1.WITH A SONG IN MY HEART 2.WHEN YOU'RE AWAY

3.LOVER   4.DANNY BOY   5.LOVE IS WHERE YOU FIND IT
6.ONE NIGHT OF LOVE   7.*GERSHWIN IN HOLLYWOOD Medley*
LOVE WALKED IN/THE MAN I LOVE/LOVE IS HERE TO STAY
8.BEYOND THE BLUE HORIZON 9.SMOKE GETS IN YOUR EYES
10.YESTERDAYS 11.JEALOUSY   12.LONG AGO AND FAR AWAY
13.ONE KISS   14.SO IN LOVE   15.SAILIN' THROUGH

161.<u>GARRETT Lesley</u> - **Soprano In Red** / Royal Phil.Orches
SILVA CLASS (Koch): SILKTVCD (SILKTVMC) 1   *1995*
WALTZ OF MY HEART / IF LOVE WERE ALL *(BITTER SWEET)*
VILJA *(MERRY WIDOW)* /SOFTLY AS IN A MORNING SUNRISE
WHY DID YOU KISS MY HEART AWAKE/WE'LL GATHER LILACS
(PERCHANCE TO DREAM) ROMANCE /LOVER COME BACK TO ME
NUN'S CHORUS / LAURA'S SONG / FINAL ARIA / CAN-CAN

162.<u>GERSHWIN George</u> **By George! Ultimate Birthday Tribute**
CARLTON CLASSICS (Technicol): 30368 01297 (2CD) 1998
CD1: 1.RHAPSODY IN BLUE (Original Jazz Band Ver) RPO
2.PIANO CONCERTO IN F RPO *with* Janis Vakarelis (pno)
3.CUBAN OVERTURE Budapest S.O. + Alicia Zizzo (pno)
4.AN AMERICAN IN PARIS RPO *with* Janis Vakarelis (pn)
5.S'WONDERFUL/THAT CERTAIN FEELING RPO 6.MAN I LOVE
RPO 7.FASCINATING RHYTHM RPO 8.LIZA RPO 9.I GOT
RHYTHM RPO *CD2:* 1.RHAPSODY IN BLUE Peter Donohue and
Martin Roscoe (pno) 2.SUMMERTIME Ruthie Henshall (v)
3.JAZZBO BROWN BLUES Richard Rodney Bennett (pno) 4.
PRELUDE NO.1 IN B.FLAT Alicia Zizzo (pno) 5.PRELUDE
NO.2 IN C.SHARP MINOR Alicia Zizzo (pno) 6.PRELUDE
NO.3 IN G.FLAT MINOR Alicia Zizzo (pno) 7.SWANNEE
Andrew Litton (pno) 8.NOBODY BUT YOU Andrew Litton
(pno) 9.PLEASE DO IT AGAIN Andrew Litton (pno) 10.
CLAP YO'HANDS Andrew Litton (Pno) 11.LULLABY Alicia
Zizzo (pno) 12.OH LADY BE GOOD Ruthie Henshall (v)
13.MELODY NO.32 IRISH WALTZ Alicia Zizzo (pno) 14.
SOMEONE TO WATCH OVER ME Ruthie Henshall (voc) 15.
PORGY AND BESS FANTASY Peter Donohoe-Martin Roscoe

163.<u>GERSHWIN George</u>

164.<u>GERSHWIN George</u> - **100th Birthday Celebration**
San Francisco Symphony / Michael Tilson Thomas pno
Audra McDonald (sop) Brian Stokes Mitchell (barit)
RCA VICTOR (BMG): 09026 68931-2 (2CD)   *1998*
CD1 CATFISH ROW / PORGY AND BESS: FUGUE-HURRICANE-
GOOD MORNIN' SISTUH-SUMMERTIME-BESS YOU IS MY WOMAN
NOW-MY MAN'S GONE NOW-THERE'S A BOAT DAT'S LEAVIN'
CD2 CONCERTO in F for Orchestra and Piano.

165.<u>GIBSON Mel</u> - **Music From The Films Of** / *featuring the*
City Of Prague Philharmonic Orch (Nic Raine-Paul
Bateman, conducting) MARK AYRES (additional synths)
SILVA SCREEN (Koch): FILMCD 195 (CD)   *1998*
GALLIPOLI-THE YEAR OF LIVING DANGEROUSLY-FOREVER
YOUNG-MAVERICK-HAMLET-MAN WITHOUT A FACE-THE RIVER-
RANSOM-THE BOUNTY-LETHAL WEAPON-CONSPIRACY BY
THEORY-BRAVEHEART-MAD MAX 1-MAD MAX 2 (premier rec)

--- <u>GODZILLA VS KING KONG</u> *see* Monster Movie Music Album

166.<u>GOLDSMITH Jerry</u> - FRONTIERS Royal Scottish Nat.Orch
VARESE (Pinn): VSD 5871 (CD)   *1997*

STAR TREK: THE MOTION PICTURE-ALIEN-LOGAN'S RUN-
TOTAL RECALL-TWILIGHT ZONE: THE MOVIE-STAR TREK:
VOYAGER-STAR TREK: FIRST CONTACT-CAPRICORN ONE-
DAMNATION ALLEY-THE ILLUSTRATED MAN

167. **GOLDSMITH Jerry** The OMEN (Essential Jerry Goldsmith
Film Music Collection) City Of Prague Philharmonic
Orchestra (Paul Bateman, Nic Raine conductors)
SILVA SCREEN (Koch): FILMXCD 199 (2CD) *1998*
FIRST BLOOD-RAMBO 2-THE FIRST GREAT TRAIN ROBBERY-
SHADOW-SWARM-THE RUSSIA HOUSE-MEDICINE MAN-
BASIC INSTINCT-MASADA-CAPRICORN ONE-UNDER FIRE-
BABY:SECRET OF A LOST LEGEND-THE BLUE MAX-BOYS FROM
BRAZIL-FIRST KNIGHT-TOTAL RECALL-POWDER-MacARTHUR-
PATTON-TWILIGHT ZONE-STAR TREK-STAR TREK: VOYAGER-
STAR TREK: FIRST CONTACT- THE OMEN

168. **GOODWIN Ron** British Light Music - New Zealand Symph
MARCO POLO (Select): 8.223518 (CD) | Orchestra *1996*
633 SQUADRON Main Theme-DRAKE 400 Suite-PUPPET SERE
NADE-NEW ZEALAND SUITE Premier-ARABIAN CELEBRATION-
THE VENUS WALTZ-PRISONERS OF WAR MARCH: The Kriegle
MINUET IN BLUE-THE TRAP Main Theme (London Marathon
Theme)-LANCELOT & GUINEVERE Main Theme-GIRL WITH A
DREAM (all composed and conducted by Ron Goodwin)

169. **GOODWIN Ron** - Conducts Film and TV Themes
FLYBACK (Chandos): FBCD 2004 (CD) *1997*
LONDON MARATHON (Theme from 'The TRAP')-HERE WHERE
YOU ARE-*MEDLEY:* KOJAK/HILL STREET BLUES/STAR TREK/
DYNASTY/DALLAS-HERE'S THAT RAINY DAY- *TRIBUTE TO
MIKLOS ROZSA:* BEN HUR main theme/PARADE OF THE CHAR
IOTEERS/LOVE THEME/THE RED HOUSE/THE FOUR FEATHERS
TROLLEY SONG- *DISNEYTIME SELECT:* ZIP A DEE DOO DAH/
SOMEDAY MY PRINCE WILL COME/I WANNA BE LIKE YOU/
LITTLE APRIL SHOWERS/WHEN YOU WISH UPON A STAR-
CARAVAN-GIRL FROM CORSICA- *STEPHEN FOSTER SUITE:*
OH SUSANNAH/SWANEE RIVER/BEAUTIFUL DREAMER/CAMPTOWN
RACES-BEAUTY AND THE BEAST-FESTIVAL TIME-CANDLESHOE
FORCE TEN FROM NAVARONE-MINUET IN BLUE-SPACEMAN AND
KING ARTHUR-GIRL WITH THE MISTY EYES-AMAZING GRACE
see also 'BRITISH LIGHT MUSIC'

170. **GOODWIN Ron** Legend Of The Glass Mountain/Adventure
EMI Studio 2 (EMI): 495 621-2 (CD) (reissues on CD)
Legend Of The Glass Mountain: 1.LEGEND OF THE GLASS
MOUNTAIN *(from GLASS MOUNAIN)* 2.THE DREAM OF OLWEN
(WHILE I LIVE) 3.INTERMEZZO *(ESCAPE TO HAPPINESS)*
4.THE WAY TO THE STARS 5.WARSAW CONCERTO *(DANGEROUS
MOONLIGHT)* 6.TO BE LOVED 7.SPITFIRE PRELUDE & FUGUE
(FIRST OF THE FEW) 8.THEME FROM LIMELIGHT 9.THEME
FROM GONE WITH THE WIND 10.RHAPSODY ON A THEME BY
PAGANINI *(STORY OF THREE LOVES)* 11.THEME FROM THE
MOULIN ROUGE 12.CORNISH RHAPSODY *(LOVE STORY)*
Adventure: 1.633 QUADRON 2.ELIZABETHAN SERENADE 3.
SONG OF THE HIGH SEAS *(VICTORY AT SEA)* 4.UNDER THE
LINDEN TREE 5.THE TRAP *(also LONDON MARATHON THEME)*
6.GIRL WITH A DREAM 7.THOSE MAGNIFICENT MEN IN

THEIR FLYING MACHINES 8.GIRL FROM CORSICA 9.THE
HEADLESS HORSEMAN 10.THEME FROM OF HUMAN BONDAGE
11.MISS MARPLE'S THEME 12.OPERATION CROSSBOW
--- **GRAINER Ron** - *see* **A-Z OF BRITISH TV THEMES** (Coll 8)
171.**GRAY Barry** - **No Strings Attached**   *1981*
   CINEPHILE (Pinn): CINCD 011 (CD) reissued 1999
   The original themes from the ATV 1960's TV series
   THUNDERBIRDS-CAPTAIN SCARLETT-STINGRAY-AQUA MARINA
   WELL DONE PARKER-JOE 90-MYSTERONS Theme / *see also*
   (TV Section) THUNDERBIRDS-STINGRAY-CAPTAIN SCARLETT
172.**GREAT BRITISH EXPERIENCE The** - Various Artists
   HMV CLASSICS: HMV 573 550-2 (2CDs)   re-issued 1999
   EMI CLASSICS: CDGB 50 (2CD) TCGB 50 (2MC)   1997
   1.DEVIL'S GALLOP *(DICK BARTON)* Charles Williams
   2.CALLING ALL WORKERS *(MUSIC WHILE YOU WORK)* Eric
   Coates 3.WESTMINSTER WALTZ Robert Farnon 4.PUFFIN'
   BILLY *(CHILDREN'S FAV.)* Edward White 5.HORSE GUARDS
   WHITEHALL *DOWN YOUR WAY* Haydn Wood 6.IN PARTY MOOD
   (HOUSEWIVES CHOICE) Jack Strachey 7.BY THE SLEEPY
   LAGOON *(DESERT ISLAND DISCS)* Eric Coates 8.GIRLS IN
   GREY *(BBC TV NEWSREEL)* Charles Williams 9.SILKS AND
   SATINS *(EMERGENCY WARD 10 Closing mus)* Peter Yorke
   10.MARCH FROM A LITTLE SUITE *(DR.FINLAY'S CASEBOOK)*
   Trevor Duncan 11.BARWICK GREEN *(THE ARCHERS)* Arthur
   Wood 12.THE RUNAWAY ROCKING HORSE Edward White 13.
   GIRL FROM CORSICA Trevor Duncan 14.NON STOP *(ITN
   NEWS 60's-70's)* John Malcolm 15.SKYSCARAPER FANTASY
   Donald Phillips 16.HEADLESS HORSEMAN Ron Goodwin 17
   ON A SPRING NOTE Sidney Torch 18.SEA SONGS *(BILLY
   BUNTER OF GREYFRIARS SCHOOL)* Vaughan Williams 19.
   CHANGING MOODS *(PC 49 THEME 'ADVENTURES OF PC 49)*
   Ronald Hanmer20.A CANADIAN IN MAYFAIR Angela Morley
   21.DANCER AT THE FAIR John Fortis 22.LAS VEGAS
   ANIMAL MAGIC Laurie Johnson 23.STARLIGHT ROOF WALTZ
   George Melachrino 24.EVENSONG Easthope Martin 25.
   KNIGHTSBRIDGE MARCH *(IN TOWN TONIGHT)* Eric Coates
   CD2: MARCHING STRINGS *(TOP OF TGHE FORM)* Ray Martin
   2.CORONATION SCOTT *(PAUL TEMPLE)* Vivian Ellis 3.
   JUMPING BEAN *SEND FOR SHINER* Robert Farnon 4.SOUND
   AND VISION *(ATV OPENING MARCH)* Eric Coates 5.YOUNG
   BALLERINA *(TV INTERLUDE:THE POTTER'S WHEEL)* Charles
   Williams 6.PARISIAN MODE *(WHAT'S MY LINE)* Wolfe
   Phillips 7.HORSE FEATHERS *(MEET THE HUGGETS)* Philip
   Green 8.PORTRAIT OF A FLIRT *(IN TOWN TONIGHT. LINK)*
   Robert Farnon 9.CAVALCADE OF YOUTH *(THE BARLOWS OF
   BEDDINGTON)* Jack Beaver 10.RUNNING OFF THE RAIL
   Clive Richardson 11.SAILING BY *(RADIO 4 LATE NIGHT
   SHIPPING FORECAST)* Ronald Binge 12.WINTER SUNSHINE
   George Melachrino 13.PARAKEETS AND PEACOCKS Jack
   Coles 14.MELODY ON THE MOVE Clive Richardson 15.
   HIGH HEELS Trevor Duncan 16.THE HAUNTED BALLROOM
   Geoffrey Toye 17.ALL STRINGS AND FANCY FREE Sidney
   Torch 18.SAPPHIRES AND SABLES Peter Yorke 19.DANCE
   OF AN OSTRACISED IMP Frederic Curzon 20.SMILE OF A

LATIN Trevor Duncan 21.BEACHCOMBER Clive Richardson
22.DREAMING Archibald Joyce 23.CONCERT JIG Ernest
Tomlinson 24.A QUIET STROLL *(TV FARMING)* Charles
Williams 25.MARCH FROM LITTLE SUITE Malcolm Arnold

173. **GREAT BRITISH FILM MUSIC ALBUM** - **Various Artists**
SILVA SCREEN (Koch): FILMXCD 309 (2CD)   *1999*
40 Tracks incl: FRENZY-OLIVER TWIST-HENRY V-HAMLET-
BATTLE OF THE BULGE-FAR FROM THE MADDING CROWD-THE
SOUND BARRIER-SINK THE BISMARCK-THE LADY VANISHES-
EMMA-THE DUELLISTS-CURSE OF THE WEREWOLF-DAMBUSTERS
STAGE FRIGHT-THE HAUNTING-COASTAL COMMAND-UNDER
CAPRICORN-A NIGHT TO REMEMBER-THE CRIMSON PIRATE-
plus the complete score for THE RED SHOES

174. **GREAT FILM SONGS** **(You Must Remember This)** Var.Arts
HAPPY DAYS-Conifer (BMG): 75605 52283-2 (CD) -4(MC)
1.AM I BLUE *(ON WITH THE SHOW-1929)* Ethel Waters
2.FALLING IN LOVE AGAIN *(BLUE ANGEL-1930)* Marlene
Dietrich 3.A BENCH IN THE PARK *(KING OF JAZZ-1930)*
Paul Whiteman Orchestra 4.GOODNIGHT VIENNA *(1932)*
Jack Buchanan 5.MEDLEY: TINKLE TINKLE TINKLE/OVER
MY SHOULDER *(EVERGREEN-1934)* Jessie Matthews 6.ONE
NIGHT OF LOVE *(1934)* Grace Moore 7.OKAY TOOTS *(KID
MILLIONS-1934)* Eddie Cantor 8.SMOKE GETS IN YOUR
EYES *(ROBERTA-1935)* Irene Dunne 9.LULLABY OF BROAD
WAY *(GOLD DIGGERS OF 1935)* Winifred Shaw 10.LOVE IS
EVERYWHERE *(LOOK UP AND LAUGH-1935)* Gracie & Tommy
Fields 11.TOP HAT WHITE TIE & TAILS *(TOP HAT-1935)*
Fred Astaire 12.ISN'T THIS A LOVELY DAY *(TOP HAT-
1935)* Ginger Rogers 13.I'VE GOT A FEELIN' YOU'RE
FOOLIN' *(BROADWAY MELODY OF 1946)* Eleanor Powell
14.WHEN DID YOU LEAVE HEAVEN *SING BABY SING-1936)*
Tony Martin 15.THIS YEAR'S KISSES *(ON THE AVENUE-19
37)* Alice Faye 16.I'VE GOT MY LOVE TO KEEP ME WARM
(ON THE AVENUE-1937) Dick Powell 17.WILL YOU REMEMB
ER *(MAYTIME 1937)* Jeanette McDonald and Nelson Eddy
18.JEEPERS CREEPERS *(GOING PLACES-1938)* Louis Armst
rong) 19.I GO FOR THAT*(ST.LOUIS BLUES-1938)* Dorothy
Lamour 20.IT'S FOOLISH BUT IT'S FUN *(SPRING PARADE-
1940)* Deanna Durbin 21.CHATTANOOGA CHOO CHOO *(SUN
VALLEY SEREANDE-1941)* Glenn Miller & His Orchestra
22.I YI YI YI YI (LIKE YOU VERY MUCH)*(THAT NIGHT IN
RIO-1941)* Carmen Miranda 23.MOONLIGHT BECOMES YOU
(ROAD TO MOROCCO-1942) Bing Crosby 24.TROLLEY SONG
(MEET ME IN ST.LOUIS-1944) Judy Garland 25.THE MORE
I SEE YOU *(DIAMOND HORSEHOE-1945)* Dick Haymes 26.
OUT OF NOWHERE*(YOU CAME ALONG-1945)* Helen Forrest

--- **GREAT MGM WESTERN MOVIE THEMES** *see* BEST OF THE WEST

175. **GREAT MOVIE SCORES FROM FILMS OF STEVEN SPIELBERG**
ERICH KUNZEL & THE CINCINNATI POPS
TELARC (BMG): CD 80495   *1999*
SUGARLAND EXPRESS-JAWS-CLOSE ENCOUNTERS OF THE
THIRD KIND-1941-RAIDERS OF THE LOST ARK-POLTERGEIST
E.T.-TWILIGHT ZONE THE MOVIE-INDIANA JONES AND THE

TEMPLE OF DOOM-COLOR PURPLE-EMPIRE OF THE SUN-
INDIANA JONES AND THE LAST CRUSADE-ALWAYS-HOOK-
JURASSIC PARK-SCHINDLER'S LIST-THE LOST WORLD-
AMISTAD-SAVING PRIVATE RYAN

176.GREAT SPORTING EXPERIENCE - Various Artists
EMI Classics: CDGOAL 1 (CD) TCGOAL 12 (MC)   1998
30 GREAT RADIO & TV SPORTS THEMES FROM 40'S-1990'S
1.GRANDSTAND current theme *(composer: K.MANSFIELD)*
2.GRANDSTAND orig theme 'News Scoop' *(L.STEVENS)* 3.
LONDON MARATHON 'The Trap' *(R.GOODWIN)* 4.SKI SUNDAY
'Pop Looks Bach' *(S.FONTEYN)* 5.TEST CRICKET 'Soul
Limbo' *(BOOKER T.& MG's)* 6.SNOOKER 'Drag Racer' *(D.
WOOD)* 7.MATCH OF THE DAY 'Offside' *(B.STOLLER)* 8.
MATCH OF THE DAY (orig)'Drum Majorette'*(A.STECK)* 9.
SPORTSNIGHT *(T.HATCH)* 10.ALLSPORTS MARCH *(R.FARNON)*
11.WIMBLEDON (opening theme) 'Light and Tuneful'
(K.MANSFIELD) 12.WIMBLEDON (closing mus.) 'Sporting
Occasion'*(A.STECK)* 13.RUGBY SPECIAL 'Holy Mackerel'
(B.BENNETT) 14.DARTS 'Cranes' *(D.WOOD)* 15.DERBY DAY
(R.FARNON) 16.BBC SPORTS PERSONALITY OF THE YEAR
'The Challenge' *(C.WILLIAMS)* 17.WORLD SERIES (1)
(R.FARNON) 18.SPORTSVIEW 'Saturday Sports'*(W.BURNS)*
19.CROWN GREEN BOWLS 'Soul Riff' *(Douglas WOOD)* 20.
INTERNATIONAL SPORTS MARCH *(S.TORCH)* 21.WORLD OF
SPORT 'World Of Sport March'*(D.HARPER)* 22.ATHLETICS
'World Series'(2) *(K.MANSFIELD)* 23.GRANDSTAND radio
(R.FARNON) 24.SPORTS REPORT 'Out Of The Blue' *(H.
BATH)* 25.GOODWOOD GALOP *(R.FARNON)* 26.SPORTSMASTER
(R.BUSBY) 27.SUPERSTARS 'Heavy Action' *(J.PEARSON)*
28.THE BIG MATCH *(K.MANSFIELD)* 29.TOUR DE FRANCE
(radio) *(E.WHITE)* 30.FOOTBALL FANFARE *(R.BURNETT)*

177.GREATEST SONGS FROM THE MOVIES 4 Movie Classic Hits
songs from Titanic / The Bodyguard / The Full Monty
/ My Best Friends Wedding - Various Artists
EXCEED-HALLMARK (CHE): 54004-2 (4CDs)   1999
CD1: TITANIC (15 Songs) CD2: FULL MONTY (13) CD3:
BODYGUARD (12) CD4: MY BEST FRIEND'S WEDDING (12)

178.GREATEST WESTERN MOVIE & TV SOUNDTRACKS VOL.2 V.Art
BEAR FAMILY (Rollercoaster): BCD 15983 (2CD)   1997
BALLAD OF CAT BALLOU Nat King Cole and Stubby Kaye
HIGH CHAPPARAL David Rose Orch THE MAN FROM LARAMIE
Al Martino LONELY MANTennessee Ernie Ford EL DORADO
George Alexander & Mellowmen THE MAN WITH TRUE GRIT
Glen Campbell FURY Prairie Chief WICHITA Tex Ritter
OLD TURKEY BUZZARD Jose Feliciano BRONCO J.Gregory
LOVE IN THE COUNTRY Limelighters SUGARFOOT Sons Of
The Pioneers STAGECOACH TO CHEYENNE Wayne Newton
GREEN LEAVES OF SUMMER Brothers Four MARMALADE MOLA
SSES & HONEY Andy Williams CIMARRON CITY Hollywood
S.O. SHERIFF OF COCHISE Prairie Chiefs WAGON TRAIN
Johnny O'Neill LEGEND OF WYATT EARP Shorty Long 26
MEN Lee Adrian WIND THE WIND Dean Martin BUTTONS
AND BOWS Bob Hope MAN WITH TRUE GRIT Glen Campbell

--- **GREENAWAY Peter** - *see* **NYMAN Michael**

179.HAMMER COMEDY FILM MUSIC COLLECTION - Var.Artists
GDI (ABM): GDICD 004 (CD)   *1999*
Themes and music cues from the Hammer Film comedies
ON THE BUSES-MUTINY ON THE BUSES-HOLIDAY ON THE
BUSES-LOVE THY NEIGHBOUR-UP THE CREEK-MAN ABOUT THE
HOUSE-GEORGE AND MILDRED-FURTHER UP THE CREEK-
NEAREST AND DEAREST-RISING DAMP-I ONLY ARSKED!-
THAT'S YOUR FUNERAL

180.HAMMER FILM MUSIC COLLECTION VOLUME 1 - Var.Artists
GDI (ABM): GDICD 002 (CD)   *1998*
1.THE DEVIL RIDES OUT *(comp: JAMES BERNARD)* 2.TWINS
OF EVIL *(HARRY ROBINSON)* 3.THE MUMMY *(FRANZ REIZENS
TEIN)* 4.CAPTAIN KRONOS VAMPIRE HUNTER *(LAURIE JOHNS
ON)* 5.DRACULA *(J.BERNARD)* 6.MOON ZERO TWO *DON ELLIS*
7.FRANKENSTEIN MUST BE DESTROYED *(JAMES BERNARD)* 8.
WHEN DINOSAURS RULED THE EARTH *(MARIO NASCIMBENE)*
9.KISS OF THE VAMPIRE *(J.BERNARD)* 10.GORGON *(J.BERN
ARD)*11.SCARS OF DRACULA *(J.BERNARD)* 12.HANDS OF THE
RIPPER*(CHRISTOPHER GUNNING)* 13.CURSE OF THE MUMMY'S
TOMB *(CARLO MARTELLI)* 14.VAMPIRE LOVERS *H.ROBINSON*
15.CREATURES THR WORLD FORGOT *(M.NASCIMBENE)* 16.THE
CURSE OF FRANKENSTEIN *(J.BERNARD)* 17.DOCTOR JEKYLL
AND SISTER HYDE *(DAVID WHITAKER)* 18.LUST FOR A VAMP
IRE *(H.ROBINSON)* 19.QUATERMASS AND THE PIT *TRISTRAM
CARY)* 20.COUNTESS DRACULA*(H.ROBINSON)* 21.SHE *(JAMES
BERNARD)* 22.BRIDES OF DRACULA *(MALCOLM WILLIAMSON)*
23.BLOOD FROM THE MUMMY'S TOMB *(TRISTRAM CARY)* 24.
LEGEND OF THE 7 GOLDEN VAMPIRES *(JAMES BERNARD)* 25.
TASTE THE BLOOD OF DRACULA *(JAMES BERNARD)*

181.HAMMER FILM MUSIC COLLECTION VOLUME 2 - Var.Artists
GDI (ABM): GDICD 005 (CD)   *1999*
1.PLAGUE OF THE ZOMBIES *(JAMES BERNARD)* 2.TO THE
DEVIL A DAUGHTER *(PAUL GLASS)* 3.DRACULA HAS RISEN
FROM THE GRAVE *(JAMES BERNARD)* 4.QUATERMASS II
(JAMES BERNARD) 5.ABOMINABLE SNOWMAN *(HUMPHREY
SEARLE)* 6.SATANIC RITES OF DRACULA *(JOHN CACAVAS)*
7.WITCHES *(RICHARD RODNEY BENNETT)* 8.FEAR IN THE
NIGHT *(JOHN McCABE)* 9.THE PIRATES OF BLOOD RIVER
(J.HOLLINGSWORTH) 10.DRACULA AD.1972 *(MIKE VICKERS)*
11.PHANTOM OF THE OPERA *(EDWIN ASTLEY)* 12.RASPUTIN
THE MAD MONK *(DON BANKS)* 13.FRANKENSTEIN AND THE
MONSTER FROM HELL *(JAMES BERNARD)* 14.MUMMY'S SHROUD
(DON BANKS) 15.LOST CONTINENT *(GERARD SCHURMANN)* 16
VENGEANCE OF SHE *(MARIO NASCIMBENE)* 17.HOUND OF THE
BASKERVILLES *(JAMES BERNARD)* 18.VAMPIRE CIRCUS
(DAVID WHITAKER) 19.DEMONS OF THE MIND *(HARRY
ROBINSON)* 20.EVIL OF FRANKENSTEIN *(DON BANKS)* 21.
FRANKENSTEIN CREATED WOMAN *(JAMES BERNARD)* 22.CURSE
OF THE WEREWOLF *(BENJAMIN FRANKEL)* 23.SLAVE GIRLS
(CARLO MARTELLI) 24.CRESCENDO *(MALCOLM WILLIAMSON)*
25.ONE MILLION YEARS BC *(MARIO NASCIMBENE)*

--- **HANNA-BARBERA** - *see* **TUNES FROM THE TOONS**
182.HARLE John - **SILENCIUM: SONGS OF THE SPIRIT**
ARGO-DECCA (UNIV): 458 356-2 (CD)   *1997*

1.MORNING PRAYER 2.SPIRITU *(BABY IT'S YOU,C4)* 3.AIR
AND ANGELS 4.FAMILY OF LOVE 5.LACRIMOSAM *(BUTTERFLY
KISS)* 6.ASTREA *(NISSAN AD)* 7.SCHOOL OF MYSTERIES
(DEFENCE OF THE REALM,BBC1) 8.LIGHT *(HMS BRILLIANT,
BBC1)* 9.HYMN TO THE SUN 10.VICES & VIRTUES 11.NIGHT
FLIGHT 12.SILENCIUM *(SILENT WITNESS theme, BBC1)*
John Harle composer/solo saxoph. Silencium Ensemble
Catherine Bott-Sarah Leonard-Nicole Tibbels (sop's)
Alexander Balanescu (viola) Paul Clarvis (perc) and
Choristers Worcester Cathedral,Academy of St.Martin
in The Fields, Children from New Brighton PS.Wirral
183.<u>HATCH Tony</u> - Hatchback
SEQUEL-CASTLE (Pinn): NEMCD 951   *1997*
1.YOU'RE THE ONE 2.ROUND EVERY CORNER 3.BEAUTIFUL
IN THE RAIN 4.LATIN VELVET 5.MUSIC 6.CROSSTOWN COMM
UTER 7.I KNOW A PLACE 8.LOOK FOR A STAR 9.HERBIN'
10.SUGAR AND SPICE 11.LOVE HUSTLE 12.WHO-DUN-IT 13.
EL PAYASO (SPANISH CLOWN) 14.WHERE ARE YOU NOW 15.
BRASILIA MISSION 16.RETURN TO THE STARS 17.SOLE
BOSS NOVA 18.BAHAMA SOUND 19.BRAZILIA 20.FINITO
184.<u>HATCH Tony</u> - The Best of Tony Hatch
SEQUEL-CASTLE (Pinn): NEMCD 920 (CD)   *1996*
1.NAKED CITY THEME *(May)* 2.JOANNA *(Hatch-Trent)* 3.
DICK POWELL THEATRE THEME *(Gilbert)* 4.SOUL COAXING
Polnareff) 5.MONDO KANE THEME (MORE) *(Ortolani-Oliv
iero-Newell)* 6.MUSIC TO WATCH GIRLS BY *Velona-Ramin*
7.CROSSROADS THEME *(Hatch)* 8.DOWNTOWN *(Hatch)* 9.MAN
ALIVE THEME *(Hatch)* 10.THE DOCTORS THEME *(Hatch)* 11
SPORTSNIGHT THEME *(Hatch)*12.SOUNDS OF THE SEVENTIES
(Hatch) 13.MEMORIES OF SUMMER (LOVE STORY THEME-TV)
(Hatch) 14.AN OCCASIONAL MAN *(Martin-Blane)* 15.THE
CHAMPIONS THEME *(Hatch)* 16.CALL ME *(Hatch)* 17.EMMER
DALE THEME *(Hatch)* 18.BIRDS *(Hatch)* 19.HADLEIGH *(Ha
tch)* 20.MAORI *(Hatch)* 21.MR.& MRS. (BE NICE TO EACH
OTHER) *(Hatch-Trent)* Jackie Trent 22.WHILE THE CITY
SLEEPS *(Hatch-Trent)* 23.WILLOW WALTZ (TIM FRAZER'S
THEME) *(Watters)* 24.BEST IN FOOTBALL *(Hatch)* 25.
DEVIL'S HERD *Anthony (Hatch)* 26.THE SURREY WITH THE
FRINGE ON THE TOP*(Rodgers-Hammerstein)* 27.LA PALOMA
Yradier(Hatch) 28.THE WORLD AT WAR *(Davis)* 29.A MAN
AND A WOMAN*(Lai-Barouh)* 30.OUT OF THIS WORLD*(Siday)*
185.<u>HAWKSHAW Alan</u> 27 TOP TV THEMES AND COMMERCIALS plus
            <u>FAHEY Brian</u> TIME FOR TV   DELETED
EMI: 498 171-2 (2CD) (orig 1970's albums)   *1999*
186.<u>HELLO CHILDREN EVERYWHERE: TOP BBC CHILDREN'S TUNES</u>
BBC Worldwide (Koch UK): 33636-2 (CD) -4 (MC) 1997
1.POSTMAN PAT Ken Barrie 2.BLUE PETER *BARNACLE BILL
orig theme* Sydney Torch Orch 3.BERTHA Ken Barrie 4.
4.FIREMAN SAM Maldwyn Pope 5.HEADS AND TAILS Derek
Griffith 6.CHIGLEY Freddie Phillips & Brian Cant 7.
HENRY'S CAT Peter Shade 8.JIM'LL FIX ITDavid Mindel
9.MOP & SMIFF *TWO OF A KIND* Mike Amatt 10.PLAY AWAY
Lionel Morton 11.RAGTIME Fred Harris-Maggie Henders
on 12.TRUMPTON Freddie Phillips 13.RUBOVIA Freddie

187.<u>**HEROES OF THE AIR**</u> - Central Band Of Royal Air Force
CFP (EMI): CDCFP 4666 (CD) TCCFP 4666 (MC)   1992
BATTLE OF BRITAIN SUITE (William Walton)-SPITFIRE
PRELUDE AND FUGUE (William Walton)-CONQUEST OF THE
AIR (Arthur Bliss)-BATTLE OF BRITAIN SUITE (Wilfred
Josephs)-COASTAL COMMAND (Vaughan Williams) *reis 95*

188.<u>**HERRMANN Bernard**</u> - **CITIZEN KANE: The Essential
     Bernard Herrmann Film Collection - Various Artists**
SILVA SCREEN (Koch): FILMXCD 308 (2CD)   1999
SYMPHONIC THEMES AND SUITES FROM:- CAPE FEAR-PSYCHO
NAKED AND THE DEAD-THE TROUBLE WITH HARRY-JASON AND
T.ARGONAUTS-TWILIGHT ZONE-SEVENTH VOYAGE OF SINBAD-
CITIZEN KANE-DAY THE EARTH STOOD STILL-GHOST AND
MRS.MUIR-OBSESSION-SNOWS OF KILIMANJARO-VERTIGO-
THE MAN WHO KNEW TOO MUCH-THREE WORLDS OF GULLIVER-
NORTH BY NORTHWEST-ON DANGEROUS GROUND-TAXI DRIVER-
MYSTERIOUS ISLAND + rejected score for TORN CURTAIN

189.<u>**HERRMANN Bernard**</u> - **CITIZEN KANE:** The Classic Film
                         Scores Of Bernard Herrmann
RCA Victor (BMG): GD 80707 (CD)   Re-issued 1991
ON DANGEROUS GROUND:The Death Hunt CITIZEN KANE:Pre
lude-Xanadu-Snow Picture-Themes and Variations-Aria
from Salammbo (with Kiri Te Kanawa)-Rosebud-Finale
BENEATH THE 12-MILE REEF:The Sea-Lagoon-Descending-
The Octopuss-Homecoming-HANGOVER SQUARE:Concerto Ma
cabre for Piano & Orchestra-WHITE WITCH DOCTOR:Talk
ing Drums-Prelude-The Riverboat-Petticoat Dance-The
Safari-Tarantula-The Lion-Nocturne-Abduction Of The
BakubaBoy-The Skulls-Lonni Bound By Ropes-Departure

190.<u>**HERRMANN Bernard**</u> - **FILM SCORES** - Los Angeles P.O.
SONY CLASSICS: SK 62700 (CD)   1996
1.THE MAN WHO KNEW TOO MUCH *PRELUDE* 2.PSYCHO *SUITE
SUITE FOR STRINGS* 3.MARNIE *SUITE* 4.NORTH BY NORTHWE
ST *OVERURE* 5.VERTIGO *SUITE* 6.TORN CURTAIN *MAINTHEME*
7.FAHRENHEIT 451 *SUITE* 8.TAXI DRIVER *MAIN THEME*

191.<u>**HERRMANN Bernard**</u> - **PARTNERSHIP IN TERROR: HITCHCOCK**
City Of Prague Philharmonic conduct: Paul Bateman
SILVA SCREEN (Koch): SILVAD 3010 (CD)   1996
digital recordings of themes & suites from ALFRED
HITCHCOCK films scored by BERNARD HERRMANN
PSYCHO / NORTH BY NORTHWEST / MARNIE / THE MAN WHO
KNEW TOO MUCH / THE TROUBLE WITH HARRY / VERTIGO
TORN CURTAIN (rejected score)

192.<u>**HERRMANN Bernard**</u> - **TORN CURTAIN:** Classic Film Music
SILVA SCREEN (Koch): FILMCD 162 (CD)   1995
CAPE FEAR-CITIZEN KANE-PSYCHO-GHOST AND MRS.MUIR-
OBSESSION-SNOWS OF KILIMANJARO-VERTIGO-TAXI DRIVER-
ON DANGEROUS GROUND *plus suite from fantasy films:-*
THREE WORLDS OF GULLIVER/THE 7TH VOYAGE OF SINBAD/
MYSTERIOUS ISLAND/JASON AND THE ARGONAUTS *+rejected
score* TORN CURTAIN *(replaced by JOHN ADDISON score)*

193.<u>**HESS Nigel**</u> - TV Themes with LONDON FILM ORCHESTRA
plus CHAMELEON and Royal Shakespeare Comp.Ensemble
CHANDOS (Chandos): CHAN 9750 (CD)   1999

1.HETTY WAINTHROP INVESTIGATES 2.BADGER 3.THE
ONE GAME "Saylon Dola" Chameleon 4.WYCLIFFE 5.WOMAN
OF SUBSTANCE 6.SUMMER'S LEASE "Carmina Valles"
Chameleon 7.DANGERFIELD 8.JUST WILLIAM 9.
EVERY WOMAN KNOWS A SECRET 10.PERFECT SCOUNDRELS
11.ANNA OF THE FIVE TOWNS 12.CAMPION 13.MAIGRET
(1992) 14.VIDAL IN VENICE 15.CLASSIC ADVENTURE 16.
ALL PASSION SPENT 17.CHIMERA "Rosheen Du" Chameleon
18.TESTAMENT 19.VANITY FAIR 20.AFFAIR IN MIND 21.
LONDON EMBASSY 22.ATLANTIS 23.A HUNDRED ACRES 24.
GROWING PAINS 25.US GIRLS 26.TITMUSS REGAINED 27.
AN IDEAL HUSBAND

----.**HILL SMITH Marilyn** - Sings IVOR NOVELLO - Chandos
Concert Orchestra conducted by Stuart Barry   *1993*
FLYBACK (Chandos): FBCD 2006 (CD) (reissued 1998)
SOMEDAY MY HEART WILL AWAKE *(KINGS RHAPSODY)*-PRIMRO
SE *(DANCING YEARS)*-LOVE IS MY REASON *(PERCHANCE TO
DREAM)*-DARK MUSIC *(ARC DE TRIOMPHE)*-THE LITTLE DAMO
ZEL-WHEN THE GYPSY PLAYED *(GLAMOROUS NIGHT)*-ON SUCH
A NIGHT AS THIS *(GAY'S THE WORD)*-FLY HOME LITTLE HE
ART *(KINGS RHAPSODY)*-KEEP THE HOME FIRES BURNING-
MUSIC IN MAY *(CARELESS RAPTURE)*-A VIOLIN BEGAN TO
PLAY *(KINGS RHAPSODY)*-SPRING OF THE YEAR-MY DEAREST
DEAR *(DANCING YEARS)*-FINDER PLEASE RETURN*(GAY'S THE
WORD)*-LOOK IN MY HEART *(VALLEY OF SONG)*-WHEN I CURT
SIED TO THE KING *(PERCHANCE TO DREAM)*-WE'LL GATHER
LILACS *PERCHANCE TO DREAM)*-FAIRY LAUGHTER-GLAMOROUS
NIGHT-WHY IS THERE EVER GOODBYE *(CARELESS RAPTURE)*

----.**HIT TV - Television's Top Themes** - Various Artists
VARESE (Pinn): VSD 5957 (CD)   *1999*
tracks include X-FILES, E.R., FRASIER, ALLY McBEAL,
SOUTH PARK, FRIENDS

194.**HITCHCOCK Alfred** - DIAL M FOR MURDER
Czech Symphony Orchestra conducted by Paul Bateman
SILVA SCREEN (Koch): FILMCD 137 (CD)   *1993*
New Digital Recordings Of Suites From A.H.Films
DIAL M FOR MURDER *(composed by DIMITRI TIOMKIN)*
UNDER CAPRICORN *(RICHARD ADDINSELL)* TOPAZ *(MAURICE
JARRE)* REBECCA and SUSPICION *(FRANZ WAXMAN)* SPELLB
OUND *(MIKLOS ROZSA)* VERTIGO-NORTH BY NORTHWEST-MAR
NIE-PSYCHO *(BERNARD HERRMANN)* FRENZY *(RON GOODWIN)*

195.**HITCHCOCK Alfred** - MASTER OF MAYHEM
San Diego Symphony Orch.conducted by Lalo Schifrin
SION (Direct): SION 18170 (CD)   *1997*
1.INVISIBLE THIRD:Overture 2.ALFRED HITCHCOCK THEME
3.VERTIGO:Suite 4.MARNIE:Suite 5.PSYCHO:Intro/The
Murder/City) 6.REBECCA:Suite 7.REAR WINDOW:Intro/
Rhumba/The Ballet/The Finale 8.ROLLERCOASTER:Theme
9.BULLITT 10.MANNIX:Theme 11.DIRTY HARRY:Suite 12.
MISSION IMPOSSIBLE: Plot/Theme * cond Lalo Schifrin

196.**HITCHCOCK Alfred** - MOVIE THRILLERS
London Philharmonic Orchestra cond.Bernard Herrmann
DECCA PHASE 4 (UNIV): 443 895-2 (CD)   reissued 1996
Suites from: PSYCHO / MARNIE / NORTH BY NORTHWEST

VERTIGO / 'A Portrait Of Hitch' : NIGHTMARE / THE
TROUBLE WITH HARRY * conducted by Bernard Herrmann
197.HITCHCOCK Alfred - PSYCHO: THE ESSENTIAL ALFRED H.
City Of Prague Philharmonic cond. by Paul Bateman
SILVA SCREEN: FILMXCD 320 (2CDs)   *1999*
27 Themes and Suites sequenced chronologically inc:
THE THIRTY NINE STEPS-THE LADY VANISHES-REBECCA-
SUSPICION-LIFEBOAT-SPELLBOUND-ROPE-UNDER CAPRICORN-
STAGE FRIGHT-STRANGERS ON A TRAIN-DIAL M FOR MURDER
REAR WINDOW-TO CATCH A THIEF-THE TROUBLE WITH HARRY
T.MAN WHO KNEW TOO MUCH-VERTIGO-NORTH BY NORTHWEST-
PSYCHO-MARNIE-TORN CURTAIN-TOPAZ-FRENZY-FAMILY PLOT
ALFRED HITCHCOCK TV SERIES THEME (Funeral March Of
A Marionette,by GOUNOD)
198.HOLLYWOOD - San Diego Symph.Orch cond:Lalo Schifrin
SION (Direct): SION 18150 (CD)   *1997*
1.SUPERMAN:March 2.RAIDERS OF THE LOST ARK:March 3.
BRIDGE OVER THE RIVER KWAI:March 4.CAPTAIN FROM CAS
TILLE:Conquest March 5.GREAT ESCAPE:March 6.PATTON:
March 7.RETURN OF THE JEDI:Parade Of The Ewoks/Impe
ial March 8.MUSIC MAN:76 Trombones 9.WHAT DID YOU
DO IN THE WAR DADDY: Statue Of Liberty March 10:
APOCALYPSE NOW: Ride Of The Valkyries 11.ARMED FORC
ES Medley 12.HUNT FOR RED OCTOBER:Hymn Of The Red
Army13.CINERAMA MARCH 14.DIRTY DOZEN:March 15.GREAT
WALDO PEPPER:March 16.JOHN PHILIP SOUSA STORY:Stars
and Stripes Forever/Liberty Bell/Washington Post/
Manhattan Beach/El Captain/Stars & Stripes Forever
199.HOLLYWOOD '96 - Various Artists
VARESE (Pinn): VSD 5764 (CD)   *1996*
INDEPENDENCE DAY-TWISTER-MISSION IMPOSSIBLE-FARGO-
HUNCHBACK OF NOTRE DAME-EMMA-A TIME TO KILL-TIN CUP
PHENOMENON-FLIPPER-COURAGE UNDER FIRE-SABRINA
200.HOLLYWOOD BACKLOT VOL.3 - Big Movie Hits - Var.Arts
Varese (Pinn): VSD 5361 (CD)   *1992*
TERMINATOR 2-MEDICINE MAN-CITY SLICKERS-FATHER OF
THE BRIDE-NAKED GUN 2.5-LITTLE MAN TATE-THE LAST BU
TTERFLY-THE GREAT MOUSE DETECTIVE-YEAR OF THE COMET
HUDSON HAWK-FINAL ANALYSIS-ARTICLE 99-DEAD AGAIN-BA
SIC INSTINCT-THE PLAYER-DOC HOLLYWOOD-MY COUSIN VIN
NY-SOAPDISH-A RAGE IN HARLEM-BLACK ROBE
201.HOLLYWOOD DIRECTORS: Music From The Films Of STEVEN
SPIELBERG - City Of Prague Philharm. (Paul Bateman)
SILVA SCREEN Treasury (Koch): SILVAD 3505 (CD) 1997
1:JAWS 2:SCHINDLER'S LIST 3:RAIDERS OF THE LOST ARK
4:INDIANA JONES AND THE TEMPLE OF DOOM 5:INDIANA
JONES AND THE LAST CRUSADE 6:1941 March 7:E.T. 8:
HOOK 9:JURASSIC PARK 10:SCHINDLER'S LIST piano vers
11:and 12: CLOSE ENCOUNTERS OF THE THIRD KIND
all music composed by JOHN WILLIAMS   *tpt: 53.55*
202.HOLLYWOOD HEROES - City Of Prague Philharmonic Orch
(Paul Bateman/Nic Raine/Kenn.Alwyn/Derek Wadsworth)
SILVA SCREEN Treasury (Koch): SILVAD 3501 (CD) 1997
1:GREAT ESCAPE *(E.BERNSTEIN)* 2:DANCES WITH WOLVES

(J.BARRY) 3:RAIDERS OF THE LOST ARK *(J.WILLIAMS)* 4:
HIGH ROAD TO CHINA *(J.BARRY)* 5:MAD MAX III BEYOND
THUNDERDOME *(M.JARRE)* 6:THE ALAMO *(D.TIOMKIN)* 7:
BORN ON THE 4TH OF JULY *(J.WILLIAMS)* 8:EL CID *(M.
ROZSA)* 9:ZULU *(J.BARRY)* 10:OUT OF AFRICA *(J.BARRY)*
11:OUTLAW JOSEY WALES *(J.FIELDING)* 12:TORN CURTAIN
(J.ADDISON) 13:ROBIN AND MARIAN *(JOHN BARRY)* 14:
CLIFFHANGER *(T.JONES)*   *tpt: 58.44*

203. HOLLYWOOD TOUGH GUYS - City Of Prague Philharmonic
(Paul Bateman/Nic Raine) / London Screen Orchestra
(Mike Townend) / Mark Ayres / Daniel Caine
SILVA SCREEN Treasury (Koch): SILVAD 3506 (CD) 1997
1:TERMINATOR *(B.FIEDEL* 2:BLADE RUNNER *(VANGELIS)* 3:
BIG TROUBLE IN LITTLE CHINA *J.CARPENTER* 4:SPARTACUS
(A.NORTH) 5:ROCKY 2 *(B.CONTI)* 6:SUPERMAN *J.WILLIAMS*
7:VILLA RIDES *(M.JARRE)* 8:CAPE FEAR *(B.HERRMANN)* 9:
MONTE WALSH *(J.BARRY)* 10: ONCE UPON A TIME IN THE
WEST *(E.MORRICONE)* 11:PROFESSIONALS *(M.JARRE)* 12:
TARAS BULBA *(F.WAXMAN)* 13:LICENCE TO KILL *(J.BARRY)*
14:SERPICO *(M.THEODORAKIS)*   *tpt: 57.36*

204. HOLLYWOOD'S GREATEST HITS VOL.1 ERICH KUNZEL cond:
Cincinnati Pops Orchestra with William Tritt, piano
TELARC (BMG-Con): CD 80168 (CD)   *1987*
20TH CENTURY FOX FANFARE-OVERTURE fromCAPTAIN BLOOD
TARA'S THEME from GONE WITH THE WIND-PARADE OF THE
CHARIOTEERS from BEN HUR-Theme from EXODUS-LARA'S
THEME from DOCTOR ZHIVAGO-THEME from LAWRENCE OF AR
ABIA-LOVE THEME from ROMEO AND JULIET-GOLDFINGER-
THEME from LOVE STORY-THEME from A SUMMER PLACE-THE
ME from JAWS-THEME from THE SUMMER OF'42-THEME from
ROCKY-THEME from TERMS OF ENDEARMENT-MAIN THEMEfrom
OUT OF AFRICA-THEME from CHARIOTS OF FIRE

205. HORNER James Essential James Horner Film Music Coll
SILVA SCREEN (Koch): FILMXCD 197 (2CD)   *1998*
GLORY-STAR TREK 2-RANSOM-LEGENDS OF THE FALL-THE
ROCKETEER-BRAVEHEART-RED HEAT-APOLLO 13-COCOON-THE
LAND BEFORE TIME-WILLOW-PATRIOT GAMES-NAME OF THE
ROSE-COMMANDO-FIELD OF DREAMS-DEEP IMPACT-TITANIC

206. HORNER James - Heart Of The Ocean
SONIC IMAGES (Cargo-Greyhound): SID 8807 (CD) 1998
TITANIC-THE ROCKETEER-APOLLO 13-FIELD OF DREAMS-
STAR TREK 2-WOLFEN-COMMANDO-THE NAME OF THE ROSE-
VIBES

207. HORNER James - Titanic and Other Film Scores
VARESE (Pinn): VSD 5943 (CD)   *1998*
TITANIC / APOLLO 13 / CASPER / COURAGE UNDER FIRE
ONCE AROUND / COCOON:THE RETURN / STAR TREK II: THE
WRATH OF KHAN / ALIENS / BRAINSTORM / BRAVEHEART

208. HORROR! - Monsters Witches and Vampires / Var.Orch
SILVA SCREEN Treasury (Koch): SILVAD 3507 (CD) 1997
1:OMEN *(J.GOLDSMITH)* 2:BRIDE OF FRANKENSTEIN *(Franz
WAXMAN)* 3:DRACULA *(J.BERNARD)* 4:TASTE THE BLOOD OF
DRACULA *(J.BERNARD)* 5:DRACULA HAS RISEN FROM THE
GRAVE *(J.BERNARD)* 6:HORRORS OF THE BLACK MUSEUM *(G.*

SCHURMANN) 7:HALLOWEEN *(J.CARPENTER)* 8:PRINCE OF DA
RKNESS *(J.CARPENTER)* 9:THEY LIVE*(CARPENTER-HOWARTH)*
10:WITCHFINDER GENERAL *(P.FERRIS)* 11:DEVIL RIDES
OUT *(J.BERNARD)* 12:HUNGER (Flower Duet from Lakme)
(DELIBES, sung by Lesley Garrett*)* 13:CURSE OF THE
WEREWOLF *(B.FRANKEL)* 14:VAMPIRE CIRCUS *(D.WHITAKER)*

209. <u>**HORROR!**</u> **- Westminster Philharm.Orch (Kenneth Alwyn)**
SILVA SCREEN (Koch): FILMCD 175 (CD)   *1996*
HORRORS OF THE BLACK MUSEUM *(GERARD SCHURMANN 1959)*
THE HAUNTING *HUMPHREY SEARLE 63)* CORRIDORS OF BLOOD
(BUXTON ORR 62) NIGHT OF THE DEMON *(CLIFTON PARKER
1957)* ABOMINABLE SNOWMAN *(HUMPHREY SEARLE 1957)* THE
WITCHFINDER GENERAL *(PAUL FERRIS 1968)* CURSE OF THE
MUMMY'S TOMB *(CARLO MARTELLI 64)* KONGA *(GERARD SCHU
RMANN 1961)* FIEND WITHOUT A FACE *(BUXTON ORR 1957)*
THE DEVIL RIDES OUT *(JAMES BERNARD 1968)* THE CURSE
OF THE WEREWOLF *(BENJAMIN FRANKEL 1961)*

210. <u>**HORROR FILM COLLECTION**</u> **Classic Italian Soundtracks**
DRG (Pinn): DRGCD 32903 (CD)   *1995*
DARIO'S THEME (musical tribute to Dario Argento)
(Marco Werba) IL TRONO DI FUOCO (**THRONE OF THE FIRE**
1970 Bruno Nicolai) /LA NOTTE DEI DIAVLOI (**NIGHT OF
THE DEVILS** *72 Giorgio Caslini)* / 7 NOTE IN NERO (**7
NOTES IN BLACK** *1977 Vince Tempera)* / LA CRIPTA E L'
INCUBO (**NIGHTMARE CRYPT** *64 Carlo Savina)* / PROFONDO
ROSSO (**DEEP RED** *1975 special suite(Giorgio Caslini)*
L'ISOLA MISTERIOSA E IL CAPITANO NEMO (**MYSTERIOUS
ISLAND OF CAPTAIN NEMO** *73 Gianni Ferrio)* /IN MONACO
(**THE MONK** *72 Pierro Piccione)* / TERRORE NELLO SPAAZ
IO (**PLANET OF THE VAMPIRES** *1965 Gino Martinuzzi Jr)*
PASSI DI MORTE PER DUTI NEL BUIO (**DEADLY STEPS LOST
IN THE DARK** *1976 Riz Ortolani)*

211. <u>**I.SALONISTI**</u> **- FILM MUSIC**
SONY CLASSICS: SK 61731 (CD) SM 61731 (MC)   *1999*
AS TIME GOES BY *CASABLANCA* / GODFATHER WALTZ /
SCHINDLER'S LIST / WEEP YOU NO MORE SAD FOUNTAINS
SENSE AND SENSIBILTY / MY HEART WILL GO ON *TITANIC*
MOON RIVER *BREAKFAST AT TIFFANY'S* / MAN AND A WOMAN
ONCE UPON A TIME IN THE WEST / MANHA DE CARNIVAL
BLACK ORPHEUS / SMILE *MODERN TIMES* / SOMEWEHERE
OVER THE RAINBOW *WIZARD OF OZ* / HOW IS THE WEATHER
IN PARIS/ LA STRADA / ZORBA'S DANCE *ZORBA THE GREEK*
FALLING IN LOVE AGAIN *BLUE ANGEL* / TITANIC MEDLEY

212. <u>**JACQUES BRELL IS ALIVE AND WELL AND LIVING IN PARIS**</u>
TER (Koch): CDTEM2 1231 (2CD)   *1997*
ORIGINAL LONDON CAST with VARIOUS ARTISTS
OVERTURE-MARATHON-ALONE-MADELEINE-I LOVED-MATHILDE-
BATCHELOR'S DANCE-TIMID FRIEDA-MY DEATH-GIRLS AND
DOGS-JACKIE-STATUE-DESPERATE ONES-SONS OF..-BULLS-
AMSTERDAM-OLD FOLKS-MARIEKE-BRUSSELLS-FANETTE-
FUNERAL TANGO-MIDDLE CLASS-YOU'RE NOT ALONE-NEXT-
CAROUSEL-IF WE ONLY HAVE LOVE

--- <u>**JAMES BOND**</u> **- see BOND James**

213.**JARRE Maurice** - DOCTOR ZHIVAGO: Classic Film Music
    City Of Prague Philharmon.Orchestra (Paul Bateman)
    SILVA SCREEN (Koch): FILMCD 158 (CD)   *1995*
    DOCTOR ZHIVAGO-A PASSAGE TO INDIA-RYAN'S DAUGHTER-
    LAWRENCE OF ARABIA-GHOST-WITNESS-IS PARIS BURNING-
    THE NIGHT OF THE GENERALS-THE MAN WHO WOULD BE KING
    FATAL ATTRACTION-VILLA RIDES-THE FIXER-EL CONDOR-
    suite from JESUS OF NAZARETH
214.**JAZZ AT THE CINEMA** - Various Artists
    SONY JAZZ: 487 460-2 (CD)   *1997*
    1.DON'T CRY FOR ME ARGENTINA *EVITA* Stan Getz 2.
    AUTUMN LEAVES *LES PORTES DE LA NUIT* Chet Baker 3.
    LAURA Ray Bryant 4.SOMETHING'S COMING *WEST SIDE
    STORY* HI-LOS 5.IT AIN'T NECESSARILY SO *PORGY & BESS*
    Aretha Franklin 6.GET ME TO THE CHURCH ON TIME *MY
    FAIR LADY* Andre Previn 7.AS TIME GOES BY *CASABLANCA*
    Supersax & L.A.Voices 8.BLUES DE LA PLUME *MILOU EN
    MAI* Stephane Grappelli 9.EXODUS SONG *EXODUS* Marion
    Williams 10.TONIGHT *WEST SIDE STORY* Ray Bryant
215.**JOHNSON Laurie The Professional (Best Of L.Johnson)**
    REDIAL (UNIVERS.): 557 210-2 (CD)   *1998*
    THE AVENGERS-DOCTOR STRANGELOVE-THIS IS YOUR LIFE-
    WHEN THE KISSING HAD TO STOP-TIGER BAY-SHIRLEY'S
    WORLD-CAESAR SMITH-HOT MILLIONS-THE PROFESSIONALS-
    JASON KING-NEW AVENGERS-AVENGERS TAG SCENE-LADY AND
    THE HIGHWAYMAN-HAZARD OF HEARTS-A DUEL OF HEARTS-
    GHOST IN MONTE CARLO-FOUR MUSKETEERS-THE FIRST MEN
    IN THE MOON-ROMANCE-I AIM AT THE STARS-ANIMAL MAGIC
    FREEWHEELERS-BOLERO-AVENGERS (Re-mix)
216.**JOHNSON, Laurie...With A Vengeance**
    SEQUEL-CASTLE (Pinn): NEMCD 935(CD) 1997 1.AVENGERS
    2.TOP SECRET 3.DR.STRANGELOVE 4.NO HIDING PLACE 5.
    BEAUTY JUNGLE 6.DOIN'THE RACOON 7.ECHO FOUR-TWO 8.
    M1 (M-ONE) 9.SOLO 10.CITY 11.LIMEHOUSE 12.WEST END
    13.LATIN QUARTER 14.GRAND CENTRAL 15.TIMES SQUARE
    16.SOUTH BEACH 17.SEVENTH AVANUE 18.STICK OR TWIST
    19.DRUM CRAZY 20.MINOR BOSSA NOVA 21.DEAR FRIEND 22
    HEATWAVE 23.TWANGO 24.WINTER WONDERLAND 25.HOE DOWN
    26.THE DEPUTY 27.DONKEY SERENADE-28.SPRING SPRING
    SPRING 29.CHAKA 30.SABRE DANCE *see also COLLECT 294*
217.**JOHNSON Laurie** - **THE ROSE AND THE GUN** - Music Of LJ
    FLY-U.Kanch (H.Mundi-FLY Dir): FLYCD 103   *1992*
    LADY AND THE HIGHWAYMAN (TVM 89)-A HAZARD OF HEARTS
    (TVM 87)-A DUEL OF HEARTS (TVM 88)-A GHOST IN MONTE
    CARLO (TVM 90)-THE AVENGERS (Theme/Tag)-THE NEW AVE
    NGERS-TIGER BAY THEME-WHEN THE KISSING HAD TO STOP
    CAESAR SMITH/THERE IS ANOTHER SONG/THIS TIME (from:
    Hot Millions)-SHIRLEY'S THEME/RICKSHAW RIDE (from:
    Shirley's World)-I AIM AT THE STARS Theme-THIS IS
    YOUR LIFE (Gala Performance)-JASON KING theme-ROMAN
    CE (The First Men In The Moon)-THE PROFESSIONALS
    LONDON STUDIO SYMPHONY ORCHESTRA (Laurie Johnson)
--- **JOPLIN Scott** King Of Ragtime *see* ZIMMERMAN Richard

218.<u>KAMEN Michael</u> - The Michael Kamen SOUNDTRACK Album
DECCA-POLYGRAM: 458 912-2 (CD) -4 (MC)   1998
extracts: ROBIN HOOD PRINCE OF THIEVES-MR.HOLLAND'S
OPUS-DON JUAN DE MARCO AND THE CENTREFOLD-CIRCLE OF
FRIENDS-CRUSOE-HIGHLANDER-NEXT MAN-WINTER GUEST-DIE
HARD-EDGE OF DARKNESS-BRAZIL *feat:* Kate Bush (voc)
Seattle Symphony Orch and London Metropolitan Orch

219.<u>KEATING John</u> - Space Experience Volumes 1 and 2
EMI Studio 2: 495 619-2 (CD)   CD reissue 1998
I FEEL THE EARTH MOVE-THE UNKNOWN PLANET-ROCKET MAN
PRELUDE TO EARTHRISE-STAR TREK THEME-JESUS CHRIST
SUPERSTAR-STAR TREK-SPACE AGENT-UPON ANOTHER EARTH-
THE SOUND OF SILENCE-SIGNAL TO SATURN Vol 2: REACH
OUT I'LL BE THERE-COUNTERGLOW-DREAMER-STEREOSKOPIA-
SOLITAIRE-STARCLUSTER-LUCY IN THE SKY WITH DIAMONDS
ASTEROID-LIFE ON MARS-EARTHSHINE

220.<u>KHACHATURIAN FILM SUITES</u> - Armenian Philharm.Orch.*
ASV (Select): CDDCA 966 (CD)   1997
ADMIRAL USHAKOV (1953)-PEPO (1934)-PRISONER NUMBER
217 (1945)-SECRET MISSION (1950) UNDYING FLAME
(1956) *conducted by L.Tjeknavorian & recorded 1995

221.<u>KORNGOLD Erich Wolfgang</u> - The Warner Bros Years
EMI ODEON: CDODEON 13   1996
CAPTAIN BLOOD-GREEN PASTURES-ANTHONY ADVERSE-PRINCE
AND THE PAUPER-ADVENTURES OF ROBIN HOOD-JAUREZ-THE
PRIVATE LIVES OF ELIZABETH & ESSEX-SEA HAWK-THE SEA
WOLF-KINGS ROW-CONSTANT NYMPH-DEVOTION-BETWEEN TWO
WORLDS-OF HUMAN BONDAGE-ESCAPE ME NEVER-DECEPTION

--- <u>KUBRICK Stanley</u> - see DOCTOR STRANGELOVE
--- <u>KUNZEL Erich</u> - *see* CINCINNATI POPS

222.<u>LADIES AND GENTLEMEN FROM</u>... - Various Artists
GREAT MOVIE THEMES (Target-BMG): CD 60019 (CD) 1998
SONGS FROM THE FOLLOWING SOUNDTRACKS:
THE KING OF JAZZ (1930) KING OF BURLESQUE (1935)
GOING PLACES (1938) CAREFREE (1938)
songs to be confirmed

223.<u>LADYKILLERS The</u> - Music From Glorious EALING Films
Royal Ballet Sinfonia conducted by Kenneth Alwyn
SILVA SCREEN (Koch): FILMCD 177 (CD)   1997
THE MAN IN THE WHITE SUIT *(1951-BENJAMIN FRANKEL)*
PASSPORT TO PIMLICO *(1949-GEORGES AURIC)*
THE TITFIELD THUNDERBOLT *(1952-GEORGES AURIC)*
THE LAVENDER HILL MOB *(1951-GEORGES AURIC)* THE
CRUEL SEA *(1953-ALAN RAWSTHORNE)* THE CAPTIVE HEART
(1946-ALAN RAWSTHORNE) SARABAND FOR DEAD LOVERS
(1948-ALAN RAWSTHORNE) WHISKY GALORE *(1949-ERNEST
IRVING)* KIND HEARTS AND CORONETS *(1949-MOZART)*
THE MAN IN THE SKY *(1956-GERARD SCHURMANN)* THE
LADYKILLERS *(1955-TRISTRAM CARY)* THE OVERLANDERS
(1946-JOHN IRELAND)

224.<u>LAI Francis</u> - A MAN AND A WOMAN / The Very Best Of
HALLMARK (Carlton): 305562 (CD) 305564 (MC)   1996
BILITIS-LOVE STORY-THE BLUE ROSE-EMOTION-HAPPY NEW
YEAR-LOVE IN THE RAIN-SEDUCTION-IMTIMATE MOMENTS-

PAR LE SANG DES AUTRES-A MAN AND A WOMAN-LIVE FOR
LIFE-AFRICAN SUMMER-SUR NOTRE ETOILE-LA RONDE-LES
UNES ET LES AUTRES-SMIC SMAC-SOLITUDE-WHITECHAPEL
225.**LANZA Mario** - **THE ULTIMATE COLLECTION**
RCA VICTOR (BMG): 74321 18574-2 (CD) -4 (MC)   1994
BE MY LOVE-DRINK DRINK DRINK-LA DONNA E MOBILE-AVE
MARIA-DANNY BOY-GRANADA-BECAUSE YOU'RE MINE-THE LOV
ELIEST NIGHT OF THE YEAR-VALENCIA-SONG OF INDIA-THE
DONKEY SERENADE-BECAUSE-O SOLE MIO-VESTI LA GIUBBA-
SERENADE-FUNICULI FUNICULA-GOLDEN DAYS-ARRIVERDERCI
ROMA-YOU'LL NEVER WALK ALONE-BELOVED-COME PRIMA-E
LUCEVAN LE STELLE-SANTA LUCIA-I'LL WALK WITH GOD
226.**LAUREL & HARDY** - **LEGENDS OF THE 2THh CENTURY**
EMI: 522 816-2 (CD)   Orig Dialogue and Music   1999
1.LAUREL & HARDY Theme music "DANCE OF THE CUCKOOS"
(Marvin T.Hatley) 2.FRESH FISH *from TOWED IN A HOLE*
3.FURNITURE PAYMENT *(THICKER THAN WATER)* 4.THE GAY
CAVIARS *(SWISS MISS)* 5.WHAT FLAVOURS HAVE YOU *(COME
CLEAN)* 6.HIGHER ENDEAVORS *(THEIR FIRST MISTAKE)* 7.
MISTAKEN IDENTITY *(PARDON US)* 8.THE TRAIL OF THE
LONESOME PINE *(WAY OUT WEST)* 9.LONG DISTANCE *(FIXER
UPPERS)* 10.WHEN THE MICE ARE AWAY *(HELPMATES)* 11.
DANGER BY CLOCKWORK *THICKER THAN WATER* 12.LAZY MOON
(PARDON US) 13.BIG SUCKER *(BEAU HUNKS)* 14.THERE'S A
DOLLAR *(BELOW ZERO)* 15.HARD BOILED EGGS AND NUTS
(COUNTY HOSPITAL) 16.WHERE WERE YOU BORN *(LAUREL &
HARDY MURDER CASE)* 17.OH GASTON *(BELOW ZERO)* 18.
STAGECOACH MANNERS *(WAY OUT WEST)* 19.AT THE BALL
THAT'S ALL *(WAY OUT WEST)* 20.TURN ON THE RADIO
(BUSY BODIES) 21.A CLEAN SWEEP *(DIRTY WORK)* 22.DUAL
DECEIT *(SONS OF THE DESERT)* 23.EVEN AS YOU AND I
(FIXER UPPERS) 24.COURT AGAIN *(SCRAM)* 25.WAY DOWN
SOUTH *(WAY OUT WEST)* 26.HAL ROACH-MGM PRESENTS
LAUREL & HARDY PARTS 1 & 2
227.**LEGRAND Michel** - **WINDMILLS OF YOUR MIND: Very Best**
HALLMARK (Carlton): 30557-2 (CD) -4 (MC)   1996
THE SUMMER OF 42-WHERE LOVE BEGINS-THEY SIMPLY FADE
AWAY-STREET WHERE THEY LIVED-OLD LOVERS NEVER DIE-
ON THE ROAD-THE WINDMILLS OF YOUR MIND-CONCERTO FOR
CABS-DO YOU COME HERE OFTEN-IN LOVE IN NORMANDY-
PARIS WAS MADE FOR LOVERS-PAVANNE FOR PEOPLE-WHERE
LOVE ENDS-SEA AND SKY *(vocal by Dusty Springfield)*-
A PLACE IN PARIS *(vocal by Matt Monro)*-I STILL SEE
YOU *(from The GO-BETWEEN)*
228.**LEVY Louis** & Gaumont British Orchestra: **MOVIE MUSIC**
EMPRESS (Koch): RAJCD 884 (CD)   1996
1.*STRIKE UP THE BAND* a)2.*IT'S LOVE AGAIN:* IT'S LOVE
b)-TONY'S IN TOWN 3.GOT TO DANCE MY WAY TO HEAVEN-I
NEARLY LET LOVE GO SLIPPING THROUGH MY FINGERS b)
4.*SWING TIME:* WALTZ IN SPRINGTIME-A FINE ROMANCE b)
5.NEVER GONNA DANCE-THE WAY YOU LOOK TONIGHT 6.
BROADWAY MELODY OF 1938: YOUR BROADWAY AND MY BROAD
WAY a)-I'M FEELING LIKE A MILLION 7.EVERYBODY SING-
YOURS AND MINE 8.*GANGWAY:* GANGWAY b)-LORD AND LADY

WHOOZELS 9.WHEN YOU GOTTA SING-MOON OR NO MOON 10.
PENNIES FROM HEAVEN: SO DO I-BUTTON YOUR SHOE 11.
PENNIES FROM HEAVEN c)-LET'S CALL A HEART A HEART
12.*GONE WITH THE WIND:* BATTLE HYMN OF THE REPUBLIC-
OLD KENTUCKY HOME-MARCHING THROUGH GEORGIA-MASSA'S
IN THE COLD COLD GROUND 13.CAMPTOWN RACES-OLD FOLKS
AT HOME-WHEN JOHNNY COMES MARCHING HOME-DIXIE 14.
PINOCCHIO: GIVE A LITTLE WHISTLE d)-TURN ON THE OLD
MUSIC BOX 15.LITTLE WOODEN HEAD-WHEN YOU WISH UPON
A STAR e) 16.*ALEXANDER'S RAGTIME BAND:* ALEXANDER'S
RAGTIME BAND-WHEN THE MIDNIGHT CHOO CHOO LEAVES FOR
ALABAM-BLUE SKIES f)-EVERYBODY'S DOING IT 17.EASTER
PARADE-NOW IT CAN BE TOLD g)-ALEXANDER'S RAGTIME BA
ND 18.*LIMELIGHT:* FAREWELL SWEET SENORITA-WHISTLING
WALTZ 19.STAY AWHILE-CELEBRATIN' 20.*SHALL WE DANCE:*
SHALL WE DANCE-LET'S CALL THE WHOLE THING OFF-THEY
ALL LAUGHED 21.THEY CAN'T TAKE THAT AWAY FROM ME a)
22.WHAT'S GOOD ABOUTGOODNIGHT-YOU COULDN'T BE CUTER
h)23.MUSIC FROM THE MOVIES MARCH a:Gerry Fitzgerald
b:Janet Lind c:Arthur Tracy e:Sam Browne f:Hazel
Jean g:uncredited h:Eve Becke
229.<u>LIVE LONG AND PROSPER</u> **CLASSIC SCI-FI & SPACE THEMES**
HALLMARK (CHE): 31152-2 (CD) 31152-4 (MC)   *1999*
1.STAR WARS main theme 2.GODZILLA 'Come With Me' 3.
DUNE 'Desert' 4.TERMINATOR 2: J.Day 5.MEN IN BLACK
6.2001 A SPACE ODYSSEY 'Also Sprach Zarathustra' 7.
STAR TREK theme 8.ARMAGEDDON 'I Don't Want To Miss
A Thing' 9.DEEP IMPACT 'Distant Discovery' 10.theme
from INDEPENDENCE DAY 11.FLASH GORDON 'Flash' 12.
LAND BEFORE TIME'If We Hold On Together' 13.LOST IN
SPACE 14.MISSION IMPOSSIBLE 15.THE X-FILES 16.FIFTH
ELEMENT 'Little Light Of Love' 17.SUPERMAN theme
tracks performed by XAVIER
230.<u>LLOYD WEBBER Andrew</u> - **Cincinnati Pops Erich Kunzel**
TELARC (BMG): CD 80405   *1996*
PHANTOM OF THE OPERA-MUSIC OF THE NIGHT-HERE AGAIN-
ALL I ASK OF YOU-ANGEL OF MUSIC-AS IF WE NEVER SAID
GOODBYE-MEMORY-I DON'T KNOW-DON'T CRY FOR ME ARGENT
INA-STARLIGHT EXPRESS-ANY DREAM WILL DO
231.<u>LLOYD WEBBER Andrew</u> - **GREATEST SONGS** - Var.Artists
SILVA SCREEN (Koch): SONG(CD)(C) 911 (2CD/2MC) 1994
Leslie Garrett-Royal Philharmon.Orch-R.P.Pops Orch-
Royal Philharmonic Concert Orchestra (Paul Bateman)
From: JOSEPH AND THE AMAZING TECHNICOLOR DREAMCOAT-
JESUS CHRIST SUPERSTAR-EVITA-TELL ME ON A SUNDAY-
SONG AND DANCE-CATS-STARLIGHT EXPRESS-REQUIEM-
PHANTOM OF T.OPERA-ASPECTS OF LOVE-SUNSET BOULEVARD
232.<u>LLOYD WEBBER Andrew</u> - **LOVE SONGS 1: Royal Phil.Orch**
with Lesley Garrett-Chris Corcoran-Sharon Campbell-
and Dave Willetts / RPO conductor: Paul Bateman
SILVA SCREEN (Koch): SONG(CD)(C)908 (CD/MC)   *1993*
ALL I ASK OF YOU-I DON'T KNOW HOW TO LOVE HIM-LOVE
CHANGES EVERYTHING-WISHING YOU WERE SOMEHOW HERE-
DON'T CRY FOR ME ARGENTINA-ONLY YOU-PHANTOM OF THE

OPERA-MUSIC OF THE NIGHT-ANOTHER SUITCASE IN ANOTHER
HALL-MEMORY-TELL ME ON A SUNDAY-THINK OF ME
233. **LLOYD WEBBER Andrew** - **LOVE SONGS 2:** Various Artists
FIRST NIGHT (Pinn): OCRCD 6044 (CD)   *1996*
1. JELLICLE BALL a) 2. MUSIC OF T. NIGHT b) 3. LOVE CHA
NGES EVERYTHING c) 4. DON'T CRY FOR ME ARGENTINA d)
5. HIGH FLYING ADORED b) 6. ANYTHING BUT LONELY c) 7.
MEMORY d) 8. CLOSE EVERY DOOR b) 9. TELL ME ON A SUND
AY c) 10. I DON'T KNOW HOW TO LOVE HIM d) 11. ALL I
ASK OF YOU b) 12. THE LAST MAN IN MY LIFE c) 13. TAKE
THAT LOOK OFF YOUR FACE d) 14. ONLY HE c) 15. JESUS
CHRIST SUPERSTAR b) a: Royal Philharm. Orch. b: Paul
Nicholas c: Marti Webb d: Stephanie Lawrence
234. **LLOYD WEBBER Andrew** - **PREMIERE COLLECTION** - **Best Of**
POLYDOR: 837282-2 (CD) -5 (DCC)   *1988*
PHANTOM OF THE OPERA *(Steve Harley-Sarah Brightman)*
TAKE THAT LOOK OF YOUR FACE *(Marti Webb)*-ALL I ASK
OF YOU *(C. Richard-Sarah Brightman)*-DON'T CRY FOR ME
ARGENTINA *(Julie Covington)*-MAGICAL MR. MISTOFFELEES
(Paul Nicholas)-VARIATIONS *(Julian Lloyd Webber)*-SU
PERSTAR *(Murray Head)*-MEMORY *(E. Paige)*-STARLIGHT EX
PRESS *(Ray Shell)*-TELL ME ON A SUNDAY *(Marti Webb)*
MUSIC OF THE NIGHT *(Michael Crawford)*-ANOTHER SUITC
ASE IN ANOTHER HALL *(Barbara Dickson)*-I DON'T KNOW
HOW TO LOVE HIM *(Y. Elliman)*-PIE JESU *(S. Brightman)*
235. **LLOYD WEBBER Andrew** - **PREMIERE COLLECTION** - **Encore**
POLYDOR: 517 336-2 (CD) -4 (MC) -5 (DCC)   *1988*
MEMORY *(Barbra Streisand)* LOVE CHANGES EVERYTHING
(Michael Ball) AMIGOS PARA SIEMPRE *(Jose Carreras-
Sarah Brightman)* ANY DREAM WILL DO *(Jason Donovan)*
CLOSE EVERY DOOR *Phillip Schofield)* OH WHAT A CIRC
US *(David Essex)* POINT OF NO RETURN *(Sarah Brightm
an-Michael Crawford)* + I AM THE STARLIGHT-WISHING
YOU WERE SOMEHOW HERE AGAIN-ARGENTINE MELODY-SEEING
IS BELIEVING-JELLICLE BALL- EVERYTHING'S ALRIGHT-
FIRST MAN YOU REMEMBER-ANYTHING BUT LONELY-HOSANNA
236. **LOST IN BOSTON IV** - Various Artists
VARESE (Pinn): VSD 5768 (CD)   *1997*
Songs composed by Alan Menken-Howard Ashman/Alan &
Marilyn Bergman/Jule Styne/Stephen Schwartz etc.
Incl: THIRTY WEEKS OF HEAVEN *(from BY THE BEAUTIFUL
SEA)* MARKING TIME *(from PIPPIN)* I'M NAIVE *(SUGAR)*
PRETTY IS *(110 IN THE SHADE)* THE JOB APPLICATION
(from BALLROOM) NOAH *(JAMAICA)* SUDDENLY THERE'S YOU
(BALLROOM) BAD *(LITTLE SHOP OF HORRORS)*+ songs from
BIG/ BEST LITTLE WHOREHOUSE IN TEXAS/ SWEET CHARITY
DRAT! THE CAT!/GOLDILOCKS/WORKING
--- **LOVE Geoff** - *see* **STAR WARS**
237. **LULLABY OF BROADWAY** - **Best Of BUSBY BERKELEY at WB**
EMI PREMIER (EMI): CDODEON 8 (2CDs)   *1996*
42 STREET: YOUNG AND HEALTHY-SHUFFLE OFF TO BUFFALO
42ND STR. GOLD DIGGERS OF 1933: WE'RE IN THE MONEY-
I'VE GOT TO SING A TORCH SONG-THE SHADOW WALTZ-REME
MBER MY FORGOTTEN MAN FOOTLIGHT PARADE: HONEYMOON

HOTEL-BY A WATERFALL-SHANGHAI LIL **WUNDERBAR:** DON'T
SAY GOODNIGHT-FASHIONS OF 1934-SPIN A LITTLE WEB OF
DREAMS **DAMES:** THE GIRL AT THE IRONING BOARD-I ONLY
HAVE EYES FOR YOU-DAMES **GOLD DIGGERS OF 1937:** WORDS
ARE IN MY HEART-LULLABY OF BROADWAY-ALL'S FAIR IN
LOVE AND WAR **IN CALIENTE:** THE LADY IN RED **HOLLYWOOD**
HOTEL: HOORAY FOR HOLLYWOOD

--- **MAGIC OF THE MUSICALS** - *see* WEBB Marti

238. **MANCINI Henry - IN THE PINK:-** Ultimate Collection
RCA VICTOR (BMG): 74321 24283-2 (CD) -4 (MC)   1995
PINK PANTHER THEME-MOON RIVER-DAYS OF WINE & ROSES
CHARADE-PETER GUNN-TWO FOR THE ROAD-THE THORN BIRDS
LOVE STORY THEME-MR.LUCKY-EXPERIMENT IN TERROR-SHOT
IN THE DARK-BLUE SATIN-BABY ELEPHANT WALK-HATARI-
PENNYWHISTLE JIG-PIE IN THE FACE POLKA-MOMENT TO
MOMENT-MOONLIGHT SONATA-DEAR HEART-SHADOW OF YOUR
SMILE-MOLLY MAGUIRE'S THEME-SUMMER OF 42-LOVE THEME
FROM ROMEO AND JULIET-AS TIME GOES BY-MISTY-TENDER
IS THE NIGHT-EVERYTHING I DO (I DO ITFOR YOU)-THEME
fr.MOMMIE DEAREST-RAIDROPS KEEP FALLING ON MY HEAD-
CRAZY WORLD-MONA LISΛ-UNCHAINED MELODY-WINDMILLS OF
YOUR MIND-TILL THERE WAS YOU-SPEEDY GONZALES-DREAM
A LITTLE DREAM OF ME-THE SWEETHEART TREE-LONESOME-
LOVE IS A MANY SPLENDORED THING-BY THE TIME I GET
TO PHOENIX-ONE FOR MY BABY-BREAKFAST AT TIFFANY'S-
THAT OLD BLACK MAGIC-EVERGREEN-MIDNIGHT COWBOY

239. **MANCINI Henry - ROMANTIC MOVIE THEMES**
RCA CAMDEN (BMG): 74321 40060-2 (CD)   1996
ROMEO AND JULIET LOVE THEME-BREAKFAST AT TIFFANY'S
(w.AMES GALWAY)-CINEMA PARADISO-THORN BIRDS THEME
(w.JAMES GALWAY)-GODFATHER THEME-MIDNIGHT COWBOY-
LOVE STORY-MISTY-THE WINDMILLS OF YOUR MIND-THEME:
THE ADVENTURERS-EVERGREEN-THE SHADOW OF YOUR SMILE
MEDLEY: DAYS OF WINE AND ROSES/MOON RIVER/CHARADE/
CAMEO FOR FLUTE-RAINDROPS KEEP FALLING ON MY HEAD-
SECRET LOVE-ONCE UPON A TIME IN AMERICA-SWEETHEART
TREE-THE MISSION-AS TIME GOES BY-THE UNTOUCHABLES

240. **MANUEL & MUSIC OF MOUNTAINS** Reflections / Carnival
EMI Studio 2: 495 622-2   CD reissue 1998
Reflections: THEME FROM A SUMMER PLACE-ROMANCE-BALI
HAI-TILL-FOLLS RUSH IN-NONE BUT THE LONELY HEART-
REFLECTIONS-EBB TIDE-BAIA-MOON RIVER-INTERMEZZOfrom
ESCAPE TO HAPPINESS-MOONGLOW and THEME FROM PICNIC
Carnival: MASCARA NEGRA-HOW INSENSITIVE-HONEYMOON
SONG-ZAMBESI-SUMMERTIME IN VENICE-LA MER-WHITE ROSE
OF ATHENS-GUANTANAMERA-RODRIGL'S GUITAR CONCERTO DI
ARANJUEZ-MANTILLA-ANGELITOS NEGROS-COME CLOSER TO
ME-MOSAIC THEME

241. **MARTIN Mary - My Heart Belongs To Daddy**
FLAPPER-Pavilion (Pinn): PASTCD 7838 (CD)   1999
tracks include LET'S DO IT-I GET A KICK OUT OF YOU-
KISS THE BOYS GOODBYE-WHAT IS THIS THING CALLED
LOVE-WHY SHOULDN'T I-THE WAITER THE PORTER AND THE
UPSTAIRS MAID-MY HEART BELONGS TO DADDY *etc.*

--- MARVELLOUS PARTY,A - *see* COWARD, Noel
242.MARVIN Hank & THE SHADOWS Play The Music Of Andrew
                              Lloyd Webber and Tim Rice
POLYGRAM TV: 539 479-2 (CD) 539 479-4 (MC)   *1997*
16 TRACKS FROM MUSICALS: EVITA-ASPECTS OF LOVE-THE
PHANTOM OF THE OPERA-CATS-STARLIGHT EXPRESS etc.
243.MEDICS: GREAT TV DRAMA THEMES - Various Artists
HALLMARK CARLTON (CHE): 30868-2 (CD) -4 (MC)   *1998*
1.CASUALTY 2.ANGELS 3.M*A*S*H* 4.MARCUS WELBY MD 5.
A COUNTRY PRACTICE 6.GENERAL HOSPITAL 7.DR.FINLAY'S
CASEBOOK 8.OWEN MD 9.CHICAGO HOPE 10.E.R. 11.SAINT
ELSEWHERE 12.SHORTLAND STREET 13.WHERE THE HEART IS
14.QUINCY 15.DOCTOR KILDARE 16.CHILDREN'S HOSPITAL
17.DANGERFIELD 18.PEAK PRACTICE
244.MIRANDA Carmen - 'The Lady In The Tutti Frutti Hat'
HARLEQUIN (Swift-Jazz Music): HQCD 133 (CD)   *1999*
Songs from Down Argentine Way / That Night In Rio /
The Gang's All Here / Springtime In The Rockies /
Weeekend In Havana *etc.*1.SOUTH AMERICAN WAY 2.MAMA
YO QUIERO 3.BAMBU BAMBU 4.I YI YI YI 5.CHICA CHICA
BOOM CHIC 6.CAECAE 7.I YI YI YI 8.WEEKEND IN HAVANA
9.REBOLA A BOLA 10.WHEN I LOVE I LOVE 11.CHATANOOGA
CHOO CHOO 12.TIC TOC DU MEU CORACO 13.PAN AMERICAN
JUBILEE 14.BRAZIL 15.YOU DISCOVER YOU'RE IN N.YORK
16.LADY IN THE TUTTI FRUTTI HAT 17.PADUCCA 18.I
YI YI YI YI 19.I'M JUST WILD ABOUT HARRY 20.
I'D LIKE TO BE LOVED BY YOU 21.GIVE ME A BAND AND A
BANDANA 22.SOUTH AMERICAN WAY 23.VOOM VOOM 24.MAMA
EN QUIERO 25.THE JIMMY DURANTE SHOW (excerpts)
--- MISSION The - *see* MORRICONE Ennio
245.MONROE Marilyn KISS + Jane Russell-Frankie Vaughan
CAMEO-TARGET (BMG): CD 3555 (CD)   *1995*
YOU'D BE SURPRISED-THE RIVER OF NO RETURN *(RIVER OF
NO RETURN)* I WANNA BE LOVED BY YOU-WHEN IF FALL IN
LOVE *(ONE MINUTE TO ZERO)* BYE BYE BABY-DIAMONDS ARE
A GIRL'S BEST FRIEND *(GENTLEMEN PREFER BLONDES)* ONE
SILVERDOLLAR-I'M GONNA FILE MY CLAIM-WHEN LOVE GOES
WRONG NOTHING GOES RIGHT *(GENTLEMEN PREFER BLONDES)*
AFTER YOU GET WHAT YOU WANT YOU DON'T WANT IT-MY
HEART BELONGS TO DADDY-SPECIALISATION-RUNNIN' WILD-
TWO LITTLE GIRLS FROM LITTLE ROCK-HEATWAVE *(THERE'S
NO BUSINESS LIKE SHOW BUSINESS)* KISS *(NIAGARA)*
246.MONRO Matt - HOLLYWOOD and BROADWAY
MFP GOLD (EMI): CDMFP 6137 (CD)   *1994*
LOOK FOR SMALL PLEASURES-STRANGER IN PARADISE-THE
IMPOSSIBLE DREAM-APPLE TREE-I'LL ONLY MISS HER WHEN
I THINK OF HER-COME BACK TO ME-HELLO DOLLY-SUNRISE
SUNSET-WALKING HAPPY-IF SHE WALKED INTO MY LIFE-PUT
ON A HAPPY FACE-TILL THE END OF TIME-CHARADE-GREEN
LEAVES OF SUMMER-THE SECOND TIME AROUND-EVERYBODY'S
TALKIN'-SHADOW OF YOUR SMILE-I'VE GROWN ACCUSTOMED
TO HER FACE-CHATTANOOGA CHOO CHOO-PRETTY POLLY
247.MONSTER MANIA - Classic Japanese Movie Music
VARESE (Pinn): VSD 5969 (CD)   *1998*

*247.*__MONSTER MANIA__ - Classic Japanese Movie Music
VARESE (Pinn): VSD 5969 (CD)   *1998*
1.GODZILLA KING OF THE MONSTERS (Main title theme)
2.DESTROY ALL MONSTERS (March) 3.GODZILLA VS MOTHRA
(Suite) 4.GODZILLA 1984 (Main title/love theme) 5/6
KING KONG VS GODZILLA (Suite) 7/8.GODZILLA VS SPACE
GODZILLA (Suite) 9.GODZILLA VS THE SEA MONSTER (The
Departure from Retch Island) 10/11.GODZILLA VS DEST
ROYER (main title/requiem) 12/13.SON OF GODZILLA
(Suite) 14/15/16.GODZILLA VS BIOLLANTE (Suite)17/18
GODZILLA VS KING GHIDORAH (suite) 19/20.GODZILLA VS
MECHAGODZILLA (m.title/G.force march) 21.GODZILLA
(requiem) 22.GOPDZILLA KING OF THE MONSTERS reprise

*248.*__MONSTER MOVIE MUSIC ALBUM__ - **'GODZILLA vs KING KONG'**
City Of Prague Philharmonic Orchestra with The
Crouch End Festival Chorus (cond: NIC RAINE)
SILVA SCREEN (Koch-S.Screen): FILMCD 196 (CD) *1998*
GODZILLA KING OF THE MONSTERS-DESTROY ALL MONSTERS-
GODZILLA VS MONSTER ZERO-KING KONG (3 SUITES by *MAX
STEINER,JOHN BARRY,JOHN SCOTT*)-MYSTERIOUS ISLAND-
THE LAND BEFORE TIME-WE'RE BACK: A DINOSAUR'S STORY
FLINSTONES-ONE MILLION YEARS BC-WHEN DINOSAURS
RULED THE EARTH-CREATURES THE WORLD FORGOT-THEODORE
REX-BABY: SECRET OF A LOST LEGEND

*249.*__MONSTER MOVIE THEMES__ - Various Artists
HALLMARK (CHE-Technicol): 31089-2 (CD)   *01/1999*
1.COME WITH ME *from GODZILLA* 2.PRESIDENT'S SPEECH
INDEPENDENCE DAY 3.MEN IN BLACK 4.THE X-FILES THEME
5.ROSEMARY'S BABY 6.BURN *THE CROW* 7.LOVE SONG FOR A
VAMPIRE *BRAM STOKER'S DRACULA* 8.TO THINK OF A STORY
FRANKENSTEIN 9.ADDAM'S GROOVE *THE ADDAMS FAMILY* 10.
JURASSIC PARK 11.CANDYMAN 12.PAZUZO *EXCORCIST 2 THE
HERETIC*13.EDWARD SCISSORHANDS 14.DEEPER UNDERGROUND
GODZILLA 15.THE LOST WORLD 16.WALK THE DINOSAUR *THE
SUPER MARIO BROTHERS* 17.IF WE HOLD ON TOGETHER *THE
LAND BEFORE TIME* 18.WE JUST WANNA PARTY WITH YOU
MEN IN BLACK

--- __MORE MUSIC TO WATCH GIRLS BY__ *see* __MUSIC TO WATCH__
                                    __GIRLS BY 2__

*250.*__MORRICONE Ennio__ - FILM MUSIC OF ENNIO MORRICONE
VIRGIN VIP (EMI): CDVIP 123 (CD) TCVIP 123 (MC)
THE GOOD THE BAD AND THE UGLY-THE SICILIAN CLAN-CHI
MAI (Life And Times Of David Lloyd George)-THE MAN
WITH THE HARMONICA (Once Upon A Time In The West)-
LA CALIFFA (Lady Caliph)-GABRIEL'S OBOE (Mission)-
A FISTFUL OF DYNAMITE-ONCE UPON A TIME IN THE WEST-
COCKEYE'S THEME (Once Upon A Time In America)-THE
MISSION remix-COME MADDELENA (Madelena)-MOSES THEME
(Moses The Lawgiver)-THE FALLS (The Mission)-
MY NAME IS NOBODY-LE VENT LE CRI (The Professional)
DEBOAH'S THEME (Once Upon A Time In America)

*251.*__MORRICONE Ennio__ - THE MISSION: Classic Film Music
City Of Prague Philharmonic Orchestra conducted by
Paul Bateman and Derek Wadsworth

SILVA SCREEN (Koch): FILMCD 171 (CD)   *1996*
THE MISSION (Suite for Orch & Choir): *The Mission/
Gabriel's Oboe/Ave Maria (Guarini)/On Earth As It
Is In Heaven/Epilogue: The Falls)* -THE UNTOUCHABLES
(Theme)-ONCE UPON A TIME IN AMERICA *Deborah's Theme*
1900 *(Romanza)*-CASUALTIES OF WAR *(Elegy For Brown)*-
TWO MULES FOR SISTER SARA-IN THE LINE OF FIRE-THE
THING-CHI MAI-MARCO POLO-ONCE UPON A TIME IN THE
WEST *(Man With The Harmonica)*-GOOD THE BAD AND THE
UGLY-A FISTFUL OF DOLLARS-FOR A FEW DOLLARS MORE-
ONCE UPON A TIME IN THE WEST-THE GOOD THE BAD AND
THE UGLY *(Ecstasy Of Gold)*-CINEMA PARADISO

252.**MORRICONE Ennio - MONDO MORRICONE: Ennio Morricone**
Orchestra featuring Edda Dell'Orsos (vocals)
COLOSSEUM (Pinn): CST 8057 (CD)   *1996*
Themes from great Italian Movies of the 60s and 70s
16 track compilation of film themes that fit neatly
into the currently hot 'Easy Listening' vogue

253.**MORRICONE Ennio** Movie Classics: Hugo **MONTENEGRO Orc**
RCA CAMDEN (BMG): 74321 44679-2 (CD)   *1997*
SIXTY SECONDS TO WHAT-GOOD THE BAD AND THE UGLY-A
FISTFUL OF DOLLARS-BATTLE OF ALGIERS-SACCO AND VENZ
ETTI-THE VICE OF KILLING-BYE BYE COLONEL-FOR A FEW
DOLLARS MORE-PAYING OFF SLOKEY-THE ADVENTURER-ONCE
UPON A TIME IN THE WEST-A GUN FOR RINGO

254.**MORRICONE Ennio - WITH LOVE**
DRG (Pinn): DRGCD 32913 (CD)   *1995*
MAIN TITLES AND RARE TRACKS FROM 21 ROMANTIC FILM
SCORES COMPOSED AND CONDUCTED BY MORRICONE BETWEEN
1960 AND 1990. Films inc. CINEMA PARADISO-BLUEBEARD
NIGHT FLIGHT FROM MOSCOW-MACHINE GUN McCAIN-RUFFIAN
TWO SEASONS OF LIFE-LADY CALIPH-THIS KIND OF LOVE-
ALIBI-DEVIL IN THE BRAIN-BLOOD IN THE STREET-SECRET

--- **MOVIE MADNESS - see SHOSTAKOVICH Dimitri**

255.**MOVIE MUSIC - THE DEFINITIVE PERFORMANCES / V.Arts**
SONY MUSIC: J2K 65813 (2CD)   *1999*
MUSIC FOR SILENT MOVIES Charlie Young 1.SINGIN' IN
THE RAIN *HOLLYWOOD REVUE 1929* Cliff Edwards 2.YOU
ARE TOO BEAUTIFUL *HALLELUJAH I'M A BUM* Al Jolson 3.
GUY WHAT TAKES HIS TIME *SHE DONE HIM WRONG* Mae West
4.TEMPTATION *GOING HOLLYWOOD* Bing Crosby 5.INKA DIN
KA DOO *JOE PALOOKA* Jimmy Durante 6.ROCK AND ROLL
TRANSATLANTIC MERRYGOUND Boswell Sisters 7.LULLABY
OF BROADWAY *GOLD DIGGERS OF 1935* Dicxk Powell 8.
WAY YOU LOOK TONIGHT *SWING TIME* Fred Astaire 9.
LOVELY WAY TO SPEND AN EVENING *HIGHER AND HIGHER*
Frank Sinatra10.SECRET LOVE *CALAMITY JANE* Doris Day
11.MAN THAT GOT AWAY *A STAR IS BORN* Judy Garland
12.GIANT *GIANT* WB Orch & Chorus 13.MARCH FROM THE
RIVER KWAI/COLONEL BOGIE *BRIDGE ON THE RIVER KWAI*
Mitch Miller Or 14.AN AFFAIR TO REMEMBER Vic Damone
15.CERTAIN SMILE Johnny Mathis 16.MY HEART BELONGS
TO DADDY *LET'S MAKE LOVE* Marilyn Monroe 17.OVERTURE
WEST SIDE STORY Johnny Green Orch 18.WITH A LITTLE

BIT OF LUCK *MY FAIR LADY* Stanley Holloway 19.TO SIR
WITH LOVE Lulu 20.MRS.ROBINSON *THE GRADUATE* Simon &
Garfunkel 21.BALLAD OF THE EASY RIDER Byrds 22.BE
JONATHAN LIVINGSTON SEAGULL Neil Diamond 23.WAY WE
WERE Barbra Streisand 24. CD2:1.SUICIDE IS PAINLESS
M.A.S.H. The MASH 2.KNOCKIN' ON HEAVEN'S DOOR *PAT
GARRETT AND BILLY THE KID* Bob Dylan 3.EVERGREEN
A STAR IS BORN Barbra Streisand 4.ON THE ROAD AGAIN
HONEYSUCKLE ROSE Willie Nelson 5.TENDER YEARS *EDDIE
& THE CRUISERS* John Cafferty & Beaver Brown Band 6.
FOOTLOOSE Kenny Loggins 7.TAKE MY BREATH AWAY *TOP
GUN* Berlin 8.IT HAD TO BE YOU *WHEN HARRY MET SALLY*
Harry Connick Jnr 9.JOHN DUNBAR THEME *DANCES WITH
WOLVES* John Barry Orch 10.STATE OF LOVE AND TRUST
SINGLES Pearl Jam 11.WHEN I FALL IN LOVE *SLEEPLESS
IN SEATTLE* Celine Dion & Clive Griffin 12.STREETS
OF PHILADEPHIA *PHILADELPHIA* Bruce Springsteen 13.
I'M FORREST *FORREST GUMP* Alan Silvestri Orch 14.
CHILDHOOD *FREE WILLY 2* Michael Jakcson 15.SWEETEST
THING *LOVE JONES* Refugee Camp AllStars-Lauryn Hill
16.MEN IN BLACK Will Smith 17.I SAY A LITTLE PRAYER
MY BEST FRIENDS WEDDING Diana King 18.SOUTHAMPTON
TITANIC James Horner Orch 19.MY HEART WILL GO ON
TITANIC Celine Dion 20.I DON'T WANT TO MISS A THING
ARMAGEDDON Aerosmith
--- <u>MOVIOLA</u> - *see* **BARRY John**
256.<u>MOZART TV</u> Favourite TV Tunes In The Style Of The
　　　　　　　Great Classical Composers - Various Arts.
DELOS USA (Nimbus): DE 3222 (CD) CS 3222 (MC) 1997
1.I'LL BE THERE FOR YOU *(FRIENDS)* (Vivaldi) 2.HILL
ST.BLUES-3.MASH-4.BRADY BUNCH (Mozart) 5.BEWITCHED
(Debussy) 6.X-FILES (Hovhaness) 7.ANGELA *TAXI*(Villa
-Lobos) 8.GREEN ACRES (Joplin) 9.LOVE IS ALL AROUND
MARY TYLER MOORE Satie 10.MR.ED Rodrigo 11.JEOPARDY
(Handel) 12.JETSONS (B.Britten) 13.WHERE EVERYBODY
KNOWS YOUR NAME *(CHEERS)* (J.Ireland) 14.I LOVE LUCY
(H.Purcell) 15.STAR TREK VOYAGER (R.Strauss)
257.<u>MUNDO LATINO!</u> - Various Artists
SONY MUSIC: SONYTV2CD (CD) SONYTVMC 2(MC) reis 1998
1.GUAGLIONE Perez Prado 2.LA CUMPARSITA (The Masked
One) Xavier Cugat 3.OYE MI CANTO Gloria Estefan 4.
SOUL LIMBO (Latino Summer Mix) Mr.Bongo 5.SOMETHING
IN MY EYE Corduroy 6.LA BAMBA Los Lobos 7.BAMBOLEO
Gypsy Kings 8.OYE COMA VA Santana 9.LIBERTANGO
Astor Piazzolla 10.SOUL SOUCE Cal Tjader 11.SOUL
BOSSA NOVA Quincy Jones 12.MAS QUE NADA Sergio
Mendes Brasil 66 13.WATERMELON MAN Mongo Santamaria
14.ESO BESO Nancy Ames 15.MORE MORE MORE Carmel 16.
HOT HOT HOT Arrow 17.CUBA The Gibson Bothers 18.
GOT MYSELF A GOOD MAN Pucho 19.CERVEZA Boots Brown
and His Blockbusters 20.TEQUILA The Champs
--- <u>**MUSIC FROM THE GOLDEN AGE**</u> - *see* **COLLECTION No.1**

*258.*__MUSIC TO WATCH GIRLS BY__ - Various Artists
SONYMUSIC: SONYTV 67(CD)(MC) (2CDs/Mc)   *1999*
CD1:1.MUSIC TO WATCH GIRLS BY Andy Williams 2.UP UP
AND AWAY Fifth Dimension 3.GOOD LIFE Tony Bennett 4
SPANISH EYES Al Martino 5.THEME FROM A SUMMER PLACE
Percy Faith 6.ON THE STREET WHERE YOU LIVE V.Damone
7.LA MER (BEYOND THE SEA) Bobby Darin 8.A CERTAIN
SMILE Johnny Mathis 9.VALLEY OF THE DOLLS Dionne
Warwick 10.JOANNA Scott Walker 11.WISHIN' & HOPIN'
Dusty Springfield 12.WICHITA LINEMAN Glen Campbell
13.MOON RIVER Danny Williams 14.GIRL WITH THE SUN
IN HER HAIR John Barry 15.MAGIC MOMENTS Perry Como
16.FLY ME TO T.MOON Julie London 17.PERHAPS PERHAPS
PERHAPS Doris Day 18.ALMOST LIKE BEING IN LOVE Vic
Damone 19.DON'T SLEEP IN THE SUBWAY Petula Clark
CD2: 1.THAT'S AMORE Dean Martin 2.DOWNTOWN Petula
Clark 3.MOVE OVER DARLING Doris Day 4.LOVE LETTERS
IN THE SAND Pat Boone 5.A SWINGIN' SAFARI Bert
Kaempfert 6.THESE BOOTS ARE MADE FOR WALKING Nancy
Sinatra 7.BLUE VELVET Bobby Vinton 8.IT HAD TO BE
YOU Vic Damone 9.MACK THE KNIFE Louis Armstrong 10
BLUE MOON Mel Torme 11.LADY IS A TRAMP Buddy Greco
12.MAMBO ITALIANO Rosemary Clooney 13.DO YOU MIND
Anthony Newley 14.SHE Peter Skellern 15.NO ONE BUT
YOU Billy Eckstine 16.FOOLS RUSH IN Brook Benton
17.SUGAR TOWN Nancy Sinatra 18.LET THERE BE LOVE
Nat King Cole & George Shearing 19.CAN'T TAKE MY
EYES OFF YOU Andy Williams
*259.*__MUSIC TO WATCH GIRLS BY__ 2: MORE MUSIC TO WATCH.....
SONYMUSIC: SONYTV 75(CD)(MC) (2CDs/Mc)   *1999*
1.CAN'T HELP FALLING IN LOVE Andy Williams 2.THE
BEST IS YET TO COME Tony Bennett 3.S'WONDERFUL Ray
Conniff 4.SOMETHIN'STUPID Frank & Nancy Sinatra 5.
THE LOOK OF LOVE Dusty Springfield 6.BORN FREE Matt
Monro 7.ALFIE Cilla Black 8.CAST YOUR FATE TO THE
WIND Sounds Orchestral 9.RAINDROPS KEEP FALLING ON
MY HEAD B.J.Thomas 10.MEMORIES ARE MADE OF THIS
Dean Martin 11.BY THE TIME I GET TO PHOENIX Glen
Campbell 12.ANYONE WHO HAD A HEART Dionne Warwick
13.WIVES AND LOVERS Jack Jones 14.I COULDN'T LIVE
WITHOUT YOUR LOVE Petula Clark 15.ON THE REBOUND
Floyd Cramer 16.QUE SEA SERA Doris Day 17.PEACEFUL
Georgie Fame 18.WHERE ARE YOU NOW Jackie Trent 19.
WONDERFUL WONDERFUL Johnny Mathis 20.ALMOST THERE
Andy Williams CD2: 1.SWAY Perez Prado feat Rosemary
Clooney 2.COME SEPTEMBER Bobby Darin Orchestra 3.
MORE I SEE YOU Chris Montez 4.IN CROWD Dobie Gray
5.COMIN'HOME BABY Mel Torme 6.CASINO ROYALE Jet Set
7.OUR DAY WILL COME Doris Day 8.IF YOU GO AWAY
Scott Walker 9.FEVER Peggy Lee 10.I LEFT MY HEART
IN SAN FRANCISCO Tony Bennett 11.WHAT A DIFFERENCE
Dinah Washington 12.CATCH A FALLING STAR Perry Como
13.WINDMILLS OF YOUR MIND Noel Harrison 14.WHAT A
WONDERFUL WORLD Louis Armstrong 15.GUAGLIANO Perez

Prado 16.59TH ST.BRIDGE SONG FEELIN' GROOVY Harpers
Bizarre 17.WINDY Association 18.STONED SOUL PICNIC
5th Dimension 19.FROM RUSSIA WITH LOVE John Barry
20.MacARTHUR PARK Richard Harris

260.**MY RIFLE MY PONY AND ME: Film Western Songs** - V.Art
BEAR FAMILY (Rollercoast/Swift):BCD 15625 (CD) 1993
MY RIFLE MY PONY AND ME:Dean Martin-Ricky Nelson fr
om *RIO BRAVO (59)* / LEGEND OF SHENANDOAH: James Ste
wart *SHENANDOAH (65)* / MONTANA *MONTANA (50)* THE SEA
RCHERS *THE SEARCHERS (56)* WAGON'S WEST/SONG OF THE
WAGONMASTER *WAGONMASTER(50)* All sung by Sons Of The
PIONEERS / NEVADA SMITH: Merle Kilgore *NEVADA SMITH
(56)* / BALLAD OF THE ALAMO: Marty Robbins *THE ALAMO
(60)* / THE HANGING TREE: Marty Robbins *THE HANGING
TREE (59)* / BALLAD OF PALADIN: Johnny Western *HAVE
GUN WILL TRAVEL (TV 57)* / THE SONS OF KATIE ELDER:
Johnny Cash *THE SONS OF KATIE ELDER (65)*/ THE REBEL
JOHNNY YUMA: Johnny Cash / RAWHIDE: Frankie Laine
RAWHIDE (TV 58) / GUNFIGHT AT OK CORRALL: Frankie
Laine *GUNFIGHT AT OK CORRALL (57)* / BALLAD OF DAVY
CROCKETT: Fess Parker *DAVY CROCKETT (55)* /RIO BRAVO
Dean Martin *RIO BRAVO (59)* / I'M A RUNAWAY: Tab Hun
ter / BONANZA: Lorne Greene *BONANZA (TV 59)* / NORTH
TO ALASKA: Johnny Horton *NORTH TO ALASKA (59)* /HIGH
NOON: Tex Ritter *HIGH NOON (52)* / AND THE MOON GREW
Kirk Douglas *MAN WITHOUT A STAR (55)* / PECOS BILL:
Roy Rogers & Sons Of The Pioneers / YELLOW ROSE OF
TEXAS/ROLL ON TEXAS MOON: Roy Rogers / DON'T FENCE
ME IN: Roy Rogers *HOLLYWOOD CANTEEN (44)* / COWBOY:
Dickson Hall

--- **MYSTERY MAGIC AND MADNESS** - *see* **SIMONETTI PROJECT**

261.**NASCIMBENE Mario** - Anthology cond: Mario Nascimbene
DRG (Pinn): DRGCD 32960 (2CD) *1996*
A FAREWELL TO ARMS-THE QUIET AMERICAN-ONE MILLION
YEARS BC-FRANCIS OF ASSISI-WHEN DINOSAURS RULED THE
EARTH-ALEXANDER THE GREAT-WHERE THE SPIES ARE-THE
BAREFOOT CONTESSA-ROMANOFF AND JULIET-ROOM AT THE
TOP-SOLOMON AND SHEBA-VIKINGS-CREATURES THE WORLD
FORGOT-SIEGE OF LENINGRAD-SCENT OF MYSTERY-SONS AND
LOVERS-LIGHT IN THE PIAZZA-BARABBAS-DOCTOR FAUSTUS-
JOSEPH AND HIS BRETHREN-VENGEANCE OF SHE-JESSICA

262.**NEW PURE MOODS** - Various Artists
VIRGIN (EMI): VTDCD 158 (2CD) *1997*
1.CACHARPAYA Incantation 2.WILD MOUNTIN THYME
(SCOTTISH TOURIST BOARD) Silencers 3.LILY WAS HERE
David A.Stewart feat Candy Dulfer 4.CHILDREN Robert
Miles 5.HARRY'S GAME Clannad 6.CAVATINA *DEER HUNTER*
John Williams 7.BRIDESHEAD REVISTED *(KELLOGG'S CORN
FLAKES/VW GOLF)* Geoffrey Burgon 8.DON'T CRY FOR ME
ARGENTINA Shadows 9.THEME FROM SCHINDLER'S LIST
Tamsin Little 10.RIVERDANCE John Anderson Concert
11.MERRY CHRISTMAS MR.LAWRENCE Ryuichi Sakamoto 12.
LITTLE FLUFFY CLOUDS The Orb 13.PLAY DEAD *(VAUXHALL
VECTRA)* Bjork w.David Arnold 14.SONG FOR GUY Elton

John 15.SWEET LULLABY Deep Forest 16.ONLY YOU *(FIAT TEMPRA)*Praise 17.ALBATROSS Fleetwood Mac 18.OXYGENE IV Jean Michel Jarre 19.CROCKETT'S THEME Jan Hammer 20.YEHA NOHA Sacred Spirit. CD2: ADIEMUS *(DELTA AIR WAYS)* Adiemus 2.CANTUS SONG OF TEARS *(CHELTENHAM & GLOUCESTER B.SOC)* Adiemus 3.TUBULAR BELLS PART ONE Mike Oldfield 4.INSPECTOR MORSE Barrington Pheloung 5.ANOTHER GREEN WORLD *(ARENA)* Brian Eno 6.ANCIENT PERSON OF MY HEART Divine Works 7.PROTECTION*(MAZDA)* Massive Attack feat Tracy 8.THE MISSION E.Morricone 9.HEART ASK PLEASURE FIRST/THE PROMISE *(THE PIANO)* Michael Nyman 10.ARIA ON AIR *(B.AIRWAYS)* Malcolm McLaren 11.RETURN TO INNOCENCE Enigma 12.SADNESS Enigma 13.CHI MAI *(LIFE AND TIMES OF DAVID LLOYD GEORGE)* Ennio Morricone 14.BLOW THE WIND/PIE JESU *(ORANGE)* Jocelyn Pook 15.WOODBROOK Micheal O'Suill eabhain 16.LAST EMPEROR David Byrne 17.PRELUDE *(B.AIRWAYS)* Yanni 18.TWIN PEAKS-FIRE WALK WITH ME Angelo Badalamenti 19.SUN RISING *(ALPEN)* Beloved 20.THEME FROM THE X-FILES DJ Dado
--- <u>**NEW WORLD ORCHESTRA**</u> - *see* **90's Movie Themes**
263.<u>**NEWMAN Alfred**</u> - **WUTHERING HEIGHTS: A Tribute**
New Zealand Symphony Orch cond: Richard Kaufman
KOCH INT.CLASSICS: 37376-2 (CD)   *1997*
WUTHERING HEIGHTS (1939) - PRINCE OF FOXES (1949) DAVID AND BATHSHEBA (1951) - DRAGONWYCK (1946) PRISONER OF ZENDA (1937) - BRIGHAM YOUNG (1940)
264.<u>**NEXT GENERATIONS**</u>: **The Very Best Of Science Fiction**
Czech Symphony Orch conducted by William Motzing
EDELTON (Pinn): 002720-2EDL (2CD)   *1997*
1.TERMINATOR *(82 B.FIEDEL)* 2.COCOON *(85 J.HORNER)* 3 STAR TREK II: THE WRATH OF KHAN *(82 HORNER)* 4.ALIEN *(1979 J.GOLDSMITH)* 5.MAC AND ME *(88 A.SILVESTRI)* 6. BILL AND TED'S EXCELLENT ADVENTURE *(88 D.NEWMAN)* 7. GHOSTBUSTERS *(84 E.BERNSTEIN)* 8.STAR TREK: THE NEXT GENERATION *(94 R.JONES)* 9.INNERSPACE *(87 GOLDSMITH)* 10.STAR TREK *(66 A.COURAGE)* 11.THE PHILADELPHIA EXP RIMENT *(84 WANNBERG)* 12.V FOR VICTORY*(84 J.HARNELL)* 13.MAD MAX 2 *(82 B.MAY)* 14.FLASH GORDON SUITE *(80 QUEEN/HOWARD BLAKE)* 15.METEOR *(79 L.ROSENTHAL)* 16. BATMAN *(89 D.ELFMAN)* 17.2010 *(84 D.SHIRE)* 18.STAR TREK VI: UNDISCOVERED COUNTRY *(91 C.EIDELMAN)* 19. TOTAL RECALL *(90 J.GOLDSMITH)* CD2: 1.SUPERMAN *(77 J.WILLIAMS)* 2.INVADERS FROM MARS *(86 C.YOUNG)* 3. STAR TREK: THE MOTION PICTURE *(79 J.GOLDSMITH)* 4. COUNTDOWN *(68 L.ROSENMAN)* 5.RETURN OF THE JEDI *(83 J.WILLIAMS)* 6.STAR TREK: THE NEXT GENERATION *(90 D.McCARTHY)* 7.MY STEPMOTHER IS AN ALIEN *(88 A.SILVE STRI)* 8.STAR TREK: DEEP SPACE 9 *(93 D.McCARTHY)* 9. EXPLORERS *(85 J.GOLDSMITH)* 10.SECONDS *(J.GOLDSMITH)* 11.STAR TREK IV: THE VOYAGE HOME *(86 L.ROSENMAN)* 12 GREMLINS 2: NEW BATCH *(90 J.GOLDSMITH)* 13.FANTASTIC VOYAGE *(66 L.ROSENMAN)* 14.DEAD ZONE *(83 M.KAMEN)* 15 RETURN OF CAPTAIN INVINCIBLE *(83 W.MOTZING)* 16.THE

FORTRESS *(93 F.TALGORN)* 17.BATTLE FOR THE PLANET OF THE APES *(73 L.ROSENMAN)* 18.ILLUSTRATED MAN *(69 J. GOLDSMITH)* 19.STAR WARS *(77 J.WILLIAMS)*

--- **NO STRINGS ATTACHED** - *see* **GRAY Barry**
--- **NORDGREN Erik** - *see* **BERGMAN SUITES**
265.**NORTH Alex** - **FILM MUSIC**
NONESUCH (TEN): 7559 79446-2 (CD) *1997*
THE BAD SEED (1956)-THE MISFITS (1961)-SPARTACUS (1960)-A STREETCAR NAMED DESIRE (1951)-VIVA ZAPATA (1952) London Symphony Orch (E.Stern) concert rec.

266.**NORTH Alex** - **NORTH BY NORTH**
CITADEL (Hot): STC 77114 (2CD) *1999*
UNCHAINED (55)/GHOST (90)-VIVA ZAPATA-THE BAD SEED A STREETCAR NAMED DESIRE-THE ROSE TATTOO-DESIREE-THE BACHELOR PARTY-13TH LETTER-I'LL CRY TOMORROW-LES MISERABLES-THE RACERS-STAGE STRUCK plus the complete score of JOURNEY INTO FEAR (1975)

--- **NOVELLO Ivor** - *see* **HILL SMITH Marilyn**
267.**NUMBER ONE SCI-FI ALBUM** - Various Artists
POLYGRAM TV (UNIV): 553 360-2 (CD) -4 (MC) *1997*
CD1: MOVIES
1.STAR WARS 2.INDEPENDENCE DAY 3.ABYSS 4.EMPIRE STR IKES BACK (Imperial March) 5.SUPERMAN (March) 6.ET (Flying) 7.BLADE RUNNER 8.RETURN OF THE JEDI (Luke and Leia) 9.APOLLO 13 10.EVE OF THE WAR (War Of The Worlds) 14.CLOSE ENCOUNTERS OF THE THIRD KIND 15. JURASSIC PARK 16.BATMAN THE MOVIE 17.DUNE Prophecy 18.DARK STAR 19.CAPRICORN ONE 20.ALIEN 21.THE BLACK HOLE 22.2001-A SPACE ODYSSEY
CD2:
TV THEMES 1.THE X FILES 2.STAR TREK NEXT GENERATION 3.DARK SKIES 4.BUCK ROGERS IN THE 25TH CENTURY 5. BATTLESTAR GALACTICA 6.TWILIGHT ZONE Theme & Variat ions 7.STAR TREK: VOYAGER 8.BABYLON 5 9.DOCTOR WHO 10.RED DWARF 11.HITCH-HIKERS GUIDE TO THE GALAXY 12 THUNDERBIRDS 13.STING RAY 14.FIREBALL XL-5 15.CAPTA IN SCARLET 16.JOE 90 17.BLAKE'S 7 18.LOST IN SPACE 1 & 2 19.THE TIME TUNNEL 20.BATMAN 21.STAR TREK TV

268.**NYMAN Michael** - **Music From Peter GREENAWAY Films**
Michael Nyman and Essential Michael Nyman Band
ARGO/DECCA (Polyg): 436 820-2 (CD) -4 (MC) *1992*
CHASING SHEEP IS BEST LEFT TO SHEPHERDS/AN EYE FOR OPTICAL THEORY/THE GARDEN IS BECOMING A ROBE ROOM *(all: The Draughtsman's Contract)* PRAWN WATCHING/TI ME LAPSE *(A Zed & Two Noughts)* FISH BEACH/WHEELBARR OW WALK/KNOWING THE ROPES *(Drowning By Numbers)* MISERERE PARAPHRASE/MEMORIAL*(The Cook The Thief His Wife And Her Lover)* STROKING/SYNCHRONISING *(Water Dances)* MIRANDA *(Prospero's Books)*

--- **NYPD BLUE - The BEST OF MIKE POST** - *see* **POST Mike**
269.**O'CONNOR Caroline** - **WHAT I DID FOR LOVE**
TER (Koch): CDVIR 8331 (CD) *1998*
1.ALL THAT JAZZ *CHICAGO* 2.WHO WILL LOVE ME AS I AM *SIDE SHOW* 3.WHAT I DID FOR LOVE *CHORUS LINE* 4.THE

NIGHT IT HAD TO END *ROMANCE ROMANCE* 5.DON'T RAIN ON
MY PARADE *FUNNY GIRL* 6.STORY GOES ON *BABY* 7.WHAT
EVER LOLA WANTS *DAMN YANKEES* 8.I GOT THE SUN IN THE
MORNING *ANNIE GET YOUR GUN* 9.THERE ARE WORSE THINGS
I COULD DO *GREASE* 10.I CAN'T SAY NO *OKLAHOMA* 11.
LIFE UPON THE WICKED STAGE *SHOWBOAT* 12.STAY WITH ME
INTO THE WOODS 13.DON'T TELL MAMA *CABARET* 14.TIME
HEALS EVERYTHING *MACK & MABEL* 15.AMERICA *WEST SIDE
STORY* 16.NOWADAYS *CHICAGO*

--- **OMEN The** - *see* **GOLDSMITH Jerry**
270.**ON THE BOX** - **Various Artists**
 K-TEL: ECD 3470 (4CD's) EMC 2470 (4MC) 1999
 THE BILL-JULIET BRAVO-BERGERAC-NO HIDING PLACE-
 POLICE WOMAN-STREETS OF SAN FRANCISCO-MAIGRET-DIXON
 OF DOCK GREEN-HEARTBEAT-VAN DER VALK-TAGGART-THE
 MAN FROM UNCLE-SWEENEY-IRONSIDE-SAINT-PERRY MASON-
 DANGER MAN-PERSUADERS-MURDER SHE WROTE-CRACKER-
 CRIMEWATCH-MAGNUM PI-KOJAK-ROCKFORD FILES-CHARLIE'S
 ANGELS-NYPD BLUE-HAWAII FIVE O-CAGNEY AND LACEY-
 HILL STREET BLUES-Z CARS-DRAGNET-MIAMI VICE-THE
 SIMPSONS-MONTY PYTHON'S FLYING CIRCUS-TALES OF THE
 UNEXPECTED-BLIND DATE-JUKE BOX JURY-GLADIATORS-
 DANGERFIELD-RUTH RENDELL MYSTERIES-LONDON'S BURNING
 THIS IS YOUR LIFE-CASUALTY-UPSTAIRS DOWNSTAIRS-THE
 ONEDIN LINE-HARRY'S GAME-SOFTLY SOFTLY TASK FORCE-
 HAMISH MacBETH-ROSEANNE-THE PRISONER-THE FUGITIVE-
 NORTHERN EXPOSURE-MASTERMIND-ALFRED HITCHCOCK PRES
 CHEERS-BEVERLY HILLS 90210-NEWS AT TEN-BAYWATCH-
 BONANZA-JEWEL IN THE CROWN-COUNTRY DIARY OF AN
 EDWARDIAN LADY-WHEN YOU WISH UPON A STAR-I'M POPEYE
 THE SAILORMAN-MUPPET SHOW-HOME AND AWAY-BROOKSIDE-
 EASTENDERS-EMMERDALE-CORONATION STREET-NEIGHBOURS-
 PRISONER CELL BLOCK H-SPORTSNIGHT-MATCH OF THE DAY
 ON THE BALL-GRANDSTAND-DAD'S ARMY-STEPTOE AND SON-
 BEVERLY HILLBILLIES-BENNY HILL SHOW-HAPPY DAYS-THE
 LAST OF THE SUMMER WINE-FAWLTY TOWERS-THE THIRD MAN
 WORLD OF SPORT-WHATEVER HAPPENED TO THE LIKELY LADS
 SESAME STREET-A TEAM-ADDAM'S FAMILY-LIFE AND TIMES
 OF DAVID LLOYD GEORGE (CHI MAI)-BLANKETY BLANK-
 DALLAS-DYNASTY-PEYTON PLACE-KNOTS LANDING-E.R.-
 ABSOLUTELY FABULOUS-WINDS OF WAR-THE THORN BIRDS-
 BRIDESHEAD REVISITED-M*A*S*H*-FLINSTONES-ONE FOOT
 IN THE GRAVE-MEN BEHAVING BADLY-ONLY FOOLS AND
 HORSES-FRIENDS-STAR TREK-TWILIGHT ZONE-DOCTOR WHO-
 MILLENNIUM-STAR TREK THE NEXT GENERATION-BABYLON 5
 THE OUTER LIMITS-STAR TREK VOYAGER-THUNDERBIRDS-
 CAPTAIN SCARLET-JOE 90-RED DWARF-QUANTUM LEAP-
 LOST IN SPACE-BLAKE'S 7-STAR TREK DEEP SPACE NINE-
 TWIN PEAKS-UFO-V THE SERIES-KNIGHT RIDER
271.**ONLY CLASSICAL ALBUM YOU'LL EVER NEED The** Var.Arts
 RCA-CONIFER (BMG): 75605 51332-2 (2CD) -4 (MC) 1998
 1.CARMINA BURANA:O Fortuna *(ORFF)* Old Spice 2.LAKME
 Flower Duet *(DELIBES)* B.Airways 3.SYMPH.NO.9: New
 World *(DVORAK)* Hovis 4.PEER GYNT: Morning *(GRIEG)*

Nescafe 5.LA BOHEME: Che Gelida Manina *(PUCCINI)*
Moonstruck 6.RHAPSODY ON A THEME BY PAGANINI: No.18
RACHMANINOV) Groundhog Day 7.CLAIRE DE LUNE *DUBUSSY*
Frankie & Johnny 8.IL TROVATORE: Anvil Chorus *VERDI*
Wranglers 9.CANON IN D.*(PACHELBEL)* Ordinary People
10.EXSULTATE JUBILATE: Alleluia *(MOZART)* Royal Wedd
ing 11.PAVANE *(FAURE)* BBC World Cup 1998 12.CARMEN:
Flower Song *(BIZET)* 13.ADAGIO IN G.MINOR *(ALBINONI)*
Galipoli 14.ROMEO & JULIET: Dance Of The Knights
(PROKOFIEV) L'Egoiste 15.ENIGMA VARIATIONS: Nimrod
(ELGAR) 16.1812 OVERTURE: Finale *(TCHAIKOVSKY)* CD2:
1.POMP AND CIRCUMSTANCE MARCH NO.1 *(ELGAR)* 2.THE
PEARLFISHERS: Au Fond Du Temple Saint (Duet)*(BIZET)*
Galipoli3.CAVALLAERIA RUSTICANA:Intermezzo *MASCAGNI*
Raging Bull 4.MESSIAH: Why Do The Nations *(HANDEL)*
5.MESSIAH: Hallelujah Chorus*(HANDEL)* 6.FOUR SEASONS
Spring *(VIVALDI)* 7.REQUIEM: Pie Jesu *(FAURE)* 8.
SPARTACUS: Adagio *(KHACHATURIAN)* Onedin Line theme
9.GYMNOPEDIE NO.1 *(SATIE)* 10.AIR ON A G.STRING *BACH*
Hamlet 11.GIANNI SCHICCHI: Oh My Beloved Daddy *(PUC
CINI)* A Room With A View 12.PASTORAL SYMPH: 5TH m/m
(ext)*(BEETHOVEN)* Fantasia 13.JERUSALEM *(PARRY)* 14.
CLARINET CONCERTO: 2nd m/m *(MOZART)* Out Of Africa
15.AGNUS DEI: Adagio *(BARBER)* 16.TURANDOT: Nessun
Dorma *(PUCCINI)* World Cup 1990. *Artists include*
LESLEY GARRETT-LUCIANO PAVAROTTI-JAMES GALWAY-BRYN
TERFEL-PLACIDO DOMINGO-ANGELA GHEORGHIU-JANICE
WATSON-JUSSI BJORLING-ROBERT MERRILL-CAMILLA OTAKI
272.**ONLY MUSICALS ALBUM YOU'LL EVER NEED The** Var.Arts
RCA (BMG): 74321 60825-2 (2CD) -4 (MC) 1999
1.SECRET LOVE *(CALAMITY JANE)* Doris Day 2.SOUND OF
MUSIC Julie Andrews 3.SOME ENCHANTED EVENING *(SOUTH
PACIFIC)* 4.ALL THAT JAZZ *(CHICAGO)* 5.LUCK BE A LADY
(GUYS & DOLLS) 6.IF I WERE A RICH MAN *(FIDDLER ON
THE ROOF)* 7.THERE'S NO BUSINESS LIKE SHOW BUSINESS
(ANNIE GET YOUR GUN) 8.SEND IN THE CLOWNS *(A LITTLE
NIGHT MUSIC)* Glenn Close 9.I KNOW HIM SO WELL *CHESS*
Elaine Paige-Barbara Dickson 10.HELLO DOLLY Carol
Channing 11.SINGIN' IN THE RAIN Gene Kelly 12.SHALL
WE DANCE *(KING & I)* Yul Brynner 13.STRANGER IN
PARADISE *(KISMET)* 14.BROTHERHOOD OF MAN *(HOW TO
SUCEED IN BUSINESS)* 15.BRING HIM HOME *(LES MISERA.)*
Colm Wilkinson 16.MUSIC OF THE NIGHT *(PHANTOM OF..)*
Michael Crawford 17.MEMORY *(CATS)* Elaine Paige 18.
OH WHAT A BEAUTIFUL MORNIN' *(OKLAHOMA)* 19.CABARET
Natasha Richardson 20.CLIMB EVERY MOUNTAIN *(SOUND
OF MUSIC)* Leslie Garrett
CD2: 1.CONSIDER YOURSELF *(OLIVER)* 2.YOU'RE THE TOP
(ANYTHING GOES) 3.LOSING MY MIND *(FOLLIES)* Barbara
Cook 4.EVERYTHING'S COMING UP ROSES *(GYPSY)* Angela
Lansbury 5.OL'MAN RIVER *(SHOW BOAT)* 6.LOVE CHANGES
EVERYTHING *(ASPECTS OF LOVE)* Michael Ball 7.AMERICA
(WEST SIDE STORY) 8.IMPOSSIBLE DREAM *(MAN OF LA MAN
CHA)* 9.OVER THE RAINBOW *(WIZARD OF OZ)* Judy Garland

10.I GOT RHYTHM *(CRAZY FOR YOU)* Ruthie Henshall 11.
IF I LOVED YOU *(CAROUSEL)* 12.AQUARIUS *(HAIR)* 13.A
COUPLE OF SWELLS *(EASTER PARADE)* Fred Astaire-Judy
Garland 14.I TALK TO THE TREES *(PAINT YOUR WAGON)*
15.BIG SPENDER *(FOSSE THE MUSICAL/SWEET CHARITY)*
16.I WANNA BE LOVED BY YOU *(SOME LIKE IT HOT)*
Marilyn Monroe 17.LULLABY OF BROADWAY *(42ND STREET)*
18.WITH ONE LOOK *(SUNSET BOULEVARD)* Michael Ball 19
MAMMY *(JOLSON)* Brian Conley 20.I COULD HAVE DANCED
ALL NIGHT *(MY FAIR LADY)* Lesley Garrett

273.**ONLY OPERA ALBUM YOU'LL EVER NEED The** Var.Artists
RCA-CONIFER (BMG): 75605 51356-2 (2CD) -4 (MC) 1999
1.BRINDISI *(LA TRAVIATA)* Lesley Garrett 2.UN BEL DI
*(MADAME BUTTERFLY/FATAL ATTRACTION)*Angela Gheorghiu
3.OMBRA MAI FU *(SERSE/DANGEROUS LIAISONS)* Judith
Malafronte 4.TOREADOR'S SONG*(CARMEN)* Robert Merrill
5.EBBEN NE ANDRO LONTANA *(LA WALLY/DIVA)* Eva Marton
6.SUMMERTIME*(PORGY & BESS)* Leontyne Price 7.O SOAVE
FANCIULLA *(LA BOHEME/MOONSTRUCK)* Luciano Pavarotti
8.SONG TO THE MOON *(RUSALKA/DRIVING MISS DAISY)*
Leontyne Price 9.UNA FURTIVA LAGRIMA *(L'ELISIR D'
AMORE/PRIZZI'S HONOR)* Placido Domingo 10.HABANERA
*(CARMEN)*Leontyne Price 11.LARGO AL FACTOTEM *(BARBER
OF SEVILLE/MRS.DOUBTFIRE)* Robert Merrill 12.FLOWER
DUET *(LAKME/BRITISH AIRWAYS AD)* Janice Watson-Ruby
Philogene 13.WHEN I A LAID IN EARTH *(DIDO & AENEAS)*
Leontyne Price 14.GRAND MARCH *(AIDA)* Kings Division
Normandy Band 15.SOAVE SIA IL VENTO *(COSI FAN TUTTE
SUNDAY BLOODY SUNDAY)* Lynne Dawson-Della Jones-
Francois Le Roux) 16.NESSUN DORMA *(TURANDOT/WORLD
CUP 1990)* Johan Botha
CD2: 1.WILLIAM TELL OVERTURE *(LONE RANGER)* Yehudi
Menuhin & Sinfonia Varsovia 2.SEGUEDILLE *(CARMEN)*
Lesley Garrett 3.E LUCEVAN LE STELLE *(TOSCA)* Johan
Botha 4.BARCAROLLE *(TALES OF HOFFMAN/BAILEY'S IRISH
CREAM)* Janice Watson-Ruby Philogene 5.CHORUS OF THE
HEBREW SLAVE *(NABUCCO)* Robert Shaw Chorale 6.VOI
CHE SAPETTE *(THE MARRIAGE OF FIGARO)* Della Jones 7.
VESTO LA GIUBBA *(I PAGLIACCI/MOONRAKER)* Placido
Domingo) 8.CASTA DIVA *(NORMA/FORD MONDEO)* Monserrat
Caballe 9.DER HOLLE RACHE *(MAGIC FLUTE)* Sylvia
Geszty 10.LA DONNE E MOBILE *(RIGOLETTO)* Placido Dom
ingo 11.CHE FARO SENZA EURIDICE *(ORFEO ET EURIDICE)*
Vesselina Kasarova 12.AU FOND DU TEMPLE SAINT *PEARL
FISHERS/GALLIPOLI)* Robert Merrill-Jussi Bjoerling
13.RIDE OF THE VALKYRIES *(DIE WALKURE/APOCALYPSE
NOW)* Netherlands Radio Philharmonic 14.NON PIU
ANDRAI *(MARRIAGE OF FIGARO)* Francois Le Rue 15.
CELESTE AIDA *(AIDA)* Placido Domingo 16.ENTR'ACTE &
WALTZ *(EUGENE ONEGINO)* Royal Opera House Chor/Orch

274.**OPERA AT THE MOVIES** - Various Artists
NAXOS (Select): 8.551164 (CD)   *1995*
TRADING PLACES: *Overture To The Marriage Of Figaro
(Mozart)* MY LEFT FOOT: *Un'aura amorosa from Cosi*

Fan Tutti **(Mozart)** SUNDAY BLOODY SUNDAY: *Soave sia
il vento from Cosi Fan Tutti* **(Mozart)** DRIVING MISS
DAISY: *Song To The Moon from Rusalka (Dvorak)* FANTA
SIA: *Dance Of The Hours from La Gioconda* **Ponchielli**
SOMEONE TO WATCH OVER ME *Flower Duet from Lakme
(Delibes)* PETER'S FRIENDS *Can-Can from Orpheus In
The Underworld (Offenbach)* THE UNTOUCHABLES *Recitar
Vesti La Giubba - I Pagliacci* **Leoncavallo** EXCALIBUR
*Siegfried's Death and Funeral March from Gotterdamm
erung (Wagner)* WITCHES OF EASTWICK *Nessun Dorma fr.
Turandot (Puccini)* A ROOM WITH A VIEW *O Mio Babbino
Caro from Gianni Scicchi (Puccini)* MOONSTRUCK *O Soa
ve fanciulla from La Boheme (Puccini)* RAGING BULL /
GODFATHER III *Intermezzo from Cavalleria Rusticana*
Mascagni DIVA *Ebben Ne Andro Lontana from La Wally
(Catalini)* A NIGHT AT THE OPERA *Anvil Chorus from
Il Trovatore (Verdi)* PHILADELPHIA *La Mamma Morta fr
om Andrea Chenier (Giordano)* APOCALYPSE NOW *Ride Of
The Valkyries from Die Walkure (Wagner)*

275.<u>OPERA GOES TO THE MOVIES</u> - Boston Pops **(A.Fiedler)**
RCA VICTOR (BMG): GD 60841 (CD)
FATAL ATTRACTION:*(Puccini: "Un Bel Di" MADAMA BUTTE
RFLY, Act.2)* WITCHES OF EASTWICK:*(Puccini: "Nessun
Dorma" TURANDOT,Act 3)* MOONSTRUCK:*(Puccini: "Quando
M'en Vo" LA BOHEME, Act 2) (Puccini: "Don de Lieta
Usci" LA BOHEME,Act 3)* DARK EYES:*(Rossini:"Una Voce
Poco Fa" BARBER OF SEVILLE, Act 1)* APOCALYPSE NOW:
(Wagner: "Ride Of The Valkyries" DIE WALKURE,Act 2)
JEAN DE FLORETTE: *(Verdi: "Overture" LA FORZA DEL
DESTINO)* PRIZZI'S HONOR: *(Rossini:"Overture" BARBER
OF SEVILLE)* A ROOM WITH A VIEW: *(Puccini: "Firenze
E Coome Un Albero Fiorito" and "O Mio Babino Caro"
GIANNI SCHICCHI) and "Chi Il Bel Sogno Di Doretta"
LA RONDINE)* GODFATHER III: *(Mascagni:"Intermezzo"
CAVALLERIA RUSTICANA)* UNTOUCHABLES: *(Leoncavallo:
"Vesti La Giubba" PAGLIACCI, Act 1)*

276.<u>ORFF Carl</u> - The Best Of CARL ORFF
RCA (BMG): 75605 51537-2 (CD)   *1999*
CARMINA BURANA - Highlights (15 trks) inc O FORTUNA
(OLD SPICE AD). feat LUCIA POPP-JOHN VAN KESTEREN-
HERNIAM PREY & MUNICH RADIO ORCH cond: KURT EICHORN
SCHULWERK (School Work) - (19 tracks) including
RUNDADINELLA *(BBC LEARNING ZONE AD)* GASSENHAUER
(VW GOLF AD) TOLZER BOYS CHOIR-GERHARDT SCHMIDT
GADEN-CHAMBER CHOIR OF THE MUNICH NATIONAL COLLEGE
STUTTGART CHORUS-HEINZ MENDA-INSTRUMENTAL ENSEMBLE
DER KLUGE (Wise Woman) DER MOND (The Moon) *extracts*

277.<u>ORIGINALS</u> - The LEVI JEANS AD Collection - Var.Arts
COLUMBIA (SONY: MOOD(C)(CD) 29   *1993*
WONDERFUL WORLD: Sam Cooke-I HEARD IT THROUGH THE
GRAPEVINE: Marvin Gaye-STAND BY ME: Ben E.King-WHEN
A MAN LOVES A WOMAN: Percy Sledge-C'MON EVERYBODY:
Eddie Cochran-MANNISH BOY:Muddy Waters-AIN'T NOBODY
HOME: B.B.King-CAN'T GET ENOUGH: Bad Company-THE JO

KER: Steve Miller Band-SHOULD I STAY OR SHOULD I GO
The Clash-20TH CENTURY BOY: T.Rex-MAD ABOUT THE BOY
Dinah Washington-PIECE OF MY HEART: (Erma Franklin)
HEART ATTACK AND VINE: Screamin' Jay Hawkins

278.PAIGE Elaine - CINEMA
WEA (TEN): 2292 40511-2 (CD)   *1989*
WINDMILLS OF YOUR MIND-OUT HERE ON MY OWN-PRISONER-
SOMETIMES-MAHOGANY-UP WHERE WE BELONG-UNCHAINED MEL
ODY-BRIGHT EYES-ALFIE-MISSING-WAY WE WERE-THE ROSE

279.PAIGE Elaine - PERFORMANCE
RCA CAMDEN (BMG): 74321 44680-2(CD) -4(MC) re: 1997
1.I HAVE DREAMED *KING AND I* 2.ANYTHING GOES 3.HEART
DON'T CHANGE MY MIND 4.ANOTHER SUITCASE IN ANOTHER
HALL *EVITA* 5.THE ROSE 6.LOVE HURTS 7.WHAT'LL I DO /
WHO 8.I ONLY HAVE EYES FOR YOU 9.HE'S OUT OF MY LIF
LIFE 10.I KNOW HIM SO WELL *CHESS* 11.DON'T CRY FOR
ME ARGENTINA *EVITA* 12.MEMORY *CATS* 13. MEMORY Repr.

280.PAIGE Elaine - STAGES
WEA: 2292 40228-2 (CD) -4MC 1983
MEMORY-BE ON YOUR OWN-ANOTHER SUITCASE-SEND IN THE
CLOWNS-RUNNIN BACK FOR MORE-GOOD MORNING STARSHINE
DON'T CRY FOR ME ARGENTINA-WHAT I DID FOR LOVE-I DO
N'T KNOW HOW TO LOVE HIM-ONE NIGHT ONLY-LOSING MY
MIND-TOMORROW

281.PERSUADERS AND OTHER TOP 70'S TV THEMES - V.Artists
SEQUEL-CASTLE (Pinn): NEMCD 424 (2CD)   *1999*
CD1: 1.PERSUADERS Cyril Stapleton Orch 2.HAWAII 5-0
Victor Silvester Or 3.RETURN OF THE SAINT Saint Orc
4.INCREDIBLE HULK Acker Bilk 5.M*A*S*H*Tony Hatch O
6.PINK PANTHER Alan Tew Or 7.KOJAK Victor Silvester
8.IRONSIDE Alan Tew Orch 9.VAN DER VALK "Eye Level"
Tony Hatch Orch 10.TAXI "Angela" Bob James 11.THE
GOODIES The Goodies 12.MORECAMBE & WISE "Positive
Thinking" Jackie Trent & Tony Hatch 13. LOVE THY
NEIGHBOUR Nina Baden-Semper 14.THE ODD COUPLE Tony
Hatch Orch 15.THE FUZZ Button Down Brass 16.AGONY
Babs Fletcher 17.BACKS TO THE LAND Anne Shelton 18.
EMMERDALE FARM Tony Hatch Or 19.UPSTAIRS DOWNSTAIRS
Victor Silvester Orch 20.MR.AND MRS.Jackie Trent &
Tony Hatch 21.SOAP Acker Bilk 22.GENERAL HOSPITAL
"Girl In The White Dress" Derek Scott Orch. 23.
BACKS TO THE LAND Anne Shelton 24.OWEN MD "Sleepy
Shores" Cyril Stapleton O 25.BUDGIE "Nobody's Fool"
Cold Turkey
CD2: 1.MATCH OF THE DAY Offside 2.SPORTSNIGHT Tony
Hatch Orch 3.BEST IN FOOTBALL Tony Hatch Orch 4.
ITV EUROPEAN FOOTBALL "World At Their Feet" John
Shakespeare Orch 5.WORLD CUP ARGENTINA 1978 Ennio
Morricone Orch 6.GAME OF THE CENTURY "Argentina
Heroes (We're On Our Way)" Moon Williams 7.MISTER
MEN Acker Bilk 8.RUPERT Jackie Lee 9.SESAME STREET
Street Kids 10.CLOPPA CASTLE Rainbow Cottage 11.
HADLEIGH Tony Hatch Orch 12.ONEDIN LINE "Love Theme
from Spartacus" (Khachaturian) Cyril Stapleton Orch

13.DUCHESS OF DUKE STREET Royal Doulton Band 14.
BOUQUET OF BARBED WIRE Acker Bilk 15.SEVEN FACES OF
WOMAN "She" Russ Conway 16.CLAYHANGER Royal Doulton
Band 17.WHO PAYS THE FERRYMAN Royal Doulton Band 18
LOTUS EATERS "Ta Trena Pou Fyghan" Manos Tacticos &
His Bouzoukis 19.MACKINNON COUNTRY Iain Sutherland
Orch 20.SAILOR "Sailing" Acker Bilk 21.NEW FACES
"You're A Star" Carl Wayne 22.COLDITZ Colditz March
Alyn Ainsworth Orch 23.WORLD AT WAR Tony Hatch Orch
24.FILM 72 etc."I Wish I Knew How It Would Feel To
Be Free" Alan Tew Orc 25.CROSSROADS "Benny's Theme"
Paul Henry and Mayson Glen Orchestra
--- **PICCADILLY DANCE ORCHESTRA** - *see* COWARD, Noel
282.**PLAY SAM PLAY...AS TIME GOES BY** - Original Artists
GREAT MOVIE THEMES (Target-BMG): CD 60018 (CD) 1997
1.AS TIME GOES BY *CASABLANCA* Ingrid Bergman-Dooley
Wilson 2.I CAN'T GIVE YOU ANYTHING BUT LOVE *JAM SES
SION* Louis Armstrong 3.STORMY WEATHER Lena Horne 4.
HONG KONG BLUES *TO HAVE AND HAVE...*Hoagy Carmichael
5.FALLING IN LOVE AGAIN *BLUE ANGEL* Marlene Dietrich
6.INKAM DINKA DOO *PALOOKA* Jimmy Durante 7.OVER THE
RAINBOW *WIZARD OF OZ* Judy Garland 8.THANKS FOR THE
MEMORY *BIG BROADCAST OF 1938* Bob Hope-Shirley Ross
9.CHICA CHICA BOOM *THAT NIGHT IN RIO* Carmen Miranda
10.NIGHT AND DAY *GAY DIVORCEE* Fred Astaire 11.MOON
OF MANAKOORA *HURRICANE* Dorothy Lamour 12.TEMPTATION
GOING HOLLYWOOD Bing Crosby 13.RHUMBOOGIE *ARGENTINE
NIGHTS* Andrews Sisters 14.LOBBY NUMBERS *UP IN ARMS*
Danny Kaye 15.SONG IS YOU *TIL THE CLOUDS ROLL BY*
Johnnie Johnstone-Kathryn Grayson 16.FOR ME AND MY
GAL J.Garland-G.Kelly-G.Murphy 17.I'LL SEE YOU IN
MY DREAMS *ROSE OF WASHINGTON SQUARE* Alice Faye 18.
DINAH *BIG BROADCAST* Bing & The Mills Brothers 19.
LET YOURSELF GO *FOLLOW THE FLEET* Ginger Rogers 20.
HOORAY FOR HOLLYWOOD *HOLLYWOOD HOTEL* Var.Artists
283.**POST MIke** - **NYPD BLUE (The Best Of Mike Post)**
SILVA SCREEN (Koch): SILVAD 3511 (CD)
22 themes including: NYPD BLUE-DOOGIE HOWSER, MD-
HILL STREET BLUES-L.A.LAW-HUNTER-LAW AND ORDER-
HARDCASTLE & McCORMACK-MAGNUM, PI-QUANTUM LEAP-THE
ROCKFORD FILES-WISEGUY-TOP OF THE HILL
284.**POWELL Dick** - **THE SINGING TROUBADOUR**
GREAT MOVIE THEMES (Target-BMG): CD 60020 (CD) 1998
SONGS FROM THE FOLLOWING DICK POWELL MOVIES:
HOLLYWOOD HOTEL (1937) GOLD DIGGERS OF 1937 (1936)
THE SINGING MARINE (1937) *tracks to be confirmed*
285.**PRADO Perez** - **OUR MAN IN HAVANA**
RCA CAMDEN (BMG): 74321 58810-2 (CD) 1998
GUAGLIONE *(GUINNESS)*-CHERRY PINK AND APPLE BLOSSOM
WHITE-PATRICIA *(ROYAL MAIL)*-MAMBO NO.5 *(FELIX CAT
FOOD/GUINNESS)*-RULETERO-PEANUT VENDOR-ONE NIGHT-
MAMBO JAMBO-IN A LITTLE SPANISH TOWN-LA FARAONA-
FLIGHT OF THE BUMBLEBEE-LA BORRACHITA-MY ROBERTA-
ADIOS MI CHAPARRITA-BEAUTIFUL MARGARET-THE FREEWAY

MAMBO-MARIA BONIA-HISTOIRE DE UN AMOR-LA RUBIA-
LEYENDA MEXICANA-ROCKAMBO BABY-OK JOE CALYPSO-
ADIOS PAMPA MIA-MAMA TEACH ME TO DANCE

286.PREMIERE - Classic Soundtracks
RCA CAMDEN (Univ): 74321 66106-2 (CD)   *1999*
1.SCHINDLER'S LIST *JOHN WILLIAMS* 2.THE UNFORGIVEN
CLINT EASTWOOD 3.DANCES WITH WOLVES *JOHN BARRY* 4.
A ROOM WITH A VIEW *PUCCINI* 'O Mio Babbino Caro' 5.
THE ENGLISH PATIENT *GABRIEL YARED* 6.GODFATHER III
MASCAGNI 'Intermezzo Cavaleria Rusticana' 7.TAXI
DRIVER *BERNARD HERRMANN* 8.YOU ONLY LIVE TWICE *JOHN
BARRY* 9.THE LIVING DAYLIGHTS *BARRY/WAAKTAR/HYNDE* 10
PLATOON *SAMUEL BARBER* 'Adagio For Strings' 11.DEATH
IN VENICE *MAHLER* '5th Symphony in C.Sharp Minor' 12
FRANKIE & JOHNNY *DEBUSSY* 'Claire De Lune' 13.THE
PINK PANTHER *HENRY MANCINI* 'The Lonely Princess' 14
BRASSED OFF *RODRIGUEZ* 'En Aranjuez Con Tu Amor' 15.
A FISTFUL OF DOLLARS *ENNIO MORRICONE* 16.DEER HUNTER
STANLEY MYERS 'Cavatina' arr.JOHN WILLIAMS

287.PRESLEY Elvis - Elvis Movies (re-mastered tracks)
RCA (BMG): 74321 68241-2 (CD)   *1999*
1.GOT A LOT 'O LIVIN' TO DO 2.LOVE ME TENDER 3.
(YOU'RE SO SQUARE) BABY I DON'T CARE 4.CRAWFISH 5.
I SLIPPED I STUMBLED I FELL 6.DOIN' THE BEST I CAN
7.FLAMING STAR 8.RETURN TO SENDER 9.LOVING YOU 10.
G.I.BLUES 11.GIRLS GIRLS GIRLS 12.I NEED SOMEBODY
TO LEAN ON 13.A LITTLE LESS CONVERSATION 14.FOLLOW
THAT DREAM 15.VIVA LAS VEGAS 16.TROUBLE 17.SWING
SWING DOWN SWEET CHARIOT 18.BOSSA NOVA BABY 19.
RUBBERNECKIN 20.THEY REMIND ME TOO MUCH OF YOU

288.PRESLEY Elvis - Can't Help Falling In Love:
                    The Hollywood Hits
RCA (BMG): 0786 367873-2 (CD)   *1999*
1.JAILHOUSE ROCK 2.LOVING YOU 3.HARD HEADED WOMAN 4
TEDDY BEAR 5.KING CREOLE 6.TREAT ME NICE 7.LOVE ME
TENDER 8.ROUSTABOUT 9.WOODEN HEART 10.ROCK-A-HULA
BABY 11.FOLLOW THAT DREAM 12.KING OF THE WHOLE WIDE
WORLD 13.SUCH AN EASY QUESTION 14.RETURN TO SENDER
15.ONE BROKEN HEART FOR SALE 16.BOSSA NOVA BABY 17.
VIVA LAS VEGAS 18.KISSIN' COUSINS 19.CLEAN UP YOUR
OWN BACK YARD 20.PUPPET ON A STRING 21.SHOPPIN'
AROUND 22.CAN'T HELP FALLING IN LOVE

289.PRESLEY Elvis - ESSENTIAL ELVIS (Film Soundtracks)
RCA (BMG): 74321 57347-2 (CD) (1991) re-issue 1998
LOVE ME TENDER (2)-LET ME-POOR BOY-WE'RE GONNA MOVE
LOVING YOU (3)-PARTY-HOT DOG-TEDDY BEAR-MEAN WOMAN
BLUES-GOT A LOT O'LIVIN' TO DO (2)-LONESOME COWBOY
JAILHOUSE ROCK (2)-TREAT ME NICE-YOUNG & BEAUTIFUL
DON'T LEAVE ME NOW-I WANT TO BE FREE-BABY I DON'T
CARE-MEAN WOMAN BLUES-LOVING YOU-TREAT ME NICE

290.PRIME TIME MUSICALS - Various Artists
VARESE (Pinn): VSD 5858 (CD)   *1997*
COPACABANA *(BARRY MANILOW)* ALADDIN *(COLE PORTER)*-
ANDROCLES AND THE LION *(RICHARD RODGERS)*-THE

CANTERVILLE GHOST *(J.BOCK-HARNICK)*-ON THE FLIP SIDE
(B.BACHARACH-H.DAVID)-OUR TOWN*(S.CAHN-J.VAN HUESEN)*
HIGH TOR *(A.SCHWARTZ-M.ANDERSON)* Charles Kimbrough-
Beth Howland-Jason Graae-Gregory Jbara-Michelle Nic
astro-Christiane Noll-Jennifer Peich-Sally Mayes...

291. **PRINCE AND THE PAUPER and other Film Music**
National Philharmonic Orch.cond by Charles Gerhardt
REIVERS-JANE EYRE-LOST WEEKEND-BETWEEN TWO WORLDS-
CONSTANT NYMPH-PRINCE AND THE PAUPER-ESCAPE ME
NEVER-SPECTRE OF THE ROSE-THE MAD WOMAN OF CHAILLOT
CLEOPATRA-JULIE-WHOSE AFRAID OF VIRGINIA WOOLF-ANNE
OF A THOUSAND DAYS-HENRY V-

--- **PSYCHO: ESSENTIAL ALFRED HITCHCOCK** *see* **HITCHCOCK**

292. **QUATERMASS AND THE PIT: Film Music of Tristram CARY**
CLOUD NINE (Silva Screen): CNS 5009 *1996*
Orchestral Suites from: QUATERMASS AND THE PIT (67)
THE FLESH IS WEAK (1957) A TWIST OF SAND (1968)
SAMMY GOING SOUTH (1963) TREAD SOFTLY STRANGER (58)

293. **QUATERMASS FILM MUSIC COLLECTION**
GDI (ABK): GDICD 008 (CD) *1999*
QUATERMASS EXPERIMENT (1955)   music: JAMES BERNARD
QUATERMASS II (1957)   music: JAMES BERNARD
QUATERMASS AND THE PIT (1967) music: TRISTRAM CARY

--- **RATTRAY Mark** - *see* **WEBB Marti**

294. **REEL LOVE** - **Great Romantic Movie Themes**
RYKODISC (Vital): RCD 10742 (CD) *1999*
Films selections include: THE MISFITS *(ALEX NORTH)*-
GOODBYE AGAIN *(GEORGES AURIC)*-TWO FOR THE SEESAW
(ANDRE PREVIN) IRMA LA DOUCE *(ANDRE PREVIN)*-VIVRE
POUR VIVRE (LIVE FOR LIFE) *(FRANCIS LAI)*-BUONO SERA
MRS.CAMPBELL *(RIZ ORTOLANI)*-CHICAGO CHICAGO (aka
GAILY GAILY) *(HENRY MANCINI)* -THE HAPPY ENDING
*(MICHEL LEGRAND-*LOVE IS A FUNNY THING *(FRANCIS LAI)*
LAST TANGO IN PARIS *(GATO BARBIERI)*

--- **RELAX...** - *see* **CLASSIC FM: RELAX...**

295. **RICE Tim** - **The TIM RICE COLLECTION**
CARLTON SOUNDS: 30362 0027-2 (CD) -4 (MC) *1996*
1.I KNOW HIM SO WELL Claire Moore and Gemma Craven
2.ONE NIGHT IN BANGKOK Carl Wayne 3.RAINBOW HIGH
Marti Webb 4.A WINTER'S TALE Peter Skellern 5.
I DON'T KNOW HOW TO LOVE HIM Claire Moore 6.ON THIS
NIGHT OF A THOUSAND STARS Carl Wayne 7.CLOSE EVERY
DOOR Dave Willetts 8.EVERYTHING'S ALRIGHT Fiona Hen
dry and Paul Jones 9.ANY DREAM WILL DO Jess Conrad
10.BUENOS AIRES Marti Webb 11.ANTHEM Ensemble 12.
ANOTHER SUITCASE IN ANOTHER HALL Stephanie Lawrence
13.GETHSAMANE Dave Willetts 14.DON'T CRY FOR ME
ARGENTINA Marti Webb 15.JESUS CHRIST SUPERSTAR Carl
Wayne 16.ONE MORE ANGEL IN HEAVEN Jess Conrad 17.
I'D BE SURPRISINGLY GOOD FOR YOU MartI Webb & Carl
Wayne 18.CIRCLE OF LIFE Carl Wayne 19.A WHOLE NEW
WORLD Stephanie Lawrence and Monroe Kent III 20.
CAN YOU FEEL THE LOVE TONIGHT Peter Skellern

296.<u>RICHARD Cliff</u> - **AT THE MOVIES 1959-1974**
EMI UK: CDEMD 1096 (2CD)   *1996*
Serious Charge (1959): NO TURNING BACK-LIVING DOLL-
MAD ABOUT YOU Expresso Bongo (1959):LOVE-A VOICE IN
THE WILDERNESS*(EP version)*-THE SHRINE ON THE SECOND
FLOOR The Young Ones (1961): FRIDAY NIGHT-GOT A FUN
NY FEELING *(alternate take)*-NOTHING IS IMPOSSIBLE-
THE YOUNG ONES*(original undubbed master)*-LESSONS IN
LOVE-WHEN THE GIRL IN YOUR ARMS-WE SAY YEAH-IT'S
WONDERFUL TO BE YOUNG *(alternate take 24)*-OUTSIDER
Summer Holiday(1963) SEVEN DAYS TO A HOLIDAY-SUMMER
HOLIDAY-LET US TAKE YOU FOR A RIDE-STRANGER IN TOWN
BACHELOR BOY-A SWINGIN' AFFAIR-DANCIN' SHOES-THE
NEXT TIME-BIG NEWS Wonderful Life (1964): WONDERFUL
LIFE-A GIRL IN EVERY PORT-A LITTLE IMAGINATION *(edi
ted vers.)*-ON THE BEACH-DO YOU REMEMBER-LOOK DON'T
TOUCH *(prev.unreleased)*-IN THE STARS-WHAT'VE I GOT
TO DO-A MATTER OF MOMENTS-WONDERFUL LIFE *(alternate
take 18)* Thunderbirds Are Go (1967): SHOOTING STAR
Finders Keepers (1966): FINDERS KEEPERS-TIME DRAGS
BY-WASHERWOMAN-LA LA LA SONG-OH SENORITA *(ext.vers)*
THIS DAY-PAELLA Two A Penny (1967): TWO A PENNY-
TWIST & SHOUT-I'LL LOVE YOU FOREVER TODAY-QUESTIONS
(film version) Take Me High (1973): IT'S ONLY MONEY
MIDNIGHT BLUE-THE GAME-BRUMBURGER DUET-TAKE ME HIGH
THE ANTI BROTHERHOOD OF MAN-WINNING bonus tracks:-
YOUNG ONES *(film vers)*-LESSONS IN LOVE *ed.film vers*
BACHELOR BOY *(film v)*-SUMMER HOLIDAY *end title film*

297.<u>ROGERS Roy</u> - **The King Of The Cowboys**
ASV/LIVING ERA (SELECT): AJA 5297 (CD)   *1998*
TUMBLING TUMBLEWEEDS-THE DEVIL'S GREAT GRANDSON-
WHEN THE GOLDEN TRAIN COMES DOWN-HOLD THAT CRITTER
DOWN-HI HO SILVER-ROUND THAT COUPLE GO THROUGH AND
SWING-ALONG THE NAVAJO TRAIL-ROCK ME TO SLEEP IN MY
SADDLE-I CAN'T GO ON THIS WAY-I'M RESTLESS-MY HEART
WENT THAT A WAY-MY CHICKASHAY GAL-DANGEROUS GROUND-
MAKE BELIEVE COWBOY-ON THE OLD SPANISH TRAIL-SAN
FERNANDO VALLEY-ROLL ON TEXAS MOON-DON'T FENCE ME
IN-YELLOW ROSE OF TEXAS-HAWAIIAN COWBOY-PECOS BILL-
BLUE SHADOWS ON THE TRAIL-BETSY-HOME ON THE RANGE

298.<u>ROMANCING THE FILM</u> **Rochester Pops Or: Lalo Schifrin**
SION (Direct): SION 18210 (CD)   *1997*
1.GONE WITH THE WIND:Tara's Theme 2.WIZARD OF OZ:
Over The Rainbow 3.CASABLANCA:As Time Goes By 4.
BREAKFAST AT TIFFANY'S:Moon River 5.LAWRENCE OF
ARABIA 6.DR ZHIVAGO:Lara's Theme 7.COOL HAND LUKE:
Symphonic Sketches 8.GODFATHER:Love Theme 9.SPACE
*MEDLEY:*2001 A SPACE ODYSSEY/STAR WARS 10.DIRTY DAN
CING:I've Had The Time Of My Life" 11.*MEDLEY:*The
LITTLE MERMAID/AROUND THE WORLD IN 80 DAYS

299.<u>ROMEO AND JULIET</u> - **Royal Scottish National Orchest**
conducted by Cliff Eidelman
VARESE (Pinn): VSD 5752 (CD)   *1997*
FEAT.*MUSIC FROM* ROMEO AND JULIET-HAMLET-HENRY V-

MUCH ADO ABOUT NOTHING-RICHARD III / *COMPOSERS:-*
Sergei Prokofiev-Dimitri Shostakovich-Miklos Rosza
Patrick Doyle-Nino Rota-Alex North-Cliff Eidelman
--- **ROSE AND THE GUN** - *see* JOHNSON Laurie
*300.***ROTA Nino** - **MUSIC FOR FILM**
SONY CLASSICS: SK 63359 (CD)   *1998*
Orchestra LA SCALA conducted by Riccardo Muti
Music inc: PROVA D'ORCHESTRA (ORCHESTRA REHEARSAL)-
THE GODFATHER-THE LEOPARD-ROCCO AND HIS BROTHERS-8½
*301.***ROTA Nino** - **SYMPHONIC FELLINI Czech Symphony Orch** *
SILVA SCREEN (Koch): FILMCD 129 (CD)   *1991*
Music Of NINO ROTA For The FEDERICO FELLINI Films
LA DOLCE VITA-LA STRADA-IL BIDONE-THE WHITE SHEIKH
ROMA-SATYRICON-CASANOVA-ORCHESTRA REHEARSAL-NIGHTS
OF CABIRIA-THE CLOWNS-I VITELLONI-AMARCORD-BOCCACC
IO 70-JULIET OF THE SPIRITS * Derek Wadsworth cond
*302.***ROZSA Miklos** - **EPIC FILM MUSIC** - City Of Prague
Philharmonic Orchestra conducted by Kenneth Alwyn
SILVA SCREEN (Koch): FILMCD 170 (CD)   *1996*
Symphonic Suites and Themes from Original Scores:
GOLDEN VOYAGE OF SINBAD *Prelude/Sinbad Battles Kali
/Finale)*-KING OF KINGS *(Prelude)*-EL CID *(Overture/
Love Scene)*-SODOM AND GOMORRAH *Overture*-QUO VADIS
(Prelude/Arabesque/Romanza/Ave Caesar-KING OF KINGS
(The Lord's Prayer)-BEAU BRUMMELL *Prelude/King's Vi
sit and Farewell)*-BEN HUR *Prelude/Love Theme/Parade
Of The Charioteers)*-ALL THE BROTHERS WERE VALIANT
(Main Title/Finale)-MADAME BOVARY *(Waltz/Bonus trk)*
KING OF KINGS *(Orchestral theme version)*
*303.***SAX AT THE MOVIES** - **State Of The Heart** (Dave Lewis
sax, Taj Wyzgowski gtr) Love Themes from the Movies
VIRGIN (EMI): CDVIP 181 (CD) (re-numbered)   *1996*
1.UNCHAINED MELODY 2.LOVE IS ALL AROUND 3.SHOW ME
HEAVEN 4.BECAUSE YOU LOVED ME 5.HOW DEEP IS YOUR LO
VE 6.KISS FROM A ROSE 7.CAN YOU FEEL THE LOVE TONIG
HT 8.SOMEWHERE OUT THERE 9.EVERYTHING I DO (I DO IT
FOR YOU) 10.GLORY OF LOVE 11.THE BEST THAT YOU CAN
DO (ARTHUR'S THEME) 12.I'VE HAD THE TIME OF MY LIFE
13.UP WHERE WE BELONG 14.WHEN A MAN LOVES A WOMAN
15.MY FUNNY VALENTINE 16.1 WILL ALWAYS LOVE YOU
17.TAKE MY BREATH AWAY 18.IT MUST HAVE BEEN LOVE
19.WAITING FOR A STAR TO FALL 20.GANGSTA'S PARADISE
*304.***SCHWARZENEGGER Arnold** **SUPER HERO (themes & scores)**
EDEL-CINERAMA (Pinn): 0022232CIN (CD)   *1998*
music from:- TRUE LIES-LAST ACTION HERO-PREDATOR-
TERMINATOR-KINDERGARTEN COP-CONAN THE BARBARIAN-
TOTAL RECALL-RAW DEAL-RED SONJA-COMMANDO-CONAN THE
DESTROYER-RED HEAT-RUNNING MAN-LAST ACTION HERO-
TERMINATOR 2
*305.***SCHWARZENEGGER Arnold** - **GRAETEST FILM THEMES**
SILVA SCREEN (Koch): FILMCD (C) 164 (CD/MC)   *1995*
CONAN THE BARBARIAN/THE DESTROYER-TOTAL RECALL-THE
TERMINATOR-TERMINATOR 2-RED HEAT-RAW DEAL-COMMANDO-
JUNIOR-TWINS-KINDERGARTEN COP-PREDATOR-TRUE LIES

306.<u>SCI-FI</u> : City Of Prague Philharmonic (Paul Bateman/ Nic Raine) / Daniel Caine
SILVA SCREEN Treasury (Koch): SILVAD 3508 (CD) 1997
1:STAR WARS 2: EMPIRE STRIKES BACK 3:RETURN OF THE JEDI *(J.WILLIAMS)* 4:TOTAL RECALL *(J.GOLDSMITH)* 5: PREDATOR *(A.SILVESTRI)* 6:DARK STAR *(J.CARPENTER)* 7: STARMAN *(J.NITZSCHE)* 8:GREMLINS II *(J.GOLDSMITH)* 9: TERMINATOR II *(B.FIEDEL)* 10:THE THING *(E.MORRICONE)* 11:APOLLO 13 *(J.HORNER)* 12:STAR TREK-THE MOTION PIC TURE *(Jerry GOLDSMITH)* 13:STAR TREK-DEEP SPACE 9 / 14:STAR TREK-GENERATIONS *(D.McCARTHY)*   *tpt: 61.48*

307.<u>SCI-FI COLLECTION</u> - Various Artists
CASTLE COMM (Pinn): MACCD 368 (CD)   1998
1.2001: A SPACE ODYSSEY 2.STAR WARS 3.RETURN OF THE JEDI 4.ET: THE EXTRA-TERRESTRIAL 5.X-FILES 6.BATMAN RETURNS 7.THE EVE OF THE WAR 8.BLADE RUNNER 9.FLASH 10.STAR TREK 11.CLOSE ENCOUNTERS OF THE THIRD KIND 12.DR.WHO 13.INDEPENDANCE DAY 14.ROBOCOP 15.STAR TREK: THE NEXT GENERATION 16.THUNDERBIRDS 17.STAR TREK: DEEP SPACE NINE 18.SUPERMAN

308.<u>SCI-FI's GREATEST HITS Vol.1</u> - 'Final Frontiers'
EDEL/TVT/SCI-FI CHANN (Pinn): 004426-2ERE (CD) 1999
1.2001 A SPACE ODYSSEY 2.STAR WARS 3.EMPIRE STRIKES BACK 4.RETURN OF THE JEDI 5.STAR TREK 6.STAR TREK THE NEXT GENERATION 7.LOST IN SPACE (1965 TV) 8. LOST IN SPACE (1967 TV) 9.LOST IN SPACE (film) 10. BATTLESTAR GALACTICA 11.SPACE 1999 12.BUCK ROGERS IN THE 25TH CENTURY 13.BABYLON 5 14.THE BLACK HOLE 15.ALIEN 16.THE ABYSS 17.VOYAGE TO THE BOTTOM OF THE SEA (TV) 18.JOURNEY TO THE CENTRE OF THE EARTH 19.LAND OF THE GIANTS 20.THE PLANET OF THE APES 21. TIME TUNNEL 22.FIREBALL XL-5 23.DOCTOR WHO 24. STARGATE 25.TOTAL RECALL 26.BLADE RUNNER 27.TRON 28.STRANGE DAYS 29.VR-5 30.SPACE ABOVE AND BEYOND 31.INSIDE SPACE 32.WELCOME TO PARADOX 33.MISSION: GENESIS

309.<u>SCI-FI's GREATEST HITS Vol.2</u> - 'The Dark Side'
EDEL/TVT/SCI-FI CHANN (Pinn): 004427-2ERE (CD) 1999
1.OUTER LIMITS 2.TWILIGHT ZONE 3.ALFRED HITCHCOCK PRESENTS 4.DARK SHADOWS 5.NIGHT GALLERY 6.KOLCHAK: THE NIGHT STALKER 7.RIPLEY'S BELIEVE IT OR NOT 8. CREEPSHOW 9.TALES FROM THE DARKSIDE 10.TALES FROM THE CRYPT 11.INCREDIBLE SHRINKING MAN 12.SCANNERS 13.THE FLY 14.VIDEODROME 15.A CLOCKWORK ORANGE 16. THE OMEN 17.HALLOWEEN 18.HELLRAISER 19.SUSPIRIA 20. POLTERGEIST 21.DRACULA THE SERIES 22.FOREVER KNIGHT 23.THE HUNGER 24.12 MONKEYS 25.THE PRISONER 26. NOWHERE MAN 27.FRIDAY THE 13TH THE SERIES 28.BEYOND REALITY 29.THE ODYSSEY 30.OUTER LIMITS (film) 31. DARK CITY 32.BEETLEJUICE 33.EDWARD SCISSORHANDS 34. LABYRINTH 35.MYSTERY SCIENCE THEATER3000 36.X-FILES

310.<u>SCI-FI's GREATEST HITS Vol.3</u> - 'The Uninvited'
EDEL/TVT/SCI-FI CHANN (Pinn): 004428-2ERE (CD) 1999
1.WAR OF THE WORLDS (radio-intro) 2.DAY THE EARTH

STOOD STILL 3.IT CAME FROM OUTER SPACEE 4.WAR OF
THE WORLDS (disturbance) 5.THE INVADERS 6.WAR OF
THE WORLDS (first attack) 7.WAR OF THE WORLDS (TV)
8.V: THE SERIES 9.MARS ATTACKS! 10.INDEPENDENCE DAY
11.WAR OF THE WORLDS (gravity of the situation) 12.
CLOSE ENCOUNTERS OF THE THIRD KIND 13.E.T.THE EXTRA
TERRESTRIAL 14.STARMAN 15.ALIEN NATION (Film) 16.
ALIEN NATION (TV) 17.THE BEAST FROM 20,000 FATHOMS
18.PREDATOR 19.JAWS 20.THE CREATURE FROM THE BLACK
LAGOON 21.THEM! 22.TARANTULA 23.JURASSIC PARK 24.
GREMLINS 25.UFO 26.WAR OF THE WORLDS (end is near)
27.KILLER KLOWNS FROM OUTER SPCE 28.ATTACK OF THE
KILLER TOMATOES!

311.<u>SCI-FI's GREATEST HITS</u> Vol.4 - **Defenders Of Justice**
EDEL/TVT/SCI-FI CHANN (Pinn): 004429-2ERE (CD) 1999
1.ASTRO BOY 2.GIGANTOR 3.SPEED RACER 4.THUNDERBIRDS
5.CAPTAIN SCARLET & THE MYSTERONS 6.CAPTAIN VIDEO &
HIS VIDEO RANGERS 7.TOM CORBETT, SPACE CADETT 8.
SPACE PATROL 9.UNDERDOG 10.ATOM ANT 11.BATMAN (TV)
12.BATMAN: THE ANIMATED SERIES 13.BATMAN (Film) 14.
BATMAN RETURNS 15.SUPERMAN (Film) 16.LOIS AND CLARK
THE NEW ADVENTURES OF SUPERMAN 17.THE GREEN HORNET
18.THE AMAZING SPIDER-MAN 19.SPIDER-WOMAN 20.WONDER
WOMAN 21.THE FLASH 22.TEENAGE MUTANT NINJA TURTLES
23.MIGHTY MORPHIN POWER RANGERS 24.THE TICK 25.THE
X-MEN 26.SIX MILLION DOLLAR MAN 27.BIONIC WOMAN 28.
INCREDIBLE HULK 29.KNIGHT RIDER 30.MAX HEADROOM 31.
THE TERMINATOR 32.ROBOCOP 33.ROBOCOP:THE SERIES 34.
QUANTUM LEAP 35.ESCAPE FROM NEW YORK 36.THE ROAD
WARRIOR (MAX MAD 2) 37.MORTAL KOMBAT

312.<u>SCIENCE FICTION & FANTASY</u> **TV SoundTrek:Perry Rhoden**
VARESE (Pinn): VSD 5865 (CD)   *1998*
tracks include: BABYLON 5 / SEAQUEST / XENA WARRIOR
PRINCESS / HERCULES / LEXX THE DARK ZONE STORIES /
CAPTAIN FUTURE etc.

313.<u>SCREEN THEMES</u> - **Royal Philharmonic Orch John Scott**
VARESE (Pinn): VSD 5208   *1998*
DIE HARD-BIG-WHO FRAMED ROGER RABBIT-BEETLEJUICE-
MILAGRO BEANFIELD WAR-CROSSING DELANCEY-COCOON THE
RETURN-MADAME SOUZATSKA-CRIMINAL LAW-NIGHTMARE ON
ELM ST.4-BETRAYED-COMING TO AMERICA-MASQUERADE-DA

314.<u>SHAKEN AND STIRRED</u>: **A JAMES BOND Film Songs Collect**
produced and masterminded by DAVID ARNOLD   1997
EAST WEST (TEN): 3984 20738-2 (CD) -4 (MC)
1.DIAMONDS ARE FOREVER *DIAMONDS ARE FOREVER* David
McAlmont 2.JAMES BOND THEME *(M.Norman)* LTJ Buckem 3
NOBODY DOES IT BETTER *SPY WHO LOVED ME* Aimee Mann 4
ALL TIME HIGH *OCTOPUSSY* Pulp 5.SPACE MARCH *YOU ONLY
LIVE TWICE* Leftfield 6.LIVE AND LET DIE Chryssie
Hynde 7.MOONRAKER Shara Nelson 8.THUNDERBALL ABC 9.
FROM RUSSIA WITH LOVE Natasha Atlas 10.YOU ONLY
LIVE TWICE Candi Staton 11.ON HER MAJESTY'S SECRET
SERVICE Propellorheads 12.WE HAVE ALL THE TIME IN
THE WORLD *ON HER MAJESTY'S SECRET SERVICE* Iggy Pop

--- **SHANE: A TRIBUTE TO VICTOR YOUNG** - *see* YOUNG Victor
315. **SHOSTAKOVICH Dimitri** - The Film Album *
DECCA (UNIV): 460 792-2 (CD)   *1999*
THE COUNTERPLAN SUITE-ALONE-TALE OF THE SILLY
LITTLE MOUSE (Op.56)-HAMLET SUITE (Op.116a)-THE
GREAT CITIZEN-SOFIA PETROVSKAYA (Op.132)-PIROGOV-
THE GADFLY SUITE (Op.97a)
* Concertgebouw Orch.of Amsterdam (Richard Chailly)
316. **SHOSTAKOVICH Dimitri** - MOVIE MADNESS - Film Music
CAPRICCIO-TARGET (BMG): 10 822 (CD)   *1997*
Score extracts from USSR films incl: HAMLET (1964,
op.116) FIVE DAYS, FIVE NIGHTS (-) GOLDEN MOUNTAINS
(1931,opus 30a) THE FALL OF BERLIN (1949,opus 82)
--- **SILENCIUM: SONGS OF THE SPIRIT** - *see* HARLE John
317. **SILENCE** - Various Artists
SONY MUSIC TV: SONYTV35(CD)(MC) (2CD/MC)   *1997*
1.ADAGIO FOR STRINGS *BARBER* 2.GREENSLEEVES *VAUGHAN*
WILLIAMS 3.PIE JESU FROM REQUIEM *FAURE* 4.CONCERTO
DE ARANJUEZ *RODRIGO* 5.INTERMEZZO FROM CAVALLERIA
RUSTICANA *MASCAGNI* 6.PIANO CONCERTO NO.21 (ELVIRA
MADIGAN THEME) *MOZART* 7.NIMROD (ENIGMA VAR.) *ELGAR*
8.IN TRUTINA(CARMINA BURANA) *ORFF* 9.ADAGIO *ALBINONI*
10.CAVATINA *MYERS* 11.PAVANE *FAURE* 12.ADAGIETTO FROM
SYMPHONY NO.5 *MAHLER* 13.ACT II SCENE FROM SWAN LAKE
TCHAIKOVSKY CD2: BAILERO (CHANTS D'AUVERGNE) *CANTEL*
OUBE 2.LARGO NEW WORLD SYMPH.9 *DVORAK* 3.CANON IN D.
PACHELBEL 4.LARGO (XERXES) *HANDEL* 5.HUMMING CHORUS
(MADAM BUTTERFLY) *PUCCINI* 6.VALSE TRISTE *SIBELIUS*
7.JESU JOY OF MAN'S DESIRING *BACH* 8.CLAIR DE LUNE
DEBUSSY 9.FLUTE CONCERTO K299 (part only) *MOZART*
10.DANCE OF THE BLESSED SPIRITS (ORFEO & EURIDICE)
GLUCK 11.MORNING (PEER GYNT) *GREIG* 12.ALLELUIA
(SONG FOR ATHENA) *TAVERNER*
318. **SIMON Carly** - FILM NOIR
ARISTA (BMG): 07822 18984-2 (CD) -4 (MC)   *1997*
YOU WON'T FORGET ME-EV'RY TIME WE SAY GOODBYE-LILI
MARLENE-LAST NIGHT WHEN WE WERE YOUNG *(Duet with*
JIMMY WEBB)-SPRING WILL BE A LITTLE LATE THIS YEAR-
FILM NOIR-LAURA-I'M A FOOL TO WANT YOU-FOOLS CODA-
TWO SLEEPY PEOPLE *(Duet with JOHN TRAVOLTA)*-DON'T
SMOKE IN BED-SOMEWHERE IN THE NIGHT
319. **SIMONETTI PROJECT The:** 'Mystery Magic And Madness'
Film and other music of CLAUDIO SIMONETTI
PRESIDENT (BMG): PCOM 1137 (CD)   *1994*
PROFONDO ROSSO (Deep Red 1977)-TENEBRAE (82)-PHENOM
MENA (Creepers 84)-SUSPIRIA (77) OPERA (87) CROWS +
I'LL TAKE THE NIGHT-SEARCHING-ALBINONI IN ROCK (Ada
gio)-CARMINA BURANA's THEME-DAYS OF CONFUSION-DEMON
320. **SINATRA Frank** - SCREEN SINATRA
EMI GOLD: 493 982-2 (CD)   *1998*
FROM HERE TO ETERNITY-THREE COINS IN THE FOUNTAIN-
YOUNG AT HEART-JUST ONE OF THOSE THINGS-SOMEONE TO
WATCH OVER ME-NOT AS A STRANGER-(LOVE IS)THE TENDER
TRAP-JOHNNY CONCHO THEME (WAIT FOR ME)-ALL THE WAY-

CHICAGO-MONIQUE (KINGS GO FORTH)-THEY CAME TO CONDU
RA-TO LOVE AND BE LOVED-HIGH HOPES-ALL MY TOMORROWS
IT'S ALRIGHT WITH ME-C'EST MAGNIFIQUE-DREAM

321. SINTRA Frank - REMEMBERS THE MOVIES 1943-1946
GREAT MOVIE THEMES (Target-BMG): CD 60016 (CD) 1997
THREE LITTLE WORDS-WHERE OR WHEN-THAT OLD BLACK
MAGIC-IF I HAD MY WAY-MY IDEAL-TILL THE END OF TIME
MAKE BELIEVE-I ONLY HAVE EYES FOR YOU-EMPTY SADDLES
SOMEBODY LOVES ME-THAT'S FOR ME-IT'S BEEN A LONG LO
NG TIME-WHITE CHRISTMAS-YOU'LL NEVER KNOW-AS TIME
GOES BY-EASY TO LOVE-I'VE GOT YOU UNDER MY SKIN-
ON THE ATCHINSON TOPEKA & SANTA FE-PEOPLE WILL SAY
WE'RE IN LOVE-DON'T FENCE ME IN-WITH A SONG IN MY
HEART-A HOT TIME IN THE OLD TOWN OF BERLIN-
I'LL REMEMBER APRIL-THERE GOES THAT SONG AGAIN

322. SLICE OF PYE - Orig British Cast MUSICALS - V.Arts
DRG (New Note-Pinn): DRGCD 13114 (CD)   1996
Musicals: ANNIE-FUNNY GIRL-BAR MITZVAH BOY-BARNARDO
THE CARD-CARRY ON LONDON-CHARLIE GIRL-MR.BURKE MP-
SONGBOOK-THE TIME OF YOUR LIFE Artists include: JOE
BROWN-LISA SHANE-ROSA MICHELLE-BARRY ANGEL-GEORGE
MITCHELL SINGERS-TONY HATCH-JACKIE TRENT-WALLY WHYT
ONS VIPERS-DIANE LANGTON-SIDNEY JAMES-GEORGE FORMBY

323. SNOW Mark - The Snow Files
SONIC IMAGES (Silva Screen): SONIC 8902 (CD)   1999
X.FILES-20,2000 LEAGUES UNDER THE SEA-OLDEST LIVING
CONFEDERATE WIDOW TELLS ALL-A WOMAN SCORNED-
CONUNDRUM-MAX HEADROOM

324. SONDHEIM Stephen: A CELEBRATION AT CARNEGIE HALL
RCA VICTOR (BMG): 09026 61484-2 (2CDs) Complete
SWEENEY TODD-FOLLIES-COMPANY-FUNNY THING HAPPENED..
DICK TRACY-MERRILY WE ROLL ALONG-INTO THE WOODS-SIN
GING OUT LOUD-PACIFIC OVERTURES-ASSASSINS-SEVEN %
SOLUTION-ANYONE CAN WHISTLE-A LITTLE NIGHT MUSIC-
SUNDAY IN THE PARK.... *see also 'TURNER Geraldine'*

325. SONDHEIM Stephen: SONDHEIM TONIGHT
TER (Koch): CDTER2 1250 (2CD)   1999
A Live Recording Of The Complete London Barbican
Centre Concert, with The London Philharmonic Orch.
conducted by David Firman and Charles Prince
Artists included: MICHAEL BALL-LEN CARIOU-DAME EDNA
EVERAGE (BARRY HUMPHRIES)-MARIA FRIEDMAN-CLEO LAINE
MILLICENT MARTIN-JULIA McKENZIE-JULIA MIGENES-CLIVE
ROWE-NED SHERRIN-ELAINE STRITCH-DAVID KERNAN etc.
Songs included: COMEDY TONIGHT-NOT WHILE I'M AROUND
MORE-COMPANY-BEING ALIVE-THE BALLAD OF SWEENEY TODD
BROADWAY BABY-LOVING YOU-BEAUTIFUL GIRLS-LADIES WHO
LUNCH-SEND IN THE CLOWNS-LOSING MY MIND-I NEVER DO
ANYTHING TWICE-BARCELONA-NIGHT WALTZ-SUNDAY IN THE
PARK WITH GEORGE-ANOTHER 100 PEOPLE

326. SOUND GALLERY - Various Artists
EMI STUDIO 2: CDTWO 2001 / 7243 832280-2 (CD) 1995
OH CALCUTTA:Dave Pell Singers BLACK RITE:Mandingo-
PUNCH BOWL:Alan Parker NIGHT RIDER *(Cadbury's Milk*

Tray):Alan Hawkshaw RIVIERA AFFAIR:Neil Richardson
JET STREAM:John Gregory HALF FORGOTTEN DAYDREAMS
John Cameron JAGUAR:John Gregory LIFE OF LEISURE
Keith Mansfield GIRL IN A SPORTSCAR:Alan Hawkshaw-
YOUNG SCENE *(ITV BIG MATCH)*:Keith Mansfield
IT'S ALL AT THE CO-OP NOW *(Co-op ad)*:Alan Hawkshaw
FUNKY FEVER:Alan Moorehouse & Bond Street Parade
SHOUT ABOUT PEPSI *(Pepsi)*:Denny Wright & Hustlers
THE HEADHUNTER:Mandingo BLARNEY'S STONED *Dave Allen
Theme)*: Alan Hawkshaw THE EARTHMEN:Paddy Kingsland
I FEEL THE EARTH MOVE:John Keating THE PENTHOUSE
SUITE:Syd Dale THE SNAKE PIT:Mandingo BOOGIE JUICE
Brian Bennett THE DETECTIVES *(Two Ronnies 'Charlie
Farley & Piggy Malone'theme)*:Alan Tew JESUS CHRIST
SUPERSTAR:John Keating MUSIC TO DRIVE BY:Joe Loss

327.<u>SOUND OF HOLLYWOOD</u> Hollywood Bowl Orch John Mauceri
PHILIPS (IMS-Poly): E.446 499-2 (CD)   *1995*
SELZNICK FANFARE *Newman* GONE WITH THE WIND *Steiner*
KING KONG *Steiner* SHALL WE DANCE *George Gershwin*
MGM FANFARE *and* WIZARD OF OZ *Stothart* GIGI *and* CHEZ
MAXIMS WALTZ *Loewe* VERTIGO *Herrmann* ADVENTURES OF
ROBIN HOOD *Korngold* SOUND OF MUSIC *Rodgers* JURASSIC
PARK *and* E.T. *Williams* DANCES WITH WOLVES *Barry*
20TH CENTURY FOX FANFARE *Newman*   STAR WARS *Williams*

328.<u>SPACE AND BEYOND</u> City Of Prague Philh.Orc.Nic Raine
SILVA SCREEN (Koch): FILMX(CD)(C) 185 (2CD/MC) 1997
2001:A SPACE ODYSSEY *(68-RICHARD STRAUSS)*-SPECIES
(94-CHRISTOPHER YOUNG)-CAPRICORN ONE *(78-JERRY GOLD
SMITH)*-APOLLO 13 *(94-JAMES HORNER)*-THE RIGHT STUFF
(83-BILL CONTI)-ALIEN*(79-JERRY GOLDSMITH)*-THE BLACK
HOLE *(79-JOHN BARRY)*-COCOON *(85-JAMES HORNER)*-THE
EMPIRE STRIKES BACK *(80)* STAR WARS *(77-J.WILLIAMS)*
ENEMY MINE *(85-MAURICE JARRE)*-LIFEFORCE *(85-HENRY
MANCINI)*-CLOSE ENCOUNTERS OF THE THIRD KIND *(77-JW)*
STAR TREK I/II/IV/V/VI/DEEPSPACE NINE/NEXT GENERATI
ON/VOYAGER/GENERATIONS/HEAVY METAL *(ALEX.COURAGE/
JERRY GOLDSMITH/DENNIS McCARTHY/J.HORNER/LEONARD
ROSENMAN/CLIFF EIDELMAN)*

329.<u>SPACE AND BEYOND 2: ALIEN INVASION</u>
City Of Prague Philharmonic Orchestra (Nic Raine) &
Crouch End Festival Chorus (David Temple)
SILVA SCREEN (Koch-S.Scr): FILMX(CD)(C)190 (2CD/MC)
CD1 1.MARS ATTACKS-2.THE DAY THE EARTH STOOD STILL
3.DUNE 4.STAR TREK: Klingon Attack 5.STAR TREK:DEEP
PACE NINE 6.STAR TREK: FIRST CONTACT 7.WHEN WORLDS
COLLIDE 8.BATTLE BEYOND THE STARS 9.THE THING FROM
ANOTHER WORLD 10.TWILIGHT ZONE: THE MOVIE Suite 11.
BATTLESTAR GALACTICA 12.STARGATE CD2 1.FORBIDDEN
PLANET 2.MARS (PLANETS) 3.CONTACT 4.STARSHIP TROOPE
RS 5.PREDATOR 6.WAR OF THE WORLDS 7.EMPIRE STRIKES
BACK: Imperial March 8.SPACE: ABOVE AND BEYOND
Suite 9.V 10.STARMAN 11.INDEPENDENCE DAY

330.SPECTACULAR MUSIC FROM THE SILVER SCREEN
City Of Prague Philharmonic Orchestra
SILVA SCREEN: ACCCD 1002 (CD)   *1998*
JAMES BOND THEME-BODY HEAT-THE ROCK-WYATT EARP-
TOTAL RECALL-MAD MAX III-THE LION IN WINTER-EL CID-
CAPTAIN BLOOD-CINEMA PARADISO-THE ENGLISH PATIENT-
TARAS BULBA-MARS ATTACKS-CAPRICORN ONE
--- **SPIELBERG Steven** - *see* **GREAT MOVIE SCORES**
--- **SPIELBERG Steven** - *see* **HOLLYWOOD DIRECTORS**

331.SPIRITS OF NATURE - Various Original Artists
VIRGIN (EMI): VTCD 87 (CD) VTMC 87 (MC)   *1996*
1.YE-HA NO-HA (WISHES OF HAPPINESS AND PROSPERITY)
Sacred Spirit 2.SWEET LULLABY Deep Forest 3.LITTLE
FLUFFY CLOUDS The Orb 4.THE SUN RISING The Beloved
5.X-FILES (DJ DADO PARANORMAL ACTIVITY MIX) DJ Dado
6.RETURN TO INNOCENCE Enigma 7.STARS (MOTHER DUB)
Dubstar 8.THE WAY IT IS Chameleon 9.PLAY DEAD Bjork
& David Arnold 10.ARIA ON AIR *BRITISH AIRWAYS AD*
Malcolm McLaren 11.ADIEMUS *DELTA AIRWAYS AD* Adiemus
12.ONLY YOU *FIAT TEMPRA* Praise 13.FALLING*TWIN PEAKS*
Julee Cruise 14.MAD ALICE LANE: A GHOST STORY *LAND
ROVER DISCOVERY* Peter Lawlor 15.SENTINEL Mike Oldfi
eld 16.THEME FROM THE MISSION Ennio Morricone 17.
THE HEART ASKS PLEASURE FIRST/THE PROMISE from THE
PIANO Michael Nyman 18.FASHION SHOW II from THREE
COLOURS RED Zbigbniew Preisner 19.CHARIOTS OF FIRE
332.STALLING Carl - **CARL STALLING PROJECT** - Warner Bros
Cartoons 1936-1958 / Various Artists
WARNER USA (Silv.Screen): 926027-2 (CD)-4 (MC) 1990
Music from WB 'Merrie Melodies' cartoons: HILLBILLY
HARE-DAFFY DOC-BEANSTALK BUNNY-SPEEDY GONZALES etc.
STALLING Carl - **CARL STALLING PROJECT Vol.2** W.Bros
Cartoons 1939-1959 / Various Artists
WARNER USA (Silv.Screen): 945430-2 (CD)   *1995*
see also 'BUGS BUNNY ON BROADWAY'!
333.STAR WARS / CLOSE ENCOUNTERS - Geoff Love Orchestra
*MFP (EMI): CD(TC)MFP 6395 (CD/MC) or 7243 857687-2
(70's albums reissued now on 1 CD first time 1997)*
STAR WARS-U.F.O.-STAR TREK-BARBARELLA-SPACE 1999-
2001 A SPACE ODYSSEY-MARCH FROM THINGS TO COME-PRIN
CESS LEIA'S THEME FROM STAR WARS-DOCTOR WHO-MARS
BRINGER OF WAR FROM PLANETS SUITE-CLOSE ENCOUNTERS
OF THE THIRD KIND-LOGAN'S RUN-THE TIME MACHINE-MAIN
TITLE & 'CANTINA BAND' FROM STAR WARS-BLAKE'S 7-
THEMES FROM THE OMEGA MAN
334.STAR WARS AND MORE - Various Artists
EDEL (Pinn): 004787-2ERE (CD)   *1999*
1.STAR WARS THEME 2.IMPERIAL MARCH *EMPIRE STRIKES
BACK* 3.FOREST BATTLE *RETURN OF THE JEDI* 4.HANS SOLO
& PRINCESS *EMPIRE STRIKES BACK* 5.STAR TREK: DEEP
SPACE NINE 6.STAR TREK IV 7.JURASSIC PARK 8.COCOON
9.INVASION FROM MARS 10.TOTAL RECALL 11.E.T.12.
METEOR 13.SUPERMAN 14.V THE SERIES 15.STAR TREK THE

NEXT GENERATION 17.STAR TREK II 18.STAR TREK VI 19.
STAR TREK THE MOTION PICTURE 20.BACK TO T.FUTURE 3

335.**STAR WARS TRILOGY Orig Soundtrack Anthology**   *1994*
ARISTA (BMG): 07822 11012-2 (4CD box set) FEATURING
'Star Wars'/'The Empire Strikes Back' + previously
unavailable expanded score 'Return Of The Jedi' and
special outtakes + unreleased mus + 50 page booklet

336.**STEINER Max Flame And The Arrow: Classic Film Music**
City Of Prague Philharmonic Orch (Kenneth Alwyn)
SCANNAN FILM (S.Screen-Koch): SFC 1502 (CD)   1998
1.SPENCER'S MOUNTAIN (1963) 2.THE DARK AT THE TOP
OF THE STAIRS (1960) 3.MILDRED PIERCE (1945) 4.ICE
PALACE (1960) 5.LIFE WITH FATHER (47) 6.NOW VOYAGER
(1942) 7.THE FBI STORY (1959) 8.SERGEANT YORK(1941)
9.HANGING TREE (1959) 10.PARRISH (1961) 11.JOHNNY
BELINDA (1948) 12.THE FLAME AND THE ARROW (1950)

337.**STONEHAM Harry High Wide & Hammond/Hits The Highway**
EMI Studio 2: 495 618-2 (CD)   CD reissues 1998
CD1 CARIOCA-COFFEE SONG-BRAZIL-YOU ARE THE SUNSHINE
OF MY LIFE-GOLDEN LADY-MY CHERIE AMOUR-OH BABE WHAT
WOULD YOU SAY-YOU WON'T FIND ANOTHER FOOL LIKE ME-
SPANISH FLEA-BEAN BAG *(IT'S A KNOCKOUT)*-BRASILIA-
CAN'T TAKE MY EYES OFF YOU-HAPPY HEART-LILY LA LUNE
WHAT DO I DO-RA TA TA-TIE A YELLOW RIBBON ROUND THE
OLD OAK TREE-SAY HAS ANYBODY SEEN MY MY SWEET GYPSY
ROSE-VADO VIA-FIRE AND RAIN-24 HOURS FROM TULSA-
ALWAYS SOMETHING THERE TO REMIND ME-HELP YOURSELF-I
COULDN'T LIVE WITHOUT YOURLOVE-OTHER MAN'S GRASS IS
ALWAYS GREENER-DON'T SLEEP IN THE SUBWAY-AFRIKAAN
BEAT-WIMOWEH-A SWINGIN' SAFARI-PREPARE YE THE WAY
OF THE LORD-DAY BY DAY CD2: DELICADO-MANANA IS SOON
ENOUGH FOR ME-SOUTH AMERICAN WAY-I LOVE YOU BECAUSE
WELCOME TO MY WORLD-BIG SPENDER-PINK PANTHER THEME-
THE STRIPPER-ACAPULCO 1922-TIJUANA TAXI-SO WHAT'S
NEW-FOR ALL WE KNOW *(LOVERS AND OTHER STRANGERS)*-
ON DAYS LIKE THESE *ITALIAN JOB)*-THOSE WERE THE DAYS
CASATSCHOK-TROIKA-LIMON LIMONERO-DANCING IN THE SUN
I WILL WAIT FOR YOU/WATCH WHAT HAPPENS *(UMBRELLAS
OF CHERBOURG)*-AQUARIUS *(HAIR)*-FREEDOM COME FREEDOM
GO-QUIET VILLAGE-THE MOGUL THEME *(TROUBLESHOOTERS)*-
I SPY-THE AVENGERS

--- **SUNSET BOULEVARD** - *see* **WAXMAN Franz**

338.**SWASHBUCKLERS** - City Of Prague Philhar.Paul Bateman
SILVA SCREEN (Koch): FILMXCD 188 (2CD)   1997
CD1: Suites & themes 1.CAPTAIN BLOOD *(E.W.KORNGOLD)*
2.PRIVATE LIVES OF ELIZABETH & ESSEX *(E.W.KORNGOLD)*
3.HOOK *(J.WILLIAMS)* 4.THE CRIMSON PIRATE *(W.ALWYN)*
5.WILLOW *(J.HORNER)* 6.ROBIN HOOD *(G.BURGON)* 7.ROBIN
HOOD PRINCE OF THIEVES *(M.KAMEN)* 8.ROBIN AND MARIAN
(J.BARRY) 9/10.ADVENTURES OF ROBIN HOOD *(KORNGOLD)*
CD2: Suites & themes 1.THE SEA HAWK *(E.W.KORNGOLD)*
2.MARK OF ZORRO *(A.NEWMAN-H.FRIEDHOFER)* 3/4/5/6 THE
DUELLISTS *(H.BLAKE)* 7.THE BUCCANEER*(E.BERNSTEIN)* 8.
ADVENTURES OF DON JUAN *(M.STEINER)* 9.MONTY PYTHON'S

THE MEANING OF LIFE *(J.DUPREZ)* 10.SEVENTH VOYAGE OF
SINBAD *(B.HERRMANN)* 11.GOLDEN VOYAGE OF SINBAD *(M.
ROZSA)* 12.SWORDSMAN OF SIENNA *(M.NASCIMBENE)* 13.
CUTTHROAT ISLAND *(J.DEBNEY)*

339.<u>SYNTHESIZER HITS</u> - Various Artists
HALLMARK (CHE-Technicolor): 30106-2 (CD)   *1998*
EVE OF THE WAR-THEME FROM TUBULAR BELLS-THEME FROM
ANTARCTICA-EQUINOXE PT.5-THE MODEL-CHARIOTS OF FIRE
MAGNETIC FIELDS PT.2-MAGIC FLY-POPCORN-MIAMI VICE-
PULSTAR-OXYGENE PT.4-AXEL F-THE CHASE FROM MIDNIGHT
EXPRESS-PEPPERBOX-CROCKETT'S THEME-MAID OF ORLEANS
(JOAN OF ARC)-AUTOBAHN

340.<u>SYNTRANCE</u>: Ambient Synth Vs. Trance Chill Out Vol.1
HALLMARK (CHE): 31169-2 (CD) 31169-4 (MC)   *1999*
1.THE OVERTURE 2.MAGIC FLY 3.TO FRANCE 4.ROTATIONS
LOGIC 5.BILITIS 6.MOUNTAIN DUST Pt.2 7.AXEL F 8.
THAT'S RIGHT 9.SEPTEMBER 10.AQUA MINERALE Part 1.
11.FIRST APPROACH 12.ECHOES OF MELODIES 13.CHASE 14
TWIN PEAKS 15.4TH RENDEZ-VOUS 16.DANCES WITH WOLVES

341.<u>TAKE A BREAK!</u> - Various Artists
COLUMBIA (Ten): 494 464-2 (CD) -4 (MC)   *1999*
1.MUSIC TO WATCH GIRLS BY Andy Williams *FIAT PUNTO*
2.PUT YOU TOGETHER AGAIN Hot Chocolate *CADBURY'S HC*
3.DOWNTOWN Petula Clark *ROVER* 4.ON THE STREET WHERE
YOU LIVE Nat King Cole *QUALITY STREET* 5.WHAT A DIFF
ERENCE A DAY MADE Dinah Washington *CROWN PAINTS* 6.
PERHAPS PERHAPS PERHAPS Doris Day *CANDEREL* 7.I CAN
HELP Billy Swan *BT* 8.CALL ME Chris Montez *BT* 9.IF I
HAD A HAMMER Trini Lopez*BARCLAYCARD* 10.SHE'S A LADY
Tom Jones *WEETABIX* 11.JUMP JIVE & WAIL Louis Prima
GAP 12.DON'T FENCE ME IN Bing Crosby & Andrews Sist
ers *CENTERPARCS* 13.YOU DO SOMETHING TO MEAlma Cogan
GALAXY 14.CAN'T SMILE WITHOUT YOU Lena Fiagbe *BT* 15
SHE'S NOT THERESantana *KFC* 16.WALK LIKE AN EGYPTIAN
Bangles *KINDER EGGS* 17.WALKING ON SUNSHINE Katrina
& The Waves *SHREDDED WHEAT* 18.THAT LADY Isley Bros.
KFC 19.LOLA Kinks *WEETABIX* 20.DON'T STOP MOVIN'
Livin' Joy *TAKE A BREAK*

342.<u>TASTE OF MUSIC, A</u> - Music from BBC TV Programmes:-
Rick Stein's Taste Of The Sea / Antonio Carlucci's
Italian Feast / Far Flung Floyd / Floyd On Italy /
Floyd on Africa. performed by CROCODILE MUSIC 1997
BBC-VOYAGER (Pinn): V.1021 (CD) V/1022 (MC)

343.<u>TATI Jacques</u> - Music From The Films Of Jacques TATI
POLYGRAM Fra (Discovery): 836 983-2 (CD) reiss 1995
1.JOUR DE FETE (1948) Mus: JEAN YATOVE 2.MON ONCLE
(1956) Mus: ALAIN ROMAINS 3. MONSIEUR HULOT'S HOLID
AY (1953) Mus: ALAIN ROMAINS-FRANCK BARCELLINI

344.<u>TEEVEE DANCE</u> - Royal Philharmonic & Mark Ayres with
11 Classic TV Themes Re-mixed by Rod Gammons
SILVA SCREEN (Koch-S.Screen): TVPMCD 406 (CD)   *1998*
THE X FILES-THE AVENGERS-THE PERSUADERS-HAWAII 5-0
DANGER MAN-DOCTOR WHO-THE PRISONER-IRONSIDE-MISSION
IMPOSSIBLE-PETER GUNN-THE SAINT etc.

345.<u>**TELEVISION'S GREATEST HITS 1**</u> - 65 Orig TV Themes
TVT-EDEL/CINERAMA (Pinn): 0022702CIN (CD) reiss 96
CAPTAIN KANGAROO-LITTLE RASCALS-FLINSTONES-WOODY WO
ODPECKER SHOW-BUGS BUNNY-CASPER THE FRIENDLY GHOST-
FELIX THE CAT-POPEYE-YOGI BEAR-MAGILLA GORILLA-TOP
CAT-JETSONS-FIREBALL XL5-HOWDY DOODY-BEVERLY HILLBI
LLIES-PETTICOAT JUNCTION-GREEN ACRES-MR.ED-MUNSTERS
ADDAMS FAMILY-MY THREE SONS-DONNA REEDSHOW-LEAVE IT
TO BEAVER-DENNIS THE MENACE-DOBIE GILLIS-PATTY DUKE
SHOW-DICK VAN DYKE SHOW-GILLIGAN'S ISLAND-McHALE'S
NAVY-I DREAM OF JEANNIE-I LOVE LUCY-ANDY GRIFFITH
SHOW-STAR TREK-LOST IN SPACE-TWILIGHT ZONE-SUPERMAN
ALFRED HITCHCOCK PRESENTS-BATMAN-FLIPPER-RIFLEMAN-
COMBAT-BONANZA-BRANDED-F.TROOP-RIN TIN TIN-WILDWILD
WEST-DANIEL BOONE-LONE RANGER-HAPPY TRAILS-MISSION
IMPOSSIBLE-MAN FROM UNCLE-GET SMART-SECRET AGENTMAN
DRAGNET-PERRY MASON-ADAM 12-FBI-HAWAII 50-77 SUNSET
STRIP-SURFSIDE 6-IRONSIDE-MANNIX-MOD SQUAD-TONIGHT

346.<u>**TELEVISION'S GREATEST HITS 2**</u> - 65 Orig TV Themes
TVT-EDEL/CINERAMA (Pinn): 0022712CIN (CD) reiss 96
3 STOOGES-MERRIE MELODIES-ROCKY & BULLWINKLE-HUCKLE
BERRY HOUND-MIGHTY MOUSE-COURAGEOUS CAT & MINUTE MO
USE-PINK PANTHER-ROAD RUNNER-GEORGE OF THE JUNGLE-
JONNY QUEST-SPIDERMAN-UNDERDOG-LOONEY TUNES-PEANUTS
THEME-MISTER ROGER'S NEIGHBOURHOOD-ODD COUPLE-COURT
SHIP OF EDDIE'S FATHER-MARY TYLER MOORE-GIDGET-THAT
GIRL-BEWITCHED-LOVE AMERICAN STYLE-HONEYMOONERS-THE
MONKEES-I MARRIED JOAN-BRADY BUNCH-PARTRIDGE FAMILY
MY MOTHER THE CAR-CAR 54 WHERE ARE YOU-IT'S ABOUT
TIME-MY FAVOURITE MARTIAN-JEOPARDY-HOGAN'S HEROES-
GOMER PYLE-RAT PATROL-TWELVE O'CLOCK HIGH-TIME TUNN
EL-VOYAGE TO THE BOTTOM OF THE SEA-SEA HUNT-DAKTARI
TARZAN-ADVENTURES OF ROBIN HOOD-RAWHIDE-BAT MASTERS
ON-MAVERICK-WAGON TRAIN-HAVE GUN WILL TRAVEL-REBEL-
THE VIRGINIAN-PETER GUNN-ROUTE 66-ISPY-THE AVENGERS
THE SAINT-HAWAIIAN EYE-GREEN HORNET-OUTER LIMITS-
DARK SHADOWS-BEN CASEY-MEDICAL CENTER-MYSTERY MOVIE
ABC'S WIDE WORLD OF SPORTS-JACKIE GLEASON-SMOTHERS
BROTHERS COMEDY HOUR-MONTY PYTHON'S FLYING CIRCUS

347.<u>**TELEVISION'S GREATEST HITS 3**</u> - 70's and 80's
TVT-EDEL/CINERAMA (Pinn): 0022722CIN (CD) reiss 97
SESAME STREET-MUPPET SHOW-ALVIN SHOW-SPEED RACER-MR
MAGOO-INSPECTOR GADGET-THE SMURFS-DASTARDLY& MUTLEY
SCOOBY DOO-FAT ALBERT & CROSBY KIDS-ARCHIES-JOSIE &
PUSSYCATS-DUDLEY DORIGHT-FRACTURED FAIRY TALES-BOB
NEWHART SHOW-CHEERS-GREATEST AMERICAN HERO-WELCOME
BACK KOTTER-ROOM 222-WKRP IN CINCINNATI-TAXI-BARNEY
MILLER-THREE'S COMPANY-HAPPY DAYS-LAVERNE & SHIRLEY
FACTS OF LIFE-GOOD TIMES-ONE DAY AT A TIME-GIMME A
BREAK-MAUDE-JEFFERSONS-ALL INTHE FAMILY-SANFORD AND
SON-DALLAS-DYNASTY-KNOTS LANDING-L.A.LAW-MARCUS WEL
BY MD-ST.ELSEWHERE-MASH-WALTONS-LITTLE HOUSE ON THE
PRAIRIE-HART TO HART-CHARLIE'S ANGELS-WONDER WOMAN-
LOVE BOAT-AMERICAN BANDSTAND-SOLID GOLD-ENTERTAINME

NT TONIGHT-MIAMI VICE-SWAT-BARETTA-STREETS OF SAN
FRANCISCO-BARNABY JONES-STARSKY & HUTCH-ROOKIES-KOJ
AK-A.TEAM-NAME O.T.GAME-QUINCY-HILL ST.BLUES-SIMON
& SIMON-MAGNUM-ROCKFORD FILES-SATURDAY NIGHT LIVE

348. **TELEVISION'S GREATEST HITS 4** Black & White Classics
TVT-EDEL/CINERAMA (Pinn): 0022732CIN (CD) 1997
ASTRO BOY-ROGER RAMJET-MIGHTY HERCULES-GUMBY SHOW-
BEANY AND CECIL SHOW-TENNESSEE TUXEDO-QUICK DRAW
McGRAW-WALLY GATOR-KING LEONARDO AND SHORT SUBJECTS
BIG WORLD OF LITTLE ADAM-KUKLA FRAN AND OLLIE-SOUPY
SALES SHOW-CAPTAIN MIDNIGHT-MAKE ROOM FOR DADDY-
FATHER KNOWS BEST-MY LITTLE MARGIE-ADVENTURES OF
OZZIE AND HARRIET-HAZEL-OUR MISS BROOKS-KAREN-THE
REAL McCOYS-LASSIE-LIFE AND LEGEND OF WYATT EARP-
GUNSMOKE-THE LAWMAN-26 MEN-COLT 45-CHEYENNE-BRONCO
LEGEND OF JESSE JAMES-HOPALONG CASSIDY-EVERGLADES-
ADVENTURES IN PARADISE-DR.KILDARE-MEDIC-BURKE'S LAW
HIGHWAY PATROL-M.SQUAD-DETECTIVES-UNTOUCHABLES-THE
FUGITIVE-CHECKMATE-TIGHTROPE-BOURBON STREET BEAT-
PETE KELLY'S BLUES-ASPHALT JUNGLE-MR.BROADWAY-NAKED
CITY-TWENTY FIRST CENTURY-FRENCH CHEF-CANDID CAMERA
YOU BET YOUR LIFE-AMOS 'N' ANDY-ABBOTT & COSTELLO-
LAUREL & HARDY-LAWRENCE WELK SHOW-TED MACK'S ORIG.
AM.HOUR-MISS AMERICA-RED SKELTON SHOW-BOB HOPE SHOW

349. **TELEVISION'S GREATEST HITS 5** - In Living Color
TVT-EDEL/CINERAMA (Pinn): 0022742CIN (CD) 1997
STINGRAY-THUNDERBIRDS-GIGANTOR-COOL McCOOL-GO GO
GOPHERS-WORLD OF COMMANDER McBRAGG-SECRET SQUIRREL-
THE ATOM ANT SHOW-WACKY RACES-HONG KONG PHOOEY-
SUPERCHICKEN-TOM SLICK RACER-H.R.PUFNSTUF-LAND OF
THE LOST-SIGMUND AND THE SEA MONSTERS-BANANA SPLITS
PLEASE DON'T EAT THE DAISIES-THE GHOST AND MRS.MUIR
NANNY AND THE PROFESSOR-HERE COME THE BRIDES-THE
FLYING NUN-FAMILY AFFAIR-DATING GAME-NEWLYWED GAME-
LET'S MAKE A DEAL-ALL MY CHILDREN-GENERAL HOSPITAL-
PEYTON PLACE-MARY HARTMAN MARY HARTMAN-GENTLE BEN-
SKIPPY THE BUSH KANGAROO-LIFE AND TIMES OF GRIZZLY
ADAMS-HIGH CHAPARRAL-THE BIG VALLEY-CIMARRON STRIP
LAREDO-THE MEN FROM SHILOH-IT TAKES A THIEF-THE
MAGICIAN-SWITCH-THE FELONY SQUAD-POLICE WOMAN-MEN-
CANNON-JUDD FOR THE DEFENSE-EMERGENCY!-POLICE STORY
SIX MILLION DOLLAR MAN-BIONIC WOMAN-THE GIRL FROM
U.N.C.L.E.-NIGHT GALLERY-KOLCHAK: THE NIGHT STALKER
INVADERS-LAND OF T.GIANTS-LOST IN SPACE-MASTERPIECE
THEATRE-WHERE THE ACTION IS-ROWAN & MARTIN'S LAUGH
IN-THE DEAN MARTIN SHOW-THE CAROL BURNETT SHOW

350. **TELEVISION'S GREATEST HITS 6** - Remote Control
TVT-EDEL/CINERAMA (Pinn): 0022752CIN (CD) 1997
FISH-NIGHT COURT-WHAT'S HAPPENING-DIFFERENT STROKES
MR.BELVEDERE-GROWING PAINS-CHARLES IN CHARGE-SILVER
SPOONS-WEBSTER-TOO CLOSE FOR COMFORT-WHO'S THE BOSS
PERFECT STRANGERS-ALICE-IT'S A LIVING-ANGIE-227-THE
GOLDEN GIRLS-ALF-MORK AND MINDY-POLICE SQUAD-BENSON
MOONLIGHTING-SOAP-BENNY HILL SHOW-THE YOUNG ONES-

THE PEOPLE'S COURT-FAMILY FEUD-THE PRICE IS RIGHT-
SISKEL & EBERT-MONDAY NIGHT FOOTBALL-LIFESTYLES OF
THE RICH & FAMOUS-FAME-PAPER CHASE-FANTASY ISLAND-
FALCON CREST-THE COLBY'S-HIGHWAY TO HEAVEN-DUKES OF
HAZZARD-B.J.& THE BEAR-THE FALL GUY-JAMES AT 15-
EIGHT IS ENOUGH-BAA BAA BLACK SHEEP-TRAPPER JOHN MD
CHIPS-VEGAS-MATT HOUSTON-CAGNEY & LACEY-T.J.HOOKER-
HARDCASTLE & McCORMICK-HUNTER-MACGYVER-KNIGHT RIDER
AIRWOLF-THE INCREDIBLE HULK-V THE SERIES-THE NEW
TWILIGHT ZONE-DOCTOR WHO-MYSTERY-HARDY BOYS & NANCY
DREW MYSTERIES-ROOTS-VIETNAM A TELEVISION HISTORY

351.<u>**TELEVISION'S GREATEST HITS 7**</u> Cable Ready 80s & 90s
TVT-EDEL/CINERAMA (Pinn): 0022762CIN (CD)   1997
THE SIMPSONS-REN AND STIMPY-BROTHERS GRUNT-DUCKMAN-
ADVENTURES OF PETE AND PETE-SPACE GHOST COAST TO
COAST-CLARISSA EXPLAINS IT ALL-BARNEY AND FRIENDS-
WHERE IN THE WORLD IS CARMEN SANDIEGO-SAVED BY THE
BELL-MAJOR DAD-MY TWO DADS-BLOSSOM-FULL HOUSE-EMPTY
NEST-FAMILY MATTERS-COSBY SHOW-DIFFERENT WORLD-ROC-
FRESH PRINCE OF BEL AIR-HOME IMPROVEMENT-ROSEANNE-
SEINFELD-MAD ABOUT YOU-IT'S GARRY SHANDLING'S SHOW-
JOHN LARROQUETTE SHOW-HUDSON STREET-THE SINGLE GUY-
DAVIS RULES-MURPHY BROWN-THE NANNY-DESIGNING WOMEN-
DOOGIE HOWSER MD-WINGS-ANYTHING BUT LOVE-SISTERS-
EVENING SHADE-THE DAYS AND NIGHTS OF MOLLY DODD-
I'LL FLY AWAY-THIRTYSOMETHING-MY SO CALLED LIFE-
BEVERLY HILLS 90210-MELROSE PLACE-HEIGHTS-21 JUMP
STREET-IN THE HEAT OF THE NIGHT-MIDNIGHT CALLER-
AMERICA'S MOST WANTED-UNSOLVED MYSTERIES-SLEDGE
HAMMER-THE EQUALIZER-N.Y.P.D.BLUE-LAW AND ORDER-
TWIN PEAKS-STAR TREK NEXT GENERATION-LOIS AND CLARK
NEW ADVENTURES OF SUPERMAN-ALIEN NATION-TALES FROM
THE CRYPT-QUANTUM LEAP-MAX HEADROOM-LIQUID
TELEVISION-HBO FEATURES-TRACEY ULLMAN SHOW-
KIDS IN THE HALL-LATE SHOW WITH DAVID LETTERMAN

352.<u>**TEMPLE Shirley** - **On The Good Ship Lollipop**</u>
PRESIDENT (BMG): PLCD 541 (CD)   1995
ON THE GOOD SHIP LOLLIPOP *(from BRIGHT EYES 1934)*
BABY TAKE A BOW *(STAND UP AND CHEER 1934)* WHEN I'M
WITH YOU/BUT DEFINATELY/OH MY GOODNESS *(POOR LITTLE
RICH GIRL 1936)* LAUGH YOU SON OF A GUN *(LITTLE MISS
MARKER 1934)* AT THE CODFISH BALL/THE RIGHT SOMEBODY
TO LOVE/EARLY BIRD *(CAPTAIN JANUARY 1936)* LOVE'S
YOUNG DREAM/THE TOY TRUMPET *(THE LITTLE COLONEL 36)*
ON ACCOUNT-A I LOVE YOU *(BABY TAKE A BOW 1934)* GOOD
NIGHT MY LOVE/THAT'S WHAT I WANT FOR CHRISTMAS/YOU
GOTTA S.M.I.L.E.TO BE H.A.P.P.Y. *(STOWAWAY 1936)*
IN OUR LITTLE WOODEN SHOES *(HEIDI 37)* PICTURE ME WI
THOUT YOU/GET ON BOARD LI'L CHILDREN/HE WAS A DANDY
HEY WHAT DID THE BLUE JAY SAY/DIXIE-ANNA *(DIMPLES
1936)* ANIMAL CRACKERS IN MY SOUP/WHEN I GROW UP
(CURLY TOP 1935) BELIEVE ME IF ALL THOSE ENDEARING
YOUNG CHARMS/POLLY WOLLY DOODLE *(LITTLEST REBEL 35)*
THE WORLD OWES ME A LIVING *(NOW AND FOREVER 1934)*

*353.*__TEST CARD CLASSICS__: The Girl The Doll The Music
FLYBACK-CHANDOS (Chandos): FBCD 2000 (CD)   1996
1.INTRODUCTION 2.ROYAL DAFFODIL *(Gordon Langford)*
Stuttgart Studio Orch 3.RIGA ROAD *(R.Egin-Mike Run)*
Westway Novelty Ensemble 4.ANGRY *(D.Mecum-J.Cassard*
H.Brunies) Oscar Brandenburg Or 5.CAPABILITY BROWN
(Ernest Tomlinson) Stuttgart Studio Orch 6.WALTZ IN
JAZZTIME *(Syd Dale)* Cavendish Ten 7.BELLA SAMBA *(J.*
Finten-R.Von Kessler) Benito Gonzales Latin Sound
8.HOLIDAY HIGHWAYMAN *(Brian Couzens)* Stuttgart Stud
io Orch 9.CORDOBA *(W.Tautz)* Orchest.Heinz Kiessling
10.MY GUY'S COME BACK *M.Powell-R.McKinley-B.Goodman*
Oscar Brandenburg Orch 11.THE LARK IN THE CLEAR AIR
(trad.arr Gordon Langford) Langford Orch 12.PANDORA
(Ray Davies) New Dance Orch 13.FIRECRACKER *(Frank*
Chacksfield) Ferdnand Terby Or 14.HEBRIDEAN HOEDOWN
*(Gordon Langford)*Stuttgart Studio Orch 15.HIGH LIFE
(Otto Sieben) Gerhard Narholz Orch 16.SAMBA FIESTA
(Heinz Kiessling) Orch.Heinz Kiessling 17.STATELY
OCCASION *(Ernest Tomlinson)* Stuttgart Studio Orches
18.CHELSEA CHICK *(Johnny Scott)* Mr.Popcorn's Band
19.GREENLAND SLEIGH DOGS (ALASKA) *(Roger)* Roger Rog
er Orch 20.THESE FOOLISH THINGS *(Jack Strachey)* Cav
endish Ten 21.MARCH FROM THE COLOUR SUITE *(Gordon*
Langford) Stuttgart Studio Orch 22.LONG HOT SUMMER
(Roger) Ensemble Roger Roger) 23.GOING PLACES *(D.Go*
ld-E.Ponticelli-G.Rees) Oscar Brandenburg 24.440Hz
*354.*__TEST CARD CLASSICS 2__: Big Band Width - Various Arts
FLYBACK-CHANDOS (Chandos): FBCD 2001 (CD)   1997
1.FING AIN'T WOT THEY USED T'BE *(Lionel Bart)* Oscar
Brandenburg Orch 2.SMILING FORTUNE *(Ronald Sekura)*
Orchestra Alexander Martin 3.THE STORY OF MY LOVE
*(Peter Voelkener)*George Winters Orch 4.LUCKY BOUNCE
(Norman Giedhill) Skymasters 5.HERE IN A SMOKY ROOM
*(Brian Fahey)*Otto Keller Band 6.WALTZ EXPRESS *(Hans*
Ehrlinger) Orch.Joe Scott 7.SLINKY *Trevor Lyttleton*
*tleton)*Brasshoppers 8.CARRY ME BACK TO OLD VIRGINNY
(Hans Conzelmann-Delle Haensch) Delle Haensch Band
9.BEAT-IN *(Pedro Gonez-Walter Waal)* Frank Pleyer &
His Orch 10.ALAMO *(Henry Mcintire-Olaf Norstad)* Orc
Joe Palmer 11.SMALL TOWN *(William Gardner)* William
Gardner Orch 12.TAKE OFF *(Erich Schneider Reinerez)*
Henry Monza Orch 13.MEET ME ON THE BRIDGE *(Brian*
Fahey) Skymasters 14.HAPPY WALK *(Ralph Heninger)*
Frank Pleyer & His Orch 15.CHARLESTON TIME *(Jimmy*
Thanner-Karl Hans Ahl) Jimmy Thanner Orch 16.APRON
STRINGS *(Ernest Ponticelli)* Hans Hatter Orch 17.
SCOTCH BROTH *(Ernest Ponticelli-Gordon Rees-Neil*
Richardson) Oscar Brandenburg Orch 18.TELE-VISION
(Hans.Conzelmann-Delle Haensch) Delle Haensch Band
19.CONCERTO GROSSO 67 *(Ernst Quelle-Rico Mares)*
Eric Landy Orch 20.HIGH BALL *(Bill Geldard)* Otto
Keller Band 21.HALLELUJAH HONEY (aka MICHAEL ROW
THE BOAT ASHORE) *(Trad.arr Frank Valdor)* Orchest

Frank Valdor 22.SOHO SWING *(Charles Kalman)* Walt
Peters & His Orch 23.DAISY *(H.Conzelmann-D.Haensch)*
Delle Haensch Band 24.WALKING ON THE SHORE *(Paul
Termi)* Orch.Franco Taomina 25.HELLO LISSY *(Fred Spa
nnuth)* Orch.Joe Palmer 26.CRAIG HILL SURPRISE *Harry
Leader-Red Budtree)* Otto Keller Band 27.POST HASTE
(Trevor Lyttleton) Brasshoppers 28.SWINGING AFFAIR
(E.Ponticelli-Gordon Rees) Oscar Brandenburg Orch.
29.JEFF'S SPECIAL *(Jeff Hasky)* Orch.Jeff Hasky 30.
INDIAN BOOTS *(Horst Bredow)* George Winters Orchest
355.THAT'S ENTERTAINMENT - Best Of MGM Musicals V.Arts
    EMI PREMIER: CDODEON 21 (CD)   *1996*
    THAT'S ENTERTAINMENT-GET HAPPY-FROM THIS MOMOENT ON
    OVER THE RAINBOW-OL' MAN RIVER-SINGIN' IN THE RAIN-
    TROLLEY SONG-VARSITY DRAG-EASTER PARADE-ALL OF YOU-
    ON THE ATCHINSON TOPEKA AND T.SANTA FE-HONEYSUCKLE
    ROSE-I LIKE MYSELF-HALLELUJAH-THERE'S NO BUSINESS
    LIKE SHOW BUSINESS *Original MGM -S/T- Recordings*
356.THEMES AND INSTRUMENTALS - Various Artists
    RCA INT (BMG): RCA(CD)(MC) 220 (2CD/MC)   *1997*
    CD1 1:ALBATROSS Fleetwood Mac 2:BABY ELEPHANT WALK
    Henry Mancini 3:GOOD THE BAD AND THE UGLY Hugo Mont
    enegro 4:PETER GUNNHenry Mancini 5:JAMES BOND THEME
    John Barry 6:STRANGER ON THE SHORE Acker Bilk 7:THE
    ENTERTAINERMarvin Hamlisch 8:LIGHT FLIGHT Pentangle
    9:HARRY'S GAME Clannad 10:ROCKET TO THE MOON Jim Br
    ickman 11:INSPECTOR MORSE 12:CROCKETT'S THEME 13:
    MIAMI VICE Jan Hammer 14:SCARBOROUGH FAYRE Intune
    15:LA SERENISSIMA (VENICE IN PERIL) Rondo Veneziano
    CD2 1:MON AMOR Frank Thore 2:PETITE FLEUR Chris Bar
    ber & Monty Sunshine 3:THEME FROM A SUMMER PLACE
    Percy Faith 4:CHERRY PINK AND APPLE BLOSSOM WHITE
    Perez Prado 5:PINK PANTHER THEME Henry Mancini 6:
    LIGHT MY FIRE Booker T.& MG's 7:BETWEEN THE LINES
    Hal Lindes 8:ARIA Acker Bilk 9:SHEPHERD'S LAMENT
    Gheorge Zamfir 10:THORN BIRDS THEME Geoffrey Burgon
    11:FROM RUSSIA WITH LOVE John Barry 12:SNOWFLAKES
    ARE DANCING Tomita 13:WINDMILLS OF YOUR MIND Michel
    Legrand 14:MIDNIGHT IN MOSCOW Kenny Ball 15:HANG'EM
    HIGH Hugo Montenegro 16:SUKIYAKI Kenny Ball
357.THEMES FROM CLASSIC SCIENCE FICTION FILMS - V.Arts
    VARESE (Pinn): VSD 5407 (CD)   *1993*
    THE MOLE PEOPLE-THE CREATURE FROM THE BLACK LAGOON-
    THIS ISLAND EARTH-THE INCREDIBLE SHRINKING MAN-IT
    CAME FROM OUTER SPACE-THE CREATURE WALKS AMONG US-
    HOUSE OF FRANKENSTEIN-HORROR OF DRACULA-TARANTULA-
    SON OF DRACULA-REVENGE OF THECREATURE-DEADLY MANTIS
358.THEMES FROM WESTERNS Nevada Sinfonia/Colorado Chor.
    HALLMARK (Carlton-Techn): 30265-2 (CD)   *1998*
    GOOD THE BAD AND THE UGLY-ONCE UPON A TIME IN THE
    WEST-RIO BRAVO-A PROFESSIONAL GUN-THE MAN WITH THE
    HARMONICA-HIGH NOON-THE RETURN OF THE SEVEN-THE
    GREEN LEAVES OF SUMMER (ALAMO)-A FISTFUL OF DOLLARS
    THE MAGNIFICENT SEVEN-HANG 'EM HIGH-JOHNNY GUITAR-

MY NAME IS NOBODY-TRUE GRIT-FOR A FEW DOLLARS MORE-
BONANZA-HOW THE WEST WAS WON-BALLAD OF THE ALAMO
*359.***THIS IS CULT FICTION** - Various Orig Artists DELETED
VIRGIN (EMI): VTCD 59 (CD) VTMC 59 (MC)   *1995*
LITTLE GREEN BAG *(Reservoir Dogs)* George Baker Sel.
MISIRLOU *(Pulp Fiction)* Dick Dale & His Del Tones
MISSION IMPOSSIBLE Lalo Schifrin / SHAFT MAIN THEME
Isaac Hayes / JUNGLE BOOGIE *(Pulp Fiction)* Kool &
The Gang / MAN FROM UNCLE THEME Hugo Montenegro Orc
EVERYBODY'S TALKIN' *(Midnight Cowboy)* Nilsson
STUCK IN THE MIDDLE WITH YOU *(Reservoir Dogs)* Steal
ers Wheel / BLUE VELVET Bobby Vinton /TOUCH OF EVIL
Henry Mancini Orch / WE HAVE ALL THE TIME IN THE WO
RLD *On Her Majesty's Secret Service* Louis Armstrong
JAMES BOND THEME John Barry 7 / JOE 90 THEME Barry
Gray Orch / THE HARDER THEY COME Jimmy Cliff / HERE
COMES THE HOTSTEPPER *(Pret-A-Porter)* Ini Kamoze /
GUAGLIONE *(Guinness / KIKA)* Perez Prado Orchestra
PLAY DEAD *(Young Americans)* Bjork and David Arnold
AVENGERS THEME Laurie Johnson Orch / YOU NEVER CAN
TELL *(Pulp Fiction)* Chuck Berry / THE RUBLE *(Pulp
Fiction)* Link Wray / SAINT THEME Les Reed Brass /
HAWAII 5-0 Ventures / STREETS OF SAN FRANCISCO MAIN
THEME John Gregory Orch / LONG GOOD FRIDAY Francis
Monkman / THE SWEENEY Power Pack Orch / HIGH WIRE
(DANGERMAN) Bob Leaper Orch / TWIN PEAKS THEME /
ALL THE ANIMALS COME OUT AT NIGHT *(Taxi Driver)*
*360.***THIS IS CULT FICTION ROYALE** - Various Artists
VIRGIN (EMI): VTDCD 151 (2CD) VTDMC 151 (MC)   *1997*
1.BULLITT MAIN TITLE Lalo Schifrin 2.THE PERSUADERS
John Barry 3.EVA Jean Jacques Perrey 4.THE PRISONER
Ron Grainer 5.SPACE 1999 Barry Gray 6.DIRTY HARRY
Lalo Schifrin 7.THE SWEENEY Harry South (perform.by
Wallace & Brint) 8.MAN IN A SUITCASE Ron Grainer 9.
JAMES BOND THEMEMonty Norman 10.GET CARTER Roy Budd
11.WHODUNNIT (PRECINCT) S.Haseley 12.THE CHAMPIONS
Tony Hatch 13.JOE 90 Barry Gray 14.PROTECTORS (THE
AVENUES AND ALLEYWAYS) Mitch Murray-Peter Callander
(performed by Tony Christie) 15.RANDALL AND HOPKIRK
DECEASED Edwin Astley 16.VAN DER VALK (EYE LEVEL)
Jack Trombey 17.AVENGERS Laurie Johnson 18.SAINT
Edwin Astley (perf: Les Reed Brass) 19.DEMPSEY AND
MAKEPEACE Alan Parker (perf: South Bank Orch) 20.
JASON KING Laurie Johnson 21.SAPPHIRE AND STEEL
Cyril Ornadel 22.UFO Barry Gray 23.THE BARON Edwin
Astley 24.THE PROFESSIONALS Laurie Johnson (special
12" Blueboy mix) CD2: MISSION IMPOSSIBLE L.Schifrin
2.DEPARTMENT S.Edwin Astley 3.MAN FROM U.N.C.L.E.
Jerry Goldsmith (perf: Hugo Montenegro) 4.RETURN OF
THE SAINT Martin-Dee (Saint Orch) 5.PROFESSIONALS
Laurie Johnson (perf: London Studio SO) 6.STINGRAY
Barry Gray 7.DANGER MAN (HIGH WIRE) Edwin Astley
(perf: Bob Leaper Orch) 8.007 John Barry 9.ON THE
WAY TO SAN MATEO (from BULLITT) Lalo Schifrin 10.

FIREBALL XL5 Barry Gray (vocal: Don Spencer) 11.
THUNDERBIRDS Barry Gray 12.STRANGE REPORT Roger
Webb (perf: Geoff Love) 13.NEW AVENGERS Laurie
Johnson 14.CAPTAIN SCARLET Barry Gray 15.SUPERCAR
Barry Gray 16.TISWAS Jack Parnell-David Lindup 17.
MAGIC ROUNDABOUT Alain LeGrand 18.TALES OF THE UN
EXPECTED Ron Grainer 19.AQUA MARINA Barry Gray (v:
Gary Miller) 20.CROWN COURT (DISTANT HILLS) Reno-
Haseley 21.HILL ST.BLUES Mike Post 22.TWIN PEAKS
Angelo Badalamenti 23.BLADE RUNNER BLUES Vangelis
361.<u>THIS IS EUROVISION</u> - Various Artists
VIRGIN (EMI): VTDCD 142 or 724384423520 (2CD) 1997
1.NE PARTEZ SANS MOI *(SWITZERLAND 1988)* Celine Dion
2.CONGRATULATIONS *(UK 1968)* Cliff Richard 3.MAKING
YOUR MIND UP *(UK 81)* Bucks Fizz 4.SAVE YOUR KISSES
FOR ME *(UK 76)* Brotherhood Of Man 5.WHAT'S ANOTHER
YEAR*(IRELAND 80)* Johnny Logan 6.BEG STEAL OR BORROW
(UK 72) New Seekers 7.A LITTLE PEACE *(Germany 1982)*
Nicole 8.APRES TOI*(LUXEMBOURG 72)* Vicky Leandros 9.
TU TE RECONNIATRAS *(LUXEMBOURG 73)* Anne-Marie David
10.WHY ME *(IREL.92)* Linda Martin 11.J'AIME LA VIE
(BELG.86) Sandra Kim 12.ROCK'N'ROLL KIDS *(IREL.94)*
Paul Harrington-Charlie McGettigan) 13.HALLELUJAH
(ISRAEL 1979) Milk & Honey and Gali Atari 14.LET ME
BE THE ONE *(UK 1973)* Shadows 15.POUPEE DE CIRE POUP
EE DE SON *(LUXEMBOURG 65)* France Gall 16.THE VOICE
(IRELAND 1996) Eimear Quinn 17.UN BANC UN ARBE UNE
RUE *(MONACO 71)* Severine 18.LOVE GAMES *(UK 84)*Belle
& The Devotions 19.JACK IN THE BOX *(UK 71)* Clodagh
Rodgers 20.LA LA LA *(SPAIN 68)* Massiel <u>CD2:</u> 1.POWER
TO ALL OUR FRIENDS *(UK 73)* Cliff Richard 2.HOLD ME
NOW *(IREL.87)* Johnny Logan 3.PUPPET ON A STRING *(UK
67)* Sandie Shaw 4.LONG LIVE LOVE *(UK 74)* Olivia New
ton John 5.BOOM BANG-A-BANG *(UK 1969)* Lulu 6.I LOVE
THE LITTLE THINGS *(UK 64)* Matt Monro 7.ALL KINDS OF
EVERYTHING *(IREL.1970)* Dana 8.DING-A-DONG *(HOLLAND
75)* Teach-In 9.A BI NI BI *(ISRAEL 78)* Izhar Cohen &
Alphabeta 10.IN YOUR EYES *(IREL.93)* Niamh Kavanagh
11.BAD OLD DAYS *(UK 78)* Co-Co 12.I BELONG *(UK 1965)*
Kathy Kirby 13.PARLEZ VOUS FRANCAIS*(LUX.78)* Baccara
14.SING LITTLE BIRDIE *(UK 59)* Pearl Carr-Teddy John
son *15.MESSAGE TO YOUR HEART (UK 91)* Samantha Janus
16.L'OISEAU ET L'ENFANT *(FRANCE 77)* Marie Myriam
17.ROCK BOTTOM *(UK 77)* Lynsey De Paul & Mike Moran
18.LONELY SYMPHONY *(UK 1994)* Frances Ruffelle 19.
ONE STEP FURTHER *(UK 1982)* Bardo
362.<u>THIS IS SCI-FI</u> - **Various Artists**
VIRGIN (EMI): VTDCDX 262 (7243 847917-2) (2CD) 1999
CD1 1.STAR WARS 2.X-FILES 3.STAR TREK 4.ROLLERBALL
(Toccata In D.Minor) 5.2001 A SPACE ODYSSEY (Also
Sprach Zarathustra) 6.TERMINATOR 7.PLANET OF THE
APES 8.FANTASTIC VOYAGE 9.ALIEN 10.THE TIME MACHINE
11.THE FLY 12.INVASION OF THE BODYSNATCHERS 13.THE
THING (Humanity part 1) 14.LOGAN'S RUN (The Dome)

15.DUNE (Prophecy) 16.WILD PALMS 17.GATTACA (The
Morrow) 18.BABYLON 5 19.BLADE RUNNER (end titles)
20.SILENT RUNNING
CD2: 1.OUTER LIMITS 2.THE DAY THE EARTH STOOD STILL
3.TWILIGHT ZONE 4.LOGAN'S RUN (TV series) 5.DR.WHO
6.STAR WARS (Cantina Band-MECO) 7.WESTWORLD THEME
8.SPACE 1999 9.THUNDERBIRDS 10.BLAKE'S 7 11.THE
TOMORROW PEOPLE 12.BARBARELLA 13.ROLLERBALL (Execut
ive Party Dance)14.UFO 15.LOST IN SPACE 16.MORK AND
MINDY 17.HITCHIKER'S GUIDE TO T.GALAXY 18.RED DWARF
19.CAPTAIN SCARLET 20.SPACE 1999 21.UFO 22.LOGAN'S
RUN 23.WAR OF THE WORLDS (EVE OF THE WAR) 24.TWIN
PEAKS 25. 'EXTREMIS' (Hal feat Gillian Anderson)
26.LOST IN SPACE Apollo 440

363.<u>**THIS IS THE RETURN OF CULT FICTION**</u> - Various Arts
VIRGIN (EMI): VTCD 112 (CD)   *1996*
1.PROFESSIONALS London Studio Or 2.ENTER THE DRAGON
Lalo Schifrin 3.STARSKY AND HUTCH *GOTCHA* Tom Scott
4.SIX MILLION DOLLAR MAN John Gregory Orchestra 5.
CHARLIE'S ANGELS theme 6.WONDERWOMAN theme 7.DR WHO
Peter Howell 8.VISION ON *ACROCHE TOI CAROLINE* Paris
Studio Group 9.TWO RONNIES *THE DETECTIVES* Alan Tew
10.MAGNUM P.I.Mike Post 11.GET SMART Ray Conniff Or
12.DAVE ALLEN AT LARGE THEME Alan Hawkshaw 13.KOJAK
14.TALES OF T.UNEXPECTED Ron Grainer 15.TAXI *ANGELA*
Bob James 16.FORD PROBE AD *FLY ME TO THE MOON* Julie
London 17.VISION ON(GALLERY) *LEFT BANK 2* Palais All
Stars 18.LAST TANGO IN PARIS Gato Barbieri 19.HILL
STREET BLUES Mike Post 20.NORTH BY NORTH WEST R.P.O
Elmer Bernstein 21.ONCE UPON A TIME IN AMERICA Enn
io Morricone 22.BUDGIE THEME Nick Harrison 23.TAXI
DRIVER Bernard Herrmann and Tom Scott alto sax 24.
WHITE HORSES Jacky 25.PERRY MASON *PARK AVE.BEAT* Bob
Crane 26.RETURN OF THE SAINT Saint Orch 27.I DREAM
OF JEANNIE 28.MAN ABOUT THE HOUSE *UP TO DATE* Hawksw
orth Big Band 29.ON THE BUSES *HAPPY HARRY* Tony Russ
ell 30.WORLD OF SPORT Don Jackson 31.BEWITCHEDtheme
32.MINDER*I COULD BE SO GOOD FOR YOU* Dennis Waterman
33.PLEASE SIR Sam Fonteyn 34.GRANGE HILL *CHICKEN
MAN* Alan Hawkshaw 35.SKI SUNDAY *POP LOOKS BACH* New
Dance Orch 36.ROOBARB & CUSTARD Johnny Hawksworth

364.<u>**THIS IS THE SON OF CULT FICTION**</u> - Various Artists
VIRGIN (EMI): VTCD 114 (2CD) VTMC 114 (2MC)   *1997*
1.REAL ME *QUADROPHENIA* Who 2.WHOLE LOTTA LOVE *TOP
OF THE POPS* CCS 3.ALL RIGHT NOW *WRIGLEY'S GUM* Free
4.LUST FOR LIFE *TRAINSPOTTING* Iggy Pop 5.A TEAM
Mike Post 6.BORN TO BE WILD *EASY RIDER* Steppenwolf
7.SMOKE ON THE WATER *STRONGBOW CIDER* Deep Purple 8.
PEOPLE ARE STRANGE *LOST BOYS* Echo and The Bunnymen
9.WEREWOLVES OF LONDON *COLOR OF MONEY* Warren Zevon
10.THE LIONS AND THE CUCUMBERS *VAMPYROS LESBOS* Vamp
iros Sounds Incorpor. 11.PORPOISE SONG *HEAD* Monkees
12.WHITE RABBIT *PLATOON* Jefferson Airplane 13.VENUS
IN FURS *DUNLOP TYRES* Velvet Underground 14.GIRL YOU

'LL BE A WOMAN SOON *PULP FICTION* Urge Overkill 15.
BE BOP A LULA *WILD AT HEART* Gene Vincent 16.GREEN
ONIONS *GET SHORTY* Booker T.& MG's 17.LOUIE LOUIE
N.L.ANIMAL HOUSE Kingsmen 18.BRING DOWN THE BIRDS
BLOW UP Herbie Hancock 19.NORTHERN EXPOSURE theme
David Schwartz 20.DUELLING BANJOS *DELIVERANCE* Eric
Weissberg-Steve Mandell 21.SUICIDE IS PAINLESS *MASH*
Jamie Mandel 22.CALLING YOU *BAGDAD CAFE* Jevetta Ste
ele 23.CAVATINA *DEER HUNTER* John Williams

*365.*THRILLER MEMORANDUM The - **Various Artists**
    RPM (Pinn): RPM 173 (CD) 1996   *reissued 1999*
    2.MEXICAN FLYER Ken Woodman & Piccadilly Brass 2.
    THE MAIN CHANCE John Schroeder Orc 3.YES AND NO Des
    Champ 4.THE PARTY Nico Mamangakis 5.FLY BY NIGHT
    Briab Marshall Orch 6.GHOST SQUAD Tony Hatch OrC 7.
    SILENCERS Patti Seymour 8.FADE OUT John Shakespeare
    9.LE TRAIN FOU Jacques Denjean 10.LIVE AND LET DIE
    David Lloyd & His London Or. 11.KISSY SUZUKI Sounds
    Orchestral 12.TWELVE BY TWO Ken Woodman Piccadilly
    Brass 13.A NIGHT WITH NUKI Brian Marshall Orch 14.
    THE SAINT Edwin Astley Or. 15.SHARP SHARKS Ingfried
    Hoffman 16.MISSION IMPOSSIBLE Mike Hurst Orches 17.
    ADVENTURE Mark Wirtz Orch 18.WEDNESDAY'S CHILD Mike
    Hurst Orch 19.THE HUSTLE Basil Kirchen 20.BIG M Des
    Champ 21.INTERCEPTION David Whittaker Orch 22.
    PENTHOUSE (MAIN TITLOE)/DANCE Johnny Hawsworth 23.
    DANGER MAN Edwin Astley Orch 24.MAN IN A SUITCASE
    Alexander Stone

*366.*THRILLERS! - City Of Prague Philharm.(Paul Bateman/
    Nic Raine/Derek Wadsworth) / London Screen Orchest
    Royal Philharmonic Concert Orch (Mike Townend) and
    Lesley Garrett w.Chamber Orch of London (Nic Raine)
    SILVA SCREEN Treasury (Koch): SILVAD 3504 (CD) 1997
    1:NORTH BY NORTHWEST *(B.HERRMANN)* 2:PATRIOT GAMES
    (J.HORNER) 3:UNTOUCHABLES *(E.MORRICONE)* 4:FUGITIVE
    (J.NEWTON HOWARD) 5:QUILLER MEMORANDUM *(J.BARRY)*
    6:NIGHTHAWKS *(K.EMERSON)* 7:IN THE LINE OF FIRE *(E.
    MORRICONE)* 8:THE FIRM *(D.GRUSIN)* 9:IPCRESS FILE
    (J.BARRY) 10:MAGNUM FORCE / 11:MISSION IMPOSSIBLE
    (L.SCHIFRIN) 12:PRESUMED INNOCENT *(J.WILLIAMS)* 13:
    INNOCENT SLEEP *(M.AYRES,* sung by Lesley Garrett)
    14:WITNESS *(M.JARRE)*   *tpt: 50.18*

*367.*THUNDERBIRDS & OTHER TOP 60s TV THEMES VOL.2 **V.Arts**
    SEQUEL-CASTLE (Pinn): NEBCD 425 (CD)   *1999*
    1.THUNDERBIRDS Cyril Stapleton & The Eliminators 2.
    AVENGERS "The Shake" (orig version) Laurie Johnson
    3.STEPTOE & SON Eagles 4.Z-CARS "Z-Cars Cha Cha"
    John Warren Orch 5.PEYTON PLACE/CORONATION STREET
    Bruce Forsyth 6.IT'S DARK OUTSIDE "Where Are You
    Now" Jackie Trent 7.FRONT PAGE STORY "The Big Beat"
    Eric Delaney Orch 8.MAVERICK Terry Young 9.WAGON
    TRAIN "Roll Along Wagon Train" Robert Horton 10.
    COMEDY PLAYHOUSE "Happy Joe" Eagles 11.DICK POWELL
    SHOW Tony Hatch Orch 12.EUROFASHION "Birds" Tony

Hatch Orch 13.AT LAST THE 1948 SHOW "Ferret Song" John Cleese & 1948 Show Choir 14.STINGRAY "Aqua Marina" (end theme) Gary Miller 15.CAPTAIN SCARLET "Mysterons Theme" Barry Gray 16.JOE 90 "Hi-jacked" Barry Gray Orch 17.THUNDERBIRDS "Parker Well Done!" Barry Gray Orch 18.THIRD MAN "Harry Lime Theme" Big Ben Banjo Band 19.DESPERATE PEOPLE "The Desperados" Eagles 20.STRANGER ON T.SHORE Eagles 21.CROSSROADS "Where Will You Be" Sue Nicholls 22.LUNCH BOX"Lunch Boxer" Jerry Allen Trio 23.MEXICO OLYMPICS "Mexico" Long John Baldry 24.HANCOCK "Spying Tonight" Derek Scott Music 25.ANDORRA Ron Grainer Orch 26.STEPTOE & SON "Junk Shop" Harry H.Corbett 27.THE SAINT Les Reed Brass 28.ROBIN HOOD Gary Miller 29.DARK ISLAND Alexander Brothers 30.BATMAN Kinks

368.TIOMKIN Dimitri Western Film World London Studio SO Laurie Johnson,John McCarthy Sing. *UNICORN KANCHANA (H.Mundi): UKCD 2011 (CD)* Suites: GIANT-RED RIVER- DUEL IN THE SUN-HIGH NOON-NIGHT PASSAGE-RIO BRAVO

369.TOP TV THEMES - Various Artists
CASTLE COMM (Pinn): MACCD 152 (CD) 1993
1.FIREBALL XL5 Flee Rekkers 2.CAPTAIN SCARLET Barry Gray Orch 3.JOE 90 Barry Gray Orch 4.THUNDERBIRDS Barry Gray Orch 5.THE AVENGERS Laurie Johnson Orch 6.THE SAINT Les Reed 7.RETURN OF THE SAINT Saint Orch 8.HIJACKED Barry Gray Orch 9.Z-CARS Johnny 8.HIJACKED Barry Gray Orch 9.Z-CARS Johnny Keating 6.THE SAINT Les Reed 7.RETURN OF THE SAINT Saint Orch 8.HIJACKED Barry Gray Orch 9.Z-CARS Johnny Keating & Z-Men 10.THE FUGITIVE John Schroeder Orch 11.HANCOCK'S TUNE (ITV) Derek Scott 12.DEPARTMENT S Cyril Stapleton Orch 13.DOCTOR WHO Eric Winstone Or 14.DANGER MAN *High Wire* Bob Leaper Orch 15.GENERAL HOSPITAL *Red Alert* Johnny Pearson Orch 16.OUR HOUSE The Piccadilly 17.CROSSROADS Tony Hatch Orchestra 18.WAGON TRAIN *Roll Along Wagon Train* Robert Horton

370.TOTALLY COMMERCIALS - Various Artists
EMI GOLD: 495 475-2 (CD) 495 475-4 (MC) 1998
1.MY SPECIAL ANGEL *(FRIZZELL INSUR)* Malcolm Vaughan 2.ANGELINA *(MASTERCARD)* Louis Prima 3.FEVER *IMPULSE* Peggy Lee 4.I'M SITTING ON TOP OF THE WORLD *(LEVI DOCKERS)* Bobby Darin 5.WILD IS THE WIND *LINDT CHOC.* Nina Simone 6.PUT A LITTLE LOVE IN YOUR HEART *MICHELOB LAGER* Jackie De Shannon 7.CALL ME IRRESPON SIBLE *VW* Dinah Washington 8.NIGHT RIDER *CADBURY'S M.TRAY)* Alan Hawkshaw 9.STOMPIN'AT THE SAVOY *P.& O. EUROPEAN FERRIES)* Benny Goodman 10.THE STRIPPER *TETLEY TEA DRAWSTRING* Joe Loss 11.I LOVES YOU PORGY *ORANGE* Nina Simone 12.STORY OF MY LIFE *GUINNESS)* Michael Holliday 13.FLY ME TO THE MOON *(FORD PROBE)* Julie London 14.IN THE MOOD *ANCHOR BUTTER* Joe Loss 15.LOVE IS THE SWEETEST THING *BLACK MAGIC* Al Bowlly 16.TEACH ME TIGER *(WHISKAS)* April Stevens 17.MELLOW YELLOW *KRAFT* Donovan 18.AIR THAT I BREATHE Hollies

371.<u>**TOWERING INFERNO: Great Disaster Movies**</u> - V.Artists
VARESE (Pinn): VSD 5807 (CD)   *1999*
Royal Scottish National Orchestra and others
TOWERING INFERNO-TWISTER-EARTHQUAKE-THE SWARM-THE
POISEIDON ADVENTURE-DANTE'S PEAK-VOLCANO-OUTBREAK-
INDEPENDENCE DAY-TITANIC
372.<u>**TRACKSPOTTING**</u> - Various Artists
POLYGRAM TV (UNIV): 553 430-2 (2CD) -4 (2MC)   *1997*
1.SAINT Orbital 2.MISSION IMPOSSIBLE Adam Clayton-
Larry Mullen 3.LOVEFOOL Tee's Club Radio Cardigans
4.SHALLOW GRAVE Leftfield 5.BORN SLIPPY Underworld
6.PAPAU NEW GUINEA Future Sound Of London 7.CRASH &
CARRY Orbital 8.SLID Fluke 9.WAKE UP Stereo MCs 10.
WILDWOOD Paul Weller 11.THIS IS NOT AMERICA David
Bowie & Pat Metheny Group 12.DOWNTOWN Lloyd Cole 13
WAIT FOR THE SUN Supergrass 14.NATURAL ONE Folk Imp
losion 15.GONE David Holmes and Sarah Cracknel 16.
PLAYDEAD Bjork & David Arnold 17.SMALL PLOT OF LAND
David Bowie 18.FORBIDDEN COLOURS David Sylvian 19.
FALLING Julee Cruise 20.HOLD ME THRILL ME KISS ME
KILL ME U2 21.36DEGREES Placebo 22.SUNSHINE SHAKERS
Reef 23.BEGGIN'YOU Stone Roses 24.LET'S ALL GO TOGE
THER Marion 25.I SPY Pulp 26.THERE SHE GOES The Las
27.YOU AND ME SONG The Wannadies 28.BAD BEHAVIOUR
Super Furry Animals 29.LUST FOR LIFE Iggy Pop 30.
THAT WOMAN'S GOT ME DRINKING Shane MacGowan & Popes
31.PERFECT CRIME Faith No More 32.SUGAR RAY Jesus &
Mary Chain 33.MISIRLOU Dick Dale & His Deltones 34.
5.15 Who 35.PET SEMETARY Ramones 36.PRETTY IN PINK
Psychedelic Furs 37.GIRL YOU'LL BE A WOMAN SOON
Urge Overkill 38.LEFT OF CENTRE Suzanne Vega 39.
STUCK IN THE MIDDLE WITH YOU Stealer's Wheel 40.HOW
HOW CAN WE HANG ON TO A DREAM Tim Hardin
--- <u>**TRUFFAUT Francois**</u> - *see* <u>**DELERUE Georges**</u>
373.<u>**TUNES FROM THE TOONS**</u> - **The Best Of HANNA-BARBERA**
MCI (MCI-THE): MCCD(MCTC) 279 (CD/MC)   *1996*
1-2 DASTARDLY & MUTTLEY 3-5 TOP CAT 6-8 YOGI BEAR 9
-12FLINTSTONES 13-14 HUCKLEBERRY HOUND 15-16 PERILS
OF PENELOPE PITSTOP 17-18 SNOOPER & BLABBER 19-21
JETSONS 22-23 HAIR BEAR BUNCH 24.SECRET SQUIRREL 25
HONG KONG PHOOEY 26-27 JOSIE & THE PUSSYCATS 28-29
SCOOBY DOO WHERE ARE YOU 30.NEW SCOOBY DOO 31-32
TOUCHE TURTLE 33-34 WALLY GATOR 35-37 PIXIE & DIXIE
38-40 QUICK DRAW McGRAW 41-42 SNAGGLEPUSS 43.HONEY
WOLF 44.AUGIE DOGGIE 45.YANKY DOODLE 46.LIPPY LION
& HARDY HA HA 47.WACKY RACES 48.BANANA SPLITS THEME
374.<u>**TURN ON! TUNE IN!**</u> - **Various Artists**
JAZZ FM/BEECHWOOD (BMG): JAZZFMCD 15 (2CD)   *1999*
1.ON THE STREET WHERE YOU LIVE Nat King Cole *TV AD:
QUALITY STREET* 2.WE HAVE ALL THE TIME IN THE WORLD
Louis Armstrong *GUINNESS* 3.I JUST WANNA MAKE LOVE
TO YOU Etta James *DIET COKE* 4.FEELING GOOD Nina
Simone *VW GOLF/COMFORT* 5.MAD ABOUT THE BOY Dinah
Washington *LEVI* 6.SPEAKING OF HAPPINESS Gloria Lynn

FORD MONDEO 7.LEFT BANK2 Noveltones*VW GOLF/AMBROSIA*
8.LET'S FACE THE MUSIC & DANCE Nat King Cole *ALLIED
DUNBAR* 9.MY SHIP HAS SAILED Sarah Vaughan *GALAXY* 10
I PUT A SPELL ON YOU Nina Simone *DIET COKE/PERRIER*
11.I WANT TWO LIPS April Stevens *PEUGEOT 306* 12.
WHEN A A MAN LOVES A WOMAN Percy Sledge *LEVI* 13.I'M
SITTING ON TOP OF THE WORLD Al Jolson *GUINNESS/RENN
IES* 14.STAND BY ME Ben E.King *LEVI* 15.MY BABY JUST
CARES FOR ME Nina Simone *CHANEL NO.5* 16.SMOKESTACK
LIGHTNING John Lee Hooker *BUDWEISER* 17.CAN'T SMILE
WITHOUT YOU Lena Fiagby *BT* 18.OCEAN DRIVE The
Lighthouse Family *ALPEN* 19.FLY ME TO THE MOON Julie
London *FORD PROBE* 20.DREAM A LITTLE DREAM Mamas and
Papas *PEUGEOT 406* 21.CALL ME Chris Montez *BT* 22.
TURN ON TUNE IN COP OUT Freakpower *LEVI* 23.
CANTELOUPE ISLAND Us 3 *KFC* 24.SOUL BOSSA NOVA
Quincy Jones *NIKE* 25.MAS QUE NADA Tamba Trio *NIKE*
26.GUAGLIONE Perez Prado *GUINNESS* 27.BIG BAMBOOZLE
Barry Adamson *BAILEY'S IRISH CREAM* 28.JUMP JIVE AND
WAIL Brian Setzer *GAP JEANS* 29.EVA Jean Jacques
Perrey *LUCOZADE* 30.MOVE ON UP Curtis Mayfield
CITROEN XSARA 31.GET DOWN TONIGHT KC & Sunshine
Band *BUDWEISER* 32.PATRICIA Perez Prado *ROYAL MAIL*

375.<u>TV ACTION JAZZ</u> - Various Artists
   RCA VICTOR (BMG): 74321 59154-2 (CD)   *1999*
   PETER GUNN / MIKE HAMMER / PERRY MASON / M.SQUAD /
   77 SUNSET STRIP / THE THIN MAN and others

376.<u>TV SOAP THEMES</u> - Various Artists
   HALLMARK (Carlton): 30624-2 (CD)   *1997*
   1.EASTENDERS 2.FALCON CREST 3.ELDORADO 4.EMMERDALE
   5.PRISONER CELL BLOCK H (THEME 'ON THE INSIDE') 6.
   MELROSE PLACE 7.CROSSROADS 8.NEIGHBOURS 9.A COUNTRY
   PRACTICE 10.CORONATION STREET 11.BEVERLY HILLS
   90210 12.BROOKSIDE 13.THE YOUNG DOCTORS 14.DALLAS
   15.DYNASTY 16.SONS AND DAUGHTERS 17.PEYTON PLACE
   18.HOME AND AWAY

377.<u>TV THEMES OF THE SIXTIES</u> - **Various Artists**
   CASTLE PIE (Pinn): PIESD 025 (CD)   *1999*
   1.THUNDERBIRDS Barry Gray Orch 2.AVENGERS Laurie
   Johnson Orch 3.THE SAINT Les Reed Brass 4.DANGERMAN
   Bob Leaper Orch 5.FUGITIVE John Schroeder Orch 6.
   THANK YOUR LUCKY STARS Peter Knight Or 7.TOP SECRET
   Laurie Johnson Orch 8.NAKED CITY Tony Hatch Orch
   9.SPIES Cyril Stapleton Orch 10.ODD COUPLE Button
   Down Brass 11.IRONSIDE Alan Tew Orch 12.WHICKER'S
   WORLD Laurie Johnson 13.MAN ALIVE Tony Hatch 14.
   CAPTAIN SCARLET Barry Gray Orch 15.MAIGRET Eagles
   16.Z-CARS Johnny Keating & Z Men 17.STEPTOE AND SON
   Ron Grainer 18.PERRY MASON Tony Hatch Orch

---   <u>TV THEMES</u> - **see HESS, Nigel**
378.<u>TV TOWN</u> - (Ultra Lounge series) - Various Artists
   EMI: CDEMS 1616 or 7243 8534 092 (CD)   *1997*
   1.BUBBLES IN THE WINE Freddy Martin 2.NAKED CITY Ne
   lson Riddle 3.ODD COUPLE Billy May 4.MAN FROM UNCLE

A.Caiola 5.THANKS FOR T.MEMORY Dave Pell 6.MUNSTERS
Jack Marshall 7.THE FUGITIVE Si Zentner 8.DICK VAN
DYKE/ALVIN SHOW Nelson Riddle 9.HUMAN JUNGLE John
Barry 10.BATMAN David McCallum 11.MANNIX Billy May
12.ONE STEP BEYOND (FEAR)/TWILIGHT ZONE Ventures 13
MOD SQUAD Al Caiola 14.MR.LUCKY Si Zentner Orch
15.MY THREE SONS Nelson Riddle 16.BURKE'S LAW Liber
ty ST 17.BEWITCHED Peggy Lee 18.MELANCHOLY SERENADE
Jackie Gleason 19.POWER HOUSE Spike Jones

379.<u>TWILIGHT</u> - Various Artists   *1999*
VIRGIN CLASS (EMI): CDDREAM2 (2CD) TCDREAM2 (2MC)
CD1: 1.EINE KLEINE NACHTMUSIK *(MOZART)* 2.TRAUMEREI
(SCHUMANN) 3.SONG TO THE MOON *DVORAK)* 4.AIR ON THE
G.STRING *(BACH)* 5.CHANSON DE NUIT*(ELGAR)* 6.CLARINET
CONCERTO IN A.*(MOZART)* 7.SERENADE *(BRITTEN)* 8.DANCE
OF THE BLESSED SPIRITS *(GLUCK)* 9.NOCTURNE NO.2 IN E
FLAT *(CHOPIN)* 10.VIOLIN CONCERTO NO.1 IN G.MINOR
(BRUCH) 11.BELLE NUIT O NUIT D'AMOUR *(OFFENBACH)* 12
ETUDE IN E *(CHOPIN)* 13.TO BE SUNG ON A SUMMER NIGHT
ON THE WATER *(DELIUS)* 14.THE SWAN *(SAINT-SAENS)* 15.
PRAYER*(HUMPERDINCK)* CD2: 1.LULLABY *(BRAHMS)* 2.PIANO
CONCERTO NO.21 IN C.*MOZART* 3.HUMMING CHORUS *PUCCINI*
CONCERTO IN A.*(MOZART)* 7.SERENADE *(BRITTEN)* 8.DANCE
OF THE BLESSED SPIRITS *(GLUCK)* 9.NOCTURNE NO.2 IN E
FLAT *(CHOPIN)* 10.VIOLIN CONCERTO NO.1 IN G.MINOR
(BRUCH) 11.BELLE NUIT O NUIT D'AMOUR *(OFFENBACH)* 12
ETUDE IN E *(CHOPIN)* 13.TO BE SUNG ON A SUMMER NIGHT
ON THE WATER *(DELIUS)* 14.THE SWAN *(SAINT-SAENS)* 15.
PRAYER*(HUMPERDINCK)* CD2: 1.LULLABY *(BRAHMS)* 2.PIANO
CONCERTO NO.21 IN C.*MOZART* 3.HUMMING CHORUS *PUCCINI*
4.NOCTURNE NO.10 *CHOPIN* 5.SERENADE IN E.MINOR *ELGAR*
6.NIGHTS IN THE GARDENS OF SPAIN *(MANUEL DE FALLA)*
7.ENT'RACTE *(BIZET)* 8.ANDANTE CANTIBILE *TCHAIKOVSKY*
9.PIANO CONCERTO NO.2 IN F.*(SHOSTAKOVICH)* 10.FOUR
SEA INTERLUDES *(BRITTEN)*11.GASPARD DE LA NUIT *RAVEL*
12.THE AQUARIUM *(SAINT-SAENS)* 13.VENUS *(HOLST)*

--- <u>**ULTIMATE COLLECTION OF CLASSIC & CULT FANTASY**</u> *see*
                                      BATTLESTAR GALACTICA

380.<u>VANGELIS</u> - GENIUS: The Music Of VANGELIS
N2 (Sound and Media): NEW 213 (CD)   *1999*
1492 CONQUEST OF PARADISE-ANTARCTICA-CHUNH KUO-
L'EFANT-MUTINY ON THE BOUNTY-BLADERUNNER-HYMN-
CHARIOTS OF FIRE-LOVE THEME FROM BLADERUNNER-TO AN
UNKNOWN MAN-MISSING-PULSTAR-CIRCLES-WILL OF THE
WORLD-DAWN-VOICES

381.<u>VANGELIS</u> - REPRISE 1990 to 1999
EAST WEST (Ten): 3984 29828-2 (CD)   *1999*
BLADERUNNER-1492 CONQUEST OF PARADISE-ANTARCTICA-
DREAMS OF SURF-OPENING-MONASTERY AT LA RABIDA-COME
TO ME-LIGHT AND SHADOW-FIELDS OF CORAL-EL GRECO
(m/m 5)-EL GRECO (m/m 6)-WEST ACROSS THE OCEAN SEA
THEME FROM BITTER MOOON-RACHEL'S SONG-EL GRECO (m/m
4)-THEME FROM THE PLAGUE-DAWN-PRELUDE

382.VENTURES - BATMAN and OTHER TV THEMES
SEE FOR MILES-C5 (Koch): C5HCD 653   1997
BATMAN THEME-ZOCKO-CAPE-GET SMART-MAN FROM UNCLE-
HOT LINE-JOKER'S WILD-UP UP AND AWAY-GREEN HORNET
00-711-VAMPCAMP-SECRET AGENT MAN-CHARLIE'S ANGELS-
MEDICAL CENTRE-STAR TREK-STREETS OF SAN FRANCISCO-
STARSKY AND HUTCH-BARRETA'S THEME-HAWAII 5.0-SWAT-
POLICE STORY-MASH-POLICEWOMAN-NADIA'S THEME FROM
THE YOUNG AND THE RESTLESS

383.VICTORY AT SEA - Eric KUNZEL & Cincinnati Pops Orch
TELARC USA (BMG-Con): CD 80175 (CD only)   1989
VICTORY AT SEA SUITE-WINDS OF WAR/WAR & REMEMBRANCE
CASABLANCA Suite-COLONEL BOGEY-WARSAW CONCERTO-THE
VALIANT YEARS-BATTLE OF BRITAIN-OVER THERE-LONGEST
DAY-GENERAL'S MARCH-ARMED FORCES Medley

384.WAR! - City Of Prague Philharmonic (Paul Bateman)
SILVA SCREEN Treasury (Koch): SILVAD 3502 (CD) 1997
1:WHERE EAGLES DARE *(RON GOODWIN)* 2:BATTLE OF THE
BULGE *(B.FRANKEL)* 3:CASUALTIES OF WAR *(E.MORRICONE)*
4: 633 SQUADRON *(R.GOODWIN)* 5:SINK THE BISMARCK!
(C.PARKER) 6:BRIDGE AT REMAGEN *(E.BERNSTEIN)* 7:
MACARTHUR / PATTON *(J.GOLDSMITH)* 8:DAS BOOT (BOAT)
(K.DOLDINGER) 9:NIGHT OF THE GENERALS *(M.JARRE)* 10:
GUNS OF NAVARONE *(D.TIOMKIN)* 11:LONGEST DAY*(P.ANKA)*
12:BATTLE OF MIDWAY *(J.WILLIAMS)* 13:IN HARM'S WAY
(GOLDSMITH) 14:IS PARIS BURNING *(M.JARRE) tpt 54.19*

--- WARNER BROS.YEARS - *see* KORNGOLD Erich Wolfgang

385.WARRIORS OF THE SILVER SCREEN City Of Prague Phil.*
SILVA SCREEN (Koch): FILMXCD 187 (2CD)   1997
Symphonic Suites: BRAVEHEART-THE THIEF OF BAGDAD-
TARAS BULBA-ANTHONY AND CLEOPATRA-FIRST KNIGHT-
HENRY V-EL CID-PRINCE VALIANT-BEN HUR-THE VIKINGS
Themes: ROB ROY-SPARTACUS-THE 300 SPARTANS-WAR LORD
LAST VALLEY-CONAN T.BARBARIAN-JASON AND T.ARGONAUTS
City of Prague P.O. and Crouch End Festival Chorus

--- WARSAW CONCERTO - *see* ADDINSELL Richard

386.WARSAW CONCERTO & OTHER FILM THEMES Bournemouth SO*
CFP (EMI): CDCFP 9020 (CD) CFP 41 4493-4 (MC) 1988
WARSAW CONCERTO from 'Dangerous Moonlight'(Film 41)
(Richard Addinsell)- THE DREAM OF OLWEN from 'While
I Live' (Film 47) (Charles Williams)-SPELLBOUND CON
CERTO from 'Spellbound' (Film 45)(Miklos Rozsa)-THE
CORNISH RHAPSODY from 'Love Story' (Film 44)(Hubert
Bath) -RHAPSODY IN BLUE (Film 45) (George Gershwin)
(K.Alwyn) feat Daniel Adni (Piano) 1980 reiss 1988

387.WARSAW CONCERTO + OTHER PIANO CONCERTOS FROM MOVIES
NAXOS (Select): 8.554323 (CD)   1998
1.WARSAW CONCERTO *(R.ADDINSELL)* 2.PORTRAIT OF ISLA
(J.BEAVER) 3.SPELLBOUND *(M.ROSZA)* 4.LEGEND OF THE
GLASS MOUNTAIN *(NINO ROTA)* 5.MURDER ON THE ORIENT
EXPRESS *(R.R.BENNETT)* 6.CORNISH RHAPSODY *(H.BATH)*
7.HANGOVER SQUARE *(B.HERRMANN)* 8.THE DREAM OF OLWEN
(C.WILLIAMS) 9.JULIE *(L.STEVENS, arr.PENNARIO)* feat
RTE CONCERT ORCH (P.O'Duinn, cond) PHILIP FOWKE pno

388.<u>**WARSAW CONCERTO**</u> - Jean Yves Thibudet (piano) with*
Romantic Piano Classics From The Silver Screen
DECCA CLASSICS (UNIV): 460 503-2 (CD)   *1998*
1.WARSAW CONCERTO *(R.ADDINSELL)* Dangerous Moonlight
2.PIANO CONCERTO NO.2 *(RACHMANINOV)* Brief Encounter
/ Seven Year Itch 3.RHAPSODY ON A THEME OF PAGANINI
(RACHMANINOV) Story Of Three Loves / Groundhog Day
4.RHAPSODY IN BLUE *(GERSHWIN)* 5.PIANO CONCERTO NO.2
(SHOSTAKOVICH) *Cleveland Orch.& BBC Symphony Orch.*

389.<u>**WATCH THE SKIES**</u> : SCI-FI THEMES - Various Artists
SONIC IMAGES (Greyhound): SID 8901 (CD)   *1999*
tracks include: ROSWELL-MEN IN BLACK-E.T.THE EXTRA
TERRESTRIAL-PREDATOR-THE TOMMYKNOCKERS-DARK SKIES-
MARS ATTACKS-THE DAY THE EARTH STOOD STILL-CONTACT-
THEY LIVE-SPECIES-X.FILES-INDEPENDENCE DAY

390.<u>**WATCHING THE DETECTIVES**</u> - Starshine Orchestra
HALLMARK (Carlton): 30726-2 (CD) -4 (MC)   *1997*
INSPECTOR MORSE-LA LAW-THE BILL-POIROT-THE SWEENEY-
LAW AND ORDER-BERGERAC-JULIET BRAVO-MAGNUM PI PRIVA
TE INVESTIGATOR-MISS MARPLE-RUTH RENDELL MYSTERIES-
STARSKY & HUTCH-TAGGART-HILL STREET BLUES-NYPD BLUE
-CAGNEY AND LACEY-KOJAK

391.<u>**WAXMAN Franz**</u> - LEGENDS OF HOLLYWOOD
VARESE (Pinn): VSD 5242 (CD)   *1990*
New recordings of Suites from Franz Waxman's scores
TASK FORCE-OBJECTIVE BURMA-PEYTON PLACE-SORRY WRONG
NUMBER-THE PARADINE CASE-DEMETRIUS & THE GLADIATORS

392.<u>**WAXMAN Franz**</u> - LEGENDS OF HOLLYWOOD - Volume 2
VARESE (Pinn): VSD 5257 (CD)   *1991*
BRIDE OF FRANKENSTEIN-MR.ROBERTS-POSSESSED-CAPTAINS
COURAGEOUS-THE NUN'S STORY-HUCKLEBERRY FINN etc.

393.<u>**WAXMAN Franz**</u> - LEGENDS OF HOLLYWOOD - Volume 3
VARESE (Pinn): VSD 5480 (CD)   *1994*
ELEPHANT WALK (6 tracks)-THE FURIES (5)-DESTINATION
TOKYO (5)-THE SILVER CHALICE (6)-NIGHT AND THE CITY
NIGHT UNTO NIGHT-HOTEL BERLIN-MR.SKEFFINGTON (2)

394.<u>**WAXMAN Franz**</u> - LEGENDS OF HOLLYWOOD - Volume 4
VARESE (Pinn): VSD 5713 (CD)   *1996*
New recordings of Suites from Franz Waxman's scores
Queensland Symphony Orch.conducted by Richard Mills
1.UNTAMED (1955) 2/3/4.ON BORROWED TIME (39) 5/6/7.
MY GEISHA (62) 8.DEVIL DOLL (36) 9.MY COUSIN RACHEL
(52) 10/11/12.STORY OF RUTH (60) 13/14/15.DARK CITY
(1950) 16/17/18/19/20.A CHRISTMAS CAROL (1938)

395.<u>**WAXMAN Franz**</u> - Sunset Boulevard: Classic WAXMAN
RCA VICTOR (BMG): GD 80708 (CD)   *Re-iss: 1991*
PRINCE VALIANT:Prelude/King Aguar's Escape/The Fens
First Chase/The Tournament/Sir Brack's Death/Finale
A PLACE IN THE SUN:Suite. THE BRIDE OF FRANKENSTEIN
Creation Of The Female Monster. SUNSET BOULEVARD:
Main Title/Norma Desmond/The Studio Stroll/The Come
back (Norma as Salome). OLD AQUAINTANCE: Elegy For
Strings and Harp. REBECCA: Prelude/After The Ball/
Mrs.Danvers/Confession Scene/Manderley In Flames.

THE PHILADELPHIA STORY: MGM Fanfare/Main Title/The
True Love. TARAS BULBA: The Ride To Dubno.
NATIONAL PHILHARMONIC ORCHESTRA (CHARLES GERHARDT)

396.<u>WEBB Marti</u> and <u>MARK RATTRAY</u> - **MAGIC OF THE MUSICALS**
MCI (Disc-THE): MCCD 149 (CD) MCTC 149 (MC)   1992
IT AIN'T NESESSARILY SO-PLENTY OF NOTHIN'-THERE'S A
BOAT-PORGY I'S YOUR WOMAN NOW-LULLABY OF BROADWAY-
I GOT RHYTHM-I GET A KICK OUT OF YOU-SUMMERTIME-LOS
ING MY MIND-BLOW GABRIEL BLOW-NOT WHILE I'M AROUND-
SEND IN THE CLOWNS-DO YOU HEAR THE PEOPLE SING-I DR
AMED A DREAM-EMPTY CHAIR AT EMPTY TABLES-LAST NIGHT
OF THE WORLD-BUI.DOI-DON'T CRY FOR ME ARGENTINA-JES
US CHRIST SUPERSTAR-MAMA-TAKE THAT LOOK OFF YOUR FA
CE-IN ONE OF MY WEAKER MOMENTS-ANTHEM-TELL ME IT'S
NOT TRUE-YOU AND I-ONLY HE-LOVE CHANGES EVERYTHING-
THE MUSIC OF THE NIGHT-MEMORY

397.<u>WEBB Marti</u> **PERFORMANCE with Philharmonia Orch.**_1989_
FIRST NIGHT (Pinn): OCRCD 6033 (CD)   reissued 1995
Introduction: I DREAMED A DREAM *Les Miserables* /
ALMOST LIKE BEING IN LOVE *Brigadoon* / MUSIC OF THE
NIGHT *Phantom* /LOSING MY MIND *Follies* /ANYTHING BUT
LONELY *Aspects Of Love* / ONLY HE *Starlight Express*
MEMORY *Cats* / LOVE CHANGES EVERYTHING *Aspects*/ ONCE
YOU LOSE YOUR HEART *Me and My Girl* /LAST MAN IN MY
Life *Tell Me On A Sunday*/BLOW GABRIEL *Anything Goes*
see also 'MAGIC OF THE MUSICALS'

398.<u>WEBB Roy</u> - **CURSE OF THE CAT PEOPLE**
The Film Music of ROY WEBB
CLOUD NINE (Silva Screen): CNS 5008 (CD)   1995
BUILD MY GALLOWS HIGH-CROSSFIRE-BEDLAM-NOTORIOUS-
SINBAD THE SAILOR-THE GHOST SHIP-MIGHTY JOE YOUNG-
CORNERED-LOCKET-DICK TRACY-CURSE OF THE CAT PEOPLE

399.<u>WEST Mae</u> **Orig Commercial Recordings and Film -S/T-**
JASMINE (BMG-Con): JASCD 102 (CD)   1996
I LIKE A GUY WHAT TAKES HIS TIME-EASY RIDER-I FOUND
A NEW WAY TO GO TO TOWN-I'M NO ANGEL-THEY CALL ME
SISTER HONKY TONK-I WANT YOU I NEED YOU-WILLIE OF
THE VALLEY-FRANKIE AND JOHNNY-THAT DALLAS MAN-WHEN
A ST.LOUIS WOMAN COMES DOWN TO NEW ORLEANS-MY OLD
FLAME-MEMPHIS BLUES-TROUBLED WATERS-HE'S A BAD BAD
MAN-MON COEUR S'OUVRE A TA VOIUX (SOFTLY AWAKES MY
HEART)-I'M AN OCCIDENTAL WOMAN IN AN ORIENTAL MOOD
FOR LOVE-MISTER DEEP BLUE SEA-LITTLE BAR BUTTERFLY
ON A TYPICAL TROPICAL NIGHT-I WAS SAYING TO THE
MOON-NOW I'M A LADY

400.<u>WESTERNS!</u> - **City Of Prague Philharm.**(Paul Bateman/
Nic Raine/Derek Wadsworth) Philharmonia Orch. (Tony
Bremner) / Westminster Philh.Orch (Kenneth Alwyn)
SILVA SCREEN Treasury (Koch): SILVAD 3503 (CD) 1997
1:BIG COUNTRY *(J.MOROSS)* 2:WILD ROVERS*(J.GOLDSMITH)*
3:UNFORGIVEN *(C.EASTWOOD)* 4: A DISTANT TRUMPET *(Max
STEINER)* 5: and 6:ONCE UPON A TIME IN THE WEST *(E.
MORRICONE)* 7:HOW THE WEST WAS WON *(Alfred NEWMAN)*
8:DANCES WITH WOLVES *(J.BARRY)* 9: MAGNIFICENT SEVEN

(E.BERNSTEIN) 10:FISTFUL OF DOLLARS *(E.MORRICONE)*
11:STAGECOACH *(arr,TOWNEND)* 12:TRUE GRIT *(E.BERNSTE
IN)* 13:TWO MULES FOR SISTER SARA *(E.MORRICONE)* 14:
SONS OF KATIE ELDER *(E.BERNSTEIN)*   *tpt* 57.44

401.**WILD WEST The** - **Essential Western Film Music Coll.**
SILVA SCREEN (Koch): FILMXCD 315 (2CDs)   *1999*
tracks: THE ALAMO-BIG COUNTRY-BUFFALO GIRLS-
THE COWBOYS-DANCES WITH WOLVES-DISTANT TRUMPET-
EL CONDOR-A FISTFUL OF DOLLARS-GETTYSBURG-GLORY-
HEAVEN'S GATE-HIGH PLAINS DRIFTER-HOW THE WEST WAS
WON-LAST OF THE MOHICANS-LONESOME DOVE-MAGNIFICENT
SEVEN-MAVERICK-MONTE WALSH-ONCE UPON A TIME IN THE
WEST-PROFESSIONALS-OUTLAW JOSEY WALES-PROUD REBEL-
RARE BREED-RED SUN-THE SEARCHERS-STAGECOACH-
SILVERADO-SHE WORE A YELLOW RIBBON-SONS OF KATIE
ELDER-TRUE GRIT-TWO MULES FOR SISTER SARA-THE
UNFORGIVEN-VILLA RIDES-WAGON TRAIN (TV)-THE WILD
BUNCH-WILD ROVERS-WYATT EARP-WILD WILD WEST (TV)

402.**WILLETTS Dave** - **On and Off Stage** - **Dave Willetts &***
SILVA SCREEN (Koch): SONGCD 902 (CD)   *1990*
Songs from: PHANTOM OF THe OPERA-LES MISERABLES-LA
CAGE AUX FOLLES-NINE-GUYS & DOLLS-PENNY MILLIONAIRE
plus the following songs: TI AMO-NIGHTS ARE FOREVER
THE ROSE-HELLO AGAIN *etc.* / *****Philharmonia Orchestra

403.**WILLIAMS John** - **CLOSE ENCOUNTERS: The Essential**
JOHN WILLIAMS Film Music Album *featuring the*
City Of Prague Philharmonic and Crouch End Festival
Chorus conducted by Paul Bateman and Nic Raine
SILVA SCREEN (Koch): FILMXCD 314 (2CD)   *1999*
SAVING PRIVATE RYAN-HOOK-COWBOYS-BORN ON THE 4TH OF
JULY-FAMILY PLOT-JFK-EMPIRE OF THE SUN-AMISTAD-THE
TOWERING INFERNO-SUPERMAN-THE RIVER-JAWS-STAR WARS-
EMPIRE STRIKES BACK-PRESUMED INNOCENT-INDIAN JONES
& THE TEMPLE OF DOOM-SCHINDLER'S LIST-BLACK SUNDAY-
CLOSE ENCOUNTERS OF THE THIRD KIND-INDIANA JONES &
THE LAST CRUSADE-RARE BREED

404.**WILLIAMS John** - **John Williams Greatest Hits 1969-99**
SONY CLASSICS: 2SK(S2T)(S2M) 51333 (2CD/MC/md) 1999
London Symph.Orch/Boston Pops Orch (John Williams)
themes & music: STAR WARS-E.T.-SUPERMAN-JAWS-SAVING
PRIVATE RYAN-STAR WARS: THE PHANTOM MENACE-INDIANA
JONES AND THE LAST CRUSADE-SUGARLAND EXPRESS-JFK-
RAIDERS OF TH LOST ARK-RETURN OF THE JEDI-REIVERS-
OLYMPIC THEME and FANFARE-EMPIRE IF THE SUN-CLOSE
ENCOUNTERS OF THE THIRD KIND-EMPIRE STRIKES BACK-
JURASSIC PARK-SCHINDLER'S LIST-HOOK-1941-STEPMOM-
ROSEWOOD-SEVEN YEARS IN TIBET-FAR AND AWAY-SUMMON
THE HEROES-HOME ALONE-BORN ON THE FOURTH OFJULY-

405.**WISDOM Norman** - **The Wisdom Of A Fool**
SEE FOR MILES (Koch): SEECD 377   *1997*
DON'T LAUGH AT ME-WISDOM OF A FOOL-DREAM FOR SALE-
UP IN THE WORLD-NARCISSUS *(with JOYCE GRENFELL)*-
BEWARE-ME AND MY IMAGINATION-SKYLARK-WHO CAN I TURN
TO-BOY MEETS GIRL *(with RUBY MURRAY)*-YOU MUST HAVE

BEEN A BEAUTIFUL BABY-HEART OF A CLOWN-I DON'T 'ARF
LOVE YOU *(w.JOYCE GRENFELL)*-BY THE FIRESIDE-JOKER-
IMPOSSIBLE-YOU'RE GETTING TO BE A HABIT WITH ME-
HAPPY ENDING-MAKE A MIRACLE *(with PIP HINTON)*-ONCE
IN LOVE WITH AMY-MY DARLING MY DARLING-LEANING ON A
LAMPOST-FOR ME AND MY GIRL-LAMBETH WALK

406.<u>**WORLD IN UNION ANTHEMS**</u> / **RUGBY WORLD CUP 1995** V.Art
POLYGRAM TV (UNIV): 527 807-2 (CD) -4 (MC)   *1995*
WORLD IN UNION 95 Ladysmith Black Mambazo featur:
P.J.Powers SWING LOW SWEET CHARIOT Ladysmith Black
Mambazo featur.China Black BREAD OF HEAVEN (Wales)
Michael Ball, Ladysmith Black Mambazo,Llanelli Male
Voice Choir BURNING IN YOUR HEART Waltzing Matilda
Union FLOWER OF SCOTLAND Barbara Dickson O CANADA
Union RUN WALLABY RUN Doug Parkinson and Wallabies
IRELAND'S CALL Andrew Strong and Irish W.Cup Squad
VA PENSIERO Union / *plus nine other Anthem tracks*

407.<u>**WORLD OF SOUND: FAVOURITE THEMES FROM BBCTV & RADIO**</u>
BBC Worldwide (Koch UK): 33635-2 (CD) -4 (MC) 1997
1.999/999 INTERNATIONAL Roger Bolton 2.CASUALTY Ken
Freeman 3.CHILDREN'S HOSPITAL Debbie Wiseman 4.BY
THE SLEEPY LAGOON *(DESERT ISLAND DISCS)* Eric Coates
5.HETTY WAINTHROP INVESTIGATES Nigel Hess 6.FAWLTY
TOWERS Dennis Wilson Quartet 7.HOWARDS' WAY Simon
May Or.8.HAVE I GOT NEWS FOR YOU Big George Webley
9.DOCTOR WHO Ron Grainer 10.RHODES MAIN THEME Alan
Parker Orchestra 11.BRING ME SUNSHINE *(MORECAMBE &*
WISE SHOW) Morecambe & Wise 12.EASTENDERS Simon May
13.MICHAEL'S THEME *(PARKINSON)* Harry Stoneham Five
14.I WISH I KNEW HOW IT WOULD FEEL TO BE FREE *(FILM*
*98)*Billy Taylor Trio 15.AT THE SIGN OF THE SWINGIN'
CYMBAL *(PICK OF THE POPS)* Brian Fahey Orchestra 16.
GOING STRAIGHT Ronnie Barker17.ON A MOUNTAIN STANDS
A LADY *(LIVER BIRDS)* Scaffold 18.MARCHING STRINGS
(TOP OF THE FORM) Ray Martin Orchestra 19.THAT WAS
THE WEEK THAT WAS Millicent Martin 20.HIT AND MISS
(JUKE BOX JURY) John Barry 21.SAILING BY *(RADIO 4*
*SHIPPING FORECAST)*John Scott 22.CALLING ALL WORKERS
(MUSIC WHILE YOU WORK) Eric Coates Orchestra 23.
IMPERIAL ECHOES *(RADIO NEWSREEL)* Band Of The R.A.F.
24.IN PARTY MOOD *(HOUSEWIVE'S CHOICE)* Jack Strachey
25.SOMEBODY STOLE MY GAL *(BILLY COTTON BAND SHOW)*
Billy Cotton Band 26.MUCH BINDING IN THE MARSH Kenn
eth Horne-Richard Murdoch BBC Radio Orch (S.Black)

408.<u>**WUTHERING HEIGHTS**</u> *see* **NEWMAN Alfred**

409.<u>**YOUNG Victor**</u> - **SHANE: A TRIBUTE TO VICTOR YOUNG**
New Zealand Symphony Orch, conduct: Richard Kaufman
KOCH INTernational (Koch): 3-7365-2H1 (CD)   *1996*
SHANE *(1952)* FOR WHOM THE BELL TOLLS *(1943)* AROUND
THE WORLD IN EIGHTY DAYS *(1956)* THE QUIET MAN*(1952)*
SAMSON AND DELILAH *(1949)* *cond.by Richard Kaufman

410.<u>**ZIMMERMAN Richard**</u> - **SCOTT JOPLIN: King Of Ragtime**
LASERLIGHT-DELTA (Targ-BMG): 55 542 (3CD Set) 1994
CD1.MAPLE LEAF RAG-HARMONY CLUB WALTZ-AUGUSTAN CLUB

WALTZ-PEACHTREE RAG-SWIPESY CAKE WALK-ORIGINAL RAGS
GREAT CRUSH COLLISION MARCH-EASY WINNERS-STRENUOUS
LIFE-RAGTIME DANCE-ELITE SYNCOPATIONS-LITTLE BLACK
BABY-PALM LEAF RAG-THE FAVORITE-THE CASCADES-SARAH
SARAH DEAR-ROSEBUD MARCH-BINKS WALTZ-ROSE LEAF RAG
WHEN YOUR HAIR IS LIKE THE SNOW CD2.THE ENTERTAINER
MARCH MAJESTIC-WEEPING WILLOW-THE SYCAMORE-COUNTRY
CLUB-SCHOOL OF RAGTIME-SOMETHING DOING-STOPTIME RAG
EUPHONIC SOUNDS-FELICITY RAG-FIG LEAF RAG-SCOTT JOP
LIN'S NEW RAG-WALL STREET RAG-PARAGON RAG-PINEAPPLE
RAG-ANTOINETTE-SNORING SAMPSON-GLADIOLUS RAG-SEARCH
LIGHT RAG-THE NONPAREIL CD3.SENSATION-FROLIC OF THE
BEARS-KISMET RAG-SILVER SWAN RAG-LILY QUEEN-HIGHLIG
HTS FROM TREEMONISHA-REAL SLOW DRAG-PRELUDE TO ACT3
THE CHRYSANTHEMUM-BREEZE FROM ALABAMA-I AM THINKING
OF MY PICKANINNY DAYS-LOVIN' BABE-PLEASANT MOMENTS-
A PICTURE OF HER FACE-CLEOPHA-LEOLA

S U B S C R I P T I O N S

T E L E - T U N E S   2 0 0 0

THE TELE-TUNES REFERENCE BOOK IS PUBLISHED TWICE A YEAR
IN JANUARY AND JULY. IN ADDITION TO THIS, MIKE PRESTON
MUSIC ALSO OPERATE A TELEPHONE DATABASE INFORMATION
SERVICE WHICH CAN BE CONTACTED MONDAY TO FRIDAY FROM
09.30am - 16.30pm. SUBSCRIBERS TO THE FULL TELE-TUNES
SERVICE HAVE ACCESS TO THIS DATABASE. THIS SERVICE
PROVIDES EXTREMELY FAST ANSWERS TO THE VERY LATEST
QUERIES ON TV AND FILM MUSIC

*PLEASE NOTE THE TELEPHONE DATABASE INFO.LINE IS FOR
SUBSCRIBERS TO THE FULL SERVICE ONLY. DETAILS FROM:-*

SUBSCRIPTION DEPT. MIKE PRESTON MUSIC THE GLENGARRY
3 THORNTON GROVE MORECAMBE LANCASHIRE LA4 5PU U.K.

T E L E P H O N E / F A X : 0 1 5 2 4 - 4 2 1 1 7 2

E.MAIL : mike.preston@ukonline.co.uk

BACK ISSUES AND SUPPLEMENTS NOTE:

TELE-TUNES MAIN BOOKS 1979-1999 ARE NO LONGER AVAILABLE
TELE-TUNES SUPPLEMENTS ARE NO LONGER AVAILABLE

SEE ALSO TELE-TUNES HISTORY PAGE 368

A CHRONOLOGICAL FILM INDEX OF THE JAMES BOND MOVIES

1) **DOCTOR NO** 1962 / *Sean Connery* / *Ursula Andress*
   Bernard Lee-Lois Maxwell-Jack Lord-Joseph Wiseman
   Title theme 'The James Bond Theme' (MONTY NORMAN)
   -S/T- *reissue: EMI Premier: CZ 558 (CD)*

2) **FROM RUSSIA WITH LOVE** 1963 / *Sean Connery* / *Daniela*
   Bianchi-Robert Shaw-Pedro Armendariz-Lottie Lenya
   "From Russia With Love" (Lionel Bart) MATT MONRO
   -S/T- *reissue: EMI Premier: CZ 550 (CD)*

3) **GOLDFINGER** 1964 / *Sean Connery* /*Honor Blackman-Gert*
   Frobe-Shirley Eaton-Harold Sakata-B.Lee-L.Maxwell
   Title song "Goldfinger" (John Barry-Leslie Bricusse
   Anthony Newley) sung by SHIRLEY BASSEY
   -S/T- *reissue: EMI Premier: CZ 557 (CD)*

4) **THUNDERBALL** 1965 / *Sean Connery* / *Claudine Auger*
   Adolfo Celi-Luciana Paluzzi-Rick Van Nutter-Martine
   Beswick "Thunderball" (J.Barry-Don Black) TOM JONES
   -S/T- *reissue: EMI Premier: CZ 556 (CD)*

5) **YOU ONLY LIVE TWICE** 1967 / *Sean Connery* / *Tetsuro*
   Tamba-Akiko Wakabayashi-Mie Hama-Karin Dor-Bern.Lee
   Title song (J.Barry-Leslie Bricusse) NANCY SINATRA
   -S/T- *reissue: EMI Premier: CZ 559 (CD)*

6) **ON HER MAJESTY'S SECRET SERVICE** 1969 *George Lazenby*
   Diana Rigg-TellY Savalas-Ilse Steppat-Gabr.Ferzetti
   Title song "We Have All The Time In The World"(Hal
   David-John Barry) sung by LOUIS ARMSTRONG
   -S/T- *reissue: EMI Premier: CZ 549 (CD)*

7) **DIAMONDS ARE FOREVER** 1971 / *Sean Connery* / *Jill St.*
   John-Charles Gray-Lana Wood-Jimmy Dean-Bruce Cabot
   Title song (John Barry-Don Black) by SHIRLEY BASSEY
   -S/T- *reissue: EMI Premier: CZ 554 (CD)*

8) **LIVE AND LET DIE** 1973 / *Roger Moore* / *Jane Seymour-*
   Yaphet Kotto-Clifton James-David Hedison-BernardLee
   Title song (Paul & Linda McCartney) PAUL McCARTNEY
   -S/T- *reissue: EMI Premier: CZ 553 (CD)*

9) **THE MAN WITH THE GOLDEN GUN** 1974 *Roger Moore* /*Britt*
   Ekland-Christopher Lee-Maud Adams-Herve Villechaize
   Title song (Don Black-John Barry) sung by LULU
   -S/T- *reissue: EMI Premier: CZ 552 (CD)*

10) **THE SPY WHO LOVED ME** 1977 / *Roger Moore* / *Barbara*
    Bach-Curt Jurgens-Richard Kiel-Caroline Munro
    "Nobody Does It Better" (Carol Bayer Sager-Marvin
    Hamlisch) sung by CARLY SIMON -S/T-
    -S/T- *reissue: EMI Premier: CZ 555 (CD)*

11) **MOONRAKER** 1979 / *Roger Moore* / *Lois Chiles-Michael*
    Lonsdale-Richard Kiel-Geoffrey Keen-Bernard Lee
    "Moonraker" (John Barry-Hal David) SHIRLEY BASSEY
    -S/T- *reissue: EMI Premier: CZ 551 (CD)*

12) **FOR YOUR EYES ONLY** 1981 *Roger Moore-Carole Bouquet*
    Topol-Lynn HollyJohnson-Julian Glover-Jill Bennett
    Title song "For Your Eyes Only" (Michael Leeson-
    Bill Conti) by SHEENA EASTON -S/T-   *DELETED*

13) **OCTOPUSSY** 1983 / *Roger Moore* /*Maud Adams-Louis Jor dan-Kristina Wayborn-Kabir Bedi-Desmond Llewellwyn* Title "All Time High" (John Barry-Tim Rice) - RITA COOLIDGE -S/T- *RYKODISC (Vital): RCD 10705 (CD)*

13a) **NEVER SAY NEVER AGAIN** 1983 *Sean Connery* / *Barbara Carrera-Kim Basinger-Klaus M.Branduaer-Max V.Sydow* Title song "Never Say Never Again" (Michel Legrand -Alan and Marilyn Bergman) and sung by LANI HALL -S/T- *Silva Screen: (Conifer): FILMCD 145 (CD)*

14) **A VIEW TO A KILL** 1985 / *Roger Moore* /*Tanya Roberts Christopher Walken-Grace Jones-Patrick Macnee* Title song "A View To A Kill" (That Fatal Kiss) by DURAN DURAN -S/T- *EMI: CDP 746159-2 (CD)* DELETED

15) **THE LIVING DAYLIGHTS** 1987 *Timothy Dalton* / *Maryam D'Abo-Jeroen Krabbe-Joe Don Baker-John Rhys Davies* Title song "The Living Daylights"(John Barry-A.HA) -S/T- *RYKODISC (Vital): RCD 10725 (CD) new issue*

16) **LICENCE TO KILL** 1989 *Timothy Dalton* / *Carey Lowell Robert Davi-Talisa Soto-Anthony Zerbe* / Title Song "Licence To Kill" (Walden-Cohen-Afansieff) GLADYS KNIGHT / M: MICHAEL KAMEN -S/T- *MCA: MCGC 6051(MC)*

17) **GOLDENEYE** 1995 *Pierce Brosnan* / *Samantha Bond-Robb ie Coltrane-Desmond LLewellyn-Judi Dench-Sean Bean* Music score by ERIC SERRA / Title song "Goldeneye" (Bono-The Edge) by TINA TURNER *Parlophone (EMI):* -S/T- *Virgin US (EMI): CDVUSX 100 (CD)*

18) **TOMORROW NEVER DIES** 1997 *Pierce Brosnan* / *Jonathan Pryce-Michelle Yeoh-Samantha Bond-Judi Dench* Music score by DAVID ARNOLD / Title song by SHERYL CROW / closing song vocal by k.d.lang -S/T- *A.& M.(Poly): 540 830-2 (CD) -4 (MC)*

19) **WORLD IS NOT ENOUGH The** 1999 *Pierce Brosnan* / *Denise Richards-Sophie Marceaux-Robert Carlisle-Judi Dench-Samantha Bond-Robbie Coltrane-J.Cleese* Music score by DAVID ARNOLD / Title song by David Arnold-Don Black and performed by GARBAGE -S/T- *UNIVERSAL: 112 161-2 (CD) -4 (MC*

20) *TO BE CONTINUED...* *(2000/2001)*

JAMES BOND MUSIC COLLECTIONS - see COLLECTION numbers 53,54,55 for track details

53. **BOND James: BACK IN ACTION!** - Various Artists *SILVA SCREEN (Koch): FILMCD 317 (CD)* *1999*

54. **BOND James: BEST OF JAMES BOND** - 30th Anniversary *EMI: 523 294-2 (CD) -4 (MC)* *1999*

55. **BOND James: THE ESSENTIAL** City Of Prague Symph.Orch cond: Nicholas Raine *(1993, revised reissue 1998)* *S.Screen (Koch): FILMCD 007 (CD)* DR.NO-FROM RUSSIA

```
1)  LOVE ME TENDER       vid: FOX 1172       5 songs-1956
2)  LOVING YOU           vid: MEDUSA         7 songs-1957
3)  JAILHOUSE ROCK       vid: WHV PES 50011  7 songs-1957
4)  KING CREOLE          vid: POLYG 6343723 12 songs-1958
5)  G.I.BLUES            vid: POLYG 6343583 10 songs-1960
6)  FLAMING STAR             vid: FOX 1173   6 songs-1961
7)  WILD IN THE COUNTRY     vid: FOX 1174   6 songs-1961
8)  BLUE HAWAII          vid: POLYG 6343703 16 songs-1961
9)  FOLLOW THAT DREAM    vid: WHV PES 99460  6 songs-1962
10) KID GALAHAD          vid: WHV PES 99335  6 songs-1962
11) GIRLS GIRLS GIRLS    vid: POLYG 6343663 14 songs-1962
12) IT HAPPENED AT THE WORLD'S FAIR vid:- 10 songs-1963
13) FUN IN ACAPULCO      vid: POLYG 6343643 11 songs-1963
14) KISSIN' COUSINS      vid: WHV PES 51148  9 songs-1964
15) VIVA LAS VEGAS       vid: WHV SO 35630   9 songs-1964
16) ROUSTABOUT           vid: POLYG 6343623 11 songs-1964
17) TICKLE ME            vid: POLYG 0858423  9 songs-1965
18) GIRL HAPPY           vid: WHV PES 51487 11 songs-1965
19) HARUM SCARUM Holiday v: WHV PES 50486  9 songs-1965
20) PARADISE HAWAIIAN STYLE v:POL 6343683 10 songs-1965
21) FRANKIE AND JOHNNY  vid: WHV PES 99666 13 songs-1966
22) SPINOUT California Holiday v:PES51489  9 songs-1966
23) EASY COME EASY GO    vid: POLYG 6347603  7 songs-1966
24) DOUBLE TROUBLE       vid: WHV PES 50485  8 songs-1967
25) CLAMBAKE             vid: WHV PES 99667  7 songs-1967
26) STAY AWAY JOE        vid: WHV PES 50525  5 songs-1968
27) SPEEDWAY             vid: WHV PES 50476  9 songs-1968
28) LIVE A LITTLE LOVE...WHV SO 35767 +26  4 songs-1968
29) CHARRO!              vid: not available  2 songs-1969
30) CHANGE OF HABIT      vid: POLYG 6347583  5 songs-1969
31) TROUBLE WITH GIRLS  v: WHV SO 35629 +3  7 songs-1969
32) ELVIS - NBC TV SPECIAL v: BMG 74321 106623    -1968
33) ELVIS - THAT'S THE WAY IT IS WHV PES 50373   -1970
34) ELVIS - ON TOUR      video: WHV PES 50153    -1972
35) THIS IS ELVIS Compil. video: WHV  SO 11173   -1981
```

```
BLUE HAWAII          SOUNDTRACK INFO    07863 66959-2 (CD)
CHANGE OF HABIT      + 28 & 29 & 31     07863 66559-2 (CD)
CHARRO!              + 28 & 30 & 31     07863 66559-2 (CD)
CLAMBAKE                 + 14 & 26      07863 66362-2 (CD)
DOUBLE TROUBLE               + 22       07863 66361-2 (CD)
EASY COME EASY GO            + 27       07863 6655-8  (CD)
ELVIS-NBC TV SPECIAL 1968                 ND 83894    (CD)
FLAMING STAR             + 7 & 9        07863 66557-2 (CD)
FOLLOW THAT DREAM        + 6 & 7        07863 66557-2 (CD)
FRANKIE & JOHNNY             + 20       07863 66360-2 (CD)
FUN IN ACAPULCO              + 12       74321 13431-2 (CD)
G.I.BLUES                               07863 66960-2 (CD)
GIRL HAPPY                   + 19       74321 13433-2 (CD)
GIRLS GIRLS GIRLS            + 10       74321 13430-2 (CD)
HARUM SCARUM                + 18        74321 13433-2 (CD)
IT HAPPENED AT THE WORLD'S.. + 13       74321 13431-2 (CD)
JAILHOUSE ROCK                          07863 67453-2 (CD)
KID GALAHAD                 + 11        74321 13430-2 (CD)
```

```
KING CREOLE                              07863 67454-2 (CD)
KISSIN'COUSINS            + 25 & 26      07863 66362-2 (CD)
LIVE A LITTLE LOVE..+ 29 & 30 & 31       07863 66559-2 (CD)
LOVE ME TENDER          4 songs on Coll 'Essential Elvis'
LOVING YOU                               07863 67452-2 (CD)
PARADISE HAWAIIAN STYLE        + 21      07863 66360-2 (CD)
ROUSTABOUT                     + 15      74321 13432-2 (CD)
SPEEDWAY                       + 23      07863 66558-2 (CD)
SPINOUT                        + 24      07863 66361-2 (CD)
STAY AWAY JOE             + 14 & 25      07863 66362-2 (CD)
THAT'S THE WAY IT IS                     74321 14690-2 (CD)
TROUBLE WITH GIRLS  + 28 & 29 & 30       07863 66558-2 (CD)
VIVA LAS VEGAS                 + 16      74321 13432-2 (CD)
WILD IN THE COUNTRY       + 6 & 9        07863 66557-2 (CD)
```

ELVIS COMMAND PERFORMANCES: Essential 60's Masters II
RCA (BMG): 07863 66601-2 (2CD)   1995
Songs from Elvis Presley Movie Musicals / <u>disc one:</u>
G.I.BLUES-WOODEN HEART-SHOPPIN'AROUND-DOIN'THE BEST
I CAN-FLAMING STAR-WILD IN THE COUNTRY-LONELY MAN-
BLUE HAWAII-ROCK A HULA BABY-CAN'T HELF FALLING IN
LOVE-BEACH BOY BLUES-HAWAIIAN WEDDING SONG-FOLLOW
THAT DREAM-ANGEL-KING OF THE WHOLE WIDE WORLD-I GOT
LUCKY-GIRLS GIRLS GIRLS-BECAUSE OF LOVE-RETURN TO
SENDER-ONE BROKEN HEART FOR SALE-I'M FALLING IN
LOVE TONIGHT-THEY REMIND ME TOO MUCH OF YOU-FUN IN
ACAPULCO-BOSSA NOVA BABY-MARGUERITA-MEXICO-KISSIN'
COUSINS-ONE BOY TWO LTTLE GIRLS-ONCE IS ENOUGH-VIVA
LAS VEGAS-WHAT'D I SAY <u>disc two:</u> ROUSTABOUT-POISON
IVY LEAGUE-LITTLE EGYPT-THERE'S A BRAND NEW DAY ON
THE HORIZON-GIRL HAPPY-PUPPET ON A STRING-DO THE CL
AM-HAREM HOLIDAY-SO CLOSE YET SO FAR-FRANKIE & JOHN
NY-PLEASE DON'T STOP LOVING ME-PARADISE HAWAIAAN ST
YLE-THIS IS MY HEAVEN-SPINOUT-ALL THAT I AM-I'LL BE
BACK-EASY COME EASY GO-DOUBLE TROUBLE-LONG LEGGED
GIRL-CLAMBAKE-YOU DON'T KNOW ME-STAY AWAY JOE-SPEED
WAY-YOUR TIME HASN'T COME YET BABY-LET YOURSELF GO-
ALMOST IN LOVE-A LITTLE LESS CONVERSATION-EDGE OF
REALITY-CHARRO!-CLEAN UP YOU OWN BACKYARD
ESSENTIAL ELVIS (Film S/Tracks) *RCA: 74321 57347-2 (CD)*
LOVE ME TENDER (2)-LET ME-POOR BOY-WE'RE GONNA MOVE
LOVING YOU (3)-PARTY-HOT DOG-TEDDY BEAR-MEAN WOMAN
BLUES-GOT A LOT O'LIVIN' TO DO (2)-LONESOME COWBOY
JAILHOUSE ROCK (2)-TREAT ME NICE-YOUNG & BEAUTIFUL
DON'T LEAVE ME NOW-I WANT TO BE FREE-BABY I DON'T
CARE-MEAN WOMAN BLUES-LOVING YOU-TREAT ME NICE
COLLECTOR'S GOLD - *RCA (BMG): PD(PK) 90574 (3CD/3MC)*
(1) Hollywood Album: GI BLUES-POCKETFUL OF RAINBOWS
BIG BOOTS-BLACK STAR-SUMER KISSES WINTER TEARS-I SL
IPPED I STUMBLED I FELL-LONELY MAN-WHAT A WONDERFUL
LIFE-AWHISTLING TUNE-BEYOND THE BEND-ONE BROKEN HEA
RT FORSALE-YOU'RE THE BOSS-ROUSTABOUT-GIRL HAPPY-SO
CLOSE YET SO FAR-STOP LOOK & LISTEN-AM I READY-HOW
CAN YOU LOSE WHATYOU NEVER HAD (2) Nashville Album
(15 Tracks) (3) Live In Las Vegas 1969 (20 Tracks)

S O U N D T R A C K S   A N D   V I D E O S
note: Some Disney Videos Have Limited Availability

ALADDIN (1993) Music & songs: ALAN MENKEN-HOWARD ASHMAN
-TIM RICE. "A Whole New World" sung by PEABO BRYSON
and REGINA BELLE *-S/T- Walt Disney (Technicol-CHE):
WD 74260-2 (CD) -4 (MC)* VHS Video: *B.Vista D.216622*
ALICE IN WONDERLAND (1951) Music score: OLIVER WALLACE
-S/T- (-)   VHS Video: *Buena Vista: D.200362*
ARISTOCATS The (1970) Songs: RICHARD and ROBERT SHERMAN
-S/T- DISNEY (B.Vista): WD 74250-2 (CD) -4 (MC)
               VHS Video: *Buena Vista: D.241902*
BAMBI (1943) Songs: FRANK CHURCHILL-E.PLUMB-LARRY MOREY
Coll. W.Disney:PDC 304 (MC) VHS Video: *D.209422*
BASIL THE GREAT MOUSE DETECTIVE (1986) Music: HENRY MAN
CINI *-S/T- (-)*   VHS Video: *Buena Vista: D.213602*
BEAUTY AND THE BEAST (1992) Songs: ALAN MENKEN-H.ASHMAN
sung CELINE DION-PEABO BRYSON Disn: WD 71360-2 (CD)
Coll: PDC 309(CD) VHS Video: *B.Vista: D.213252*
BEDKNOBS AND BROOMSTICKS (1971)   Songs by R.& R.SHERMAN
-S/T- (-)   VHS Video: *Buena Vista: D.200162*
BLACK HOLE The (1979) Music Score: JOHN BARRY.Suite on
FILMXCD 185 (CD) VHS Video: *Buena Vista: D.200112*
BLACKBEARD'S GHOST (1967)   Music score: ROBERT BRUNNER
-S/T- (-)   VHS Video: *Buena Vista: D.200622*
BUG'S LIFE, A (1998) Music & songs: RANDY NEWMAN / "The
Time Of Your Life" performed by RANDY NEWMAN *-S/T-*
DISNEY-EDEL (Pinn): 010634-2DNY (CD) -4DNY (MC)
CINDERELLA (1950)   Music and songs: OLIVER WALLACE-PAUL
J.SMITH-MAC DAVID-AL HOFFMANN and JERRY LIVINGSTON
Coll Walt Disney: PDC 300 (MC) VHS Video: *D.204102*
DUCKTAILS THE MOVIE (1991)   Music score: DAVID NEWMAN
-S/T- (-)   VHS Video: *Buena Vista: D.210822*
DUMBO (1941)   Music: F.CHURCHILL-O.WALLACE-N.WASHINGTON
-S/T- (-)   VHS Video: *Buena Vista: D.202472*
FANTASIA (1940) featuring: The Philadelphia Orchestra
(Leopold Stowkowski) *-S/T-* (dig.remastered in 1990)
Disney: DSTCD 452D (2CD) DSTMC 452MC (2MC) deleted
       VHS Video: *Buena Vista: D.211322 (deleted)*
FANTASIA 2000 (2000) *information to be confirmed*
FLUBBER (1997) Music score: DANNY ELFMAN / Disney Music
and Stories on *DISNEY (Technicol): WD 77566-2 (CD)*
FOX AND THE HOUND The (1981) Songs: RICHARD & R.SHERMAN
-S/T- (-)   VHS Video: *Buena Vista: D.220412*
GOOFY MOVIE The (1995) Music: DON DAVIS + V.Artsists
-S/T- Disney (Technic-CHE): WD 76400-2 (CD) -4 (MC)
       VHS Video: *Buena Vista: D.274512*
HERCULES (1997)   Music score: ALAN MENKEN
-S/T- DISNEY (Technic/Carl): WD 60864-2 (CD) -4(MC)
       VHS Video: *Buena Vista: D.270832*
HUNCHBACK OF NOTRE DAME The (1996)   Music: ALAN MENKEN
Lyr STEPHEN SCHWARTZ song "Someday" sung by ETERNAL
-S/T- W.Disney (Technicol): WD 77190-2 (CD) -4 (MC)
       VHS Video: *D.610058 (VHS)*

JAMES AND THE GIANT PEACH (1995) M/Songs: RANDY NEWMAN
  -S/T- *W.DISNEY (B.Vista): WD 68120-2 (CD) -4 (MC)*
                                    VHS Video: *Guild: G 8870S*
JUNGLE BOOK (1967) Songs: RICHARD and ROBERT SHERMAN
       with LOUIS PRIMA-PHIL HARRIS-STERLING HOLLOWAY
  -S/T- *Walt Disney Records: WD 70400-2 (CD) -4 (MC)*
  Children's Coll on Walt Disney (Pinn): PDC 305 (MC)
                                    VHS Video: *Buena Vista: D.211222*
LADY AND THE TRAMP The (1956)   Songs: PEGGY LEE-J.BURKE
    Mus: OLIVER WALLACE songs sung by **Peggy Lee** -S/T-
    WALT DISNEY (Technicolor): WD 6021328 (CD)
    Spoken Word & Songs Coll Walt Disney: PDC 301 (MC)
                                    VHS Video: *Buena Vista D.205822*
LION KING The (1994) Music sco: HANZ ZIMMER) songs incl
    "Circle Of Life" (TIM RICE-ELTON JOHN) ELTON JOHN
    -S/T- *DISNEY (Technic) WD 60802-2 (CD) also on*
       Rocket (Polyg): 522690-2 (CD) 522690-4 (MC)
                                    VHS Video: *Buena Vista: D.229772*
LITTLE MERMAID The (1990) Songs by ALAN MENKEN & HOWARD
    ASHMAN. Disney's Sounds & Stories Recordings on
    DISNEY (Technic) WD 60628-2 (CD) WD 60628-4 (MC)
    DISNEY (Technic) WD 60946-2 (CD) WD 60946-4) and
    DISNEY (Technol) WD 775840 (CD)(sing-a-long ser)
                                    VHS Video: *Buena Vista: D.209132*
MARY POPPINS (1964) Songs by RICHARD and ROBERT SHERMAN
    with JULIE ANDREWS-DICK VAN DYKE-DAVID TOMLINSON
    -S/T- *Walt Disney WD 77572-2 (CD) WD 77572-4 (MC)*
                                    VHS Video: *Buena Vista: D.200232*
MICKEY'S CHRISTMAS CAROL (1983) -S/T- *W.Disney Records*
    PDC 312 (MC)   VHS Video: *Buena Vista: D.201882*
MULAN (1998) Mus: JERRY GOLDSMITH. songs by MATT WILDER
    DAVID ZIPPEL -S/T- *DISNEY (Silva Screen):60631 (CD)*
                                    VHS Video: *(-)*
OLIVER AND COMPANY (1989) Music score by J.A.C.REDFORD
    -S/T- *Disney (Techn): WD 608902(CD) PCD 450(CD/MC)*
                                    VHS Video: *Buena Vista: D.240302*
101 DALMATIONS (1996) Music score: MICHAEL KAMEN -S/T-
    DISNEY (B.Vista): WD 69940-2 (CD) WD 69940-4 (MC)
                                    VHS Video: *Buena Vista: D.212632*
101 DALMATIONS (1961)   Songs: MEL LEVIN m: BRUNS/DUNHAM
    -S/T- *(-)*   VHS Video: *Buena Vista: D.212632*
PETER PAN (FILM 1953) Music: OLIVER WALLACE-PAUL SMITH
    DISNEY'S MUSIC & STORIES *DISNEY (Technicol-CHE):*
       WD 77583-2 (CD) WD 77583-4 (MC) and PDC 306 (MC)
                                    VHS Video: *Buena Vista: D.202452*
PETE'S DRAGON (1977) Mus.dir: IRWIN KOSTAL with V.Arts
    -S/T- *(-)*   VHS Video: *Buena Vista: D.200102*
PINOCCHIO (1939) M: LEIGH HARLINE-P.SMITH-N.WASHINGTON
    -S/T- *Disney: WD 75430-2 (CD) -4(MC) + PDC 302 (MC)*
                                    VHS Video: *Buena Vista: D.202392*
POCAHONTAS (1995) Music sco ALAN MENKEN Songs (A.Menken
    Stephen SCHWARTZ) inc "Colours Of The Wind" sung by
    VANESSA WILLIAMS -S/T- *DISNEY: WDR 75462-2 (CD) -4*
    (MC) PDC 316 (CD) VHS Video: *Buena Vista: D.274522*

RELUCTANT DRAGON The (1941) VHS Video: *Disney: D.205332*
RESCUERS The (1976) 'Story Of The Rescuers'
  -S/T- *(-)*   *VHS Video: Buena Vista: D.240642*
RESCUERS DOWN UNDER The (1990) Mus sco: BRUCE BROUGHTON
  -S/T- *Silva Screen Imp: 60613-2 (CD) / PDC 308 (CD)*
              VHS Video: *Buena Vista: D.211422*
RETURN OF JAFAR (1994) VHS Video: *Buena Vista: D.222372*
ROBIN HOOD (1973) Songs: GEORGE BRUNS-FLOYD HUDDLESTON
  with ROGER MILLER-PHIL HARRIS-TERRY THOMAS-P.USTINOV
      -S/T- *(-)*   *VHS Video: Buena Vista: D.202282*
SLEEPING BEAUTY (1959) Mus: GEORGE BRUNS -S/T- *DISNEY:*
  WDR 75622-2 (CD)   *VHS Video: Buena Vista: D.204762*
SNOW WHITE & THE SEVEN DWARFS 1937 Songs: FRANK CHURCHI
  LL-LEIGH HARLINE-PAUL SMITH feat: ADRIANA CASELOTTI
    -S/T- *Disney: WD 74540-2 (CD) -4 (MC) PDC 303 (MC)*
              VHS Video: *Buena Vista: D.215242*
SONG OF THE SOUTH (1946) Music by: DANIEL AMFITHEATROF
  CHARLES WOLCOTT-PAUL SMITH-ALLIE WRUBEL-RAY GILBERT
    -S/T- *(-)*   *VHS Video: Buena Vista: D.201022*
SUMMER MAGIC (1963)   Songs: RICHARD and ROBERT SHERMAN
    w:BURL IVES-HAYLEY MILLS -S/T- *(-)*   *VHS: (-)*
SWORD IN THE STONE (1963) Songs: RICHARD/ROBERT SHERMAN
  -S/T- *(-)*   VHS Video: *Buena Vista: D.202292*
TARZAN (1999) Music: MARK MANCINA Songs by PHIL COLLINS
  -S/T- *DISNEY-EDEL (Pinn): 010247-2DNY (CD) -4DNY MC*
          also 010248-2DNY (CD) 010249-4DNY (MC)
THREE CABALLEROS The (1945) Music: CHARLES WOLCOTT-PAUL
  J.SMITH-EDWARD PLUMB   VHS Video: *B.Vista: D.200912*
TOY STORY (1996) Music/songs RANDY NEWMAN
  W.Disney (Technicol): WD 77130-2(CD) WD 77130-4(MC)
              VHS Video - *Disney: D.272142*
TOY STORY 2 (1999) Music & Songs by RANDY NEWMAN
  -S/T- *DISNEY (USA): 60647 (CD)*
WIND IN THE WILLOWS The   VHS Video: *B.Vista: D.204272*
WINNIE THE POOH 'The Many Songs of WINNIE THE POOH'
  DISNEY (Carlton-Polyg): WD 11564-2 (CD) -4 (MC)
WINNIE THE POOH AND A DAY FOR EEYORE (-) Music & Songs
  RICHARD & ROBERT SHERMAN *featur:* STERLING HOLLOWAY
    -S/T- *(-)*   *VHS Video: Buena Vista: D.205322*
WINNIE THE POOH AND CHRISTMAS TOO *VHS Vid: BV: D.241232*
WINNIE THE POOH AND THE BLUSTERY DAY (1968)   Songs by
  RICHARD & ROBERT SHERMAN *featur:* STERLING HOLLOWAY
    -S/T- *(-)*   *VHS Video: Buena Vista: D.200632*
WINNIE THE POOH AND THE HONEY TREE (1966)   Songs by
  RICHARD & ROBERT SHERMAN *featur:* STERLING HOLLOWAY
    -S/T- *(-)*   *VHS Video: Buena Vista: D.200492*
WINNIE THE POOH AND TIGGER TOO (1964) Songs:RICHARD and
  ROBERT SHERMAN *feat:* STERLING HOLLOWAY-PAUL WINCHEL
    -S/T- *(-)*   *VHS Video: Buena Vista: D.200642*
WINNIE THE POOH: THE GREAT RIVER RESCUE (New Adventures
          Of)   VHS Video: *Buena Vista: D.241032*

DISNEY'S HIT SINGLES AND MORE! -   SEE COLLECTION 130

BRITISH SONG CONTEST (SONG FOR EUROPE) 1999

BBC Television Centre 07 March 1999 / Terry Wogan
Winning Order / Song Title / Performing Artist / Points

```
1 - SAY IT AGAIN              - PRECIOUS    - 52457
2 - SO STRANGE                - ALBERTA     - 51708
3 - UNTIL YOU SAVED MY LIFE   - SISTER SWAY - 51398
4 - YOU'VE TAKEN MY DREAMS    - JAY
```

"SAY IT AGAIN" (Paul Varney) performed by PRECIOUS
then went on to represent the UK in The 44th...

EUROVISION SONG CONTEST 1999

*From the Int.Conference Centre,Jerusalem 29th May 1999
and Transmitted By BBC1 TV and BBC Radio 2*

Country	Song	Artist	Points
1.SWEDEN	"Take Me To Your Heaven"	CHARLOTTE NILSSON	163
2.ICELAND	"All Out Of Luck"	SELMA	146
3.GERMANY	"Journey To Jerusalem"	SURPRIZ	140
4.CROATIA	"Maria Magdalena"	DORIS	118
5.ISRAEL	"Happy Birthday"	EDEN	93
6.ESTONIA	"Diamond Of Night"	EVELIN SAMUEL and CAMILLE	90
7.BOSNIA-HERZ	"Passengers"	DINO & BEATRICE	86
8.DENMARK	"This Time I Mean It"	TRINE JEPSEN and MICHAEL TESCHI	71
8.HOLLAND	"One Good Reason"	MARLAYNE	71
10.AUSTRIA	"Reflection"	BOBBIE SINGER	65
11.SLOVENIA	"For A 1000 Years"	DARJA SVAJGER	50
12.BELGIUM	"Like The Wind"	VANESSA CHINITOR	38
12.U.K.	"Say It Again"	PRECIOUS	38
14.NORWAY	"Living My Life Without You"	STIG VAN EIJK	35
15.MALTA	"Believe In Peace"	TIMES 3	32
16.TURKEY	"Immortal Love"	TUGBA ONAL	21
17.IRELAND	"When You Need Me"	THE MULLANS	18
18.POLAND	"Hold Me Tight"	MIECZYSLAW SZCZESNIAK	17
19.FRANCE	"I Want To Give My Voice"	NAYAH	14
20.LITHUANIA	"The Songthrush"	AISTE	13
21.PORTUGAL	"Take My Hand"	RUI BANDEIRA	12
22.CYPRUS	"It Will Be Love"	MARLAIN	2
23.SPAIN	"I Don't Want To Listen"	LYDIA	1

see also previous EUROVISION SONG CONTESTS pages 98-100

L O N D O N   T H E A T R E   M U S I C A L S

*   *CURRENT AND FORTHCOMING WEST END SHOWS*   *

*BLOOD BROTHERS - *PHOENIX Theatre from 28 JULY 1988*
LYN PAUL-MARK HUTHCINSON-DEBBIE PAUL-ANDY SNOWDEN
recording 1995 First Night (Pinn): CASTCD 49 (CD)
see also page 64,

*BUDDY - *STRAND Theatre (or.Palace Theatre.19 OCT 1989)*
ANGUS MacGREGOR-MILES GUERRINI-SIMON RAWLINGS & Co.
1995 'Live' Rec: First Night (Pinn): CASTCD 55 (CD)
1989 Orig London Cast: First Night: QUEUECD 1 (CD)
see also page 69,

*CATS - *NEW LONDON Theatre from 11 MAY 1981*
NEW LONDON THEATRE CAST
1981 Orig London Cast: Polydor: 817 810-2 (2CD)
Highlights Recording: Polydor: 839 415-2 (CD)
see also page 75,

*CHICAGO - *ADELPHI Theatre from 18 NOVEMBER 1997*
CHITA RIVERA-MICHAEL SIBERRY-VALARIE PETTIFORD-
NORMAN PACE *prev:* RUTHIE HENSHALL-NICOLA HUGHES-
CLARKE PETERS-JOEL GREY *orig* UTE LEMPER-HENRY
GOODMAN-NIGEL PLANER-MEG JOHNSON-CLARKE PETERS
recording (1998) RCA (BMG): 09026 63155-2 (CD)
see also page 77,

*FOSSE THE MUSICAL - *PRINCE OF WALES from 26 JAN 2000*
MUSIC FROM VAR.MUSICALS CHOREOGRAPHED BY BOB FOSSE
recording unconfirmed

*GREAT BALLS OF FIRE - *CAMBRIDGE from 06 OCTOBER 1999*
JERRY LEE LEWIS STORY with BILLY GERAGHTY-JOHN
BANNISTER-KIM BRETTON-AMELDA BROWN-EDDIE BURTIE
recording unconfirmed

*KING AND I, The - *LONDON PALLADIUM from 03 MAY 2000*
ELAINE PAIGE and JASON SCOTT LEE and Company
recording unconfirmed / see also page 142,

*LES MISERABLES - *PALACE Theatre from 4 DECEMBER 1985*
PALACE THEATRE CAST Production
1985 Orig London Cast - First Night: ENCORECD 1
for other recordings see page 148

*LION KING The - *LYCEUM from 19 OCTOBER 1999*
inc.music by ELTON JOHN-TIM RICE *and others*
O.Broadway Cast: DISNEY-EDEL (Pinn): 010 455-2DNY
O.London Cast: CURRENTLY UNAVAILABLE
see also page 150,

LONDON   THEATRE   MUSICALS

* CURRENT AND FORTHCOMING WEST END SHOWS *

*MAMMA MIA! *PRINCE EDWARD Theatre from 23 MARCH 1999*
MUSICAL BASED ON THE SONGS OF ABBA
recording: POLYDOR (Univ): 543 115-2 (CD) -4 (MC)

*PAJAMA GAME *VICTORIA PALACE from 04 OCTOBER 1999*
RICHARD ADLER-JERRY MOSS (songs) dir: SIMON CALLOW
feat: LESLIE ASH-GRAHAM BICKLEY-ANITA DOBSON-ALISON
LIMERICK-JOHN HEGLEY and Company
recording unconfirmed / see also pages 180, 181,

*PHANTOM OF THE OPERA *HER MAJESTY'S from 9 OCTOBER 1986*
MIKE STIRLING-CHARLOTTE PAGE and Company
1986 Orig London Cast - Polydor: 831 273-2 (CD)
see also pages 184, 185

*SAINT SHE AIN'T, A *- APOLLO,SHAFTESBURY AVE. 22 SEP 99*
DENIS KING (music) DICK VOSBURGH (lyrics/book) *feat*
RAE BAKER-BARRY CRYER-PAULINE DANIELS-BRIAN GREENE
recording: unconfirmed

*SATURDAY NIGHT FEVER *LOND.PALLADIUM 5/5/1998-26/2/2000*
ADAM GARCIA-TARA WILKINSON-ANITA LOUISE COMBE & Com
recording: POLYDOR: 557 932-2 (CD)
see also page 204,

*SPEND SPEND SPEND *- PICCADILLY - 05 OCT 1999 -*
BARBARA DICKSON-RACHEL LESKOVAC-STEVEN HOUGHTON
recording: unconfirmed

*STARLIGHT EXPRESS *- APOLLO VICTORIA from 27 MARCH 1984*
New Re-Vamped 1993 Show - LON SATTON-RAY SHELL & Co
1984 Orig London Cast - Polydor: 519 041-2 (CD)
see also page 219,

*TESS OF THE D'URBERVILLES *- SAVOY from 30 OCT.1999*
POPPY TIERNAY-PHILIPPA HEALEY-JONATHON MONKS & Co.
recording: unconfirmed

*WHISTLE DOWN THE WIND *- ALDWYCH from 01 JULY 1998*
ANDREW LLOYD WEBBER-JIM STEINMAN NEW MUSICAL
record: Really Useful-Poly: 559 441-2 (CD) -4 (MC)
see also page 244,

CHECK WITH THE THEATRE BOX OFFICE FOR LATEST DETAILS

TELE-TUNES WAS FIRST PUBLISHED IN 1979 AND IS NOW IN IT'S 21ST YEAR. THE ORIGINAL EDITION WAS PUT TOGETHER AS A RESULT OF CONSTANT REQUESTS FROM THE RECORD RETAIL SECTOR IN WHICH MIKE PRESTON WAS WORKING IN AT THE TIME. FIRST ISSUE TOTALING 108 PAGES, CONSISTED OF A 61 PAGE TV THEME SECTION, 5 PAGES OF TV COMMERCIALS, 17 PAGES OF FILM SOUNDTRACKS AND A FEW ODDITIES SUCH AS COMMERCIAL TV VOICE OVERS, TV ADVERTISED ALBUMS AND TV THEMES THAT MADE THE CHARTS!

A SECOND EDITION APPEARED ALMOST A YEAR LATER AND INCREASED ITS SIZE TO 152 PAGES. THE PUBLICATION WAS THEN PUT ON ICE FOR A FEW YEARS WHILE THE BUSINESS CHANGED DIRECTION AND RELOCATED TO THE SOUTH COAST. A THIRD SMALLER EDITION OF 104 PAGES WAS ISSUED IN 1984 AND AT THE SAME TIME IT WAS DECIDED THAT THE MAIN BOOK SHOULD BE COMPLIMENTED BY QUARTERLY SUPPLEMENTS.

IN 1988 THE COMPANY RELOCATED TO THE PRESENT ADDRESS AND THE TELE-TUNES INFORMATION DATABASE WAS SET UP. SINCE THEN THE BOOKS HAVE BEEN PRODUCED ANNUALLY WITH THE BACK-UP OF THE INFO DATABASE WHICH IS EXCLUSIVELY OWNED AND RUN BY MIKE PRESTON MUSIC. T-T SUBSCRIBERS NOW HAVE THE BENEFIT OF SUPERFAST INFORMATION AT THE END OF A PHONE-LINE.

WHILE INFO.TECHNOLOGY MOVES AT THE SPEED OF LIGHT, THERE IS STILL NEED FOR A FAST, RELIABLE, ACCURATE AND FRIENDLY MUSIC INFORMATION SERVICE, AND IN THIS REPECT TELE-TUNES HAS ALWAYS PRIDED ITSELF IN BEING ABLE TO BRING A PERSONAL AND APPROACHABLE TOUCH TO SUBSCRIBERS OF THIS PUBLICATION.

FROM YEAR 2000 THE TELE-TUNES REFERENCE BOOK WILL BE PUBLISHED TWICE DURING THE YEAR, EACH EDITION BEING COMPLETELY REVISED AND REPRINTED. THESE BOOKS WILL COMPLEMENT THE DATABASE PHONE LINE OPERATION WHICH CONTINUES TO BE THE MOST POPULAR PART OF THE TELE-TUNES SUBSCRIPTION SERVICE.

INFORMATION ABOUT THE TELE-TUNES WEBSITE WILL BECOME AVAILABLE AT A LATER DATE, IN THE MEANTIME FEEL FREE TO CONTACT US VIA PHONE, FAX OR E.MAIL

MIKE PRESTON MUSIC, THE GLENGARRY, THORNTON GROVE
MORECAMBE, LANCASHIRE LA4 5PU. TEL / FAX: 01524 421172
E-MAIL: mike.preston@ukonline.co.uk

E.& O.E.